ed the b

Due

IRD

THE PUBLIC SERVANT

DOUGLAS HURD

THE
PUBLIC SERVANT

An Authorised Biography
MARK STUART

MAINSTREAM
PUBLISHING

EDINBURGH AND LONDON

Copyright © Mark Stuart, 1998
All rights reserved
The moral right of the author has been asserted

First published in Great Britain in 1998 by
MAINSTREAM PUBLISHING COMPANY (EDINBURGH) LTD
7 Albany Street
Edinburgh EH1 3UG

ISBN 1 84018 125 7

A catalogue record for this book is available from the British Library

Typeset in Perpetua
Printed and bound in Great Britain by Butler and Tanner Ltd

For Julie

Contents

Illustrations

Douglas Hurd's christening, 1930

Douglas (centre) with his parents, brothers Julian and Stephen, rabbit and dogs, 1936

Douglas Hurd (third from right) before the Eton Wall Game, 1947 (© Sport & General Press Agency Ltd)

The aftermath (© Keystone Press Agency Ltd)

Rainscombe Farm, c.1947, memories of which caused all the fuss in the Conservative leadership contest of November 1990

Douglas Hurd (second row, extreme right) at Mons Officer Cadet School, 1949

A young Douglas Hurd, c.1950 (© Bassano Ltd)

Cambridge Union Society. Change of Officers Debate, 10 March 1952. Newly elected president, D.R. Hurd, Trinity College, takes the chair from the retiring president, Greville Janner, Trinity Hall (© Stearn & Sons)

Douglas with his parents, c.1952

The young diplomat, Western Hills, Peking, 1956

Douglas with his son Nicholas in Rome, 1965

With the Prime Minister, Edward Heath, at Mid-Oxon Rally, 1973. The late Michael Wolff is on the right (© Oxford Mail & Times)

Douglas Hurd with Edward Heath and Teng Hsiao Ping, China, 1974. (William Waldegrave is on Hurd's left)

At the Great Wall of China with Mrs Thatcher leader of the opposition, 1977.

Douglas Hurd with the Queen and Francis Pym (right), Foreign Office, 1982

Douglas, Judy and their son, Philip. Philip was born on election night, June 1983, causing Hurd to miss his count

New Year's Day on the mountains of Mourne in Northern Ireland, with sons

Tom and Alexander, 1985

In County Down with the Bradley family, 1985

On the lake at Chevening° with Philip, 1991

In Sarajevo with President Izetbegovic, 1992

Enjoying Argentinian hospitality on the Gibson estançia, 1993

Rajasthan, India, 1994

In Vitez, Bosnia, with British troops 1994

Hurd sports a new coat, admired by John Sawers (Principal Private Secretary)

Enjoying a relaxed walk along the Rhine with the German Foreign Minister Klaus Kinkel and his family, 1995

At Westwell with Judy and their daughter, Jessica, 1977

Preface

My reasons for writing this book were two-fold. At a personal level, I was interested in authority and deference. Hailing from a close-knit farming background in the north-east of Scotland, where very little ever changed, perhaps I was slow to notice that deference had mostly disappeared. Douglas Hurd reminded me of a primary school headmaster (known in the north-east of Scotland as a 'dominie') who was still able to exercise authority. I was also brought up as a Conservative. Since Douglas Hurd had served under three Conservative Prime Ministers — Heath, Thatcher and Major — I chose Hurd as a way of explaining recent Conservative history and how this relates to the decline of deference. He seemed to me to be a figure of authority in an age when respect for authority had disappeared. The modern Conservative Party had always been about a balance between continuity and change. Had Mrs Thatcher so embraced the free market and meddled with British institutions that the Conservative Party went off balance, and ultimately lost its hold on power?

I first met Douglas Hurd in May 1995 when he was still Foreign Secretary. He could not disguise his alarm at the prospect of someone writing a book about him. I found him cautious and lacking a certain warmth. After reflecting on the matter, the Foreign Secretary agreed not to stand in the way of my interviewing several dozen people associated with his life. Then, in the autumn of 1995, I received an invitation to lunch and found Hurd more relaxed, charming even. Perhaps it was in his interests to be so. Soon after, he agreed to co-operate fully with the biography.

Central to this co-operation were the diaries which Douglas Hurd has kept since the age of nine. The quality of the diaries has improved over time. They began as jottings in small notebooks. From 1979, however, Hurd took to buying a more substantial W.H. Smith 'page-a-day' diary. As Foreign Secretary, he got into the habit of writing at the top of his diaries where he was at any given point, which is helpful, given the frenetic pace of modern international diplomacy. Throughout, the diaries are written in note form, rather than complete sentences. Unfortunately, Douglas Hurd was unwilling to allow unrestricted access to his diaries. While being more open than the average Tory, he is not a freedom-of-information radical. Instead, we agreed upon a system where I would pre-select over 300 moments from his political career. The evidence which I requested from the diaries was mainly drawn from Hurd's sixteen years as a minister, from 1979 until 1995. We then sat down together over seven meetings, lasting about an hour-and-a-half each. I read out the date and Hurd looked up the diary entry. Douglas Hurd did not prepare for our meetings. Judging from the transcripts, Hurd seems to have been summarising his diaries off-the-cuff. The main problem we encountered in this exercise was Hurd's dislike of excessive detail and my desire, as an academic, to discover minute points of interest. Indeed, his only interference (that itself is too strong a word) in the writing of the biography was to warn that the book would be too long. He was proved right; nearly half the first draft has fallen on the cutting room floor. His own memoirs will be broad-brush and much shorter. But there was little censorship. I can recall only three occasions where he refused to read out the next line, not wishing to engage in personal attacks against former Cabinet colleagues. Frequently, Hurd stopped and explained the context of his remarks. So, whereas the diary entries are listed in the endnotes as 'Diary Readings with Douglas Hurd', context and comment appear as 'Interview with Douglas Hurd'. So extensive are the endnotes in this book that I decided against a bibliography.

In Hurd's view, the value of diary evidence is limited. He sees them as an aide-mémoire, but little else. He believes there is a tendency for ministers to use their diaries as a safety-valve, exaggerating the importance of the day's events and the disagreements which emerge. Ministerial meetings are described as 'stormy' or 'disastrous', but the fact that these comments are written straight away guards against hindsight, retrospective calm. Understandably, the diaries concentrate in detail on matters close to the minister, but other issues are given scant coverage. In itself, this tells one how little most ministers – unless they are generalists like William Whitelaw or Nigel Lawson – know about the detailed plans of their Cabinet colleagues.

My own view is that, within the constraints of the diary readings, one does gain a feel for what it is like to be a Cabinet minister. It is not possible for a senior minister to examine issues in a neat row, in isolation from one another; the tyranny of time and the pell-mell of politics – the tendency for events to crowd-in on top of one another – gets in the way. The trivial and the important jostle for a Cabinet minister's time. The diaries provide a valuable personal insight into the characters of the three Conservative Prime Ministers with whom Douglas Hurd served at close quarters.

Ultimately, the diaries tell us more about what Douglas Hurd has done and witnessed, than what Douglas Hurd is really like. The only way of discovering more was to get to know him better. With each meeting, Hurd's natural reserve diminished, but never entirely disappeared. I found him persuasive, perhaps too persuasive – most of the time he convinces. On a visit to Hurd's Westwell home, my wife and I were given a tour of the village. We peered inside the Anglican church where he worships on Sundays, and around the graveyard and monuments – the nooks and crannies. My original view of him remained: Douglas Hurd is the quintessential village headmaster.

As to the value of oral evidence – interviewing over thirty individuals connected with Hurd's career – there was little discernible pattern, except to note three things. First, long-serving former senior ministers and officials who do not keep a diary are less likely to remember specific events, because their political life has been overlain with so many similar problems. There is a tendency to confuse one issue with another or to have forgotten an issue completely, unless it triggers a specific memory of something else. Their evidence, as with all oral evidence, needs to be checked against specific dates. Second, sometimes the person at one remove, the junior minister or the friend who has not kept in touch, can provide the best insight. Third, I regret not having the time or the resources to interview any of the international statesmen with whom Hurd worked so closely.

Having looked through almost every press cutting relating to Douglas Hurd from *The Guardian* and *The Times* from 1967 to 1995, I noticed a marked deterioration in the quality of reporting on Parliament. This deterioration can be dated to within a month – November 1990. By coincidence, at the same time as the Conservative Party was unseating Mrs Thatcher, the press stopped reporting accounts of what was said in Parliament. Instead, they started using quotations which bear only a passing resemblance to what appears in *Hansard*. For the next seven years, the press coverage focused almost exclusively on politics from the point of view of opinion polls and the speculation about the Conservative leadership. After Black Wednesday, *The Times* turned Euro-sceptical and the rest of the papers concentrated almost entirely on the Government's difficulties. This was partly because the second Major Government lost control of the political agenda, but objective reporting of the news suffered, as did reporting of international issues. Basing modern political biographies largely on press cuttings is a mistake. As a corrective to this skewed coverage, where possible, I have tried to quote directly from *Hansard* for domestic issues and I consulted *Keesing's Contemporary Archives* (which continues as *Keesing's Record of World Events* from 1975) which provides a straight, objective account of international-relations issues.

There is one vital historical source which is only alluded to in this biography

– transcripts of telephone conversations between ministers and international statesmen. The diary readings give some indication of the sheer number of calls involved. Many of the vital decisions in modern diplomacy and government policy are decided on the telephone. This is a major problem for the historian or biographer of the modern era.

Mark Stuart
May, 1998

Acknowledgements

The list of people I need to thank is legion, and this summary will not do proper justice. To those who were willing to be interviewed, I accord my heartfelt thanks. I would especially like to mention the following: Sir Antony Acland, John Barton, Edward Bickham, Sir Kenneth Carlisle, Baroness Chalker, Kenneth Clarke, Sir Patrick Cormack, Sir Alan Donald, Maurice Fraser, Tristan Garel-Jones, Richard Gozney, David Heathcoat-Amory, MP, Lord Howe of Aberavon, Lord (Greville) Janner, Lord Jenkins of Hillhead, Gerald Kaufman, MP, Stephen Lamport, Lord Lawson of Blaby, Lord Lloyd of Berwick, Andrew Osmond, Chris Patten, Sir Timothy Raison, Dr Timothy Ryder, Jacky Shaw-Stewart, Lord Wakeham, William Waldegrave, Sir Dennis Walters, Viscount Whitelaw, Timothy Yeo, MP, and Philip Ziegler. Many thanks to all those who were interviewed but preferred not to be mentioned by name.

Thanks are due to Alan Clark and Weidenfeld and Nicolson for granting permission to quote from Alan Clark's *Diaries*, and to HarperCollins Publishers Ltd for permission to reproduce a quote from Martin Gilbert's *In Search of Churchill*.

Letters from Sir Charles Powell, Mary Moore, Richard Ollard, Jane Norton, Sir Richard Evans and Sir Robert Rhodes James provided valuable insights. As for the subject himself, I greatly appreciated his openness, the tolerance which he showed by sitting through long interview sessions, as well as by kindly supplying photographs for this book. Many thanks to Judy Hurd for her hospitality during a visit to Westwell. To Julia Broad, Douglas Hurd's Diary Secretary at NatWest Markets, I send my heartfelt thanks for setting up all the interviews.

On a practical level, I would like to express gratitude to Brendan Casey, Peter and Sue-Anne Grant, Dr Alan Templeton and Dr Lindsey Allan, for providing free accommodation during my frequent visits to London. Many thanks are also due to Sandie Pinnock-Burland and Stephen Burland for their advice and kindnesses during my two years residing with them in Hull, and to Brent Collins, Samantha Mackereth, and Paul, Alicia and Bethany Monks for their support in Lancaster. The advice and support of Brian Gorman is warmly appreciated.

Philip Cowley at the University of Hull provided a constant stream of press cuttings and was also on hand to comment on drafts. I am particularly indebted to him for providing expert advice on the Conservative leadership contest of November 1990. I would also like to thank Professors Philip Norton and David Denver, both leading British political scientists, for allowing me the freedom to research this biography during my periods working for them. Professor Norton was instrumental in suggesting politicians to be interviewed and David Denver provided succinct advice on the book proposal and editing. Dr Ian Jackson at Lancaster kindly agreed to comment on the Northern Ireland chapter. At Aberdeen University, I would like to thank Professor Roy Bridges for making himself available to offer advice. The staff at the British Newspaper Library at Colindale deserve a special mention for their efficiency in hunting down copies of the *Witney Gazette* and the *Belfast Telegraph*. May I also thank Mrs Eileen Burr for her help in masking my woeful knowledge of Latin and the Classics. Lord Windlesham, Principal of Brasenose College, Oxford offered sage advice on Chapter 12 (criminal justice policy), while Michael Crick's comments on Chapter 5 (novels) were much appreciated.

Closer to home, I would like to thank my mother, Mrs Hazel Stuart, who video-taped endless political programmes and helped out financially, and to my father, Mr Alfie Stuart, for setting such high standards. Thanks are also due to my uncle, who will be too embarrassed to be mentioned by name, for helping to fund this project. Special affection is accorded to my two cats, Alfie and Audrey, who brightened my days during the writing of this biography. Most importantly, may I thank my wife, Julie, for her love and unfailing support as well as her tolerance, which was, I fear, not always reciprocated. On a practical level, credit is due for her advice on the passages relating to Douglas Hurd's novels and her extensive work in correcting my grammatical errors. Responsibility for any remaining mistakes rests solely with the author.

Lastly, I would like to thank Mr Harry Smith, the Dominie, who inspired this biography by his authoritative and disciplined teaching at Cultercullen Primary School.

1

Confusion Over Class

Douglas Richard Hurd was born on 8 March 1930, the eldest son of Anthony Hurd, a tenant farmer, who tended five hundred acres of not particularly good downland at Rainscombe Farm, near the town of Oare in Wiltshire. The farm was ploughed up during the Second World War, but in peacetime it was a mixed farm, with Sussex cattle, sheep and poultry. Life on the farm seems to have been happy for Douglas and his two younger brothers, Julian and Stephen. To this day, he retains a fondness for that particular rim of hills in Wiltshire: a painting of Douglas Hurd as a small boy sitting on a horse with his two brothers, with the hill above the farm brought closer than real life by artist Keith Henderson, has pride of place above the mantelpiece at Hurd's present home, 'Freelands' in the village of Westwell on the edge of the Cotswolds. Hurd acknowledges that his memories of an idyllic childhood on the farm got him into 'a real muddle' during the November 1990 Conservative leadership contest, when he tried to counter claims that he was a patrician:

> It was the recollections of Rainscombe and my father as a tenant farmer, never able to conjure up enough money to buy the farm. We weren't poor at all, but the idea that this was in some way an aristocratic background wasn't the case at all. Later, he became a life peer, but people get hopelessly mixed up about these things.[1]

In November 1990, in his attempt to become leader of the Conservative Party and Prime Minister, Hurd tried and failed to convince his contemporaries and the general public that he was of humble origins, saying that he had 'planted potatoes fifteen inches apart for nine pence an hour'.[2] One of the obstacles which Hurd had in convincing the electorate was that his public image was of an old-fashioned grandee with a safe pair of hands: he looked and sounded like an aristocrat.

There is little doubt that Hurd mishandled the question of his background. His friend and ally from the 1990 leadership contest, Kenneth Clarke, would have handled it differently:

> My opinion was he should have handled that by saying, yes, he admitted he'd had a very advantaged start in life. That was no crime. His father had been an MP and a farmer, he had been to Eton. He was conscious of that, but it made him all the more aware of plenty of people who did not have advantage, made him very much socially aware of the need not to have a socially-divided society.[3]

However, John Barton, a contemporary at Eton:

> It never occurred to me until a few years ago when the press started writing, that he had an aristocratic background at all. I thought of him as middle class. He had great intellectual authority, dignity, a certain nobility, but not of the class sort which was apparent in many of our contemporaries.[4]

From the standpoint of someone like William Waldegrave, who hails from a genuinely aristocratic family, Douglas Hurd's background is firmly middle class:

> It is an absurd misunderstanding of modern journalists to think that Douglas Hurd, because he has a dignified manner, should be described as a Tory patrician. My father knew his father quite well. He is quite something else. His father was not a great hereditary aristocrat with rolling acres. His father was a meritocrat, in British class terms, in the middle of the middle class.[5]

Douglas Hurd's father had never been destitute, and arguments about not having enough money to go to one of the top public schools might seem remote to those struggling to live on low incomes. But in terms of the strata of English life, Hurd's father, despite being a well known figure in farming, journalistic, and political circles, hailed from the ranks of the middle classes, as did most of his recent ancestors. In fact, Douglas Hurd's family background and ancestry is far more interesting and varied than the confusing label with which he was lumbered for most of his political career would imply. The present Hurd family can be traced back to the younger sons of yeomanry stock in the Somerset and Wiltshire area, who joined the ranks of the professional middle class.

Tracing Hurd's ancestry back to the reign of George III, we discover a Dr Richard Hurd, who became Bishop of Worcester. Bishop Hurd was a favourite of George III, and the King would ask for him to deliver the sermon at Bath Abbey when the Royal Court was touring the West Country. The Bishop's sermons, however, were declared 'dull stuff' by Boswell, but Dr Samuel Johnson replied indignantly, 'Dull stuff? Let me tell you that Hurd is a man whose acquaintance is a valuable acquisition.'[6] George III did ask the Bishop of Worcester to become Archbishop of Canterbury, but Richard Hurd, by then over seventy years old, declined the offer, declaring 'my next palace, your Majesty, will be in heaven.'[7] The Bishop also published a collection of North Country ballads and poetry. His likeness is preserved in two portraits by Gainsborough painted in 1788, one of which now hangs in the Hurd library in Hartlebury, where the Bishops of Worcester still reside.

While Douglas Hurd's own religious beliefs mirrored those of his Anglican ancestor Bishop Hurd, for the most part his ancestors belonged to the dissenting tradition. Douglas Hurd's great grandfather, William, was a congregational preacher, before he became a solicitor. Unfortunately, he became embroiled in a costly partnership law suit, and here perhaps is the source of the Hurd family's comparative lack of money. Because of William Hurd's misfortune, both Douglas Hurd's grandfather and father were forced to earn a living as journalists.[8] Although the surname Hurd is held to mean 'Keeper of Treasure', very few of the Hurds have been very wealthy. Dr Philip Hurd, a Somerset lawyer, appears to be the main exception. He made considerable sums of money through land speculation around the suburbs of London at the beginning of the nineteenth century. The streetname Hurdwick Place in Mornington Crescent owes its origin to Dr Hurd. The present Douglas Hurd has peered into the 'nooks and crannies' of Kentish Town parish church, where a brass tablet marks the pew of this Anglican lawyer and speculator.

Douglas Hurd's grandfather, Sir Percy Angier Hurd – who was of Huguenot stock on his mother's side – was brought up in the dissenting tradition in the market town of Berkeley in Gloucestershire, but subsequently became an Anglican. In his unpublished memoirs, Sir Percy Hurd recounts an occasion when, as a schoolboy aged seven or eight, Douglas was shown round Westminster Roman Catholic Cathedral. After witnessing the genuflexions of the worshippers and gazing at the many ornate symbols in the side chapels of the cathedral, the young Douglas was asked by his grandfather what he thought of it. 'Very idolatrous,' was his laconic reply.[9]

Sir Percy Angier Hurd became the first member of the family to become a Member of Parliament in 1918. The trend was carried on by Hurd's father, Anthony Hurd, in 1945. Although Douglas could claim to come from a political family, neither his father nor grandfather attained or indeed would seem to have sought high office. Both were in the mould of respected backbenchers who represented an interest in the House of Commons, in their case, the farming interest.

Sir Percy began his career as a journalist in the London office of the *Toronto*

Globe. He wrote articles for the weekly journal, the *Canadian Gazette* and later was made editor. His involvement in other Canadian publications continued when he became London Correspondent (and later editor) of the *Montreal Gazette* and later for Sir Hugh Graham's (later Lord Athelstan's) journal, the *Montreal Daily Star,* writing distinctive cablegrams under the pen-name of 'Windermere'. Percy Hurd's interest in Canada nearly took the Hurd family across the Atlantic, but he declined Sir Hugh Graham's offer to work as a journalist in Montréal. Several other Hurds have gone across to the New World, including two professors. Hurd's great, great uncle John became a hydrographer to the Navy: part of the English Channel is named after him, and there is a 'Cape Hurd' in Hudson's Bay, Canada.[10] After his retirement from the Foreign Office, Douglas Hurd revived his grandfather's association with the Canadian newspaper industry and now writes an occasional foreign affairs column for the *Globe and Mail*.

As his interest in Canada perhaps suggests, Percy Hurd became a strong supporter of the cause of Empire Unity and Imperial Preference – in marked contrast to his grandson's later staunch defence of free trade. In 1898, Percy Hurd established the *Outlook*, a weekly review, whose main purpose was to promote Joseph Chamberlain's cause of Empire Unity. Among the well known contributors to the review were George Wyndham, later Chief Secretary for Ireland, the poet W.E. Henley, and the novelist H.G. Wells. In 1903, Percy became Assistant Secretary and later Secretary of Chamberlain's Tariff Commission, through which the concepts of tariff reform and imperial preference were developed under Arthur Balfour, Andrew Bonar Law and Neville Chamberlain.

The Hurd family suffered greatly in the war of 1914 to 1918. Two of Percy Hurd's four sons fell on the Somme, both aged twenty-one. Percy Hurd's eldest son, Douglas William, fell in 1916, and Angier Percy (known as Jack), a Lieutenant in the Hertfordshire regiment, suffered the same fate in 1918.

In 1918, Andrew Bonar Law – Canadian born and sharing Hurd's passion for tariff reform – persuaded Percy Hurd to stand as a Conservative candidate in the Liberal stronghold of Somerset and Frome. Surprisingly, Hurd won the seat and held it until 1923, when the Conservatives were heavily defeated in the General Election. However, Sir Percy was only to suffer a year out of Parliament, since an old friend, Sir Edward Goulding (later Lord Wargrave), was about to retire as Member for the Devizes Division of Wiltshire, in the days when outgoing Conservative MPs held considerable sway in the selection of their successor. Douglas Hurd remembers accompanying his grandfather as a young boy around the Devizes constituency during the 1935 General Election campaign. He also fondly recalls the moment when, aged seven, he presented Lady Baldwin, wife of the Prime Minister, with a bouquet of flowers.[11]

Percy Hurd was a jovial, but active backbencher, who defended the interests of Empire and agriculture. He served as Honorary Secretary of the Conservative Backbench Agriculture Committee for four years and published several volumes on Empire issues.[12] In 1932, he was knighted for his public service, on the recommendation of Ramsay MacDonald. The honour was given in recognition of his work in local government. A resident of Highgate, he represented the ward on Hornsey Council for over twenty years, before becoming an Alderman in 1940. He was also President (unpaid) of the Rural District Councils Association of England and Wales for twenty years. Percy Hurd was a great promoter and defender of civic space, initiating the campaign which made a public park of Queen's Wood, Highgate, promoting the purchase of Ken Wood and becoming the first President of the Highgate Village Preservation Society.

In later life, Douglas Hurd developed a similar sense of civic duty, a belief in the idea of service to the community and a pride in civic space. Although much of the local government reforms of the Thatcher years centralised power away from local government, Hurd remained, at heart, a village Tory. He would strongly agree with his grandfather's defence of the idea of public service, written in 1948:

> These municipal and rural experiences made me realise how much public spirit and managing powers are devoted, generally without money reward, to upholding the high traditions of local life in this country.[13]

Sir Percy travelled the continent of Europe, first as a journalist, then as a delegate to the regions of France devastated in the Great War – Allied Relief Committee of Royal Agricultural Society – and finally as a member of the Empire Parliamentary Association in the inter-war years. His unpublished memoirs are laced with anecdotes of his encounters with European leaders. On one occasion, during a visit to Kaiser Wilhelm's Germany, Percy Hurd attended a sumptuous luncheon by Chancellor von Bulow in the belief that, as a journalist acquainted with Canada, he might impart information on Germans who had settled in Ontario. As was his habit (and that of the French), Percy tucked his serviette under his chin awaiting the arrival of his soup. Whereupon, he heard a click of heels and a resplendent soldier standing behind him:

> 'Excuse me', said this German officer, 'but a French guest of the Kaiser was seated here last week and used his serviette as you have done, and His Majesty directed me to inform him that this is not a barber's shop.' Needless to say my serviette remained beneath my chin.[14]

Looking back on his long parliamentary career, Sir Percy could also recall memorable but disturbing visits to Hitler's Germany, Mussolini's Italy, and Franco's Spain, where he detected the 'growing menace of continental militarism'.[15]

Sir Percy's brother, Sir Archibald Hurd, was thoroughly receptive to the warnings of German militarism, having been strongly influenced by the famous Sir John (later Lord) Fisher, before the Great War. Sir Archibald was for thirty years naval correspondent to the *Daily Telegraph* and an historian of some repute on the subject of the Merchant Navy. His works include the *Official History of the Merchant Navy*, published in three volumes between 1921 and 1929. But Sir Archibald's career as a naval expert had been entirely unplanned. Like his brother, he began as a journalist with the *Surrey Times* and the *Western Morning News*, which owned a subsidiary called the *Naval Military Record*. Unexpectedly, the editorship of the paper fell vacant and Archibald Hurd, despite protestations of his ignorance of such matters, was made editor at the age of only twenty-two. An illustrated article in the *Windsor Magazine* attracted the attentions of John Le Sage and Hurd became lead writer on naval matters for the *Daily Telegraph*. In 1928, Archibald Hurd was knighted and acquired a controlling interest in the *Shipping World*. The main theme of his volumes on the merchant navy was the heroic conduct of masters and men in the First World War. According to *The Times*:

> . . . he [Sir Archibald Hurd] showed they occupied an almost unique position in military history since, although untrained in loyalty to any service or corps and uninstructed in the use of arms, they were animated with a fighting spirit of a crack corps. Their heroic obstinacy was, he showed, the equivalent of a great strategic victory. [16]

Despite his failing eyesight in later life, he remained forever figuratively on the look-out against threats to the supremacy of the British Navy, publishing *The Eclipse of British Sea Power: An Increasing Peril* in 1933.[17]

Douglas Hurd's father was Anthony Richard Hurd, born in 1901, the third son of Sir Percy Hurd. Anthony attended Marlborough College and, after reading Agriculture at Cambridge, he combined the occupations of tenant farmer and journalist on agricultural matters. In 1924, he became farm editor of *The Field* and, by 1932, had succeeded the doyen of agricultural journalists, C.J.B. Macdonald, as Agricultural Correspondent of *The Times*. Over the next twenty-five years, Anthony Hurd would gain a reputation as an authority on all matters agricultural, making several farming broadcasts for the BBC. At local level, he joined the Council of the National Farmer's Union (NFU), representing the county of Wiltshire. During the Second World War, Anthony Hurd was appointed Assistant Agricultural Adviser at the Ministry of

Agriculture. His experiences were recorded in a *A Farmer in Whitehall*, published in 1951.

In 1945, Anthony Hurd emulated his father by becoming Member of Parliament for Newbury in Berkshire. This eventually necessitated a move from the five hundred-acre family farm in Wiltshire to a house at Winterbourne, just north of Newbury, in 1947. Because of the tiny nature of his holdings, he joined forces with the lands of his neighbour, Godfrey (later Sir) Nicholson, Member of Parliament for Farnham. Anthony Hurd formed a close friendship with his neighbour and fellow MP as was shown in 1966 when Sir Godfrey read the lesson at Anthony Hurd's memorial service. As a boy Douglas Hurd knew Emma Nicholson, one of Godfrey Nicholson's four daughters, who went on to become Conservative MP for Devon West and Torridge in 1987 until her defection to the Liberal Democrats during the New Year of 1996.[18] Taken together, Winterbourne Holt and Home Farm comprised only half a dozen fields, hardly qualifying Anthony Hurd or his eldest son, Douglas, as members of the landed gentry. Although he was always nostalgic for his farming background, Douglas Hurd decided not to go into farming. The family tradition was carried on instead by his youngest brother, Stephen, who returned to farm in the Marlborough Downs in Wiltshire, and was later made a director of several farming companies and building societies.

In 1951, Anthony Hurd's parliamentary career reached a crossroads when Winston Churchill offered him the post of Parliamentary Secretary to the Ministry of Agriculture, but he turned it down, feeling he could best represent the farming interest from the backbenches. In the same year, he was made Chairman of the Conservative Agriculture Committee, a post he filled with distinction until his retirement in 1964.

Anthony Hurd's wide knowledge of farming matters made him an excellent choice for fact-finding visits abroad. From 1948 onwards, he visited various parts of the globe, including an investigation into the notorious groundnut scheme in Tanganyika. In 1956, he became the first ever British Member of Parliament to visit the Falkland Islands, later becoming a director of the Falkland Islands Company Ltd, bringing his knowledge of sheep and grassland improvement to the role.[19] Further directorships were added in the shape of Massey Ferguson Holdings, Fison Fertilisers and the Muar River Rubber Company. Anthony Hurd was also appointed Chairman of the Westbourne Park Building Society and Thames Valley Eggs Ltd, but in those days the fees from these directorships were modest. He was knighted in 1959 and after the 1964 General Election he was made a life peer.

His premature death on Antigua in the West Indies in February 1966 robbed the farming industry of a great champion and his wife, Stephanie, of a loving husband.

Born Stephanie Corner, her father had been a surgeon. Her mother came from Blairgowrie in Perthshire. Douglas had two Scottish grandmothers, since his father's mother, Hannah Hurd, was a Cox of Dundee, daughter of a Congregationalist minister. He remembers his mother as being 'very unassertive, but nevertheless a strong character'.[20] As a young married woman, she had been even more shy, but after her husband's death, she became much more of a matriarchal figure. In the last twenty years of her life – she died in 1985 – Douglas saw a lot more of his mother and grew to know her better. Another consequence of Anthony Hurd's untimely death was that Stephanie had to support herself on her husband's limited capital for another twenty years: Douglas Hurd's oft-heard remark about being 'a bit thin' financially was never far from the truth.

Anthony Hurd's rather orthodox character was in marked contrast to the eccentricity of his younger brother, Robert Hurd. Douglas Hurd's bachelor uncle had been christened Philip Andrew Hurd (after the aforementioned London lawyer of Georgian days), but young Philip detested the name, and changed it by deed poll to Robert. Douglas Hurd remembers his uncle as being 'unpredictable and was just slightly eccentric by the standards of the day'.[21] Despite his foibles, Robert rose to prominence in Scotland as an architect, receiving the Saltire Society Award in 1958 for his redevelopment of the Royal Mile and the Civic Trust Award in 1961. In 1963, he died in Switzerland aged only fifty-eight. Although renowned for his sympathetic redevelopment of historic sites – particularly Lamb's House in Leith and Culross Abbey House – his primary achievement was the design of some eleven hydro-electric power stations in the Highlands and Islands of Scotland in the late 1940s. It was at this time that Robert Hurd introduced Douglas to the north-west Highlands of Scotland, where eccentricity was (and is) tolerated, and often cultivated. Douglas Hurd also remembers his first ever visit to Scotland as a boy, when he went to stay with his Uncle Robert at 49, George Square, Edinburgh. As was typical of his 'wicked' uncle, Robert Hurd produced a box of Monopoly, rather than taking his nephew to evensong at St Giles's Cathedral.[22]

Perhaps fortunately for Douglas Hurd, his uncle was not left in charge of his schooling. Douglas attended Twyford Preparatory School, a small school which normally sent boys to Winchester, just a few miles away. All three boys, Douglas, Julian and Stephen, attended Twyford. Among Hurd's contemporaries was Jock Bruce-Gardyne, who later became MP for Knutsford and was a close ally of Mrs Thatcher on the right-wing of the Conservative Party.[23] That apart, Hurd made few lasting friends at Twyford. He was a shy boy and the chief achievement of his preparatory school was, according to Hurd, to make him good at passing exams.[24] He remembers receiving a good grounding in French from 'a very tough master who used to tap a pencil on your head when you got your verbs wrong.'[25] As a diplomat, Hurd would become fluent in both French and Italian.

The vital exam which Hurd passed was the scholarship competition for Eton, known as the King's Scholarship. Hurd claims his father could not have afforded to send his son to the top public school in the country unless he had won a scholarship. But financial restrictions did not stop his youngest brother, Stephen, from attending Winchester, one of the Clarendon Schools.

Boys were permitted to sit the King's Scholarship exam between the ages of twelve and thirteen, but most of them sat the examination nearer the age of thirteen. Douglas Hurd was a very young twelve when he passed the exam with flying colours and went to Eton as a Colleger, where he would henceforth appear on the school roll as Hurd, K.S. Whilst Hurd had already proved himself as a scholar, the prospect of going to Eton was a daunting one for this shy, abrupt young boy.

Notes

1. Interview with Douglas Hurd, 26 Nov. 1996.
2. *The Guardian*, 26 Nov. 1990.
3. Interview with Kenneth Clarke, 16 Dec. 1996.
4. Interview with John Barton, 22 Jul. 1997.
5. Interview with William Waldegrave, 17 Dec. 1996.
6. Sir Percy Hurd, *The Hurds: A Note by Sir Percy Hurd* (unpublished, 1948).
7. Ibid.
8. Sir Percy Hurd, *Recollections of Sir Percy Angier Hurd* (unpublished, 1948), p. 18.
9. Ibid., p. 14.
10. Percy Hurd, *The Hurds*.
11. Philip Roth, *Parliamentary Profiles* (1989), p. 750.
12. Publications by Sir Percy Hurd include: *The Empire: A Family Affair; The New Empire Partnership: Defence, Commerce, Politics* (in conjunction with his brother, Sir Archibald Hurd); *The War and the Future; Canada, Past, Present and Future; The Fighting Territorials* (2 vols.).
13. Percy Hurd, *Recollections*, p. 26.
14. Ibid., pp. 27–8.
15. Ibid., p. 29.
16. *The Times*, 22 Jun. 1959.
17. Sir Percy Hurd's other publications included: *Sea Traders* (1921); *Ocean Tramps* (1922); *The Reign of the Pirates* (1925). He was also joint editor of *Brassey's Naval and Shipping Annual*, from 1922 to 1928.
18. Emma Nicholson, *Secret Society* (Indigo, London: 1996), p. 31.

19. *The Times*, 14 Feb. 1966.
20. Interview with Douglas Hurd, 17 Dec. 1996.
21. Interview with Douglas Hurd, 26 Nov. 1996.
22. Douglas Hurd, 'British Interests and the Inter-Governmental Conference', Speech to Scottish Council of European Movement, 26 Apr. 1996.
23. Jock Bruce-Gardyne served in the Foreign Service before becoming Paris correspondent of the *Financial Times* from 1956 to 1960. He was MP for South Angus from 1964 to October 1974. From 1970 to 1972, he was Parliamentary Private Secretary to the Secretary of State for Scotland. His ministerial career really took off under Mrs Thatcher when he was made Minister of State at the Treasury in 1981, and then as Economic Secretary to the Treasury, from 1981 to 1983.
24. Interview with Douglas Hurd, 26 Nov. 1996.
25. Ibid.

2

A Gentleman and a King's Scholar:
Eton, September 1942–July 1948

For a young Colleger¹ of only twelve-and-a-half, like Douglas Hurd, arriving in the September 1942 'Election',² wartime Eton meant occasional air raids and food rationing. Despite the threat of bombs landing on the school, Claude Elliot, Headmaster of Eton, had decided not to evacuate the boys during the Second World War. On the whole, the decision worked to the benefit of the boys and the unity of the College. In doing so, he avoided the difficult adjustments which London-based public schools like Westminster suffered in the post-war period. Douglas Hurd's time at Eton spanned the end of one Provost's tenure and the beginning of another: Lord Hugh Cecil was succeeded in 1945 by Henry Marten, a former history master, then Vice Provost at Eton. Lord Hugh Cecil, former Member of Parliament for Oxford University, and son of the nineteenth-century Prime Minister, the Marquess of Salisbury, was ennobled in 1942 by Winston Churchill, becoming Lord Quickswood. Together with Claude Elliot, they gave uninspiring leadership to the College, but Elliot's grasp of finance, his bureaucratic skill in balancing the books, presaged a later trend in education.

Despite the wartime rationing, 'Hurd, K.S.' and the other boys were well-fed thanks to the formidable efforts of the Matron-in-College, Miss Elsie Iredale-Smith. She was in effect the domestic bursar in charge of the health and feeding of the Collegers. Nicknamed 'The Airedale', she could be very fierce at times, as Douglas Hurd recalls:

> To the young Colleger she might, at first, seem intimidating, with her small, dumpy figure, sharp nose, and strict insistence on the rules. Nothing good came to the scholar caught unwashed in bed, or preparing for early school with a torch under the bedclothes.³

But she was also capable of remarkable acts of kindness. Hurd recalls that she took immense trouble to ensure he was able to sit the Newcastle examination in March 1947 while he was suffering from chickenpox.[4] Miss Iredale-Smith eventually retired to a flat near Sloane Square in Chelsea, where according to Hurd, 'she used to buy huge quantities of food from Harrods'.[5] All manner of former boys, who had gone on to become civil servants, generals and judges, called round for tea at her flat. Douglas Hurd was among the most assiduous of visitors and he felt moved to pen an affectionate obituary in *The Times*, when she died at the grand old age of ninety-six. Miss Iredale-Smith had inherited a considerable amount of money, and again demonstrated her generosity to Douglas Hurd by giving him a small sum to help him put his three boys from his first marriage through Eton. Nicholas, Thomas and Alexander were all educated at Eton and Philip, Hurd's son from his second marriage, also followed his father's example.

In their first year at Eton, new Collegers were obliged to sleep in a long, thin hall called 'Long Chamber', sometimes known simply as 'Chamber'. Housing around fifteen boys, Chamber was laid out like an open dormitory, but partitioned into stalls where the boys slept. At the end of Long Chamber were the 'Red Rooms'. These were usually reserved for the Captain of Long Chamber, normally a boy from the year above, and his deputy. In his second year, Hurd became Captain of Chamber, but during his first year, he fell seriously ill with tuberculosis, and because of this, was permitted to sleep for a time in one of the Red Rooms.

A key influence on Hurd at this difficult time was the Master-in-College,[6] Dr Walter Hamilton. Having started his academic career as a fellow at Trinity College, Cambridge, Hamilton subsequently found his true forte was as a schoolmaster. A close friend in the same Election as Hurd remembers Walter Hamilton quickly identifying Douglas as a favourite. Perhaps it was because Hurd and Hamilton were both highly intelligent but fundamentally shy in nature that they became friends. Many former pupils testify to Walter Hamilton's special gift of being able to earn their friendship, by disarming himself in a manner not unlike the philosopher Socrates. Hamilton was often 'down in the dumps' and his moods, often sending himself up, reminded many of A.A. Milne's character Eeyore. His scowl was also legendary, and as he became more rotund, this only added to the comic effect. Writing the foreword to a special portrait of Walter Hamilton compiled by Donald Wright (former Headmaster of Shrewsbury School), Douglas Hurd brought out the paradox of 'someone whose appearance and expressed outlook on life were often wreathed in gloom, but who was one of the happiest men I have known.'[7]

After 1950, Walter Hamilton was never quite so melancholy again, having found remarkable happiness in his young wife, the exceptionally beautiful Jane

Burrows, whose brother Tim was two years above Hurd at Eton. The closeness between Douglas and Walter was revealed when Douglas became godfather to one of the Hamilton's sons.

Hamilton's influence on Hurd lay not so much in his academic skills, as in his intellectual personality.[8] Although Hurd was extremely bright as a boy of twelve, at that age he found in Walter Hamilton someone who helped shape his character by imbuing him with a strong sense of moral principle, teaching him what was the right way and the wrong way to do things, when to laugh and when not to, how to conduct one's relations with other people: in a word, how to be civilised. In Douglas Hurd's words, he 'helped to form the tastes of a shy and abrupt boy'.[9]

Hamilton was also able to broaden Hurd's outlook on life beyond books and exams. Hurd recalls that Walter Hamilton would invite the boys into his study on Sunday evenings to listen to readings of Jane Austen, Trollope or his favourite, P.G. Wodehouse.

Walter Hamilton's capacity for eccentricity and mirth was most evident during his regular holidays in the north-west Highlands. Douglas, who had already been introduced to the area by his equally eccentric Uncle Robert, was friends with – and in the same Election as – Jacky Shaw-Stewart, whose parents owned Morar Lodge, near Arisaig on the north-west coast of Scotland. Walter Hamilton and Douglas Hurd were regularly invited to stay with the Shaw-Stewarts during the Easter and Summer holidays in the late 1940s. Walter rented the Gatehouse of Traigh from the Shaw-Stewarts, which looked out onto the islands of Rhum and Eigg. Hurd has fond memories of 'shark-fishing with Gavin Maxwell (a friend of Hamilton's) on the Minch, Chateau Yquem in profusion, Monopoly, extraordinary golf in the rain, sunsets over Skye, gossip, a constant coming of young and old'.[10] In 1954 Walter Hamilton bought a house on the island of Mull, and Hurd would go up to visit his old Master-in-College. Douglas Hurd retained a love of the Highlands, using it as a kind of sanctuary from the rigours of ministerial life. He would stay with the Shaw-Stewarts and enjoy Scottish Country dancing on the Isle of Skye or perhaps help out with a spot of hay-making on the farm: even when he was on holiday, it was characteristic of Douglas Hurd not to idle about.

In later life, Hurd kept in touch with Walter Hamilton. In those days, it was the custom for Old Etonians to correspond with their former schoolmasters, but the sheer weight of correspondence between Walter Hamilton and his former boys reveals the respect and affection in which he was held. It is clear that Walter Hamilton influenced not only Douglas Hurd but a whole generation of boys at Eton.

In 1938, Hamilton admitted in a letter to his great friend James Duff that 'politics are not really my thing'.[11] However, many of the principles which Hurd has espoused throughout his life have their roots in Walter Hamilton. He taught Hurd to be on his guard against ideology, extremes and the sloganising of the Sophists, stressing instead the Socratic belief that problems could be solved by rational argument between like-minded people.[12] Neither had time for rabble-rousing populists. Even a cursory analysis of Hurd's speeches as a senior minister reveals constant references to 'balance', 'rational argument' and 'good sense' or 'commonsense'.

Despite being only twelve-and-a-half – and being ill – Hurd thrived in the highly competitive atmosphere of College, and zoomed up his Election, doing well in the end-of-term exams, which were called 'trials'. When it came to 'final order', Hurd finished third in a highly distinguished academic year. Final-order exams were crucial (they no longer exist) because at the end of their sixth term (or 'half' as school terms were known at Eton), boys would sit their Schools Certificate (their equivalent of 'O' level), and thence might go on to specialise in subjects like English or History. Because this was the last occasion when the boys could be compared with each other, final order determined their place in College, and whether one could become Captain of the School, which denoted the highest ranking Colleger remaining in the school from final order.

The highest-placed Colleger in Douglas Hurd's Election was Charles (later Sir) Willink, whose father, 'Happy' Harry Willink, was Churchill's Minister of Health. Charles Willink was extremely good at passing exams and became Captain of the School, but went on to become an unexceptional housemaster at Eton. Just above Douglas Hurd in final order was Hurd's friend Raef Payne. He too went back to Eton from Trinity College, Cambridge, becoming a brilliant schoolmaster and a much-loved Eton figure, and also emulated Walter Hamilton by becoming Master-in-College. Raef Payne was a talented artist and painted portraits of both Douglas Hurd and Sir Antony Acland, which now hang in the Provost's Lodge. It is a good likeness of the young Hurd. His appearance is upright, pensive with flushed cheeks – which were quite noticeable in his youth – but with a certain nobility about him.

During his time at Eton, Douglas made friends with Acland, an Oppidan who went on to become Permanent Under-Secretary of State at the Foreign Office and Head of the Diplomatic Service from 1982 to 1986. Sir Antony was made Provost of Eton in 1991 at the time when Hurd was a Fellow. He recalls being very impressed, in view of the Foreign Secretary's hectic schedule, at how often Hurd was able to attend the meetings of the governing body: out of six meetings a year, Hurd regularly attended four, rather in the same way as Peter Carrington had done before him. The issues addressed, such as the College accounts, could be fairly mundane, but Hurd did not stint during his visits, often staying on afterwards for lunch. One such occasion was right in the middle of the Qualified Majority Voting row of March 1994, when Hurd felt, after several weeks hard pounding on this issue, the need to spend a day away from it. Sir Antony has suggested that this was for Hurd 'a sort of relaxation. He was back on his familiar ground . . . and felt that he was at home.'[13] Sometimes, Hurd would fly in to RAF Northolt from a foreign visit, arrive at the College without much warning, have a quick bath and change, before making the trip down to Oxfordshire for a constituency engagement. No one minded Hurd using Eton as a staging-post; he never expected any special treatment because he was Foreign Secretary. Hurd's continued association with the College as a Fellow, and the fact that all his sons have been sent there, illustrate just how important a part the College has played in his life.

The most handsome young man in the September 1942 Election was Hurd's friend Tony Lloyd, who finished just below him in final order. Lloyd and other contemporaries confirm the story which appeared in the newspapers, that as young boys, Hurd used to say he wanted to be Foreign Secretary, whilst Lloyd said he wanted to be Attorney-General.[14] As things turned out, whilst Douglas had his schoolboy dream fulfilled, Lord Lloyd did not quite achieve his, although he became a distinguished high court judge, and in 1993 was made Lord Appeal in Ordinary. Intellectually, Willink, Payne, Hurd and Lloyd made a formidable foursome, and some boys further down final order and younger boys in the 1943 Election, had an inferiority complex about them. One member of the 1943 Election recalls, 'Douglas Hurd and those three exuding an air of brilliance.'[15] All four decided to go to Trinity College, Cambridge, partly because they regarded it as the blue ribbon College at Cambridge, partly reflecting their desire to go on together, and partly following the advice and example of Walter Hamilton, who went back to Trinity in 1945 (but had left for Westminster before the four arrived in 1950).

Although Douglas excelled at passing exams, he was not a good athlete, except for a game exclusive to Eton called 'The Wall Game'. Hurd himself admits that The Wall Game 'did not require a great deal of dexterity'.[16] It consisted of pushing the other side almost ceaselessly and then advancing, often with little result. Hurd was quite large physically for his age and according to his life-long friend Timothy Raison (from the 1943 Election), 'very tenacious' when it came to shoving back the Oppidan opposition.[17] A photograph appeared in *The Tatler and Bystander* of Hurd playing The Wall Game for the Collegers against the Oppidans on St Andrew's Day, 1947. During his days at Cambridge, Hurd returned to Eton to play in one of the scratch sides put together in order to give the College Wall Game team practice for their game against the Oppidans.

However, when it came to most ball games, Hurd moved rather clumsily around the field of play. This may in part have been due to his deteriorating eyesight. When he first went to Eton, Hurd only wore his spectacles for reading; by his final year he was wearing them continuously, but it was not so bad as to prevent him doing his National Service. Neither did it prevent him from becoming a mean hand at table tennis, which he used to play on the narrow polished oak table in the upper boys' common room. During his National Service training at Oswestry, Hurd would also play ping-pong at the local NAAFI Club.[18]

Despite not being good at games, Hurd was not regarded by his contemporaries as a 'sap' or a swot. True, there was an element of compulsion about games at Eton, but Hurd showed emerging self-discipline by his willingness to participate in activities at which he did not excel. Eventually, Hurd became Captain of the College 'A' Field Game team. Contemporaries recall Hurd as being a strict captain.[19]

On the question of Douglas Hurd as a disciplinarian, a myth has grown up in recent years that he delivered regular beatings to younger boys, earning him the sobriquet, 'Hitler Hurd'. No evidence has emerged to suggest that Hurd earned a reputation for beating boys. As Captain of Long Chamber, in his second year, he was in charge of the younger boys, and could administer a disciplinary beating with a length of stout rubber hose known as 'the siphon'. Later on, as Captain of the School, it was occasionally Hurd's responsibility to administer beatings with a cane. The tales of 'Hitler Hurd' seem to be almost entirely the invention of *Private Eye*. Certainly, Hurd has a strong sense of self-discipline, and years later, as a senior minister, especially in Northern Ireland and the Home Office, he proved to be tough when dealing with the brutalities of power. But it was part of Hurd's duty as a senior to administer beatings to younger boys, and it seems he neither did so regularly nor gained any morbid satisfaction from the task. To suggest otherwise is to misunderstand his character.

Hurd's greatest academic achievement at Eton came in March 1947 when he won the Newcastle Scholarship. This examination was competed for by the top twenty-five or so Classicists at Eton, and involved gruelling tests in Latin, Greek and Divinity. Winning the Newcastle meant that Hurd was the best classical scholar in his year. When he gained a Major Scholarship to Cambridge, his university entry was secured. This success presented Hurd with something of a difficulty because he wanted to stay on beyond his normal spell of five years to become Captain of the School, and yet he had achieved the highest accolade in classics. Hurd therefore had a year in hand, with which to specialise in something else. He decided to switch to history, although he remembers there was 'a certain amount of clucking about that'.[20]

The most influential figure in persuading Hurd to switch to history was, paradoxically, a classics master. Richard Martineau was a brilliant classics beak who taught the headmaster's top division, known as 'A1'. He persuaded a reluctant Douglas Hurd to read Macaulay's *History of England*. Soon after, Hurd was to be seen sitting under a tree in Martineau's garden, ploughing his way through the great episodes in English history.[21] Hurd found the experience rewarding, and at the end of his year of history, he finished runner-up for the Rosebery Prize, pipped only by his new friend, Simon Barrington-Ward, who went on to become Bishop of Coventry. Both produced very good answers – Hurd's was commended as being worthy of a top civil servant, but Barrington-Ward's answer was regarded by the examiners as outstanding.[22]

As part of their education, boys in the Sixth Form were obliged to learn texts from world literature or politics or history in a language of their choice, and recite long passages in front of their peers on the big day of 4 June. The custom of 'speeches' seems to have had a major impact on boys in later life. It gave them the chance to develop their public-speaking skills, and an interest in language, text, rhetoric and political argument. Hurd's close friend, Tony Lloyd, learned passages of English prose, which he still remembers to this day.[23] The recollection of his contemporaries is that Douglas chose Cicero and spoke in Latin. As a senior minister, Douglas Hurd would often use classical, literary and artistic references in his speeches. Sometimes it was an allusion to Cicero or Homer, at other times a comparison with a painting by Landseer.

As Captain of the School, he came into more contact with Oppidan boys. It was a feature of life at Eton that until a boy's later years, he did not know many boys outside his own house, unless he shared the same tutor.[24] In this way, Hurd became friends with Philip Ziegler, an Oppidan, who went on to become a noted biographer of Mountbatten and Harold Wilson.

In his final year, Hurd edited the *Eton College Chronicle*, a position traditionally held jointly by an Oppidan and a Colleger. Hurd was succeeded by Timothy Raison, whose father knew Anthony Hurd after a brief partnership in establishing the agricultural journal, *Farmer's Weekly*.[25] As part of the 1943 Election, Tim had first got to know Douglas when Douglas was Captain of Chamber. Sir Timothy Raison went on to become Minister of State at the Foreign Office from 1979 to 1983, and then Minister for Overseas Development until 1986. By a quirk of fate, just as Hurd moved from the Foreign Office to the Home Office, Raison moved in the opposite direction, so their ministerial contact was limited. However, they remained close friends, and holidayed together at Arisaig with the Shaw-Stewarts in the summer of 1980. While picnicking in the middle of the north-west Highlands, they were to be found debating light-heartedly whose responsibility it was to handle immigration cases; the Minister at the Home Office or the Minister at the Foreign Office.

Hurd succeeded another very close friend, Tony Lloyd, as head of the Political Society at Eton. Because of the College's proximity to London, coupled with the enticement of an agreeable dinner afterwards, it was relatively easy to persuade often quite famous men to come to speak. Notable speakers at the time included Peter Thorneycroft, the Foreign Secretary, Ernest Bevin, and the Archbishop of Canterbury, Lord Fisher of Lambeth.

It was also during his final year that Douglas befriended John Barton, a gifted Oppidan, who was to become one of the founders of the Royal Shakespeare Company and director of many fine productions, mostly Shakespearian, in the 1960s, 1970s and 1980s. The threat of air raids is often held up as the reason why there were no plays staged at Eton until after the Second World War. In reality, in contrast to the thriving theatrical scene at Eton in the 1990s, in the 1940s, Claude Elliot, the Headmaster, disapproved of plays. Despite bureaucratic resistance from on high, Barton persisted, and, with the aid of a theatre-loving housemaster named E.P. Hedley, persuaded Elliot to give the go-ahead, provided their were no 'tarts' in the company![26] Barton made his directorial début with a truly fine production of Shakespeare's *Henry IV, Part I*. The motivation for the play was not Barton's wish to pursue a career in theatre – for he had no preconceived plan to become a theatre director – it was that he, along with several other boys, was deeply interested in literature, political argument and public speaking. Moreover, they had the freedom as senior boys to try out things which they had not done before.[27] The reason for selecting *Henry IV, Part I* was that many of them had been to London to see Laurence Olivier and Ralph Richardson star in a very great production of the play.

The final cast list comprised John Barton as Hotspur; Raef Payne as Falstaff; Julian Slade (of *Salad Days*, renowned then for his amusing caricatures of schoolmasters and their wives) as Prince Hal; Tim Raison as Henry IV; Antony Acland was Bardolph; Robin Tuck as Owen Glendower; and Tony Lloyd as Lady Mortimer. There was much amusement as Tony Lloyd had to dress up as Lady Mortimer and sing a song in a supposedly Welsh accent. Not knowing any Welsh, Lloyd made up some words in gobbledegook.[28] In an inspired piece of casting, Barton chose the modern day Earl of March to play one of his ancestors, Edmund Mortimer, the Earl of March.

Douglas Hurd was cast as the Earl of Worcester. In one scene, Douglas, as the Earl of Worcester, has a stand-up row with the King, played by Tim Raison. It is one of Shakespeare's great political attack speeches, and it is understandable why an aspiring politician like Douglas Hurd was keen to play the part. The Earl of Worcester accuses the King, who has deposed Richard II, of seeking political advantage. But Worcester has a treacherous side to him as well. The part of Worcester is not a major role, but he also has another important scene where he restrains the mad-brained Hotspur, telling him to stop waffling and talk serious politics. All round, it is an appealing part for a politician to play.

A close friend and member of the cast claims Douglas Hurd was 'rather stiff',[29] but John Barton recalls that Douglas Hurd brought the right amount of steel to the part and possessed the rare gift of being able to play irony.[30] An old '78 record was made of some of the scenes by five of the boys and a copy survives to this day. Later, at Cambridge, Barton cast Hurd in the first ever play he wrote. It was about a medieval cricket match and was entitled *That's All One*. Douglas Hurd played the part of the rebel leader who kills the Lord of Misrule, and puts a cold, realistic political hand across the proceedings.

That final year at Eton was enormously enjoyable for Hurd. He made new friends and broadened his interests. Eton had been not unlike a university for boys, where most of their time was their own and where they had their own room. It was indeed a place of privilege, which opened doors to Hurd, but in later years the media, the electorate and some of his fellow politicians were to fail to understand that, although he was from a comfortable, middle-class family, he had risen to near the top in terms of academic excellence through merit alone. Among a group of very able contemporaries, he stood out as one of the most able. Not only was Hurd considered by his peers to be in the first flight of intelligence, they perceived him as having judgement, commonsense and a certain noblity. But while his character was noble, his background was not. Eton had also taught Hurd, despite his natural shyness, to be a robust and self-disciplined young man with a strong sense of duty. Essentially, he has always been the same sort of person. Obviously he matured, but what he was as a young man was implicit in what he became. The fact that he said he wanted to be Foreign Secretary from an early age indicates a clear-sightedness, but throughout his life, he would never allow himself to be changed or corrupted by power: each step on the ministerial ladder was unplanned. However, after he left Eton, two tough experiences tested his reserves of self-discipline and robustness to the full.

Notes

1. The boys at Eton were divided into 'Collegers' and 'Oppidans'. Collegers were those boys who had passed a scholarship examination in May/June, while Oppidans, originally called 'Commensuals', had done 'Common Entrance'. Oppidans were normally the sons of wealthy individuals, although Oppidan scholars existed.
2. Collegers arrived in September or January, depending on where they finished on the scholarship list. Each entry of boys was known as an 'Election'.
3. Douglas Hurd, 'Obituary. Miss Elsie Iredale-Smith', *The Times*, 20 Jan. 1988.
4. Ibid.
5. Interview with Douglas Hurd, 26 Nov. 1996.

6. The post of Master-in-College dated from the sixteenth century when the headmaster, needing more time to deal with his wider duties, appointed a deputy to be master in, but not of, College. The 1862 Royal Commission Report into Eton College summarised the post of Master-in-College as 'an ill-paid young gentleman, specially deputed by the Head Master to live familiarly among Collegers and to act as their guide and friend, but not their tutor', quoted from Robert Bourne, 'The Way He Should Go', in Donald Wright (ed.), *Walter Hamilton, 1908–1988: A Portrait* (James & James [Publishers] Ltd: London, 1992), p.39.

7. Douglas Hurd, 'Foreword', in Wright (ed.), *Walter Hamilton*.

8. Walter Hamilton left Eton in 1945, three years before Hurd, to become again a Fellow at Trinity College Cambridge. He went on to become a distinguished headmaster first of Westminster then of Rugby, and finally Master of Magdalene College, Cambridge. He served with distinction on the Committee of the Headmaster's Conference, the body representing the interests of public schools, from 1953 to 1966, and was its Chairman for four years.

9. Douglas Hurd, 'Foreword', in Wright (ed.), *Walter Hamilton*.

10. Ibid.

11. James Duff became Warden of Durham University and later became a Fellow of Trinity College, Cambridge; *see* 'Letter from Walter Hamilton to James Duff, 2 October 1938', in Wright (ed.) *Walter Hamilton*, pp. 66, 59.

12. *See* a lecture given by Walter Hamilton in Guildford Cathedral, entitled 'Education and the Search for Truth', reproduced in Chapter Nine, Wright (ed.) *Walter Hamilton*, pp. 157–70.

13. Interview with Sir Antony Acland, 17 Mar. 1997.

14. Interview with Lord Lloyd of Berwick, 25 Nov. 1996.

15. Private information.

16. Interview with Douglas Hurd, 26 Nov. 1996.

17. Interview with Sir Timothy Raison, 23 Jul. 1996.

18. NAAFI stands for Navy, Army and Air Force Institutes. They are used as canteens and places of basic entertainment for servicemen.

19. Private information.

20. Interview with Douglas Hurd, 26 Nov. 1996.

21. Ibid.

22. Conversation with Douglas Hurd, 22 Jul. 1996.

23. Interview with Tony Lloyd, 25 Nov. 1996.

24. Ziegler and Hurd shared the same history tutor, Mr Routh, an amiable bachelor who was also Ziegler's housemaster.

25. Interview with Sir Timothy Raison, 23 Jul. 1996.

26. Interview with John Barton, 22 Jul. 1997.
27. Ibid.
28. Interview with Lord Lloyd of Berwick, 25 Nov. 1996.
29. Private information.
30. Interview with John Barton, 22 Jul. 1997.

3

The Mast: National Service and Cambridge, 1948–1952

At the end of July 1948, Douglas Hurd found himself catapulted from the enclosed, often idyllic world of Eton, into the army. Like many other intelligent young men of his generation, he did not relish the prospect. As he attended a dinner with Richard Martineau and a few other boys one pleasant summer's evening, he thought for a moment that the cloud on the horizon had been blown away, albeit temporarily. A few days before, word had reached him that his call-up, originally set for 26 July, had been postponed for a fortnight. Alas, a contemporary arrived with the news that the War Office had changed their minds. Perhaps in order to avoid accusations of favouritism, the authorities insisted that University entrants would have to arrive as previously stated. On hearing the news, Douglas Hurd wished knowledge could have been deferred until after that happy evening. On the following Monday, the boys from Eton would be off to the army to become men after all.

In reality, school leavers who had already secured a place at University were treated relatively leniently by the War Office. Provided they agreed to be called up immediately, the army agreed to release them in time to take up their University places in the autumn of the following year. This meant that those like Douglas – who joined in July 1948 – could expect to be out of the army by October 1949. Hurd's year were lucky: their successors were caught by the advent of the Korean War in 1950, which raised the basic minimum of National Service from eighteen months to two years.

In deciding to go into the Royal Artillery, Douglas revealed something about his lack of enthusiasm for National Service. Had he been more willing, perhaps he would have joined the Brigade of Guards or the Rifle Brigade. Instead, his diary entries from the time are peppered with fractions, one tenth, one eighth, etc., representing the proportion of time he had served.¹ At the beginning at least, he was counting the days before he would be able to go to Trinity College, Cambridge.

On 26 July 1948, a reluctant Hurd arrived at Oswestry for his scheduled eight weeks of basic training. It was a warm summer, and the new recruits were extremely uncomfortable as they marched up and down the parade ground. There were even press reports at the time of men going out on runs in full kit and collapsing and dying! In the first week, Tim Ryder – a member of the 1943 Election who entered the Royal Artillery on the same day as Hurd – recalls being sent out with Hurd on a fatigue to scythe grass along a railway siding between Shrewsbury and Oswestry. It was terribly hot and everyone was exhausted by the end of the day.² There was no comforting news from the outside world either. This was also the lamentable week when England set Australia over four hundred in their second innings at Headingley, only for England to lose the match, with Don Bradman scoring a hundred.

There were, however, one or two compensations in the early days. The men could go down to Oswestry town where there was a NAAFI Club and a table-tennis table where Hurd could brush up on his skills. Because those with University places had arrived a fortnight earlier than originally planned, when the full batch of recruits arrived to start their training, Hurd and a few others were given a day's leave. They were rounded up in a big truck and allowed to visit Chester for the day. Evensong in a peaceful village church was another solace.

After three-and-a-half weeks, Hurd's group moved on for another eight weeks in a different regiment at Oswestry. At this time, things started to go badly wrong for Douglas. In the first few weeks, he had been suffering from a poisoned right index finger, and found he could not polish his boots with his right hand, and so was forced to clean them left-handed. Then he had the misfortune to become ill with pneumonia. One contemporary remembers being on the parade ground one morning when suddenly a figure came into sight, staggering along with all his kit on his back. When the figure came into fuller view, the parade party realised it was Douglas on his way to the medical room. He had just reported sick and had to go through the inhumane task of carrying all his kit.

His friend, Tony Lloyd, then in the Coldstream Guards, went to visit Hurd in hospital. He kept in touch with friends by letter. Hurd admits 'it wasn't a desperate period, but certainly it was one of the less happy times.'³ He had to draw on his deep reserves of self-discipline and his strong sense of duty. After a stint of officer training at Mons, in Surrey, he obtained a commission in March 1949 as a Second Lieutenant, joining the Fifth Regiment of the Royal Horse Artillery at Larkhill on Salisbury Plain. He was comforted by the fact that his

Oppidan friend Antony Acland was in the same regiment, although not in the same battery. However, they were able to meet in the officer's mess in the evenings.

After his unfortunate illness, Hurd began at least to tolerate his National Service. At Larkhill, he was in charge of 25-pounders, and his job was to take the artillery pieces out onto Salisbury Plain, set them up on the correct firing range, and fire them off onto a designated piece of downland. He admits he was not exactly a born soldier, but the time passed more quickly than it had at Oswestry. The experience seemed to toughen Hurd mentally and temperamentally. He responded to the discipline of the army, and in later life drove himself quite hard, organising his life with remarkable self-discipline. After completing his National Service, Douglas Hurd did something odd. In 1952, he volunteered for a scheme where ex-servicemen could return to the army for a few weeks of refresher training. Hurd claims he did it 'partly because I wanted to show myself that I could do it, even though I was quite glad to be out of the army'.⁴ The episode illustrates two very important facets of Hurd's character. He is imbued with a very strong sense of duty and self-discipline, but just sometimes, he has a tendency to take the duty and the self-discipline a shade beyond the human norm; there is a touch of the Captain Oates about Douglas Hurd.

Whilst his experience of National Service was apparently too short to have any major influence on his life, something happened at Cambridge connected with the army which affected him far more deeply. During Douglas's second year at Trinity College, his younger brother Julian committed suicide. He was just nineteen. Perhaps the driving force behind Julian's decision to shoot himself was his detestation of army life. Recently, Hurd has found a number of letters from his father to senior army figures, questioning what was done to help National Servicemen who had this difficulty. Some months after the tragedy, Anthony Hurd asked the Commanding Officer of the Mons Officer Cadet School (where Julian had been training) to dinner to discuss this. Douglas Hurd remembers the occasion. The conversation was friendly, but did not get far.⁵ The circumstances surrounding the death of his brother may partly explain Douglas's decision to go back into the army for refresher training in 1952. Perhaps he wanted to prove that a Hurd was tough enough to handle the rigours of army life. Hurd's mother, Stephanie, was a great source of strength at the time, but close friends at Cambridge understandably found it difficult to talk to Douglas about his grief. One or two contemporaries had been killed in Malaya while serving in the army, but this was the first time anyone had come face to face with this sort of tragedy.

Hurd's robust nature pulled him through, and he went on to become a successful undergraduate, succeeding Greville Janner – later Labour MP for

Leicester West – as President of the Cambridge Union, and Geoffrey Howe as Chairman of the Cambridge University Conservative Association. Other near-contemporaries included Norman St John-Stevas, who later became Mrs Thatcher's first Leader of the House of Commons and Chancellor of the Duchy of Lancaster. In his memoirs, St John-Stevas recalls first hearing about his hero, Walter Bagehot, through a Cambridge Union debate about the reform of Parliament when Douglas Hurd quoted him.[6] Percy Cradock, who became Ambassador to China and later a foreign policy adviser to Mrs Thatcher and John Major, was another near-contemporary as was Simon Barrington-Ward, who, although he was at Magdalene College, remained good friends with Hurd. However, Hurd did not make any notable new friends at Cambridge. It was the core of friends at Eton with whom he continued to keep in touch: Tim Raison and Antony Acland went to Christ Church, Oxford, and he remained firm friends with Tony Lloyd who was in Trinity College and read classics initially, before switching to law.

The end of the war and the long summer holidays provided Hurd with the opportunity to go abroad. In 1950, Tim Raison and Douglas visited Italy. At Lake Garda, they were inspired by 'Frater Ave Atque Vale', a Tennyson poem, to row from Desenzano to Sirmione, though half-way they got tired and turned the boat around. But his most memorable trip abroad occurred in the late spring of 1951. By coincidence, Antony Acland's twenty-first birthday fell on 12 March – only four days after Douglas Hurd's. Antony Acland's father gave him a return air ticket to Athens as a birthday present. Acland had the idea of asking Douglas Hurd and Tony Lloyd if they would like to accompany him on holiday. A magical six weeks ensued, in which the three hitch-hiked their way around Greece.

In the early 1950s, there were very few tourists – they had the stadium of Delphi entirely to themselves. When they reached the horseshoe-shaped theatre at Epidaurus, Tony Lloyd – forever the actor – insisted on declaiming from the stage while Douglas and Antony sat up at the back stalls to determine if he was audible from there. Lloyd's recital of Greek verse could indeed be heard from the back of the fourth century theatre. Late twentieth-century Greece is linked up by impressive roads, paid for by the European Union's Regional Development Fund. In 1951, the three travellers often had to choose more primitive ways of getting around. On one occasion they hitched a lorry carrying a load of sheep, but there was only room for two in the front cab with the driver. Douglas Hurd drew the short straw, riding with the sheep in the back, a fate which Acland would tease him about in later life when, as Foreign Secretary, Hurd became accustomed to being driven about in ambassadorial Rolls Royces flanked by police escorts. On another occasion, they reached a river in flood and had to hold onto the tail of a donkey to make the crossing, up to their shoulders in the cold water.

Towards the end of their holiday, the three young men took in the Greek islands of Mikonos, Dhilos and Tinos. After visiting Dhilos, they needed to hire a little boat to get them to the other side of the island to catch the big boat back to Mikonos. Douglas Hurd and Tony Lloyd tried to use their knowledge of Homeric Greek to negotiate with the fishermen, but in the end, Antony Acland's passable grasp of German as a modern-languages student proved more useful. As a consequence of the German occupation of Greece in the Second World War, a number of the local population spoke German.[7]

Academically, Trinity College was not as seminal for Hurd as Eton had been. He had entered Cambridge as a Major Scholar, which placed him in the top four or five students, and entitled him to stay in College accommodation rather than in digs. During his first year, his home was New Court, Trinity, before moving across to Great Court for his second year. His history tutors included George Kitson Clark and John Gallagher. Gallagher was then a young don, and became Professor J.A. Gallagher, distinguished historian of Navy and Empire, who wrote *The Imperial Idea and Its Enemies*, and famously collaborated with R.E. Robinson on the subject of imperialism in Africa to propound the 'Robinson-Gallagher thesis' in *Africa and the Victorians* (1961). Other history tutors included Michael Vyvyan and Walter Ullmann, the latter a medievalist and expert on ecclesiastical history. Hurd's specialised subject was the Second French Republic. He enjoyed reading in the University library and finished with first class honours.

Hurd's main regret at Cambridge was spending so much time running the Union and the Conservative Association. As President of the Union, Hurd describes the process of organising speakers to come to Cambridge as 'a bit of a chore'.[8] The most memorable speaker was Enoch Powell, renowned even then for his gifts of oratory. To this day, Hurd has a recurring nightmare that a speaker has let him down at the last minute, and another, of a looming examination for which he had done no work.[9]

During Hurd's three years at Cambridge, there were two General Elections: one in February 1950, which Labour won narrowly, and one in October 1951, which the Conservatives won narrowly with more seats, but less of the popular vote. The constituencies of Cambridge and Cambridgeshire were both marginal Labour seats which were recaptured by Conservative candidates William Hamilton Kerr and Stephen Gerald Howard respectively. Hurd recalls helping with the Conservative campaign: distributing leaflets and heckling the Labour candidates from the back of village halls. In later life, he retained a great love of electioneering, especially the idea of old-fashioned meetings in town halls, but he still regrets spending so much of his University time in political activities. Could he have his time again, he would prefer to devote more time to other pursuits, such as music and painting.

Above all, Hurd's time at Cambridge had been overshadowed by the death of his brother, Julian. He wrote letters to friends trying to set out his feelings about it, but it was often easier to talk with more recent associates than with his close friends from Eton. Whilst walking with a fellow diplomat one winter's evening in Peking in the mid 1950s, Hurd – fond of analogies from an early age – compared friendship to a mast. A tall flag pole, he said, could only stand up to the wind if it was properly anchored with halliards. If one had a large number of tethers (friends), one could withstand the wind. Douglas needed friends as anchorages. Far from conforming to his later public image as a supremely confident statesman exuding an air of detached competence, Douglas Hurd is a deeply thoughtful, intelligent man, who, like most of mankind, harboured doubts about his own abilities and valued friendship throughout his ministerial career.

Notes

1. Diary Readings with Douglas Hurd, 26 Nov. 1996.
2. Interview with Dr Timothy Ryder, 17 Feb. 1996; Tim Ryder later became a Lecturer and finally Reader in Classics at the University of Hull, before taking up a similar appointment at Reading University in 1990. After their first few weeks of army training, Hurd and Ryder did not keep in touch.
3. Interview with Douglas Hurd, 26 Nov. 1996.
4. Ibid.
5. Letter from Douglas Hurd to the author, 25 May 1998.
6. Norman St John-Stevas, *In Two Cities* (Faber & Faber, London: 1984), p. 52.
7. Interview with Sir Antony Acland, 17 Mar. 1997.
8. Interview with Douglas Hurd, 26 Nov. 1996.
9. Ibid.

4

The Diplomatic Life, 1952–1966

On leaving Cambridge, Douglas Hurd was very keen to pursue a political career, but in the early 1950s there were only a limited number of routes into Parliament. Conservative candidates were usually drawn from the army, or through one of the professions, or via the business and financial sectors. There was, as Hurd was often heard to remark in later life, 'no ladder leading student politicians straight into politics'.[1] Douglas's father was the key influence at this juncture in persuading him that before he considered standing for Parliament, he needed to earn a living in the real world.[2]

In deciding which career path to follow, Hurd was fortunate to meet with Sir Roger Makins, then a senior Foreign Office official, with whom he conversed on the terrace of the House of Commons. Makins – who was made a hereditary peer in 1964, becoming Lord Sherfield – was a tall, commanding figure of a man who became Ambassador to Washington in 1953. Hurd was suitably inspired, and emulated Makins by finishing top of the Foreign Office exam. Although Hurd is excessively modest by inclination, he is extremely proud of this achievement.[3] Finishing in first place helped to banish some of the lingering doubts about his own abilities.

Hurd was interviewed by an unnamed admiral about the possibility of joining MI6, but declined the offer. In 1952, Douglas did not want to be an unsung hero. With his mind set on a political career, he needed his achievements to be recognised by the outside world.

On taking up his Foreign Office job in London, Hurd found a flat in central London, along with two of his closest friends, Jacky Shaw-Stewart and Tim Raison. Shaw-Stewart worked in the City of London while Raison was beginning his career as a journalist. Eventually, they rented an upstairs flat in 78, Tufton Street. Conveniently situated within walking distance of the Foreign Office, the flat has since been demolished, but in those days, it was let out by two Welsh sisters, the Howell-Davis's, who ran a dairy shop beneath. Philip Ziegler, who later joined the flat when Jacky Shaw-Stewart moved back up to Scotland, describes it as 'an incredibly squalid establishment'.[4] Tim Raison is rather more charitable, acknowledging that although it was 'scruffy', it was not unclean.[5] There were only two proper bedrooms in the flat and the three friends developed a system of rotating rooms fortnightly, with one of them sleeping in the dining room at any given time.

Hurd's career has been conspicuous for the absence of jobs related to business and finance. Only his first and his most recent job (with NatWest Markets) have had any real connection with economics. Even then, both were primarily diplomatic rather than economic: Hurd is not someone who particularly enjoys studying statistics or concerning himself with the minutiae of macroeconomic policy. But that does not mean he does not understand facts and figures; merely that his attention tends to wander when turgid statistics, which have little relevance to the wider picture, are churned out. In his first job at the Economic Relations Department of the Foreign Office, Hurd had to tackle highly technical matters relating to Britain's trade relations with Latin America. Even by 1952, meat rationing had not been phased out, and consequently, Britain was forced to import vast quantities of beef, most especially from Argentina. Although Hurd found the work dull, it was important in the sense that, if one got the quantities wrong, serious consequences might follow.

At that time, a typical day's work for Foreign Office civil servants would not start before ten o'clock. This was part of a tradition dating from the last century, when the old coaches arriving at Dover laden with telegrams did not arrive in London until ten. Officials could expect to work until six or seven at night (all night during a crisis) and also every Saturday morning. New recruits did not undergo any formal training; they were merely thrown into an office and learned as they went along. In the Foreign Office, officials originated everything. Even the most insignificant paper on tractor numbers in Poland had to be summarised by a lowly official, filed correctly with a pink or white ribbon, and sent up to the next senior official. In the vast majority of cases, the file would disappear into the system. But, very rarely, one's minute might go right up, past the Permanent Secretary and come back down signed 'A.E.', denoting Anthony Eden, the Foreign Secretary. But such moments of excitement were rare. A high priority was given to observing time-honoured formalities and procedures. Douglas Hurd recalls that you never knocked on the door of a superior and one never called him 'sir', since this title was reserved for Ambassadors.[6]

One important skill which the Foreign Office taught Hurd was to draft clearly, concisely and quickly. During his years as a senior minister, several

Cabinet colleagues noted Hurd's deftness in compiling elegant summaries which required very little subsequent re-drafting.[7] However, in his first year at the Foreign Office, Hurd's foreign-language skills were found wanting. Believing himself to have a firm grasp of French from his days at Twyford Prep. and Eton, he foolishly told his superior that he could translate during a meeting with a French delegation. Hurd was given the task of compiling an account of the meeting, but his eventual report to the head of department was, in his own words, 'scanty and inaccurate'.[8]

In the Economic Relations Department, Hurd learned most of his skills from his immediate superior, Peter Ramsbotham. But during Hurd's first few weeks, Ramsbotham was preoccupied in the wake of Iran's decision to nationalise the assets of the Anglo-Iranian Oil Company. As with Sir Roger Makins, Peter Ramsbotham later became British Ambassador in Washington. In 1977, David Owen, the Foreign Secretary, saw fit to appoint James Callaghan's son-in-law Peter Jay (then Economics Editor of *The Times*), as Ambassador, and Ramsbotham received little consolation in his new post as Governor of Bermuda. In May 1977, Hurd was among those who signed an Early Day Motion in the House of Commons congratulating the Ambassador 'on his distinguished period of service and deeply regrets that the appointment of his successor should have to be justified by attacks on a public servant who cannot defend himself'. Some rather nasty comments had been made about Sir Peter at that stage, suggesting that he was snobbish, old-fashioned in style and had become rather a figure of fun. One story alleged that when Sir Peter was asked on an official form to report the number of his staff 'broken down by sex', he wrote 'None'.[9] In reality, Sir Peter established an enviable range of high-level contact in Washington. Throughout his career, Hurd has showed enormous respect and deference towards those senior to him, and because he had worked under Sir Peter, he felt it his duty to come to his defence. In March 1974, Hurd mounted a similar defence of Sir Donald Maitland when Harold Wilson appointed the defeated Labour MP Ivor Richard as British Ambassador to the United Nations.[10] In an age when deference has all but disappeared, behaviour like this appears somewhat overdone, but Hurd has always stuck to an older way of doing things, which can leave him open to a certain amount of ridicule.

Outside the world of work, Hurd and his friends socialised a great deal. As with most people in their early twenties, they led a highly collective existence. Groups of people would flow in and out of the Tufton Street flat, which became a hub for their network of friends. Douglas Hurd admits to 'parties all over London and repeated efforts to fall in love,'[11] but at this stage, it appears he was unsuccessful. A close friend describes Hurd as being 'gauche' with women.[12] No one can recall Hurd having any serious girlfriends at Eton or Cambridge, and his friends found it hard to imagine Douglas dating girls at all, because he was awkward, shy, and unable to take the lead in female company. He would have to wait until he was posted to New York before his repeated efforts to fall in love bore fruit.

Late in the night, after such an aforementioned party, Tim Raison, Philip Ziegler and Douglas would occasionally find themselves walking back to their flat in the shadow of Big Ben. If the light was shining in the tower, Philip Ziegler recalls Douglas and Tim becoming 'transfused by a desire to get in there and see what was going on'.[13] On several occasions, Ziegler would weakly agree to accompany them into the Stranger's Gallery of the House of Commons. Whilst Ziegler tried to keep his eyes open during some obscure debate, there was, he remembers 'a look of fixed delight on their faces'.[14] It was clear to Ziegler that both Douglas and Tim, but especially Douglas, wanted to go into politics. Neither Tim nor Douglas knew at the time what route they would take to become Members of Parliament – there was no preconceived plan – but they were both captivated by the workings of the House of Commons.

In May 1954, Hurd's life changed dramatically with his posting to China – his first posting abroad. In the second of his *Letters from a Diplomat* series on Radio Four, entitled 'Parades and Peking Picnics', Hurd recounts that, since the Foreign Office did not require him to take up his position in Peking until June, he decided to take the slow boat to China.

On his arrival in Peking, Hurd witnessed the high tide of Chairman Mao's revolution. Only five years before, Mao had overthrown the nationalists, and the revolution was still popular amongst the people. The biannual military parades down Tiananmen Square were spectacular events. China's sense of superiority over all other races was combined by an excessive hostility for all things Western. Diplomats who were posted out to Peking in the 1950s could expect to experience two years' hard labour. Entry permits were required to enter China and exit permits to leave. Hurd's movements within mainland China were also restricted: British diplomats were not allowed to travel more than twenty-five miles outside Peking without the permission of the Chinese authorities. In 1954, Britain was not even permitted to have an Embassy in Peking. In January 1950, the British Government decided to recognise the People's Republic of China, but the Chinese did not treat Britain as a diplomatic equal. From 1950 to 1953, the British were only allowed a diplomatic presence in Peking in the form of 'The Office of the Negotiating Representative of the British Government'. Between 1950 and 1952, Britain was in effect 'at war' with China due to the involvement of Chinese 'volunteers' in the Korean War. At the Geneva Conference of 1954, called to end the civil war in Laos, Zhou En Lai and Anthony Eden agreed that Britain should exchange diplomatic representatives at the level of chargé d'affaires. Even then, Britain was at or near the bottom of the diplomatic list. The British office remained in the old

Legation Quarter of Peking, alongside the Dutch, who were also limited to the level of chargé d'affaires. The only other Western missions, namely the Norwegians, the Danes, the Swedes, the Finns and the Swiss, enjoyed full diplomatic relations. In 1958, the British Chargé d'Affaires Office quitted the Legation Quarter and moved to a new diplomatic area in the East of Peking. The two governments exchanged ambassadors in 1972 after Britain agreed to close its Consulate in Taiwan.

But back in the 1950s, Hurd's diaries recall many tedious days spent passing the time in the magnificent compound of the old Legation Quarter in Peking, scene of the Boxer rebellion at the turn of the century. The graves of those who died were still there, adding to the embattled feel of the place. He spent a lot of time corresponding with his friends, particularly Tim Raison, Tony Lloyd and Philip Ziegler (who was then a diplomat in Laos).

The monotony of life in Peking was relieved, according to Hurd, by 'amateur theatricals, Scottish dancing, carol singing in its appointed season and too much eating and drinking'.[15] In winter, there was also the pleasure of skating on the moat of the Forbidden City. Only occasionally was Hurd able to escape from the tedium of life in Peking. In particular, Hurd has fond memories of autumn visits to the Western Hills and the Valley of the Ming Tombs. At the weekends, friends – including pretty Scandinavian secretaries – would meet up, fill a couple of cars, pack a picnic and head off for the Western Hills. Among the Swedish secretaries in Peking was Barbro Sonander, who later married Francis Noel Baker, son of Philip Noel Baker, who had been made Clement Attlee's Minister of Fuel and Power in 1950.

Another friend at the time was Alan Donald, then Third Secretary to Peking, who climbed the diplomatic ladder to become British Ambassador to China in 1988. Hurd also shared a house with John Fretwell, who became British Ambassador to France in 1982 and Deputy to the Permanent Under Secretary of State at the Foreign Office in 1987. He, Donald and Fretwell, had lunch together every day, along with another Third Secretary, Richard Evans, who served as British Ambassador to China from 1984 to 1988. In the 1950s, the Foreign Office sent officials to China to learn Chinese after a year of grounding in London rather than sending out people already proficient in the language as now. Evans and Donald were language students in China for a year, before joining the Embassy's Chinese Secretariat which dealt mainly with domestic politics. Douglas Hurd and John Fretwell worked in the Chancery, dealing with trade, consular and external affairs. Richard Evans remembers several weekend visits to Chinese temples, describing the group of young diplomats as 'temple haunters'.[16]

In 1956, Douglas Hurd and Alan Donald spent five days in the Shandong province, visiting the Temple of Confucius by train before spending two days climbing up Taishan mountain, a feat which they would relive together thirty-five years later. It is a pity that the disagreements between Alan Donald and Douglas Hurd over the final stages of the handover of Hong Kong seem to have temporarily dented the friendship of those happy early years together. Hurd still has the little black and white snaps of China which he took in the 1950s.

Above all, Hurd was struck by the puritanical nature of the Chinese:

> A simple puritanism prevailed. No prostitutes, no gambling halls, no tips. A hotel porter sprinted down the railway platform with two used razor blades which I had left in my bedroom − in case the hotel should be accused of theft. Another went to great pains to give me back about a farthing in Chinese currency which I had overpaid − in case he should be accused of taking a tip.[17]

Despite being in the Chancery Section, Hurd learned to speak Mandarin during his time in Peking, but steered clear of Chinese sources later when writing his non-fiction book *The Arrow War* in 1967. Mandarin is notoriously difficult to write, but Hurd became fluent in the language thanks to the efforts of a pretty Chinese woman called Miss Yu. In the tradition of the times, Hurd's language teacher was also puritanical, wearing a 'severe Mao tunic' although she eventually revealed that she 'kept at home a camphorwood chest full of bright dresses with slit skirts, which she hoped one day to wear again'.[18]

In contrast to Peking, Hurd found Hong Kong a much more exciting place. In 1954, he remembers taking the Star Ferry across to Hong Kong to dine with the then Governor, Sir Alexander Grantham:

> A highly nervous young diplomat, I was instructed by Sir Alexander's ADC that after dinner at twenty-three minutes past nine precisely, I would sit by the wife of the Korean Consul-General, and eight minutes later would be taken to meet on the next sofa the Commander of the United States Seventh Fleet.[19]

Since then, Hurd has felt an 'electric charge' every time he visits 'the most stimulating city in the world'.[20]

Before returning to London in 1956, Hurd travelled on part of the Trans-Siberian railway (he missed his train and lost his luggage at the start of the journey) stopping off in Ulan-Bator, the capital of Mongolia. Sir Alan Donald recalls receiving a postcard from Douglas Hurd, who quoted the Chief Lama as asking after a fellow Lama at 'Cantersbelly' in Britain.[21]

In August 1956, again travelling by ship, this time the *Queen Mary*, Hurd arrived in the harbour of New York − a city with an equally vibrant feel. Hurd was about to take up his post as Second Secretary to the British Mission to the United Nations. He could not have known that he would start his job in such a whirlwind of international crisis or that he would at last fall in love. Only a few days earlier, on 26 July 1956, President Nasser of Egypt had nationalised the Suez Canal, and from then on, the United Nations became the focus of frenetic international diplomacy. Because of the diplomatic hubbub caused by Nasser's action, Hurd was largely ignored in his first few days at the UN. However, he soon settled into his job as Private Secretary to Sir Pierson Dixon, the British Ambassador to the United Nations. Sir Pierson had played a key role in the setting up of the United Nations. Prior to that, he had been Principal Private Secretary to Anthony Eden (whom he accompanied to Potsdam) and Ernest Bevin, before being appointed British Ambassador to Prague when the Iron Curtain was coming down over Eastern Europe. He was a quiet fellow, and like Hurd later, he enjoyed writing in his spare time, producing a number of novels and a notable portrait of Napoleon's favourite sister, Pauline Borghese.

In October 1956, Sir Pierson Dixon was preoccupied with the diplomatic fall-out caused by Britain's secret plan with the French and the Israelis to invade Egypt, of which he had been given no prior knowledge. Hurd recalls how the whole official apparatus of the Foreign Office was circumvented by the Prime Minister, Anthony Eden, and his Foreign Secretary, Selwyn Lloyd. On the dramatic night of 29 October, when Israel attacked Egypt, Douglas Hurd played the role of messenger to Sir Pierson. It was the beginning of the Metropolitan Opera season in New York, and both the British Ambassador and his American counterpart, Henry Cabot Lodge, had boxes reserved to hear the great Maria Callas singing *Norma*. On hearing the news from Egpyt, Cabot Lodge hastily convened a meeting with Sir Pierson during the interval, in order to agree to an emergency session of the UN Security Council for the following morning to condemn the Israeli action. However, Douglas Hurd had handed Sir Pierson a telegram with strict instructions from London not to follow this course of action. Sir Pierson was as baffled as Cabot Lodge, but had to try to make excuses for not co-operating, without any explanation from London for the change of policy. Having got to know the personal characteristics of his superior, Douglas Hurd saw Sir Pierson's neck turn 'a bright shade of pink' as his discomfort mounted.[22]

A few days later, the unthinkable happened. The British cast their first veto at the United Nations. The British officials at the United Nations were downcast, with Douglas Hurd noting in his diary on 1 November, 'The world is crumbling around us.'[23] Matters were made worse by the news that the Soviet Union had crushed rebellion in Hungary. After much delay, the British and French troops landed in Egypt. Hurd's view of Suez has always been that the action was morally defensible, but that it should have been accompanied by a well thought-out plan to carry the policy through. Officials at the time assumed there would be some master plan in the Foreign Office about which they had not been informed and which would get them out of the mess. But it never came; it did not exist. Britain was forced, under economic pressure from the United States, to hand the Suez area over to UN control. Hurd is an admirer of Anthony Eden, and as Foreign Secretary commissioned a bust of him to stand at the bottom of the main staircase in King Charles Street. But Suez was Eden's big mistake – an uncharacteristic rush of blood.

Hurd is critical of Selwyn Lloyd's abrupt manner when visiting the United Nations in New York. Very few superiors are ever singled out for harsh criticism by Hurd. Reading his book on the Heath government, *An End to Promises*, one is struck by his tendency to find something good to say about everyone, even if he combines this with an acute eye for the absurd and a love of eccentric characters. From his time in New York, Hurd reserves his greatest admiration for Dag Hammarskjöld, the United Nations Secretary General: 'I do not know whether he was a saint, but he was certainly a remarkable, selfless man.'[24]

Hurd admired the way that Hammarskjöld would converse with a junior official in the same friendly way as he would an ambassador. But the Secretary General's enigmatic, elliptical style meant that Sir Pierson required Douglas to sit quietly memorising what had been said in the ambassador's discussions with Hammarskjöld in order to work out its meaning afterwards. Sadly, Hammarskjöld was killed in mysterious circumstances during the war in the Congo in 1960.

This was the period in the United Nations history of stalemate between the two superpowers, with the UN's role being to keep the Cold War cold. The United Nations General Assembly became a safety valve for international disputes. Hurd sat through long and exhausting debates when much hot air was expounded in the condemnation of Western colonialism by the African or Asian caucus. The most memorable speaker of the age was Krishna Menon of India:

> On Kashmir, the star performer was Krishna Menon of India, with his grey mane, hook nose, walking stick and deep glaring eyes. His speeches were immense, long and virulent, particularly against Britain. For hour after hour, regardless of relevance, he would run through a list of viceroys, denouncing the shortcomings of each. Once when he had exhausted the viceroys, he turned on my most amiable master, and denounced Sir Pierson Dixon. At the end of this particular oration, Krishna collapsed in the manner of the Earl of Chatham, and was carried to a side room of the Security Council. In a faint voice he asked to see Sir Pierson Dixon. My amiable master entered

the room amid a flutter of Indian doctors and officials, expecting to receive some apology. 'I forgive you, I forgive you', murmured the great man and closed his eyes.[25]

As he had done in China, Hurd spent a great deal of time socialising, except that the vibrant atmosphere of New York was in marked contrast to the restrictive, puritanical mood of Peking. He broadened his mind, absorbing the feel of Central Park, visiting museums, going to opera and theatre, while continuing to enjoy Scottish country dancing in yet another incongruous setting. Besides the people he knew from the United Nations, there was a large and youngish British community in Manhattan, and this group provided a number of friendships. In the summer of 1959, he and some of these friends bought a 1953 Chevy and drove across the United States to San Francisco.

Among Hurd's contemporaries during his posting to New York was Mary Galbraith (later Mary Moore). As the two most junior members of the British permanent mission to the United Nations, Douglas and Mary shared an office for nearly three years, and have remained friends. After her marriage a few years later, Mary went on to write a number of plays for radio and television, under the name Helena Osborne, and, like Hurd, was a relatively successful novelist. In the 1980s, she was Principal of St Hilda's College, Oxford.

It was also in New York that Douglas met Tatiana Eyre. A stockbroker's daughter, she was social secretary to Lady Dixon, Sir Pierson Dixon's wife. In many respects, Douglas and Tatiana were opposites. While he was very intellectual and cerebral, she was highly athletic and very good at games, especially tennis and skiing. On one occasion they went skiing with the Aclands in Switzerland. While Tatiana was whizzing down the black slopes, Douglas was floundering about on the nursery slopes because his spectacles continually kept misting up with condensation. Upon Douglas's return to London to become Private Secretary to the Permanent Under Secretary of State at the Foreign Office in 1960, Tatiana and Douglas were married. One of Hurd's best friends, Tony Lloyd, was his best man and, just three weeks later, Hurd was on duty as best man at Lloyd's own wedding. Tatiana and Douglas set up home at 27, Cheyne Row, near the river. Although they had three boys together, the early years of happiness did not last. Tatiana was not suited to playing the role of the dutiful wife of a diplomat or the wife of a politician. The couple were separated in 1976. Even though they subsequently remained good friends, the break-up of their marriage caused Douglas much lingering anguish.

From the mid 1970s, Hurd retreated into his shell, becoming markedly more taciturn and unwilling to reveal his inner feelings to others. He had always been reserved and shy, but he developed a thicker layer, a carapace, which – until he met his second wife, Judy – no one was allowed to penetrate. It was a bleak, unhappy time of his life and a great pity, because it masked his wry, witty, sardonic side.

During his three years in London at the beginning of the 1960s, Douglas Hurd worked under two very different Permanent Under Secretaries of State. 'Derick' Hoyer-Millar, who became Lord Inchyra in 1961, was a calmer operator than his successor Harold (later Lord) Caccia. Hoyer-Millar had served as British High Commissioner in Germany, before returning to London in 1957. His style of work and tendency to play things down (initially at any rate) ensured that he got on well with senior ministers, especially Alec Douglas-Home and Harold Macmillan. The Prime Minister (Harold Macmillan) always referred to him as 'Sir Frederick' and was said to have remarked affectionately of the Permanent Under Secretary: 'Whenever I want Sir Frederick, he's always on the night train to Scotland.'[26]

His successor was different. Harold Caccia was a good looking man of action, who had gained a rugby blue at Eton and enjoyed playing squash and tennis. Ernest Bevin had chosen him to modernise the Foreign Office as Assistant Under Secretary of State, even though Harold Macmillan said of him he was 'more wrapped up in his old school tie' than most of his contemporaries.[27] Caccia was renowned for telling exciting stories of his wartime adventures with Ian Fleming – creator of James Bond – behind enemy lines. His strong contacts in Washington, particularly with Bedell-Smith, acting US Secretary of State (when John Foster Dulles was ill), helped heal the rift with the United States over Suez. On returning from Washington, Caccia's main career achievement was to organise the merger of the Colonial Office and the Foreign Office into the unified Foreign and Commonwealth Office in 1964, which he went on to head. In contrast to his predecessor, Caccia was a more hectic and hands-on Permanent Under Secretary.

Unlike Douglas Hurd, Caccia was an opponent of Britain's entry into the EEC. Even though Edward Heath, as Lord Privy Seal, was attempting to negotiate Britain's entry during Hurd's time in London, they did not get to know each other well at this stage. Hurd knew Heath only slightly, through his father. His only abiding memory of Edward Heath is being a member of the audience when Heath played the piano in the British Embassy for matins in Moscow during the visit when the Nuclear Test Ban Treaty was signed in August 1963.[28] Although his views on Europe had not really crystallised at this stage, in retrospect, Hurd takes the line of Macmillan, Heath and other pro-Europeans, that Britain made the mistake of not being a member of the European Community from the very beginning. Instead, Britain left herself isolated and unable to influence the development of the institutions of the European Community.

In 1963, Douglas and Tatiana rented out their house in Cheyne Row and packed their bags for Rome, where Hurd took up his new post as First Secretary (Political) at the British Embassy. Despite his promotion, Hurd found the work in Italy monotonous and, again, much of the time was spent socialising. But Hurd was becoming bored and unsure whether he wanted to carry on much longer as a diplomat. However, someone arrived at the British Embassy in Rome who was to create a welcome diversion.

Notes

1. Douglas Hurd, 'A Bowler Hat and a Tightly Furled Umbrella',
   Letters from a Diplomat, Radio 4, 3 Jun. 1996 (original transcript).
2. Interview with Douglas Hurd, 26 Nov. 1996.
3. Ibid.
4. Interview with Philip Ziegler, 21 May 1996.
5. Interview with Sir Timothy Raison, 23 Jul. 1996.
6. Hurd, 'A Bowler Hat and a Tightly Furled Umbrella'.
7. Kenneth Baker, *The Turbulent Years: My Life in Politics* (Faber & Faber: London, 1993), p.417. Interview with Lord Wakeham, 19 Dec. 1995. Interview with William Waldegrave, 17 Dec. 1996.
8. Hurd, 'A Bowler hat and a Tightly Furled Umbrella'.
9. *The Times*, 13 May 1977.
10. Douglas Hurd, 'Letter to the Editor', *The Times*, 22 Mar. 1974.
11. Hurd, 'A Bowler hat and a Tightly Furled Umbrella'.
12. Private information.
13. Interview with Philip Ziegler, 21 May 1996.
14. Ibid.
15. Hurd, 'Parades and Peking Picnics', *Letters from a Diplomat*, Radio 4, 10 Jun. 1996 (original transcript).
16. Conversation with Sir Richard Evans, 25 Feb. 1997. Evans borrowed the phrase from Banquo's ghost in *Macbeth*, Act 1, Scene 6 about Macbeth's castle.
17. Hurd, 'Parades and Peking Picnics'.
18. Ibid.
19. Ibid.
20. Ibid.
21. Conversation with Sir Alan Donald, 25 Feb. 1997.
22. Hurd, 'The Centre of the Storm', *Letters from a Diplomat*, Radio 4, 17 Jun.1996 (original transcript).
23. Ibid.
24. Ibid.

25. Ibid.
26. Interview with Sir Antony Acland, 17 Mar. 1997.
27. Sir Roderick Barclay, *The Independent*, 2 Nov. 1990.
28. Interview with Douglas Hurd, 22 Jul. 1996.

5

Writing for Fun

At the time of Andrew Osmond's arrival in Rome in 1965, Douglas Hurd had reached the rank of First Secretary (Political) at the British Embassy there.

Back in 1961, Osmond had been amongst the co-founders of the satirical magazine *Private Eye*, which was subsequently sold to Peter Cook. Somewhat surprisingly, Osmond joined the Diplomatic Service a year later, serving in France and West Africa, before being posted to Rome as Third Secretary (Economic).

In some respects, it was an unusual combination for a friendship: the conventional, mainstream diplomat with a first class career record – eight year's Osmond's senior – getting to know the satirically-minded writer who freely admits that he fitted into the Foreign Service 'like a square peg in a round hole'.[1] However, Osmond's sense of fun helped bring out Hurd's wry, sardonic, slightly mischievous side. Their wives got on well too, and all four would go off for weekends together, taking houses by the sea along the Italian coast. Also, for some odd reason of internal geography, Hurd and Osmond found themselves sharing an office and so had plenty of time to get to know each other better still; there was relatively little to do at the Rome Embassy during the long, hot Italian summer.

Late one night, Hurd and Osmond had a heart-to-heart in contemplation of their respective future careers. Hurd revealed that he wanted to 'go where the meat was',[2] meaning that the days when an ambassador had real power were over, and that he must therefore go into politics. In reply, Osmond intimated his desire to become a novelist. In that moment, Hurd suggested that they write a book together.

Whilst 'drinking whisky and watering endless geraniums'[3] on the veranda of Hurd's flat in Rome, they began to explore ideas for writing a novel. Osmond admits he was heavily influenced by *Seven Days in May*, a thriller by Fletcher

Knebel and Charles W. Bailey — which was eventually made into a film by John Frankenheimer — about American generals taking over the White House. Osmond wanted to write a similar type of novel, which he came to call '"what would happen if" books'.[4] The three books which they wrote together in the 1960s all followed a similar pattern. Hurd and Osmond would choose a likely crisis set in the near future. Around this Hurd would compose a wonderfully elegant three-page summary, written in the style of a Foreign Office paper — outlining a 'scenario of maximum probability'.[5]

In the case of the first book, *Send Him Victorious* (1968), the plot involves a Rhodesian declaration of independence from Britain. Hurd worked out how the British Government might react to such a crisis, what the likely reaction at the United Nations would be, and how the Russians would respond. Rhodesia was just the trigger. Hurd and Osmond wanted to tell the story of a British *coup d'état*, and in such circumstances, they agreed that loyalty to the British Crown would be the key to the whole crisis. Osmond would then make up scenes arising from these 'reaction points'[6] with the action shifting like a hand-held camera, from one reaction point to another, as the crisis unfolded. Thus the characters arose from necessary points of view. If Hurd and Osmond needed a journalist to appear in a scene, then the character of Jack Kemble would appear. If the British Cabinet was making a decision, the action would follow Patrick Harvey, the Prime Minister. These creations, Kemble and Harvey, are the omnipresent characters in the four books which Hurd and Osmond wrote together. Although one can criticise Hurd and Osmond for creating stereotypes, characterisation was not the primary motivating force behind the books. They were fast-moving and, according to both, fun to write. Unlike Hurd's later short stories (which he wrote as Foreign Secretary), they reveal very little about his inner feelings and doubts.

The process of making up scenes was akin to a scenario in a film script, with numbered sections outlining in four or five lines what was to happen in a particular scene or chapter. The chapters would be divided up according to each other's experience: Hurd would write Cabinet scenes and Foreign Office telegrams, whereas Osmond would write about drunken journalists and wild goings-on. Each would tend to follow the characters they had created. Both would work through a 'shopping list', sending the material back and forth by post (by 1967 both had left the Foreign Service and were living in England) over a period of six to eight months, and meeting up occasionally to discuss progress. Most importantly, they adhered to the maxim of good co-authorship (something which rarely succeeds in fiction): that each would have the final say on the other's work.

After they had completed a few chapters, they sent them to Collins, with the knowledge that they would receive a helping hand. By 1967, Hurd had already published a non-fiction book, entitled *The Arrow War: An Anglo-Chinese Confusion, 1856–1860* (Collins, 1967). Hurd had sent the typescript to his future editor at Collins, Richard Ollard[7] at the suggestion of Philip Ziegler, who had married Sarah, daughter of Sir William Collins, who was then Chairman and Managing Director of the publishing house. *The Arrow War* was a scholarly account of James Bruce, the eighth Earl of Elgin, who was sent to China by the British Government as a plenipotentiary, to press British rights to trade as an equal nation upon an unwilling Chinese Emperor. Hurd was fortunate to gain access to the diaries of the eighth Lord Elgin because his late uncle, Robert Hurd (the Edinburgh architect), had been friends with the present Lord Elgin, Andrew Bruce. Hurd spent the summer of 1966 in Lord Elgin's estate at Broomhall in Fife wading through James Bruce's diaries and subsequently wrote *The Arrow War* in the pleasant surroundings of the library in the Travellers' Club, Pall Mall.[8]

Richard Ollard, another old Etonian, was very impressed by the early chapters of *Send Him Victorious* and gave Hurd and Osmond a contract. The novel was moderately successful in Britain and elsewhere, and had the distinction of being serialised in the French newspaper *Le Monde,* with some amusing consequences! Osmond recalls a friend of his, whose mother was holidaying in the South of France, being telephoned to ask if she was all right, given that the French press were full of reports of the British army engaging in mutiny!

The book's greatest strength, and that of the two which followed, is the ring of authenticity with which the language of officialdom is used. As one reviewer observed in *The Spectator* in 1968:

> The trick lies in the documentary approach, the coating of surface realism. They know how politicians talk, how diplomats react and government departments work.[9]

Stylistically, the first three books owe something to the work of Lionel Davidson, author of several best-selling thrillers, such as *The Rose of Tibet* (1962) and *A Long Way to Shiloh* (1966). The dialogue is in short bursts, without pause to tell the reader who is talking, like little film clips on paper. Indeed, the books read like film scripts, with short chapters as the action shifts from one crisis point to another.

Hurd and Osmond adopted a similar approach when writing the second book, *The Smile on the Face of the Tiger* (1969); again with a 'what would happen if' scenario, this time a Chinese threat to invade Hong Kong. Drawing on Hurd's experiences in Peking and Osmond's service with the Gurkhas in Malaya, they weave a story about Laurence Pershing (Minister of State at the

Foreign Office responsible for Asian Affairs), who is racked with guilt over the shooting of a young Chinese Communist girl in Malaya in 1957. In the story, the death was witnessed by one Chiang Li-shih, who later becomes a Chinese official able to compel Pershing into leaking US plans for Cambodia to the Chinese. The book, which was written long before Mrs Thatcher became Prime Minister, has an innocent reference to a character called Mrs Thatcher being worried because 'her boy's out there [in Hong Kong] with the Blue Funnel line'.[10] Robert Rhodes James, the former Conservative MP for Cambridge, used to tease Douglas Hurd about this unintended reference.[11] Although there is a danger of reading too much into the writing of the novels, there are occasional clues about the early political philosophy of Douglas Hurd. On one occasion, the fictional Prime Minister, Patrick Harvey, listens in Cabinet with growing irritation to his Health Secretary, Broom:

> There is a market for medical services as far as for any other commodity.
> We must let the demand find its own level by the free play of the market.[12]

Harvey/Hurd's response under his breath is, 'Ignorant claptrap'.[13]

The third novel, *Scotch on the Rocks* (1971), stretched credulity a little too far, by describing as it does an alliance of students, Highlanders and Glasgow hardmen who stage a military coup and declare Scottish independence. In terms of characterisation, there is little apology made for stereotyping: we find a huntin', fishin' and shootin' Scottish lord; a flame redhead, headstrong daughter of the revolution; a working-class radical from Glasgow Green; and a verbose SNP matriarch. The novel was made into a five-part BBC drama serial by James McTaggart and shown in full. However, the series incurred the wrath of the SNP who protested to the BBC's 'Watch Committee', a body of independent worthies, who upheld the complaint and ordered the film destroyed. One feels the Scottish nationalists took themselves rather too seriously and missed the point that Hurd and Osmond were writing with their tongues firmly in their cheeks. However, not all copies of the series were destroyed. Andrew Osmond retains a copy of the first ten minutes of the first episode (which was shown on 11 May 1973). Intriguingly, on the evening of Hurd's resignation from the Foreign Office on 23 June 1995, the BBC's *Newsnight* programme showed a short clip from *Scotch on the Rocks*. According to the journalist Michael Crick, the BBC archives retain only three of the original five episodes.[14]

Andrew Osmond also fell foul of a member of the Scottish National Liberation Army (SNLA) who wrote to him complaining about the inaccuracy of a number of the book's 'Scottishisms'. They had a point. It is rare to find Glaswegian 'fellers' who head to the pub for a Bacardi and coke.[15] In his reply to the terrorists, Osmond apologised, but asked 'why it took a couple of

Englishmen to write a book about how Scotland gained its independence'.[16] By way of rejoinder, he was sent a perfectly serious military plan by the SNLA activist.

Despite the views of the radical fringe of the Scottish nationalist movement, Hurd and Osmond overestimate the revolutionary staying power of the Scots. However, if logic can be suspended, it is a well-written, pacy yarn. Once again, the most realistic pieces of writing are the segments written as *The Times* editorial, and a piece in the magazine *Private Eye*.

The first three books proved a reasonable commercial success initially – all three were in the top ten fiction lists – and were reprinted. *Scotch on the Rocks*, in particular, continues to be borrowed in considerable numbers from libraries, especially in Scotland: Hurd and Osmond still earn a modest annual return from the Public Lending Right (PLR).[17]

In the 1970s, Hurd chose to write two books on his own. *Truth Game* (1972) was a warning against the declining standards of the British press – a theme which later became a favourite of Douglas Hurd's during his years as a senior minister. The story-line culminates with the Conservatives losing an election due to press distortion of events during a revolutionary coup in a fictitious African country called 'Rajnaya'. Rajnaya was very loosely based on Oman, which Hurd had visited in March 1969, accompanying Edward Heath (then Leader of the Opposition) on a trip to the Gulf states. The opening chapter of *Truth Game* draws heavily on Hurd's earlier encounter with the real Sultan of Oman, and is later repeated almost word for word in Hurd's non-fiction account of the Heath years, *An End to Promises* (1979).[18]

In *Vote to Kill* (1975) Hurd made good use of his experiences whilst political secretary to Edward Heath: the similarity between this fictional account and reality is again quite striking. Using the backdrop of an ageing Prime Minister facing calls to withdraw troops from Northern Ireland, the book's greatest strength is the way it describes the minutiae of life at Number 10, Downing Street. But the plot falls down absolutely by virtue of the implausibility of its ending. In the early 1970s, although Hurd's political views were not yet fully formed, we do see a marked disdain for the politics of populism and extremism on the one hand and his preference for moderation, good sense and consensus on the other. Despite the efforts of the rebel Tory demagogue, Jeremy Cornwall, to carry the country with a national crusade to 'Bring the Boys Home', it is the elderly Prime Minister, Sir James Percival, who keeps a cool head and wins the General Election: the good sense of the British people prevails after one of their sporadic dalliances with populism. It is a similar theme to the very first novel, *Send Him Victorious*, where the pragmatic, non-ideological Prime Minister, Patrick Harvey, calmly weathers the storm to see off the Rhodesian rebels in his own party.

In 1978, Osmond was living in Hurd's constituency in Mid-Oxfordshire and they decided to resume their partnership. The omens seemed good. Neither Hurd nor Osmond had achieved as great a success in their subsequent solo writing careers as they had had together, although Osmond's own novel *Saladin* (1976) had been a modest success. The first three books had been written for fun. There had been no agonising and very few differences of view. It seemed a good idea to repeat a winning formula. The plot was another near future crisis. This time, a European car firm merger is disrupted by international terrorists and the kidnapping of their old favourite, Patrick Harvey. However, two problems prevented *War Without Frontiers* (1982) from becoming another success. Firstly, there was a difference of concept which did not emerge immediately. Osmond explains:

> I said to Douglas, 'our public have lapped up the first three. Those are just
> the appetisers. What they will love is a great big main course of Hurd and
> Osmond.' All of which, I'm afraid, turned out to be a ghastly mistake.[19]

Instinctively, Hurd preferred to stick to the original formula. This difference of opinion was put to one side as Hurd and Osmond signed contracts with Hodder and Stoughton. Then, in May 1979, Hurd was given a post in Mrs Thatcher's new government as Lord Carrington's number three at the Foreign and Commonwealth Office. Hurd's increased workload meant that he decided to let Osmond pursue his own concept of the book. In the end, Hurd had very little input into the final product, except for the passages dealing with the character of Otto Riemeck, the President of the European Commission, and the last scene where Patrick Harvey is reunited with his wife.[20]

The novel is flawed by its scope and length: large sections lack dramatic relevance, diverting the reader's attention away from the main drama of the kidnap – which itself is actually very well written. The book was a commercial flop. At one stage, Granada Television adapted it into a script for a six-part television series, but the plans were subsequently shelved. Osmond describes the experience of the fourth book as 'an unhappy episode'[21] which strained their friendship (but never to breaking point), and which made Hurd feel very uncomfortable when it came to publicising a book which he did not like. As a Minister of State at the Foreign Office, coping with issues related to international terrorism, most notably the Iranian hostage siege, the novel did appear to lean a little too favourably towards the terrorist viewpoint. For Osmond, who had devoted three years to the book, its failure was a financial calamity. He abandoned novel writing and switched to a career in writing the corporate literature of international companies, in which he had more success.

Perhaps Hurd and Osmond lost the essential ingredient of co-authorship –

the need for a close personal chemistry – when Hurd's ministerial career started in 1979. Or perhaps the artistic rift began after they completed *Scotch on the Rocks*. Although they continued to see each other (and still do), their writing partnership only flourished when they had time on their hands, when they wrote purely for fun.

In any case, by the time *War Without Frontiers* was published in 1982, Hurd had acquired a new writing partner. Stephen Lamport had become Hurd's Private Secretary at the Foreign Office in the summer of 1981, having previously spent four years with the Diplomatic Service in Tehran. It was whilst on a train journey from Brussels to the European Parliament in Strasbourg in November 1981, that Hurd and Lamport first discussed the possibility of writing a novel together. Ironically, Hurd happened to be reading the proofs of *War Without Frontiers* at the time. Hurd aired the idea to Lamport, and they both agreed to think about ideas for a plot over Christmas. Lamport recalls walking his dog one wet December afternoon during the Christmas holiday, and coming up with the idea for a story about a junior minister who takes up a cause, which in the end destroys him.[22] This was to become the basic plot of *The Palace of Enchantments* (1985). During some long flights on a ministerial visit to India in early January 1982, Hurd and Lamport developed their ideas for the plot.

As with Osmond, Hurd and Lamport agreed to vet each other's scripts and divide up the writing fairly equally. Hurd concentrated on the parts dealing with Whitehall, Cabinet, and scenes in the House of Commons. Lamport wrote the African scenes, and those involving the central character, Edward Dunsford – including the stormy relationship with his wife, Rosemary and the difficulties with his local constituency association. By this stage, Hurd had become a Home Office minister and despite the constraints of time, spent lunchtimes in St James's Park with Lamport, looking at and revising draft chapters. But, in Hurd's view, the exercise was primarily to keep his hand in, awaiting a time when he could concentrate more fully on writing.[23] With the end of the Cold War, the novel seems rather dated, but the overall result is an extremely accurate guide to the machinations of government at Whitehall, Cabinet, parliamentary, and local level. More intriguing is the way in which Stephen Lamport was able to portray the marital breakdown of Edward Dunsford, the junior minister who goes off the rails. The character of Rosemary Dunsford, his wife, at times horribly real, is the unsung strength of the book.

However, the novel suffered a blow when the Foreign Office refused Hurd and Lamport permission to set their African scenes in the Sudan. Lamport was forced to relocate the action to the fictitious 'Meridia' and the capital city from Khartoum to his invention of Mangara. Whilst Lamport maintains that the enforced change did not affect the commercial success of the book, one questions whether fictitious African countries provide the necessary realism for political novels.

The novel's plot also bears a striking resemblance to C.P. Snow's *Corridors of Power* (1964). Set at the time of the Suez Crisis, Snow's work documents the rise and fall of an ambitious Conservative junior minister who becomes convinced that Britain should adopt a policy of unilateral nuclear disarmament. Roger Quaife, secretly unfaithful to his wealthy wife, favouring a mousy secretarial mistress, reaches beyond his powers as a junior minister. In the final page of *The Palace of Enchantments*, Hurd refers to the cleaning ladies covering 'the corridors of power with soapy water'.[24] Unfortunately, this has the unintended effect of reminding the reader where he has read a similar plot before, even if the similarity is an entirely unconscious one.

The fact that Hurd has written a series of political thrillers has done no serious harm to his ministerial career. He was occasionally teased in the House of Commons and in the press for the sexual content of some of his novels, but his co-authors are responsible for most of the sexy bits. His two solo efforts, *Truth Game* and *Vote to Kill* are far less racy than the earlier collaborations. But Hurd always refers to 'pretty girls' rather than women and his writing would be considered sexist in our politically correct world.

Hurd's writing skills were referred to during the Conservative leadership contest in November 1990. If anything, perhaps he should have stressed them more in order to raise his profile, and demonstrate that he had a another facet to his character beneath the surface of the Foreign Secretary. Away from the formal, aloof, high-browed style to which the public has become accustomed, he has always possessed a wry, humorous, sardonic side. The politicians in Hurd's books are always engaging in intrigue and scheming. Andrew Osmond believes:

> Hurd has a sharp eye for humbug in public figures and likes to unmask the baser motivations. His dislike of ideologues comes close to condemning idealism of any sort, in others or himself. Thus, his heroes are always ordinary folk – quiet, unpretentious, decent, modest, industrious, pragmatic, with no illusions about themselves. [Is this] an unconscious self portrait?[25]

But it would be a mistake to claim – as Patrick Cosgrave does – that Hurd's writings reveal him as a cynic about human nature.[26] Douglas Hurd – unlike John Major, who allowed himself to become cynical – is an optimist, willing to give people the benefit of the doubt until proven otherwise. He is, believe it or not, something of a romantic at heart and likes nothing more than reading a weepy Victorian novel before bedtime. When asked by the *Times Literary Supplement* in 1985 to select a piece of neglected fiction which deserved to become better known, Hurd chose Disraeli's *Lothair*,[27] a story about Victorian high society in which three women, representing the Roman Catholic and Anglican faiths and Italian nationalism, vie for the love of a handsome lord. There is also a slightly sentimental, dreamy side to Douglas Hurd. His choice of favourite authors – Waugh, Trollope and Wodehouse – shows a love of England and its institutions, a quiet patriotism.

Hurd, along with his co-authors, has proved to be a writer of admirably readable, fast-moving political thrillers. The fact that he can write well demonstrates the breadth as well as the depth of his abilities. He has certainly been better received than the former French President, Valery Giscard D'Estaing, whose romantic novel *Le Passage* (1994) was viciously lampooned in the French press.[28] However, before his latest novel, *The Shape of Ice*, was published, Hurd had yet to prove that, given more time, he could emulate either the mastery and depth of C.P. Snow, or indeed the literary gifts of his hero, Benjamin Disraeli.

Notes

1. Interview with Andrew Osmond, 26 Oct. 1995.
2. Ibid.
3. Ibid.
4. Ibid.
5. Ibid.
6. Ibid.
7. Interview with Philip Ziegler, 21 May 1996.
8. Conversation with Douglas Hurd, 25 Oct. 1995.
9. Matthew Coady, 'Bodies Politic' in *The Spectator*, 2 Feb. 1968.
10. Douglas Hurd & Andrew Osmond, *The Smile on the Face of the Tiger* (Collins: London, 1969), p. 49.
11. Conversation with Sir Robert Rhodes James, 22 Jul. 1996.
12. Hurd & Osmond, *The Smile on the Face of the Tiger*, p. 63.
13. Ibid.
14. Conversation with Michael Crick, 8 Jul. 1996.
15. Douglas Hurd & Andrew Osmond, *Scotch on the Rocks* (Collins: London, 1971), pp. 78, 29.
16. Interview with Andrew Osmond, 26 Oct. 1995.
17. Ibid.
18. Interview with Douglas Hurd, 22 Jul. 1996; Douglas Hurd, *An End to Promises* (Collins: London, 1979), p. 41.
19. Interview with Andrew Osmond, 26 Oct. 1995.

20. Interview with Douglas Hurd, 22 Jul. 1996; interview with Andrew Osmond, 26 Oct. 1995.

21. Interview with Andrew Osmond, 26 Oct. 1995.

22. Interview with Stephen Lamport, 19 Dec. 1995.

23. Interview with Michael Sissons, 21 May 1996; interview with Douglas Hurd, 22 Jul. 1996.

24. Douglas Hurd & Stephen Lamport, *The Palace of Enchantments* (Hodder & Stoughton: London, 1985), p. 320.

25. Letter from Andrew Osmond to the author, 2 Jun. 1998

26. Patrick Cosgrave, 'Diplomat with a Touch of Acid', *The Times*, 12 Sept. 1985.

27. Douglas Hurd, 'Neglected Fictions', *Times Literary Supplement*, 18 Oct. 1985.

28. *The Sunday Times*, 20 Nov. 1994.

6

The Pell-Mell of Politics:
Working For Edward Heath,
1966–1974

The experience of writing novels with Andrew Osmond had been a welcome diversion, but after three years of diplomatic service in Rome, Douglas Hurd considered it was time for a change of career. He may have identified with Alan Selkirk, the hero of his first novel, *Send Him Victorious*: the bright young diplomat finds himself in a rut and is told by the daughter of an ageing ambassador, 'Don't be so dim and bureaucratic. If you go on like this you'll be just like my father. He's wanted for so long for someone to ask his opinion that now he hasn't got one.'[1]

Having earlier expressed a desire to enter politics, Hurd remained unclear how, or even if the opportunity would arise. Guarding against the possibility of failure, a letter to Edward Heath – whom he knew through his father, but only slightly – was only one of six speculative letters which he sent off from Rome: another of the six was sent to Warburg's, the merchant banking firm. It was only after receiving a telegram from Edward Heath asking him to return to London that Hurd learned that, had he stayed on in the Foreign Office, he would have been offered a post in Chile. Instead, Michael Fraser, Head of the Conservative Research Department, offered Hurd the post of Foreign Affairs Officer, which he accepted.

The main task of the Conservative Research Department, then located in Old Queen Street, was to produce propaganda literature for the Conservative Opposition – promoting aspects of Conservative policy and, of course, finding useful quotations with which to denounce Harold Wilson's Government. Hurd's most notable party political paper of the time was an assessment of the limitations of the UN, entitled *The United Nations: A Conservative Analysis*.[2] Referring closely to Sir Alec Douglas-Home's Oxford speech of November 1967, Hurd declared:

> The United Nations should not be called on to deal with every situation regardless of the circumstances or the prospects of success . . . The way to build up its reputation is to encourage it to take on those activities it can do, and refuse those things which are at present beyond its power.[3]

The main accusation levelled at the Labour Government was that it had progressively handed over colonial problems to the United Nations. In phraseology typical of the paper, Labour were accused of using the UN 'as a waste-paper basket into which they toss problems, like those of Aden and Rhodesia, which they themselves have lamentably failed to solve.'[4]

The Conservative Research Department tends to be more active in Opposition than in Government, but even so, Hurd did not find the work hugely stimulating. Moreover, there was a slightly awkward spell early on when he was being summoned to Heath's Albany flat – Heath tended to use his own flat as a place of work, rather than his office at the House of Commons – on a fairly regular basis. This created a certain tension with Guy Hadley, ostensibly Hurd's boss as head of the Foreign Affairs section, who saw his junior going off to meetings with the Prime Minister. It seems Edward Heath very quickly saw Hurd as one of his bright, young 'Albany set'. These tensions were resolved when Hadley retired and Hurd succeeded him.

Hurd brought to the Albany set a vast knowledge of foreign affairs upon which Heath could draw, but he had yet to establish contacts in the House of Commons. His key mentor and facilitator at this time was Dennis (later Sir) Walters. They were already acquainted, having met in Rome when Walters was a governor of the British Institute in Florence.

As joint secretary of the Conservative Backbench Foreign Affairs Committee, Dennis Walters was particularly helpful in introducing Hurd to the more influential figures on the Conservative backbenches. In 1967, the Conservative Backbench Foreign Affairs Committee was important in two respects. First, in those days, there were no House of Commons Select Committees, merely party committees whose influence was considerable. Second, the Backbench Committees were a valuable source of research and experience, and in some respects fulfilled the role of civil servants for a party which was then in Opposition. Part of Hurd's remit was to brief and keep the minutes of the Conservative Foreign Affairs Committee. He also had to brief the Shadow Foreign Secretary, Sir Alec Douglas-Home, on the views of the Committee's members. Hurd and Walters cemented their friendship. Much later, during his years as a senior minister, Hurd spent quiet holidays at Walters's Tuscan villa, relatively free from press intrusion.[5]

Hurd recorded his period as political secretary to Edward Heath in the aforementioned elucidating account of the Heath Government from 1970 to 1974, *An End to Promises*. Hurd intended the book to be a personal memoir, based on his diaries of that period and drawing from the considerable number of minutes which he wrote to his leader, Edward Heath. Not only did Hurd wade through his diary entries from 1970 to 1974 for *An End to Promises*, but he also incorporated snippets from the period when Heath was having difficulty establishing his authority as Leader of the Opposition, and a full account of the Conservative Party's unexpected 1970 General Election victory.

In August 1968, Hurd succeeded John MacGregor as head of Edward's Heath's private office. There were a few weeks' overlap when MacGregor was settling into his new job with Hill Samuel in the City of London, while Douglas Hurd was familiarising himself with the procedures in his new post. Hurd recalls one morning when MacGregor went off to Hill Samuel, leaving Hurd in charge of sorting out Edward Heath's mail. A fine sifter of dross from gems, Hurd carefully looked through his leader's correspondence, consigning about one quarter of it immediately to the waste-paper basket. On MacGregor's return, Hurd could only watch in silence as his predecessor diplomatically went over to the bin and lifted all the junk mail back onto a desk. The creased letters were then carefully flattened out, while MacGregor announced that Mr Heath liked to see all his correspondence. It now seems incredible that in 1968, the quantity of mail was modest enough for the technocratic Heath, the Leader of the Opposition, no less, to look through all of his own letters.[6]

Of the many foreign trips made by Edward Heath as Leader of the Opposition the most interesting was a visit to the Gulf states in March 1969. Heath was then firmly of the view that Britain should retain a role east of Suez, and had been appalled by Harold Wilson's decision in 1968 – following sterling's devaluation in November 1967 – to withdraw from the region. In contrast, even after devaluation, Heath continued to believe it was possible for Britain to maintain a role in the Middle East. Writing in October 1967, along with Eldon Griffiths, Peter Tapsell and Dennis Walters, Hurd had been of the opinion that Britain had no option but to remain in the Persian Gulf until Saudi Arabia, with the support of Iran, was in a position to take over the role which Britain had performed since the turn of the century.[7] But this was a Conservative Party document written before the devaluation of the pound. Only Enoch Powell had the foresight to air the possibility of Britain's withdrawal from the Persian Gulf in his Conservative Party Conference speech of October 1965. While Heath returned from his visit still adamant that Britain should retain a presence in the Middle East, Hurd claims the visit clarified in his own mind that events had moved on. 'We had simply lost the will to continue the effort and Mr Heath was unable to revive it.'[8]

Once in office, Heath was persuaded by the Foreign Office to abandon the policy, but Hurd remembers the visit with fondness, and went on to enjoy his subsequent visits to the Gulf, first as Minister of State and then as Foreign Secretary. In return, the Arab leaders grew to admire Douglas Hurd, the archetypal English gentleman. Heath also retained a deep interest in the region, and during Hurd's tenure as Foreign Secretary in 1990 he decided – against Hurd's advice – to go on a humanitarian mission to Iraq to ask Saddam Hussein to release the British hostages being held there (see Chapter 14).

Heath abhorred racism – he sacked Enoch Powell after his 'Rivers of Blood' speech and allowed Ugandan Asians to enter Britain in 1972 – but did feel increasingly alienated by the constant carping of Black Africa at the biennial meetings of the Commonwealth Heads of Government (CHOGMs). On the eve of the Singapore CHOGM, Hurd noted in his diary on 13 January 1971, 'The prospect of nine days in the dock was not attractive.'[9]

At the time, Heath was being vilified for his decision to sell arms to South Africa; Foreign Office officials were opposed to Heath's line on the issue. Hurd's account of the episode is fairly scant, but he reminds us in the introduction to An End to Promises that, as Heath's political secretary, he gained only a 'snapshot' of each issue.[10]

During his years as Leader of the Opposition, Heath had tried unsuccessfully to breathe new life into Britain's position in the Middle East and the Far East.[11] He was always suspicious of the 'Special Relationship', despite being on good personal terms with Richard Nixon. Having explored the remaining options for Britain's future world role and found them wanting, Heath embarked upon his central purpose: the modernisation of Britain by securing its entry into the European Economic Community. But first he needed to convince his own party.

When Edward Heath became Leader of the Opposition in July 1965, he faced almost immediate and vociferous opposition to his pro-European stance from critics within his own party. In An End to Promises, Hurd cites several other issues which split the Conservative Party at this juncture: sanctions against Rhodesia; Heath's central role in abolishing Resale Price Maintenance in 1964; the issue of immigration; and the persistence of snobs within the parliamentary party who sneered at Heath's background.[12] Subsequently, Heath would neglect the parliamentary party in government and pay the ultimate penalty when he lost the leadership contest in 1975, but there were many in his parliamentary party who sought to make his life difficult from the very outset of his leadership, as Hurd described on the verge of the 1970 General Election. 'Trouble within the ranks had been at least brought under control. The authority of its leader had been painfully established.'[13]

The central figure in establishing Heath's authority in the Conservative Party was Sir Alec Douglas-Home. The traditional right-wing of the Conservative Party, particularly the supporters of Ian Smith, identified closely with Sir Alec, but he was always supportive of Edward Heath. Like many of the younger Conservative politicians in the late 1960s and early 1970s, Douglas Hurd found in Sir Alec Douglas-Home, a political mentor and means of introduction. The former Prime Minister, a fellow old Etonian, allowed Douglas Hurd to use his name when he first started looking for a seat to contest.

There has been considerable debate over Hurd's assertion that, during its years in Opposition, the Conservative Party had become 'equipped with policies more elaborate and better researched than any Opposition had ever attempted'.[14] For one thing, Rab Butler's reform exercise after the Conservative's 1945 defeat, culminating in the Industrial Charter of 1948, had been formidable. In reality, although Heath was extremely assiduous in setting up a plethora of policy groups, the central issue of an incomes policy was fudged. John Campbell, a biographer of Heath has concluded:

> The débâcle of February 1974 had its roots in the fudge of 1965-1970. With this central failure it has to be concluded that the whole policy exercise, for all its substantial marginal achievements, essentially failed.[15]

On the central question of the Selsdon Park Conference of 1970, Hurd is silent. William Waldegrave, Hurd's successor as Political Secretary to Heath, remembers the then Prime Minister as a consensus politician who did not set out to create confrontation with the unions.[16] Mrs Thatcher and her supporters have sought to portray Heath's Government as a betrayal of the promises made at Selsdon. Hugo Young avers that Heath's betrayal became an essential part of the Thatcherite mythology: Heath was the pariah figure who let the Conservative Party down by recourse to corporatism, Thatcher the phoenix who rose triumphant from the ashes.[17] Geoffrey Howe, on the other hand, who likes to see himself as being a Thatcherite before Thatcher, sees many similarities between Heath's agenda of 1970 and the 1979 manifesto.[18] The weight of the evidence seems to suggest that the Selsdon conference reflected the optimism in the Conservative Party on the eve of the 1970 General Election — the hope that Britain's problems could be tackled by sweeping away outmoded practices and thereby improving Britain's competitiveness — rather than revealing any free-market zealotry on the part of Edward Heath.

There is a distinctly puritanical tone about *A Better Tomorrow*, the Conservative Party manifesto for the June 1970 General Election. Hurd helped write the foreword to the manifesto, which was signed by Edward Heath. Hurd, who reproduces the foreword in *An End to Promises*, describes it as 'a key document' which signalled 'a note of genuine puritan protest'.[19] Hurd shared Heath's dislike of Harold Wilson's partisan style of politics, with its point-scoring and 'government by gimmick' (though recent biographies by Philip Ziegler and Ben Pimlott have sought to counter Harold Wilson's unprincipled image). Edward Heath is by nature a curmudgeonly man, with whom sections of the Conservative Party found it difficult to deal, but his neglect of his party was partly drawn, as Hurd points out, 'from his belief that the government of Britain was too serious a matter to be carried forward in the style of Harold Wilson.'[20] Unfortunately, as John Campbell concludes, Heath's disdain of party political advice in favour of civil servants left him exposed in government.[21]

Hurd enjoys the cut and thrust of political campaigning. More than the dour press conferences and the television appearances, he thrives out on the campaign trail, speaking in crowded village halls, tackling the odd heckler, reminiscent of his grandfather's days in Frome back in 1918. He reserves a particular fondness for the 1970 General Election campaign because the Conservative victory came against the predictions of the pollsters. Writing many years later, after his resignation as Foreign Secretary, Hurd drew a comparison between the General Elections of 1970 and 1992:

> In 1992, as in 1970, a leader entered a contest on unfavourable terms. In both cases the opinion polls and therefore the commentators gave him up for lost. In both cases the Labour Party began to act as if they had won. In both cases, they [the leaders] changed tack, abandoned elaborate plans based on American campaigning concepts and discovered to their surprise that the leader of their Party actually did quite well when confronted with ordinary electors. Neither John Major's soapbox nor Ted Heath's walkabouts were part of the original plans. They changed the nature of the Election and helped to bring success against the odds.[22]

As well as explaining the troubles of Edward Heath's latter period as Leader of the Opposition, *An End to Promises* has three other valuable features. First, it is an insider's account of the workings of government; second, it is a first-hand account of the character and style of Edward Heath as Prime Minister; but most importantly, as its title suggests, *An End to Promises* identifies the need for a new realism among politicians and the electorate about what governments could achieve in the field of economic policy. Similarly, in 1977, William Waldegrave's book *The Binding of the Leviathan* cast doubt on the value of state intervention.

Excerpts of Hurd's book were printed in *The Observer* in 1979 to mixed reviews. One critic, writing in the *New Statesman* called it 'a slight book in every respect and often bland to the point of prissiness'.[23] Richard Ollard – who had been responsible for publishing Hurd's novels – was not even keen for the book to be published by Collins, but Hurd's new agent, Michael Sissons, was insistent that a man of Hurd's literary skill should be retained as a client.[24]

The book is, as Hurd admitted, a personal memoir, not a comprehensive history of events. Some areas, such as Northern Ireland, are given scant coverage, but this is a reflection of Hurd's minimal involvement in the issue. Others issues, like industrial relations, where Hurd was deeply involved, provide a rich vein for historian and biographer alike. Many of the themes in *An End to Promises* recur in his novels *Truth Game* and *Vote to Kill*, but seasoned observers of Hurd will already be aware of his tendency to repeat the same themes over several years, dusting them off, freshening them up and dressing them in a new guise each time.

Hurd is very charitable when referring to his contemporaries. Qualifying phrases are used a little too often; the overall meaning is lost in his attempt to be complimentary about everyone. Criticisms of blandness are probably close to the mark. There is little gossip in Hurd's account of Heath's Government; readers will find no Alan Clark here. Hurd does have an eye for the ridiculous – the full diaries contain amusing observations of his political contemporaries – but in *An End to Promises*, they are largely absent. Writing in 1978–79, Hurd was probably wary of rocking the boat, either with his former boss or with his own party, then on the verge of government.

Despite being a personal memoir, the book reveals very little about Douglas Hurd the man. We learn a great deal about what Hurd observed, but far less about what he is like. Hurd's account is far more revealing about the personality and style of Edward Heath. Perhaps this was good sense. As Heath's political secretary, Hurd was more an observer than a major participant in policy making, and described himself, with characteristic modesty, as 'a base mechanic'.[25] In contrast to most politicians, Hurd has virtually no vanity, no sense of his own importance. He sees himself as a public servant performing his duty to the nation. That in itself may sound trite, pompous or old-fashioned, depending on one's viewpoint, but duty and service are fundamental to the way he has conducted his political career. Throughout *An End to Promises*, the outer layer of Hurd's carapace is all that is exposed; the tortoise remains firmly in its shell. But the book is both a good insider's view of the workings of government, and an aid to understanding the transition of the modern Conservative Party from Edward Heath to Margaret Thatcher, helping chart his own political journey from one leader to the other *en route*.

The real importance of Hurd's book from a historical point of view is its perceptive analysis of the industrial relations conflicts of the Heath Government and the contention that, after the defeat at the hands of organised labour, Britain would require, as Hurd puts it, 'a new mandate for harsh measures'.[26] Hurd argued, following the failed dash for economic growth under Heath, that it was no longer possible for governments to make economic promises to their electorates:

> The public expenditure cuts of December 1973 were only the first of these adjustments which would be needed. We were entering a period of lean years, perhaps many years of really harsh scarcity and impoverishment. The lean years would need new policies and a new vocabulary. There would have to be an end to promises. People would have to understand, because only with that understanding could their government do what was needed.[27]

The unity and sense of purpose of the modern Conservative Party in the early Thatcher years was forged by its perception of the defeat at the hands of the miners, not so much in 1973–74, but at Saltley Gates in February 1972. To date, much of the focus for historians of the Heath Government has been on the impact of the Yom Kippur War and the miners' dispute of 1973–74, when in fact Douglas Hurd sees 1972 as the key influence. In his meticulous biography of Edward Heath, John Campbell avers that Saltley Gates was not a turning point in the mining dispute. It seems clear that, given the perilous state of coal stocks in 1972, Edward Heath's Government was already on the verge of giving in before Saltley. But symbolism was everything. The union movement had, at a stroke, erased the memory of 'Black Friday', the day in 1926 which broke the General Strike. Conversely, for Conservative politicians, the memory of defeat at the hands of the miners would be etched in memory, simmering away until they regained power. Fifteen thousand 'flying pickets' led by Arthur Scargill had prevented the police from securing the passage of lorries from the coke depot in the Midlands. Hurd's most memorable passage from this period is now a standard quote:

> 11 Feb. 1972: The Government now wandering vainly over the battlefield looking for someone to surrender to – and being massacred all the time.[28]

Defeat at Saltley Gates in 1972 meant that the Conservative Party's own supporters would not stomach another humiliating reversal at the hands of the miners. This was the conclusion of a paper written to Heath by Hurd and William Waldegrave – then moving from the Central Policy Review Staff (CPRS) to succeed Hurd as Heath's political secretary – on 6 December 1973:

> A settlement in manifest breach of Stage 3 would not be possible for this Government, because it would destroy the authority and break the morale of the Conservative Party beyond the hope of restoration in the lifetime of this Parliament.[29]

A similar memo could have been written in 1984. The Conservative Party still could not have borne another defeat at the hands of the miners. The Conservative Party's *raison d'être* in the late 1970s and during the 1980s became the defeat of organised labour. Next time, the interests of the nation had to win; inflation had to be brought down at all costs, and the unions had to be defeated.

In the longer term, Saltley Gates dried out the economic views of the parliamentary Conservative Party. Whilst political opportunism undoubtedly played a part in the speed with which former Heathites like Douglas Hurd, William Waldegrave, Kenneth Baker, Chris Patten and John MacGregor dissociated themselves from Edward Heath when Mrs Thatcher became leader in 1975, they were all sure that they should not – and could not – face another defeat at the hands of organised labour. Even 'wets' like Peter Walker, had no desire to return to the miserable experience of 1972. Indeed, as Energy Secretary under Mrs Thatcher, Walker was at the forefront of defeating the Miners' Strike of 1984-85. Douglas Hurd, too, became acutely aware of trade union challenges during his period as Minister of State at the Home Office in 1984. Hurd was in charge of policing operations during the Miners' Strike, although the erstwhile Home Secretary, Leon Brittan, encouraged from behind by Mrs Thatcher, took most of the important decisions (see Chapter 9). As Home Secretary during the Wapping Dispute of 1986-87, Hurd did not flinch from taking a tough line against strikers (see Chapter 13).

During the 1980s, Hurd's own economic views, however incomplete, dried out. He may have shied away from worshipping at the altar of the free market, but he was always clear in his own mind that it was not the job of Government to intervene in industry to prop up so called 'lame ducks', or to spend vast sums of money on the social services – which he later termed the 'hungry giants'.[30] In short, Hurd went along with Mrs Thatcher, because large parts of her agenda, particularly the policies to curb trade union power, started to work. But in doing so, the Conservative Party moved further to the right than he would ideally have wished.

Even in the 1990s, although the Conservatives were divided on the issue of Europe, they were almost at one – apart from Edward Heath – in their opposition to the relatively modest Social Chapter provisions in the Maastricht Treaty. Again, this all stemmed from a belief that, after struggling in the 1980s to restore the balance of industrial power towards business, it was unacceptable to allow the European Community to give back any power to the workers. This attitude was seen by Britain's European partners as verging on the irrational, but it was the unifying belief which had held the Conservative Party together for more than a decade.

There are caveats to this argument. It assumes that Mrs Thatcher had a preconceived plan to defeat the unions, and a clear idea of how she was going to achieve this. In fact, she moved cautiously in her first term, edging in the dark in the fields of trade union reform and privatisation. The difference between Hurd's view and that of Mrs Thatcher remains the question of whether or not the Heath Government made a valiant attempt – in Hurd's words, the 'rough work of pioneers' – to modernise Britain and reform industrial relations, failing because of exogenous shocks, or whether Edward Heath is the man to blame for performing a series of U-turns from the policies put forward at the Selsdon Park conference in 1970.

The real success behind the Conservative Party in the latter half of the 1980s rested on its confident interpretation of British political history since 1970. Thatcher was perceived as the first Prime Minister to tackle the trade unions, when in fact Heath made a fairly honourable attempt. However, there is a historical case for claiming that Harold Wilson and Barbara Castle were the first to recognise the need to tackle trade union power with their *In Place of Strife* document in 1969.[31]

An End to Promises added to the historical debate about British politics, but Hurd was only half correct in his analysis. Yes, there would be harsh measures, but his advocacy of a coalition government as the means to achieve cuts in public expenditure turned out to be wrong. Writing in 1979, he saw two parties who appeared to be moving to the extremes and who appeared to disagree about everything. By 1981, it looked to most political observers as if Mrs Thatcher might not survive, and the growing appeal of the Social Democratic Party (SDP) opened up, for a fleeting moment, the opportunity of a national government. Ever since that brief moment in February 1974 following the Conservatives' narrow defeat, when Heath had entered into negotiations with the Liberals to try to form a coalition government, Hurd has been in favour of parties co-operating on the vital issues of public spending, preserving NATO and ensuring Britain's membership of the European Community.

As a backbench MP in the mid 1970s, Hurd became a brief convert to proportional representation.[32] His support has since waned, partly for party political reasons, but mostly because the two major parties have shifted closer together on many of the national-interest issues which affect Britain. The need for coalition governments has passed, for the moment at least. As with many issues, Hurd has no ideological attachment to the cause of proportional representation, but if a new system of voting is needed in the future as a means of preserving moderate policies in the national interest, he may drift back to support some form of proportional representation.

Hurd has been inconsistent on PR, but he has remained consistent since the 1970s about his dislike of adversarial politics. He believes that politicians should be able to engage in rational argument, without resorting to the argy-bargy of political debate. A comparison between his views expressed in 1979 in *An End to Promises* and one of his speeches after resigning as Foreign Secretary in 1995 reveals Hurd's dislike of partisan politics to be a consistent, if somewhat well-worn, theme. The former states:

> People simply do not take seriously the toy drums and tin whistles of ordinary party politics as practised on the floor of the House.[33]

And in November 1995:

> There is I think a real danger that, egged on by the media, all parties in this House, all of us, may play out the old play, not realising that beyond the footlights half the audience has crept away and the other half is sitting there in mounting irritation.[34]

An End to Promises is also valuable for its in-depth insight of how the executive works, and the relationship between the various bodies which make up the Prime Minister's retinue. Hurd did not share the view of his predecessor as political secretary, Marcia Williams (Lady Falkender), that the Civil Service is Conservative with a large 'C'.[35] Lady Falkender's view was expressed both in the Richard Crossman and Tony Benn diaries, which depict set-piece battles between Conservative permanent secretaries against incoming socialist-minded ministers. Neither does Hurd share the view of Joe Haines, Harold Wilson's, chief press officer, that the Civil Service resents political change.[36] In Hurd's experience, Whitehall officials take the line that ministers must decide, though their preference is for the minister, of whatever party, to follow a clear direction and adhere to policies once they are embarked upon.[37]

At Number 10, Heath was served by his Political Office, led by Hurd, and his Private Office, staffed by career civil servants working at Number 10. Edward Heath's own preference for Civil Service advice was illustrated when he appointed Donald Maitland, a career diplomat, to run his Press Office – in contrast to Harold Wilson, who had made political appointments in the shape of Joe Haines and Gerald Kaufman. Heath also relied a great deal on the advice of Sir William Armstrong, Head of the Home Civil Service.

Despite being the Prime Minister's political secretary, Hurd was not permitted to attend Cabinet meetings, but largely thanks to the influence of his predecessor, Marcia Williams, his office at Number 10 was adjacent to the Cabinet room. Before and after full Cabinet, ministers would congregate in clusters outside chatting unrestrainedly, enabling Hurd to play the role of fly-on-the-wall. Tea was taken in the junior of the two Private Office rooms, which meant Hurd was given security clearance (from Robert Armstrong, Heath's

Senior Private Secretary, who succeeded Sandy Isserlis) to skim through the papers filling up in the senior of the Private Offices, destined for the ministerial red boxes.[38] Combined with his speech-making role, Hurd was, in one respect, an embryonic political adviser, except that he was serving a Prime Minister who preferred to take Civil Service advice. William Waldegrave, then with the Central Policy Review Staff (CPRS), did not see Douglas Hurd as a political adviser with a capital 'P'. If Heath was seeking advice on short-term political tactics – 'spin doctoring' in modern jargon – or liaison with Conservative Central Office, he tended to turn to his personal policy adviser and principal speech writer, Michael Wolff. If he wanted to gain a broader strategic picture, he would listen to, or read a memo from, Douglas Hurd. Throughout this period, Waldegrave felt that Hurd was very careful and modest in his role as head of Heath's private office.[39]

One of Hurd's most pointed observations from his time working at Number 10 was that senior ministers were overworked, weighed down by a mass of paperwork, and becoming increasingly cut-off from the political aspect of their role. Meanwhile, junior ministers, who could assist their minister, were 'kept in a separate cocoon of minor engagements and paperwork'.[40] One of Hurd's suggested improvements to the workings of the executive was for senior ministers to have political advisers to act as the minister's eyes and ears, thereby keeping them acquainted with the party political side of ministerial office. In his frustration, Hurd wrote a memo to Heath in August 1971, entitled *The Party as Auxiliary to Government*, in which he identified a growing 'difficulty in getting Ministers to think politically about their daily problems'.[41] The difficulty about relying so heavily on Civil Service advice was that it tended to fall silent during crises. Douglas Hurd cites the aftermath of Bloody Sunday on 30 January 1972, the inflation talks of the summer of 1973 and the November 1973 coal crisis as occasions when Civil Service advice 'fell below what was required'.[42]

Heath, however, did launch one brave experiment to try to give the Government a strategic outlook. The CPRS was intended to be an independent source of advice to Cabinet, free of Whitehall influence and departmental loyalties. Headed by the outspoken, but highly intelligent Victor Rothschild, it did try to give coherence and shape to the Government, even if, according to Geoffrey Howe, it did not have much influence over policy formulation.[43] John Campbell describes the CPRS as 'a unique episode, a brief heady moment of creative energy and one of the most notable achievements of Heath's premiership.'[44] The Cabinet were to be given regular presentations charting future trends, acting as an early-warning system, predicting policy difficulties in the future. Hurd's main criticism was that the CPRS 'rubbed ministers' noses in the future'.[45] It was seen as meddling by other Government departments. Its success, as William Waldegrave recalls, 'mirrored the confidence of the

Government. Governments that are confident are willing to think ahead, think the unthinkable; Governments that are beginning to become embroiled in the short term, are not.'[46]

The 'Think Tank', as it quickly became known, enjoyed its maximum period of influence from 1971 to 1972, but fell out of favour with Heath in the autumn of 1973, when Lord Rothschild made a speech predicting that, if the economy carried on in its present path, Britain would end up poorer than the Spanish or the Portuguese. The Think Tank remained in limbo until Mrs Thatcher performed the last rites in 1983. Hurd, along with many other observers, still identifies a need for a source of independent advice to the Prime Minister, but acknowledges the case for a relatively informal structure so that each new Prime Minister has the freedom to introduce his or her own *mode d'emploi*.

Of all his views on politics, Hurd gives particular prominence to the idea that events, both important and apparently trivial, have a tendency to pile on top of ministers, crowding in on one another. Even if an issue seems relatively unimportant, it may take up a great deal of time, jostling with the more pressing matters of state. Time is a precious commodity for a senior minister. Because of its scarcity, the Whig view of government, that ministers should be held to account for every decision, is, in Hurd's view, unsustainable. The business of government must go on, not free from, but also not weighed down by, the need to justify every action in retrospect. Hurd is convinced that this fact of government is not sufficiently understood by the chattering classes, and his most recent novel, *The Shape of Ice*, reinforces this point.[47] The Major premiership of 1990 to 1997 and the Heath Government of 1970 to 1974 both suffered from the tyranny of events, like a Shakespearian tragedy — troubles coming not singly but battalion-fold:

> Because historians tend to analyse one subject at a time they sometimes lose sight of the pell-mell of politics. Problems crowd in on top of each other, competing for scarce time. The principal actors thrive for a time on the excitement of this way of life. They do not notice the onset of fatigue. But if they allow themselves no respite, the pace slows, they increasingly miss their stroke, they begin without realising it to move through a fog of tiredness. This happened to Ministers in the winter of 1973. Certainly the events were already crowding in.[48]

But civil servants from Edward Heath's Government deny that the central machinery of government was breaking down at the end of December 1973. Lord Croham, then Permanent Secretary at the Treasury, and Lord Armstrong of Illminster (Heath's Principal Private Secretary), accept that there were strong pressures on ministers and officials at the time. Geoffrey Howe, then Minister for Trade and Consumer Affairs, acknowledges that the external pressure of the oil-price shock and the coal strike were 'debilitating', but maintains 'people were not burying their heads in their pillows and weeping'.[49]

Against this, one should bear in mind that the influential Sir William Armstrong, Head of the Home Civil Service, to whom Heath deferred a great deal, came under immense strain and was forced to retire through ill health in January 1974. Viscount Whitelaw admits in his memoirs to feeling the strain on returning from the collapse of the Sunningdale Agreement in Ulster, only to be faced with a state of emergency.[50] In addition, Lord Hunt of Tanworth, who succeeded Burke Trend as Secretary to the Cabinet in the Autumn of 1973, felt there was 'a smell of death hanging over the government with very tired ministers not making the best decisions.'[51] Perhaps the whole apparatus of government was not at breaking point, but probably Hurd's description of 'a fog of tiredness' was fair of a number of officials and ministers in late 1973 and early 1974. However, the real source of the Government's malaise was the strength of worker power. Hurd does not go as far as this, but he did observe in *An End to Promises* that 'the facts of power in Britain were against the Government',[52] and with hindsight, that one of the reasons that Heath lost 'had to do with the brutal exercise of trade union power'.[53]

Nevertheless, compared with the Thatcher and Major cabinets, the Heath Cabinet remained extremely united throughout. Douglas Hurd was one of those who remained loyal, and indeed, *An End to Promises* is dedicated to Edward Heath. However, Heath made known he was unhappy with the book. Partly this was because he found it difficult to forgive those who had accepted Shadow Cabinet posts from Margaret Thatcher after being so closely connected with him. Unlike many of the Thatcherites, Hurd never joined in the chorus of name-calling which went on against his former boss whom, at the beginning of the book, he describes as 'a remarkable patriot'. But it is not at all certain that they ever became very close friends and confidants, in the way that Heath was close to Michael Wolff and Sara Morrison.[54] The diaries refer to Heath as 'Mr Heath'. Later, this softens to 'E.H.', but there is no indication of Hurd referring to his leader as 'Ted'. Perhaps this came down to Hurd's strong sense of deference and propriety towards those he worked for (when he became a senior minister, Hurd began regularly to refer to Edward Heath as 'Ted'). Just occasionally, Hurd cannot resist seeing the humorous side of Heath's conscientious and technocratic mind. During Heath's painstaking preparation for the crucial Anglo-French summit with President Pompidou in May 1971, there is a sketch by Hurd of Heath studying like a student under a tree, dunking his biscuits in his tea. One of Hurd's strengths as a writer is the rough sketch. This forte is displayed in his novels, when we are given potted descriptions of an Arab desert or a crowded political rally at a village hall. This is not altogether surprising: Hurd's life, especially as a diplomat and as Foreign Secretary, has been dominated as much by fleeting observations of people and places as by participation in actual events.

A great deal of Hurd's time was spent writing memos and scripting speeches for Edward Heath, as Churchill's biographer Martin Gilbert discovered in 1972 during tea with Edward Heath in the garden of 10 Downing Street:

> The Prime Minister was accompanied by his Political Secretary. At one point Heath asked me how Churchill prepared his speeches, how did his speechwriters work? I interrupted keenly to say that Churchill did not use speechwriters, but dictated all his own speeches, even on occasion writing them out in longhand. As I spoke, I noticed the young man go somewhat red, and Heath look a little put out. I realised at once that I was in the presence not only of a Prime Minister but of a speechwriter. Twenty years later the young man, Douglas Hurd, was Foreign Secretary.[55]

However, Hurd was only one component of a speech-writing team which was headed by Michael Wolff and Geoffrey Tucker, Director of Publicity at Central Office. There was also a varying group of paid speech writers, including James Garrett, Barry Day, Ronald Millar and, latterly, Andrew Neil, who became editor of The Sunday Times and then, in 1996, Editor-in-Chief of The Scotsman. One of Hurd's major criticisms of Heath in An End to Promises was his failure to communicate his ideas effectively: either to his own party at Conferences or to the electorate on television. Chapter six of Hurd's book is entitled 'Speeches and Silences'. Drafting speeches at speed is a skill at which Hurd excels. His years in the Foreign Office had taught him to draft a paper at speed, but it was a task which he grew to detest:

> I seem to have spent all my working life drafting speeches for other people, and I hate it. It becomes almost intolerable when one has no clear guidance on what is needed.[56]

Hurd vents his frustration on several occasions in his diaries. An entry for 20 November 1970 is typical:

> Torquay: Lunch, and he [Heath] sleeps and reads yachting papers, and only in Somerset does he for the first time read the draft. Speech is Okay, just, without much of him in it, and he is tired.[57]

This is not to suggest that Heath was an idle Prime Minister. Hurd makes several references to the fact that Heath drove himself very hard indeed,[58] and, as Hurd puts it, that the Prime Minister was a perfectionist without the time to perfect.[59] Speeches for conferences would be drafted at the very last minute, and there would be no time for Heath to practise his emphasis. Part of the problem – not identified by Hurd at the time – was that Heath performed best when he spoke extempore. After Heath lost the Tory leadership, he chose to speak in the House of Commons without notes, developing a speaking style which came to be admired by his fellow MPs. Had Heath been left entirely to his own devices, he may have developed more quickly into a better speaker. But as Prime Minister, Heath was extremely wooden on television. Both Hurd and Geoffrey Tucker, Director of Publicity at Central Office, tried to persuade Heath to speak in shorter sentences, but the overall effect on camera was that he appeared to bark in staccato fashion at the electorate. The material Heath wanted to include in his speeches reflected his desire to run a government free from gimmickry. But as Hurd puts it, 'Mr Heath believed that people deserved the evidence, and, by God, they were going to get it. It sometimes made for hard pounding.'[60]

Hurd believed that the failure to communicate extended beyond the Prime Minister to ministers and the heads of the nationalised industries, especially during industrial disputes:

> On industrial and economic matters the caution of Ministers and the silence
> of the employers were often during 1970-74 no match for the concerted
> effort of the Labour opposition and the trade union movement.[61]

Time and time again, Hurd complained that the employers conceded all their bargaining power at the beginning of a pay round by making their opening offer their final offer. The unions, aware of their power, refused and went on strike. The pay dispute was then handed over to outside arbitrators, who caved in to union demands. In the case of the February 1972 dispute, Lord Wilberforce's over-generous recommendation in Hurd's view made it impossible for ministers in party political terms to concede another victory to the miners in 1973-74. During the Heath Government, ministers stayed ineffective and silent during industrial disputes. The mistakes of the Heath period were learned during the Thatcher years, when ministers became politically involved in disputes. Hurd predicted the public backlash to industrial disputes accurately:

> Unless public sector disputes subside into insignificance, a counterforce
> will eventually be created. It may be ugly, or it may be sensible, but the

public will not remain forever content to suffer as innocent victims of
disputes over which it has no control.[62]

By 'the public', Hurd really meant the Government. His prediction in 1979 that
the interests of the taxpayer and the consumer had to be defended by ministers
became a favourite rhetorical theme of ministers during the struggles of the 1980s.

Hurd cites Heath's winning-over of President Pompidou, and Britain's
consequent entry into the European Community, as being the greatest single
achievement of the Heath premiership.[63] True, Heath was serendipitous in the
sense that General de Gaulle had fallen from office and was replaced by
someone more amenable to Britain's point of view, but Heath deserves credit
for realising that winning over the French was the key to securing Britain's
entry. The Prime Minister took a gamble by playing a highly personal role –
developing a good personal rapport with Georges Pompidou during the first
Anglo-French summit in May 1971.

The much more difficult hurdle lay in persuading Parliament to pass the
European Communities Bill, a task which was performed with considerable skill
by the Chief Whip, Francis Pym. In June 1971, however, Hurd was worried
that the Conservative Party might not pass the Bill if the Government waited
too long. In a minute to the Prime Minister on 7 June, he urged a quick vote.
Hurd describes himself as 'a hothead'.[64] Instead, Heath launched a massive
publicity campaign in July 1971 to persuade Conservative Party members of the
merits of joining the Community, thus exerting considerable constituency
association pressure on anti-European Conservatives. The key vote on the
principle of the Bill was held on 28 October 1971.[65] Francis Pym's astute
tactical move in calling a free vote on the Conservative side, encouraged sixty-
nine Labour rebels to vote with the Government (because they were not facing
a strongly whipped Conservative lobby). The Government carried the motion
with a comfortable majority of 112.[66]

However, there were tense votes ahead, including the Second Reading vote
on 17 February 1972, which the Government won by only eight votes.[67] It seems
certain that Edward Heath would have resigned as Prime Minister had he lost
this vote. We know this because, after Michael Wolff's death, William
Waldegrave was put in charge of Wolff's personal and political papers by the
executor, Geoffrey Howe. Amid the pile of papers, Waldegrave uncovered a
resignation speech, drafted by Michael Wolff.[68] On a vital matter of this kind, it
was Michael Wolff rather than Douglas Hurd who would be called upon to
compile a draft. This was as it should have been; Wolff was senior to Hurd.

Hurd falls short of blaming Heath for causing the U-turns of 1972, or at least,
he seeks to explain Heath's decision to prop up lame ducks through the Industry
Bill and introduce a statutory incomes policy. He was deeply affected by the

news on 20 January 1972 that unemployment had risen above one million. Combined with his puritanical streak, Heath disliked the go-ahead, gung-ho side of capitalism and Hurd's views at that stage were very similar. But Douglas Hurd denies penning the famous phrase which Heath used about Lonrho, 'the unacceptable face of capitalism'. Heath initially made the unscripted comment at Perth on 12 May 1973 at a dinner on the eve of the Scottish Conservative Party Conference. During Prime Minister's Questions on Tuesday, 15 May 1973, Heath replied to a question by Jo Grimond, the Liberal leader about Lonrho. 'It is the unpleasant and unacceptable face of capitalism, but one should not suggest the whole of British industry consists of practices of this kind.'[69]

Despite the fact that Hurd did not invent the phrase (Michael Wolff seems to have added the phrase after he first heard it from Heath), he was never a strong believer in the rigid doctrine of monetarism. In *An End to Promises*, Hurd quotes an article by T.E. Utley reviewing Professor Hayek's book on monetarism:

Why then do the ancestral voices of Toryism persistently warn me against Dr Hayek? In a nutshell, because his rigid ideology, which rests firmly on the view that the free market is a panacea for nearly all the politically curable ills, exaggerates one of the great truths about politics at the cost of neglect in the other. In its concern for liberty, it disparages the importance of social cohesion.[70]

We might as well attribute T.E. Utley's quotation to Hurd because this is exactly the strand of Toryism from which Hurd derives his views. Although his experiences during the Heath years caused him to see the need for tough economic measures, Hurd stopped short of supporting Mrs Thatcher's brand of individualism. Somehow, Hurd still believes it is possible for the Conservative Party, which espouses inequality, simultaneously to promote social cohesion, by those with wealth and power taking responsibility and becoming 'active citizens'. His views would become much clearer in his speech to the Peel Society in February 1988, but even in 1979 he warned against the dangers of monetarism:

The danger of this theory is the implication that another Conservative Government will have a straightforward and not too difficult task if only it holds to its orthodoxy. The truth is different. Britain cannot be governed dogmatically or by the exercise of will-power. However well-founded the dogma, however strong the will, Britain can only be governed with the consent of people of widely differing opinions.[71]

Contrary to his expectations, someone possessing the necessary will-power was able to use political dogma against the wishes of the majority of the nation to pursue her political ends. Hurd grew to admire Mrs Thatcher for being able to achieve something which in 1979 he did not believe could be achieved.

Hurd is most critical of Edward Heath's decision not to call an election three weeks earlier than he did. During the months of December 1973 and January 1974, there was a battle going on for the ear of the Prime Minister. Hurd was only one of many officials and ministers, including Nigel Lawson, William Waldegrave and Peter Carrington, who were trying to persuade Heath to call an election for 7 February. At a steering committee meeting at Chequers on 12 January 1974, Hurd and a number of others thought they had got through to Heath, but the next day he threw cold water over their ideas. Heath believed he could make a deal with the TUC and expended a great deal of effort, wasted in Hurd's opinion, trying to secure agreement.[72]

On 15 January, Hurd wrote a note to the Prime Minister, putting the case for an early election. If they called an election on 7 February, it would be against the background of the miners' overtime ban, not a strike, but if they appeared to cling on, the Government's authority would ebb away:

> We are gradually getting nearer the time when the Government will be forced, by a revolution of business and public opinion and by the damage done to the nation, to accept a settlement clearly and substantially outside Stage 3.[73]

Hurd went on:

> I suppose that such a settlement would provoke in the Party and outside a violent sense of betrayal, directed personally at you, and the Government would be broken-backed for the remainder of its time.[74]

The real case against Heath, perhaps, was not so much that he called an early election, but that, having set himself against an early poll and then being forced into calling one three weeks later, smacked of ineptitude. Could Heath have won any election regardless of the date? Hurd recalls that, on 11 January 1974, Humphrey Taylor from the Opinion Research Centre (ORC) – the only pollster who correctly predicted a Conservative victory in 1970 – was forecasting a narrow Conservative win if an early election was called. Setting aside the unreliability of opinion polls, could Heath really have made a deal with the miners after an election victory? Or did the electorate (Wilson actually won the largest number of seats with less of the popular vote than the Conservatives) sense that only a Labour Government with some identification with the workers had the influence to seek an accommodation with them? Hurd would disagree but he did argue that any abandonment of the Government's incomes policy before an election would have been politically disastrous:

The Government would have limped on in a broken-backed way for a year or so, probably under a different PM. The defeat at the hands of the miners and Lord Wilberforce in 1972 is crucial to this argument. In retrospect, I do not doubt that we were right to advise against a second surrender on the same ground.[75]

Given that it was politically impossible for Heath to have made a second deal with the miners before the election, it does not seem credible to claim that he could have done so after the election, despite an electoral mandate. The balance of power in favour of the trade unions was too great for a Conservative Government to have succeeded in such a climate and the Conservative Party would not have been able to swallow giving in to the miners again. Only after the débâcle of the Winter of Discontent in 1978-79, was the electorate willing to contemplate a different approach to industrial relations.

During the February 1974 campaign, the Pay Board put out a new set of figures on relative pay, which appeared to show the miners had a genuine case. Hurd noted in his diary:

22 Feb. 1974: We are cruelly savaged by the Pay Board, putting out entirely new figures on relative pay for miners, more favourable to their case. E.H. simply retires in a cloud of stubborn and unconvincing negatives.[76]

Six days later, Heath lost the election; even though the Conservatives polled more votes than Labour, they had five fewer seats. But Hurd was not involved in the central campaign, apart from half a day at Chequers:

17 Feb. 1974: To Chequers. Cautious mood. We are just ahead in the polls, but Liberals show much vitality; mortgages are a major worry. There may be a slippage in the last 48 hours.[77]

For the most part, Hurd was out campaigning in the mud and rain of Mid-Oxfordshire, where he had been selected as a candidate in February 1972. Unlike the 1970 Election, Hurd was fighting his own campaign away from the glare of the media. 'I'm completely divorced from radio, TV and national happenings.'[78]

On his successful election on 28 February 1974, Hurd wrote, 'The one real aim of my working life realised. Don't really have to go any higher.'[79]

So, Hurd was a new Member of Parliament, but he did not go to London until 4 March. Instead, he spent the weekend at home in Oxfordshire recovering. Although he talked to Heath on the telephone, he was not involved in the abortive negotiations with Jeremy Thorpe, about a possible coalition with the Liberals. By the time Hurd returned to Number 10, it was simply a matter of packing up his sacks and belongings:

> 4 Mar. 1974: I said my own goodbyes today. The cameras are not looking.
> Ted said goodbye to us all . . . It will be a long road back.[80]

During his years as Heath's political secretary, Hurd had acquired great experience and knowledge of the workings of government, but as a backbench MP, whose party was now in Opposition, he was suddenly bereft of the benefits of power. The next five years of Douglas Hurd's life would be lean years, not only in political terms, but also financially and emotionally.

Notes

1. Hurd, *Send Him Victorious*, (Collins: London, 1968) p. 31.
2. Douglas Hurd, *The United Nations: A Conservative Analysis*, Old Queen Street Papers, CRD, No. 4, 18 Dec. 1967. (Part of *Notes on Current Politics Series*).
3. Ibid., p. 463.
4. Ibid., p. 463.
5. Private information.
6. Conversation with Douglas Hurd, University of Hull, 8 Nov. 1996.
7. Eldon Griffiths et al., *The Middle East and Britain*, CPC, Sept. 1967.
8. Douglas Hurd, *An End to Promises: Sketch of a Government, 1970–74* (Collins: London, 1979), p. 46.
9. Ibid., p. 53.
10. Ibid., p. 51.
11. In August 1968, Heath aired the idea of a defence pact between Britain, Australia, New Zealand, Singapore and Malaysia during a trip to the Far East.
12. Hurd, *An End to Promises*, p. 12.
13. Ibid., p. 10.
14. Ibid., p. 10.
15. John Campbell, *Edward Heath: A Biography* (Jonathan Cape: London, 1993), p.234.
16. Interview with William Waldegrave, 17 Dec. 1996.
17. Evidence by Hugo Young, Michael Kandiah (ed.), 'Witness Seminar. The Heath Government', in *Contemporary Record*, vol. 9, no. 1, (Summer 1995), p. 192.
18. Evidence by Lord Howe of Aberavon, Kandiah (ed.), op. cit., p. 192.
19. Hurd, *An End to Promises*, p. 14.
20. Ibid., p. 14.

21. Campbell, *Edward Heath*, p. 291.
22. Douglas Hurd, 'To listen or decide?', *Daily Telegraph*, 14 Oct. 1995.
23. R.V. Johnson, 'Jolly Firm', *New Statesman*, 23 Feb. 1979; *see* also Alan Watkins, 'Come and go', *The Spectator*, 24 Feb. 1979.
24. Interview with Michael Sissons, 21 May 1996.
25. Hurd, *An End to Promises*, p. 63.
26. Ibid., p. 129.
27. Ibid., p. 130
28. Ibid., p. 103.
29. Ibid., p. 119.
30. Ibid., p. 86.
31. *See* Barbara Castle, *The Castle Diaries, 1964–70* (Weidenfeld & Nicolson: London, 1984).
32. Douglas Hurd, 'Electoral Reform: A True Tory Cause', *The Spectator*, 24 January 1976; Hurd favoured a hybrid system between first-past-the-post (FPTP) and the single transferable vote (STV).
33. Hurd, *An End to Promises*, p. 71.
34. H. of C. Deb. (6th Series), 15 Nov. 1995, vol. 267, col. 9.
35. Marcia Williams, *Inside Number 10* (Weidenfeld & Nicolson: London, 1972).
36. Joe Haines, *The Politics of Power* (Jonathan Cape: London, 1977).
37. Hurd, *An End to Promises*, p. 31.
38. Ibid., pp. 34–5.
39. Interview with William Waldegrave, 17 Dec. 1996.
40. Hurd, *An End to Promises*, p. 31.
41. Ibid., pp. 94–5.
42. Ibid., pp. 117–18; p. 36.
43. Lord Howe of Aberavon, quoted in Kandiah (ed.), op. cit., p. 209.
44. Campbell, *Edward Heath*, p. 319.
45. Hurd, *An End to Promises*, p. 39.
46. Interview with William Waldegrave, 17 Dec. 1996.
47. Douglas Hurd, 'The Tyranny of Time', *Letters from a Diplomat*, Radio 4, 24 June 1996 (original transcript).
48. Hurd, *An End to Promises*, p. 113.
49. Kandiah (ed.), op. cit., pp. 212–14.
50. William Whitelaw, *The Whitelaw Memoirs* (Aurum Press: London, 1989), p. 124.
51. Kandiah (ed.), op. cit. p. 213.
52. Hurd, *An End to Promises*, p. 103.
53. Ibid., p. 150.
54. Sara Morrison was the former wife of Charles Morrison, (Devizes), whom Heath made a Vice Chairman of the Conservative Party in 1970.

According to John Campbell, 'she was one of the few people who could tell him [Heath] when he was behaving intolerably,' Campbell, *Edward Heath*, p. 257.

55. Martin Gilbert, *In Search of Churchill* (Harper Collins: London, 1994), p. 268.

56. Hurd, *An End to Promises*, p. 76.

57. Ibid., p. 76.

58. Although both Edward Heath and William Whitelaw confessed to needing eight hours of sleep every night.

59. Hurd, *An End to Promises*, p. 76.

60. Ibid., p. 82.

61. Ibid., p. 80.

62. Ibid., p. 106.

63. Ibid., p. 64.

64. Hurd, *An End to Promises*, p. 65.

65. According to Britain's leading authority on parliamentary dissent, Professor Philip Norton, twenty-one rebel Conservative MPs came under some kind of constituency pressure between October 1971 and February 1972. Philip Norton, *Conservative Dissidents: Dissent Within the Parliamentary Conservative Party, 1970–74* (Temple Smith: London, 1978), pp. 177–200.

66. The voting was 356 votes to 244. Thirty-nine Conservative MPs voted against the Government while two abstained. On the Labour side around 120 Labour MPs abstained.

67. The voting on Second Reading was 309 votes to 301. Fifteen Conservative MPs voted against, with four abstaining. Five Liberal and five Labour MPs also abstained. I am indebted to Professor Philip Norton for the information in this and the previous footnote.

68. Interview with William Waldegrave, 17 Dec. 1996.

69. H.of C. Deb. (5th Series), 15 May 1973, vol. 856, col. 1243.

70. Hurd, *An End to Promises*, p. 91.

71. Ibid., p. 140.

72. Ibid., p. 125.

73. Ibid., p. 128.

74. Ibid., p. 128.

75. Ibid., p. 135.

76. Diary Readings with Douglas Hurd, 26 Nov. 1996.

77. Ibid.

78. Ibid.

79. Ibid.

80. Ibid.

7

The Lean Years, 1974–1979

On 28 February 1974, the returning officer declared Douglas Richard Hurd the duly elected Member of Parliament for the new constituency of Mid-Oxfordshire. At the time, it seemed difficult to believe that the same man had struggled for years to win selection for any seat, let alone one with a reasonably comfortable majority of nearly eight thousand. Hurd had begun his quest for a seat as early 1967, but his candidature was handicapped by the perception of him amongst Conservative associations as the 'Central Office' candidate. Hurd's position as Heath's political secretary marked him out as a Smith Square imposition.

Conservative associations also dislike showy publicity in support of applicants, and Hurd's case was hampered not only by his high profile role with Edward Heath, but also by *The Times* 'Diary', which adopted him as a kind of unlucky mascot. When Christopher Rowland died in December 1967, Hurd's application to stand in the Meriden by-election was given unwelcome backing by *The Times*.[1]

Due to his new responsibilities as Heath's political secretary, Hurd promised his leader that he would not apply for any seats until after the 1970 General Election.[2] His hopes of being selected were revived in August 1970, when Quintin Hogg was re-elevated to the peerage, becoming Lord Chancellor,[3] and thereby forcing a by-election contest in St Marylebone. When Hurd was revealed as one of a shortlist of twenty, *The Times* 'Diary' depicted him as 'already a warm favourite' who had 'appeared at the front of the field'.[4]

However, Douglas Hurd reached the final four in the race for the prosperous London seat. The other candidates were John Cope, then personal assistant to the Conservative Party Chairman;[5] Ross McWhirter, a libertarian right-winger who, along with his brother, Norris, compiled the *Guinness Book of Records*, until Ross was murdered by the IRA in November 1975; and the eventual winner,

Kenneth Baker.[6] Hurd's own memory of the final selection evening is nebulous, but Kenneth Baker recalls Hurd's moment of cruel disappointment in his memoirs.[7]

Baker credits his wife, Mary, with winning him the contest, but although candidates' wives were expected to turn up for selection meetings, it is more likely, as Baker admits, that Hurd was unsuccessful because of his identification as the imposed Central Office candidate.[8] In 1974, when they were both Members of Parliament, Baker and Hurd employed the same constituency secretary, Judy Smart. After several years of hesitation, Hurd eventually asked her out and in 1982 she became Hurd's second wife.

In February 1971, Douglas Hurd was still married to his first wife, Tatiana. Convention dictated that the wives of Tory applicants were expected to accompany their husbands to selection meetings. The death of Sir Henry Kerby, a well-known supporter of the Rhodesian whites, had created a vacancy in the ultra-safe Conservative seat of Arundel and Shoreham in Sussex. Again, Hurd was short-listed.[9] As the candidates and their wives arrived for the selection meeting at the Beach Hotel in Littlehampton, they were greeted by half-a-dozen women demonstrators, protesting about the fact that Tory wives had to be assessed for their suitability along with their husbands. The protesters carried banners reading, 'Tory wives – are you women or chattels?' and 'This is 1971 not 1871.'[10] The selection committee, safely ensconced inside the hotel, compounded Hurd's miserable evening by selecting Richard Luce as their candidate.[11] Hurd describes these unsuccessful attempts to be selected as 'rather dispiriting'.[12]

Events took a turn for the worse in May 1971, when Hurd was forced to pull out of the race for the Macclesfield seat, which had fallen vacant after the death of Sir Arthur Vere Harvey. The *Manchester Evening News* ran a story publicising Hurd's trip to Paris with Edward Heath, during the Anglo-French summit which paved the way for Britain's entry into the Common Market. Anti-Marketeers in the Macclesfield Conservative Association objected to what they regarded as unfair coverage, and Hurd withdrew 'because it just got too difficult'.[13] By this time, *The Times* 'Diary' felt it was putting a jinx on Douglas Hurd.[14]

Hurd's hopes were raised in December 1971 when he was short-listed for two seats, one in Eastbourne and one in the new seat of Mid-Oxfordshire. The new constituency had been carved mainly out of Neil Marten's old Banbury seat,[15] along with rural areas to the south of the city of Oxford in the old division of Henley. This time, Hurd had the advantage of not being publicised as the front runner. That unhelpful mantle was placed on the considerable shoulders of Michael Heseltine, who fell ill and did not even make it to the final selection evening. Heseltine was MP for Tavistock in Devon at the time, but was on the hunt for a new seat since Tavistock was disappearing in the boundary changes. Ironically, he later found a safe seat in Henley, right next door to Mid-Oxfordshire. The final four competitors in Mid-Oxfordshire were: William Shelton, the Member for Clapham, another MP affected by boundary changes; Timothy Whiteley, who was to cast around in vain for a seat; Christopher Ward, a solicitor, who had won Swindon for the Conservatives at the October 1969 by-election, but lost it to Labour at the General Election in 1970; and Douglas Hurd, who this time refused to build up false hopes, as his diary entry for the evening reveals:

> 20 Jan. 1972: The luck turns. British Legion Hall. The three others were Ward, Shelton and Whiteley. We drive down very gloomily. I performed second. Great weight off my mind.[16]

Given that Hurd had secured a relatively safe seat, the biggest obstacle – that of actually being selected as a Conservative candidate – had been surmounted. He remembers that night as 'the real turning point' in his political career.[17] But, at his formal adoption meeting at Witney on 11 February 1972, Hurd's mind was preoccupied with the disastrous impact of the Wilberforce Report which had recommended a massive wage increase for the miners:

> 11 Feb. 1972: Adoption meeting at Witney. 250 attended. Sore throat. No disappointments so far. They don't know yet what has hit us. The Government now wandering vainly over the battlefield looking for someone to surrender to and being massacred all the time.[18]

Heath's Government never really recovered from the events of February 1972, and in February 1974 Hurd entered Parliament as a backbench MP on the Opposition side. In his maiden speech, he remarked upon the characteristics of his constituency. Although predominantly a rural seat, Hurd reminded his fellow MPs that the town of Witney was famous for one industry:

> It is no good talking to my constituents about an energy policy which is based just on coal, oil, gas and nuclear energy. No energy policy will satisfy the people of Witney unless it includes maximum support and encouragement for the manufacture and use of blankets.[19]

Unsurprisingly, given his diplomatic background, the main thrust of Hurd's maiden speech was devoted to foreign affairs. Hurd criticised Harold Wilson for replacing Sir Donald Maitland, a professional diplomat, with Ivor Richard, the defeated Labour politician, to head the United Kingdom permanent delegation at the United Nations Headquarters in New York. The rest of Hurd's speech attacked the Government's decision to reconsider stopping aid to Chile because of the emergence of a fascist dictatorship under General Pinochet.[20]

After he had spoken, Hurd recalls being summoned by Edward Heath, who was still Leader of the Conservative Party. Heath was not amused. Hurd remembers him saying, 'Quite a good speech. I never want you to speak in the House of Commons again with your coat button undone.'[21]

Although a new MP, from his years as Heath's political secretary Hurd had the distinct advantage of knowing about Prime Minister's Questions.[22] Hurd would later be respected as a statesmanlike figure who tried to use the power of reasoned argument rather than partisan point-scoring, but as a backbench MP, he could not afford the luxury of being above the fray; he needed to get himself noticed. William Waldegrave, who had succeeded Douglas Hurd as Heath's political secretary, recalls that during this period 'he [Hurd] did quite explicitly seek to go and make his own frontline career.'[23] There is considerable evidence to support this impression. Between March 1974 and January 1976, Hurd's period as a backbencher, he made numerous attacks on Harold Wilson at PMQs, at least thirteen of which received coverage in *The Times*. In the same period, he penned roughly an equal number of letters to the editors of *The Times* and the *Sunday Times*. The paradox was that the bulk of Hurd's partisan attacks on Harold Wilson at Prime Minister's Questions were on the subject of Wilson's failure to consider co-operation between the parties in a non-partisan coalition government. The MP for Mid-Oxfordshire's question to the Prime Minister on 4 July, 1974 (referring to a radical speech by Tony Benn, Secretary of State for Industry at Great Yarmouth on 19 June), was typical:

> Will the Prime Minister say what his choice will be if, in the autumn, he has to decide between sticking to the highly divisive policies announced by the Secretary of State and taking part in a national government designed to deal with an increasingly serious economic situation?[24]

But Hurd reserved his biggest attack on Harold Wilson for June 1976, after Wilson's resignation honours were announced. Speaking at Blandford in Dorset, Hurd described those on Wilson's so-called 'lavender list' as 'a bizarre collection of individuals', and argued that the honours system ought not to be a means 'by which a Prime Minister buys popularity in Fleet Street or in the kingdom of sport and entertainment. It should not be a means of giving fresh time to individuals just because they are already famous, or because they are already rich.'[25]

Although Hurd's speech was partly intended as a serious-minded attack on the abuse of the honours system, it also revealed a Wilsonian eye for a newspaper headline. He was privately pleased to have secured his first lead headline on the front page of the *Daily Mail*: a piece by the journalist Gordon Grieg was headed 'THE QUEEN, HONOUR AND SIR HAROLD: TORY MP's SENSATIONAL ATTACK ON TITLES.' Douglas Hurd has always believed very strongly that the honours system should reflect the unsung feats of those performing public service for the good of the community and the nation. Much later in his career, during the Major Government, he would have preferred that the Prime Minister had gone even further in reforming the honours system, cutting back honours for sporting and entertainment celebrities and increasing rewards for service to the community. As Foreign Secretary, Hurd recalls having great difficulty in explaining to officials that there would not be so many honours for Foreign Service as a result of John Major's reforms.[26]

The most serious divisions within both major parties in the 1970s occurred over Britain's membership of the Common Market. Edward Heath had secured Britain's entry in 1973, but in the interests of Labour Party unity, James Callaghan, the Foreign Secretary, sought to renegotiate the terms of entry. The then German Chancellor, Helmut Schmidt, has since admitted that the Labour Government's renegotiation was 'a cosmetic arrangement'.[27] The 'new' terms which Callaghan negotiated at Dublin Castle were no significant advance on those secured by Heath in 1971. The Labour Party remained bitterly divided on the issue of Europe and Harold Wilson was forced to allow members of the Cabinet to exercise their own free will during the referendum campaign.

The Conservative Party line in 1975 was to oppose a referendum. By February 1975, Margaret Thatcher had deposed Edward Heath as leader of the Conservative Party. Hurd definitely voted for Heath in the first ballot, switching to William Whitelaw in the second ballot, but by then Mrs Thatcher had gained an unstoppable momentum from the first round, in which she had decisively defeated Edward Heath. The first ballot result was, according to Nigel Lawson, 'primarily a vote against Ted Heath, rather than a vote for Margaret Thatcher'.[28] Heath lost the leadership primarily because he had lost three out of four general elections; he was perceived as a loser by his colleagues, in a party which, in the second half of the twentieth century, was not used to losing general elections.

As the new leader of the Conservative Party, Mrs Thatcher inherited from Edward Heath a strongly pro-European line, though, according to Hurd, at that stage 'Margaret Thatcher did not have a feel for Europe.'[29] On 11 March 1975, she made a highly partisan maiden speech as Leader of the Opposition arguing against a referendum on Europe, a speech which Hurd believes refutes entirely her later claim that she had always perceived the Common Market as merely a free-trade area.[30]

Douglas Hurd played only a supporting role in the 1975 referendum campaign and was an assiduous if junior member of the all-party umbrella 'Britain in Europe' executive, which ran the 'Yes' campaign. Meanwhile, Mrs Thatcher confined herself to making a few speeches at the beginning and the end of the campaign, allowing the pro-Europeans in her own party, and especially Edward Heath, to put the case for Britain's membership.[31]

In contrast to the 'No' campaign, which was starved of resources,[32] the 'Britain in Europe' executive met most mornings during the campaign in the opulent surroundings of the Waldorf Hotel:

> 13 May 1975: From 8 to 12 at the Waldorf. Ate a scrappy breakfast with the apparatchiks – Robin Harris, Roy Jenkins, Geoffrey Tucker. 9.30 steering committee. 10.45 press conference. Jenkins and [Jeremy] Thorpe. Thinly attended, but they performed well. Servitor, as in the old days, carrying the bag and the hand-out, which was very dull.[33]

The main flash points of the campaign were on the question of jobs and prices. At a press conference on 18 May 1975, Tony Benn claimed that as a result of the trade deficit with the Common Market, half-a-million jobs in Britain would be lost.[34] Meeting again at the Waldorf for a planning meeting, the executive of 'Britain in Europe' all agreed that 'Benn has scooped us on Sunday [25 May 1975] with a scare about jobs.'[35] However, a press conference followed in which William Whitelaw was very effective. Such calm, prosperous-looking establishment figures like William Whitelaw were able to convince the country that it was safer economically for Britain to join the Common Market. Conservatives like Whitelaw were themselves converted to Community membership because they saw it as an economic bulwark against Communism, complementing the military structure of NATO. If one was not a member of the Community, one would not have the clout inside NATO to preserve the Atlantic Alliance.[36]

During the campaign, Hurd mostly performed an auxiliary role as a carrier of bags and convener of meetings. Near the end of the campaign, he was worried that 'our campaign has flagged. The media are bored', but on the eve of polling his mood was more upbeat:

> 4–5 Jun. 1975: Last day of this extraordinary campaign. Talked briefly to E.H. [Edward Heath], who has done stupendously well. Essex with the Wakehams [John and Roberta]. Rather stilted at the Oxford eve of poll meeting in Wheatley with the Liberal candidate. In the campaign bus around the West with Andrew [Osmond, who joined Hurd for the campaign] very cheerfully. In the constituency. Polling slowish. Win clearly by 2-1, carrying

Scotland, Wales and Northern Ireland – a very remarkable result, which would have been incredible six months back.[37]

Two important points emerge from this diary entry. First, the major achievement of the referendum campaign was to turn around a fairly hostile anti-European mood in the country into at least a reluctantly pro-membership majority within six months. Second, both at the time and in retrospect, Hurd acknowledges that Edward Heath 'played a blinder'[38] during the referendum campaign. Heath's enthusiasm for Europe had shone through, and free from the constraints of party leadership (and his coterie of speechwriters), he spoke well, most notably at the Oxford Union debate.[39]

The referendum campaign marked the high tide of co-operation between the parties, something which alarmed Mrs Thatcher, but pleased establishment figures like Heath, Whitelaw and Reginald Maudling, who were seen sharing platforms with moderates from the Labour Party like Shirley Williams and Roy Jenkins, as well as Jeremy Thorpe from the Liberal Party. In contrast, it appeared to the electorate that the extremes of left and right were represented in the 'No' campaign: Michael Foot, Barbara Castle, Tony Benn and Enoch Powell were, in Powell's own words, seen as 'a motley crew'.[40] Given Britain's poor economic performance and the perceived danger of a lurch to the left under Benn, the electorate voted for entry into the Common Market, if only because they saw little alternative.

For a brief period after the 1975 referendum, it seemed that there might be a coalition government comprising moderate figures from the three main political parties. The two greatest obstacles to this were the attitudes of the two party leaders. Harold Wilson believed he could introduce a moderate social democratic consensus without the need for a coalition government. Despite Hurd's – and others' – continued dislike of Wilson's political style, in his last Government, from October 1974 until March 1976, Wilson was primarily concerned with putting Britain on a firmly social democratic rather than a socialist path.

Whereas Mrs Thatcher was obdurately opposed to any form of cross-party co-operation, Edward Heath had been trying to promote the idea of a national government ever since his abortive talks with the Liberals in the aftermath of the February 1974 Election. In the run-up to the October 1974 Election, Hurd was one of those strongly supporting the idea.

After the 1975 referendum campaign was over, Hurd led calls for a national government in a speech to the Oxford Conservative Women's Club on 10 June 1975:

Many of us have worked cheerfully with others of different parties to bring about the right and reasoned response to the question of Europe. It is natural that our constituents should want us to do the same in tackling the much more desperate problem of inflation, and we should not underestimate the deep unpopularity of our present system of adversarial politics.[41]

His arguments were very much couched in terms of moderate politicians from all sides occupying the centre ground to ward off the threat of a left-wing faction of the Labour Party.

Throughout the latter half of 1975, Hurd repeated his calls for a coalition government, but the prospects foundered partly on differences between the parties over industrial strategy. Whilst the Labour Government was willing to use the National Enterprise Board (NEB) to support ailing industries (such as the American-owned Chrysler Corporation), the Conservative Party's demoralising experiences during Heath's premiership created a deep hostility among most Conservative MPs toward any return to a featherbedding strategy.

As backbench Member of Parliament for Mid-Oxfordshire, Hurd defended the interests of his constituents on a number of issues of local concern. Throughout his political career, and especially during his sixteen years as a minister, Hurd remained acutely aware of the need to stay in touch with the views of his constituents. This was not hot air, but reflected his genuine roots as a village Tory – his mother and grandfather had been local councillors – who wanted to preserve the idea of community. From expressing concerns about the dumping of low-level radioactive waste at North Leigh, to opposing the closure of Burford's cottage hospital, Hurd was as assiduous as any Member of Parliament in defending the interests of his constituents.

The main issue concerning Mid-Oxfordshire in the period from 1974 to 1979 was the upheaval associated with RAF Brize Norton, in the heart of Hurd's constituency. Despite some victories for Hurd's constituents in their campaign to prevent noise pollution on their patch, it remained a live issue in Hurd's constituency throughout the 1980s.

One issue which surfaced in the mid 1970s was the debate over state funding of political parties. Hurd was opposed to any use of taxpayer's money. In July 1975, Hurd presented written evidence – along with his friend Nigel Lawson – to the Houghton Committee, which was then investigating state finance of political parties. Lawson and Hurd knew each other quite well, having first met in the late 1960s at a Königswinter conference in Germany,[42] when Hurd worked in the Conservative Research Department and Lawson was the editor of *The Spectator*. In September 1973, Douglas Hurd persuaded Edward Heath to recruit Nigel Lawson – then a journalist research fellow at Nuffield College – as a special political adviser.

In their joint evidence to the Houghton Committee, Hurd and Lawson argued that, even if high inflation made it more difficult for political parties to raise funds, their experience was not unique; other more deserving voluntary organisations, like the Red Cross and the National Trust, were struggling to raise revenue. Moreover, there were two essential differences between voluntary organisations and political parties:

> The first difference is that many people rightly regard the political parties as partly responsible for the inflation. The second is that unlike other voluntary organisations they have the power through their representatives in Parliament to vote themselves taxpayer's money to see them through their difficulties.[43]

The message was austere and puritanical, reflecting their belief that the poor state of the British economy required belt-tightening by everyone, and that included political parties. But, their efforts were unsuccessful. The 'Short Money', as it became known (named after Ted Short, Lord President of the Council and Leader of the House of Commons), provided for partial state funding of political parties.

Hurd and Lawson were similarly unsuccessful when they joined forces in December 1974 over the issue of the Public Lending Right (PLR). They argued in favour of a system of library charges for books, rather than the PLR system which gives a small percentage to authors based on the frequency with which their books are borrowed from libraries.[44]

The idea of charging for borrowing library books provoked a sizeable correspondence in *The Times*, stirring Hurd and Lawson to reply in January 1975, expressing surprise at the 'mountain of false analogy [which] has been heaped upon us'.[45] The two remained good friends, and had few differences of opinion in the Thatcher years, notable exceptions being the issues of broadcasting and the poll tax.

By speaking out against state funding of political parties and airing the controversial idea of charging for library books, there may have been an element of Hurd demonstrating to the new leadership that he no longer agreed with the failed policies of his former boss, Edward Heath.

After a period of almost two years waiting on the backbenches, Hurd was made a front-bench spokesman on European Affairs by Mrs Thatcher. Douglas Hurd's reaction to his appointment is captured in his diary entry from the time:

> 15 Jan. 1976: Lunch with Robin Oakley. PMQ [Home Office Questions]. Goes well. He [Roy Jenkins] becomes cross. Straight out to Mrs T. [Thatcher], who offers me the European job, briskly, but pleasantly. It's the success that I wanted and in happier circumstances, I'd be walking on air.[46]

When he arrived, his immediate superior was Reginald Maudling, but only for a short time; Maudling, unable to get on with Mrs Thatcher, was soon replaced by John Davies, who died tragically of a brain tumour in 1978.

The circumstances to which Hurd referred concerned the break-up of his marriage to Tatiana. In personal terms, the latter half of the 1970s was a dark period in Douglas Hurd's life. He had very conventional views on marriage and was deeply hurt when he separated from Tatiana. Hurd rented a cottage in the village of Westwell to be close to his three young sons, who lived with their mother in the village of Black Burton. No one else liked the modest cottage, but for some reason Douglas Hurd became rather attached to it. Despite the break-up of their marriage, Tatiana and Douglas remain close friends, markedly so, for a former couple. But friends of Douglas Hurd recall him withdrawing into his shell. Always an emotionally reserved person, from the mid 1970s onwards, he became even more guarded and wary of expressing his inner feelings. When he became a minister, the necessary formalities disguised the wry humour, and the public came to see him as a remote, aloof figure. It was only when he met his second wife, Judy, that he began to enjoy a happier personal life.

The 1970s were also lean years for Hurd in financial terms. Prior to the 1980s, an MP's wages were relatively poor. That is not to say that a person living on an average income would have regarded Hurd as anything other than well off. But in terms of the political circle to which he belonged, Hurd had no significant capital. He therefore needed to seek an additional source of income to supplement his salary as a Member of Parliament.

Hurd was fortunate in receiving help from Geoffrey Rippon, the man who had been at the forefront of the negotiations which led to Britain's entry into the Common Market. Rippon was Chairman of the European League for Economic Co-operation (ELEC), a long-established multi-party organisation which sought to promote the case for Europe inside Britain. Douglas Hurd also remembers Alistair McAlpine, who was then the Treasurer of ELEC (and also Honorary Treasurer of the Conservative Party from 1975 to 1990) being supportive at the time. This seems rather odd in the present context given McAlpine's conversion to Euro-scepticism and his very rude comments in January 1995 about Douglas Hurd's competence as Foreign Secretary.[47] Rippon appointed Douglas Hurd and David Steel as research directors of ELEC. Operating from a small office off Regency Street, in Westminster, their role was to organise meetings, arrange pro-European publications, and establish links with Britain's European partners. As Hurd points out, his part-time post served a double purpose. 'It gave me some contacts in European circles, and gave me, not a large sum, but it just topped up my parliamentary salary.'[48]

The post with the ELEC lasted until 1979, when Hurd was appointed

Minister of State at the Foreign and Commonwealth Office. During his years in Opposition, Hurd broadened and deepened his knowledge of Europe, as a result of several visits, sometimes with ELEC, and sometimes on behalf of his party. The visits extended his appreciation of the countries he would later deal with as a minister.

This was the period in Hurd's political life when he listened and learned, and deferred a great deal to those higher up the political ladder. He was fortunate enough to attend a conference at Ditchley Park in April 1976, at which he remembers listening for hours to Harold Macmillan reminisce about his political career. Macmillan was then writing his memoirs, and so had plenty of stories to tell:

> Harold Macmillan talks until after midnight, drinking brandy and smoking cigars. Thinks himself more archaic than he really is. He tells me a story about Churchill having an argument with Lord Moran [consulting physician to Winston Churchill; author of *Winston Churchill: The Struggle for Survival*, 1966]. He's not feeling well. He's got a temperature:
>
> Churchill: I shall get up.
> Moran: No. No, you'd do much better to stay in bed.
> Churchill: I shall get up. There are many people from the press and television outside.
> Moran: What will you say to them?
> Churchill: I shall say that I regret to have to inform you gentlemen that the life of Lord Moran is drawing peacefully to its close.[49]

Hurd's main preoccupation as Front Bench Spokesman on European Affairs was to respond to the proposals to transform the European Assembly from a nominated legislature into a directly elected European Parliament.[50] But it was to be a long drawn out saga before the European Assembly (Elections) Bill eventually became law in 1978 and the first direct elections were held in 1979.[51]

As a firm pro-European, Douglas Hurd was quite hopeful that a directly elected European Parliament would be able to hold the European Commission to account and that the new MEPs would establish a bond with their constituents akin to that of Westminster MPs.[52] In a speech to the Swinton Conservative College in June 1975, he said Britain 'should aim at a pincer movement of parliamentary control,' with the Council of Ministers being responsible to national parliaments and the Commission being held to account by the newly elected European Parliament.[53] He was to be disappointed.

As with most issues concerning Europe, there were divisions within the two major parties. The main debate in the House of Commons was over the system of voting for the direct elections. Hurd argued against Labour's preferred option of a regional-list voting system for the new body. Personally, Hurd was in favour of a hybrid system of proportional representation, akin to the German system, but retaining the single-member constituency. However, as his party's spokesman on Europe, he attacked the regional-list method on the grounds that such a system was not practised by the bulk of the Community's member states, and hence would not be the system which the Community adopted. Therefore, he argued, Britain would have to change their system of voting twice.[54] In a free vote on 13 December 1977, Labour backbenchers went against the advice of Merlyn Rees, the Home Secretary, allying with the Conservatives (who were whipped) to defeat the regional-list proposals.[55]

Margaret Thatcher and Douglas Hurd never became close allies; she was never regarded by him as 'one of us'. In her eyes, he was too tainted by his association with Edward Heath, even if she had shown a certain amount of grace by appointing Hurd to a junior front-bench position within two years of his becoming an MP. In any case, Hurd never wanted to be an intimate. He did not share her view of society, and in the 1980s advocated his own separate vision of Toryism. None the less, from a very early stage the two formed a sound working relationship. Hurd developed a very quick understanding of how Mrs Thatcher's mind operated, and was fortunate in that he got to know her early on: in April 1977, she asked him to accompany her on a visit to China and Japan. Hurd was taken on the trip ostensibly because of his knowledge of the area from his days as Third Secretary in Peking in the 1950s. He was joined on the visit by Mrs Thatcher's daughter, Carol, and John Stanley, her PPS. Hurd christened the group 'the Gang of Four'.[56] As Leader of the Opposition, Mrs Thatcher was relatively inexperienced in foreign affairs. It was her first visit to China and only her second visit ever to a Communist country. Hurd recalls her being genuinely appalled at the thought-control operating in China:

> She asked one Chinese in Peking what he thought about Stalin and he said: 'On reflection, I think Stalin was 60 per cent right and 40 per cent wrong.' And then we travelled to the South-west and she asked the same question and got exactly the same answer. 'I think on the whole Stalin was 60 per cent right and 40 per cent wrong.' She was horrified by that.[57]

Hurd performed an awkward role as a stooge. The demands of protocol meant that Mrs Thatcher could not argue with any of the Chinese she met, so Hurd found himself, if not defending them, then trying to account for their behaviour. 'How could they say that?' she would remark to Douglas. But above all, the trip enabled Hurd to learn about Mrs Thatcher's character and style of working.

Of the many other trips abroad which Hurd made in this period, perhaps the most interesting was his visit to southern Africa in October 1978, again with

John Stanley. The trip was organised by the non-governmental, but pro-white, South Africa Foundation. In order to see a balanced view of the politics of southern Africa, Hurd and Stanley tried to combine meetings with South African businessmen in prosperous Johannesburg with a visit to the Soweto township to meet Dr Nthalo Motlana, then a physician and African National Congress (ANC) activist.

On 17 October, Hurd and Stanley went to Pretoria for talks with the South African Prime Minister, P.W. Botha, whom Hurd describes in his diary as 'sallow, friendly and powerful'.[58] From there, they visited Ulundi, the Zulu capital, where they were granted an audience with Chief Gatsha Buthelezi:

> 19 Oct. 1978: Smart, fluent, humorous, tolerant of words. Explains how he rides the two horses; Leader of Inkatha and Chief Minister of Kwazulu.[59]

After listening to a long diatribe from Pik Botha, South Africa's Foreign Minister against his British opposite number Dr David Owen, the two British MPs were taken off on an unscheduled visit to Namibia, one of the frontline states at war with South Africa. They soon found themselves in the Namibian bush, watching young black soldiers using sniffer dogs to detect South-West African Peoples Organisation (SWAPO) landmines.

Later in the visit, Hurd and Stanley flew to Lusaka for a meeting with the Zambian President, Kenneth Kaunda. He was angered by the lukewarm support of the Conservative Party on the question of sanctions against neighbouring Rhodesia, which had declared Unilateral Declaration of Independence (UDI) from Britain in November 1965. By 1978, guerrilla forces under Joshua Nkomo and Robert Mugabe were operating from Zambia, and to a much greater extent from Mozambique.[60] When Hurd and Stanley visited Rhodesia, therefore, it was suffering from a growing number of incursions on two fronts, to the south and to the north. After a meeting with General Walls, the Rhodesian Commander, Hurd described the security situation in his diary as 'basically deadlocked'.[61]

Hurd and Stanley were granted an audience with Ian Smith, whom Hurd described as 'Glacial – not in a hostile manner, but simply distant'.[62]

At this time, the Rhodesian whites were forced to live in protected compounds. As Hurd and Stanley arrived by police escort at just such a village compound, the usual token blacks were put on show by the Rhodesian authorities to give the impression of racial integration. Hurd flew home to London, strongly of the view that the Rhodesian whites had to settle with the African nationalists in the medium term.

Mrs Thatcher was virtually alone among Western politicians in her support for the Smith/Muzorewa internal settlement.[63] Her instinctive sympathies were with the Rhodesian whites. She despised the actions of terrorists, even if the bulk of the international community saw the Rhodesian blacks as freedom fighters.

The Rhodesian issue was one which divided the Conservative Party from top to bottom.[64] The key point at issue was whether the Conservative Party should support the continuation of economic sanctions against Rhodesia. The Conservative Party's line since Edward Heath, had been to offer lukewarm support for sanctions, but Mrs Thatcher was very reluctant to continue the policy. At the Conservative Party Conference in October 1978, John Davies, the Conservative's chief spokesman on Foreign Affairs, made an uncertain, rambling speech, during which he was heckled by sympathisers of Ian Smith. He later complained of a severe headache and was taken to hospital; a few months later he died of a malignant brain tumour. Hurd recalls the occasion as being 'truly awful' to watch.[65]

However, in government, Mrs Thatcher deferred to the views of Peter Carrington, her Foreign Secretary, the Queen (who was privately insistent), and Sir Sonny Ramphal, Secretary-General of the Commonwealth, in bringing about an independent Zimbabwe as a result of the Lancaster House Conference in 1979. One of Mrs Thatcher's traits, which Hurd identified at an early stage, was that she would argue, and then she would sign, with the reluctance and the regrets coming later. Hurd was also conscious of her many contradictory views, but he stayed loyal and was rewarded with the post of Minister of State at the Foreign Office after the election victory of May 1979. Hurd set out from the start to become a front-bench politician, but above all, his years on the Opposition benches were lean years when he watched and listened and deferred.

Notes

1. 'Times Diary', *The Times*, 19 Dec. 1967. Keith Speed won the Meriden by-election and held the seat until February 1974. In October 1974, he was elected the member for Ashford in Kent, where he served until his retirement in 1997.
2. Interview with Douglas Hurd, 26 Nov. 1996.
3. In October 1963, Lord Hailsham had renounced his peerage, to improve his chances of succeeding Harold Macmillan as leader of the Conservative Party. It was widely considered to be a rash move, as was the famous bell-ringing episode at the Conservative Party Conference in 1963. Hailsham was Lord Chancellor from 1970 to 1974 and again from 1979 to 1984.
4. 'Times Diary', *The Times*, 15 Aug. 1970.
5. John Cope went on to become Conservative Deputy Chief Whip, 1983–1987.

6. Kenneth Baker had won a by-election contest in Acton before narrowly losing the seat by 660 votes at the 1970 General Election.

7. Kenneth Baker, *The Turbulent Years: My Life in Politics*, pp. 32–3.

8. Ibid.

9. Hurd was short-listed alongside both John Stanley, a financial analyst, who later became Mrs Thatcher's PPS when she was Leader of the Opposition, and then served as her Minister of Housing and Construction in the first Thatcher Government before being made Minister of State for the Armed Forces in 1983; and Richard Luce, who had unsuccessfully contested Hitchin at the 1970 General Election, losing to Shirley Williams.

10. *Shoreham Herald*, 19 Feb. 1971; *The Times*, 15 Feb. 1971.

11. Richard Luce served as MP for Arundel and Shoreham until February 1974, before the seat became Shoreham in the boundary changes. Along with Peter Carrington and Nicholas Ridley, Luce resigned as a Foreign Office minister after Argentina invaded the Falkland Islands in 1982, but he was reappointed as a Minister of State at the Foreign Office in June 1983.

12. Interview with Douglas Hurd, 26 Nov. 1996.

13. Ibid.

14. 'Times Diary', *The Times*, 15 May 1971. In September 1972, Nicholas Winterton, a firm opponent of the Common Market, was elected in the by-election as Conservative Member of Parliament for Macclesfield, where he has remained ever since.

15. Neil Marten, a notable opponent of the Common Market, served as MP for Banbury from 1959 to 1983, although the boundaries of his constituency were substantially altered in February 1974.

16. Diary Readings with Douglas Hurd, 26 Nov. 1996.

17. Interview with Douglas Hurd, 26 Nov. 1996.

18. Diary Readings with Douglas Hurd, 26 Nov. 1996.

19. H. of C. Deb. (5th Series), 19 March 1974, vol. 870, cols 912–13.

20. Ibid., cols 914–15.

21. Interview with Douglas Hurd, 26 Nov. 1996.

22. Ibid.

23. Interview with William Waldegrave, 17 Dec. 1996.

24. H. of C. Deb. (5th Series), 4 Jul. 1974, vol. 876, col. 599.

25. *The Times*, 4 Jun. 1976.

26. Interview with Douglas Hurd, 20 Jan. 1997.

27. Hugo Young, interview with Helmut Schmidt, *The Last Europeans*, Channel 4, 3 Dec. 1995.

28. Interview with Lord Lawson of Blaby, 6 Dec. 1995.

29. Interview with Douglas Hurd, 26 Nov. 1996; *see* Margaret Thatcher, *The*

Path to Power (Harper Collins: New York, 1995) pp. 330–33.

30. Interview with Douglas Hurd, 26 Nov. 1996; for Mrs Thatcher's maiden speech, *see* H. of C. Deb. (5th Series), 11 Mar. 1975, cols 304–17. The House of Commons subsequently agreed to the referendum vote by 312 votes to 248.

31. Thatcher, *The Path to Power*, p. 331.

32. The 'No' campaign gathered £8,629.81 while the 'Yes' fund's war chest amounted to £1,356,583; Phillip Whitehead, *The Writing on the Wall: Britain in the Seventies* (Michael Joseph: London, 1985), p. 138.

33. Diary Readings with Douglas Hurd, 26 Nov. 1996.

34. Footnote, Tony Benn, *Against the Tide: Diaries 1973–1976* (Arrow Books: London, 1989), p. 382.

35. Diary Readings with Douglas Hurd, 26 Nov. 1996.

36. Interview with Viscount Whitelaw of Penrith, 10 Mar. 1993.

37. Diary Readings with Douglas Hurd, 26 Nov. 1996.

38. Interview with Douglas Hurd, 26 Nov. 1996; David Butler and Uwe Kitsinger agree in their volume, *The 1975 Referendum* (Macmillan: London, 1976), p. 77.

39. For an account of Heath's performance, *see* Barbara Castle, *The Castle Diaries, 1974–76*, p. 406 (3 Jun. 1975).

40. Whitehead, *The Writing on the Wall*, p. 137.

41. *The Times*, 11 Jun. 1975.

42. Annual Anglo-German conferences for politicians, journalists and businessmen to discuss matters of common interest. The conference later alternated between Königswinter in Germany and Cambridge.

43. *The Times*, 3 Jul. 1975.

44. Douglas Hurd and Nigel Lawson, 'Letter to the Editor', *The Times*, 20 Dec. 1974.

45. Douglas Hurd and Nigel Lawson, 'Letter to the Editor', *The Times*, 7 Jan. 1975.

46. Diary Readings with Douglas Hurd, 26 Nov. 1996.

47. Alistair McAlpine, 'The Man for all Seasons Whose Time has Finally Run Out', *The Mail on Sunday*, 22 Jan. 1995.

48. Interview with Douglas Hurd, 26 Nov. 1996.

49. Diary Readings with Douglas Hurd, 26 Nov. 1996. The phrase 'drawing peacefully to its close' refers to the final bulletin on the illness of George V in 1935.

50. Hurd had been a member of the Select Committee on Direct Elections to the European Parliament, which recommended direct elections in their report of 19 Aug. 1976.

51. H. of C. Deb. (5th Series), 13 Dec. 1977, vol. 941, cols 320–21. The

Labour Government gave priority to its devolution plans for Wales and Scotland, leaving the European Assembly (Elections) Bill to make a slow passage through the House of Commons.

52. H. of C. Deb. (5th Series), 24 Nov. 1977, vol. 939, col. 1878.

53. *The Times*, 16 Jun. 1975.

54. H. of C. Deb. (5th Series), 13 Dec. 1977, vol. 941, col. 319.

55. Ibid., cols 417–22. The voting was 319 to 222.

56. For Mrs Thatcher's account of the visit to China, *see* Thatcher, *Path to Power*, pp. 388–93.

57. Interview with Douglas Hurd, 26 Nov. 1996.

58. Diary Readings with Douglas Hurd, 17 Dec. 1996.

59. Ibid.

60. The Portuguese – who had formerly controlled Mozambique – had lost control in 1976 following the fall of the fascist government in Portugal.

61. Douglas Hurd, *Diary*, 24 Oct. 1978.

62. Ibid., 27 Oct. 1978.

63. In 1978, Mrs Thatcher sent Viscount Boyd of Merton to head a Conservative Party mission to observe the Muzorewa election, which he pronounced as fair.

64. *See* M. Stuart, 'Conservative Party Rupture and the Rhodesian Crisis, c.1964 to c.1970' (University of Aberdeen: unpublished M.Litt thesis, January 1994).

65. Interview with Douglas Hurd, 17 Dec. 1996.

8

A Junior Minister's Lot:
Minister of State at the Foreign and
Commonwealth Office,
May 1979–June 1983

For Douglas Hurd, the 1979 General Election brought two pieces of good news. He had doubled his majority: from just over 7,300 in October 1974 it had risen to nearly 15,500, largely due to a slump in support for the Liberals. The second piece of news, hearing that he had been made Minister of State at the Foreign and Commonwealth Office, came as no surprise. He had been an opposition front-bench spokesman for the three years previously, and had fully expected to be made a minister by Mrs Thatcher.

Having served fifteen years as a diplomat, Douglas Hurd found himself in familiar surroundings when he arrived at King Charles Street to take up his first ministerial post. Ostensibly, his ministerial remit covered defence matters, arms control and disarmament, the Middle East, North Africa, economic matters relating to the developing world and the United Nations. As Minister of State, he was equal to number three in the ministerial pecking order.[1] Because Lord Carrington was Foreign Secretary, Sir Ian Gilmour, as Lord Privy Seal, deputised for the Foreign Secretary in the House of Commons and occupied a seat in Cabinet.

Despite being expected to cover a wide range of ministerial responsibilities, the area which occupied a disproportionate amount of Hurd's time as Minister of State was the Middle East. Between May 1979 and February 1983, Hurd made fourteen ministerial visits to the area,[2] reflecting the turbulence of the region in the late 1970s and early 1980s. In 1979, the Shah of Iran was deposed by an Islamic fundamentalist revolution led by Ayatollah Khomeini, with fifty hostages being taken at the American Embassy in Tehran. By the end of the year, the Soviet Union had invaded Afghanistan, establishing a puppet regime under Barbak Karmal.

As the Minister of State responsible, Hurd was asked by the Prime Minister to chair an Afghan Conference in London on Monday, 31 December 1979. This was the first in a long series of meetings intended to try to formulate a co-ordinated Western response to the Soviet invasion. In early January 1980, the Foreign Secretary, Lord Carrington, toured countries closely connected with the crisis, while Douglas Hurd delivered his first major statement in the House of Commons as a Minister on 14 January 1980, which 'considering I have nothing to say goes quite well'.[3]

Working out a co-ordinated Western response to the Soviet invasion of Afghanistan was a lengthy, unrewarding process. Hurd records a 'very dreary'[4] four-hour meeting of the NATO Council on 15 January, where the member countries agreed to differ on the question of sanctions, largely due to objections from the French. It was left to each individual nation to agree their own level of response. Hurd returned to London to attend a meeting with the Prime Minister to agree an outline of British sanctions. On Peter Carrington's return, Hurd became involved in his neutrality plan for Afghanistan. Under the Foreign Secretary's plan, in return for a Soviet withdrawal, Afghanistan would have become a neutral and non-aligned country. However, the proposal foundered.[5]

A great deal of Douglas Hurd's time was taken up with the forthcoming Olympic Games, due to be held in Moscow in the summer of 1980. Mrs Thatcher and the Americans were very keen to stage an alternative Olympics as a propaganda event to counter the Moscow Games, but it quickly became clear to Hurd that British politicians were not going to be able to prevent many individual athletes from competing at the Games. Hurd had particular difficulties with Peter Coe, Sebastian Coe's father, who managed his son's affairs. Peter Coe argued that British athletes were being asked to pay the ultimate price, giving up their chance of glory.

In March 1980, Hurd went to Geneva to discuss plans for an alternative Olympics with international Olympic officials. He quickly saw the idea as a non-starter:

17 Mar. 1980: Two concepts. The Americans want a TV spectacular. The Dutch and we are very cautious and in favour of private approaches to particular types of athlete.

18 Mar. 1980: Breakfast with Lloyd Cutler. Not a bad list of suggestions which are approved. Fed up with the subject which I fear is a loser.[6]

If Hurd was reluctant then he was being pushed from behind by Mrs Thatcher, who claimed in a letter to Sir Denis Fellows, Chairman of the British Olympic Association (BOA), that if British athletes took part, it would 'seem to condone an international crime'.[7] The Prime Minister's main foreign policy objective in the early 1980s was to offer succour and support to the United States. In her statement to the House of Commons on the Soviet invasion, the Prime Minister said the United States 'must not be alone in its firmness'.[8] Throughout the early 1980s, Hurd shared Mrs Thatcher's firmness on the Atlantic Alliance, even if his choice of language was invariably more diplomatic than hers.[9]

However, on the question of the Olympic Games, he simply took the view, along with the British press at the time, that 'of all the things I was asked to do as a Minister of State that was the only one that struck me at the time and strikes me now as deeply foolish.'[10]

The Moscow Games went ahead. The West German Government and the Americans ordered their athletes not to take part. The British Government advised rather than compelled their athletes not to compete – a plea which went unheeded, as athletes like Seb Coe, Steve Ovett and Alan Wells won gold medals in Moscow.

The turbulence in the Middle East spilled over onto Britain's doorstep at the end of April 1980. A group of armed Iranians, calling themselves the Group of the Mohieddin al-Nasser, stormed the Iranian Embassy in London, taking twenty-six people hostage, including four Britons.[11]

Very quickly, an operations room was formed downstairs in the Cabinet Office. Ostensibly, the Home Secretary, William Whitelaw, was in charge of policy, with the operational side being left to the Metropolitan Commissioner of Police, David McNee. As Minister of State at the Foreign Office, Hurd's role was to try to persuade Arab ambassadors to negotiate with the terrorists to surrender. However, the talks foundered because Hurd was not able to offer safe conduct for the terrorists. Hurd's diary entries from the time show his admiration for William Whitelaw's handling of the crisis and his frustration at the *laissez-faire* attitude of the Arab ambassadors:

30 Apr. 1980: Operations room fills with people. Willie Whitelaw in charge. Does well . . . Back to the Ops room. Prime Minister appears in purple, but she doesn't interfere as much as I expected.[12]

Over the next two days, the situation was deadlocked:

2 May 1980: Four sessions on 2 May. Nothing notable happens at Princes

Gate. Terrorists' demands shift all the time. Willie Whitelaw took me back to the Home Office to talk to the [Metropolitan] Commissioner [David] McNee. Reveals his determination not to let the gunmen go, even if they release their hostages.[13]

In these sort of crises, Hurd feels Mrs Thatcher was far less gung-ho and far more wary than most people imagine. According to Hurd, she took a lot of persuading from William Whitelaw and Peter Carrington (who telephoned her from Washington) that, if the terrorists shot any hostages, the Special Air Service (SAS) should be sent in, but the final decision to hand over to the army rested with the Metropolitan Commissioner, David McNee.

On the Saturday, 3 May, two hostages, a pregnant woman and an Iranian were released, but Sunday was the vital day for Hurd. He had a meeting with the Arab ambassadors at the Foreign Office, but without the offer of safe conduct for the terrorists they refused to appear in person outside Princes Gate. The end of the siege came the next day, a Bank Holiday Monday:

5 May 1980: Into the bunker at nine. All calm. Saw the Jordanian Ambassador. They all coalesced round the view they can't act unless we offer safe conduct. The terrorists harp continuously on the need to see Ambassadors, and cannot be ridden off onto the Red Cross or the imam of the mosque.[14]

The last sentence refers to a Muslim imam who tried to negotiate with the terrorists, but to no avail. Hurd tried all day to persuade the ambassadors. He rang the Jordanian Ambassador again, then a shot rang out from the Iranian Embassy, but no body appeared. By this stage in the crisis, the Cabinet Office had too many people milling about, so William Whitelaw, Hurd and a few others retired to a much smaller meeting of ministers and officials. Here, David McNee made the decision to call in the army. The Metropolitan Commissioner of Police is not under the control of the Home Secretary and he, not the Government, had to decide when to call in the army. McNee said that in effect he had done all he could and called on the civil power represented by Whitelaw who could then call in the army. It was agreed on the Monday that a second shooting and/or body would trigger the SAS, which would then move to readiness:

5 May 1980, continued: Then a body was moved out and the attack is ordered and we watch it on the telly. Immense relief. Peter Carrington was in Washington [at the Pentagon, seeing Dr Harold Brown, the US Secretary of Defence]. I rang him up. Prime Minister appears radiant and enthusiastic.

> Steak and whisky appear. Leave the bunker just after ten. Bloody
> ambassadors![15]

With the embassy siege in London resolved, the British Government came under renewed pressure from its American allies to take measures against Iran, which was still holding American hostages in the Iranian capital, Tehran. The British reluctantly agreed to impose limited sanctions against Iran in May 1980. Douglas Hurd and Cecil Parkinson, then Minister for Trade, were jointly responsible for securing the passage of the Iran (Temporary Powers) Bill. As a result of working together on the Bill, they got to know each other reasonably well.[16] The Bill was taken through all its stages in only thirty-six hours, with Hurd opening his first debate on Second Reading:

> 12 May 1980: Get bogged down and ramble. Rally at end. Longest speech
> yet. Many interruptions. [Peter] Shore hedges, [Enoch] Powell attacks me.
> It's a tiresome, negative business. I'm sick of it by midnight, but the debate
> doesn't go too badly. Cecil Parkinson winds up well. Good majority.[17]

There was no enthusiasm for sanctions amongst MPs: the experience of Rhodesia had split the Conservative Party and embarrassed the Labour Government after the Bingham Report revealed that British oil companies had contravened the oil sanctions order.[18] In May 1980, the sanctions against Iran did not include oil, but they were not really designed to be a comprehensive, enforceable set of measures. One of their main purposes, as sanctions often are, was to send a signal to the Iranian Government that it was on the wrong track. But the overriding reason for the sanctions was spelled out clearly by Hurd to the House of Commons during his opening remarks:

> If we were to say 'No' to the President [of the United States], if we were
> to say that our experience of Rhodesia was miserable and that we did not
> believe that such action would have the desired effect, however able our
> arguments, we would be administering a major rebuff on the most sensitive
> point of our major ally.[19]

Around the same time as the Iranian Embassy siege in May 1980, a crisis flared up with yet another Middle East country, this time Saudi Arabia. On 1 May 1980, the Saudis asked Britain to withdraw its Ambassador, James Craig, after Anglia Television screened the drama documentary film, *Death of a Princess*. The film revealed that, in 1977, Princess Misha, the granddaughter of Prince Mohammed ibn Abdul Aziz (the elder brother of King Khaled) had been found guilty of committing adultery under Islamic law and had been publicly executed, along with her lover.[20]

The Saudi Arabian Government had expressed its deep concern prior to the screening of the drama, but the British Government decided to permit its broadcast on the grounds of freedom of speech. Despite apologies from Lord Carrington, the British Ambassador was summoned to Riyadh on 23 April and asked to leave. The British Government was extremely worried about the economic implications of any deterioration in relations with the Saudis. In an attempt to restore diplomatic ties, Douglas Hurd was sent out to Jedda on 26 July 1980. The decision to send a Minister of State was in some senses a gamble, but as Hurd points out:

> I went first as a kind of John the Baptist to Peter Carrington, precisely because it wouldn't terribly matter if I was snubbed or given the cold shoulder.[21]

Hurd had no idea how he would be received by the Saudis. But his fears were soon to be eased: as his plane touched down at Jedda airport, he spotted police cars on the tarmac and a line of policemen ready to salute him. The Saudis, like the Chinese, are renowned for using every nuance of diplomatic protocol to deliver diplomatic signals.

From Jedda, Hurd was flown to Taif, a town in the hills to the north. On his arrival, Hurd was shown to a room in the huge Intercontinental Hotel, set in the middle of the Saudi desert. He was told that Prince Saud al Faisal, the Saudi Foreign Minister, would hold a meeting in his office in an hour's time, and used the spare time to take a shower. While he was in the shower, someone tapped on the shower curtain and told him that the Foreign Minister wanted to see him straight away. Rushing out of the shower, he dressed too hastily and broke the zip of his trousers. Douglas Hurd, Minister of the Crown, on the verge of a crucial meeting with a senior member of the Saudi royal family, was without a change of clothes and no way of mending his zip! His only option was to try to hide the fact. Hurd's diary entry reveals the full embarrassment of the occasion:

> 28 Jul. 1980: My zip breaks at crucial moment. My suit is old, tight and shiny. He [Prince Saud] is tall, quick, with a touch of creativeness. Clear at once they had decided to forget the film and exchange ambassadors. Trade resumption less automatic but should not be long. Seems genuinely anxious to confirm with P.C. [Peter Carrington].[22]

Hurd's trip made the lead headline on the front page of *The Times* the following morning.[23] However, he is the first to admit that the Saudis had decided in advance of his visit to resume normal relations with Britain. Trade relations with Saudi Arabia, especially the sale of arms, were boosted after Mrs Thatcher's visit to the area in April 1981. Hurd accompanied Mrs Thatcher on that occasion, but his abiding memory of Saudi Arabia from that period will be of the 'zipper incident'; for a Foreign Secretary who later became known for his immaculately quiffed hair and the cut of his suits, it remains an embarrassing personal collection.

Despite the occasional crises, Douglas Hurd enjoyed his visits to the Middle East. He got to know the leaders of the Gulf States very well. Their unreformed political systems inclined towards stability, so that most of the Foreign Ministers he met as Minister of State were still in office when he became Foreign Secretary in October 1989. However, one issue in the Middle East blighted Hurd's whole time as Minister of State; the controversy surrounding the death of Nurse Helen Smith.

On 20 May 1979, after an illegal drinks party in Jedda hosted by Mrs Penelope Arnot and her husband Dr Richard Arnot, Nurse Helen Smith, aged twenty-three, died along with Jonannes Otten, a Dutch sea captain, after falling, jumping or being pushed from a block of flats. Nurse Smith's father, Ronald Smith, refused to accept official explanations that his daughter had died as a result of falling from a sixth floor apartment building. Instead, he became convinced that his daughter had been murdered and embarked upon a long-running campaign to reveal the truth. In three successive editions of the satirical magazine *Private Eye*, allegations were made that Gordon Kirby, British Vice-Consul in Saudi Arabia, had been responsible for ordering a Foreign Office cover-up over the death of Miss Smith. No evidence was ever found to substantiate the claims – and Mr Kirby eventually won damages from *Private Eye* in 1984. Hurd felt particular sympathy for the diplomat and his family who were treated in a shabby way by the magazine.

The Helen Smith saga spanned the whole time that Hurd was a Minister of State and beyond. One official who worked closely with him at the time recalls that the case 'wasn't high politics in ordinary international-relations terms, but was high politics in terms of the personal drama.'[24] From Hurd's point of view, the issue tested his powers of patience. The proverb says, 'There's no smoke without fire,' but Hurd felt this was one case where 'there wasn't any fire, just a lot of smoke.'[25]

Mr Smith felt aggrieved because he had been denied access to the Foreign Office report into the case on his arrival in Saudi Arabia. Hours after the deaths, Gordon Kirby had been sent out to the scene of the incident and subsequently compiled a twenty-four-paragraph confidential report to his superior, Francis Geere, the British Consul, based on Mrs Arnot's account of the incident. Kirby also compiled a second report based on rumours circulating among staff at the

Bahksh hospital where Nurse Smith had worked. Mr Smith, a former policeman, started to look into the case for himself. He became suspicious when he was refused access to a Foreign Office typewriter to write up his notes, but actually this was because it was Foreign Office policy to lock up typewriter ribbons at night. This aspect of Foreign Office procedure was unfortunately not explained to Mr Smith at the time. Otherwise, the British officials in Saudi were remarkably tolerant: Ronald Smith was permitted to stay at the Consul's house to save on hotel bills where he borrowed a typewriter from Mr Geere's housekeeper. Another official kindly agreed to put him up for a while longer, but he was asked to leave after a couple of days because he was proving too much of a handful.[26]

Smith became suspicious because of what he saw as the lack of openness on the part of the Saudi authorities and the refusal of British officials to hand over the first Foreign Office minute compiled by Kirby. However, the Foreign Office could not release the report because an illegal drinks party had just been held; revealing the contents of the report might have incriminated people on drinks charges. Mrs Penelope Arnot and her husband Dr Richard Arnot, along with several others, spent five months in a Saudi jail, where they faced a public flogging for serving alcohol. Low level diplomatic efforts by the British Government, and clemency by King Khalid, saved the Britons from this ordeal. But Hurd strenuously denies a link between the row over *Death of a Princess* and the Helen Smith affair:

> The Saudis were deeply offended by the showing in Britain of a television film which, in their view, was insulting to their own Royal family. They never at any stage had any such interest in the Helen Smith case. To them the death of Helen Smith was an event arising from a sleazy party between immoral foreigners. Because the death occurred in their jurisdiction, it was their duty to investigate it and this they did. But they never showed any political interest in the case and there was never any suggestion that the case would affect our relationship with them. At any given moment there are several dozen British citizens in jail in Saudi Arabia as in other foreign countries and it is normal for British ministers from time to time to ask that their cases be reviewed or clemency shown. We did this for Mrs Arnot, as we have done for many others. Here again there was nothing which the Saudis would have found remarkable.[27]

Ronald Smith's actions became increasingly rash and desperate. In September 1980, he appeared unannounced at the Foreign Office in King Charles Street, demanding to see Lord Carrington. Naturally, the Foreign Secretary was unavailable, but Hurd agreed to see Mr Smith, by appointment, the following week:

> 25 Sept. 1980: He [Ronald Smith] produces no evidence, but is adamant that
> he can prove all. Suggested he went to the Ombudsman. This rocks him
> momentarily.[28]

Mr Smith had not heard of the procedure whereby allegations of maladministration by British consular officials overseas could be investigated privately by a Parliamentary Commissioner, known as an Ombudsman. Such a person would have had full access to the Foreign Office papers. However, Mr Smith turned down the offer and pursued his cause publicly through the courts. The Leeds coroner, Philip S. Gill, rejected Smith's demand for an inquest in November 1981. Smith took his case to the Divisional Court which ruled in April 1982 that the coroner did not have to hold an inquest because a coroner's jurisdiction only arises when a body is found in his or her area. A British subject who dies abroad has no call on the coroner because he or she is concerned with bodies and not with incidents.[29] Still dissatisfied, Smith took his case to the Court of Appeal which overturned the Divisional Court ruling on 30 July 1982.[30] This in turn opened the way for a highly publicised inquest which ran from August to December 1982, which returned an open verdict. Hurd claims the Foreign Office would have welcomed an inquest, but could not say so publicly in case it seemed as if they were influencing the decision of the courts. Throughout, he believes the Foreign Office was prevented from laying the issue to rest because it refused to break its own procedures.[31]

Ronald Smith briefly received support from three local Labour MPs – Stanley Cohen (Leeds, South East), Martin Flannery (Sheffield, Hillsborough) and Bob Cryer (Keighley) – who were among those who signed an Early Day Motion, calling on the Home Secretary to institute a comprehensive inquiry into the case. But overall, there was no groundswell of parliamentary interest. Hurd would have welcomed an adjournment debate in which he could have explained more fully the Foreign Office's position.[32]

Undaunted, Mr Smith demanded a full public inquiry and was supported by John Gunnell, the leader of the West Yorkshire County Council, who claimed he had received photographs which proved Nurse Smith was murdered.[33] In May 1997, after the General Election, Ronald Smith wrote to the new Home Secretary, Jack Straw, demanding a full public inquiry. Nothing it seems, will succeed in laying the issue to rest.

In the aftermath of the Argentinian invasion of the Falkland Islands in April 1982, Hurd was the only Minister of State at the Foreign Office who decided not to resign. It was only right that he should stay on; he had no ministerial responsibility for the Falkland Islands. When the crisis first erupted, on Thursday 1 April, Hurd was attending the Anglo-German Königswinter Conference at St Catherine's College, Cambridge. At the last moment, Lord Carrington had to call off due to the crisis, so Douglas Hurd stood in for him, giving an off-the-cuff speech on the Falklands. Hurd's diary entries from the time show his unsuccessful efforts to persuade Lord Carrington not to resign:

> 2 Apr. 1982: Peter Carrington told me in the lobby of the House of Commons [there was an Emergency Debate] that he had decided to resign. Off he goes to the Prime Minister who talks him out of it.[34]

The next day, Hurd attended a meeting of Foreign Office ministers, where the atmosphere, according to his diary, was 'very subdued'.[35]

On Sunday, 4 April, Hurd was struck by the attitude of his mother to the Falklands conflict. Unlike her son, Stephanie Hurd had visited the Falklands: on several occasions in the early 1960s, she accompanied her husband, Anthony Hurd, on trips there when he was a director of the Falkland Islands Company.[36] Douglas fully expected his mother to be resolute in her support for the Falkland islanders. Her view was that the war was going to wreck forever the way of life of the islanders; there would be no turning back the clock to the happy lives she had seen them lead before the invasion. In April 1994, Hurd would visit the Falkland Islands as Foreign Secretary. There, he donated to the island's museum a collection of letters written by his mother in which she had described the people and the wildlife on the island. After the visit, Hurd was inspired to write a short story entitled 'Sea Lion', about an historian who discovers that Mrs Thatcher did not engineer a war to influence the outcome of the 1983 General Election.[37]

But back in 1982, Hurd was again trying to persuade Peter Carrington not to resign:

> 4 Apr. 1982: Press on the Falklands Islands as bad as could be. Mother anxious to avoid bloodshed and destruction. I talked to Peter Carrington on the telephone. Tried to argue him out of resignation, using the argument about his influence abroad, saying he couldn't resign because there was some leader in *The Times* or some *Panorama* programme tomorrow; even talked about the Duke of Omnium.[38]

The Duke of Omnium was a conscientious character from Trollope's novel, *The Prime Minister*, who was always very sensitive to criticism. Hurd urged Lord Carrington not to be like him. But this time, Carrington's decision was unalterable. On the Monday, Hurd went to see him again, but:

> 5 Apr. 1982: We do not this time, try to dissuade him [Carrington]. Much
> gloom and demoralisation. First day of new regime. Francis Pym very steady
> and sensible. I am to be his deputy, take over EEC.[39]

Hurd was not heavily involved in policy-making during the operation to retake
the Falklands, and the diplomatic negotiations were left to the new Foreign
Secretary, Francis Pym. In retrospect, Hurd takes the view that Mrs Thatcher
was right about the substance of the Falklands. To him, it was was another
example of how she showed that things which had been perceived as impossible
could be done if the necessary political will and leadership were brought to
bear. He later praised her chapter on the Falklands in her memoirs.[40] However,
at a meeting during the Falklands campaign in April 1982, Hurd once again
witnessed at first hand her tendency to assume extreme positions:

> 19 Apr. 1982: She [Mrs Thatcher] believes that the Foreign Office error
> consisted in not seeing how far Argentina was slipping into the Soviet orbit
> . . . how fascism, communism are alike, etc . . . all implore her, Willie
> Whitelaw, fortissimo, not to develop this line in public.[41]

In retrospect, Hurd gently pokes fun at Mrs Thatcher, but characteristically
qualifies his remarks with a compliment:

> There was a great deal to be said against General Galtieri, but not that he
> was a Communist, but she was very worked up, understandably . . . I think,
> and I felt at the time that she handled it extremely well.[42]

Outwardly, Hurd remained loyal to the Prime Minister, but occasionally his
body twisted and contorted to betray his discomfort as he listened to another
over-the-top comment. His strong sense of the ridiculous meant he could not
resist noting down these moments in his diary in the evening.

Hurd's wide experience in the Foreign Office since 1979, and the fact that
all the other key ministers with experience had resigned, meant he became the
point of continuity in the reshaped Foreign Office ministerial team. After the
reshuffle, Hurd was promoted as Deputy Foreign Secretary in all but name.
However, the Foreign and Commonwealth's representation in Cabinet was cut
from two to one as the overall Cabinet size decreased by one; Hurd had
narrowly missed out on a place in Cabinet. Whether Mrs Thatcher seized the
opportunity to reduce the influence of the Foreign Office – her antipathy
towards it was legendary – is not clear, but the overall changes still represented

a small step up the ministerial ladder for Douglas Hurd. His new responsibilities covered the Middle East, the Indian sub-continent and Europe (geographically as well as the European Community). He was firmly in the Number Two spot ahead of fellow Ministers of State.[43] Because of Francis Pym's preoccupation with the Falklands and his relative inexperience in foreign affairs, Hurd was given significantly more responsibility than a Minister of State could normally have expected. Even after the Falklands campaign, he retained some of the level of work which he had shouldered during the conflict. From April 1982 onwards, Hurd's diary started to fill up with accounts of more meaningful meetings.

During the Falklands campaign, Hurd attended one important event of a different kind. On 7 May 1982, he married his former secretary, Miss Judy Smart. After a brief ceremony in Wantage, a service of blessing was held at St Andrew's Church, Chaddleworth in Berkshire. Hurd's marriage to Judy marked the beginning of a much happier phase in his personal life. Judy, an unfussy, practical person, slotted perfectly into the role of minister's wife. Moreover, Hurd had found someone in whom he could confide. Their love and friendship remains visible to those who see them together.

Douglas Hurd watched the way Peter Carrington conducted his relationship with Mrs Thatcher, and in a sense, was able to imitate that style, although he was not as outspoken in her presence as Peter Carrington sometimes was. In contrast, Pym was much less self-assured and less at ease in the Prime Minister's company. As Hurd diplomatically recalls, 'the relationship never really took root'.[44] Hurd, conversely, had a good working relationship with Pym, although the latter had a tendency to be gloomy about everything. During the 1983 General Election campaign, Pym unwisely commented that 'landslides on the whole don't produce successful governments,'[45] and this gave Mrs Thatcher her excuse to sack him.

Hurd assumed responsibility for the affairs of the European Community at the height of Britain's row with her partners over her budget contributions. On 20 June 1982, Britain vetoed plans for a budget settlement. However, the major European negotiations had already been conducted by Ian Gilmour and Peter Carrington, and were settled primarily by Geoffrey Howe, the Foreign Secretary, and Margaret Thatcher at the Fountainebleau Summit in June 1984.[46] During the early 1980s, Douglas Hurd was solidly pro-European, without ever being federalist in outlook. He strongly supported the idea of a free trade rather than a protectionist Europe and began to formulate his own ideas on European Political Co-operation (known as EPC). In an article which appeared in *International Affairs* in the summer of 1981, Hurd began to suggest ways of improving the effectiveness of a common rather than a single European foreign policy. Up until this point, there had been limited progress in agreeing common positions between the ten members of the European Community – except for the Venice Declaration in 1980, and the co-operation between the ten at the Conference on Security and Co-operation in Europe (CSCE), known as the Madrid process[47] – but Hurd wanted to see the ten work together gradually, brick by brick, developing the habit of co-operation. It was a consistent theme of his ministerial career.

In 1982 and 1983, Douglas Hurd's main preoccupation on day-to-day European issues concerned the delayed negotiations for an enlarged European Community, encompassing the new democracies of Spain and Portugal. The obstacle which most concerned the British Government was the question of Spanish restrictions on the frontier crossing with Gibraltar. Douglas Hurd insisted at the Brussels and Stuttgart meetings of foreign ministers in 1982 that, before Spain joined, it would have to lift such restrictions. Also, the Northern members believed the accession of two more Mediterranean countries with inefficient agricultural sectors would put more pressure on the finance of the Community, and tip the institutional balance of the Community towards the Southern states.[48] Finally, there was a problem over Spain's high car tariffs. However, Douglas Hurd believed it was important to bolster democracy in Spain and Portugal.[49] Moreover, if Spain was welcomed into the European Community, her people would be more likely to vote in favour of joining NATO's political structure, a valuable prize for the Western Alliance.

During 1982 and 1983, events in the Middle East continued to occupy most of Douglas Hurd's attention. On 7 June 1982, Hurd's diary recorded the Israeli invasion of Southern Lebanon:

> 7 Jun. 1982: Israelis storming into Lebanon. See Francis Pym. He is, as usual, very gloomy about everything, especially the Anglo-American relationship.[50]

Britain condemned the Israeli invasion and deployed troops to Lebanon as part of a multi-national force, comprising the British, the French, the Dutch and the Americans. Hurd never liked the city of Beirut, but on 29 March, he flew in by helicopter to visit the British troops:

> 29 Mar. 1983: By helicopter to the Queen's Dragoon Guards. In a fearful slum outside. Guard of honour. Up to the roof. Look over the Sidon Road which is the main Israeli supply route. Competent briefing. They want to stay on another three months. They enjoy their welcome and the patrolling. Lunch at Embassy last visited autumn 1979. Foreign Minister very gloomy. Went to his cocktail party.[51]

In October 1983, a suicide bomber would kill 170 US and French troops, leading to the withdrawal of the whole operation.

The issue of Palestinian self-determination became entangled in the war in Lebanon. As a whole, the British Government supported the principles of the EEC's Venice Declaration of June 1980, which backed Palestinian rights to self-determination, whilst recognising Israel's right to exist. However, Mrs Thatcher's pro-Israeli stance often caused problems with the Foreign Office. Given the large number of Jewish people in her constituency, the Foreign Office had to contend with what became known as 'the Finchley factor'. Douglas Hurd recalls debating with her, arguing whether Britain should meet with PLO leaders. Hurd argued that the PLO had to be distinguished from other terrorists groups like the IRA because they represented a majority, and if a majority was denied freedom, then what rights did these people have? Whilst this fact did not give terrorists the right to blow up other people, could Britain deny all contact with the PLO? With much reluctance, Hurd was given permission by the Prime Minister to meet with the head of the PLO's political department, Mr Farouk Kaddoumi, ostensibly the PLO's Foreign Minister-in-waiting. However, in a move to reassure both Mrs Thatcher and the Israeli Government, Kaddoumi saw Hurd as part of a wider Arab League delegation:

> 8 Jul. 1982: Very controversially see Arab League delegation, consisting of the Prime Minister of Bahrain . . . Kaddoumi. This last is a shift in policy, only dragged out of a reluctant Prime Minister. Conversation on Lebanon itself is unremarkable.[52]

As Hurd points out, the substance of the meeting was far less important than the fact that the meeting actually took place. This first meeting paved the way for the Prime Minister to see Kaddoumi in April 1983, again as part of an Arab League delegation:

> 18 Apr. 1983: London. Meeting with PLO. Farouk Kaddoumi . . . delegation led by the King of Jordan . . . Prime Minister deals with them with much charm and firmness. Big lunch. A great relief to have it all over.[53]

By this stage in his ministerial career, Hurd was slowly building up a stock of respect on both sides of the House of Commons. His ability to deal calmly and in a non-partisan way with foreign affairs questions was widely admired. Stephen Lamport, then his Private Secretary, characterises Hurd as possessing an 'air of detached confidence'.[54] As a witness to his performances in the House of Commons, Lamport never saw Hurd lose that sense of calm authority, although if roused, he was capable of producing a sharp set of claws. On 5 November 1981, when Michael Foot, Leader of the Opposition, mocked a passage of his speech on NATO strategy with an audible 'Oh', Hurd fired back with a headmasterly rebuke:

> Please do not let us hear 'ohs' and 'ahs' when a junior Minister describes NATO strategy. It is the strategy which the Right Hon. Member for Leeds, East [Denis Healey] helped to form and with which the Leader of the Opposition lived as an approving member of the Cabinet for many years. Let us have no nonsense about that.[35]

As a Minister of State, Hurd was highly respected by Foreign Office officials, but because he hailed from a diplomatic background, he always made a conscious effort to distance himself slightly from his officials. This was probably a wise move in relation to his political reputation outside King Charles Street. Younger officials were always on their mettle because Hurd was known not to suffer fools gladly. If an official did not have an informed answer at a meeting, or was found to be 'winging it', they would invariably be found out. Long-winded contributions would be received with a look skyward or a bout of fidgeting. Hurd ran his department like an old-fashioned headmaster, who could, if need be, be firm and tough – although never rude – with his pupils. A civil servant working under Hurd at the time recalls several instances of meetings at the Foreign Office which officials would regard afterwards as something of an ordeal. Above all, Hurd's sharp and ordered mind meant he was able to cut through detail, quickly identifying the essence of a problem. This made him a good chair of a meeting. Officials recall him transacting business briskly, but very much as the politician operating at arm's length.

Internally, Douglas Hurd was the minister who sat on the Senior Promotions Board as deputy secretary. His old friend from Eton, Sir Antony Acland, the Permanent Under Secretary, was its chairman. The task of the Board was to make recommendations to the Foreign Secretary for the senior ambassadorial appointments. While the Foreign Secretary discussed the most senior appointments with the Prime Minister, the knowledge that a respected Minister of State like Douglas Hurd was providing input on the committee made it more likely that the Foreign Secretary would heed the committee's advice.[36]

However, certain weaknesses in Hurd's armoury had yet to be exposed. Whilst his broad-brush approach suited the demands of the Foreign Office, where he was rarely called upon to guide legislation through the House of Commons, he did did not altogether enjoy getting involved in lots of detail for detail's sake. Neither did Hurd have any real experience, apart from his time with Edward Heath, of issues outside the realm of foreign affairs. This meant that Hurd's rise up the ministerial ladder was always going to be vulnerable if he was asked by the Prime Minister to take on a ministerial portfolio relating to domestic policy. While most of his colleagues tended to engage in political intrigue, Hurd tended to stand back from the grubbier side of politics. In that sense, the cliché 'above the fray', is reasonably apposite. This reluctance to court popularity meant that, although Hurd was respected on the Conservative backbenches, he never had a significant following in the way that someone like Michael Heseltine later had. Neither has Douglas Hurd ever been a thrusting, passionate, emotional advocate of a cause. His natural reserve and certain lack of warmth with people he does not know prevented him from being a party politician with popular appeal.

Hurd proved to be a competent Minister of State, largely because he already knew the territory and his personal qualities suited the role of foreign minister. However, on the question of his next ministerial move, Hurd was pessimistic about his chances of reaching the Cabinet:

> 26 Apr. 1983: Call on Lord Carrington, who's off to Lebanon. He asks me if I want to be Secretary General of NATO. (That was his way of telling me that he thought he was going to be Secretary General.) He thought that Margaret Thatcher would put me in the Cabinet, inside the Foreign Office, as Number 2, which I very much doubt.[37]

Hurd's gloomy assessment of his own chances of reaching Cabinet proved correct, but he was to be distracted from political concerns in dramatic fashion on the night of 9–10 June 1983.

Notes

1. Peter Blaker (Blackpool, South), Nicholas Ridley (Cirencester and Tewkesbury), and Neil Marten (Banbury) – Minister for Overseas Development – were the Ministers of State, with Richard Luce (Shoreham) as Parliamentary Under Secretary of State. H. of C. Deb. (5th Series), 21 May 1979, vol. 967, written answers, col. 61.
2. H. of C. Deb. (5th Series), 9 Mar. 1983, vol. 38, written answers, cols 424–5.
3. Diary Readings with Douglas Hurd, 17 Dec. 1996.
4. Ibid.
5. Three founder members of the non-aligned movement – India, Yugoslavia and Algeria – all rejected the idea. Keesing's Contemporary Archives, p. 30380.
6. Diary Readings with Douglas Hurd, 17 Dec. 1996.
7. Keesing's Contemporary Archives, p. 30386.
8. H. of C. Deb. (5th Series), 14 Jan. 1980, vol. 976, cols 1222–33.

9. Douglas Hurd, Speech to Western European Union Assembly, 3 Jun. 1980.

10. Interview with Douglas Hurd, 17 Dec. 1996.

11. For alternative accounts of the Iranian Embassy siege, *see* William Whitelaw, *The Whitelaw Memoirs*, pp. 178–85; Margaret Thatcher, *The Downing Street Years* (Harper Collins, paperback edn: London, 1995), pp. 89–90.

12. Diary Readings with Douglas Hurd, 17 Dec. 1996.

13. Ibid.

14. Ibid.

15. Ibid.

16. Cecil Parkinson, *Right at the Centre* (Weidenfeld & Nicolson: London, 1992), p. 171.

17. Diary Readings with Douglas Hurd, 17 Dec. 1996.

18. *Report on the Supply of Petroleum and Petroleum Products to Rhodesia* (Bingham Report), 1978.

19. H. of C. Deb. (5th Series), 12 May 1980, vol. 984, col. 926.

20. *Keesing's Contemporary Archives*, p. 30429.

21. Interview with Douglas Hurd, 17 Dec. 1996.

22. Diary Readings with Douglas Hurd, 17 Dec. 1996.

23. *The Times*, 29 Jul. 1980.

24. Private information.

25. Interview with Douglas Hurd, 17 Dec. 1996; 'Smoke without Fire' formed the title of a draft article written by Hurd while he was Minister of State at the Foreign Office. It was checked by his Private Secretary, Stephen Lamport.

26. 'Helen Smith: The Real Cover-Up', the *Sunday Times*, 12 Dec. 1982.

27. Douglas Hurd, *Smoke Without Fire*, Draft Article (undated), p. 6.

28. Diary Readings with Douglas Hurd, 17 Dec. 1996.

29. Regina versus West Yorkshire Coroner, Ex parte Smith, 'Law Report', *The Times*, 5 Apr. 1982.

30. Lord Lane, Lord Chief Justice, and Lord Justice Donaldson ruled (with Lord Justice Walker dissenting) that the coroner was obliged to hold an inquest even though the death occurred outside the jurisdiction of the English courts, Regina versus West Yorkshire Coroner, Ex parte Smith, 'Law Report', *The Times*, 31 Jul. 1982.

31. Douglas Hurd, *Smoke Without Fire*, p. 4.

32. Ibid.

33. *The Times*, 18 May 1983.

34. Diary Readings with Douglas Hurd, 17 Dec. 1996.

35. Ibid.

36. Anthony Hurd was the first British Member of Parliament to visit the Falkland Islands, and introduced a type of grass, called 'Yorkshire Fog', for the islanders' sheep.
37. *Sea Lion* was published in the *Daily Telegraph* on 31 Dec., 1994.
38. Diary Readings with Douglas Hurd, 17 Dec. 1996.
39. Interview with Douglas Hurd, 17 Dec. 1996.
40. Douglas Hurd, 'Chairing From the Front', *The Spectator*, 6 Nov. 1993.
41. Diary Readings with Douglas Hurd, 17 Dec. 1996.
42. Interview with Douglas Hurd, 17 Dec. 1996.
43. Hurd's fellow ministers were Lord Belstead, Cranley Onslow (Woking), Neil Marten (Banbury) – still at Overseas Development – and Malcolm Rifkind (Edinburgh, Pentlands) who joined the the ministerial team as Parliamentary Under Secretary of State. *Keesing's Contemporary Archives*, pp. 31538–9.
44. Interview with Douglas Hurd, 17 Dec. 1996.
45. Thatcher, *Downing Street Years*, p. 294.
46. Ibid., pp. 541–5.
47. Douglas Hurd, 'Political Co-operation', *International Affairs*, Summer 1981, vol. 57, no. 3, pp. 383–93.
48. *The Times*, 16 Apr. 1983.
49. H. of C. Deb. (5th Series), 21 Jul. 1982, vol. 28, col. 421.
50. Diary Readings with Douglas Hurd, 17 Dec. 1996.
51. Ibid.
52. Ibid.
53. Ibid.
54. Interview with Stephen Lamport, 19 Dec. 1995.
55. H. of C. Deb. (6th Series), 5 Nov. 1981, vol. 12, col. 209.
56. Interview with Sir Antony Acland, 17 Mar. 1997.
57. Diary Readings with Douglas Hurd, 17 Dec. 1996.

9

Doom and Gloom:
Minister of State at the Home Office,
June 1983–September 1984

The boundary changes had created the new parliamentary constituency of Witney in time for the June 1983 General Election.[1] The bald statistics of Hurd's poll in the 1983 General Election were reasonably satisfactory. His actual majority fell slightly from 15,491 in 1979 to 12,712 in 1983, but his overall percentage share of the vote hardly shifted. The main cause of this apparent contradiction was a strong challenge from the Liberal/SDP Alliance candidate, John Baston, at the expense of the Labour candidate, Carol Douse. However, on Election night, Hurd had far more important matters on his mind. That night, his wife, Judy, gave birth to their baby son at the John Radcliffe Hospital in Oxford.

The birth of his son on election night caused him to miss his own count and declaration. Hurd's place at the count, held in Langdale Hall, Witney, was taken by Tom Ponsonby, the Chairman of the West Oxfordshire Conservative Association, and the news of his election victory was relayed on a 'hot line' by his personal campaign manager, Mrs Sheila Coles. Judy had given birth only twelve minutes after the election declaration. Hurd's diary entry reveals the drama of the day:

> 9 Jun. 1983: Up early. Back to the John Radcliffe. Stayed there, cutting short the tour. Miss my count, my declaration, and my party. 55 per cent of poll, which is good. Caesarian. Philip is born at 2.30. Cope with reporters. Drive home as dawn comes.[2]

In the morning, he recalls turning on the radio 'in a fuzzy sort of way' to listen for the General Election results.[3] Instead of that, he heard the national anthem being played. It was Prince Philip's birthday. This was one reason why Douglas and Judy decided to name their son Philip. Also, there had been two Philips in the Hurd family tree: Dr Philip Hurd, the lawyer and speculator of the previous century, and of course, Douglas Hurd's eccentric uncle, who so detested the name, that he changed it by deed poll to Robert.

A few days later, Hurd was the recipient of some less happy news from the Prime Minister:

> 13 Jun. 1983: Prime Minister rings at 12.30. A rumour relayed by Stephen [Lamport] proves correct. Briefly, and civilly, she asks me to go to the Home Office, praising my work at the Foreign Office and Home Office experience would do me good later. Accept, though not with a high heart.[4]

Hurd has described the following few weeks as 'the most daunting time in the sixteen years that I was a minister'.[5] The work at the Home Office was completely unfamiliar to him. He knew nothing about the police, and yet he became responsible for all the police forces in England and Wales, as well as betting and gambling, civil defence and broadcasting. In addition, he was made the minister responsible for the Police and Criminal Evidence Bill – a highly controversial piece of legislation which had been carried over from the previous Parliament. Douglas Hurd and his Parliamentary Under Secretary of State, David Mellor, were the ministers charged with the day-to-day task of guiding the Bill through the House of Commons.

At only forty-three, the new Home Secretary, Leon Brittan, was nearly ten years younger than Douglas Hurd, and it took an adjustment on Hurd's part to get used to taking orders from a much younger man. Hurd's recollection is that 'L.B.' was extremely considerate in helping him through his first few weeks.[6] According to Douglas Hurd, Leon Brittan, like Geoffrey Howe, possessed a QC's 'huge appetite for detail'.[7] But in contrast to ministers like Keith Joseph, who were unable to cut through the detail to make decisions, Hurd feels that Leon Brittan was able to accommodate that.[8] Douglas Hurd, on the other hand, was often bored by the mass of detail, and the endless meetings, clogged with boring legal jargon, seemed to get him down.

After a few months, Hurd replaced the staff in his private office – having found them well below standard – and then began visiting police stations; in July 1983 he noted in his diary a pleasing visit to Hendon Police College. Hurd is an establishment figure who will always support established authority. Throughout his two spells at the Home Office, he showed a marked readiness to supply the police with the resources which they felt they needed: in

December 1983, Hurd revealed in a written answer that 20,000 plastic bullets had been supplied to fifteen police forces in England and Wales.[9]

But, back in July 1983, a typical diary entry shows Hurd was still in a morose mood:

> Another good meeting with L.B. [on the Police and Criminal Evidence Bill].
> Tired and depressed. Seems below the level of a humdrum job.[10]

In terms of responsibility, Hurd's job did not have an unduly burdensome workload, it was just that at the time he did not feel a match for it. From the autumn of 1983 to the spring of 1984, his ministerial life was dominated by the controversial and tortuous passage of the Police and Criminal Evidence Bill. The Committee Stage of the Bill lasted for a total of fifty-nine sessions (then a record), running from the Second Reading debate on 7 November 1983 until 29 March 1984. Hurd recorded the end moment of the Bill in his diaries with a note of satisfaction:

> 29 Mar. 1984: We finish the Bill at 7.40. This is a big achievement. I'm well
> pleased. Labour issue badges recording the record of 59 sessions.[11]

During the 1980s, the Labour Party's attitude on Home Office issues was dominated by a passionately libertarian defence of the rights of the individual. Unsurprisingly, the Opposition opposed most of the provisions of the Police and Criminal Evidence Bill. In this, it was seconded by the Greater London Council (GLC) which, under the leadership of Ken Livingstone, launched its 'Kill the Bill' campaign. Although the Bill had originally flowed from a Royal Commission Report on Criminal Procedure by Sir Cyril Philips, established by the previous Labour Government, the Labour Party vigorously opposed the clauses which proposed to extend police powers of stop-and-search, and search-and-seizure. Most controversially, the Bill sought to give the police the power to detain suspects for questioning without charge for a new maximum of ninety-six hours. Gerald Kaufman, then Labour's Shadow Home Secretary, singles out Douglas Hurd for criticism for his handling of the Bill. He believes Hurd did not understand all the legal aspects of the legislation and would have been lost without the help of David Mellor.[12] During the passage of the legislation in committee and then at report stage, the Labour Opposition were able to force a number of significant concessions. Throughout, one is forced to concur with Gerald Kaufman's opinion: Douglas Hurd was far from inspiring in his performances at the Dispatch Box.

During the Committee Stage, Labour's Shadow Home Affairs Spokesman, Robert Kilroy-Silk, challenged Hurd on the Bill's definition of police access to 'a public place'. Did a person's garden, he asked, constitute 'any place where as a matter of simple and practical fact the public have ready access?'[13] Floundering about with the legal concepts, Hurd's only response was that was 'something we ought to look at again'.[14] In December 1983, David Mellor was forced to tidy up the mess left by Douglas Hurd by tightening up the definition of a public place.

The Opposition was also worried that the new powers of stop-and-search would discriminate against black people, citing a Policy Studies Institute report of the time, which identified a marked tendency for police officers to stop-and-search young black males. Moreover, as Clare Short, MP for Birmingham, Ladywood argued, if the police were suspicious of someone, then they should arrest a suspect. Hurd argued during the Report Stage that 'stop-and-search is a real alternative to arrest'; arrest was more coercive than stop-and-search.[15]

Labour also attacked the Government's proposals to give the police powers to seize confidential documents from the houses of suspects. The original provisions in the Bill would have given the police the power to obtain warrants without first having to explain to a magistrate how the evidence could help their inquiries. The clause in the Bill was intended only for what were known as 'serious arrestable offences', typically dealing with cases of terrorist so-called 'safe houses'. Hurd's defence of the clause was that a further tightening of the law would render the investigations of the police unworkable.[16]

It was the Government's plan to set a legal maximum of ninety-six hours for police to detain suspects without charge which provoked the greatest opposition. Many civil rights groups and members of the legal profession joined Labour in their opposition, fearing miscarriages of justice if corrupt police officers used the new detention provisions to obtain a confession when they lacked prima facie evidence. On 20 February 1984, in an article in *The Times* entitled '96 HOURS: TIME TO THINK AGAIN', Geoffrey Bindman, a solicitor, argued that the ninety-six-hour provisions were a new departure in the law, creating for the first time the notion of detaining persons for questioning.

Hurd responded to Mr Bindman in a letter to *The Times* the following day (21 February), claiming that the existing law in England and Wales set no absolute fixed limit for which an arrested person might be detained before being charged. Hurd tried to soothe worries about the clause by arguing that the normal maximum for detention without charge would be twenty-four hours and that a person would only be held beyond that time if he was being held in connection with a 'serious arrestable offence and if his further detention is necessary to secure, preserve or obtain evidence for an investigation which is being diligently and expeditiously conducted.'[17]

Hurd went on to argue there were a small number of important instances where the police needed more time to complete their investigations:

> The question is whether in such cases, however valid the police case for
> further detention, however serious the offence, the investigation should have
> to be broken off and the detained person set free. We believe that this would
> expose the public to unreasonable risk.[18]

One can argue that the Police and Criminal Evidence Act of 1984 tilted the
balance too far in favour of protecting the public at the expense of the rights
of the individual. Few citizens had much faith in the new Police Complaints
Authority, even if the 1984 Act established the laudable safeguard of the tape-
recording of police interviews with suspects. Besides, it only served to increase
the burden of paperwork on police forces across England and Wales.

Winding up the debate on Third Reading, Hurd tried to peddle the line that
he was glad that the House of Commons had considered carefully such a
complex piece of legislation:

> When the pamphlets are pulped and the speeches forgotten, this will be seen
> as solid, sensible and necessary legislation. I am glad, looking back, that we
> had a record number of Committee sittings. I am glad that we secured the
> Bill in Committee without a guillotine, and without a single government
> defeat. The Bill clears away cobwebs in this part of our law.[19]

Although the remarks reflected Hurd's long-held view that Parliament should
scrutinise legislation carefully rather than legislating in haste, his closing rhetoric
was perhaps a cloak to disguise the raft of concessions which he and his party
were forced to concede to the Labour Party. Most significantly, safeguards were
introduced on the new ninety-six hours detention without charge rule. At
thirty-six hours, the suspect would have recourse to a hearing before a
magistrate's court with a lawyer present. The rocky passage of the Police and
Criminal Evidence Bill marked one of the least impressive periods in Hurd's
ministerial career.

On 31 March 1984, Hurd's diary records that he was still bleak and gloomy,
and now he had to contend with the policing of the Miners' Strike. With the
memory of defeat at the hands of the miners, especially in February 1972, still
fresh and sore in his mind, Hurd was determined to play his own small part in
facing down the challenge posed by Arthur Scargill and the National Union of
Mineworkers. There was a general feeling, even among wets like Peter Walker,
the Energy Secretary, that this time they could not fail; ministers had a kind of
messianic zeal about the necessity of winning the coal dispute. Although Hurd
was the minister responsible for the police, Leon Brittan, the Home Secretary,

and, of course, Margaret Thatcher took the lead in the decisions over policing:

> 16 Mar. 1984: Picketing crisis in Nottinghamshire . . . L.B. [Leon Brittan] does deftly in the House of Commons. No mistakes. I am on the sidelines.[20]

Hurd recalls that the Prime Minister was always pressing for greater and greater police resources as the dispute wore on.[21] During the dispute, Hurd's task was to ease local-authority fears of increased financial burdens resulting from the costs of policing the dispute.

Hurd also replied to several oral and written questions from Labour MPs, promising to look sympathetically on those police authorities, particularly in Nottinghamshire, which were suffering from stretched police resources, and ultimately, the Government agreed to exempt from grant claw-back the additional local-authority expenditure arising from the miners' industrial action.[22]

In parliamentary terms, the debates over the Miners' Strike were muted by the equivocal attitude of the Labour leadership. It was left to Labour MPs from mining constituencies and the hard left to request emergency debates:

> 10 Apr. 1984: Wind up with emergency debate on police operation in coalfields. This is six minutes. Goes well, better than anything for a long time. A good debate. L.B. [Leon Brittan] effective, David Owen more so, Benn mad.[23]

Tony Benn's allegations at the time were that army officers were regularly used to supplement police numbers. In his diaries, Benn can only produce anecdotal evidence to support his claims.[24] Although striking miners did witness police officers without code numbers on the lapels of their uniforms, this suggests they were police officers drafted in from other forces across the country, co-ordinated by a special national reporting centre at New Scotland Yard. It does seem as though the Miners' Strike 1984–85 saw the emergence of a national police force in Britain rather than one based on the control of local police authorities.

The most brutal clashes between striking miners and police occurred outside the Orgreave Coking Depot in South Yorkshire during late May and early June 1984. Journalist Gerry Northam, in his book *Shooting in the Dark: Riot Police in Britain*, claims that 'Orgreave represented the unveiling of colonial policy tactics in mainland Britain.'[25] The tactics used at Orgreave set the pattern for police responses to the inner city riots in 1985, the Wapping dispute from 1986 to 1987, and various gatherings at Stonehenge and Glastonbury during Hurd's later period as Home Secretary.

The events at Orgreave sparked an angry response from Labour MPs representing mining constituencies. Allen McKay, MP for Barnsley, West and Penistone, an ex-miner, identified the real significance of Orgreave:

> After the defeats in 1972 and 1974, in 1981 when the Prime Minister backed down on the proposed twenty colliery closures, after Saltley and all the other incidents, the Conservatives said that it would never happen again. The reason for the vast police presence on the picket lines is the Prime Minister's determination that there should not be another Saltley.[26]

Whilst being careful to condemn the violence, Gerald Kaufman, Labour's Shadow Home Secretary, joined his backbenchers in calling for an impartial public inquiry to determine whether the police exercised excessive powers or infringed civil liberties.[27] Douglas Hurd rejected such calls, and said the proper procedure was via the Police Complaints Board. Instead, he defended the police tactics, accusing the pickets of violence and mass intimidation, and called on the opposition front bench to 'use their influence with the leaders of the strike and persuade them to change their bullying and undemocratic tactics.'[28]

Hurd was equally unyielding in his support for civil-defence measures against nuclear attack. As the Minister of State responsible for civil defence, he argued that it was a necessary part of deterrence that Britain should have civil defence measures in place.[29] The British Medical Association (BMA) and the Royal College of Nursing (RCN) disagreed, along with many Labour local authorities, especially the GLC, arguing that in the aftermath of a nuclear war, the devastation would be so great, that efforts to save lives would be relatively meaningless. In October 1983, faced with Labour authorities which had declared themselves 'nuclear-free' zones, Hurd pushed through draft regulations compelling local authorities to allocate resources for civil defence, announcing his measures on the eve of Britain's biggest ever nuclear demonstration by the Campaign for Nuclear Disarmament (CND).

During the Commons debate on the draft regulations in October, Hurd was perhaps a shade overearnest in putting the Government's case:

> Much of the research and evidence comes from the United States and should be examined in the light of British conditions – for example, British houses tend to be somewhat more solid than American houses. [Interruption] Why the giggles? Let us try to deal with facts.[30]

The Government did not put a great deal of money into funding voluntary groups who carried out civil defence exercises, but their efforts fitted in with Hurd's strong belief in service in the national interest:

> 15 Jul. 1983: Inspect summer camp at Royal Observer Corps. A long parade, classroom speech in a hangar. Agreeable and interesting group.[31]

In retrospect, Hurd is unrepentant about taking a strong line against CND or supporting civil defence measures, believing that the West's decision to deploy Pershing and Cruise missiles played a part in ending the Cold War.[32] Nowadays it is easy to mock the stances taken during the Cold War era because most of its concepts are now badly dated or defunct – like the threat of nuclear attack from the Warsaw Pact.

On a more mundane domestic level, Hurd played an important part in tightening up the law on television-licence evasion – initiating the age of the sophisticated licence-detector van – and the law on drink driving, but he got into a considerable amount of difficulty with intoximeters. In April 1983, the Home Office had issued police forces with breathalysers. In March 1984, the Government faced demands to change drink-driving laws when two former employees of the machine's manufacturers, Lion Intoximeters, revealed to the Daily Express that the 'Lion Intoximeter 3000' machine was prone to error and had a high failure rate. The motoring organisations were joined by the Association of Police Surgeons and the Magistrates Association in calling for drivers to have the right to a blood or urine test if they were found to be over the legal limit. Under the law at that time, only drivers found by the machine to be 15 microgrammes over the legal alcohol limit of 35 microgrammes per 100 millilitres of alcohol had the right to a blood or urine test. Initially, Hurd argued that returning to the old system would lead to bureaucratic delays, but the Daily Express revelations and the adverse publicity surrounding the attempt by Lion Intoximeters to halt publication of the revelations, forced him to reconsider.[33]

Hurd had not greatly enjoyed the experience of being Minister of State at the Home Office. He was simply not suited to the legal content of the department and became gloomy and disillusioned. There were even rumours at the time that he became an idle Minister of State, which if it is true, bore no comparison with his self-discipline and impressive work rate as Home Secretary and Foreign Secretary. However, he had gained experience of Home Office matters which was to prove of immeasurable value when he was appointed Home Secretary by Mrs Thatcher in September 1985. But in September 1984, Hurd had forgotten the Prime Minister's words of advice in June the previous year, when she had said that experience in the Home Office would stand him in good stead later on in his ministerial career. His mood on 8 September was, once again, one of Eeyorish gloom:

Feel a bit low. No house. No promotion. Not enough money, but not desperate.[34]

Notes

1. In the boundary changes implemented in the June 1983 General Election, the Bartons, Tackley and Woolton were excluded from the new seat of Witney, while the villages of Kidlington, Begbroke, Yarton, Gosford and Water Eaton were added.
2. Diary Readings with Douglas Hurd, 17 Dec. 1996.
3. Interview with Douglas Hurd, 17 Dec. 1996.
4. Diary Readings with Douglas Hurd, 17 Dec. 1996.
5. Interview with Douglas Hurd, 17 Dec. 1996.
6. Ibid.
7. Ibid.
8. Ibid.
9. H. of C. Deb. (6th Series), 5 Dec. 1983, vol. 50, written answers, cols 7–8.
10. Diary Readings with Douglas Hurd, 17 Dec. 1996.
11. Ibid.
12. Interview with Gerald Kaufman, 13 Nov. 1996.
13. *The Times*, 30 Nov. 1983.
14. *The Times*, 25 Nov. 1983.
15. H. of C. Deb. (6th Series), 15 May 1984, vol. 60, col. 193.
16. *The Times*, 21 December 1983.
17. Douglas Hurd, 'Letter to the Editor', *The Times*, 22 Feb. 1984; *see* also Douglas Hurd, 'Why we are sticking on 96', *The Times*, 5 Jul. 1984.
18. Ibid.
19. H. of C. Deb. (6th Series), 16 May 1984, vol. 60, col. 411.
20. Diary Readings with Douglas Hurd, 17 Dec. 1996; Mrs Thatcher established a committee of ministers under her chairmanship, to monitor the strike. Its membership comprised William Whitelaw (Deputy PM), Peter Walker (Energy), Leon Brittan (Home Department), Nigel Lawson (Treasury), Norman Tebbit (DTI), Tom King (Employment), Nick Ridley (Transport) and George Younger (Scotland). Occasionally, Michael Havers, the Attorney-General, was called in. The committee met once a week, but proved unwieldy. Thereafter, Peter Walker arranged smaller meetings; Thatcher, *Downing Street Years*, pp. 340–7.
21. Interview with Douglas Hurd, 17 Dec. 1996.
22. H. of C. Deb. (6th Series), 2 Apr. 1984, vol. 57, written answers, col. 375.

23. Diary Readings with Douglas Hurd, 17 Dec. 1996.

24. Tony Benn, *The End of an Era: Diaries 1980–90*, edited by Ruth Winstone (Arrow Books: London, 1994), p. 346.

25. Gerry Northam, *Shooting in the Dark: Riot Police in Britain* (Faber & Faber: London, 1989), p. 59. Northam reveals that these tactics were based on an advisory Association of Chief Police Officer's (ACPO) document entitled *Public Order Manual of Tactical Options and Related Matters*.

26. H. of C. Deb. (6th Series), 23 Jul. 1984, vol. 47, col. 797.

27. Ibid., col. 799.

28. Ibid., col. 804.

29. Douglas Hurd, 'Letter to the Editor', *The Times*, 7 Dec. 1983.

30. H. of C. Deb. (6th Series), 26 Oct. 1983, vol. 47, col. 338.

31. Diary Readings with Douglas Hurd, 17 Dec. 1996.

32. Interview with Douglas Hurd, 17 Dec. 1996.

33. On 26 March 1984, the Court of Appeal ruled that there was a wider public interest involved in the information leaked to the *Daily Express* by Philip Evans and Robert Smith, two former employees of Lion Intoximeters. Lord Justice Stephenson (presiding), Law Report, *The Times*, 27 Mar. 1984.

34. Diary Readings with Douglas Hurd, 17 Dec. 1996.

10

Proceeding with Caution: Secretary of State for Northern Ireland, September 1984–September 1985

Only two days after expressing pessimism over his promotion prospects, and after five years as a Minister of State, Hurd finally entered the Cabinet when Mrs Thatcher appointed him Secretary of State for Northern Ireland:

> 10 Sept. 1984: Prime Minister asks me to go around about noon. She looks tired. Sits me down in the drawing room, shutting off one section [Hurd comments on Mrs Thatcher's habit of getting up when people entered the room, to move furniture and shut doors]. She [Mrs Thatcher] wants someone of intellect and toughness in Northern Ireland, which Peter Carrington always said.[1]

Hurd recalls her saying:

> Peter always says you're very tough. You've got a smooth manner, but you're very tough inside.[2]

In actual fact, Mrs Thatcher had narrowed down her choice for the post of Northern Ireland Secretary to Douglas Hurd and Patrick Mayhew, the Solicitor General. Hurd had been chosen in preference to Mayhew because the former was considered, on balance, to be drier on economic policy.[3] Hurd's path up the ministerial ladder had undoubtedly been slowed by his prior association with Edward Heath, but Mrs Thatcher came to recognise his strengths of competence, loyalty and toughness. She retained her suspicions of Hurd because of his Heathite past and his Foreign Office background, but she was fair in her dealings with him, and even her apparent demotion of him in 1983 to the Home Office had been a blessing: it ensured Hurd gained a proper grounding in a domestic department before his promotion to Cabinet.

In the wake of Jim Prior's resignation as Secretary of State for Northern Ireland, there were strong rumours that Hurd might be in the running for the job, and he discussed the possible security implications with Judy. Even so, as his diary entry for 8 September suggests, he was not very optimistic about his chances. Mrs Thatcher was not entirely sure that Hurd would accept – because of the security aspect and the fact that his son, Philip, was only two years old. However, Hurd accepted the offer immediately. William Whitelaw, the Deputy Prime Minister, and John Wakeham, the Government Chief Whip, appeared in the room to congratulate Douglas Hurd, and Mrs Thatcher opened a bottle of wine – German hock – to celebrate. According to Peter Carrington, with whom Hurd conversed later that day, this had never happened before in his experience.[4]

Realising he would soon be surrounded by security guards, Hurd slipped away from the celebrations, hoping to catch a few final hours of freedom. But, as he drove down the lane at Westwell, there they were:

10 Sept. 1984: Slavery begins. They are many but courteous.[5]

The next morning, Hurd told waiting reporters that he could hear the police guards 'crunching on the gravel' outside his Oxfordshire home.[6] Perhaps the remark about slavery was an exaggeration, but ever since, Hurd has been surrounded by police. For a brief moment during the IRA ceasefire in 1995, he expressed the hope that his security might be scaled down, but that proved to be a false dawn. Privately, he describes the sensation of their omnipresence as 'very bizarre'.[7]

On taking up his new job, Hurd could boast very little prior experience of Ulster, with two notable exceptions. An attempt to kill the Prime Minister by IRA terrorists had been the plot of his 1975 novel, *Vote to Kill*. The British and Irish press trawled the text of the novel for any vague clues about Hurd's attitudes on Northern Ireland, but they searched in vain. Hurd's only previous visit to the Province caused much more of a stir. In January 1978, he had agreed to take part in a *Spotlight* programme for the BBC. The original plan had been to send two MPs – one Labour and one Conservative – with no prior experience of Ulster, across to the Province on a fact-finding mission. Before going, Hurd had been scrupulous in consulting Roy Mason, then the Labour Secretary of State for Northern Ireland, and the Shadow Spokesman for the Opposition, Airey Neave, neither of whom raised any objection to the trip.

However, at the last minute, the Labour MP pulled out and Hurd went to Northern Ireland alone. As part of a background briefing away from the cameras, Hurd toured West Belfast to assess political attitudes among the predominantly Nationalist community. It was at this point that he had a private discussion with Gerry Adams:

> 13 Jan. 1978: Ballymurphy Community Centre [West Belfast]. A bleak, bare room. Argue for an hour with Gerry Adams, PSF [Provisional Sinn Fein]. An intelligent young man with a black beard and a thick voice.[8]

There is no doubt that the man Hurd spoke to was Gerry Adams. It seems that Danny Morrison, later convicted for terrorist offences, was also present at the meeting but Hurd would not have known at the time what Morrison looked like. This was the first and only time that Adams and Hurd met. Although there is no indication from the diaries, Hurd remembers Adams as being uncompromising; a disagreeable argument ensued which led nowhere. On learning of Hurd's appointment to Northern Ireland, Sinn Fein revealed that the meeting had taken place, and claimed, somewhat predictably, that Hurd was coming to the Province, as 'an apologist for British violence, to take responsibility for a corrupt administration dependent on British guns for its existence.'[9] At an impromptu press conference on the steps of Stormont Castle, Hurd responded to the press reports of his 1978 meeting with Sinn Fein by stressing its unfruitful nature and that the visit had been approved in advance by Roy Mason and Airey Neave. This helped ensure that the revelations sparked media interest for only one day.

Although Hurd used his first few weeks in the post to listen to and consult with the various constitutional parties in the Province, rather than pronouncing on issues, he did make a point of quickly ruling out any talks with Sinn Fein.[10] The IRA and their supporters, were in Hurd's eyes, 'destroyers' rather than 'doers', rogues rather than men of goodwill. They wished to upset the existing order of things rather than seeking to reform it by gradual, peaceful means; they offended his Tory, establishment instincts.

Almost immediately, Hurd faced a crisis involving a hunger strike by ten loyalist prisoners at Magilligan jail. The prisoners were campaigning for segregation from IRA prisoners. Douglas Hurd, along with the minister responsible for prisons, Nicholas Scott, successfully defused the issue by agreeing to send thirteen loyalist prisoners from the Maze to Magilligan and twenty-six republicans in the opposite direction, thereby achieving a better balance between loyalist and republican prisoners.[11]

Despite the pressures of the new job, Hurd's initial feelings were of excitement and exhilaration at being promoted to the Cabinet after it seemed his political rise had ground to halt at Minister of State level. Writing three weeks after being promoted, he observed:

> A great change for the better. A job with real responsibility . . . sweeps away most of the misgivings building up in my own mind about my own capacity. Of course, a run of bad luck or mistakes could bring this back . . . After three weeks, the excitement and the pleasure still win.[12]

Hurd was fortunate in being served by a solid ministerial team at the Northern Ireland Office, particularly two very able Parliamentary Under Secretaries of State. Nicholas Scott had the difficult task of dealing with prisons and internal security as well as education, whilst Chris Patten dealt with a large portfolio comprising housing, local government, transport, planning, health and social security, Home Office regulatory issues (e.g. vehicle licensing), and a great deal of the day-to-day administration of the Province. In effect, Patten was responsible for two departments: Health and Social Security, and the Department of the Environment. Patten's role occasionally went beyond his official brief. In the run-up to the Hillsborough Summit of November 1984, Hurd asked Chris Patten to look at the possibilities of the 'twin track' strategy: developing not only the relationship between London, Belfast and Dublin, but also an attempt to persuade the political parties to work together in some form of devolved institution in Northern Ireland.[13] The Northern Ireland team was complemented by Lord Lyell, who was the minister responsible for agriculture, and dealt with matters relating to Northern Ireland in the Lords. Junior ministers and officials alike quickly grew to admire Hurd's intellectual authority, which made him very comfortable about delegating decisions. Chris Patten even goes as far as to describe him as 'incomparably the best delegator I have ever worked with'.[14]

Hurd's Number Two was Dr Rhodes Boyson. An eccentric former headmaster with right-wing views on economics and 'Orange' leanings on Northern Ireland, his portfolio comprised mainly economic issues such as employment, industrial policy and agricultural matters raised in the House of Commons. Boyson was a favourite of Mrs Thatcher and he may have felt he had been sent to Northern Ireland to keep an eye on Hurd from an 'Orange' point of view. Whether or not this was actually the case is debatable. Hurd and Boyson worked together on a perfectly amicable basis. In any case, Boyson had nothing to worry about; Hurd would describe himself as a Unionist with a small 'u'. Although he brought a relatively open mind to the Province, he had more natural sympathy for the Unionists than his predecessor. James Prior had found the nationalists more genial company than the Unionists, especially Enoch Powell, his traditional foe from his Heathite days. The irony was that it was the nationalist refusal to participate in the Northern Ireland Assembly which wrecked Prior's devolution plans.

Even if the Unionists continued to be suspicious of his Foreign Office background – which they automatically equated with conspiracy and intrigue with the Irish Republic – Hurd was relatively orthodox in his views on the future course of constitutional talks. Whilst he supported the right of the Republic to be consulted on matters relating to Northern Ireland, he was not in favour of joint authority. In his view, any future peace agreement would combine a limited Irish dimension with an assembly along the lines of the Sunningdale Agreement of 1973. That agreement had failed due to a strike by Protestant workers, and direct rule had been imposed by London ever since. James Prior's plans for a devolved assembly in 1982-83 were scuppered by the blanket refusal of the Social Democratic and Labour Party (SDLP) to participate. When Douglas Hurd arrived, he was not as committed, though not hostile, to the remnants of Prior's assembly. It had clearly failed. On the other hand, because he was filled with all the excitement and zest one might expect from a politician newly appointed to the Cabinet, he did not want to be seen as a political do-nothing. Possessing the mind of a Whitehall administrator, he always wanted to explore the alternative option, the plan 'B'. So, as well as continuing talks with the Irish Government under the auspices of the Anglo-Irish Inter-Governmental Council and trying to drive down the level of terrorist violence, he actively sought ways of softening certain aspects of direct rule.

The steering committee of the Anglo-Irish Intergovernmental Council worked in secret, free from security concerns. The British team was headed by Sir Robert (now Lord) Armstrong, the Cabinet Secretary. Sir David Goodall, a senior Foreign Office Official on secondment to the Cabinet Office and Sir Alan Goodison, British Ambassador to Dublin, completed the trio of British negotiators.[15] Douglas Hurd quickly identified Sir Robert Armstrong as the key man on the British side:

27 Sept. 1984: Robert Armstrong came and briefed me about his secret dealings in Dublin. As a result, my own mind clears. I think the answer may be an Irish dimension, as the SDLP want, plus majority rule as a safeguard, which is what the Unionists want.[16]

The general rule of thumb since the imposition of direct rule is that most Secretaries of State for Northern Ireland, along with the officials at the Northern Ireland Office, have adopted a more guarded attitude to closer relations with the Republic – understandably, for it is they that have to deal with a possible Unionist backlash. Meanwhile, the Foreign Office has been generally enthusiastic about co-operation with the Republic. Although Hurd brought with him a Unionist tinge, he quickly became attuned to the importance of the talks process. His role in the shaping of the Anglo-Irish Agreement was not so much in the detailed negotiations as in his being a mediating force within the British Government – between Downing Street which was the more sceptical, and the Foreign Office which was the more adventurous.

After making his first major public speech in Enniskillen, Co. Fermanagh, Hurd quickly learned the importance of language and symbols in the politics of Northern Ireland. At a passing-out parade of new Royal Ulster Constabulary (RUC) officers, Hurd praised the Chief Constable of the RUC, Sir John Hermon, and said he was encouraged by the 'increasing support which the police enjoy among the public at large'.[17] Peter Barry, the Irish Foreign Minister, who was in Luxembourg at the time, telephoned a senior official in the Department of Foreign Affairs to make a complaint. Dr Garrett Fitzgerald, the Irish Taioseach, then telephoned Alan Goodison, British Ambassador in Dublin to express his reservations about the remarks. Hurd's comments were also branded as 'seriously misleading' by Seamus Mallon, Deputy Leader of the SDLP.[18] However, when Barry actually took the time to read the transcript of Hurd's remarks he found them to be more balanced than the initial reports had suggested. Soon afterwards, Garrett Fitzgerald admitted on Irish television (RTE) that he had been 'a bit too hasty'.[19] Hurd feels there was a pattern in the response of Irish political figures to his remarks:

> It did happen quite often . . . I said something, looking at it again still thought it was very conciliatory, which produced considerable commotion. This could happen either way. Usually, it was the nationalist side which took offence. Phrases are taken up and run with in a way which it is very difficult to foresee.[20]

Something which was impossible to foresee was the IRA's bomb attack on the Grand Hotel in Brighton early on the final day of the Conservative Party Conference. Luckily, Hurd was not staying at the Grand, but with his ex-wife's parents, who lived near the village of West Burton, near Arundel. Hurd was woken at about 5 a.m. by the police to be told about the attack. Initially, the police were reluctant to take Hurd to Brighton in case of further blasts; it was considered too risky to have too many senior Cabinet ministers exposed to further injury. Realising that he was due to speak in the first debate that morning, Hurd hastily rewrote his speech on the kitchen table of his former in-laws' house. When he arrived at the scene, Hurd records seeing 'shocked people, dishevelled, full of rumours'.[21] No one it seemed, knew quite what had happened. However, the Prime Minister decided it was to be business as usual, and the Conference agenda went ahead as planned. John Gummer, as Conservative Party Chairman, was responsible for Conference arrangements and Hurd recalls him performing well in keeping the Conference on track.

The opening debate on Northern Ireland was a subdued affair, interrupted by bemused delegates trickling into the Conference hall, as people spoke from the platform. Hurd played a straight bat in his own speech, warning against the word 'initiative', which he claimed aroused hopes in one community and anxieties in the other. There would, he said, be no change in Northern Ireland's constitutional position within the United Kingdom without the freely given consent of the majority of its people.[22]

After the Prime Minister's closing speech, Hurd had hoped to return to his London home in Redan Street. But, by this time, the police were naturally very edgy and they advised him to stay at Westwell, which was, given its remote location, far more defensible than his home in Hammersmith. That night, Hurd reflected on his friend John Wakeham who had been badly injured and had lost his wife Roberta in the blast.

However, the IRA attack did not deal a fatal blow to the talks process between the British and Irish Governments. If anything, it merely hardened Mrs Thatcher's resolve, that although she did not want joint institutions established between North and South, co-operation was needed with the Republic in order to combat the menace of terrorism. Throughout the bumpy talks process, Dr Garrett Fitzgerald and Geoffrey Howe in particular, tried to keep her on board by pursuing this line. Unfortunately, at the Anglo-Irish Summit at Chequers on the weekend of 18-19 November 1984, Douglas Hurd was witness to Mrs Thatcher's tendency to make over-the-top remarks, both in public and in private. On the first day of the summit, out of earshot of the Irish delegation, she resurrected one of her more bizarre ideas, namely repartition: the concept that the border could be redrawn and the nationalists repatriated to the Republic. On the night of 18 November, Douglas Hurd categorised Mrs Thatcher as 'an anti-Unionist Unionist', meaning that although she was sympathetic to maintaining Ulster as part of the United Kingdom, she often found the Unionists themselves difficult to deal with.

The following day (19 November), Hurd described how the 'Prime Minister and Taioseach exchange misunderstandings.'[23] In personal terms, Mrs Thatcher and Garrett Fitzgerald got on reasonably well (although she had been charmed much more by his predecessor, Charlie Haughey), but they did not really listen to what the other was saying. The closest relationship was between Geoffrey Howe and Garrett Fitzgerald. Every time Mrs Thatcher blew a gaping hole through the talks process with her outlandish comments, Howe and Fitzgerald, both patient and considered men, would repair the damage, when they met at European level.[24]

At the press conference held in Number 12 Downing Street after the Chequers Summit, Mrs Thatcher rejected each of the three proposals made by the Irish Forum on the future status of Northern Ireland. The New Ireland Forum was originally the idea of John Hume, leader of the Catholic SDLP, but it had been intended by Dr Fitzgerald to act as a moderate nationalist think-tank. The New Ireland Forum Report of May 1984 listed three possible options for constitutional change: a united Ireland, a federal Ireland, and joint authority between London and Dublin. Although the moderate nationalists retained the long-term goal of a united Ireland, they accepted the principle of consent. To each of these three proposals, Mrs Thatcher dismissively bellowed 'that's out'. Even though Hurd's predecessor, James Prior, had rejected all three options on 4 July, as became her trait, it was Mrs Thatcher's tone which rankled with the Irish. As so often happened in Hurd's experience, it was not the talks with international leaders which caused difficulties, but the bravura press conferences afterwards. It is to Garrett Fitzgerald's credit that he did not allow his anger to smoulder for long, although at the time, he found Mrs Thatcher's comments 'gratuitously offensive'.[25]

The following day (20 November), Hurd gave a separate press conference in Belfast, insisting that the Irish republic could not exercise any executive authority in the affairs of the North, offering only a consultative role via the concept of a joint security council. From Hurd's point of view, he was starting the process of lowering Irish expectations about the scope of a future agreement. Still smarting from the undiplomatic comments of Mrs Thatcher, nationalist politicians reacted badly. Dick Spring, the Irish Deputy Prime Minister, or 'Tanaiste', refused to accept Hurd's limited ideas and accused him of referring selectively to the Chequers talks. Hurd's own recollection was rather different:

> 21 Nov. 1984: Press Conference in Belfast. This goes reasonably well . . .
> By evening, it appears the SDLP react badly . . . I get the transcript. It's harmless and conciliatory.[26]

Hurd sees this as another example of the over-blown indignation from nationalist politicians to apparently conciliatory remarks.

Hurd's vision of politics is of moderate people from all sides of the community, practical people of good sense, coming together to produce sensible policies by a process of reasoned argument. His latest novel, *The Shape of Ice*, details a plan by business leaders from both communities in Northern Ireland, who begin participating in party politics. The initiative succeeds in fiction, but the political reality of megaphone politics in Northern Ireland never showed signs of matching Hurd's vision of reasonableness and rational argument. Hurd's view that it was not unrealistic to find ways in which the minority could feel part of the country of Northern Ireland did not go far enough. There was a fundamental difference between entrenching the majority in a devolved assembly, which the Unionists wanted, and recasting all of Northern Ireland's institutions, stripping them of connotations of the British Crown and flag, and involving the Republic in the day-to-day running of the affairs of the North, as the Catholic minority wanted.

Since the imposition of direct rule, there appears to have been marked reluctance amongst the majority of Secretaries of State for Northern Ireland to deal with the high level of discrimination and alienation experienced by the minority Catholic community in the North. However, during his brief spell in Northern Ireland, Hurd did come to see that Catholics were under-represented and that the Unionists had to be more ready to accommodate change. He was a prime mover in ensuring that the report of the Fair Employment Agency was acted upon. His decency in this regard helped prepare the way for the Fair Employment (Northern Ireland) Act of 1989, which started the process of equality of employment for Catholics.

Away from the cut and thrust of politics, Douglas and Judy Hurd grew fond of living in Hillsborough Castle, joined at weekends by Philip, who was then only a toddler. With his eye for all things cultural and historical, Hurd admired the numerous portraits by John Lavery in the dark rooms of the Castle.[27] Outside, he enjoyed the garden, which sports the largest rhododendron in Europe. But political life demanded that Hurd led 'a four-toothbrush' existence.[28] There would be occasional overnight stays in the flat in Stormont Castle if his work ran late into the evening; weekends were often spent at Westwell; and the Hurd's London house in Redan Street was convenient for the Westminster commitments. By this time, Hurd had moved out of his rented cottage in Westwell, into a bigger house in the same village. However, the Hurds gazed longingly over their fence at 'Freelands' – the large, upright manorial farmhouse next door. Fearing that the house would never come on the market, the Hurds bought Home Farm, near Longworth, some thirty miles from Westwell, in the winter of 1985. It was a house they would never inhabit. One Sunday, at church in Westwell, the owner unexpectedly offered to sell 'Freelands' to the Hurds, who hastily accepted.

Security considerations demanded that Hurd take a different route to Belfast each time he visited the city. He enjoyed the drive in and out of Belfast, especially St Anne's Cathedral. Hurd attended services in the parish church at Hillsborough, with its original eighteenth-century pews, when spending weekends in Ulster. He became good friends with Dr Robin Eames, Archbishop of Armagh and head of the Church of Ireland. Much later, during the behind-the-scenes talks which led to the Downing Street Declaration in December

1993, Eames became a line of contact between Albert Reynolds, the Taioseach, and senior Unionists.[29]

Hurd spoke in St Anne's Cathedral on Ash Wednesday, 20 February 1985. The tone of his speech was optimistic and conciliatory:

> After five months here, a short time, I know, I believe that it is possible to gradually soften the edges of conflict and distrust, to dissolve the suspicion and to drain the poison of the body politic.[30]

Referring to the constitutional parties, he expressed regret at their lack of willingness to make progress in talks, and their tendency 'to denigrate every good idea, every new policy, and every opportunity'.[31] They were, he claimed, too reluctant to move out of the trenches for fear of losing the support of those who elected them. That night, Hurd could not help noting in his diary with wry amusement that members of the Special Branch were dotted around the church, forced to sit through his speech, all trying in vain to blend into the congregation.[32] He would return to St Anne's alone to pray on his last day in Northern Ireland.[33]

At the turn of the year, there was a lull in terrorist violence. The RUC was able to report a fall in the death toll from 101 in 1981 to 64 in 1984 – still high, but apparently on a downward path.[34] It seemed that Hurd's strategy of 'grinding down' terrorist violence was succeeding.[35]

On New Year's Day 1985, Hurd relaxed by taking a memorable walk across the snowy wastes of the Mountains of Mourne. As a senior minister, he became renowned for his eye for topography, his love of walking and his voracious stride. He enjoyed making regional tours of the Province, meeting people and seeing things for himself. There was a pleasant trip to the Antrim coast at the end of October 1984, when the Hurds took in the Giant's Causeway and visited the old Bushmills distillery at Portballintrae.[36] There were visits to some of the finest farmers in the British Isles, including in July 1985, a Catholic family called the Bradleys who farmed above Warrenpoint, in County Down. Hurd was encouraged by the moderately nationalist viewpoint he encountered. There were afternoons spent with Judy watching the horse-racing – Judy's brother-in-law is the racing trainer, Jeremy Hindley – at Downpatrick and Down Royal. In February 1985, Hurd enjoyed a visit to Whitla Hall, at Queens University, Belfast, where he opened an exhibition of academic books. Some of his own novels were on display at one of the stands. In July 1985, Hurd would publish his novel *The Palace of Enchantments* with Stephen Lamport, his former Private Secretary at the Foreign Office. There was also the happy news that Judy was expecting another child in August. When baby Jessica arrived, she became the first girl to be born in the Hurd family for four generations. In short, there was an enjoyable life outside the immediate hurly-burly of party politics.

Conversely, on the political front, Hurd continued to be on the receiving end of gesture politics, particularly from the nationalist community. After one meeting with a delegation of Catholic priests, he was once again downbeat:

> 11 Feb. 1985: Met the priests at Stormont. Very depressing. No sign of any appreciation of terrorism . . . starts well on unemployment, steadily deteriorates. I am exposed and am accused of being Paisley's tool.[37]

By acting as the honest broker, Hurd discovered that he could not win with any side of the political debate. However, by the end of February, he was feeling optimistic that the Irish were 'nibbling at our modest proposal' as a result of talks in London with Peter Barry, the Irish Foreign Minister.[38] Then, on 28 February, during discussion with Geoffrey Howe on the Anglo-Irish talks, news began to come in of a fearful attack on the RUC station at Newry. Experienced observers of the Province had been rightly wary of the apparent lull in terrorist violence. First reports came in that eight men had been killed. During dinner that evening with Ronnie Grierson and the great Irishman Tony O'Reilly, Chairman of Heinz Foods, the telephone rang four times with news of fresh disasters, this time in South Belfast.

The next day, Hurd decided to cancel his plans in London, and flew to Newry:

> 28 Feb. 1985: Away in a deep gloom. Meeting [with security advisers at Stormont]. RUC explain how, by atrocious luck, nine were killed by the mortar. Drive to the area. Small, crowded room upstairs in police station overlooking the shattered portacabin canteen. Walk to the fatal lorry with tubes still fitted. Meet councillors, etc., call in to the hospital to see young wounded. My first security disaster.[39]

Other terrorist atrocities did take place during Hurd's year in Northern Ireland, but the bombing at Newry constituted Hurd's only major terrorist incident. During a visit to Londonderry in July 1985, he made the mistake of making favourable comments about the security situation. Four days later, the IRA launched an attack on a commercial target. No one was seriously injured, but politicians claimed that the bombing had occurred solely because of Hurd's remarks. Most Secretaries of State for Northern Ireland have fallen into that trap since. It was a no-win situation: pessimism was greeted with opprobrium, and expressions of optimism with bomb blasts.

After Newry, Hurd's security advisers were edgy about his personal security – as they had been after the Brighton bombing – and felt that the Hurds should vacate their home in Hammersmith, which was considered indefensible from terrorist attack. A safer location in central London was found, at South Eaton Place.

Three weeks after Newry, Hurd was in Dublin for talks with Fitzgerald, Spring and Barry ahead of Mrs Thatcher's informal meeting with Dr Fitzgerald at the Milan European Council in June. In front of a roaring peat fire in Iveagh House, he talked with Barry and Spring before having lunch with Fitzgerald and Barry:

> 22 Mar. 1985: They're perfectly friendly, but depressing. I don't want to expand our original proposal . . . the truth is we want a minimalist agreement, because we don't accept their basic analysis, which is that their involvement will rally the minority in a few months.[40]

As part of the drive against terrorism, Hurd visited the United States to meet with leading political and business figures interested in Irish affairs. His predecessor, Jim Prior, had made a similar visit and the tour of the United States became a regular fixture in the Secretary of State for Northern Ireland's political calendar. The tour took in Washington DC, New York, Chicago, San Francisco and Los Angeles. Hurd's day in Washington included lunch with American journalists and editorial writers, and meetings with Tip O'Neill, Speaker of the House of Representatives, and William Webster, Director of the Federal Bureau of Investigation (FBI). The guest list at the British Embassy dinner that evening ran like a roll-call of everyone on Capitol Hill with an interest in Irish issues: Senators Gary Hart, Daniel Moynihan and Howard Metzenbaum were joined by Congressmen Tom Foley, Edward Feighan and Benjamin Gilman.

The main purpose of the trip was to promote American corporate investment in Ulster. Hurd realised that Irish-American businessmen, who sympathised with the minority community, were wary of investing in Ulster, when there were perceived inequalities of employment opportunities for Catholics, particularly in companies likes Shorts and Harland & Wolff. Throughout his year in Northern Ireland, Hurd was always aware of the considerable economic pressure being exerted by the Americans on the British Government to create a fair employment agency.

The other great economic pressure being exerted was from the Treasury, which was trying to find ways of cutting the high level of British Government spending in Northern Ireland. However, throughout the 1980s, the Thatcherite vision of privatisation and cutting public spending wherever and whenever possible was unable to extend its tentacles as far as Northern Ireland. The announcement of the privatisation of Shorts in November 1984 was a rare exception. Hurd may have made reassuring noises to the Annual Confederation of British Industry (CBI) dinner in February 1985, that 'the economy of Northern Ireland would be on a sounder long-term basis if the role of the public sector were somewhat reduced,'[41] but little was done to curb the vast subsidies which the Province enjoyed in this period. The news in July 1985 of the precarious financial state of the Lear Fan project was a typical example of the substantial levels of Government subsidy which were ploughed into high-profile and sometimes questionable projects.[42] The last rites were performed on the De Lorean car company only after £77 million had been ploughed in by the Industrial Development Board. Some of the job losses in traditional industries were partly offset by inward investment and European Community money. In October 1984, Hurd opened the New Foyle Bridge in Derry, which had been partly financed by the EEC's Regional Development Fund.[43] However, unemployment remained persistently high, standing at 127,089 in October 1984, some 21.9 per cent of the insured working population.[44]

Northern Ireland was viewed increasingly by the British Government as a burden, not just economically, but strategically and politically. This feeling escalated much more rapidly after the collapse of the Berlin Wall in 1989, when Northern Ireland's strategic importance to Britain diminished dramatically. However, even by 1985, there was a perceptible decline in the parliamentary Conservative Party's identification and affection for the Union with Northern Ireland. This was evident in November 1985 when only twenty-one Conservatives voted against the Anglo-Irish Agreement in the House of Commons.[45]

As news began to leak out in the spring and the summer of 1985 of a possible impending agreement with the Republic, it was the turn of the Unionist politicians to hurl insults at Hurd. In March 1985, Revd Ian Paisley publicly attacked Hurd for not attending the funerals of those killed at Newry and a month later called him an 'arrogant dictator'. And yet, on 27 April, Hurd had a perfectly courteous private discussion with Paisley on the telephone. The Democratic Unionist Party (DUP) leader asked after Hurd's mother, who was very ill. She died a few weeks later and Paisley sent a very kind letter of condolence. Hurd remembers the marked contrast between the courteous meetings in private with all the major constitutional leaders, 'which didn't prevent them throwing the most amazing adjectives in between whiles.'[46] All the constitutional parties had constituencies to answer to, and were wary of breaking free from the tired old rhetoric.

Most of the spring was taken up with trying to develop ways of softening the effects of direct rule on the Province. Since the collapse of the Sunningdale Agreement in 1974, Northern Ireland had been governed by direct rule from London, with Orders in Councils being passed in the House of Commons.

These orders were non-amendable and a limited time – usually one-and-a-half hours – was allowed for debate. Often, the debates took place late at night and were characterised by thin attendance. Hurd wanted to give a measure of power back to local councils. But as he noted in his diary, officials at the Northern Ireland Office preferred to preserve the status quo:

> 9 May 1985: Long, important meeting at the Northern Ireland Office to chart the way forward. Officials are negative. Only Chris Patten and Edward Bickham [Hurd's special adviser] have constructive minds. Nick Scott is tired, Rhodes Boyson not tuned in. Officials like direct rule without Dublin or devolution. Chair rather wearily.[47]

Later the same day Hurd had a rare meeting with Enoch Powell:

> 9 May 1985: Then a long session with Enoch [Powell] in my room. He was courteous. Drinks plain tonic. A stately joust on basic principles . . . accommodating minorities. He regards security co-operation as a myth. The Republic irremediably bent on unity. Over 40 per cent of South Down Catholics assimilable . . . acknowledges [West] Belfast is different, but the UDI is flawed. Declines to discuss his conspiracy theories.[48]

These conspiracy theories could be summed up as believing that there was an on-going plot by the Foreign Office to hand everything over to the Republic. Generally, Hurd preferred to deal with James Molyneaux, leader of the Ulster Unionists, but Powell considered himself to be Molyneaux's mentor, and it was often difficult for Hurd to see Molyneaux without Powell wishing to be present. As the pieces of the Anglo-Irish Agreement jigsaw came together, Hurd decided to offer Molyneaux and Powell privileged prior knowledge of the Agreement, via their membership of the Privy Council. He invited them both to look at the text of the Agreement in advance, but in a memorable moment, as Molyneaux was about to agree, Powell shrewdly stopped his leader from looking at the text. It was essential for the Unionist's case against the deal to create a myth of betrayal by the British Government against the Unionists. By reining in Molyneaux, Powell left the Unionists completely free to denounce the Anglo-Irish Agreement in its entirety.

The Orange marching season, running from late June into the month of July, has posed difficulties for every Secretary of State who has served in the Province. In attempting to be all things to all men, the minister in charge is always open to attack from all sides. Up until the new Parades Commission came into force in 1998, the Secretary of State had the power to ban parades, but the Chief Constable of the RUC, Sir John Hermon, had control of re-routeing parades if necessary. Hurd's line was that parades should continue if they were limited to historical or traditional routes, but that if the nature of the parades was changed, then he might have to intervene. But, according to Chris Patten, one could never totally guarantee that if one took a tough line in banning marches the police would be able to deliver.[49]

The most sensitive decision concerned the proposed march through the village of Portadown, a village north-west of Armagh. This parade had a long tradition, but the route no longer ran through a green field site, but through a predominantly Catholic area. At a meeting of the Northern Ireland Assembly's Security Committee on 2 July 1985, Gregory Campbell, a DUP representative, deliberately provoked trouble by calling Hurd a liar. Hurd was having none of it, and walked out of the meeting. It was a rare show of frustration from Hurd.

During Northern Ireland questions on 11 July 1985, Hurd voiced his frustration with the lack of reasonableness among the opposing groups over his stance on marches. Surely, it was possible 'to celebrate a battle or a tradition without provoking or humiliating those who do not belong to that tradition'.[50] He then put his finger firmly on the reason for many of the difficulties in Northern Ireland: 'There are many symbols in Northern Ireland and many people in both communities who are determined to provoke and be provoked.'[51]

Despite these public expressions of frustration, the sensitive marching season passed off without too much incident, except for violent clashes between loyalists and the RUC at Cookstown at the end of June.[52] Chris Patten – who from this period on became a firm admirer of Douglas Hurd – has 'never seen a difficult political operation carried off as well as Douglas managed that summer marching season in Ulster.'[53]

Hurd's last two months in Northern Ireland were much quieter than the high tension of July. Unfortunately, at the end of August, he broke his ankle while walking in a friend's garden. His foot was in plaster for over three weeks, meaning he had to hobble round on crutches during his last few weeks as Secretary of State. Hurd's injury attracted the concern of Mrs Thatcher when she telephoned to offer him the job of Home Secretary:

> 1 Sept. 1985: After lunch, slowly and sleepily to house in London. Galvanised by a wholly unexpected call from Chequers. 'Are you sitting down? Please listen carefully.' She offers me the Home Secretary. Mixed feelings, as job in Northern Ireland is hardly begun, and there are many things which we have become fond of, especially of Hillsborough . . . The pattern of life is hard to predict.[54]

So, Hurd was not hugely excited about the change of job. Writing two days, later, he wrote with regret:

3 Sept. 1985: I definitely wish I had stayed in Northern Ireland, not because we were poised for success, but I was on top of the job, and ready for danger.[55]

A week later Hurd would get all the excitement he needed as he visited the scene of the Handsworth riots in Birmingham, but he missed out on the final stages of the Anglo-Irish Agreement. The balance of credit (if that is the word) for the Agreement on the British side seems to lean towards Sir Robert Armstrong and Geoffrey Howe. Hurd downplays his own role and identifies Robert Armstrong as the key negotiator alongside Sir David Goodall. One should not underestimate the value of Geoffrey Howe's good working relationship with Garrett Fitzgerald, which helped to soothe the Irish Taioseach after Mrs Thatcher's periodic outbursts. However, given Geoffrey Howe's often uneasy relationship with Mrs Thatcher, Douglas Hurd played an important role in persuading her to sign up to the Agreement. As such, he was one of the architects of the Agreement. The Prime Minister herself deserves credit for making the pragmatic decision to sign against her instincts. On the other side, the Irish civil servants displayed a sureness of touch, while Messrs Fitzgerald, Barry and Spring showed considerable tolerance and flexibility in accepting a deal which was well below their initial expectations.

The Anglo-Irish Agreement represented an historic shift in the attitude of the British Government towards the status of Northern Ireland. For the first time ever, London had challenged Unionist strength by establishing the Intergovernmental Conference, chaired by the Secretary of State for Northern Ireland and the Dublin Minister for Foreign Affairs. Co-operation with Dublin was now seen by the British as part of the political landscape, even if the British had stopped far short of joint authority. Meanwhile, the Agreement plunged Unionism and the IRA into crisis. Both were forced to rethink their long held positions. The Unionists could no longer rely on the British as guarantors of the Union and the IRA began at least to debate whether Britain was still behaving as an imperial power. But the conflict renewed in its intensity. Apart from the Newry bombing, Hurd's year in Northern Ireland represented the calm before the storm. After the Agreement, the Ulster Unionist MPs resigned en masse[56] and the IRA, bolstered with Libyan arms, embarked upon a terrifying bombing campaign.

Overall, Douglas Hurd will be remembered as a cautious, low-key Secretary of State, who performed the role of honest broker, whilst attracting abuse from all sides of the political spectrum. If anything, he underestimated the level of discrimination and alienation being experienced by the nationalist community, but with limited room for manoeuvre, he at least began a process of trying to introduce some measure of fairness into employment law and attempted, largely in vain, to persuade the Unionist side to have more regard for the minority community. Officials and junior officials admired his intellectual authority, his ability to delegate, and the outward ease with which he seemed comfortable in dealing with the brutalities of wielding power; Peter Carrington had been correct in his assessment of Hurd as possessing the necessary toughness to be a senior minister. Above all, Hurd should be remembered for his sense of history and his considered analysis of the basic problem of politics in Northern Ireland – that politicians, tied down by symbolism and tradition, were afraid to free themselves of gesture politics. Hurd tempered his excitement of being appointed a Cabinet minister, with due caution.

Notes

1. Diary Readings with Douglas Hurd, 17 Dec. 1996.
2. Interview with Douglas Hurd, 17 Dec. 1996.
3. Private information.
4. Diary Readings with Douglas Hurd, 17 Dec. 1996.
5. Ibid.
6. *Belfast Telegraph*, 11 Sept. 1984.
7. Conversation with Douglas Hurd, Westwell, 13 Jun. 1997.
8. Diary Readings with Douglas Hurd, 17 Dec. 1996.
9. *Belfast Telegraph*, 11 Sept. 1984.
10. Ibid., 12 Sept. 1984.
11. Ibid., 5 Oct. 1984.
12. Diary Readings with Douglas Hurd, 20 Jan. 1997.
13. Interview with Chris Patten, 22 Jul. 1997.
14. Ibid.
15. Eamonn Mallie & David McKittrick, *The Fight for Peace: The Secret Story Behind the Irish Peace Process* (Heinemann: London, 1996), p. 26; the Irish team comprised Michael Lillis, Sean Donlon, Dermot Nally and Noel Dorr.
16. Diary Readings with Douglas Hurd, 20 Jan. 1997.
17. *Belfast Telegraph*, 3 Oct. 1984.
18. *The Times*, 5 Oct. 1984.
19. *Belfast Telegraph*, 8 Oct. 1984.
20. Interview with Douglas Hurd, 20 Jan. 1997.
21. Diary Readings with Douglas Hurd, 20 Jan. 1997.
22. *The Times*, 13 Oct. 1984.
23. Diary Readings with Douglas Hurd, 13 Oct. 1984.

24. Geoffrey Howe, *Conflict of Loyalty* (Macmillan: London, 1994), pp. 417, 420, 423.
25. *The Times*, 23 Nov. 1984.
26. Diary Readings with Douglas Hurd, 20 Jan. 1997.
27. Sir John Lavery, 1856–1941, British painter, born in Belfast, member of the 'Glasgow School'.
28. Interview with Douglas Hurd, 20 Jan. 1997.
29. Mallie & McKittrick, *The Fight for Peace*, p.222.
30. *Belfast Telegraph*, 20 Feb. 1985.
31. Ibid.
32. Diary Readings with Douglas Hurd, 20 Jan. 1997.
33. Letter to the Author from Douglas Hurd, 25 May 1998.
34. *Belfast Telegraph*, 2 Jan. 1985.
35. Ibid., 9 Jan. 1985.
36. Ibid., 29 Oct. 1984.
37. Diary Readings with Douglas Hurd, 20 Jan. 1997.
38. Ibid.
39. Ibid.
40. Ibid.
41. *Belfast Telegraph*, 7 Feb. 1985.
42. The Lear Fan company had developed a new specification of a carbon-fibre turbo-prop engine at their Carmoney plant, but the firm's failure to gain an air-worthiness certificate in the United States led to the winding up of the company in January 1986.
43. *Belfast Telegraph*, 17 Oct. 1989.
44. Ibid., 4 Oct. 1984.
45. H.of C. Deb. (6th Series), 27 Nov. 1985, vol. 87, cols 969-973.
46. Interview with Douglas Hurd, 20 Jan. 1997.
47. Diary Readings with Douglas Hurd, 20 Jan. 1997.
48. Ibid.
49. Interview with Chris Patten, 22 Jul. 1997.
50. H.of C. Deb. (6th Series), 11 Jul. 1985, vol. 82, col. 1247.
51. Ibid., col. 1248.
52. *Belfast Telegraph*, 29 Jun. 1985.
53. Interview with Chris Patten, 22 Jul. 1997. It is ironic that Patten is now a member of the RUC Parades Commission.
54. Diary Readings with Douglas Hurd, 20 Jan. 1997.
55. Ibid.
56. All fifteen Unionist MPs resigned their seats and stood in a mini-election in January 1986. However, the Offical Unionist, James Nicholson, lost Newry and Armagh to Seamus Mallon of the SDLP. On their return to

the House of Commons, the Unionists mounted a partial boycott which was broken on 14 April 1986 when they voted against the Government on the Second Reading of the Shops Bill [Lords]. The gradual decline in the Unionist vote was shown at the 1987 General Election when Enoch Powell lost his South Down seat to Eddie McGrady, again of the SDLP.

11

Coping with Contradictions: Douglas Hurd's Relationship with Mrs Thatcher as Home Secretary, 1985–1989

As Home Secretary, Hurd became very conscious of the susceptibility of the Home Department to the tyranny of unexpected events. In December 1987, he likened this elegantly to the poet Horace's description of a 'thunderbolt hurled from a clear sky'.[1] As early as his second week at Queen Anne's Gate, Hurd experienced his first thunderbolt. On 9 September 1985, news started to arrive of riots in the Handsworth area of Birmingham. The following day, with the permission of the Prime Minister, Hurd went to Birmingham to assess the situation. In retrospect, he believes that he went there too early. It was a difficult balance for a Home Secretary to strike: if one waited until it was all over, then one could be accused of not caring, but if one went too early – as Hurd did – there was the danger that his presence at the scene would stir up further trouble. On his arrival, he was anxious, despite the fact his ankle was still in plaster, not to hang around in the Chief Constable's office. Perhaps his desire for danger got the better of him as he hobbled to the scene of the rioting:

> 10 Sept. 1985: As I'm arguing with young blacks, missiles begin to fly. I'm not hit, but I'm hussled on. Talked to disgruntled Asians on a corner, then in a side street to frightened whites. Visit the firemen, community leaders; Jeff Rooker [local Labour MP] is helpful.[2]

Apart from the tragedy at Hungerford,[3] the other thunderbolt from a clear sky during Hurd's tenure as Home Secretary occurred at Hillsborough Football Stadium on Saturday, 15 April 1989, when 94 people were killed and 174 injured. The Sheffield Wednesday ground was due to stage a Football Association (FA) Cup semi-final between Nottingham Forest and Liverpool, when, at around 2.45 p.m., an unexpectedly large number of Liverpool fans converged on the turnstiles at the Leppings Lane end. The police appeared to panic at the sheer number of Liverpool fans converging outside the ground. There appears to have been a failure of communication between the police monitoring the entrance to the ground and those monitoring the front of the terraces, resulting in a crush of fans at the front of the Liverpool end as the police refused to open the gates of the security fencing.

The following day, Hurd paid a visit to the scene of the disaster along with the Prime Minister and the Minister for Sport, Colin Moynihan. Hurd described the scene vividly in his diary. Hurd's initial assessment was that the police were at fault — a conclusion which was not shared by the subsequent coroner's inquest or the Taylor Report:

> 16 Apr. 1989: To Sheffield, miserably in cold helicopter with M.T. [Margaret Thatcher]. Earpads, so no speech. Briefing with chief constable, who is pale and inarticulate. To the dreary, litter-strewn ground at Hillsborough, with the fearful little gate and bent banners. Enter the two hospitals. In intensive care, youngsters fight against death or brain damage. Relations sit round. More youngsters, bruised, but revived and talkative, tell stories. Young special constable of nineteen breaks down. Clearly, there is one, perhaps two, major police blunders. M.T. shaken, but remorseless in her compassion.[4]

At the time, Douglas Hurd was filled with admiration for the forthright way in which Mrs Thatcher comforted the injured fans and their families in hospital. He recalls the moment when the Prime Minister came upon the bed of a dying boy, surrounded by his family:

> My whole instinct would have been to steer clear. Here is a family in great anxiety. One would perhaps smile and go on. The last thing you would want is a politician around this. Not at all. She went straight up, took the mother's hand, put the mother's hand on the boy's hand, and said: 'You feel him, touch him. It will do him good and it will do you good too.' She took control of the situation, talked to them, in a way I wouldn't have dreamt of doing. But she was right. They will remember that all their lives; not just a bossy Margaret Thatcher coming in and making a nuisance. She just got the feel of it right. I was impressed.[5]

Overall, during his four years as Home Secretary, Douglas Hurd did not suffer from a high degree of Prime Ministerial interference in his running of Home Office policy. This was in marked contrast to their later relationship between October 1989 and November 1990 when Hurd was Foreign Secretary. Mrs Thatcher would have regular bilateral meetings with Hurd as Foreign Secretary; at the Home Office, these occurred on average, only about once a month. But, there were a number of issues where she did interfere, sometimes intentionally, as over broadcasting and secrecy, sometimes unintentionally, in the case of the capital punishment issue.

Mrs Thatcher was strongly in favour of reintroducing the death penalty, but she was always very conscious of the need not to express this opinion too openly, perhaps believing that there would be too many complications in trying to change the law. From the viewpoint of every Conservative Home Secretary since the abolition of the death penalty in 1965, the capital punishment debates in Parliament and at the Conservative Party Conference became awkward events requiring careful handling.[6] In his memoirs, William Whitelaw acknowledges that his over-emotional response to the capital punishment debate at the Conservative Party Conference in 1981 damaged his standing in the party, making it more difficult to propose sensible reforms in sentencing policy.[7] During his time as a Minister of State at the Home Office, Douglas Hurd also recorded in his diaries the impact of Leon Brittan's ill-judged House of Commons speech in July 1983 in favour of capital punishment for terrorist offences but not other categories of murder:

13 Jul. 1983: Performs competently, but has chosen an indefensible line. Hanging crashes decisively by far larger majorities than predicted.[8]

Despite changing his mind on several other issues during his political career, Hurd was always consistent in his opposition to capital punishment. He admits to being influenced by Roy Jenkins, whose speech as Home Secretary in 1965 against the death penalty Hurd regards as 'one of the best I have ever heard'.[9]

Unlike Leon Brittan, Hurd did not stumble during the two debates on capital punishment – in successive years, 1987 and 1988 – in the House of Commons. His approach was to set out a number of statistics on the subject, then analyse the difficulties associated with the clauses proposed, before expressing his personal views.[10] During his second speech in June 1988, Hurd claimed that restoration of the death penalty would do little to tackle the inexorable rise in violent crime since the mid-1950s because offences involving murder formed a very small proportion of total violent crime. Reintroducing the death penalty for terrorism would, he claimed, only create more sympathy for the IRA. Restoration would mean not private executions, but protracted legal disputes and executions in the full glare of publicity as had been the experience in the United States.[11]

Hurd's real difficulties occurred, not in the House of Commons, but at the notoriously volatile annual debates on law and order at the Conservative Party Conference. On such occasions, he had to contend with emotive speeches from retired police sergeants who were capable of stirring the Conference delegates into a froth. Mrs Thatcher felt she had to attend the law and order debates, even though she disagreed with Hurd on capital punishment.[12] As delegates spoke in favour of the death penalty, she would clap her hands under the platform table, out of sight of the delegates. One year, the Conference Chairman inadvertently allowed too many pro-hangers to speak in the debate. Hurd recalls her saying to him afterwards, 'They shouldn't have done that. It was quite wrong. Not the way to hold a debate.'[13]

The law and order debate at the October 1987 Conservative Party Conference exposed the contradiction between the Prime Minister's personal views and the desire not to humiliate Hurd. Coming after a summer of crisis over prison overcrowding (see Chapter 12), Hurd was privately anxious as he stood up to speak:

> 7 Oct. 1987: A difficult speech. Nervous, coming after three months of tension. No way to live a life. Monday Club in full voice calling for capital punishment. No criticism on prisons. Start poorly, but on capital punishment, they heckle and I respond. This goes well. Then the middle section on knives and lenient sentences a success. Peroration fades a bit, but good applause. The Prime Minister remains seated, and so do others. She says afterwards, it couldn't have been better done. She's scared of the capital punishment issue.[14]

Hurd achieved the trick at Party Conferences of balancing his opposition to capital punishment with a stout defence of the police and a series of tough-sounding announcements. At the 1986 Conference at Bournemouth, he announced proposals to use video links in child-abuse cases, and measures to tackle fraud, the proceeds from drug trafficking, anti-terrorist and extradition agreements.[15] The following year at Blackpool, he announced tough measures on the ownership of firearms, the carrying of knives and measures to curb sex and violence on television.

Hurd was even able to advance the debate on criminal-justice policy at the 1987 Party Conference, cutting himself free from the defensive style of previous Tory Home Secretaries:

> With the start of the Autumn term, a new generation in our schools came

into that critical age group of 13 to 15. We see them every day, waiting at the bus stop, hurrying along a pavement, chatting at the school gates.

For some of them, the critical moment is approaching – the critical choice will be made. Will the tree grow straight or crooked? Is it a choice for teenagers, a choice which is actually more difficult than it was for most of us in our time. Do they say 'Yes' to drugs and to the crime that goes with drugs? Are they led into violence by stupid drinking or by a mindless appetite for excitement? But it is surely a choice for us too. Do we let them slide downhill into the slovenly society or do we, their elders, set the right standards of behaviour in schools, on television, and in public life? In truth, this can't be for us a matter of choice; it must be a matter of course.[16]

It was a brave speech and, in Conservative terms, probably warranted a standing ovation. However, the law and order debates at Party Conferences do not show the Conservative Party membership in its best light. Baiting the Home Secretary on the issue of the death penalty is an annual sport. After the 1988 Conference in Brighton, Matthew Parris wryly pointed out that:

. . . Tories love being shocked by crime. When the Home Secretary spoke of reductions in crime, the conference simply didn't want to listen. For the persistence of vice is a comfort as well as an outrage to true Conservatives. The root of their philosophy is an unshakeably low opinion of human nature, including their own.[17]

Mrs Thatcher shared this low view of human nature, believing in the notion of 'public harm'. It was a contradiction for someone who was an economic libertarian to be authoritarian on social issues. These contradictions led to a deeply flawed piece of legislation in the shape of the Broadcasting Act of 1990.

The Prime Minister was determined to break the BBC and ITV's duopoly of television programming. The Prime Minister never liked the BBC, seeing it as a source of political bias and old establishment attitudes. During her premiership, she, along with her Party Chairman, Norman Tebbit, had several spats with the BBC, most notably over its coverage of the Libyan bombing in April 1986. However, as Home Secretary, Hurd tried to remain impartial and, using his diplomatic skills, endeavoured to steer clear of the controversy stirred up by his Party Chairman.

From the outset, Mrs Thatcher wished to introduce advertising to the BBC, but her wings were clipped in July 1986, when the Peacock Committee Report – established by Leon Brittan in March 1985 and chaired by Professor Alan Peacock – decided against advertising. A majority of the Committee recommended that existing ITV contracts then awarded by the Independent Broadcasting Authority (IBA) should be put out to competitive tender. This appealed greatly to the Prime Minister's instincts for ending the apparently arbitrary share-out of contracts by the IBA, which seemed to her to be free from transparency and competition.

Douglas Hurd's views on broadcasting differed greatly from those of Mrs Thatcher. Given the flaws in the 1990 Act, should Hurd have used the authority of his office to oppose the Prime Minister's plans? Two important factors prevented this. First, Hurd was outnumbered on the key Cabinet sub-committee, 'Miscellaneous 128', which eventually shaped the White Paper of November 1988, entitled *Broadcasting in the '90s*.[18] Nigel Lawson, the Chancellor of the Exchequer and Lord Young of Graffham, Trade and Industry Secretary, shared Mrs Thatcher's aim of breaking the duopoly of programme production held by the BBC and ITV. Second, Douglas Hurd was slightly more radical economically than his Conservative colleagues and the political commentators gave him credit for. He did, for instance, see that the cosy duopoly of programme production had led to indefensible restrictive practices.

Hurd wanted to maintain a high quality of broadcasting output, but he was occasionally irritated by the self-righteous way in which the leading figures in broadcasting talked about themselves and their programmes. For instance, he never sought to defend the vague notion of public service broadcasting – 'the must carry rule' – as a holy grail. On 19 September 1985, during a speech to the Royal Television Society, he said he found it difficult to see Saturday night television as being a 'temple of culture'.[19]

Standing behind Douglas Hurd was a Home Office Department which was overwhelmingly in favour of preserving the status quo. By a quirk of history, responsibility for broadcasting originally belonged to the office of the Postmaster General, but in 1979 it shifted to the Home Office. Initially the move seemed to work: relations between the broadcasting establishment and the conciliatory William Whitelaw were generally good. But, during the latter half of the 1980s, there were moments of inter-departmental rivalry between the Home Office and the DTI (backed by the Treasury), the latter wanting the television companies to be more commercially orientated. When, eventually, in 1992, as a result of a report by Sir David Calcutt, QC two years earlier, responsibility for broadcasting shifted from the Home Office to the new Department of National Heritage, in reality it ended an unhappy marriage between broadcasting and the Home Office.[20]

Realising that he was outnumbered in Misc. 128, Hurd conceded considerable ground to the views of the Prime Minister, Nigel Lawson and David Young. However, neither Hurd nor the Chancellor shared Mrs Thatcher's drive to combat 'moral degradation' on television.[21] Mrs Thatcher was a great supporter of Mary Whitehouse, leader of the Viewers and Listeners Association. It was she who pushed for the establishment of the Broadcasting Standards Council under William Rees-Mogg, established in June 1988 to monitor and conduct research into the effects of sex and violence on television.[22] Hurd had begun negotiations with the broadcasting authorities with a view to establishing a non-statutory body, but Mrs Thatcher came back from the scene of the Hungerford massacre in August 1987 firmly of the view that the new body should be given statutory powers.[23]

Privately, Douglas Hurd was uneasy about the sheer scale of censorship which Mrs Thatcher was seeking to impose, even though the Conservative Election Manifesto of 1987 committed the party to 'bring forward proposals for stronger and more effective arrangements to reflect [public] concern [about] the display of sex and violence on television.' During her second term, a wave of moral panic about video violence had led to the Conservative MP Graham Bright's Video Recordings Bill becoming law in 1985.[24] But it was the third Thatcher term which saw the real attempts belatedly to impose a bygone morality. With Mrs Thatcher pushing from behind, Hurd introduced an unrivalled series of measures to control 'taste and decency'.

Further contradictions in Mrs Thatcher's approach were shown by her odd affection for the *News at Ten* which she felt had to be preserved because she approved of its coverage and admired its regular presenter Alastair Burnet, who later received a knighthood. So when it came to designing the so-called 'quality threshold' for ITV franchise applications, the requirement that the news on ITV remain inside peak time viewing hours was retained.

Nor did Mrs Thatcher's image as a strong, decisive leader who efficiently dispatched business extend to discussions on broadcasting issues. On 24 April 1989, Hurd noted in his diary, 'Misc. 128: PM wayward, all over the place.'[25]

With the majority of the Cabinet subcommittee in favour of radical change, Hurd was not prepared to go into battle against David Young, Nigel Lawson and Mrs Thatcher. Instead, Hurd did two things. The first was to seek to change attitudes within the Home Office to broadcasting, which were generally conservative with a small 'c'. He impressed upon officials that it was time to move on in the debate, otherwise the DTI might increasingly take over the responsibility for broadcasting. The second part of the strategy was to begin to air some of the Government's most controversial plans in high-profile speeches.

In a speech to the Tory Coningsby Club on 22 June 1988, Hurd created a considerable stir by claiming that he did not regard the BBC licence fee as immortal.[26] Hurd was airing the new heresies in advance of the Government's White Paper in November 1988. By talking-up the possibility of subscription television before the White Paper was published, he was able to make his eventual proposals sound less radical than originally feared. In the event, the plans for subscription television were kicked into touch, to be considered at the end of the BBC's Charter, which was due to expire in 1996. It was a favourite Whitehall way of appearing to concede ground in the belief that, several years down the line, ambitious plans would stay on the shelf gathering dust.

After a summer of consultation and debate,[27] the White Paper was published in the autumn of 1988. In effect, the big two televison companies would act as publishing houses, commissioning programmes from independent producers, rather than retaining complete control over programme production. Most significantly, the Government proposed the introduction of competitive tender for ITV contracts, ending the arbitrary control of the IBA, which would be replaced by the Independent Television Commission (ITC). The new body would have a lighter regulatory touch, but with the safeguard of a 'quality threshold'. The debate during the passage of the Broadcasting Bill centred on two questions: at what level should the quality threshold be set; and should the new ITC be given the power to reject the highest bid if it was felt that a company had failed to meet the threshold requirements?

White Papers are meant to set out the principles rather than the detail of reform, but too much was left vague and open about the Government's initial proposals, especially on censorship. Terrestrial channels would not be able to broadcast material which was 'inherently unacceptable' and 'offensive to public feeling'. Exactly how these two phrases were to be defined in legal terms was not made clear. All types of broadcasting would be subject to the Obscene Publications Act of 1959. British output on satellite services would be subject to the same censorship as terrestrial services. The British Government would enter into consultations with the Council of Europe Convention on Transfrontier Broadcasting to seek agreement on European output. 'Unacceptable output' from non-European countries would lead to complaints from national governments and advertisers being penalised.

In private, Hurd was opposed to the privatisation of Channel 4, believing that if it was exposed to competition and forced to provide a return to shareholders, its remit for providing innovative programmes might be jeopardised.[28] The 1988 White Paper merely listed three options on the future of Channel 4: privatisation, trust status and the status quo. However, in June 1989, Hurd announced that the Government had decided not to make Channel 4 an independent commercial company competing with other broadcasters. Instead, after 1993, subject to parliamentary approval, Channel 4 would become a public trust, selling its own advertising, underpinned by the ITC.[29] Hurd had successfully defended one corner of the broadcasting industry from the free market, but gave ground elsewhere.

In a sea full of contradictions, the Government's proposals to liberalise the radio industry were an island of commonsense, and represented the strongest

TOP: Douglas Hurd's christening, 1930

LEFT: Douglas (centre) with his parents, brothers Julian and Stephen, rabbit and dogs, 1936

Douglas Hurd (third from right) before the Eton Wall Game, 1947

The aftermath

Rainscombe Farm, *c.* 1947, memories of which caused all the fuss in the
Conservative leadership contest of November 1990

Douglas Hurd (second row, extreme right) at
Mons Officer Cadet School, 1949

A young Douglas Hurd *c.* 1950

TOP: Cambridge Union Society. Change of Officers Debate, 10 March 1952. Newly elected president, D.R. Hurd, Trinity College, takes the chair from the retiring president, Greville Janner, Trinity Hall

LEFT: Douglas with his parents, *c.* 1952

The young diplomat, Western Hills, Peking, 1956

Douglas with his son Nicholas in Rome, 1965

With the Prime Minister, Edward Heath, at Mid-Oxon Rally, 1973. The late
Michael Wolff is on the right

part of the White Paper. Hurd always felt more comfortable talking about radio than television, and enjoyed appearing on the *Today* programme and *The World at One* on Radio Four. When it came to discussing the future of radio, Hurd felt on surer ground. His plans for another two national BBC radio stations were widely welcomed. Coupled with a rapid growth in independent commercial radio, these proved to be highly successful policies. The proposals for an expansion of community radio also appealed to Hurd's belief in active citizenship and social cohesion.[30]

Hurd's overall approach was to encourage a wide range of representations on the White Paper. Several backbench Conservative MPs, notably George Walden, MP for Buckingham, and Sir Giles Shaw, MP for Pudsey, voiced fears of a decline in the quality of programmes on offer if ITV franchises were hived off to the highest bidder.

Responding to these representations in June 1989, the Home Secretary announced a series of significant changes to the Government's plans. In addition to laying specific plans for Channel 4, three major alterations were made to strengthen the quality threshold. First, Hurd added a requirement 'to provide a reasonable proportion of programmes (in addition to news and current affairs) of high quality, and to provide a diverse programme service calculated to appeal to a wide variety of tastes and interests.'[31] Hurd added to this the exceptional power of the ITC to award a franchise to a company other than the highest bidder. The ITC would have to make its reasons public and its decision would be subject to judicial review. Third, applicants would have to post a performance bond with the ITC. Successful bidders would then lose a proportion of the bond if they failed to meet the quality threshold.

These changes still proved unsatisfactory to a number of Conservative backbenchers during the Bill's extensive Committee Stage (38 sittings) and Report Stage (the eventual Bill produced 170 clauses and 12 schedules). By this time, Hurd had left the Home Office and David Mellor, the new Minister of State, was forced to concede even more ground on the franchise system and the quality threshold. The exceptional-circumstances provision was tightened still further so that exceptionally high quality could displace the highest-money bid. The quality threshold was bolstered, and teletext and subtitling services for the hard of hearing were also entrenched.[32]

The concessions which David Mellor announced were ones which Hurd would have been only too happy to make. It is ironic that David Mellor had, for the second time, rescued a piece of legislation which Hurd had mishandled if one recalls Hurd's tenuous grasp of the legal concepts during the passage of the Police and Criminal Evidence Bill of 1983-84. Hurd's image as a 'safe pair of hands' does not always hold true, especially when handling legal detail.

The first round of auctions for the franchises ended in high farce in 1991.

Mrs Thatcher wrote a rather odd letter of apology to Bruce Gyngel, Chairman of TV-AM, commiserating with him on the loss of his franchise. She had greatly admired Gyngel's tough policies against the trade unions and was dismayed at the failure of the legislation. The simplistic picture of her as a free-market demon does not fit. Often unintentionally, she produced contradictory policies, despite the efforts of her ministers to tone them down.

Throughout his ministerial career, Hurd greatly admired the way Margaret Thatcher was able to show that things which the Conservative Party has previously thought were impossible – like tackling trade union power and introducing privatisation – were in fact possible, with sheer will and strong leadership. However, he never shared the same views of society and the individual. As Home Secretary, whilst remaining loyal in policy terms, Hurd felt able to put forward his own vision of Conservatism.

On 5 February 1988, Hurd spoke to the Peel Society's dinner, celebrating the bicentennial of the birth of Sir Robert Peel. In front of several previous Home Secretaries, Hurd acknowledged that, while the Conservative Government had successfully encouraged economic enterprise in the 1980s:

> The fruits of economic success could turn sour unless we can bring back greater social cohesion. Social cohesion is quite different from social equality: indeed the two are ultimately incompatible. But social cohesion alongside the creation of wealth through private enterprise: these are the two conditions of our future progress.[33]

Hurd rejected the accumulation of private wealth as the final goal of society. As people acquired wealth, he argued, it was their duty to become 'active citizens'.[34]

In essence, Douglas Hurd was seeking to update the High Tory views of Edmund Burke. Writing in response to a *New Statesman* editorial in April 1988 accusing him of 'neo-feudalism', Hurd fleshed out his philosophy of Citizenship in the Tory Democracy.[35] He rejected the Fabian view of citizenship as merely an obligatory relationship between the state and the citizen. People had ties of allegiance to their family, neighbourhood and nation. The key to responsible citizenship was to hand power back down to the citizen. He quoted Edmund Burke's idea of 'little platoons':

> No cold relation is a zealous citizen. To be attached to the subdivision, to love the little platoon we belong to in society is the first principle (the germ as it were) of public affections. It is the first link in the series by which we proceed towards the love of our country, and of mankind.[36]

In effect, Hurd was attempting to reinvent little groups of élites along the lines of the village squire, the Anglican parson, the Justice of the Peace, which existed in the time of Edmund Burke. Central to Hurd's argument was his strong belief in voluntary and public service:

> The English tradition of voluntary service is, of course, not new. Justices of the Peace from the fifteenth century to the present, the school and vestry boards of the Victorian age, councillors in modern local government represent a long-standing tradition of public service. School governors are unpaid, so are jurors, so are residents', ratepayers' and tenants' leaders, so are neighbourhood watch co-ordinators, so are the thousands of people who give their time freely to the huge and thriving number of British charities. What is new is the rediscovery that schemes based on this tradition are often more flexible and more effective than bureaucratic plans drawn up on Fabian principles and inevitably bound by rules of accountability and universality which narrow their range. Perhaps even in these columns one can suggest that the WRVS [Women's Royal Voluntary Service] has worn rather better than the Webbs.[37]

By the late 1980s, Hurd began to focus on the idea of delivering a higher quality of public service in order to improve the quality of life of the citizen, calling for 'good stewardship within the public services': [38]

> When we ask for good stewardship we are not damaging a profession but asking it to add a dimension to its strength. The Conservative Government needs and respects the professions, though not always the antique rules and procedures within which they are encased.[39]

In effect, Hurd was trying to place a High Tory gloss on the Government's controversial reforms to education, health, housing and crime prevention, by saying that they were improving the efficient delivery of public services and devolving power downwards to the people. As Foreign Secretary, in the early 1990s, Hurd developed this into the idea of an 'enabling state'. Governments, he argued, should be flexible in choosing which bodies, public or private, could deliver better public services and a better quality of life.[40]

However, the idea of the enabling state was flawed. First, it was highly undemocratic. The National Health Service Trusts, self-governing schools and Housing Associations took power away from democratically elected councillors and placed power in the hands of unelected local appointees, modern local élites. Second, the Conservative reforms to local government which Hurd endorsed saw a massive centralisation of power in Britain. Third, Hurd's belief that active citizenship was compatible with free-market economics because private property gave the citizen a stake in the economic power of the country, simply did not work during the 1980s. The middle classes, liberated by Mrs Thatcher's economic policies, opted for piling up their bank balances and focusing their lives on their families to the exclusion of their neighbours. The 1980s cult of the individual and the accumulation of wealth served to undermine the very institutions which Hurd was seeking to defend. Economic liberalism led to greed and socially irresponsible behaviour on the part of those who acquired the wealth, and social tensions amongst the new underclass.   Douglas Hurd was thoughtful enough to try to address the moral questions raised by these dramatic social and economic changes, but as the *New Statesman* pointed out, his attempt 'to graft a sub-Disraeli appendix onto Thatcherism's body politic is plainly doomed'.[41]

Mrs Thatcher missed a historic opportunity to lay out a credible ethical case for Conservatism when she made her famous speech to the General Assembly of the Church of Scotland in May 1988. She went over-the-top by trying to claim to the Kirk that part of the obligation of a Christian was to accumulate private wealth ('It is not the creation of wealth that is wrong, but love of money for its own sake'), and by downplaying the role of society:

> We are all responsible for our own actions. We cannot blame society if we disobey the law. We cannot simply delegate the exercise of mercy and generosity to others.[42]

Hurd saw, as Thatcher did not, that it is simply not possible to build a fence around one's neighbours. They will always scale the fence. The experiment was tried and failed in South Africa, Rhodesia and Northern Ireland. The day after Mrs Thatcher's speech to the Kirk, speaking on ITV's *Weekend World*, Hurd stressed his own belief in active citizenship, while delivering a coded critique of Mrs Thatcher's speech:

> I do think that we need to emphasise more than we did at the beginning that individualism is not just a narrow or selfish thing. The reason why we put stress on individual achievement is not just so that we can pile up little mountains of wealth but so that the country is a more decent place. We have got to say to people who are doing well: 'Look, there is a community to which you also belong. Be an active citizen within it.'[43]

However, both Hurd's vision of society and Mrs Thatcher's had some common ground in the area of personal responsibility. In particular Hurd's belief in the notion of voluntary service. The two visions were able to co-exist without Hurd appearing disloyal.

Around this time, Douglas Hurd was also involved in dialogue with the Church, but from his own Anglican perspective. On 10 February 1988, he became the first Cabinet minister of any party to address a fringe meeting of the Church of England General Synod in London. With the Archbishop of Canterbury, Dr Robert Runcie, in attendance, the Home Secretary called on the churches to take the lead in the realm of personal morality:

> Those who commit violent crime seem genuinely to have no sense of the consequences of their actions. To them it is as if the old lady whom they assault, the young boy whom they abduct, the rival whom they stab is simply a target, a stuffed doll without human emotions. There is no sense in many of them of the suffering which their violence can cause. This can only be because neither from their parents, nor their school, nor from the television at which they goggle hour after hour, nor from any influence upon them, have they gained the simplest inkling that every human being is worthy of respect and that the infliction of suffering is a sin whether or not the offender is caught. The only moral principle to which they respond is the comradeship of the jungle. It is as if, for them, neither the Old nor the New Testament had been written.[44]

In effect, Hurd was linking the decline of moral values in Britain to the concomitant decline of religious belief. He was not saying that all non-believers were violent criminals, but if no one reinforced ideas of right and wrong, then there would continue to be a decline in moral standards. As a traditional Anglican – Hurd later became a Trustee of the Prayer Book Society – he wanted the Church and State to co-operate in trying to rebuild moral values. But, even by 1988, it was too late to deliver moral homilies; society was going off in an entirely different direction.

Apart from attempts to impose censorship on broadcasting, the new moral drive was witnessed in the area of homosexuality when the Government pushed through a clause in the Local Government Bill (known as Clause 28) forbidding local government from 'intentionally promoting' homosexuality. Hurd's own voting record on the subject of homosexuality is non-liberal, contrasting with his more liberal views on divorce and capital punishment. However, when the second attempt was made by the Conservatives to reimpose moral values in the 'Back to Basics' drive of 1993, Hurd was one of the siren voices warning against the hijack of the Conservative Party by Michael Howard, Peter Lilley and John Redwood. As Hurd had remarked to the congregation at St Martin-in-the-Fields in February 1988, politicians 'are at their least attractive when they don the mantle of the Pharisee'.[45]

On economic issues, it is a myth to claim Douglas Hurd is a 'wet'. He describes himself as 'dead centre': while he does not believe that the free market is miraculous, he is a strong advocate of free trade rather than protection, is against big government and believes in sound money. For the most part, Hurd is 'dry' on economic issues; only in the area of tax cuts are there damp patches. In his later period as Foreign Secretary, Hurd became known for his support of what he called 'responsible tax cuts', that is, the Government should only cut taxes if this is not at the expense of cuts in the number of teachers, doctors and nurses. As early as June 1986, at a speech to party workers in Nottingham, Hurd called for a balance between the provision of good quality public services and tax cuts.[46] He pays particular attention to the views of those working in the professions, whom he genuinely respects.

In electoral terms, it was useful for the Conservative Party to have someone who, in the words of the New Statesman, is 'the dry who pretends to be a wet pretending to be dry'.[47] His disdain of the adversarial system of British politics appeals to the so-called 'centre ground', the 'floating voters' who might be tempted to vote for the centre parties. In the year running up to the 1987 General Election, about a quarter of his speeches concentrate on countering the threat posed by the SDP/Liberal Alliance.[48] In January 1987, he warned Basingstoke Conservatives to 'show ourselves as the Party of good citizens and good neighbours.'[49] Although it is hard to quantify the impact Douglas Hurd had on the electorate, his personal vision of citizenship may have had an impact at the margins in stopping some Conservative doubters from shifting to the Alliance. Professional people seemed to respect the fact that Hurd is well read, civilised and moderate.

Despite being given considerable operational freedom as Home Secretary, Douglas Hurd did find himself signing up to a number of measures where he disagreed with the Prime Minister. Hurd's announcement of the broadcasting ban on terrorist groups in Northern Ireland in October 1988 was the most notable. In order to forestall measures which Hurd and his successor at Northern Ireland, Tom King, believed would be counter-productive in the fight against terrorism, they agreed to the broadcasting ban. Hurd's diaries reveal his misgivings at the time:

> 19 Oct. 1988: Make statement barring Sinn Fein etc. from the media. Goes well enough in the House, but media themselves scratchy and I'm not proud of it. Did it to help Tom King.[50]

And the following day, his sense of regret increased:

20 Oct. 1988: Poor press on yesterday's announcement of Sinn Fein etc. Indeed, it is a poor decision. My contribution to Ulster.[51]

Despite his private misgivings, Hurd argued that the terrorists were drawing support and sustenance from the radio and television and that the victims of those killed and injured suffered considerable distress when the Sinn Fein justified their actions on the media immediately after the atrocities.[52] However, as Roy Hattersley, Labour's Shadow Home Secretary, made clear in reply to Hurd's statement, the broadcasting ban was of immense propaganda value to the IRA because they were able to present themselves, especially in the United States, as victims denied freedom of expression.[53] Moreover, there were gaping loopholes in the broadcasting ban because it only applied to direct statements and not to reported speech. News reporters circumvented the ban by showing a film of the terrorist spokesperson, accompanied by an actor's voice describing, verbatim, what he or she was saying. When the peace process showed signs of working during John Major's premiership, Douglas Hurd, then Foreign Secretary, encouraged the Secretary of State for Northern Ireland, Sir Patrick Mayhew, to lift the ban as quickly as was prudent.

Unlike the more sycophantic Cabinet ministers of the time, Hurd was not afraid to argue his case with the Prime Minister. Kenneth Clarke recalls that Hurd has 'a frosty air which he adopts when he feels he has to say something, and will not allow himself to be silenced'.[54] The best example of the genuine negotiation which took place between Mrs Thatcher and Douglas Hurd occurred during the formulation of the Official Secrets legislation.

As a participant and onlooker, John Wakeham, the Leader of the House of Commons at the time, recalls that the negotiations between Douglas Hurd and Mrs Thatcher over the Official Secrets legislation were tough and:

. . . formidable stuff, equalled only in different ways in my time in government – which was most of the time with Mrs Thatcher there – with Geoffrey Howe over the South African policy and Kenneth Baker over education, where the committee became a dialogue between the two, where the minister, who knew his stuff – which Douglas did – held his own, kept his cool and battled through and got her to concede. She acted as a very good foil – if you like as a prosecutor – and he defended himself very well. These were real tests.[55]

Margaret Thatcher and Douglas Hurd were not as far apart on Official Secrets legislation as has sometimes been made out. Mrs Thatcher had begun her premiership with surprising openness, by revealing that Anthony Blunt had been a Soviet spy. However, as her premiership wore on, she became increasingly annoyed by Whitehall leaks and obsessed with Government secrecy, revealed by her attempts to ban Peter Wright's book *Spycatcher*. The phrase 'economical with the truth', uttered by her former Cabinet Secretary, Sir Robert Armstrong, in the Australian courts, seemed to sum up her antipathy to open government. On 27 January 1987, Hurd noted in his diary:

> 27 Jan. 1987: Filled by ludicrous security meetings. Chasing in vain the hares of various publications as they scamper across the scene . . . Ludicrous meeting in the Prime Minister's room to review incoherently this confused field. Big bangs outside which we suppose are bombs but turn out to be fireworks from British Airways prematurely saluting privatisation.[56]

Douglas Hurd was dragged into a series of spats with the BBC on the issue of secrecy, which were not of his own making. Before he arrived at the Home Office, a programme entitled *Real Lives: At the Edge of the Union* had been withdrawn by the BBC Board of Governors, but Hurd was relaxed about its eventual showing on 16 October, 1985.[57] However, he could not avoid the row which erupted in early 1987 over a Special Branch raid on the BBC's Glasgow offices and the home of the journalist Duncan Campbell. Documents were seized relating to a film about the Zircon spy satellite, due to be shown as part of the BBC's *Secret Society* series. As Douglas Hurd explained to the House of Commons, the Attorney-General, Sir Michael Havers, in his prosecuting capacity, asked the Metropolitan police to launch an investigation. That evening, Hurd noted in his diary:

> 2 Feb. 1987: The world of semi-secrets blows up again with Special Branch raids on the BBC in Glasgow. Malcolm Rifkind [Secretary of State for Scotland] handles PMQs well. There is much noise and pointing of fingers and an SO 20 [Standing Order 20] which I'll have to deal with tomorrow. All this rather a penance.[58]

That night, he dictated the text of his speech himself. The following day, Hurd was reasonably happy with his opening speech. Unusually the Prime Minister and the Leader of the Opposition wound up for their respective sides:

> 3 Feb. 1987: Make a reasonable job of it. PM and our lads were pleased but I'm alarmed at the unreality of her zest for secrecy and the party's growing obsession against the BBC . . . Kaufman starts well. Spoils it as ususal. Kinnock in permanent passion. M.T. [Margaret Thatcher] shouts her way through questions.[59]

Whilst there was clear evidence of bungling on the part of the Scottish police, no evidence was ever found to suggest that any Government minister had ordered the raids. Throughout, the Attorney-General had debarred himself (as was convention) from consulting colleagues on matters relating to prosecutions. Nevertheless, the incident created the general impression of a non-liberal Prime Minister who was trampling on freedom of information. The episode led to a further deterioration of relations between the Government and the BBC, evidenced by the resignation on 29 January of Alasdair Milne, the BBC's Director General.[60] Hurd sought to dampen down the furore by appearing relaxed over the eventual screening of the film about the Zircon spy satellite.[61]

Mrs Thatcher's public pronouncements had clearly shown that, as Douglas Hurd recalls, 'she really hung on very tight to anything to do with secrecy.'[62] But, after the failure to prosecute Clive Ponting in 1985, even she was willing to concede that the existing legislation was no longer credible. Hurd came to the same view, particularly with regard to Section 2 of the Official Secrets Act of 1911, which he thought was a broken reed. Section Two stated that the unauthorised disclosure of any official information, significant or trivial, was a criminal offence. The catch-all nature of the 1911 Act – its failure to discriminate between matters of national security and general government information – meant that it had become widely regarded as oppressive whilst making the Government appear more Draconian than it actually was. The 1911 Act no longer commanded jury and therefore public support. Cautious and considered reform was needed to repair the law and avoid the leaks.

Previous attempts to reform the law had failed,[63] and it was not until April 1987 that Hurd reopened the book on the subject of reforming the law on official secrets.[64] By complete coincidence, while the Government was deliberating its proposals, Douglas Hurd came under pressure from Richard Shepherd, Conservative MP for Aldridge-Brownhills, a libertarian radical, who, after finishing top of the ballot, introduced his own Private Members' Bill on secrecy. The Cabinet decided to stop Richard Shepherd's Protection of Information Bill by issuing overtly a three-line whip, something which has not happened before or since. On the Bill's Second Reading, Hurd made an uncomfortable but necessary defence of the right of the executive rather than Parliament to legislate on a sensitive matter of this kind.[65]

Hurd brought forward his White Paper proposals in the summer of 1988.[66] Section 2 of the Official Secrets Act 1911 was to be reformed such that the unauthorised disclosure of a large proportion of official information would no longer be a criminal offence. The relaxation of the law would cover economic information (including Budget proposals), Cabinet documents, ministerial correspondence, and information from firms or individuals. However, the Home Secretary announced six categories of information which would be subject to the criminal law. The new categories carried the safeguard that the disclosure had to meet a specified test of harm, which would be for the courts to determine, rather than the old system whereby the minister issued a certificate. Initially, Hurd proposed that the disclosure of information relating to defence matters and international relations would only result in prosecution 'if it is likely to result in specified damage to the national interest'.[67] Disclosure of security and intelligence information outside the security services would only be a criminal offence if it damaged the operation of the security services. In contrast, members of the security services would be bound by a lifelong duty of confidentiality. Information relating to interception of communication (for example phone tapping) and information received in confidence from other governments (especially matters relating to terrorism) would be absolute offences. The sixth category, that of information concerning the commission of a crime or leading to a prisoner escaping from custody, would carry the safeguard of a test of harm.

Between the White Paper stage in June 1988 and the Second Reading on 21 December 1988, Hurd made a number of concessions, which basically relaxed some of the rules relating to discloures.[68] He argued that having made these concessions, it was time for Members to realise that his proposals were the most sensible and the right balance:

> However, there is a little bit of a change, is there not? Surely fair-minded hon. Members will accept there is a little change . . . [the measures] are certainly conservative measures in that they have at their heart the effective protection of the citizen from specific and grave dangers. However, they are also radical reforms because they open windows that have remained closed and cobwebbed, because they define clearly what has been confused for a long time, and because they strike in 1988 a balance that is designed for today.[69]

Opposition MPs, especially the relentless Tam Dalyell (Linlithgow), along with libertarian Conservatives, particularly Jonathan Aitken (Thanet, South) and Richard Shepherd (Aldridge-Brownhills) remained unconvinced. They believed that civil servants and members of the security services should have the safeguard of a public-interest defence. This was the right of someone to claim it was necessary to disclose to the wider public something which the Government had done wrong. In Hurd's view, civil servants were bound by a lifelong duty of confidentiality. If they had anxieties or grievances, then the proper course was for him or her to seek internal redress. The major flaw in this argument, as Richard Shepherd pointed out, was that the idea of internal redress assumed that a civil servant should place absolute trust in the honesty of his or her superiors.[70]

Another bone of contention in the Bill was the provision which made it a criminal offence to publish confidential information in Britain when the same information had already been published lawfully in another country. The clause appeared to have the fingerprints of the Prime Minister all over it. She was still smarting from the decision of the Australian courts to permit publication in Australia of the *Spycatcher* book by Peter Wright. Sir Ian Gilmour supported a defence of prior publication, so that a person charged with publishing secrets would be able to argue that his or her information had already been published in the United Kindgom or elsewhere. His commonsense argument was that once a secret is known, it is no longer a secret.[71] Hurd's line was that it was simply too risky to say that in all circumstances second publication would not be harmful. He seemed to be tying himself in knots in order to accommodate the Prime Minister's insistence on this point.

Throughout the various stages of the Bill, Hurd had been heavily criticised by a distinguished group of MPs, including Roy Jenkins, Edward Heath, Sir Ian Gilmour, Merlyn Rees, David Owen, and Sir Bernard Briane (Father of the House). On Third Reading, Hurd acknowledged that he had witnessed 'a devoted and articulate band of critics from all parties,'[72] but stressed that, for the first time, the vast bulk of official information would not be subject to the criminal law. The law could not be based around the Opposition's 'vision of the whistleblower, the conscientious civil servant who is asked to do something wrong'.[73]

Hurd concluded by claiming that 'the critics have not been able to mobilise more than a certain level of support'.[74] It is a favourite Hurd tactic when debating to use phrases like 'things have gone our way', or 'the argument has moved on', or 'the steam seems to be going out of the other side's argument', even if this is not the case.

Hurd opted to legislate separately for the security services. The Prime Minister was persuaded by the arguments of Sir Anthony Duff, then Head of MI5, and earlier, the man who had helped negotiate the Rhodesian settlement in 1980. Sir Anthony argued that the security operatives themselves wanted a proper legal framework within which to work.

On 23 November 1988, Douglas Hurd used the Home Affairs Debate on the Address to outline the principles behind the Security Services Bill. The proposals sought to establish in law the functions of the security services: foreign espionage, and tackling terrorism and subversion. For the first time, the Director General of the Security Service would be personally responsible in law for the service's neutrality. The Home Secretary would have the power to apply for warrants to search a property only if they were of 'substantial value' and his actions would be reviewed by an independent commissioner, who would report annually to Parliament (subject to security excisions). Also, there would be a tribunal which would receive and consider complaints from citizens. In an attempt to give civil servants some form of redress, Hurd revealed that Sir Philip Woodfield had been a staff counsellor since November 1987, charged with the job of listening to grievances from civil service staff.

Hurd realised that the capacity of a government to function effectively required that certain parts of the system be conducted in secret. It was the job of Government to propose and Parliament to dispose.[75] Ministerial responsibility could not be 'devolved or shared with others'.[76] It was for this reason that Hurd opposed parliamentary scrutiny of the security services:

> Such a piece of parliamentary machinery would either demolish the barrier of secrecy, which is essential to the working of the service, or try to straddle it – with predictably painful results. If the body knew all, it would know it could say little to the rest of parliament without damaging results. If it knew little, it could say nothing with any conviction.[77]

Hurd claimed that the Security Services Bill, together with the Official Secrets Bill and the growing openness of Government, represented 'an essay in openness that has no parallel in the history of our Government since the war.'[78] But the reforms which Hurd introduced as Home Secretary need to be seen in the wider context of his further reforms as Foreign Secretary. After the 1992 General Election, he introduced a series of liberalising measures on the issues of secrecy and open government. In May 1992, Hurd ordered the release of a considerable number of historical documents held beyond the thirty-year rule, saying that 'the culture of secrecy had gone too wide'.[79] This was followed in 1994 by the Intelligence Services Act, which, for the first time, acknowledged the existence of SIS, or MI6, and the Government's Communication Centre at GCHQ, Cheltenham. MI6 was put on the same statutory basis as the home security service, MI5, following the pattern of the Security Services Act of 1988.[80]

Douglas Hurd also played a decisive part in persuading the Cabinet to support William Waldegrave's plans to introduce the Citizen's Charter and more open government.[81] At the last Cabinet discussion on the Conservative manifesto before the 1992 General Election, Hurd led a move, co-ordinated beforehand with the Prime Minister and William Waldegrave, to include in the manifesto a commitment that the Government would publish the membership of Cabinet Committees.[82]

After the Election, Hurd supported Waldegrave in Cabinet when ministers had to decide whether to introduce much greater publication of Government background papers and reports and establish a code of practice with an ombudsman.[83] For a while, it looked as if the Cabinet pragmatists favouring continued Government secrecy would carry the day. They were worried that if the Government commissioned a report which it subsequently disapproved, then it needed to retain the power to suppress it. The day was saved by two interventions, one by Douglas Hurd and the other by the Lord Chancellor, James Mackay. The Foreign Secretary, in an ironic intervention, said he could not understand why these arguments were being deployed; since everything leaked anyway, was it not better to publish? At this point, another Cabinet doubter asked whether the Government could not just suppress the information, to which Lord Mackay is said to have replied in his gentle Scottish voice, 'I don't think that would be quite honest.'[84]

Throughout his four years at the Home Office, Hurd remained loyal to Mrs Thatcher. Despite his continuing loyalty, Hurd had private doubts over Mrs Thatcher's style of leadership, particularly her careless disregard of collective Cabinet responsibility, which was exposed during the Westland crisis.

Michael Heseltine, the Defence Secretary resigned from the Cabinet on 9 January 1986 over the failure of Mrs Thatcher to consider a European takeover bid of the ailing Westland Helicopter company based in Yeovil. In doing so, he sparked off a series of events which nearly lead to the downfall of the Prime Minister.[85] As Home Secretary, Douglas Hurd recalled, after the crisis was over, that once Heseltine had walked out of Cabinet, ministers carried on routinely as if nothing had happened. No one was quite sure whether Heseltine had left 'this Cabinet', meaning just that or had actually resigned from the Government. Hurd became anxious after Mrs Thatcher's statement to the House of Commons on Friday, 23 January 1986. The Prime Minister professed her complete ignorance over the selective leaking of a letter, originally written by the Solicitor General, Patrick Mayhew, in which he had criticised the conduct of Michael Heseltine. In his diaries, Hurd describes her statement as 'Horrific. Makes Leon Brittan's position impossible and her own precarious.'[86]

The following day (Saturday), Leon Brittan was forced to resign as Trade and Industry Secretary. That day, Hurd was on a regional tour of Lancashire and it was not until the Sunday that the Home Secretary became more closely involved in the crisis:

> 26 Jan. 1986: Came down on sleeper from Euston. Bumped through the night. To Number 10 for talks with Nigel Wicks [Prime Minister's Principal Private Secretary] and Charles Powell. Prime Minister appears for five minutes, tired and talkative. They all claim there are answers on all the points outstanding to close this fiasco. But I fear these are complicated.[87]

Hurd was due to speak on Brian Walden's *Weekend World* programme. In the background, his officials and advisers worked extremely hard to ensure he gave a good performance. The Prime Minister was anxious that he should use the opportunity to attack Michael Heseltine, something which Lord Whitelaw had already done in the Lords.[88]

However, Hurd was never the type to engage in personal attacks on colleagues. Instead, in a frank interview with Brian Walden, the Home Secretary said that Mrs Thatcher's performance on the Thursday needed amplifying and it was in the national interest that she should do so. He compared the Westland affair to 'a little stream which suddenly flash-flooded its banks and swept away two ministers and did a lot of damage'.[89] Candidly, he admitted, 'We have paid the price as a Government for the temporary collapse of collective responsibility, so we need to ensure that it does not happen again.'[90]

Colleagues rang him up to congratulate him on his handling of the interview, although his remark that 'the worst thing for the country would be to lurch into some kind of discussion of the leadership' may only have served, as Hugo Young argues, to heighten speculation about the Prime Minister's future.[91] There was even a story at the time, confirmed by officials since, that the reaction in Number 10 half-way through the Walden interview was one of 'Well done, Douglas', but by the end the programme, it was more a case of 'This man is dangerous.'[92] But the overall impression was of a loyal Cabinet firefighter, capable of damping things down when the Government was in difficulty.

The following day (Monday 27 January), Hurd was a participant in one of the most curious episodes of the Thatcher Government. The Opposition had tabled an emergency debate for that evening in the House of Commons. Leon Brittan's resignation had not eased the Prime Minister's position, but left her directly in the firing line. It was therefore necessary to save the Prime Minister by preparing a watertight series of answers to the outstanding points. It was in this context that a meeting took place at Number 12, Downing Street attended by William Whitelaw, Geoffrey Howe, John Biffen, John Wakeham, Sir Robert Armstrong and Nigel Wicks. In his diaries, Hurd christened the group 'the greybeards':

> 27 Jan. 1986: Without the Prime Minister, we go through her draft speech, rewriting important passages to give fuller information.[93]

As the greybeards deliberated downstairs, an unseen Prime Minister sat in a room upstairs receiving a series of changes to the original drafts of her speech. Meanwhile, Leon Brittan was anxious to see an advance copy of Mrs Thatcher's speech. His loyalty was conditional at this point. Ministers knew that he still had the capacity to sink the Prime Minister if he pinned responsibility for the leaked letter directly on the door of Number 10.

As it turned out, the Leader of the Opposition, Neil Kinnock, came to Mrs Thatcher's rescue as he delivered one of the most verbose and mistimed performances the House of Commons saw during the Thatcher era. All Mrs Thatcher had to do was to stick carefully to her prepared draft, and refuse to take interventions from the floor. After the debate, Hurd sensed correctly that the crisis was dying down:

27 Jan. 1986: Kinnock poor. It's a clumsy story, but it's out now, and its very clumsiness convinces.[94]

It was at this point that the two Pattens, John and Christopher, and William Waldegrave said to Douglas Hurd that, if Mrs Thatcher fell, he should stand for the leadership. Hurd immediately rejected the idea. His own view was that the crisis was over: his diary entry for that day closes with the phrase, 'Life will now subside.'[95]

In contrast to Nigel Lawson and William Whitelaw – the two best Cabinet generalists from the Thatcher governments – Douglas Hurd did not normally intervene as Home Secretary on matters outside his departmental brief. On the issue of the poll-tax, Hurd was a member of the E (LF) Cabinet sub-committee (Economic (Local Finance)), which comprised two-thirds of the full Cabinet. Hurd had some private reservations about the new tax, but remained loyal, despite being lobbied hard by Nigel Lawson, the Chancellor of the Exchequer, who was opposed to the measure. It was, according to Lord Lawson, 'the only disappointment I had with him during his time as Home Secretary.'[96] Hurd's post-mortem on the poll-tax is that ministers never saw the wood for the trees:

I did come in occasionally on the poll-tax, but more on the detail of it. In retrospect, we all should have come in more strongly on the principle of it. I think it was one of those moments when you never identify the decisive moment. You're always dealing with the detail. The basic decision has been taken. You're constantly in the business of limiting the damage.[97]

The introduction of the poll-tax presented Douglas Hurd with a constituency problem in Witney which formed a large part of the West-Oxfordshire district council. In February 1990, eighteen West-Oxfordshire councillors resigned over rent rises for council tenants following the withdrawal of £2.7 million in housing benefit from central government grants. In May 1990, the rebel Tory leader, David Walker, stood as an Independent Conservative and won the Curbridge and Brize Norton ward at the local elections. One of the major difficulties with the poll-tax was that the bills arriving on the doorsteps were much higher than the Government had anticipated. In Oxfordshire, the bill was nearer £400 than the £237 predicted. During the Conservative leadership contest in November 1990, Hurd understandably found it difficult to repudiate a policy which had, after all, been agreed by the whole Cabinet, of which he was a key member.

The main conclusion to be drawn from Hurd's experiences as a Cabinet Minister working at the Home Office under Mrs Thatcher are that, for the most part, he remained a loyal Cabinet Minister. The Prime Minister did not interfere in the daily running of the Home Department, except over hanging and broadcasting, where Hurd had to tolerate her contradictary views, in the former toughing it out and in the latter giving ground. There is sometimes a perception that Cabinet ministers all know each other intimately, discuss matters regularly, and are acquainted with the policy details of each other's departments. At least as far as Douglas Hurd's period as Home Secretary was concerned, this was not generally the case. For the bulk of the time, he was preoccupied with the running of his own department, and as with most effective ministers during the Thatcher Government, he discovered that the best way of dealing with Mrs Thatcher was à deux, where he was able to argue his case effectively. In the wider forum of the Cabinet subcommittees, he was renowned for being in commmand of his brief and for a willingness to argue his case effectively without being intimidated by the Prime Minister, especially during the formulation of the Official Secrets legislation. However, Douglas Hurd never became 'One of Us'. He never sought that status, and correspondingly, the Prime Minister never felt he was a committed Thatcherite. Specifically, she was never sure that Hurd could be entirely relied upon over the issue of Europe, because of his background in the Foreign Office and his close association with Edward Heath. But despite their lack of closeness, Mrs Thatcher did respect Douglas Hurd's competence and loyalty.

Hurd and Thatcher offered differing visions of Conservatism, but were able to co-exist without allowing those differing visions to develop into major arguments over policy. However, his diaries reveal his private reactions towards Mrs Thatcher's style: sudden amusement at her mannerisms, incredulity as she aired some of her over-the-top, contradictory views; and then equally sudden disapproval of her style of Government, interspersed with moments of admiration. Throughout, Hurd's natural reserve, entrenched by his diplomatic training and his deep sense of loyalty, ensured that only the occasional raised eyebrows gave away anything of his inner emotions.

Notes

1. Douglas Hurd, 'Statutes of Liberty', The Spectator, 5 Dec. 1987.
2. Diary Readings with Douglas Hurd, 20 Jan. 1997.

3. The tragedy in August 1987 when Michael Ryan ran amok killing sixteen people.

4. Diary Readings with Douglas Hurd, 26 Feb. 1997.

5. Interview with Douglas Hurd, 20 Jan. 1997.

6. The Murder (Abolition of Death Penalty) Act of 1965 initially suspended rather than abolished capital punishment. After a five year experiment, abolition was made permanent in 1969.

7. William Whitelaw, *The Whitelaw Memoirs*, pp. 195–200.

8. Diary Readings with Douglas Hurd, 17 Dec. 1996; for Leon Brittan's speech, *see* H. of C. Deb. (6th Series), 13 Jul. 1983, vol. 45, cols 885–92.

9. Interview with Douglas Hurd, 17 Dec. 1996.

10. For Hurd's first speech as Home Secretary on capital punishment see H. of C. Deb. (6th Series), 1 Apr. 1987, vol. 113, cols 1124–30.

11. For Hurd's second speech against the death penalty *see* H. of C. Deb. (6th Series), 7 Jun. 1988, vol. 134, cols 747–54.

12. In 1989, Hurd was relieved when Mrs Thatcher decided not to attend the law and order debate at the Conservative Party Conference.

13. Interview with Douglas Hurd, 17 Dec. 1996.

14. Diary Readings with Douglas Hurd, 26 Feb. 1997.

15. Douglas Hurd, Speech to 103rd Conservative Party Conference, Bournemouth, 8 Oct. 1986 (Conservative Party News Service: 552/86).

16. Douglas Hurd, Speech to 104th Conservative Party Conference, Blackpool, 7 Oct. 1987 (Conservative Party News Service: 656/87).

17. Matthew Parris, 'Erring Hurd and the Demon Todd', *The Times*, 13 Oct. 1988.

18. *Broadcasting in the '90s: Competition, Choice and Quality, Cm. 517.*

19. *The Times*, 20 Sept. 1985.

20. Sir David Calcutt, QC, Home Office. *Report of the Committee on Privacy and Related Matters, Cm. 1102*, HMSO, 1990. The Home Office also lost responsibility for safety at sports grounds and press freedom and privacy.

21. Nigel Lawson, *The View From No. 11: Memoirs of a Tory Radical* (Corgi Books: London, 1993), p. 722.

22. H. of C. Deb. (6th series), 16 May 1988, vol. 133, cols 689–98.

23. Martin Durham, 'The Thatcher Government and Moral Rights', *Parliamentary Affairs*, 1989, vol. 42, p. 61.

24. For a fuller account, *see* D. Marsh, P. Gowin and M. Read, 'Private Members Bills and Moral Panic: The Case of the Video Recordings Bill (1984)', *Parliamentary Affairs*, Apr. 1986, vol. 39, no. 2, pp. 179–96.

25. Diary Readings with Douglas Hurd, 7 Oct. 1997.

26. *The Times*, 23 Jun. 1988.

27. *See* H.C. 262, Home Affairs Committee, *The Future of Broadcasting*, vol. I,

Session 1987–88, 22 June 1988.

28. Channel 4 had been established by William Whitelaw in 1982, acting on the recommendations of the Annan Report of March 1977.
29. H. of C. Deb. (6th Series), 13 Jun. 1989, vol. 154, col. 712.
30. H. of C. Deb. (6th Series), 8 Feb. 1989, vol. 146, col. 1014.
31. H. of C. Deb. (6th Series), 13 Jun. 1989, vol. 154, col. 710.
32. See David Mellor's Third Reading speech, H. of C. Deb. (6th Series), 10 May 1990, vol. 172, cols 412–18.
33. Douglas Hurd, Speech to Peel Society Dinner, Tamworth, 5 Feb. 1988.
34. Ibid. This was not the first occasion when Hurd had spoken of the concept of the 'active citizen'. On 26 February 1987, the Home Secretary developed the theme during the Bow Group's annual dinner.
35. Douglas Hurd, 'Citizenship in the Tory democracy', New Statesman, 29 Apr. 1988.
36. Ibid.
37. Ibid.
38. Douglas Hurd, Speech at Lee Ford Fair, Honiton, 8 Jul. 1989.
39. Ibid.
40. Douglas Hurd, 'Conservatism in the 1990s', CPC Party Conference Lecture, Nov. 1991.
41. Editorial, 'Citizen Hurd', New Statesman, 15 Apr. 1988.
42. Ibid.
43. The Times, 23 May 1988.
44. Douglas Hurd, Speech to a Fringe Meeting of the General Synod of the Church of England, Church House, London, 10 Feb. 1988.
45. Douglas Hurd, Lenten Address on Theme of 'Suffering Servants', Church of St Martin-in-the-Fields, 18 Feb. 1988. In January 1994, on hearing of the Tim Yeo affair, Hurd noted in his dairy 'We are becoming a nation of Pharisees.' Diary Readings with Douglas Hurd, Westwell. 13 Jun. 1997.
46. The Times, 7 Jun. 1986.
47. Editorial, 'Citizen Hurd', New Statesman, 15 Apr. 1988.
48. Douglas Hurd, Extract, Speech to Great Rollright Conservatives, 25 Jul. 1986.
49. Douglas Hurd, Extract, Speech to Basingstoke Conservatives, 9 Jan. 1987.
50. Diary Readings with Douglas Hurd, 26 Feb. 1997.
51. Ibid.
52. H. of C. Deb. (6th Series), 19 Oct. 1988, vol. 138, col. 893.
53. Ibid., col. 894.
54. Interview with Kenneth Clarke, 16 Dec. 1996.
55. Interview with Lord Wakeham, 19 Dec. 1995.
56. Diary Readings with Douglas Hurd, 7 Oct. 1997.

57. *The Times*, 16 Oct. 1985.
58. Diary Readings with Douglas Hurd, 7 Oct. 1997.
59. Ibid.
60. Alasdair Milne was succeeded by Michael Checkland, who had been deputy Director-General of the BBC since 1985.
61. *The Times*, 5 Mar. 1987.
62. Interview with Douglas Hurd, 7 Oct. 1997.
63. A committee under Lord Franks reported in 1972 and eventually led to a White Paper by the Labour Government in 1978, but its plans were interrupted by the 1979 General Election.
64. H. of C. Deb. (6th Series), 15 Dec. 1987, vol. 124, written answers, col. 435.
65. H. of C. Deb. (6th Series), 15 Jan. 1988, vol. 125, cols 581–87.
66. H. of C. Deb. (6th Series), 29 Jun. 1988, vol. 136, col. 365.
67. Ibid., col. 365.
68. H. of C. Deb. (6th Series), 21 Dec. 1988, vol. 144, cols 460–1.
69. Ibid., cols 468–9.
70. H. of C. Deb. (6th Series), 2 Feb. 1989, vol. 146, col. 469. The Government won the vote on the public-interest defence by 267 votes to 179; cols 533–6. However, seventeen Conservatives dissented from the Government line – the largest case of dissent during the passage of the Official Secrets Bill.
71. H. of C. Deb. (6th Series), 16 Feb. 1989, vol. 147, col. 545.
72. H. of C. Deb. (6th Series) 22 Feb. 1989, vol. 147, col. 1079.
73. Ibid.
74. Ibid., col. 1080.
75. H. of C. Deb. (6th Series), 15 Jan. 1988, vol. 125, col. 584.
76. H. of C. Deb. (6th Series), 23 Nov. 1988, vol. 142, col. 122.
77. Ibid., col. 123.
78. H. of Ć. Deb. (6th Series), 23 Nov. 1988, vol. 142, col. 125.
79. *The Guardian*, 15 May 1992.
80. For Hurd's speech on the Second Reading of the Intelligence Services Bill [Lords] *see* H. of C. Deb. (6th Series), 22 Feb. 1994, vol. 238, cols 153–65.
81. Hurd and Waldegrave's quiet advocacy of open government had been going on since the 1970s. Waldegrave recalls being asked by Lord Rothschild's CPRS to write a paper on open government. When the paper was received by Douglas Hurd, it went up to the Prime Minister unchanged. Interview with William Waldegrave, 17 Dec. 1996.
82. Ibid.
83. Under Waldegrave's plans, policy-making decisions and advice to ministers

would still be kept confidential under the thirty-year rule.

84. Interview with William Waldegrave, 17 Dec. 1996.

85. For an unrivalled account of the Westland crisis, *see* Hugo Young, *One of Us* (Pan Books: London, 1993), pp. 431–57.

86. Diary Readings with Douglas Hurd, 26 Feb. 1997; for Mrs Thatcher's speech, *see* H. of C. Deb. (6th Series), 23 Jan. 1986, vol. 90, cols 449–60.

87. Diary Readings with Douglas Hurd, 26 Feb. 1997.

88. H. of L. Deb. (5th Series), 23 Jan. 1986, vol. 470, col. 341.

89. *The Times*, 27 Jan. 1986.

90. Ibid.

91. Young, *One of Us* (Macmillan: Final edn., London, 1993) p. 454.

92. Private information.

93. Diary Readings with Douglas Hurd, 26 Feb. 1997.

94. Ibid.

95. Ibid.

96. Interview with Lord Lawson of Blaby, 6 Dec. 1995.

97. Interview with Douglas Hurd, 20 Jan. 1997.

12

Watching One's Back:
Reforming the Criminal Justice System

In general, Mrs Thatcher did not interfere in matters relating to the running of criminal justice policy. She did have her own personal Home Office policy unit,[1] but it never exerted a powerful influence on behalf of Number 10. In some respects, this was par for the course. As Hurd later remarked, 'I've worked with three Prime Ministers quite closely. I can't remember a Prime Minister ever going near a prison.'[2]

More than most offices of state, the Home Secretary's policies derive more from his (but not yet her) own judgement and that of his officials, than the collective decisions of the full Cabinet or Cabinet subcommittees. When it comes to responsibility for day-to-day operational matters or managing periodic crises, the Home Secretary is out on his own. He must demonstrate to his Cabinet colleagues and the Prime Minister that he is, in the words of the cliché, a safe pair of hands. The bulk of the Home Secretary's time is spent not formulating new policy, but in the daily implementation of existing policy:

> The Home Secretary . . . is constantly required to decide appeals against disciplinary findings affecting police officers: to cope with protests against decisions of immigration officers at the port about the entry of particular individuals: to decide proposals that individual foreigners should be deported from this country: to decide proposals that particular individuals should be detained under the Prevention of Terrorism Act.[3]

Besides the sheer workload, Prime Ministerial power and the influence of the Conservative Party Conference as described in the previous chapter, other factors exist which constrain any Conservative Home Secretary's room for manoeuvre.[4]

One of the most alarming features of criminal justice policy in the 1980s and 1990s has been the rise in influence of the media, particularly the written press. The need to explain and justify one's decisions to the media became as important as the content of the policies themselves. Hurd was lucky in having an excellent head of information at the Home Office in the shape of the late Brian Mower. By nature a reserved man, he was none the less very astute in cultivating the media. Whenever a new policy initiative was in the pipeline, Mower would ensure that the issues would be trailed in articles in the middle-market Conservative newspapers — the *Daily Telegraph*, *The Times*, the *Daily Express*, the *Daily Mail* — as well as the other serious broadsheets. If the Home Secretary was promoting a new Neighbourhood Watch scheme or signing a new extradition treaty, it was almost certain to be trailed in the press. Douglas Hurd's special adviser, Edward Bickham, also played a central role in briefing the press, particularly on those issues with a strongly political bent.

Hurd could draw on a close working knowledge of the press lobby system from his days with Edward Heath. He would take the trouble of dining regularly with the main political commentators and the editors of the broadsheet newspapers, especially his friend Max Hastings, then Editor of the *Daily Telegraph*.

The most constraining influence exerted by the press during Hurd's period as Home Secretary and since was the rise of the populist tendency most vociferously represented by the *Daily Mail*. Hurd was always averse to responding to populist demands for tougher sentences and to sloganising from this section of the press, but could not ignore entirely their opinions because there was always a real danger that they would whip up a fuss, thereby undermining what he was trying to do. Lord Windlesham has accurately described the tabloids as 'the stocks of the modern age'.[5]

Closely allied with the populism of the press on criminal justice policy was the influence of the muscular or punitive brand of Conservatism, as represented by the Tory right and populist wings on the Tory backbenches. If Hurd was seen to be moving too far in a liberal direction or perceived as not handling an issue with sufficient firmness, the rumblings could be detected from the influential Conservative Home Affairs Committee. Hurd had weekly meetings with the officers of the Committee in his room in the House of Commons. In between times, his Parliamentary Private Secretaries, David Heathcoat-Amory (Wells) (until July 1988) and Timothy Yeo (Suffolk, South), along with the Government whips, were his eyes and ears on the ground. Hurd favoured a liberal approach to sentencing policy, but as Home Secretary, he was always acutely aware of the need to watch his back for signs of trouble.

In the House of Commons as a whole, the system for holding the Home Secretary to account was formidable. Hurd was subject to about three quarters of an hour of Home Office questions every month. If these occasions were handled badly, they could deal a blow to the whole course of the Home Office's programme for several months ahead. Apart from the necessity of courting the Conservative Home Affairs Committee, Hurd was subject to occasional grillings from the Select Committee on Home Affairs. Also influential was the Parliamentary All-Party Penal Affairs Group.[6] Fortunately for Hurd, the Chairman of both these groups for the bulk of his time as Home Secretary was Sir John Wheeler, a former Assistant Governor in the Prison Service. Wheeler was usually sympathetic to the views of the Home Secretary and later helped steer doubting Conservative backbenchers into accepting non-custodial sentences.

Outside Parliament, there existed a whole host of penal reform groups and special-interest pressure groups who tried to influence the debate during the run-up to new Government legislation. The Howard League for Penal Reform, the Prison Reform Trust and the National Association for the Care and Resettlement of Offenders (NACRO), all conducted important studies based on empirical research from which a Home Secretary could chose to draw for his legislative ideas. Victims of crime, probation officers, prison governors and wardens, and the police all had their own pressure groups. In September 1986, Douglas Hurd caused something of a stir by claiming the growing role of pressure groups was getting in the way of efficient Government. Delivering a lecture to the Royal Institute of Public Administration, he observed that as pressure groups interposed themselves more and more between the executive on the one hand and Parliament on the other, they were making it more difficult to reach decisions which were properly balanced and in the general interest. They were, he said, 'like serpents constantly emerging from the sea to strangle Laocoön and his sons in their coils'.[7]

Despite the commotion caused by his speech, Hurd learned to live with all these conflicting constituencies. His line of approach when formulating new policies remained akin to a senior Whitehall official asking himself, 'How can I get this thing through?' Careful attention to all the groups in the House of Commons and outside made them feel that they had been informed. Hurd saw himself as having three main roles as Home Secretary: as a commander, a conciliator and a constituency MP. In an especially burdensome department, he adopted his characteristic broad-brush approach when dealing with policy papers and meeting with officials, and used his ordered mind to cut through the mass of paperwork, identifying the essence of a problem. He was a good chairman: meetings would be conducted smoothly and briskly. He was not afraid of making decisions. Hurd listened to the arguments of the various groups which made up the criminal justice system: the judges, the magistrates, the probation officers and the police.

As well as dining regularly with chief constables, on his arrival at the Home Office, Douglas Hurd was the first Home Secretary to instigate meetings with the Chairman and Joint Secretaries of the Metropolitan Police Federation. Ken Exworth, Secretary of the Joint Executive Committee of the Police Federation from 1988 to 1992, was of the view that 'Douglas Hurd was the only Secretary of State who really took any interest in what we had to say. The handshake on arrival drew you into the room and the one at the end pushed you out.'[8] Mr Exworth, did, however, have cause to comment on what he perceived to be Douglas Hurd's lack of table manners:

> My favourite memory is of a Christmas lunch where Douglas Hurd picked up his soup bowl by the two handles and downed the last drop of soup — much to the surprise of the Receiver, who was in full flow on some subject at the time.[9]

Hurd also adopted a conciliatory approach in his dealings with the Opposition Front Bench. In contrast to his predecessor, Leon Brittan, Hurd would make a special point of consulting on a regular basis with the Shadow Home Affairs Spokesman. It was part of Hurd's view of politics that it was in the national interest that the Opposition should be consulted on the bulk of the issues affecting the Home Office. But Hurd was not above playing party politics himself. He believed there might be an advantage to be gained if his opposite numbers had prior access to privileged information in private, resulting in them being forced to curtail their public attacks on the Home Secretary in the House of Commons.

During Hurd's four years at the Home Office, he sparred with Gerald Kaufman and Roy Hattersley. Of the two, Hurd found the former easier to deal with. Kaufman was, like Hurd, a cultured man, and widely read. Although Kaufman found that Hurd's briefings told him nothing new that he could not have gleaned from the press, he appreciated the fact that he was consulted. It was, Kaufman recalls, a 'refreshing change' from the 'inflexible, arrogant and unimaginative' approach of Leon Brittan.[10]

In his public exchanges with Hurd in the House of Commons, Kaufman's caustic, confrontational style was legendary. At the beginning of the prison officers' dispute in late April 1986, Kaufman warned the Home Secretary 'with his intransigent bungling in this exceptionally delicate area he is recklessly playing with fire'.[11] Hurd's diaries as Home Secretary are peppered with references to Kaufman going 'O.T.T.' Kaufman is willing to concede that Hurd's markedly different style of attempting to 'smother everything in cotton wool' sometimes worked effectively against his more direct approach.[12]

Kaufman, hailing from the libertarian strand of the Labour Party, genuinely opposed the Government's non-liberal agenda, particularly its attitudes towards secrecy, the curbing of immigration, and proposals which limited the rights of the accused. Despite regarding Douglas Hurd as a decent and likeable man with whom he mixed well in private, Kaufman is critical of Hurd for caving into Mrs Thatcher over broadcasting, and for his insufficient grasp of legal concepts which resulted in the slovenly drafting of government legislation.[13]

Hurd found Roy Hattersley 'elusive'.[14] Hattersley's style of debating with Douglas Hurd was effective, because he would depict the Home Secretary, accurately as it happens, as a decent, liberal man, 'trapped between logic and the 1922 Committee'.[15] During a statement on prisons, Hurd noted the difference between the two men:

> The right hon. Gentleman's [Roy Hattersley] technique is very different from
> that of his predecessor. He is trying to kiss me into oblivion, whereas his
> predecessor never made such an attempt.[16]

Hattersley was more successful than Kaufman in getting under Douglas Hurd's skin. His passionate, egalitarian instincts jarred with the traditional Tory views of his opposite number. Hattersley regarded Hurd as a patrician figure who felt that the ruling élite knew what was best for the people. But because of the comfortable Conservative majorities at this time, Hurd's main concern was not with the attitudes of those opposite him. Roy Hattersley was correct in saying that Hurd wished to move criminal justice policy in a more liberal direction, but that he constantly had to look over his shoulder, in order to avoid losing the confidence of his backbenchers.

At the end of April 1986, an industrial dispute by prison officers sparked a rash of unexpected riots in Britain's prisons. The dispute started on 17 April when the members of the main prison officers' union, the Prison Officers' Association (POA), voted in favour of industrial action over the Government's attempts to exert more managerial influence over the running of the prisons.

The situation escalated when prison officers took control of Gloucester prison. Hurd met with a delegation of prison officers on 28 April, but said he could not resume full talks until the prison officers called off their action. The following day:

> 29 Apr. 1986: Make statement on the prisons dispute. There is unease behind
> me. Depressed by the prospect of long, damaging dispute, with occasional
> dangers.[17]

During his statement, the unease came from three Conservative backbenchers – Sally Oppenheim (Gloucester), Peter Bruinvels (Leicester, East) and John Hannam (Exeter) – who were concerned at the impact of the dispute on the security of prisons in their constituencies.[18]

On Wednesday, 30 April, news began to come in of a series of riots across Britain's jails. At Northeye prison near Bexhill, the inmates set the jail alight; disturbances were reported at Lewes in East Sussex, at Bristol prison, and at Erlestoke youth custody centre near Devizes, where forty detainees launched a mass breakout. Hurd captured the drama in his diary entry that evening:

> 30 Apr. 1986: Disastrous day. Prisons riot and burn as inmates make excitement out of the prison officers' work to rule. Volunteer a statement to the House at 10 p.m. A wise decision. [Gerald] Kaufman, as usual, overdoes it and I get by. Very gloomy to Ops room in Cleland House.[19]

Earlier that day, initial reports from Lord Glenarthur, the prison's minister, indicated that people had been killed. By the time Hurd stood up in the House of Commons at ten o'clock to deliver his statement, he had learned that these reports were false. But the intervening few hours were 'the most dramatic and anxious I experienced as Home Secretary, worse than the [Handsworth] riots which had come before'.[20]

The next morning, it seemed to Hurd that there was a mountain to climb:

> 1 May 1986: A very daunting day. About a dozen battered and smouldering prisons . . . Prime Minister anxious.[21]

Mrs Thatcher was surprised, not that the prison officers' dispute had started (the points at issue were clear in her mind), but that the Home Office had not received any intelligence reports indicating that the prisoners might take advantage of the situation. Later that day, Hurd was relieved to hear the news that the POA had suspended their action:

> 1 May 1986: Drama begins to drain out of the situation. By the time I get up at 4 p.m., clearly the situation is past its worst. Senior MPs helpful. Kaufman changes his tune and is statesmanlike.[22]

Five days later, Douglas Hurd asked Her Majesty's Chief Inspector of Prisons, Sir James Hennessy, to conduct an inquiry into the disturbances. In addition, Hurd and Simon Glenarthur, with the aid of Eric Caines, Director of Personnel and Finance in the Prison Department, began formulating and then implementing the policy known as Fresh Start. Prison officer overtime was slashed and special allowances were scrapped in return for higher salaries and a unified grading structure.

The hasty implementation of the Fresh Start was later criticised by Lord Justice Woolf in his 1991 report into disturbances at Strangeways prison,[23] but it is difficult to see what other means could have been found to modernise the antiquated pay-and-conditions structure of prison officers without a once-and-for-all radical overhaul.[24]

The prison riots of May 1986 also highlighted the growing problem of prison overcrowding. William Whitelaw had set in motion a substantial programme of prison building and improvements, but on average, it took seven years to plan, design, build and open a prison. In the meantime, Hurd faced a seemingly inexorable rise in the prison population. By July 1987, it stood at 51,000 – 4,000 more than the previous year and 9,300 above the Certified Normal Accommodation (CNA).[25] Matters eventually came to a head in the summer of 1987. On 4 July, Hurd noted in his diary:

4 Jul. 1987: Prison problem weighs on me. I think three years of this (i.e., being Home Secretary) will be ample.[26]

On 6 July, Hurd presented a package of proposals to the Prime Minister, designed to place a sticking plaster over the problem until longer term measures could be brought to bear. Incidentally, at the same meeting Douglas Hurd persuaded Mrs Thatcher to put the Security Service on a statutory footing. Hurd proposed to relax parole conditions for non-serious offenders (serving up to and including twelve months) by increasing the amount of remission dependent on good behaviour from one-third to one-half of their sentence. In addition, as a stop-gap measure, he proposed to open an old army camp at Rollestone in Wiltshire to provide temporary accommodation for 360 inmates. In the medium term, Lord Carlisle of Bucklow, QC, a former Education Secretary and Home Minister, would report on a review of the workings of Parole and Remission.[27] After visiting Brixton Prison to assess the overcrowding problem at first hand, Hurd attended a series of meetings with Home Office officials to go over the detail of his proposals:

9 Jul. 1987: Complete the prison package. Realise how desperately difficult it will be to accomplish over the next seven or ten days.[28]

Hurd's prediction of difficulties ahead proved accurate on 13 July when *The Guardian* newspaper leaked his prison proposals. There was a fear of executive release at this time, a power which permits the Home Secretary to let prisoners out before they have completed their sentences. Such a policy would have enraged the right of the Conservative Party and undermined the Conservative Government's message of being tough on criminals and protecting the public. Hurd's proposals for relaxing parole were designed to prevent executive release:

> 13 Jul. 1987: The usual sort of difficulties crackle around my prison package. Surprisingly, the Prime Minister is not dismayed about remission [relaxing of parole] but she is alarmed by the public expenditure side and the cost of more prisons.[29]

Alongside the safety aspect of overcrowded prisons, the issue of cost was the main impetus for reform of the criminal justice system in the period from 1987 to 1989.

More immediately, Hurd faced a secondary issue of how to staff his temporary camp at Rollestone. Due to a shortage of prison officers, Hurd tried to persuade George Younger, Secretary of State for Defence, to provide soldiers to help with security at the camp. However, Younger refused on the grounds that it was against the army's principles:

> 16 Jul. 1987: George Younger unable to produce a single cook or bottle washer for Rollestone. Fortunately, this issue, on which we have spent much time, is secondary.[30]

Hurd would later use the episode with the army camp in his novel *The Shape of Ice*. His plan for soldiers was rejected by Cabinet.

On 16 July 1987, Douglas Hurd faced explaining his proposals to David Evans, Secretary of the POA, and then the wrath of his backbenchers in the House of Commons. Hurd's statement was one of those occasions when confidence in a minister can very quickly drain away:

> 16 Jul. 1987: Shaken by hostile reception of backbenchers in my room. PMQs go well, then a statement on prisons. Goes as well as could be expected, except for Leon Brittan, who leads the attack, which is odd given his own action on parole. Other hostile backbenchers are predictable. David Heathcoat-Amory [Hurd's Parliamentary Private Secretary], said that was the most difficult statement to make. John Major congratulates me on courage, but it isn't really courageous. I just feel relief.[31]

On this occasion, Leon Brittan attacked the measures on the grounds that some of those released would be sexual offenders, and that there was a danger of releasing prisoners, not on the basis of individual consideration of cases, but on the basis of a new and more liberal penal policy.[32] Of the predictable backbenchers to whom Hurd referred,[33] Ivor Stanbrook (Orpington) was the most outspoken:

Is my right hon. Friend aware that the general public will not understand how it is that a Conservative Government, faced with overcrowded prisons, are about to release on to the streets thousands of convicted criminals and hundreds of violent criminals before their time is up? Is there not a strong argument for providing additional prison accommodation rather than doing what my right hon. Friend proposes? Is this not an error of political judgement?[34]

Considering that, behind his back, a large number of Conservative MPs not only had their knives sharpened, but one or two were making a few stabs directly at him, Hurd's performance had indeed been as courageous as John Major had described. However, the episode was thoroughly unwelcome to any Home Secretary, especially a Conservative Home Secretary whose Government was committed to protecting the public. As if to make matters worse, that night, Hurd's youngest son from his first marriage, Alexander, was hurt after a fight at a party at Meriden. For the next two days, Hurd received a bad press, most notably a short but damaging lead article in the *Daily Telegraph*.[35]

Even though overall prison numbers fell between 1988 and 1989 (including a slight fall in the remand population), there was an omnipresent danger of further outbreaks of prison violence. In May 1989, Hurd would experience another headache, this time over roof-top protests and rioting prisoners at the Risley Remand Centre near Warrington in Cheshire.[36] The Strangeways riot erupted in May 1990 after Hurd departed from the Home Office.[37]

After the 1987 General Election, Hurd gained a reputation as a liberal reformer on sentencing policy. This is not quite accurate. Simply put, Hurd wanted to avoid a return to the prisons crises of 1986 and 1987. His chastening experiences also led him to oppose changes in sentencing policy made by Michael Howard between 1993 to 1997. Speaking in 1997, Hurd reflected on the impact of the events of 1986 and 1987 on his subsequent thinking:

It is a thing which is held against me. I just felt and feel that we must never get into that position again, which was one reason why I am anxious about the present situation [1997]. Overflowing prisons, which was the state we were at — we were really using every possible means — means insecure prisons. We had just seen the dangers of violence, and something had to be done.[38]

A crucial supporter of Douglas Hurd's attempts to secure more resources for the prisons in his last two years at the Home Office was the Chief Inspector of Prisons, Judge Stephen Tumim. Tumim's appointment on 1 October 1987 came as something of a surprise: he was not from the upper echelons of the legal establishment, serving as a judge at Willesden Crown Court. He was better known as the author of *Great Legal Disasters* (1983) and *Great Legal Fiascos* (1985), and as a witty raconteur in the Garrick Club. However, the decision to appoint Tumim turned out to be an inspired choice. He used his excellent communication skills in the media to highlight the case for better prison conditions. Tumim became a high profile figure who proved a useful lever in the Home Office's quest for more Treasury funds for the prison-building programme. While Tumim was clearly liberal on criminal justice policy, Douglas Hurd believes he was never a raving liberal and – delivering the highest Hurd compliment – always took a 'balanced' and 'sensible' view.[39]

Hurd's legislative record on criminal justice policy can be divided into two distinct phases. The first concerned the largely inherited raft of measures brought in by the Criminal Justice Acts of 1987 and 1988. The second concerned the pause for breath between 1987 and 1989, which paved the way for the Criminal Justice Act of 1991.

The General Election of 11 June 1987 had interrupted the passage of the Criminal Justice Bill of 1986-87. It was therefore decided to push through those aspects of the Bill which stood a reasonable chance of being agreed with the Opposition before the dissolution of Parliament – forming the 1987 Act – leaving another series of measures to be debated in the new Parliament.

The greater part of the original Bill was contained within the Criminal Justice Act of 1988. The main change from the original Bill was to increase the Attorney-General's power to refer unduly lenient sentences to the Court of Appeal. Originally, the offender's sentence could not be increased by the Court of Appeal, but Clause 34 of the 1988 Act granted that power in exceptional cases where damage was done to public confidence in the legal system resulting from unduly lenient sentences.

The most contentious part of the 1988 Act was Douglas Hurd's decision to abolish the right of defendants to challenge jurors without cause in trial proceedings, a concept known as 'peremptory challenge'.[40] Hurd argued that giving defendants the right to challenge up to three jurors in a trial gave a 'substantial tilt' in favour of the defendant in court proceedings. Secondly, peremptory challenge went against the principle that juries should be selected at random. The Opposition argued that the random selection principle was a myth. They regarded peremptory challenge as a vital safety valve, enabling the defendant at least to feel that he or she was getting a fair trial. The Labour

Party's stance was supported by the Criminal Bar Association and by six Conservative MPs, five of whom were barristers.[41]

In reply to the Report Stage debate in March 1987, Douglas Hurd attacked the underlying current of the speeches of two barristers – Alex Carlile (SDP/Liberal Alliance Member for Montgomery), and Ivan Lawrence (Conservative: Burton) – that the law should be made by lawyers:

> If we were to rely solely on the advice and opinions of lawyers in forming the statute book of this country, it would be very different from what it is today, and I do not believe that it would be better.[42]

As Home Secretary, Hurd was impatient of the tyranny of the lawyers. He believed that the criminal justice system had become weighted to the advantage of the defendant and was keen to reduce the number of games which could be played by defence counsels.

Ever since 1979, successive Conservative Home Secretaries had pursued a dual-track approach to sentencing, which aimed to secure tougher sentences for serious crimes, while introducing more non-custodial sentences for non-serious offences. By the summer of 1987, however, it appeared that too much emphasis had been placed on the former and not enough on the latter. The point had been reached where non-custodial sentences were no longer perceived as credible by public opinion, the media or Conservative backbenchers. There was a need to rework sentencing policy to make it more credible in the eyes of these groups.[43] Hurd's Minister of State, John Patten, deserves much of the credit for achieving this.

As Lord Windlesham, the expert on criminal justice policy, points out, Hurd had the advantage, shared by the two most successful Home Secretaries since the Second World War – Rab Butler (in 1959) and Roy Jenkins (1966) – of being reappointed to the Home Office after a General Election victory.[44] Like these two distinguished predecessors, Hurd had established sufficient authority and standing within the Home Department by 1987. He also had the time to survey the scene, and the flexibility to draw on different studies from inside and outside the Home Office, looking afresh at ways of reducing prison overcrowding. New measures would be announced on parole, prison privatisation and crime prevention, culminating in the Criminal Justice Act of 1991. But one can overstate the importance of the careful research studies, policy meetings and seminars as well as the legislation which followed.[45] All the time, the tyranny of events – the crowding of one issue on top of another – affected the final course of the reform process.

In other areas of sentencing policy, Hurd discovered there were limits as to how far he could move in a liberal direction. The bulk of legislation relating to sentencing rested on the concept of judicial sentencing, namely that Parliament laid down the maximum penalties for offences, but it was for the courts to determine the appropriate punishment. Discretionary life sentences existed for all serious crimes, with the exception of cases involving murder, which carried a mandatory life sentence. In 1988, Hurd responded to strong parliamentary pressure in the Upper House, including the Lord Justice Lord Lane and several Law Lords, by supporting the establishment of a House of Lords Select Committee under Lord Nathan to review the law on mandatory sentencing.[46] The Nathan Report's recommendation to end mandatory sentences for murder fell victim to the rising tide of populism in the country and the idea was dropped by Kenneth Baker.

In a similar way, Hurd's plans to abolish the right to silence were later swept away by public concerns over miscarriages of justice. In May 1988, Hurd moved cautiously, establishing a Working Group under Bill Bohan, who was then Head of the Criminal Policy Department of the Home Office.[47] He was worried about possible opposition from Conservative lawyers in the House of Commons (more so than on peremptory challenge where he took them on). By the time the Home Office Working Group reported a year later, the Court of Appeal had quashed the convictions of the 'Guildford Four'. The Home Secretary could not ignore deep public concern over the methods used by police to secure confessions. Kenneth Baker was compelled to establish a Royal Commission to look into the whole question of criminal procedure. In 1993, by a majority of nine to two, the Commission recommended that the right of silence be retained.[48] They were supported by the Bar Council, the Criminal Bar Association and the Law Society, but Michael Howard ignored all their advice and diminished the right of silence in the Criminal Justice and Public Order Bill in 1994.

Hurd demonstrated a surprising degree of radicalism, but always tempered by prudence. He would only move ahead with a policy idea if he was convinced of the merits of the proposal and saw it as having a reasonable chance of securing support in the House of Commons. In the case of evidence given by children in criminal proceedings, Hurd proceeded with caution, but in one sense broke new ground with Section 32 of the Criminal Justice Act of 1988 which enabled children under fourteen to give evidence via a live televised link in cases of cruelty or sexual assault. The impetus for Section 32 came from the Fraud Trial Committee's Report of Lord Roskill in 1986 which proposed television links in fraud trials. Among the enthusiasts in this area of policy was Edward Bickham, Douglas Hurd's special adviser, who saw that the use of television link-ups could be transferred to cases involving children. There was a general consensus that children needed to be spared the harrowing ordeal of court appearances, but this needed to be balanced with protecting the legitimate rights of the accused to a fair trial.[49]

By contrast, Hurd moved very slowly in his first two years as Home

Secretary on the question of private-sector involvement in the prison system. Like Leon Brittan and William Whitelaw before him, he tended to see the disadvantages as Home Secretary of handing over responsibility for aspects of the prison to a private-sector which had very little track record of providing such services. Institutionally, there was also the natural conservatism of the Home Office, jealously guarding their areas of responsibility from the other departments or predators from outside. Hurd's first announcement in the area of private-sector involvement was very canny indeed. Under pressure from the Conservative right wing on the day of his parole announcement on 16 July 1987, the Home Secretary announced a review of private-sector involvement in the construction of prisons, via the Prison Buildings Board. However, he appeared to rule out any further moves in this area:

> I do not think that there is a case, and I do not believe that the House would accept a case, for auctioning or privatising prisons or handing over the business of keeping prisoners safe to anyone other than Government servants. However, I do not think we can afford to sit back and say that the way in which we have been doing things in the prison building programme is absolute and cannot be improved.[50]

However, in the course of the next year, Hurd came under increasing pressure from a variety of quarters to reconsider the case for privately run prisons and the ferrying of parole prisoners by private security firms.

Douglas Hurd recalls that he was persuaded of the merits of prison privatisation by John Wheeler,[51] who had visited the United States in the autumn of 1986 to assess the value of 'contract provision' for the running of pre-trial detention units, known as New Remand Units or NRUs. In their majority report (all three Labour members opposed), the Home Affairs Select Committee recommended private-sector bidding for the construction and management of NRUs.[52]

Hurd's policy U-turn on the privatisation of prison services needs to be seen in the context of the rising prison population. It was highly significant that his earlier than expected announcement of a Green Paper to look at private-sector involvement in all aspects of the prison system[53] was part of a package of further measures to stem prison overcrowding.[54] The unpalatable possibility of executive release continued to weigh heavily on his mind as he stood up in the House of Commons on 30 March 1988:

> We must be ready to think imaginatively to ensure that the prison service can meet its obligations. In that context, the possibility of involving the private-sector more closely in aspects of the prison system should be urgently considered.[55]

David Heathcoat-Amory (Wells), Hurd's Parliamentary Private Secretary, was very helpful in mobilising support on the Tory backbenches for Hurd's change of policy. The Somerset MP's firm right-wing credentials were important in this regard.

In addition to the Green Paper, Hurd had commissioned a team of management consultants from Deloitte, Haskins and Sells to examine the feasibility of privately run NRUs as well as the escorting of remand prisoners from custody to court and back again. This feasibility study reported back in March 1989 and led to a major parliamentary statement from the Home Secretary in which he said he was satisfied that, in these two limited areas, a triple safeguard could be put in place to ensure accountability from the private-sector:[56] a monitor directly accountable to the Home Secretary; an inspectorate along the lines of Her Majesty's Inspector of Prisons; and a board of visitors.[57]

On grounds of pragmatism rather than ideology, Douglas Hurd had changed his mind. He believed that the case in favour of relieving the police and prison services of the time-consuming escorting task for parole prisoners only was 'compelling'.[58]

Symbolically at least, Hurd had conceded something wider:

> The introduction of the private-sector into the management of the prison system in the way I have outlined would certainly represent a bold departure from previous thinking and practice. It offers the prospect of a new kind of partnership between the public and the private-sectors of our national life. We should not be scornful of new ideas which, if successful, will make an important contribution to the Government's programme of providing decent conditions for all prisoners at a reasonable cost . . . The contracting-out of services does not diminish in this or other areas the contracting authority's responsibility for the quality of service provided; it is simply using a different method to deliver the service.[59]

His opposite number, Roy Hattersley, believed that Hurd was 'prepared to swallow any item of Conservative ideology no matter how distasteful'.[60] Hattersley deployed the traditional arguments against private-sector involvement in the prison system, claiming that it was wrong in principle to profit financially from those imprisoned by the state.

From December 1988 to December 1989, the prison population fell by 2,100 to just under 47,000 and the number of prisoners on remand fell by 900 as Hurd's stopgap measures began to take effect and the seeds sown by Whitelaw's prison-building programme finally started to bear fruit. By October 1989, Hurd had shifted to the Foreign Office. It seemed that his successor, David Waddington, along with David Mellor, his Minister of State at the Home Office, were showing signs of stalling the process of reform. But the Prime Minister's personal intervention was crucial in saving the plans to proceed with private-sector involvement.[61] In another twist of the plot, Waddington's successor, Kenneth Baker eventually secured an amendment to the Criminal Justice Bill at Report Stage on 25 February 1990 (which became Section 84 of the Criminal Justice Act of 1991), which expanded the provision of escort far beyond that envisaged by Hurd. He filed loyally through the division lobby in support of the amendment, despite the fact that in July 1987 he had specifically ruled out ferrying convicted prisoners. There was now no distinction between escorting remand prisoners – always a special category of prisoner – and all convicted prisoners.[62] The over-zealous move resulted in a series of high-profile prisoner escapes after Group 4 Securitas started escorting prisoners. Hurd's triple safeguard in a limited area of policy switched to wholesale privatisation across a broad front.

So far from this account, it might appear that all Hurd did as Home Secretary was stimulate a vast quantity of measures designed to legislate crime out of existence. On the contrary, Hurd was always aware that legislation alone would not combat the rise in crime. As Home Secretary, he did not ignore the area of crime prevention. Although many of the initiatives were not his original idea, he was able to draw on existing ideas and research to enhance what was already in place. A Ministerial Group on Crime Prevention was established. Chaired first by Giles Shaw (Pudsey) and then by John Patten, it involved officials from eleven other Government departments. The aim of the Group was to press individual departments to introduce crime-prevention policies.[63]

'Neighbourhood Watch' and 'Home Watch' schemes had sprung up all over the country since 1982, but it was Douglas Hurd who presided over a massive expansion of these locally-based initiatives. To their critics, they were middle-class self-defence organisations. It is all too easy to be cynical about the public posturing of politicians about tackling crime, but Douglas Hurd was genuinely enthused when visiting new crime-prevention projects up and down the country. To him, Neighbourhood Watch schemes were real-life examples of active citizens, 'doers' rather than 'destroyers', joining together in 'little platoons' to re-create a sense of community. On 20 March 1987, in a speech to Conservatives in Wantage (next door to his Witney constituency), he made the link between crime prevention and civic duty:

> I am quite sure from visits to some of our inner cities that crime prevention
> in its widest sense is the key to bringing some spirit and civic sense back to
> the grisly housing estates which disfigure the heart or the outskirts of many
> of them.[64]

In practical terms, Hurd saw the Government's job as kick-starting the process from the Home Office crime-prevention centre at Stafford, but that local and specific projects stood the best chance of flourishing.

Hurd established a charitable organisation called Crime Concern, which was designed to publicise steps the public should take to tackle crimes in their communities. On the suggestion of John Patten, Hurd asked Steven Norris, the former Conservative MP for Oxford East who had been defeated at the 1987 General Election, to become Chairman.

In other areas of Home Office policy, Hurd took a more traditional Tory line, particularly with regard to immigration. On 16 November 1987, the Home Secretary opened the debate on the Second Reading of the Government's Immigration Bill. His remarks summarised the views of all Conservative Home Secretaries since Rab Butler:

> The Act [1971] was introduced in the belief that there is a limit to the extent to which a society can accept large numbers of people from different countries without unacceptable social tensions. That remains our view. It is not an anti-immigrant view; it is a realistic view.
>
> It would not be in the interests of the ethnic minorities themselves if there were a prospect of further mass inward movement. That prospect would increase social tensions, particularly in our cities. That is why we say that firm immigration control is essential if we are to have good community relations.[65]

The Immigration Act of 1988 was merely the concluding piece in a series of measures announced by Douglas Hurd designed to tighten the existing law on immigration. In 1986, Hurd imposed visa restrictions on citizens of Bangladesh, Ghana, India, Nigeria and Pakistan. His aim was to cut the volume of people clogging up the immigration system at Heathrow. The passengers from the five countries constituted over 50 per cent of those sent home.[66] Hurd argued it was sensible for operational reasons to assess claimants in their country of origin before they arrived in the UK.

Hurd's opposite number at the time, Gerald Kaufman, genuinely felt that Hurd's policy was 'personally humiliating for the visitors and shaming to this country's reputation'.[67] He believed the Conservatives were playing the race card in the run-up to the 1987 General Election, although on a personal level, Kaufman never saw Hurd resort to racism. In Kaufman's libertarian, non-racialist eyes, it seemed unfair that predominantly white visitors from Australia, New Zealand and Canada constituted three times the number of visitors from the five countries and yet Britain was picking on the most vulnerable group.

In March 1987, Hurd closed another immigration loophole by imposing charges of up to £1,000 on air carriers who brought people into the United Kingdom without a valid passport or identity documents. The move was precipitated by the case of sixty-four Tamils who had been duped by a group of racketeers into believing they could enter Britain without valid documents. Hurd made an exception with the Tamil case, but the new rules put the onus on carriers not to allow on board people who did not have the correct documents. Hurd claimed there was a clear distinction between people with a genuine and well-founded fear of persecution covered by international convention, and those seeking a materially higher standard of living.[68] However, as Gerald Kaufman pointed out, how would the carriers under the new Immigration (Carriers') Liability Act be able to distinguish between bona fide and bogus refugees?[69]

Hurd stood firm over the case of Viraq Mendis. Mendis was a Sri Lankan citizen who had arrived in the United Kingdom as a student in 1973 and had been granted visa extensions until August 1975. It appeared that Mr Mendis had failed his university examinations on three occasions and decided to overstay, disappearing without trace until May 1984, when he was arrested. Mendis then applied for political asylum, claiming that, as a Tamil separatist, his life would be in danger if he was deported to Sri Lanka. After being served with a deportation order, Mendis sought sanctuary in a church in the Hulme area of Manchester. On 18 January 1989, Mendis was seized from the Manchester church and the following day he lost two more hearings in the courts. Douglas Hurd's diary entries from the time indicate he was more concerned with the possible court reversals than the outcry from Church groups and Opposition MPs.[70] Under international pressure, Hurd stood his ground and Mendis – whose Tamil views later proved to be fabricated – was deported to Colombo. This stance on immigration whilst Home Secretary would strengthen his hand during the later row in the Conservative Party in 1989 and 1990 over the granting of Hong Kong passports (see Chapter 19).

In the case of the Muslim reaction to the publication of Salman Rushdie's *The Satanic Verses*, Hurd was faced with a race-relations problem requiring a more conciliatory tone. In February 1989, he entered the lion's den by addressing a meeting of Muslim leaders in Birmingham. Hurd recalls it as 'a very awkward occasion because it was trembling on the edge of a great deal of noise and it was just controlled.'[71] Hurd's diaries reflect this:

24 Feb. 1989: Central mosque, crowd, tension. TV lights and heat. Muslims explain the nature of the insult from *The Satanic Verses*. I expound arguments about freedom. Some disappointment, and tendency to shout, but well handled [by Muslim chairman].[72]

In his speech, Hurd said he was not seeking to offend the religious beliefs or cultural traditions of those who had come to settle in Britain, but no one in Britain was above the law. He acknowledged that British Muslims had been grieved and hurt by *The Satanic Verses*, but that did not give them the right to use violence or the threat of violence.[73]

In July 1987, Douglas Hurd received evidence from the Los Angeles-based Wiesenthal Centre pressing him to begin prosecutions against alleged Nazi war criminals living in the United Kingdom. Although the widespread perception at the time amongst Hurd's colleagues was that he was opposed to such a move, the actual story is rather different. It is correct to say that Hurd was initially reluctant to proceed further with an investigation into the alleged crimes. It was not so much political caution, but a worry about the accuracy of statements based on events which had occurred over forty years before. However, he admits to having been genuinely shaken by the weight of the horrors described in the Wiesenthal Report, and recalls having long arguments on the subject with Judy and with Max Hastings. He realised that it was perfectly possible to enact the legislation and not secure a conviction, because of the difficulty of getting evidence, but in his view that was no excuse for forgetting that crimes of this exceptional and horrific nature had taken place.[74]

In February 1988, Hurd proceeded with caution by asking Sir Thomas Hetherington, the former Director of Public Prosecutions, and Mr William Chalmers, formerly Crown Agent for Scotland, to investigate the allegations.[75]

In July 1989, Hetherington and Chalmers reported back, recommending that there should indeed be a change in the law to permit the prosecution in the United Kingdom of those accused of war crimes. English law did not then have jurisdiction to try offences of murder and manslaughter abroad when the accused was not a British citizen at the time of the offence. Therefore, there was a need for legislation to extend the jurisdiction of the courts.[76] The normal procedure was extradition, but all the alleged crimes took place in countries controlled by the Soviet Union, with which Britain had no extradition treaty.

The War Crimes Tribunal recommended retrospective legislation on the moral grounds that:

> The crimes committed are so monstrous that they cannot be condoned . . .
> To take no action would taint the United Kingdom with the slur of being a
> haven for war criminals.[77]

Hurd's subsequent statement to the House of Commons was delivered in a measured and non-partisan way, in recognition that the issue cut across the normal party lines – Hurd's own PPS, David Heathcoat-Amory, was strongly opposed to reopening the war-crimes cases.[78] Hurd resisted the temptation to widen the legislation to make possible the prosecution of criminals from any war found to be sheltering in Britain, believing correctly that this would complicate the issue still further. He drew back from rushing ahead with the legislation at the tail end of the 1988-89 session.

By the time the new session was under way, Hurd had been moved to the Foreign Office, and the responsibility for the legislation shifted to the new Home Secretary, David Waddington. The legislation eventually produced a constitutional crisis with the House of Lords. The Government subsequently invoked the Parliament Act of 1911 to force its will on the Upper House. After the second Lords rejection on 4 June 1990, Geoffrey Howe, Leader of the House of Commons, thought he had the support of Douglas Hurd and Malcolm Rifkind, Secretary of State for Scotland (most of the suspected war criminals were said to be in Scotland) in opposing the measure.[79] However, given Hurd's revelations that he was a quiet supporter of the war-crimes legislation, one doubts whether he would have backed Howe against David Waddington and Margaret Thatcher, who, given the 'Finchley factor', wanted to press ahead and overturn the Lords decision. At the Cabinet meeting on 21 June 1990, the view of David Waddington and the Prime Minister prevailed.

The subsequent failure to prosecute any of the alleged war criminals residing in Britain does not negate the fact that Hurd felt it was right in principle to pursue the cases because of the horrific nature of the crimes involved. It was important to show that Britain did not regard these crimes as in any way more acceptable with the passage of time.

Part of the reason for the onerous and burdensome nature of the post of Home Secretary is that there are certain areas of criminal-justice policy which are his sole responsibility – which he can neither discuss in Cabinet nor, in making the final decision, delegate to junior colleagues. During Hurd's period as Home Secretary, the most time-consuming and agonising examples of this isolation occurred in the area of miscarriages of justice.

Section 17 (1) of the Criminal Appeal Act of 1968 gave the Home Secretary the power to refer cases to the Court of Appeal's criminal division. The law appeared to give the Home Secretary unfettered powers of referral in every case – the wording was 'if he thinks fit' – but in practice every Home Secretary since 1968 restricted referral where fresh evidence had come to light, which had not been available to the original jury.

On 20 January 1987, in a statement to the House of Commons, Douglas Hurd elaborated at length on the proper role of the Home Secretary in deciding whether to refer miscarriages of justice to the Court of Appeal. In particular, he had in mind the three major cases of alleged miscarriages of justice dating back to the IRA's bombing campaign in mainland Britain in the 1970s: the Birmingham pub bombings, the Guildford and Woolwich pub-bombing cases and the conviction of the Maguire family (often known as the Maguire Seven). Since the 1970s, successive Home Secretaries had come under differing sorts of pressure from the general public, media and politicians to review individual cases. But, as Hurd said in his statement:

> In responding to these pressures, a Home Secretary must never allow himself to forget that he is an elected politician and that, under our system, the process of justice must be kept separate from the political process. It is open to others to say: 'If I were trying that case as a judge, I would have given a different summing up' or, 'If I had been on that jury, I would have reached a different verdict.' But it is not open to the Home Secretary simply to substitute his own view of the case for that of the courts. It would be an abuse of his powers if he were to act as though he or those who might advise him constituted some higher court of law.
>
> A different situation arises, of course, if new evidence or some new consideration of substance is produced which was not available at the trial or before the Court of Appeal. In any civilised system of justice, there must be a means whereby a case can be reopened so that new matters can be assessed alongside the old evidence by due process of law. This distinction between new evidence and differences of opinion about old evidence has governed the way in which my predecessors have used the power under section 17 of the 1968 Criminal Appeal Act to refer cases to the Court of Appeal.[80]

On this occasion, Hurd drafted the statement entirely on his own. Whatever the eventual weaknesses of the system (which Hurd himself would later acknowledge as Foreign Secretary) the clarity and logic of the statement is impressive. It became the *locus classicus* for cases of this kind, quoted by Home Office officials and judges alike.

Adhering closely to the criteria of new evidence, the Home Secretary decided to refer the cases of the 'Birmingham Six', on the grounds that there was new evidence casting doubt on the scientific test used during the trial – the Griess test – which had led the original jury to conclude that two of the men had handled nitroglycerine.

However, Hurd decided not to refer the two other major cases of alleged miscarriages of justice: the Guildford Four and the Maguire family.[81] Hurd argued that no new evidence had come to light in either of these cases, despite the evidence of the investigative journalist Robert Kee in his book *Trial and*

Error, published back in October 1986. The prosecution case against the Maguires had been based almost entirely on the results of thin-layer chromatography (TLC) tests which indicated that all seven defendants had handled nitroglycerine. Although Robert Kee claimed that the evidence had been contaminated, Hurd concluded there was no supporting evidence.

In the case of the Guildford Four, the convictions rested almost entirely on the confessions which the four men gave to the police. The 'Balcombe Street gang' of IRA terrorists claimed that they had carried out the bombings, but Hurd argued that this evidence was not new since the Court of Appeal in July 1977 had already concluded that the IRA had engaged in 'a cunning and skilful attempt to deceive the Court by putting forward false evidence'.[82]

Throughout the next six months the Home Secretary came under intense political pressure to refer the cases of the Guildford Four and the Maguire Seven to the Court of Appeal. Ever since 1979, Cardinal Basil Hume, Archbishop of Westminster, had campaigned vigorously on behalf of the Guildford Four. On 23 July 1987, Hume led a distinguished delegation to try to persuade Douglas Hurd to reopen the Guildford case. Prior to the meeting, Hume had sent Hurd a compendium of legal and factual material which, in the Cardinal's opinion, constituted new and substantial evidence. The prestigious group comprised two former Home Secretaries, Roy Jenkins and Merlyn Rees, and two distinguished judges, Lords Scarman and Devlin, together with Robert Kee. Hurd could not wholly escape from the issue even on holiday. Roy Jenkins recalls having dinner with Douglas Hurd in Italy in August 1987, and rather spoiling the occasion by saying that Basil Hume would never leave these cases alone as long as he was alive.[83]

After a leading article in *The Times* of 28 July 1987, criticising Hurd for stalling on the Guildford case, the Home Secretary penned a letter to the Editor, repeating his line about new and substantial evidence.[84] But he showed signs of movement by revealing that, since his decision not to refer in January, he was considering the possibility that new evidence had come to light. In particular, he mentioned testimony by Mrs Yvonne Fox, purporting to provide an alibi for Paul Hill, one of the accused, on the night of the Woolwich bombings which was revealed on the *First Tuesday* programme on 3 March.[85] Hill's confession was crucial to the Guildford case because it was his confessions which implicated the other three men.

There were other factors in Hurd's deliberations. One concerned the fate of Carole Richardson. Hurd did not think she was the sort of person who should be in prison:

> Part of my worry was that if I referred it, and the Court of Appeal confirmed the verdict, which I thought they would, the chances of getting Carole Richardson out a bit early, would have been very much reduced.[86]

Amongst the upper echelons of the judiciary, there was great sensitivity about the Guildford case. The Lord Chancellor in 1987 was Lord Havers, who as Sir Michael Havers, QC had been prosecuting counsel in both the original trials. The Master of the Rolls, Sir John Donaldson (later Lord Donaldson of Lymington), was the judge at both trials.

Another extremely important factor in Hurd's deliberations was the output of his officials in 'C3', the Home Office Division responsible for miscarriages of justice cases. Throughout his time at the Home Office, Hurd was aware of the power of the officials who filtered the evidence, the people who sifted the information before it arrived on his desk. Although he praised the work of his officials throughout, C3's reports were, in effect, at two removes from the actual raw evidence. Hurd became increasingly irritated by the procedures of C3 rather than the officials themselves. Also, C3 was constrained by the fact that its work was paid for out of the relevant police force budgets, and interminable debates took place over which force footed the bill.

On 14 August 1987, Hurd decided to order a special police investigation into the Guildford case under James Sharples, deputy Chief Constable of Avon and Somerset police. The purpose was to establish the extent of the evidence provided by Mrs Yvonne Fox giving an alibi for Paul Hill and another woman, Moira Kelly, who claimed she was with Carole Richardson in London at the time she was supposed to be preparing for the Guildford bombing.

Another ever-present consideration which played on Douglas Hurd's mind was that he risked receiving a bloody nose if the Court of Appeal threw a referral back in his face. His caution in referring the Guildford case was partly justified when the Court of Appeal threw back the case of the Birmingham Six on 28 January 1988. Lord Lane delivered a stinging rebuke to Hurd implying that the case should not have been referred in the first place: 'The longer the hearing has gone on the more this court has been convinced the jury was correct.'[87]

During the Christmas recess of 1988-89, Hurd took the Guildford files home to Westwell, as he had done in late 1986-early 1987 with the Birmingham cases. This was about the only time of year that he could look through the files for hours in succession without fear of interruption:

> 29 Dec. 1988: Pore over Guildford case for the umpteenth time and decide to refer.[88]

On 16 January 1989, the Home Secretary announced in a written answer to the House of Commons his decision to refer the case of the Guildford Four back to the Court of Appeal.[89] Shortly before Hurd moved to the Foreign Office, the Court of Appeal quashed the convictions of the Guildford Four on

19 October 1989.[90] On the instructions of the Court of Appeal, criminal investigations were launched by the Director of Public Prosecutions into alleged malpractice by Surrey police officers. The Home Secretary responded immediately by ordering a judicial inquiry into the Guildford case and the Maguire cases under Sir John May, a newly retired Lord Justice of Appeal.[91] Although Hurd expressed regret at the wrongful convictions, a week later he created a row in the House of Commons by saying:

> I hope that Opposition Members in their pursuit of this matter, will take into account the fact that the people who suffered most from it were not those who were wrongfully imprisoned but those who were murdered at Guildford.[92]

Despite being asked by Clare Short, Labour MP for Birmingham, Ladywood, to retract his comments, Hurd said he was merely making a statement of fact. Fact maybe, but the remark was uncharacteristically insensitive, and did not chime with his sense of fairness throughout his deliberation of the three cases.

The collapse of the Guildford case inevitably led to the collapse of the case against the Maguire family. On 14 March 1991, the Court of Appeal quashed the convictions against the Birmingham Six. The Government responded to the public disquiet by launching a Royal Commission under Lord Runciman to review all stages of the criminal appeals process, including the Home Secretary's power to refer cases to the Court of Appeal.

By this time, Sir John May's own inquiry had been delayed by the need to proceed against three Surrey police officers accused of fabricating evidence (no cases were ever brought to trial). His final report recommended the establishment of a Criminal Cases Review Authority.[93] Sir John May then became a member of the Royal Commission which accepted his original recommendation. Although Hurd had become Foreign Secretary in October 1989 shortly after he had established the May inquiry, he retained a close interest in Home Office policy, and took the bold step of giving evidence before the May Inquiry on 2 October 1991.

When asked by Sir John May what had gone wrong in the Maguire case, Hurd replied:

> I think in this case and other cases, the system and the way it was handled turned out to be inadequate for the purposes of justice . . . There is a strong case for having a standing body, outside of political pressures, which has an investigative facility and which would have the right to refer cases direct to the Court of Appeal.[94]

It could be argued that Hurd moved a little too cautiously on the individual cases, particularly the Maguire Seven. Perhaps he was too ready to accept official versions of events. This is certainly the view of Gerald Kaufman.[95] However, if a Home Secretary fails to give the police and the judiciary the benefit of the doubt, he undermines the credibility of his own office. There was the delicate matter that many of the figures in the judiciary had presided over the original verdicts. Furthermore, if Hurd was to blame for being too slow to react, then he shares the blame with successive Home Secretaries since 1974; at least they developed an objective criteria by which to judge such cases. The painstaking way in which Hurd reviewed the cases suggests strong public-service instincts, and a sense of fairness. Throughout, Hurd showed a willingness to listen to representations. The eventual change to the independent Criminal Cases Review Commission in April 1997 as a result of the Criminal Appeal Act of 1995 owed in large part to Hurd's evidence to the May inquiry.[96]

After his retirement from the Foreign Office in June 1995, Hurd watched with mounting private irritation as the Home Secretary, Michael Howard, began to dismantle the liberal aspects of sentencing policy. It was not so much that Hurd's policies were deliberately designed to be liberal, but that their aim had been to prevent the dangers associated with overcrowded prisons. Michael Howard's recourse to populism, beginning at the notorious Conservative Party Conference of October 1993, eventually roused even the most emollient and tolerant former diplomat into revolt. Even then, Hurd would refrain from attacking Howard personally. But the contrast between the two politicians' styles as Home Secretary could not have been greater: while one man listened to advice, the other repeatedly ignored it in the quest for votes.

Notes

1. The Number 10 Home Office unit was headed by Hartley Booth, the lawyer and expert on extradition who was to succeed her as MP for Finchley in 1992.

2. Robert Crampton, interview with Douglas Hurd, 'I am not afraid of being called a liberal', *The Times*, 15 Jan. 1997.

3. Douglas Hurd, Lecture to Royal Institute of Public Administration, 13 Sept. 1986 (Draft copy).

4. Windlesham, *Responses to Crime: Penal Policy in the Making, vol. 2*, (Clarendon Press: Oxford, 1993), p. 209. I am particularly indebted to Lord Windlesham, Principal of Brasenose College, Oxford, for his advice and assistance for this chapter. He served as Minister of State at the Home Office from 1970 to 1972 and was Chairman of the Parole Board of England and Wales from 1982 to 1988. For those seeking a fuller account

of criminal justice policy in Britain from a liberal viewpoint, his three volumes entitled *Responses to Crime* (1987, 1993, 1996) are unparalleled in their insight.

5. Windlesham, *Responses to Crime: Penal Policy in the Making*, vol. 2, p. 21.

6. Robert Kilroy-Silk was MP for Ormskirk from Feb. 1974 to May 1983, then Knowsley, North from June 1983 to November 1986. He was Chairman of the Parliamentary All-Party Penal Affairs Group from 1979 to 1986. After a prolonged battle with Militant supporters, he left politics to become a television presenter.

7. Douglas Hurd, Lecture to Royal Institute of Public Administration, 19 Sept. 1986 (Draft copy); Laocoön was a priest in Greek legend who warned the Trojans against the wooden horse.

8. 'Secretaries on Home Secretaries', *Metline: Magazine of the Metropolitan Police Federation* (10th anniversary edn.), June 1997, p. 12.

9. Ibid.

10. Interview with Gerald Kaufman, 13 Nov. 1996.

11. H. of C. Deb. (6th Series), 29 Apr. 1986, vol. 96, col. 794.

12. Interview with Gerald Kaufman, 13 Nov. 1996.

13. Ibid.

14. Interview with Douglas Hurd, 17 Dec. 1996.

15. H. of C. Deb. (6th Series), 30 Mar. 1988, vol. 130, col. 1086.

16. H. of C. Deb. (6th Series), 17 Jul. 1987, vol. 119, col. 1299.

17. Diary Readings with Douglas Hurd, 26 Feb. 1997.

18. H. of C. Deb. (6th Series), 29 Apr. 1986, vol. 96, cols 795–8.

19. Diary Readings with Douglas Hurd, 26 Feb. 1997.

20. Interview with Douglas Hurd, 26 Feb. 1997.

21. Diary Readings with Douglas Hurd, 26 Feb. 1997.

22. Ibid. *see* also H. of C. Deb. (6th Series), 1 May 1986, vol. 96, cols 1110–24.

23. *Prison Disturbances: April 1990: Report of an Inquiry by Lord Justice Woolf and Judge Stephen Tumim, Cm. 1456*, HMSO, 1991.

24. Douglas Hurd, Speech to Prison Governors' Association, Queen Elizabeth II Centre, London, 23 Mar. 1988.

25. The prison system was near breaking-point with around 5,000 prisoners crammed three to a cell, 14,000 doubled up and a further 650 being held in unsatisfactory conditions in police cells; H. of C. Deb. (6th Series), 16 Jul. 1987, vol. 119, col. 1296.

26. Diary Readings with Douglas Hurd, 26 Feb. 1997.

27. *The Parole System in England and Wales, Report of the Review Committee, Cm. 532*, HMSO, 1988.

28. Diary Readings with Douglas Hurd, 26 Feb. 1997.

29. Ibid.

30. Ibid.

31. Ibid.

32. H. of C. Deb. (6th Series), 16 Jul. 1987, vol. 119, col. 1300.

33. Ivan Lawrence (Burton), Sir Eldon Griffiths (Bury St Edmunds), Nicholas Budgen (Wolverhampton, South West) Sir Nicholas Bonsor (Upminster), and Teddy Taylor (Southend, East) were among the others who voiced concern.

34. H. of C. Deb. (6th Series), 16 Jul. 1987, vol. 119, col. 1309.

35. *Daily Telegraph*, 18 Jul. 1987.

36. *The Times*, 4 May 1989.

37. *Prison Disturbances: April 1990: Report of an Inquiry by Lord Justice Woolf and Judge Stephen Tumim [Part II only]*, Cmnd. 1456, HMSO, 1991.

38. Interview with Douglas Hurd, 26 Feb. 1997.

39. Ibid.

40. The best description, in layman's terms, of peremptory challenge came from the Conservative Ivan Lawrence (Burton). Speaking in March 1987: 'At the beginning of a trial a jury is brought in. The jurors take the oath and stand in the witness box. If nobody challenges them, the twelve become the jury, but if counsel for the defence gets up and says "Challenge" that juryman stands down and somebody else comes forward, takes the oath and, if unchallenged stays.' H. of C. Deb. (6th Series), 31 Mar. 1987, vol. 132, col. 992.

41. The six Conservative MPs who voted against peremptory challenge were David Ashby (Leicestershire, North West), Nick Budgen (Wolverhampton, South West), Patrick Ground (Feltham and Heston), Ivan Lawrence (Burton), Jim Lester (Broxtowe) and Peter Thomas (Hendon, South). Of these, only Jim Lester was not a barrister, *see* H. of C. Deb. (6th Series), Div. No. 131, 31 Mar. 1987, vol. 113, col. 1000.

42. Ibid., col. 996.

43. For a fuller account *see* Windlesham, 'The Quest: Punishment in the Community', in *Responses to Crime. Penal Policy in the Making*, vol. 2, pp. 209–54.

44. Ibid., p. 210.

45. On 28 September 1987, Douglas Hurd chaired a one-day seminar at Leeds Castle in Kent. Ministers and officials discussed possible ways of improving crime prevention, enhancing the credibility of non-custodial sentencing and the probation service, tackling young reoffenders and ways of reducing prison overcrowding.

46. *Select Committee on Murder and Life Imprisonment*, H.ofL. Papers, 78 – I, HMSO, 1989.

47. H. of C. Deb. (6th Series), 18 May 1988, vol. 132, written answer, col.

466. The Home Office also sponsored more research on the topic at the University of Kent

48. *Cmnd. 2263*, HMSO, 1993.

49. The controversial area of pre-trial video evidence was explored by an Advisory Group on Video Evidence under Judge Pigot which reported in December 1989. The Pigot Report concluded that pre-trial evidence was appropriate in trials for sexual assaults and cases of cruelty and neglect in children under fourteen. It recommended extending video evidence in sexual cases to all children under seventeen.

50. H. of C. Deb. (6th Series), 16 Jul. 1987, vol. 119, col. 1303.

51. Interview with Douglas Hurd, Westwell, 13 Jun. 1997.

52. *HC 291, Home Affairs Committee, Fourth Report, Session 1986–87: Contract Provision of Prisons*, HMSO, 1987.

53. *Private-sector Involvement in the Remand System, Cm. 434*, HMSO, 1988.

54. H. of C. Deb. (6th Series), vol. 130, 30 Mar. 1988, cols 1083–98; Douglas Hurd first hinted at a change in policy over prison privatisation on 23 March 1988 during a speech to the Prison Governors' Association held at the Queen Elizabeth II Conference Centre in London.

55. Ibid., col. 1084.

56. H. of C. Deb. (6th Series), 1 Mar. 1989, vol. 148, col. 277.

57. Ibid., col. 282.

58. Ibid., col. 278.

59. Ibid., col. 278, 280.

60. Ibid., col.279.

61. Windlesham, *Responses to Crime: Penal Policy in the Making*, vol. 2, p. 295–6.

62. Ibid., pp. 298, 422–7.

63. H. of C. Deb. (6th Series), 8 May 1986, vol. 97, col. 278.

64. Douglas Hurd, Extract, Speech to a Conservative Lunch at Wantage, 20 Mar. 1987 (Conservative Party News Service, 188/87).

65. H. of C. Deb. (6th Series), 16 Nov. 1987, vol. 122, col. 779.

66. H. of C. Deb. (6th Series), 21 Oct. 1986, vol. 102, col. 948.

67. Ibid., col. 949.

68. H. of C. Deb. (6th Series), 3 Mar. 1987, vol. 111, col. 740.

69. Ibid., col. 742.

70. Douglas Hurd, Diary, 18–20 Jan. 1989.

71. Interview with Douglas Hurd, 26 Feb. 1997.

72. Diary Readings with Douglas Hurd, 26 Feb. 1997.

73. Douglas Hurd, Race Relations and the Rule of Law, Birmingham Central Mosque, 24 Feb. 1989.

74. Interview with Douglas Hurd, 20 Jan. 1997.

75. For Hurd's initial statement on War Crimes, *see* H. of C. Deb. (6th Series), 8 Feb. 1988, vol. 127, cols 28–36.

76. Tom Bower, 'Should we make the Nazis pay?', *The Times*, 20 Oct. 1989.

77. War Crimes, *Report of the War Crimes Inquiry, Cm. 744*, HMSO, 1989. The second half of the report, detailing the merits of individual cases, was not published in order to avoid prejudicing any future proceedings. H. of C. Deb. (6th Series), 24 Jul. 1989, vol. 157, col. 733.

78. Interview with David Heathcoat-Amory, 22 Jul. 1996.

79. Geoffrey Howe, *Conflict of Loyalty* (Macmillan: London, 1994), pp. 626–7.

80. H. of C. Deb. (6th Series), 20 Jan. 1987, vol. 108, col. 735.

81. The 'Guildford Four' comprised Patrick Armstrong, Gerard Conlon, Paul Hill and Carole Richardson. The Maguire family referred to Mrs Maguire and her husband Patrick, two of their sons, Vincent and Patrick, their brother-in-law Patrick 'Guiseppe' Conlon (who died in jail), Patrick O'Neill and Sean Smyth.

82. H. of C. Deb. (6th Series), 20 Jan. 1987, vol. 108, col. 737.

83. Interview with Lord Jenkins of Hillhead, 12 Nov. 1996.

84. Douglas Hurd, 'Letter to the Editor', *The Times*, 30 Jul. 1987.

85. Ibid.

86. Interview with Douglas Hurd, 20 Jan. 1997.

87. *The Times*, 29 Jan. 1988.

88. Diary Readings with Douglas Hurd, 26 Feb. 1997.

89. H. of C. Deb. (6th Series), 16 Jan. 1989, vol. 145, written answers, cols 8–10.

90. Court of Appeal, Law Report, *The Times*, 20 Oct. 1989.

91. H. of C. Deb. (6th Series), 20 Oct. 1989, vol. 158, cols 278–80.

92. H. of C. Deb. (6th Series), 26 Oct. 1989, vol. 158, col. 1039.

93. H.C. 296, *Second Report on the Maguire Case*, HMSO, 1992.

94. *The Guardian*, 3 Oct. 1991. On giving evidence to the full Royal Commission, Kenneth Clarke, the new Home Secretary, concurred with Douglas Hurd's view. Windlesham, *Responses to Crime*, vol. 3, p. 395.

95. Interview with Gerald Kaufman, 13 Nov. 1996.

96. Windlesham, *Responses to Crime: Legislating with the Tide*, vol. 3 (Clarendon Press: Oxford, 1996) p. 393; *see* also 'Criminal Appeals: An Orderly Reform' Chapter Ten, pp. 385–432.

13

The State Versus the Citizen:
A Question of Balance

'The bonds of words are too weak to bridle men's ambitions, avarice, anger and other passions without the fear of some coercive power.'
– Thomas Hobbes, *Leviathan* (Everyman edition: London, 1914)

Throughout his ministerial career, the overriding public and media impression of Douglas Hurd has been of a politician with a safe pair of hands. Much more than any other minister in the Thatcher and Major Governments, Hurd has suffered from an unusually high number of clichés. He is variously known as the Tory grandee, who keeps himself above the fray, or as the cool, headmasterly statesman or mandarin, who deals with crises in a detached, authoritative manner. In some senses, the image conforms to reality. As Home Secretary, Hurd did display an air of calm authority in crises such as Westland in January 1986, and the prisons dispute in the spring of 1986. He was quiet but effective in cultivating the press; he enjoyed the respect of most of the political commentators. The Prime Minister continued to admire his overall competence and, despite a few rough patches of media criticism, the clichés about competence always returned.

In another sense, Hurd's reputation for competence had to do with his style of presenting himself in the media and the House of Commons. Despite being naturally very reserved, he deliberately cultivated a statesmanlike air. The paradox was that, despite being scornful of the growth of image makers and sound-bite politicians,[1] Hurd took great care over his choice of words and his appearance: his immaculate quiff of hair, the herring-bone shirt with matching tie and handkerchief, and nicely tailored suits. As Foreign Secretary, he became renowned for his oddly-shaped German Loden overcoat. But, it was never a natural, comfortable style. Some commentators found it high-minded and detached, somehow lacking in warmth or passion. They disliked his droning voice with its odd vowel sounds, and the awkward use of hand gestures as he spoke – characteristics which were not so apparent when talking to friends in private. Alan Clark, the roguish erstwhile Minister of Trade, famously remarked that Douglas Hurd had a split personality:

> *A deux* he [Douglas Hurd] is delightful; clever, funny, observant, drily cynical. But get him anywhere near 'display mode', particularly if there are officials around, and he might as well have a corncob up his arse. Pompous, trite, high-sounding, cautiously guarded.[2]

It was as though Hurd deliberately slipped into this ministerial 'display mode' whenever he appeared in public. The whole approach looked and sounded confident and competent and therefore it was perceived as such. But was this perception of ministerial competence justified?

Unlike the Foreign Office, which is rarely required to pilot legislation through the House of Commons, the Home Office is normally responsible for the passage of at least one major bill per session, plus two or three other minor bills. During Hurd's period as Home Secretary, there were an unusually burdensome number of controversial bills, especially in the 1987 to 1992 Parliament. Even at the time, Douglas Hurd felt that there was a growing tendency for ill-considered legislation to be rushed through the House of Commons without proper scrutiny, which resulted in Parliament subsequently having to alter flawed legislation. Did this apply to some of the major bills which Hurd piloted through the House of Commons from 1985 to 1989?

One of Hurd's early mistakes occurred on the Second Reading of the Shops Bill [Lords]. In an off-the-cuff exchange with Ted Rowlands, in which the Labour MP for Merthyr Tydfil and Rhymney asked the Home Secretary for a guarantee that at no stage after Second Reading would he seek to move a guillotine, Hurd unwisely replied, 'I gladly give that guarantee.'[3] Hurd was clear in his own mind that the Government did not have the votes to secure a guillotine (a parliamentary procedure designed to curtail debate), but he acknowledges in his diary:

> 14 April 1986: It was ruled out in my mind, but it wasn't ruled out by the whips.[4]

In fact, his unscripted remarks did not make a difference to the final result – the vote was by that time lost – but Hurd admits it was an error which 'showed parliamentary inexperience'.[5]

In his diary that evening, he vented his feelings:

14 Apr. 1986: We lose by 14. Something of a relief to see the damn bill buried.[6]

The remarks were perhaps an exaggeration, a spur-of-the-moment reaction to the defeat. But Hurd is right to concede that, at that point in his ministerial career, he was inexperienced in piloting legislation through the House of Commons. Even by April 1986, most of Hurd's ministerial experience had been confined to the Foreign Office. Although he had spent sixteen months as a Minister of State at the Home Office, his handling of the Police and Criminal Evidence Bill had not shown him in his best light. His year in Northern Ireland had not involved a great deal of contact with the House of Commons, despite the continuation of direct rule.

Hurd could comfort himself that, his error apart, the dramatic defeat of the Government on the Second Reading of the Shops Bill [Lords] on 14 April 1986, represented a collective failure of the Government: the entire Cabinet had supported the deregulation of Sunday trading, only to be thwarted by a large group of their own backbenchers who felt that the issue was one of conscience which should have been subject to a free vote and not a three-line whip. Defeats of this kind were exceptionally rare. It was only the second time since 1924 that a Government had lost a vote on Second Reading.

Intellectually, Hurd accepted the need for reform, since the existing legislation had become indefensible.[7] The 1950 Act was being widely flouted by DIY stores, with some councils attempting to prosecute errant companies while others turned a blind eye. The Act had also become riddled with anomalies: Chinese takeaways could open on Sundays (because they were not foreseen in 1950), but fish and chip shops could not. Despite the near unanimous view that the law needed to be changed, Hurd soon discovered widely differing views within the Conservative Party about the nature of the change which should be made.

On 20 May 1985, the House took note of the findings of the Auld Committee,[8] voting by a majority of twenty in favour of its findings.[9] The warning signals should have been apparent. Despite a three-line whip, twenty-five Conservative backbenchers voted against the Auld proposals and a further eighty abstained or were not present.[10] On reflection, the Government decided not to tamper with the law in Scotland, which was already more deregulated than England, but the Auld Committee's proposals for total deregulation appeared in the Queen's Speech of November 1985 as the Shops Bill [Lords].

By starting the Bill in the House of Lords, the Government hoped to avoid burdening the House of Commons with yet another controversial piece of legislation in the 1985-86 session. In the House of Commons, Douglas Hurd was already responsible for piloting three other major bills through the House of Commons – on animal experimentation, public order and drug trafficking. During the debate on Home Affairs at the beginning of the session, the Home Secretary confessed to having 'some mixed feelings about the load of legislation which we in the Home Office have put on ourselves in the coming Session'.[11] With the benefit of hindsight, the Home Office's legislative programme was too congested in the 1985-86 session, and the same could be said for the next two sessions.

Apart from one Government defeat on an amendment securing shopworker protection,[12] the Bill gained its Third Reading in the House of Lords with little opposition on 25 February 1986. However, the Government had made the mistake of giving the opponents of the Bill, inside and outside Parliament, time to organise their campaign. From a disparate band of Church groups emerged a powerful coalition in the shape of the 'Keep Sunday Special' campaign.

In contrast to the determined efforts of the anti-Sunday trading lobby, those groups which supported the Shops Bill were initially complacent, believing that because they had secured the Government's support for the Bill, given its large majority, they were assured of success. As the Government became embarrassed by the tiny numbers of letters being received by the Home Office in favour of the Bill, groups such as the National Consumer Council (NCC) and 'Open Shop', comprising five major retailers – Woolworths, Asda, W.H. Smith, Harris Queensway and Habitat/Mothercare – encouraged their customers to write to the Home Office expressing support for a change in the law.

In February 1986, Hurd responded to the concerns of backbenchers by sending them a briefing paper, outlining the anomalies of the existing system and putting the case for total deregulation.[13] But, the alarm bells started ringing in the Whips Office in late March when a large number of MPs, mostly Conservative, signed two early day motions, one calling for a free vote on the Bill (attracting eighty-five Conservative signatures) and the other calling on the Government to have regard for the special character of Sunday (which attracted the support of sixty-five Conservative MPs). It was decided at Cabinet on 10 April that a three-line whip would be issued on Second Reading, with free votes being promised at committee and report stages. In addition, a Special Standing Committee would be set up to take oral and written evidence. Douglas Hurd hoped that the existence of a standing committee would allow all sides a say over the details of the Bill. However, he underestimated the Conservative rebels' anger over the Government's decision to issue a three-line whip on an issue which they considered to be one of personal conscience. In effect, the existence of a three-line whip encouraged the rebels to kill off the Bill on Second Reading.

The Government's overall handling of the Bill had hardly been astute. The Auld Report had outlined a perfectly rational case in favour of reform, but it was not a political document. In retrospect, more time should have been spent analysing how best to find a way through the political opposition to the Bill. Also, the Cabinet were not willing to make compromises on worker protection or legislation which fell short of total deregulation – moves which might have given Hurd a chance of reducing the number of Conservative rebels. The Government used the wrong method of legislating on Sunday trading. When the Conservative Party tentatively returned to the issue in 1994, the House of Commons was presented with a series of free votes on three main options, total deregulation, modification, and partial deregulation. It was the last of these three which became the favoured option in the Sunday Trading Act of 1994.[14]

The defeat of the Shops Bill occurred at a bad time for the Government, coming soon after the Westland Affair. More significantly, on the very evening that the Shops Bill fell, American F-111 bombers were taking off from British airbases to launch air strikes on Tripoli. Douglas Hurd was not among the small group of senior ministers consulted about the merits of the raid, whereas Geoffrey Howe, the Foreign Secretary, George Younger, the Defence Secretary, Michael Havers, the Attorney-General and William Whitelaw, the Deputy Prime Minister, were. In effect, Mrs Thatcher presented her other Cabinet ministers with a *fait accompli*. She had already given President Reagan permission before the Overseas and Defence Committee met. Hurd describes the meeting in his diaries as 'quite rough'.[15] According to Hugo Young, Douglas Hurd was among those who voiced criticism of the American raid, along with Nigel Lawson, Norman Tebbit, John Biffen and Kenneth Baker.[16] This has since been confirmed by Douglas Hurd.[17]

Before his error over the Shops Bill, Hurd had enjoyed the best period of media coverage in his ministerial career thus far. There was a widespread perception amongst the political commentators that his handling of the Handsworth riots and the prison officers' dispute had been calm and authoritative. His reputation was further enhanced by good media performances during the Westland crisis. In these respects, he was seen as a rising political star in the potential Conservative leadership stakes amongst backbenchers and political commentators alike. But his slip over the Shops Bill checked that rise and from then on until the outbreak of the Gulf War in 1990, he became embroiled in piloting a particularly heavy raft of Home Office legislation through the House of Commons.

After experiencing months of tension over prison overcrowding in the summer of 1987, Douglas Hurd and Judy welcomed the chance to holiday with

Woodrow Wyatt and his wife in Italy. However, the end of their holiday was interrupted with the news on 19 August 1987 that Michael Ryan had run amok with a self-loading Kalashnikov rifle, killing sixteen people in the Berkshire village of Hungerford. On the Sunday after the killings (23 August), Hurd went to Hungerford to survey the scene of the massacre, visiting Mrs Brereton, the widow of the police constable who was shot, and then called in to see some of the survivors recovering in hospital at nearby Swindon. On 27 August, he also attended the dignified funeral of PC Brereton at the village of Shaw near Newbury. Almost immediately, Hurd launched a Home Office inquiry into possible changes to the gun law, but he resisted those urging for emergency legislation to be rushed through before Parliament reassembled in the autumn.

On 2 December 1987, Hurd brought forward his White Paper to the House of Commons. It proposed to extend the types of firearms prohibited under the Firearms Act of 1968 to include full-bore, self-loading rifles, burst-fire weapons and short-barrelled, self-loading or pump-action shotguns – weapons which he viewed as having no legitimate sporting use. An amendment would be added to the Criminal Justice Bill (which was going through Parliament at the time) to increase to life imprisonment the maximum penalty for carrying firearms in furtherance of crime. A clause was also added which raised the maximum penalty for possession of a shotgun without a certificate to three years or a fine or both.

The Home Secretary announced he was tightening the requirements for the ownership of shotguns. The police would be required to keep a detailed register of all shotgun owners, and would have new powers to refuse a shotgun certificate if a gun owner could not provide a good reason for possession. All shotguns would be required by law to be held in a secure place in the home when not in use, subject to inspection by the police. No shot-gun ammunition could be purchased without the production of a valid certificate, although a third party could buy ammunition on behalf of the gun holder. Firearms dealers would have to keep detailed records of gun transactions, which would be made available to the police in order to trace illegal firearms.[18]

Immediately, Hurd faced criticism, not so much from the Opposition members who generally wanted to tighten gun laws still further, but from supporters of the wildfowl lobby. Led by Hector Monro, Conservative Member for Dumfries and Galloway, they claimed that the Home Secretary's proposals would create resentment in the shooting world.[19]

Hurd fully intended to consult as widely as possible with interested parties before Second Reading, but the only thing which was clear from his statement was its woolly drafting. When former Home Secretary Merlyn Rees queried Hurd as to the exact requirements of a 'fit and proper person' to run a gun club, Hurd replied lamely, 'We shall have to refine and develop that matter.'[20]

There was a lack of firearms expertise in the Home Office at the time. The Bill did not specify the number of rounds of ammunition, its provisions excluded Northern Ireland, and there was inadequate provision for compensation.[21] The Bill was effectively rewritten at Report Stage, when the Government finally introduced a new clause to extend its scope to Northern Ireland. The time for debate was curtailed three times at Report Stage, which ended in high farce as forty-seven amendments in a row were passed with MPs voting in their 'places' or seats, instead of voting in the division lobbies.[22]

Perhaps there were mitigating circumstances. Any attempt to alter the firearms legislation would have provoked a rebellion from libertarians and the wildfowl lobby. Moreover, the Bill was always going to be influenced by the moral panic, the knee-jerk reaction to the events at Hungerford. On later reflection, could one really legislate against a madman? Douglas Hurd at least resisted the temptation to legislate before the summer recess and took time to listen to the various pressure groups. He did make concessions after a succession of defeats in Committee, endured by Douglas Hogg, the Parliamentary Under Secretary of State at the Home Office. Hogg was faced with a genuine backbench revolt, supported by a well-organised firearms lobby, conducted via such organisations as the British Shooting Sports Council (BSSC) and the British Association for Shooting and Conservation (BASC).[23]

The ranks of the rebels were swelled by Conservatives offended by the use of guillotines to curtail debate, and libertarians like John Biffen, MP for Shropshire North. The old sage made a mischievous reference to the Conservative Government's interference in the liberties of the individual:

> I want to speak on behalf of what I believe to be the silent majority in the House – the publicans and sinners. We have been given some welcome respite from the foghorn of conscience that has been blasted through the chamber over the past few days.[24]

Outside the House of Commons, Auberon Waugh launched personal attacks on the Home Secretary, christening him 'Nanny Hurd' in a series of articles in *The Spectator* magazine.[25] The gist of Waugh's argument was essentially the same as that which John Biffen was making: that the Conservatives were making moral homilies, and legislating in areas where the individual should be left to his or her own devices. Waugh argued that Hurd had betrayed his class – Hurd's father was a farmer and Editor of *The Field* – by infringing the rights of traditional Conservative supporters to engage in their favourite sport, whilst alienating them from the police.

At the end of his speech on Second Reading, Douglas Hurd expressed the hope that his reform of firearms law would 'last at least another twenty years'.[26] .

His aspirations were shattered when another madman, Thomas Hamilton, massacred eleven schoolchildren in the Scottish town of Dunblane on that dreadful day on 13 March 1996. In response to the public outcry after the massacre, the Government established an inquiry under Lord Cullen, which led to the introduction of the Firearms (Amendment) Act of 1997, banning 80 per cent of hand-guns and heavily regulating the remainder. The main difference between the two tragedies was that, after Dunblane, unlike Hungerford, the relatives of the victims launched a vigorous campaign ('Snowdrop') to seek a complete ban on hand-guns. After receiving many letters from owners of hand-guns, Hurd expressed concern that Parliament was rushing through an unworkable piece of legislation. Was the House of Commons listening to the arguments in a dispassionate way or were they responding to the emotional demands of the aggrieved relatives?[27]

During his four years as Home Secretary, Douglas Hurd presided over a large number of measures which sought to curb the rights of the individual. The best-forgotten football identity card scheme was a case in point.

The impetus for the introduction of the Football Spectators Bill [Lords] came from the final report of Mr Justice Popplewell into crowd safety and control at football grounds, which was published on 16 January 1986. In his final report,[28] Popplewell's main recommendation was the introduction of a club membership card scheme which would only apply to the supporters of the visiting team. This marked a reversal from his interim report which had recommended a full membership scheme. In January 1986, the Home Secretary accepted the main recommendations of the Popplewell inquiry relating to safety at sports grounds.

On the wider issue of compulsory identity cards for all citizens, Hurd asked the police in July 1988 for an assessment of their viability. Their view was that the advantages outweighed the diasadvantages. Although the police subsequently changed their view during the Michael Howard era, Douglas Hurd remained firmly opposed to compulsory identity cards. During the Major Government, Hurd formed an atypical alliance on the issue with Cabinet ministers from the libertarian right, such as Peter Lilley, to block the move.

After Popplewell, football clubs failed to respond to Douglas Hurd and Margaret Thatcher's urgings to introduce a voluntary scheme.[29] The failure of the clubs to respond was used as one of Hurd's arguments for introducing a football identity card scheme.

The passage through Parliament of the Football Spectators Bill [Lords] was the joint responsibility of the Department of the Environment – in particular the Minister for Sport, Colin Moynihan – and the Home Office. The muddle which followed demonstrated a lack of understanding of football supporters and the needs of the game in general on the part of both the police and that of most ministers, including Douglas Hurd, Colin Moynihan and the Prime Minister.

As previously described (see Chapter 11), Hurd's first impression on visiting the scene of the Hillsborough disaster on 16 April 1989 was that there had been one or possibly two police blunders. In particular, Hurd had in mind the decision of Superintendent Roger Marshall of South Yorkshire police, who gave the order to let thousands of supporters into the stadium because he feared a wall was about to collapse on them. Secondly, there appears to have been a clear breakdown in communication between the police outside the ground and those inside. It remains a mystery why the on-the-spot judgement of an experienced Home Secretary was not taken into account during the Taylor Report into the stadium tragedy.

After visiting the scene of the tragedy, Hurd acted swiftly by establishing an inquiry under Lord Justice Taylor of Gosforth to look into the question of crowd control and football safety.[30] But, on 17 April 1989, Hurd announced in the House of Commons the Government's decision to proceed with the Football Spectators Bill [Lords] after what he termed 'a pause for the sake of seemliness'.[31] One must seriously question the initial decision to proceed with the Bill. During the Home Secretary's statement, not a single Conservative MP spoke in support of Hurd's decision to proceed. In particular, Hurd faced criticism from three distinguished Conservative backbenchers: Sir Neil Macfarlane, the former Minister for Sport, John Carlisle, Chairman of the Tory Backbench Sports Committee and Sir Fergus Montgomery, a long-serving member of the Select Committee on the Environment.[32] However, Conservative backbenchers and ministers were divided between those who wanted to abandon the Bill altogether, those who wanted to abandon the Bill but legislate afresh on the basis of the Taylor Report (Douglas Hurd's view), and other senior ministers (including, eventually Mrs Thatcher) who wished to push on with the whole Bill after a seemly pause. Earlier in the day, Hurd had asked to see the Prime Minister and other relevant ministers attended:

> 17 Apr. 1989: We try to move her out of the trenches. Broadly, I say, she should aim to get rid of terraces, appoint a supremo, and sublimate the bill. Nick Ridley supported me. She reacts stormily. The others are not much help. She eventually relents a bit, so we now have some postponement of the bill. It's a question of how we make use of this pause. Then I made a statement at 3.30. Doesn't go particularly well because I'm hooked on the bill. Let it soldier on. Prime Minister and the ranks quite pleased but no real runs.[33]

The next day, Hurd had more discussions with the Department of the Environment:

> 18 Apr. 1989: Ebb and flow all day on the subject as DOE views change. Ends with Nick Ridley evidently planning to push the bill right through in May, which I doubt will work.[34]

Then the following day:

> 19 Apr. 1989: I rang Nick Ridley at breakfast and find that he is indeed thinking of pushing ahead with football bill in May. This is [Colin] Moynihan pushing from below and the PM from above, but the backbench and the PPSs' revolt now pervasive. By tea-time, when we meet with Wakeham, Waddington etc., we agree we must postpone to spillover or new session. But shall we move the Prime Minister? If not we shall go smash into the buffers.[35]

In the middle of these discussions, a row was going on over the Lord Chancellor's legal reforms: one issue piled itself on top of another.

On Thursday, 20 April, a meeting was held by senior ministers before the full Cabinet[36] to discuss how to keep the Bill afloat:

> 20 Apr. 1989: More ministerial meetings. M.T. all over the place. Constantly interrupting. Not a full storm, but exasperating. [Bernard] Ingham and Moynihan egg her towards intransigence. Gradually, we wear her down from an Act in July to an Act in November, which might give time for Taylor's interim report, which is the crucial point.[37]

That afternoon, John Wakeham, Leader of the House, standing in for the Prime Minister, hinted at a change of policy by saying that no new date had been set for the Third Reading of the Bill in the Lords. But, at a meeting that evening between Douglas Hurd and Nicholas Ridley (Environment Secretary), the line about a seemly pause was dropped. Eventually, a compromise was hammered out, despite resistance from Mrs Thatcher, delaying Royal Assent for the Bill so that the findings of Lord Taylor's interim report, due out in the autumn of 1989, could be incorporated into the final Bill. However, this compromise came unstuck on 25 April when Hurd was informed at a private meeting with Taylor that the interim report would not be ready before the spillover. Hurd commented that night:

> 25 Apr. 1989: So the cat will be back among the pigeons.[38]

Hurd's prediction proved right. At a meeting next day with senior ministers, he noted:

> 26 Apr. 1989: We're back on the old horns now that Taylor is unlikely to give an opinion before September on the membership scheme . . . DOE ministers now in retreat. Business managers braver.[39]

The Government – and most especially the Prime Minister – remained anxious to pursue the fight against football hooliganism. Part II of the Bill gave the courts powers to impose restriction orders on convicted hooligans to prevent them from travelling to matches abroad. Despite the doubts hanging over the membership-card scheme contained in Part I, the Government pushed through a Second Reading vote on 27 June 1989. Because of the shared responsibility for the Bill between the Home Office and the Department for the Environment, Nicholas Ridley (opening the debate) and the Minister for Sport, Colin Moynihan (winding up) were left with the task of placating the Conservative rebels. In the end, the Government survived with a comfortable majority of seventy-eight, but fifteen Conservative MPs rebelled on a three-line whip.[40] After the summer recess, the Bill was passed into law with the national membership scheme intact.[41]

In January 1990, Lord Justice Taylor expressed 'grave doubts' about the impact on public safety of a national membership scheme.[42] The Government accepted his view, and abandoned the scheme, but instead of apologising to the football authorities and football fans everywhere, David Waddington, Hurd's successor at the Home Office, said that he might come back to the scheme at a future date.[43] It is often forgotten that the provision for a national membership scheme still exists in law and, technically at least, can be introduced without the approval of Parliament.

Curiously, given Mrs Thatcher's genuine empathy with and concern for the injured victims and their families at Hillsborough, her memoirs make only a passing reference to the Heysel stadium disaster, and no mention whatever of the worst disaster in British sporting history. She showed instransigence by deciding not to withdraw the Football Spectators Bill, despite pressure from the Conservative backbenches and from Douglas Hurd. The failure to implement Part I of the Football Spectators Bill was yet another example of Mrs Thatcher's tendency to take up half-formed, contradictory views on subjects about which she knew little. In her third term, she seemed obsessed with trying to eliminate wrongdoing by producing legislation which curbed civil liberties.

As Home Secretary, Hurd was not so much socially authoritarian, as deeply worried about the collapse of social responsibility and self-discipline on the part of the young. This was particularly the case when Hurd responded to the rise in drunken behaviour by 'lager louts' in market towns across Britain:

> You do not find much poverty or social deprivation there. What you find are too many young people with too much money in their pockets, too many pints inside them, but too little self-discipline and too little notion of the care and responsibilities which they owe to others.[44]

In an attempt to tackle the wider problems associated with alcohol misuse, Hurd established a new ministerial group chaired by John Wakeham, the Leader of the House. The group was extremely effective in changing society's perceptions towards drink-driving: attitudes shifted from seeing such behaviour as a silly mistake to the view that it was totally unacceptable.

However, attempts to cut overall alcohol consumption came up against the bulwark of the Treasury. In his memoirs, Nigel Lawson recalls that in 1989 Douglas Hurd led a deputation of ministers from the group urging him to increase taxes on alcohol in the following Budget in order to tackle the problem of drunken behaviour among the young. The Chancellor ignored their advice on the grounds that the move would be inflationary, that the demand for alcohol was inelastic and that determined drinkers would merely switch to drinking products which carried a lower duty.[45]

Journalist Michael Trend penned an article entitled 'Losing Our Liberties – By Law' in *The Spectator* magazine on 21 November 1987, in which he accused the Home Office of responding too readily to events by introducing a host of new laws which restricted the liberties of the citizen.[46]

Hurd responded in *The Spectator* two weeks later in a piece entitled 'Statutes of Liberty'. In his defence, Hurd returned to one of his favourite words, balance:

> The citizen wants protection against the criminal, and most citizens are willing, I would judge, to see the balance tilted in favour of the police and the power of the law in order that criminals might more readily be deterred and punished. But the Home Office and Parliament have to remember the balance between the need of the citizen to be protected against crime, and the liberties of the citizen as an individual faced with the coercive power of the State and the courts. Every major piece of legislation needs to be tested in that balance.[47]

Hurd's measures in relation to police powers, public order, combatting terrorism and drug trafficking, demonstrate a tendency to lean far more in the direction of centralising power in the hands of the state than protecting the civil liberties of the citizen. As Home Secretary, Hurd never fell shy of using words like discipline, order and punishment. The pattern was for him to give the police and the courts whatever powers they needed to protect the citizen and the State from perceived threats.

At one level, the Public Order Act of 1986 was a much-needed modernisation of an outdated area of English law, and, although the White Paper was the child of Hurd's predecessor, Leon Brittan, the eventual Act fitted very much into Hurd's belief in reforming laws and institutions which had fallen into disrepair.

A new offence of riot was created, carrying a maximum penalty of life imprisonment — a notable change from the White Paper which suggested ten years.[48] The offence of violent disorder replaced the old law of unlawful assembly and carried a maximum penalty of five years in prison or an unlimited fine. Clause five of the Act created a new offence of disorderly conduct, which was defined as behaviour which was not violent but which is 'threatening, abusive, insulting or disorderly and is likely to cause alarm, harrassment or distress'.[49] Again, this represented a departure from the White Paper which would have required proof of alarm, involving the victim going to court. Hurd made this alteration after listening to the advice of the Magistrates' Association, the Association of Metropolitan Authorities and the Society of Prosecuting Solicitors, who believed that victims would be reluctant to go to court.[50]

Part II of the Public Order Act sought to deal with processions and assemblies. Clause eleven required the police to be informed seven days in advance of a march, with certain exceptions, and was backed up by the extension of police power to contain marches subject to three tests: prevention of serious damage to property; serious disruption of the life of the community; and intimidation of others.

The change was a direct response to the problems of picketing during the Miners' Strike of 1984 to 1985:

> Assemblies and static demonstrations may just as often be the occasion of
> public disorder as marches and the Government believe that it is unacceptable
> for gatherings, such as those at Greenham Common, or the mass pickets of
> the miners' strike, to be outside the framework of controls.[51]

The police were now allowed to relocate the site of a demonstration, change its date or time and limit the numbers attending. In effect, the right of assembly was determined henceforth by the police commander on the ground, within flimsy safeguards.

In response to growing complaints about New Age festivals, the Government introduced a new law of trespass to prevent convoys of hippies from straying onto private land. The only liberalising measure in the Public Order Act created a new offence of incitement to racial hatred which was opposed by Tory right-wingers and the Police Federation. Gerald Kaufman, responding to the Second Reading debate, added another entry to Hurd's tasteful anthology of comments from his opposite number:

> The trouble is that the Bill goes a long way towards turning the reluctant and unwilling police into Maggie's boot boys.[52]

Even before the provisions of the Public Order Act came into force, Douglas Hurd obliged whenever the police requested equipment and resources from the Home Secretary. During the riots on the Broadwater Farm estate in Tottenham in October 1985, the police were deployed with plastic bullets and CS Gas for the first time on the British mainland (against the wishes of some Labour-run police authorities), although they were not in fact used. In May 1986, Hurd issued a Home Office circular to the effect that Chief Constables could draw stocks of CS Gas and plastic bullets from central stores if local police authorities refused to authorise their purchase.[53] In effect, Hurd had unchecked power to provide central services for the police.

Throughout his time as Home Secretary, Hurd developed a good working relationship with the Police Federation and the Association of Chief Police Officers (ACPO). On 22 May 1986, his address was well received at the Police Federation Conference at Scarborough. The *Police Review*, the magazine of the Police Federation, commented on the poor performance of Hurd's predecessor, Leon Brittan, the year before, regarding Hurd as 'an altogether more astute platform speaker'.[54]

On 10 June 1986, Douglas Hurd also gave a reassuring performance at the ACPO Conference at Torquay. In marked contrast to Kenneth Clarke, who later attempted to shake up the structures of police pay and conditions with the Sheehy proposals, Hurd fostered a more cosy relationship with the police. At the ACPO, he almost cuddled up to the delegates:

> I congratulate you on the positive response which you have made in improving effectiveness and efficiency in the police service. You have been plying your brooms energetically, showing no mercy to the cobwebs or the dusty corners which you sometimes found.[55]

In fact, police pay under the Conservatives was allowed to go through the stratosphere. As Kenneth Clarke came to realise, it was one of the areas into which the cold wind of Thatcherite cutbacks had not been able to reach. The central reason for this was that the Conservative Government needed to keep the police on board to ensure that they enforced their new Draconian laws.

In the face of criticisms of police brutality, Hurd placed complete faith in the operational independence of chief police officers on the ground:

> It is rather too easy afterwards for critics to say either that the police should
> have done more or that they should have done less. These operational
> judgements lie at the heart of modern policing, and I know that they can be
> desperately difficult. I also know that they must be left to the decision of the
> professional on the spot, subject to the law and its principle of reasonable
> force. That is the legal position, and I am sure it is the commonsense position
> as well.[56]

Douglas Hurd was equally supportive of the police during the year-long
Wapping dispute from March 1986 to February 1987. Rupert Murdoch,
Australian magnate and Chairman of News International, decided to move his
newspaper operation out of Fleet Street and onto a new site at Wapping in East
London. Murdoch wanted to eliminate restrictive practices amongst the print
workers and introduce new computer technology at his new printing plant in
Wapping. His decision to sack 5,500 printers from the two main print unions,
the National Graphical Association (NGA) and the more moderate general print
union, Sogat '82, headed by Brenda Dean, sparked a series of violent clashes
between print workers and socialist militants on the one hand, and police using
riot tactics on the other.

Unlike 1972, when Hurd identified in his diaries the reluctance of ministers
to become involved in industrial disputes, as Home Secretary, he kept a high
profile during the Wapping dispute. His resolve was maintained by the memory
of the industrial reverses under Edward Heath. In a speech to the Coningsby
Club in February 1986, he recalled those bleak days:

> In those days it seemed that whatever the Government did, whomever the
> elected representatives of the people voted, the vital power in this country
> rested with the trade union leadership. After the Conservative Government
> had been defied by the NUM in 1972 and 1974, and had lost the first
> election of 1974 to Labour, it was commonplace among the commentators
> that the Tories were out for the foreseeable future because they could never
> achieve a reasonable relationship with the trade union barons. How long ago
> that age of grovel seems. That particular shadow has been lifted from the
> land.[57]

One of the real difficulties was that the legitimate mass picketing of the
Wapping plant by print union members and their families was increasingly
hijacked by militant groups out to cause trouble. Hurd issued a statement in
which he compared the demonstrators to 'a honey-pot around which insects

buzz. Worse than that they provide a focus for all kinds of people with all kinds of violent inclinations.'[58] The decision of Sir Kenneth Newman, the Metropolitian Police Chief Constable, to use riot tactics to disperse the crowds resulted in innocent civilians and reporters being injured. One of the worst incidents occurred on Saturday, 3 May 1986, when 1,700 police confronted 10,000 demonstrators leaving 175 policemen and eighty-three civilians injured, including two reporters from ITN.[59] The Wapping riots occurred right in the middle of the prison riots. One issue piled on top of another.

Douglas Hurd maintained throughout the dispute that Sir Kenneth Newman exercised operational independence. In contrast to non-Metropolitan areas which are controlled by local police authorities, in the capital, the Home Secretary is the Metropolitan Police Authority and is accountable to Parliament for their actions, but the Metropolitan Police Commissioner is supposed to retain complete independence over all operational matters.

Hurd steadfastly resisted calls from the Opposition for a full public inquiry, and took the line that the proper procedure for investigating complaints against the police was through the Police Complaints Authority as established by the Police and Criminal Evidence Act of 1984. It remains open to question whether a body dominated by police should be called upon to investigate the allegations of misdemeanours by the police.

During the Wapping dispute, Douglas Hurd demonstrated both a loyalty to Mrs Thatcher's agenda of crushing organised labour and the ability to cope with the brutalities of wielding power as a senior minister. There was one point, however, when Hurd believed that he should call in Brenda Dean of Sogat '82 for talks but the Prime Minister 'demurred'.[60]

The critical stance of the Labour Front Bench to the dispute put Douglas Hurd at an advantage because he was able to accuse the Labour Party of implying that Wapping should be left unprotected. Meanwhile, the Labour Front Bench and the TUC increasingly tried to distance themselves from the behaviour of the Labour militants and the print workers. On Saturday, 24 January 1987, a further night of demonstrations took place outside the Wapping plant.[61] Hurd tried to keep in touch with developments from his home at Westwell, but his telephone was out of order. Ministerial meetings with the Prime Minister were also dominated by discussion of the Zircon affair. No issue could be discussed in isolation – each swirled around competing for Hurd's limited time.[62]

By the beginning of 1987, Hurd was in a stronger position to deal with the violence. First, there was some evidence of outside infiltration: of the sixty-seven people arrested, only thirteen were found to be members of the print unions. During the clashes, it was claimed that an attempt was made by the protestors to string wire across a road to unseat mounted police. Second, the use of violence weakened the position of the TUC and the Labour leadership.

Norman Willis, the General Secretary of the TUC, the Leader of the Opposition, Neil Kinnock, and Gerald Kaufman were forced to condemn the violence, whilst Dennis Skinner's comment that Labour must 'win the streets' was roundly condemned in the House of Commons.[63]

Third, and most importantly for the outcome of the dispute, the provisions of the Public Order Act of 1986 came into force on 1 April 1987, giving the police advance knowledge of static demonstrations, and new powers to determine the site of the demonstration and the numbers taking part. Hurd was able to warn of the imminent implementation of the new legislation as a stick with which to bludgeon the unions into making concessions. A combination of the prospect of the new public-order legislation and the divisions in the Labour movement caused by the level of violence led to the dispute being ended unconditionally by the NGA and Sogat '82 on 5-6 February 1987.

In other areas of criminal justice policy – tackling drug trafficking, improving extradition procedures and introducing anti-terrorist measures – Hurd's approach was equally tough. The Drug Trafficking and Offences Act of 1986, gave the courts in effect a *carte blanche* to seize any assets accrued in the five years previous to arrest, all of which it was assumed would have been derived from pedalling drugs. The Act also reworked English law, enabling international agreements to be signed with other countries to enhance mutual enforcement.[64] The extradition provisions in the Criminal Justice Act of 1988 further enhanced the ability of the authorities to bring to trial persons living abroad accused of offences in the United Kingdom. Between 1988 and 1991, Douglas Hurd was extremely active in securing extradition bilateral agreements with foreign countries to combat the drug traffickers.

Extradition policies were on the whole successful, with the major exception of the Irish Republic. In March 1986, the flaws in security co-operation with the Republic were exposed by the failure to extradite Evelyn Glenholmes, who was suspected of terrorist offences on the British mainland from 1981 to 1982. Normally in such matters responsibility rested with the Attorney-General, Sir Michael Havers, but for some unclear reason – Hurd claims he was 'trying to be helpful'[65] – the Home Secretary decided to make a statement to the House of Commons on 24 March 1986. Hurd's diary records him changing the original draft statement which he had been given:

> 24 Mar. 1986: The draft statement in my box last night [Sunday] stated that neither the police nor the DPP [Director of Public Prosecutions] had erred on the Glenholmes in any respect. This I reject. Of course, it quickly proves false. There was negligence, tiny negligence by Met.[ropolitan] policemen

and greater by the DPP's office in automated form . . . Statement on
Glenholmes. Quite fiercely attacked. No runs to be made, but not out.[66]

The reaction to Hurd's statement was indeed fierce. While the Home Secretary
could have predicted Gerald Kaufman's description of the episode as a
'discreditable botch-up', he would not have expected Robert Maclennan, the
SDP/Liberal Alliance's Home Affairs Spokesman, to call for the resignation, if
not of the Home Secretary, then at least of the Attorney-General.[67]

The facts of the case were that a set of warrants were first issued on 31
October 1984, but the Irish courts requested fresh warrants on 6 November
1984, by which time Glenholmes had disappeared. She was subsequently
arrested in Dublin on 12 March 1986, but the District Court of Dublin ruled
that her extradition papers were defective, and Glenholmes was discharged. The
information for both sets of warrants (31 October and 6 November) was
identical, but the 6 November information was not resworn by the magistrate
in London (a point missed by the DPP's office), so the Irish court was able to
rule on a purely technical point that the relevant information contained had not
been resworn.[68]

Hurd's tone throughout his statement was apologetic. Had he casually
adopted an arrogant tone and accepted the findings of the original draft
statement given to him in his red box late at night, this minor episode could
have easily led to his resignation, and probably the resignation of several others,
including the DPP, the Attorney-General, and the magistrate who failed to
ensure that the 6 November 1984 document was resworn. As it was, Hurd
deserves credit for being alert to the errors, but it does seem odd, as Merlyn
Rees pointed out in the course of questioning, that the Attorney-General, who
was responsible for extradition warrants and the DPP's office, was not the
minister giving the statement.[69]

The other main issue at stake over the Glenholmes case, which was only
raised by Ivan Lawrence (Burton) at the time, was the less than helpful attitude
of the Irish courts towards the extradition of suspected IRA terrorists. It only
served to strengthen Enoch Powell's argument that security co-operation with
the Republic was a myth. In a very vague hint that he was annoyed with the
obstructive attitude of the Irish courts, Hurd said 'everyone who has studied
the case knows that even then there were further difficulties further down the
road.'[70]

In the wider European context, greater strides were made by Hurd and his
European partners to combat the growing threat of international terrorism. The
main impetus for international co-operation came after the American bombing
on Libya in April 1986. Although many European states disapproved of the
American action (and Douglas Hurd shared some of these reservations), the

Home Secretary wanted to heal the rifts in the Community and to use the opportunity to co-ordinate inter-governmentally an anti-terrorist crackdown. On 23 April, Hurd flew across to The Hague for a meeting with Edwin Meese, the United States Attorney-General, William Webster, Director of the FBI, and Robert Oakley, Head of the State Department's Counter Terrorist Unit. A meeting then took place between the EEC Interior and Justice ministers under the auspices of the Trevi Group.[71] This rather loose process, which existed outside the provisions of the Treaty of Rome, had begun in Italy in 1976 but had lain more or less dormant until 1985. Its aim was to co-ordinate information and measures between European countries – primarily at security-service level – relating to terrorism, drug trafficking and football hooliganism.[72]

At a domestic level, Hurd further entrenched the provisions of the Prevention of Terrorism Act (PTA) which was designed to combat all forms of international terrorism, but especially IRA terrorism. The Act was originally introduced by the Labour Government in November 1974 in response to public outrage following a massive IRA bombing campaign on mainland Britain. Throughout his tenure as Home Secretary, Douglas showed he would not flinch from confronting the IRA, even if that meant, in a personal sense, consigning himself to the company of bodyguards for the rest of his life, and in a wider sense, curbing individual liberties and creating resentment within the Catholic community in Northern Ireland.

In 1986, Hurd had asked Lord Colville of Cross to conduct an independent review of the operation of the Prevention of Terrorism Act, widening his net in 1987 to consider the overall effectiveness of the legislation. Hurd published a White Paper in December 1987 which recommended that the Act, due to expire in 1989, be made permanent, subject to annual review by Parliament.[73] Hurd disagreed with Lord Colville's recommendation that the Home Secretary's power of exclusion be abolished. In cases where the Home Secretary had evidence of an active IRA terrorist cell or prisoners due for release were heard talking about resuming bombing, Hurd felt he needed to retain the power, with the aid of three special advisers, to restrict the movement of such terrorist suspects. In 1987, he introduced some 111 exclusion orders in Britain and twenty-three in Northern Ireland.[74] Anti-terrorist measures like these – and many more made in secret – placed Hurd near the top of the IRA's hitlist.

Even though the Home Office has traditionally been a burdensome department, Douglas Hurd presided as Home Secretary over the passage of a huge swathe of legislation. Throughout, Hurd claimed to be modernising outdated laws and trying to strike, in his favourite words, a sensible balance between protecting the public through the powers of the State and preserving the individual rights of the citizen. On balance, however, Hurd's measures were weighted in favour of the State. This was partly related to the Government's agenda of confronting the power of organised labour – a task from which Hurd did not flinch, because of the reverses he had experienced in 1972 and 1974. There was a clear contrast to be drawn between Hurd's liberal views on sentencing and his markedly non-liberal approach to public order and tackling terrorism. Whenever he was called upon, Hurd upheld the interest of established order. However, Hurd's general reputation for liberalism survived relatively unscathed, despite the predominantly non-liberal nature of the measures which he introduced. His reputation for competence also remained largely intact in spite of the notable mistakes which he made when guiding Home Office legislation through the House of Commons. On most occasions, Hurd's emollient political style reassured the bulk of his critics.

Notes

1. Douglas Hurd, 'What became of all the passion?', *The Independent on Sunday*, 22 May 1994.
2. Alan Clark, *Diaries* (Weidenfeld & Nicolson: London, 1993), p. 198 (29 Jan. 1988).
3. H. of C. Deb. (6th Series), 14 Apr. 1986, vol. 95, col. 593.
4. Diary Readings with Douglas Hurd, 26 Feb. 1997.
5. Interview with Douglas Hurd, 20 Jan. 1997.
6. Diary Readings with Douglas Hurd, 26 Feb. 1997.
7. H. of C. Deb. (6th Series), 7 Nov. 1985, vol. 86, col. 121.
8. *The Shops Acts. Late-Night and Sunday Opening. Report of the Committee of Inquiry into Proposals to Amend the Shops Act* (The Auld Committee), *Cmnd. 9376*, Nov. 1984, para. 291.
9. The House of Commons voted by 304 votes to 184 in favour of the Auld Report, H. of C. Deb. (6th Series), 20 May 1985, vol. 79, cols 827–30.
10. The evidence which relates to the Shops Bill [Lords] has been largely based on two excellent accounts of its ill-fated passage: see Francis Bown, 'The Defeat of the Shops Bill, 1986', in Michael Rush (ed.) *Parliament and Pressure Politics* (Study of Parliament Group, Clarendon Press: Oxford, 1990), Chapter 9, pp. 213–33. This account is an edited version of Bown's thesis submitted to the University of Hull and includes extracts of an interview with Douglas Hurd conducted by Bown on 15 Dec. 1986; also see Paul Regan, 'The 1986 Shops Bill', *Parliamentary Affairs*, vol. 4 (1988), pp. 218–35.
11. H. of C. Deb. (6th Series), 7 Nov. 1985, vol. 86, col. 121.
12. H. of L. Deb. (5th Series), 11 Feb. 1986, vol. 471, cols 121–2. The voting was Contents 121, Not Contents 120.

13. *The Sunday Times*, 16 Feb. 1986.
14. Philip Cowley and Mark Stuart (1997), 'Sodomy, Slaughter, Sunday Shopping and Seatbelts. Free Votes in the House of Commons, 1979 to 1996', in *Party Politics*, vol. 3, no. 1, pp. 141–52.
15. Diary Readings with Douglas Hurd, 7 Oct. 1997.
16. Hugo Young, *One of Us*, pp. 476–7.
17. Interview with Douglas Hurd, 7 Oct. 1997.
18. H. of C. Deb. (6th Series), 2 Dec. 1987, vol. 123, cols 933–45.
19. Ibid, col. 939.
20. Ibid.
21. During the passage of the Bill, a second money resolution was required when the Government belatedly considered the issue of compensation.
22. The Deputy Speaker, Harold Walker, felt that divisions were being unnecessarily claimed, and used Standing Order Number 39 to allow MPs to vote standing in their places. H. of C. Deb. (6th Series), 25 May 1988, vol. 134, cols 473–91.
23. For a fuller account of the Committee Stage of the Firearms Bill see David Melhuish and Philip Cowley, 'Whither the "New Role" in Policy Making? Conservative MPs in Standing Committees, 1979 to 1992', *The Journal of Legislative Studies*, vol. 1, no. 4, Winter 1995; dissent occurred on all eleven of the Standing Committee's divisions; six of those saw four Conservative MPs dissenting, pp. 60–1. The bulk of Conservative rebels in the House of Commons were prominent members of the wildfowl lobby, had farming connections and/or represented rural constituencies. Sir Hector Monro (Dumfries), Jerry Wiggin (Weston-Super-Mare), Henry Bellingham (Norfolk, North West) and Paul Marland (Gloucestershire, West), were the main dissenters in Standing Committee. During the Bill's Report Stage, these four rebels were joined regularly by Sir Nicholas Bonsor (Upminster), Alick Buchanan-Smith (Kincardine and Deeside), Bill Walker (Tayside, North) and Michael Colvin (Romsey and Waterside). In the House of Lords, Earl Ferrers, the Home Office minister responsible, faced criticism from a group of Conservative peers led by Lord Swansea, the former Olympic shot.
24. H. of C. Deb. (6th Series), 25 May 1988, vol. 134, col. 398; The largest Conservative rebellion on the Firearms (Amendment) Bill occurred on 23 May 1988 on a recommittal motion by Jerry Wiggin (Weston-Super-Mare). Nineteen Conservatives voted against the Government line: Henry Bellingham (Norfolk, North West), William Benyon (Milton Keynes), Sir Nicholas Bonsor (Upminster), Alick Buchanan-Smith (Kincardine and Deeside), Sir Anthony Buck (Colchester, North), Michael Colvin (Romsey and Waterside), Barry Field (Isle of Wight), Peter Griffiths (Portsmouth,

North), Michael Grylls (Surrey, North West), Richard Holt (Langbaurgh), Dame Elaine Kellett-Bowman (Lancaster), Paul Marland (Gloucestershire, West), Robin Maxwell-Hyslop (Tiverton), Peter Rost (Erewash), Bill Walker (Tayside, North), and Jerry Wiggin (Weston-Super-Mare). The two tellers were Sir Hector Monro (Dumfries) and Robert Hicks (Cornwall, South East). The other Conservative rebels during the Bill were Ray Whitney (Wycombe), Ann Winterton (Congleton), Nicholas Winterton (Macclesfield) and Nicholas Budgen (Wolverhampton, South West).

25. Auberon Waugh, 'When the risk of lions is less than the nuisance of keeping hold of Nurse', *The Spectator*, 28 Nov. 1987; 'Who will rid us of this demented Nanny in the attic?', *The Spectator*, 12 Dec. 1987; 'Further reflections of the Nanny Hurd terror', *The Spectator*, 9 Jan. 1988.

26. H. of C. Deb. (6th Series), 21 Jan. 1988, vol. 125, col. 1118.

27. Interview between Sir David Frost and Douglas Hurd, *Breakfast with Frost*, 15 Dec. 1996.

28. Popplewell had been asked to investigate the causes of the fire at Bradford City Football Ground on 11 May 1985 and football hooliganism at the Birmingham City match the same day. Shortly after the inquiry was underway, another tragedy occurred at the Heysel Football stadium in Brussels on 29 May, and Popplewell was asked to widen the scope of his inquiry.

29. On 6 July 1988, the Prime Minister had met with the President of the Football League and the Chairman of the Football Association to ask them if they would introduce a voluntary scheme.

30. *The Hillsborough Stadium Disaster, 15 April 1989, Inquiry by Lord Justice Taylor, Final Report, Cm. 962*, HMSO, 1990; Lord Taylor of Gosforth succeeded Lord Lane as Lord Chief Justice in April 1992.

31. H. of C. Deb. (6th Series), 17 Apr. 1989, vol. 151, col. 26.

32. Ibid., cols 25, 26, 34.

33. Diary Readings with Douglas Hurd, 7 Oct. 1997.

34. Ibid.

35. Ibid.

36. The meeting was attended by Mrs Thatcher; John Wakeham, Leader of the House; David Waddington, Chief Whip; Nicholas Ridley, Secretary of State for the Environment; Colin Moynihan; and Douglas Hurd.

37. Diary Readings with Douglas Hurd, 7 Oct. 1997.

38. Ibid.

39. Ibid.

40. H. of C. Deb. (6th Series), 27 Jun. 1989, vol. 155, cols 925–30. The fifteen Conservative rebels on the Second Reading of the Football

Spectators Bill [Lords] were William Benyon (Milton Keynes), Dr Rhodes Boyson (Brent, North), Terry Dicks (Hayes and Harlington), Sir Ian Gilmour (Chesham and Amersham), John Greenway (Ryedale), Robert Hicks (Cornwall, South East), Michael Irvine (Ipswich), David Knox (Staffordshire, Moorlands), Jim Lester (Broxtowe), James Pawsey (Rugby and Kenilworth), Hugo Summerson (Walthamstow), John Watts (Slough), Ray Whitney (Wycombe), John Wilkinson (Ruislip, Northwood) and Nicholas Winterton (Macclesfield).

41. H. of C. Deb. (6th Series), 30 Oct. 1989, vol. 159, cols 144–7.

42. *Cmnd. 962*, p.75.

43. H. of C. Deb. (6th Series), 29 Jan. 1990, vol. 166, col. 26.

44. Quoted from Peter Riddell, *The Thatcher Decade* (Basil Blackwell: Oxford, 1989) p. 174.

45. Nigel Lawson, *The View From No. 11*, pp. 876–7.

46. Michael Trend, 'Losing our Liberties', *The Spectator*, 21 Nov. 1987, pp. 9–11.

47. Douglas Hurd, 'Statutes of Liberty', *The Spectator*, 5 Dec. 1987.

48. White Paper, *Review of Public Order Law, Cmnd. 9510* (16 May 1985).

49. H. of C. Deb. (6th Series), 13 Jan. 1986, vol. 89, col. 793.

50. Ibid., col. 794.

51. Ibid., col. 797.

52. Ibid., col. 810.

53. Northumbria Police Authority took Hurd to court, arguing unsuccessfully that the Home Secretary had gone beyond the provisions of the Police Act of 1964. In December 1986, the courts ruled that the Home Secretary exercised general prerogative power. In November 1987, the Court of Appeal confirmed this ruling by stating there was no conflict between statute and Royal prerogative. Gerry Northam, *Shooting in the Dark: Riot Police in Britain* (Faber & Faber: London, 1989), pp. 148–51.

54. Ibid., p. 29.

55. Douglas Hurd, Speech to ACPO Summer Conference, Torquay, 10 Jun. 1986.

56. Ibid.

57. Douglas Hurd, Speech to the Coningsby Club, 19 Feb. 1986.

58. *The Times*, 7 May 1986.

59. For a passionate, if one-sided account of the events of 3 May 1986 at Wapping, *see* Tony Benn, *The End of An Era: Diaries 1980-90* (Arrow Books: London, 1994), pp. 448–50.

60. (27 Jan. 1987) Diary Readings with Douglas Hurd, 7 Oct. 1997.

61. Benn, *The End of an Era*, p. 490.

62. Diary Readings with Douglas Hurd, 7 Oct. 1997.

63. *The Times*, 27 Jan. 1986; H. of C. Deb. (6th Series), 26 Jan. 1987, vol. 109, cols 21–32.
64. H. of C. Deb.(6th Series), 21 Jan. 1986, vol. 90, cols 241–6.
65. Interview with Douglas Hurd, 26 Feb. 1997.
66. Diary Readings with Douglas Hurd, 26 Feb. 1997.
67. H. of C. Deb. (6th Series), 24 Mar. 1986, vol. 94, cols 613, 617, 618.
68. As a side issue which did not affect the case, a Metropolitan police officer made another error (to which Hurd refers in his diary entry) when referring to the dates on which the warrants were issued.
69. H. of C. Deb. (6th Series), 24 Mar. 1986, vol. 94, col. 614.
70. Ibid., col. 620.
71. Trevi is short for Terrorism, Revolution and Violence.
72. *Keesing's Contemporary Archives*, Jan. 1987, p. 34883.
73. H. of C. Deb. (6th Series), 16 Feb. 1988, vol. 127, cols 925–31.
74. Ibid., col. 928.

14

Walls Come Tumbling Down, July 1989–October 1990

On 24 July 1989, Douglas Hurd received – with remarkable forbearance – the news that Mrs Thatcher had offered Geoffrey Howe his job as Home Secretary. His diary entry for that day records that 'I stay somewhat wearily but surviving.'[1] Mrs Thatcher rang Hurd that morning to announce that the only change at the Home Office was that Douglas Hogg, Parliamentary Under Secretary of State, was leaving Queen Anne's Gate to become a Minister of State at the Department of Trade and Industry, and she complimented him on his handling of matters at the Home Office, something which was very unusual for her. Hurd recalls:

> I was relatively at ease with it all. I really wasn't too fussed. She'd have made me Leader of the House. I wouldn't have welcomed that. I knew she wouldn't drop me altogether.[2]

Immediately after the damaging news began to break that Thatcher had offered Howe his job, Hurd moved swiftly to lobby journalists in the House of Commons, spreading the line that he was relaxed about the revelations; the Prime Minister was perfectly entitled to offer his job to someone else. By staying calm, Hurd not only killed off a damaging story, but, as he remarked a few days later, 'It's fine. I've got credit in the bank.'[3] Mrs Thatcher owed him one.

Three months later, his assessment proved right.

> 26 Oct. 1989: Amazing day . . . Nigel Lawson silent, but not morose [in Cabinet] . . . sit beside Prime Minister for her questions and statement on

the Commonwealth Conference [Malaysia]. Back to the Home Office. More routine meetings and then news that Nigel Lawson has resigned over [Sir Alan] Walters. All flabbergasted. PM rings up about six to offer me the Foreign Office. She's still in shock. She was reluctant. She said 'You won't let those Europeans get on top of you, will you now Douglas?'[4]

On the recommendation of Kenneth Baker, then Conservative Party chairman, and Charles Powell, her Private Secretary, Mrs Thatcher agreed to Hurd's appointment without dissent.[5]

For Hurd, the news fulfilled a lifelong dream first shared with his friend Tony Lloyd at Eton as a boy, although he denies he had any pre-conceived blueprint for reaching the doors of King Charles Street.[6]

Hurd's appointment as Foreign Secretary was greeted with an element of relief by officials at the Foreign Office in view of his predecessor's short but uncomfortable summmer in the job. While Major had felt ill at ease among the bright, self-confident Oxbridge educated officials, Hurd fitted into the culture immediately; they were welcoming back one of their own. Despite – or perhaps because of – this, Hurd tried to make sure that he stayed at one remove from officials, playing the role of the politician rather than the Whitehall mandarin. However, largely because of Hurd's diplomatic background, he never entirely succeeded, especially with the Prime Minister.

Officials quickly discovered Hurd's dislike of jargon. Junior officials would have their letters redrafted and cut down to a single page by the Foreign Secretary. Certain words were banned – 'currently' and 'appropriate' were especially frowned upon because they told the reader nothing new. Hurd disliked intensely sentences packed with nouns. Why did a crisis need to be described as a 'crisis situation'? Were meetings really 'key strategic meetings'? An internal video was even produced by Hurd in an attempt to cut out jargon.

Hurd was a self-disciplined Foreign Secretary who did his homework. Because meetings dominated his day and dinner engagements the early evening, the only time he could tackle the paperwork was after eleven at night. Hurd would not over-indulge in food or alcohol over a dinner and made a point of getting on with his ministerial red boxes. Aware of the tyranny of time, he used his time well, but did not become completely immersed in detail or stay up into the small hours like Geoffrey Howe. As a postscript, when the present Foreign Secretary, Robin Cook, stumbled over Arms to Sierra Leone, he was given a headmasterly rebuke from Lord Hurd for not doing his homework:

These may be tedious matters of housekeeping to the architects of lofty ethical foreign policy; but in fact they are at the heart of any worthwhile policy. If the engine is not running properly then the course set by the captain on the bridge becomes irrelevant.[7]

In contrast to the Home Office, where Mrs Thatcher had bilateral meetings with Hurd once a month, the Prime Minister met with Hurd at least every week, often twice a week. With the possible exceptions of Baldwin and Attlee, successive twentieth-century British Prime Ministers have, in the words of George Brown, wanted to 'play at being Foreign Secretary'.[8] In Mrs Thatcher's case, she was obsessed with the view that the Foreign Office was the source of all evil, forever scheming to undermine British national interests in favour of appeasement towards European federalists. On his arrival, Hurd made a special point of ensuring that no Foreign Office official was to contact Number 10 except through the Permanent Under-Secretary. Despite the potential for tensions, relations between Charles Powell, Mrs Thatcher's Private Secretary, and Douglas Hurd were good. The Prime Minister and Douglas Hurd continued to work reasonably well together, although the new Foreign Secretary defined his relationship with her at the time as 'loyal and co-operative but not subservient'.[9]

Very soon after entering the Foreign Office, Hurd faced the dramatic consequences of the fall of the Berlin Wall, but the issue which generated the most letters in his mailbag concerned the allegations of United Kingdom military backing for Khmer Rouge guerrillas in Kampuchea (formerly known as Cambodia). Allegations that the British Government was secretly training guerrillas in camps on the Thai side of the border with Cambodia surfaced in September 1989 and were repeated a month later in a film by the journalist and thorn-in-the-side of Douglas Hurd, John Pilger, which received coverage in the *Daily Mirror*.[10] On 8 November, in reply to a question by James Lester, the Conservative Member for Broxtowe, who took an active interest in the Cambodian issue,[11] Hurd gave a detailed written statement in the House of Commons. He denied the allegations, but stated he believed that events had changed in Cambodia so as to warrant a change in British Government policy. The Vietnamese had withdrawn their combat units from Cambodia, but the failure in August 1989 of the Paris International Conference on Cambodia to reach a political settlement meant there was an increasing need for humanitarian relief. He announced a small increase in humanitarian aid (£250,000 via the charity UNICEF) to help refugees on the Thai/Cambodian border, and wrote of his intention to send a diplomat from the British embassy in Bangkok to the Kampuchean capital, Phnom Penh. However, the US administration was firmly opposed to the British move and this resulted in the British abandoning their plans to dispatch the diplomat.[12]

The disagreement between London and Washington stemmed from the

United States' refusal to resume any form of diplomatic contact with Vietnam. Every US policy in the region stemmed from this fact. The Americans were opposed to the Vietnamese-backed Hun Sen Government in Cambodia and (as shown in Chapter 19) opposed the British plans at this time for the involuntary repatriation of Vietnamese boat people from Hong Kong, which would have involved diplomatic contact with the Government in Phnom Penh. It was an irrational policy based on bitterness dating from the Vietnam War. Eventually, a way through was found on the Cambodian question, when the Australians unveiled a plan, later taken up by the United Nations Security Council, resulting in the signing of a peace agreement in Paris in October 1991.

The main difference between Mrs Thatcher and Douglas Hurd arose over Britain's entry into the Exchange Rate Mechanism (ERM) and the issue of German reunification. On the former issue, Douglas Hurd did collude with John Major in trying to persuade the Prime Minister to join the ERM. The hand of the Foreign Secretary and the Chancellor of the Exchequer had been strengthened by the demotion of Geoffrey Howe and the resignation of Nigel Lawson. Having lost a Foreign Secretary and a Chancellor, Mrs Thatcher could ill afford to lose another two senior ministers. If Mrs Thatcher had absolutely refused to enter the ERM and offered her resignation, would Hurd and Major have backed down? The answer would have depended on the level of the Prime Minister's support within her parliamentary party at the time. Had she become isolated in Cabinet and unpopular on the backbenches, she might have been cornered into retreat. Conversely, it was not so much that a threat by Mrs Thatcher to resign would have been taken seriously by Hurd and Major, merely the fact that, backed by a large majority, if she meant 'no', the power of her office was such that her two senior colleagues would have been forced to draw back. As it turned out, by October 1990, Mrs Thatcher saw she was isolated in Cabinet and able only to carry a significant minority of the backbenches with her on the issue. She went along with ERM reluctantly, but without threatening to resign.

Douglas Hurd's own role in fashioning Britain's entry into the ERM has been overstated.[13] From October 1989, John Major and the Foreign Secretary met for a series of private working breakfasts at Carlton Gardens. Their close working relationship was later dubbed the 'Hurd-Major axis'. Hurd and Major kept in touch more than their predecessors, Geoffrey Howe and Nigel Lawson. Even though Mrs Thatcher later perceived a conspiracy between Howe and Lawson against her, what emerges from both their memoirs is that, if anything, they had failed to conspire with sufficient regularity or force to persuade Mrs Thatcher to join the ERM. In no sense did either Major or Hurd conspire against the Prime Minister. The word 'axis' is correct if it is taken to mean that the two senior ministers formed an alliance which gently sought to persuade the Prime Minister to adhere to the Madrid conditions framed by Lawson and Howe in May 1989. The only conspirator in the Government was Mrs Thatcher herself, who, in increasingly strident tones, sought to undermine carefully formulated Government policy.

The Foreign Secretary was not closely involved in the detail of setting the conditions for Britain's entry into the ERM. This task had been fashioned by Nigel Lawson and his Treasury team and picked up by John Major. Hurd's backseat approach was both tactical and strategic. Tactically, he judged it unwise for the Prime Minister to have grounds to think that the Foreign Office's fingerprints were all over the Treasury's plans for Britain's entry, given her deep-seated suspicions of everything which emanated from King Charles Street. In contrast, John Major was liked by Mrs Thatcher and it was thought his method of gentle but persistent persuasion would be more effective with the Prime Minister. The Chancellor was therefore left to wear down the Prime Minister over the summer of 1990, gradually coaxing her towards entry, and once he made progress, locking her into the decision quickly, before she had second thoughts. Strategically, Hurd shared Major's view that, unless Britain joined the ERM, she would be unable to influence the future course, not only of economic and monetary union, but also of political integration. While Major concerned himself with ERM entry, Hurd focused on the debate over political union.

Ten days after Hurd became Foreign Secretary, the Berlin Wall came tumbling down (or rather it was chipped away bit-by-bit by students and tourists armed with small picks), marking the end of the Cold War division of Germany. At this crucial juncture in European history, Hurd realised that the reunification of Germany was inevitable. As he later commented, he was obeying one of the oldest rules of foreign policy 'don't stand unnecessarily in the path of an avalanche'.[14]

In contrast, Mrs Thatcher harboured a deep-seated fear of a resurgent Germany which might dominate Europe, if not militarily then economically. Somehow, she believed the process of German reunification could be controlled by the four old Allied powers: Britain, France, the Soviet Union, and the United States within the two-plus-four talks (the aforementioned countries plus the two Germanies) process. Her memoirs tell of abortive attempts to create a Franco-British axis to contain German power.[15] Unfortunately, her delusions were reinforced by President Mitterrand and Mikhail Gorbachev, but as Hurd recalls, they were only playing with the idea; Mrs Thatcher was not.[16]

Mrs Thatcher's mistake was to underestimate the strength of the Franco-German partnership, especially the French desire to bind Germany forever into the European Community. In a BBC television series, *The Poisoned Chalice*, Douglas Hurd recalls his disagreement with the Prime Minister:

> I thought this was something which was unreal. It was something which British Governments of all parties had backed, favoured for donkey's years — German unification. Here was Chancellor Kohl. This was the objective of his life. And it was quite clear that she [Mrs Thatcher] was doing her best to make it difficult.[17]

Unlike the Prime Minister, Hurd did not bring any prejudicial baggage with him to the issue of German reunification. Indeed, his predilection for flexibility and compromise suited a diplomatic environment in which events shifted with enormous speed, sweeping away many of the old fixed points of international relations which had been frozen by the Cold War. Hurd's role *vis à vis* Chancellor Kohl and the Prime Minister was to act as a kind of go-between or emissary. Because relations between Kohl and Thatcher had deteriorated so badly during 1990, Hurd would regularly visit the German Chancellor with the full authority of the Prime Minister.

During the last months of Mrs Thatcher's premiership, Hurd could only repair the fissures caused by the upset she created at successive European summits. It was not so much her arguments — in many cases Britain had a valid case to press — but the belligerent way in which she went about the task. The Dublin Summit of 25 and 26 June was a case in point. A major area of contention at the summit was the problem of how best to supply the Soviet Union with aid. Hurd shared Mrs Thatcher's view that it would be unwise to supply President Gorbachev with massive and immediate assistance (a policy which the German Government conversely supported). However, Hurd described the Prime Minister in his diary on 25 June as being 'belligerent and exhausted', a comment which would recur from then to her nemesis at the first Rome Summit at the end of October 1990.[18]

Mrs Thatcher's belligerent style at Dublin was in contrast to the diplomatic way Hurd dealt with his own difficulties on the subject of Cyprus. Hurd resisted moves by other members of the European Community to get involved in the Cyprus question, believing that it was 'a complication to the efforts which the UN, the Americans and we were making'.[19] The meeting became a classic set-piece debate on the issue, in which Hurd was forced to cede ground. Despite the vigorous debate, there was no bitterness in the air, no suggestion that Hurd had been bludgeoning his European partners into submission. Of course, it is worth pointing out that, while Mrs Thatcher's stance on aid to the Soviet Union was accepted, Hurd's tactics over Cyprus resulted in a compromise.

There was a limit to how long Britain's European partners would continue to bear Mrs Thatcher's abrasive way of conducting European business. Privately, Hurd became increasingly concerned by this. The fact that Hurd had ceded ground in one area did not mean he was a soft touch; it gave him credit in the bank for the Maastricht negotiations. In a more general sense, the European leaders grew to admire Hurd's conciliatory approach; it conformed to the way European politics worked.

The following month, Nicholas Ridley, Trade and Industry Secretary, made one unscripted remark too many when he claimed that European integration was 'a German racket designed to take over the whole of Europe' in an interview with Dominic Lawson, Editor of *The Spectator* magazine. On reading the article, Hurd records:

> 10 Jul. 1990: Read like drunken ramblings, but weren't.[20]

The Foreign Secretary had in mind Ridley's comment:

> I'm not against giving up sovereignty in principle, but not to this lot. You might as well give it to Adolf Hitler, frankly.[21]

Douglas Hurd considered the issue closed when Charles Powell extracted a complete retraction from Ridley, and the Prime Minister read the apology in front of the whole Cabinet on 12 July. There was a suggestion then and since that Hurd wanted Ridley to resign. Several pieces of evidence appear to contradict this view. First, on 12 July, Hurd recorded in his diary, 'He is not an enemy nor I an executioner.'[22] The two ministers knew each other relatively well, having worked together as Ministers of State at the Foreign Office under Peter Carrington in the early 1980s. While they found much to disagree about, especially on the question of Europe, they were on good personal terms. Judy Hurd had previously worked as Nicholas Ridley's secretary. Indeed, Ridley had gifted Judy Hurd a number of his paintings – he was something of an artist – which hang on the walls at Westwell. Moreover, by 12 July, Hurd believed that Ridley would survive despite backbench pressure:

> 12 Jul. 1990: Backbenchers surge around. There is a wide view that he [Ridley] should go. But I bet PM will stick with him.[23]

Not for the last time, Hurd's skills of political punditry were found to be wide of the mark. It was events of the following day, Friday, 13 July, which created the misleading impression that Hurd was manoeuvring for Ridley's resignation. The Foreign Secretary gave the vote of thanks in reply to the annual Ditchley Lecture given by his former boss, Lord Carrington. In his remarks, Hurd added some fairly innocuous comments about Europe:

> Our alliance, our partnership and our friendship with France and Germany

lie at the heart of modern British foreign policy. Lingering memories of the past do not prevent us from strengthening, month by month, the practical proofs of that friendship. . . . Nothing will now put these processes in doubt.[24]

Two journalists at the meeting – Hella Pick, Diplomatic Editor of *The Guardian*, and Edward Mortimer, Foreign Affairs Editor of the *Financial Times* – galloped away with Hurd's comments on tape and wrote up articles in the Saturday press to the effect that Hurd was pressing for Ridley's resignation. For example, Anthony Bevins, the political editor of *The Independent* wrote that 'the reputation of Mr Ridley was rubbed in by Douglas Hurd'.[25] The episode was a classic instance of Hurd's view that the press can run with a story in an entirely different way from that intended by politicians. In reality, it was Conservative backbench pressure, not Douglas Hurd, which determined Ridley's fate. Once Ridley had resigned, Hurd continued to try to defuse the affair, describing it as 'a five-day wonder'.[26]

Thus, by July 1990, there were no remaining members of Mrs Thatcher's original 1979 Cabinet, except an increasingly agitated Geoffrey Howe. However, no sooner had the Foreign Secretary defused one row with Germany than another appeared: the leaking of a secret memorandum of a Chequers meeting. The seminar was attended by a group of eminent historians, including Norman Stone, Timothy Garton-Ash, and – crucially – Charles Powell. In the chair, Mrs Thatcher raised a series of provocative questions such as 'Have the Germans changed?' while Charles Powell mischievously compiled the minutes of the meeting. The experts listed typical German characteristics such as egotism, superiority, angst and excess. But, the historians were not an anti-German cabal. According to Timothy Garton-Ash, they concluded that, although the German people had not changed, Germany had changed after forty years of democracy.[27] In the words of Philip Stephens, Associate Editor of the *Financial Times*, 'Kohl wanted a European Germany, but Thatcher feared a German Europe.'[28] Hurd's own view was that Germany and the German people – at least in the Western half of the country – had changed. For him, there were no nightmare images of a resurgent Germany reclaiming in peace what it had failed to achieve in war.

In early August 1990, Hurd was looking forward to a holiday when he turned on the radio to discover that Iraq had just invaded Kuwait. Because Mrs Thatcher was with President Bush in Aspen, Colorado, Hurd was effectively put in charge until the Prime Minister's return.

Britain had previously leant towards Iraq during the Iran-Iraq war. However, in March 1990 there was universal condemnation of the execution of Farzad Barzoft, an Iranian-born journalist working for *The Observer*, who had been convicted of spying, and Hurd was still concerned about the case of Ian Richter, jailed for life in Iraq, also on spying charges. Hurd entrusted William Waldegrave, his Minister of State, with much of the responsibility in this area of policy.

Relations between Britain and Iraq had improved to such an extent that Hurd had chaired a Cabinet subcommittee meeting on 19 July 1990 where senior ministers considered the possibility of lifting all embargoes on Iraq.[29]

With the exception of the cloud hanging over the British hostages held in Iraq and Kuwait, and, unlike his later dilemmas over the Bosnian conflict, Hurd did not encounter any major intellectual, operational or moral obstacles to the decisions taken in the Gulf.[30] As he wrote in his diary on the morning of 2 August, the Iraqi invasion of Kuwait was a 'clear case of aggression'.[31]

Hurd's first response to the Iraqi invasion was to freeze Kuwaiti assets held in Britain. The following day, he spoke at length with the Prime Minister by telephone, and she expressed gratitude for the way he had deputised thus far. Hurd is one of those who believes that she 'quite substantially stiffened Bush on the subject. I think that Bush would not have come to the conclusion so early that aggression had to be reversed if he hadn't been in Colorado with Margaret.'[32]

Hurd was a member of the War Cabinet, comprising the Prime Minister, Tom King at Defence, and John Wakeham, who was there ostensibly on the grounds that he was Energy Secretary. In reality, Mrs Thatcher wanted a trusted political ally, her former Chief Whip, at her side to ensure she would not be outnumbered should any controversial decision arise. The membership of the War Cabinet reflected a careful balance of the competing forces inside the Thatcher Government and was another example of Mrs Thatcher's continual fear that the Foreign Office influence should not be allowed to hold sway on matters of this kind.

Hurd's task was to preserve two fragile alliances: one internationally in the shape of the coalition with the Arab states; and the other in parliamentary terms with the Opposition parties in order to preserve a bipartisan approach to the crisis.

The need to preserve the coalition of Arab states ranged against Saddam Hussein prompted Hurd's tour of the Gulf States at the beginning of September 1990. The visit to Ali Saleh, the President of the Yemen, was fraught with difficulty because, while not actually siding militarily with Saddam Hussein, he joined King Hussein of Jordan and Yasser Arafat of the PLO in refusing to side with the allied coalition. Hurd recalls having 'a terrific argument' with the Yemeni President:

3 Sept. 1990: Ali Saleh. Brisk, jokey, combative. We have a real set-to on Iraq.[33]

The most poignant moment of the trip came the following day when Hurd called on the exiled Kuwaiti Government. For a month, they had been residing at a hotel in Taif in Saudi Arabia. Hurd described the Emir in his diary as 'forlorn and fairly silent',[34] but that told one little because he was, Hurd recalls, renowned for being of a generally gloomy disposition. Hurd then had discussions with James Baker, the US Secretary of State, with whom he kept in close touch throughout the crisis. Hurd was a confirmed admirer of Baker. He always respected the judgement of his American counterpart, although he sometimes found him quite brisk to deal with.

The final leg of Hurd's Middle East shuttle diplomacy was reserved for the most difficult task of all; tempering the Jordanian King's support for Saddam Hussein. As with the President of Yemen, Hurd had another long argument with King Hussein of Jordan:

5 Sept. 1990: We go over it all. Perhaps he has moved a little. Certainly, against the annexation of Kuwait. Flying to Baghdad to say so, but still wants Saddam Hussein to have access to the sea.[35]

Hurd was particularly understanding of the Jordanian position because he knew they faced economic and humanitarian problems as a result of the Iraqi invasion. With Turkey and Egypt, Jordan would bear the brunt of the imposition of the trade embargo imposed on Iraq, and therefore needed to be propped up financially. In humanitarian terms, Jordan had to accommodate a flood of mostly Asian refugees fleeing Saddam Hussein. King Hussein also had to answer to a large and volatile Palestinian population which, along with Yasser Arafat, the PLO leader, saw Saddam Hussein as their champion. The King was walking a tightrope between cutting off links with the West, thereby crippling his economy, and angering the Palestinians within his own country.

From Jordan, Hurd flew back to London to wind up the debate on the Gulf Crisis, following the emergency recall of Parliament. In contrast to the Congressional and public opinion in America which was fairly evenly divided on the issue – the Senate only voted by fifty-two votes to forty-seven in favour of military action on 13 January 1991 – the unity of the House of Commons was impressive throughout the conflict. Neil Kinnock, and Labour's Shadow Foreign Secretary, Gerald Kaufman, agreed with the Government that aggression should not pay, although Labour placed greater emphasis than the Government on securing United Nations authorisation under Article 42 of the Charter for any further action (such as an air blockade) rather than the role of the American,

British and other forces deployed in Saudi Arabia under Article 51.[36] In the words of Gerald Kaufman, 'We will not be voting to give a blank cheque for whatever action may be taken in the future.'[37]

However, Hurd and Kaufman worked very closely to ensure a bipartisan approach in the House of Commons. They were able to draw on the habit of consultation which they had enjoyed when Hurd was Home Secretary. All debates on the Gulf War were arranged in advance with the full agreement of the Opposition, mostly using a procedure known as the adjournment. Kaufman recalls that his aim throughout was to ensure that as few Labour members as possible voted against the Labour front-bench line.[38]

Apart from the pacifist left, the only other leading dissenting voice in the House of Commons was Edward Heath. He contradicted Hurd's line, and claimed that military action by the allied coalition would need the further authority of the United Nations.[39] But even Heath voted with the Government in the final vote.[40]

According to Mrs Thatcher's memoirs, after the debate, the Prime Minister discussed the imposition of sanctions with Douglas Hurd. At this stage, Hurd felt sanctions might succeed if the alliance formed against him could convince Saddam Hussein that he would be militarily defeated if he stayed in Kuwait. Mrs Thatcher, on the other hand, was worried that leaving the troops too long in the Saudi desert might lead to the break up of the fragile Arab coalition.[41] Hurd recollects that there were nuances of difference between himself and the Prime Minister. The pattern was repeated across the Atlantic where James Baker was, like Hurd, more instinctively cautious. Hurd recalls that '[George] Bush and Margaret Thatcher were just slightly impatient to get on with it.'[42] Baker and Hurd were insistent that each stage of the escalation should require a UN Security Council resolution, providing an additional political basis for military action:

> It was a mistake simply to say that international law makes it possible to do these things without a specific resolution – legally that was correct – but you needed to carry people with you in a way that we actually managed to do.[43]

Hurd had in mind the support of China and the Soviet Union. As permanent members of the Security Council, they held vetoes over further United Nations involvement in the Gulf. James Baker and Douglas Hurd met for talks at the United States Embassy in Moscow on 11 September. They talked for an hour in the so-called 'funny room', where a series of taped voices are played so that eavesdroppers cannot listen in. Hurd describes the effect as 'like having a conversation at a cocktail party in an ocean liner'.[44]

The following day, Hurd visited President Gorbachev. Almost each time they met, Hurd encountered Gorbachev in fine form. This occasion was no exception:

> 12 Sept. 1990: Gorbachev sparkles. Gives us an informal Q & A about the
> state of the Soviet Union, especially economic reform, the state of the
> republics. So self-confident that he persuades us within the four walls, but
> outside all is slipping.[45]

In contrast, after his first meeting with Boris Yeltsin (then leader of the Russian Federation), Hurd was struck by his authoritarian manner:

> 12 Sept. 1990: A dictator in waiting. Unsighted on detail, vigorous and
> entirely confident. Enjoy the joust and learn that he will win over
> Gorbachev.[46]

Later, he dined with Eduard Shevardnadze, the Soviet Foreign Minister with whom Hurd always had good relations. In 1996, after his resignation from the Foreign Office, Hurd kept in touch by visiting the former Russian Foreign Minister, by this stage President of Georgia. Looking back, Hurd was struck by the extent of Shevardnadze's flexibility on whether a reunified Germany should be in NATO, the extent of Russian co-operation during the Gulf War and the Russian attitude to the collapse of the Warsaw Pact.

The only blot on Hurd's landscape was the attempts of his former boss, Edward Heath (and also Tony Benn), to intervene on behalf of the British hostages held in Kuwait. The Conservative Party leadership certainly did not appreciate the timing of Heath's announcement – during the Conservative Party Conference in Bournemouth – that he was going to Baghdad.[47] John Campbell, a biographer of Edward Heath, sees the former Prime Minister's initiative over the Gulf hostages as his last attempt to reoccupy the world stage.[48] Leading figures in the Conservative Party felt that Hurd should have done more to try to block Heath's visit, but his instincts were to refrain from attacking Heath. This made sense. Hurd could not really stop Heath from going. Heath's visit to Iraq went ahead on 19 October, but he only succeeded in bringing home thirty-three hostages (in an aeroplane supplied courtesy of Richard Branson).[49]

However, these were minor irritants for Douglas Hurd. The British Foreign Secretary was probably at the peak of his standing in the Conservative Party and in the country. But the profession is a precarious one: shares in Hurd dipped a few days later when he made a trip to Israel which he admits was 'in a way the most unsuccessful foreign visit that I did in the whole time I was Foreign Secretary.'[50]

Hurd fell victim to the gesture politics of Israel in much the same way as he had suffered at the hands of the conflicting political groups in Northern Ireland as Secretary of State. On arrival on 15 October, the British press entourage were snubbed at the airport by the Israeli authorities, putting them in a bad mood from the very outset. The following day, when Hurd went to the Knesset and saw Yitzshak Rabin[51] and the members of the Foreign Affairs Committee, the Foreign Secretary was reported by some of the Knesset members as having said that he was opposed to a Palestinian state. In fact, Hurd never said that. The careful line he took was that Israel had the right to secure borders and the Palestinians had the right to self-determination. The exact words Hurd used were that he 'did not particularly favour' a Palestinian state. However, members of the Israeli Knesset leaked the content of the private conversation to Israeli television, which picked up the story that Hurd had ruled out a Palestinian state. Hurd tried to repair the damage by saying the British position had not changed 'one jot or tittle', but the following day (17 October) the Palestinians boycotted a meeting scheduled with the Foreign Secretary. It was a humiliating moment: Hurd was kept waiting in the full glare of publicity and was subsequently snubbed. In a final attempt to recoup something from the visit, Hurd met with the Israeli Foreign Minister, David Levy. However, Levy spoke no English, and Hurd was forced to converse with him in French, resulting in a very long-winded discussion. The meeting with Levy also exposed, to Hurd's fury, the glaring lack of Foreign Office officials who spoke Hebrew.

Hurd describes the episode as 'a deliberate attempt, not by the Israeli Government, but by Knesset members, to make mischief and they succeeded.'[52] The British press reacted badly to the visit. A lead article in *The Times* on 18 October criticised the Foreign Secretary.

Assessing the motives of the Knesset members is difficult. Hurd's visit included the opening of a British Council centre in Gaza which had been built without the permission of the Israeli authorities. Gaza was then still part of the Occupied Territories, although the British Government had a long-established policy of refusing to recognise the area as Israeli territory. Even more pressing was the instability caused by the Temple Mount massacre. On 8 October, less than a week before Hurd's visit, Israeli soldiers had shot dead twenty-one Palestinians on the Dome of the Rock or the Temple Mount area of Jerusalem. Before Hurd left for Israel, he penned an article in the *Sunday Express* in which he condemned the Israelis for the incident. Although Israel had a right to secure borders they did not have a right to deny the Palestinians basic freedoms:

> Their schools are closed at a whim. Their water sources are siphoned away. Illegal settlements are built on their lands. They are subject to collective punishment for the violence of individuals.[53]

There was a real danger that the Iraqi President would succeed in decoupling the Arab coalition ranged against him by trying to link his withdrawal from Kuwait with the settlement of the question of the Israeli Occupied Territories This was summed up by Hurd's pithy comment that 'we must not allow him [Saddam] to throw sand in our eyes.'[54] But in order to retain a line to the Palestinians, Hurd supported the UN Secretary General's proposals to investigate the Temple Mount killings and expressed the hope that when Saddam Hussein had been ousted from Kuwait, there would be 'a new opportunity for fresh thinking' on the Palestinian question.[55]

Within a week, Douglas Hurd had recuperated sufficiently to focus on the forthcoming Rome Summit at the end of October. The main historical argument over the 'First Rome Summit', as it became known, was whether Mrs Thatcher and Douglas Hurd had been ambushed by the chairman of the summit, the Italian Prime Minister Giulio Andreotti, who introduced a specific starting date for Stage Two of the Delors Plan for European Economic and Monetary Union (known as EMU).[56]

Douglas Hurd was surprised at the Italian proposal because of a reassuring conversation he had had with Chancellor Kohl in Bonn only twenty-four hours before the summit. This was another visit organised with the full knowledge of the Prime Minister, with Hurd acting as an emissary. During the meeting on 26 October, Hurd claims Kohl gave no prior indication that he would press during the Rome Summit for a firm date for Stage Two. Hurd claims he was led to believe that all the main proposals would come to the table at the Inter-Governmental Conference (IGC) scheduled for December.

There appears to be a considerable weight of evidence leaning the other way. Chancellor Kohl had said publicly two weeks earlier that he wanted a start date for Stage Two of January 1994. In his biography of Mrs Thatcher, Hugo Young claims that London received a telegram from the British Embassy in Rome reporting that several of the other members states were coalescing around a fixed date for Stage Two.[57] While Mrs Thatcher and Douglas Hurd may not have been cruelly deceived by their European partners, it is unlikely that Hurd would have misread the line being taken by Chancellor Kohl — information which the Foreign Secretary faithfully reported to the Prime Minister.[58] It is not being disingenuous to claim that the Italian political leaders at this time had a reputation for cunning and engaging in gesture politics. Goaded by the European press for their inaction over their presidency, they may have desired to launch a *coup de théâtre*. It is difficult to trust the word of the then Italian Foreign Minister, Gianni de Michelis, a man who was jailed in July 1993 for accepting bribes from Italian businessmen eager to win lucrative road-construction contracts. In July 1995, the former Prime Minister, Giulio

Andreotti, was charged with murder. What may have happened is that Chancellor Kohl, who had been warming to the idea of a firm date for Stage Two, jumped on board the Italian bandwagon at the summit.

What is certain is that Mrs Thatcher had clearly expected to push the British agenda of completing the Uruguay round of the General Agreement on Tariffs and Trade (GATT) and securing measures against Saddam Hussein. The Prime Minister and Douglas Hurd do seem to have been genuinely shocked by the content of the Italian draft conclusions. At every summit, the heads of the delegation receive the draft conclusions early on the morning of the final day and have to wade through them quickly, safeguarding their positions, highlighting where they disagree. Over breakfast on the morning of 28 October, Hurd and Margaret Thatcher looked through the draft summit conclusions:

> 28 Oct. 1990: They are bad. Andreotti is pressing beyond what we hope. Palazzo Madama [sixteenth-century building previously owned by the Florentine Medici family; became the seat of the Italian Senate in 1871] to concert with officials. I handle political union. Six objections.[59]

Meanwhile, the Prime Minister handled EMU. Hurd recalls the real damage was done, as always, with Mrs Thatcher's unscripted remarks at the subsequent press conference. In his diary entry for 28 October, he describes the Prime Minister's performance as 'assertive and angry'.[60]

On his return to London the following day, 29 October, Alan Clark, then Minister of State for Defence, paid a visit to Hurd:

> 29 Oct. 1990: I must be prepared to lead the party at once. It couldn't go on any longer. I was the only person who could take over. Disabuse him.[61]

The following day (30 October), Mrs Thatcher made her famous 'No, No, No' comments to the House of Commons. Once again, it was not the meticulously scripted Foreign Office statement which caused the difficulty, but Mrs Thatcher's answer to the supplementary remarks. Hurd recollects his reaction:

> She [Mrs Thatcher] was very offensive to her European partners. She carried it off, but I disliked the way she did it intensely.[62]

In Hurd's opinion, Mrs Thatcher's irresistible desire for the theatrical had begun to wear thin. While it may have excited her backbenchers, it upset the Cabinet's carefully agreed policy and upset Britain's European partners. Her 'No, No, No' comments also sparked Geoffrey Howe's resignation from the Government, tipping the Conservative Party over the precipice into a leadership contest.

Notes

1. Diary Readings with Douglas Hurd, 26 Feb. 1997.
2. Interview with Douglas Hurd, 26 Feb. 1997.
3. Philip Stephens, *Politics and the Pound: The Conservatives' Struggle with Sterling* (Macmillan: London, 1996), p. 128.
4. Diary Readings with Douglas Hurd, 26 Feb. 1997.
5. Hurd was preferred over Cecil Parkinson (Secretary of State for Transport) and Tom King (Secretary of State for Defence). Kenneth Baker, *The Turbulent Years*, p. 308.
6. Douglas Hurd, 'The Tyranny of Time', *Letters from a Diplomat*, Radio 4, 24 Jun. 1996 (original transcript).
7. Douglas Hurd, 'Has Cook Run Out of Time?', *Daily Telegraph*, 14 May 1998.
8. *The Times*, 19 Jan. 1978. George Brown had been giving evidence to the Defence and External Affairs Subcommittee of the Commons Expenditure Committee the previous day.
9. Stephens, *Politics and the Pound*, p. 143.
10. 'Thatcher orders the SAS into Cambodia's killing fields', *Daily Mirror*, 1 Nov. 1989.
11. James Lester was a long-standing member of the Foreign Affairs Select Committee, and more pertinently, was Chairman of the all-Party Parliamentary British-Vietnam Group as well as chair of the Overseas Development and Refugees Group. On 1 November 1989, he raised the issue of Cambodia in an adjournment debate. H. of C. Deb. (6th Series), 1 Nov. 1989, vol. 159, cols 439–44.
12. *The Guardian*, 29 Nov. 1989.
13. *See* Alan Watkins, *The Fall of Margaret Thatcher: A Conservative Coup – A Post-Election View* (Duckworth, Second Edition: London, 1992), p. 132. To be fair, Watkins did go on to comment that, 'It seems a little hard to treat Mr Hurd as if he were a sixteenth-century Jesuit – or a twentieth-century Scientologist – bringing innocent minds to the service of strange faiths.', p. 133.
14. Douglas Hurd, 'Wars and Peacemakers', *Letters from a Diplomat*, Radio 4, 1 Jul. 1996 (original transcript).
15. Margaret Thatcher, *The Downing Street Years*, pp. 796–9.
16. Douglas Hurd, 'Wars and Peacemakers'.
17. Douglas Hurd interviewed by Michael Elliot, *The Poisoned Chalice*, 'Nemesis – The Enemy Within', Part 4, BBC2, 30 May 1996.

18. Diary Readings with Douglas Hurd, 18 Mar. 1997.

19. Interview with Douglas Hurd, 18 Mar. 1997.

20. Diary Readings with Douglas Hurd, 18 Mar. 1997.

21. Quoted in Watkins, *The Fall of Margaret Thatcher*, p. 133.

22. Diary Readings with Douglas Hurd, 18 Mar. 1997.

23. Ibid.

24. *The Independent*, 14 Jul. 1990.

25. Anthony Bevins, 'Tory MPs say Ridley must go', *The Independent*, 14 Jul. 1990.

26. *The Times*, 17 Jul. 1990.

27. Timothy Garton-Ash interviewed in Hugo Young, *The Last Europeans,* 'The Crunch', Part 2, Channel 4, 3 Dec. 1995.

28. Stephens, *Politics and the Pound*, p. 150.

29. H. of C. Deb. (6th Series), 23 Feb. 1993, vol. 219, cols 776–7.

30. Douglas Hurd, 'Wars and Peacemakers'.

31. Diary Readings with Douglas Hurd, 18 Mar. 1997.

32. Interview with Douglas Hurd, 18 Mar. 1997.

33. Diary Readings with Douglas Hurd, 18 Mar. 1997.

34. Ibid.

35. Ibid.

36. Article 51 of the UN charter says that states have a right to self-determination 'until the Security Council has taken measures necessary to maintain international peace and security.'

37. H. of C. Deb. (6th Series), 7 Sept. 1990, vol. 177, col. 892.

38. Interview with Gerald Kaufman, 13 Nov. 1996.

39. H. of C. Deb. (6th Series), 6 Sept. 1990, vol. 177, cols 751–3.

40. On a technical motion moved by Tony Benn – an adjournment of the House of Commons – only thirty-seven Labour MPs backed the move against 437 in the Government lobby. Ibid., cols 903–6.

41. Thatcher, *Downing Street Years*, pp. 824–5.

42. Interview with Douglas Hurd, 18 Mar. 1997.

43. Ibid.

44. Ibid.

45. Diary Readings with Douglas Hurd, 18 Mar. 1997.

46. Ibid.

47. George Jones, 'Ted's Party Trick', the *Sunday Times*, 14 Oct. 1990.

48. Campbell, *Edward Heath*, p. 780.

49. Tony Benn also went to Baghdad at this time. For a fuller account, *see* Tony Benn, *The End of An Era*, pp. 616–24.

50. Interview with Douglas Hurd, 18 Mar. 1997.

51. Rabin had just been ousted as leader of the Labour Party by Shimon Peres in July 1990.

52. Interview with Douglas Hurd, 18 Mar. 1997.

53. Douglas Hurd, 'Why I condemn Israel's actions', *Sunday Express*, 14 Oct. 1990.

54. Ibid.

55. Ibid.

56. The Delors Committee on EMU had, unwisely in retrospect, been agreed by Mrs Thatcher at the Hanover Summit in 1988. The committee consisted of a group of central bankers chaired by the European Commission President, Jacques Delors. Its report recommended a three-stage plan on the road to monetary union. Stage One envisaged all the countries of the European Community joining the Exchange Rate Mechanism (ERM), with the abolition of capital controls and greater use of the European Currency Unit (ECU). This would be followed by the creation of a European Monetary Institute, which in Stage Three would be transformed into a European Central Bank running a single currency with fixed exchange rates.

57. Young, *One of Us*, p. 575.

58. Thatcher, *Downing Street Years*, p. 765.

59. Diary Readings with Douglas Hurd, 18 Mar. 1997.

60. Ibid.

61. Ibid.

62. Interview with Douglas Hurd, 18 Mar. 1997.

15

A Good, Solid Deputy:
The Conservative Leadership Contest
of November 1990

Before announcing his resignation, Geoffrey Howe telephoned Tim Renton, the Chief Whip, and also Douglas Hurd, since 'it was on his patch that any policy backlash was most likely to come'.[1] Surprised at Howe's decision, Hurd tried to dissuade him, claiming 'it would make the position of the pro-Europeans in the Cabinet more difficult'.[2] Even by early November 1990, Hurd still believed that with the help of John Major (then Chancellor of the Exchequer), he could tie Mrs Thatcher into an agreed policy on Europe. In a speech to the CBI in Glasgow on 6 November, Hurd moved to discount talk of a leadership contest, but set out his pragmatic approach to the single currency and political union. He argued that a common currency might in time evolve into a single currency, but that it had to come about as a result of the economic choices of consumers, not through political imposition. Indirectly, Hurd warned Mrs Thatcher about her increasingly aggressive language on European matters:

> There is no dread conspiracy against us, there is simply an argument, and no reason why we should be scared or defeatist in that argument . . . We must continue to fight our corner for British interests, but we can do that without frightening ourselves with ogres.[3]

However, what became known as Hurd's 'ogres speech' was undermined by Michael Heseltine's open letter to his Henley constituents published in the *Sunday Times*. The letter was widely interpreted as an opening shot in his long-awaited leadership bid. The Foreign Secretary quickly assumed his by now

251

familiar role of a firefighter, appearing on the *Walden* programme, and pronounced Heseltine's letter 'not particularly wise'.[4]

Such was the hostility heaped on Heseltine by the Tory press that the crisis might have blown over had not Geoffrey Howe delivered his stinging resignation speech of Tuesday, 13 November. This gave Michael Heseltine the 'unforeseen set of circumstances' for which he had been waiting. After Howe's speech, Hurd saw the Prime Minister alone and had a frank discussion about her future:

> 13 Nov. 1990: She's wounded. She's hard to work with, but most of us want to try, even though she finds it difficult to argue without causing offence.[6]

The next morning, Hurd had breakfast with John Major:

> 14 Nov. 1990: He's grey, with a heavy cold and a bad abscess in his tooth. Obviously, he has at the back of his mind [that] he might stand after Margaret withdraws if she does. I still think she will win, but the 'mad house' is producing a swing against her after Geoffrey Howe's speech. The two Pattens, William Waldegrave, Tim Yeo (my PPS) urge me to be brave and come in if she quits.[7]

Hurd's name had been touted as a possible candidate as far back as 1986. After the Westland crisis, three 'Blue Chips'[8] – Chris and John Patten and William Waldegrave – had approached Douglas Hurd, asking him to stand as a candidate if Mrs Thatcher fell. Tristan Garel-Jones said words to the effect, that if Mrs Thatcher fell, a number of colleagues would come knocking at his door. Hurd's reply is said to have been, 'You'll have to knock very hard.'[9]

In November 1989, when Anthony Meyer challenged Mrs Thatcher, a contingency plan was floated involving Douglas Hurd. If Mrs Thatcher had fallen, Hurd would have been wheeled in as a party unity candidate. The move was supported by a wide cross-section of the party; demonstrated by the fact that Alan Clark on the right of the party, and Nicholas Scott on the left, were willing to act as proposer and seconder. Garel-Jones, John Major and Chris Patten would also have given their backing to the idea.[10] When Hurd was approached, however, he refused to have anything to do with the plan, but was seen as the 'Number Eleven Bus' candidate: the most likely successor should anything happen to Mrs Thatcher.[11]

There was one flaw in this view of Hurd; no one is sure whether Hurd ever wanted to be leader of the Conservative Party and Prime Minister. As William Whitelaw commented in November 1990, 'the trouble with Douglas was the same with me in 1975. He doesn't really want the job.'[12] Alan Clark's diary entry of 13 November 1990 described Hurd as 'deeply reluctant'.[13] Clark drew the analogy with Lord Halifax (Douglas Hurd), Churchill (John Major) and George IV (the Queen), suspecting that Hurd would step aside in favour of Major as Halifax had done in favour of Churchill.[14] On Tuesday, 20 November, Peter Jenkins, political columnist of *The Independent*, shared this view:

> Mr Hurd, far from edging forward, is holding back, uncertain about entering the fray at all, although he will likely be prevailed upon to do so if second ballot there is and she [Mrs Thatcher] withdraws.[15]

On Friday, 16 November, speaking at a Conservative businessmen's lunch in Batley, Yorkshire, Hurd appeared to make his continued loyalty conditional on Mrs Thatcher sticking to an agreed policy on Europe:

> When this contest is over, the Prime Minister and the Cabinet will want to draw the threads of our policy on Europe together unmistakably, and rally the party and the country behind us.[16]

He repeated his support for Geoffrey Howe's view of Europe, but added:

> I part company with him over his conclusion that our party's policy cannot be effectively carried through with Mrs Thatcher as our party's leader.[17]

Later that day, at a press conference in Leeds, Hurd stated that he was confident that Mrs Thatcher would win on the first ballot. Kenneth Baker, then Conservative Party Chairman, also remembers Hurd saying there was a 'pricking in my thumbs'[18] that she would win on the first ballot.

But at the Leeds press conference, Hurd was provoked by the press when he revealed that he would not stand 'against her'[19] — strongly inferring that he might stand in a possible second ballot. Hurd was later blamed by Mrs Thatcher's supporters for undermining her position during the first round. Actually, Hurd was genuinely annoyed that his comments had been taken out of context. His overriding objective in this phase of the leadership contest was to piece the party back together in time for the general election. Despite his policy differences with Mrs Thatcher over Europe, the quickest means of achieving that was a Thatcher victory in the first ballot.

Michael Heseltine seized on Hurd's comments, using them as a way of enticing potential Hurd supporters into voting for Heseltine on the first ballot. This, Heseltine teased, would ensure Mrs Thatcher's demise, in turn opening the way for a second ballot to take place in which figures like Douglas Hurd would be freed to stand. This mischievous ploy carried obvious dangers for

Heseltine because if he and his team talked up Hurd's chances too much, Hurd might win a possible second ballot. But the important point is that Hurd observed too many of the proprieties, instructing Tim Yeo, his PPS, not to go canvassing on his behalf before the first ballot. At this point, private approaches were made by senior backbenchers who might have initially preferred to back Hurd rather than Heseltine, but once Hurd had sent them on their way, they supported Heseltine and did not come over to Hurd in the second ballot.[20] Hurd's attitude was honourable, but not what was required to win.

Hurd agreed to sign Mrs Thatcher's nomination papers for the first ballot. On Sunday, 18 November, he began canvassing colleagues on Mrs Thatcher's behalf. Conversations with Chris and John Patten, Malcolm Rifkind and William Whitelaw brought him to the view that he would stand if Mrs Thatcher was beaten or withdrew from the contest.[21] That day, Douglas Hurd was irritated by Mrs Thatcher's comments in an interview with Charles Moore, Associate Editor of the *Sunday Telegraph,* in which she refused to rule out a referendum on the single currency.[22] Once again, Hurd's careful plan to unite the party on Europe was showing signs of cracking. Hurd also disliked the manner in which the Prime Minister attacked Michael Heseltine in *The Times* on the following day, accusing him of 'interventionism, corporatism, everything that pulled us down'.[23]

If John Major was hampered by his wisdom-tooth operation (although one could argue that by staying away from the seamy events, Major avoided creating enemies for himself), Hurd was unable to influence events at Westminster, because he was to accompany Mrs Thatcher to the Conference of Security and Co-operation in Europe (CSCE), being held in Paris to mark the end of the Cold War in Europe.

The result of the first ballot was relayed to Mrs Thatcher in Paris on the Tuesday night. She had failed to clear the first hurdle by only four votes. Hurd had only been told about Mrs Thatcher's prepared statement minutes before the result. It had been decided at a meeting on Monday morning between John Wakeham, Kenneth Baker, George Younger and Cranley Onslow, that if she narrowly failed to clear the hurdle posed by the first ballot, she would go straight into the second round.

According to second-hand accounts, Charles Powell, Mrs Thatcher's adviser on Foreign Affairs, exerted unnecessary pressure on Hurd to sign Mrs Thatcher's nomination papers for the second ballot.[24] In fact, Hurd did not hesitate in backing Mrs Thatcher.[25] Hurd asked Peter Morrison, Mrs Thatcher's PPS, if he should make a statement. Morrison concurred, but they both decided that Hurd should answer no questions. Twenty minutes after the initial result, Hurd stood on the steps of the British Embassy:

The Prime Minister continues to have my full support and I am sorry this destructive and unnecessary contest should be prolonged in this way.[26]

That evening in Paris, Hurd was filled with genuine admiration for his Prime Minister:

> She carried herself magnificently at Versailles that evening. All eyes were upon her as dinner followed banquet, and course followed course at the immense table in the Galerie des Glaces. They looked upon her as some wounded eagle, who had herself wounded many in the past, but whom no one wished to see brought down, unable to soar again. Thanks to her own style and courage she was not humiliated. During the eleven years in which I served in her Government I felt many emotions towards our Prime Minister. Admiration was rarely far away. But I never felt so admiring as on that last night in Paris in November 1990.[27]

That night, Hurd also kept in touch with opinion amongst MPs in Westminster via his PPS, Timothy Yeo, who attended a meeting of ministers at Tristan Garel-Jones's flat in Catherine Place. Yeo also spoke that evening on the phone to Judy Hurd, who had not gone with Hurd to Paris. Although Judy had been very loyal to Mrs Thatcher, she was, according to Yeo, 'less reluctant than Douglas was, at the thought of him being a candidate'.[28] This view has been confirmed by Chris Patten, who remembers that it was a problem getting Hurd to stand but that he was persuaded by Judy.[29]

The following morning, it emerged that Mrs Thatcher wanted to cling on to office. Cabinet unity was to form the basis of Mrs Thatcher's second round campaign, and she agreed to see the members of the Cabinet individually to confirm their support. Meanwhile, Hurd had been having his lunch with Chris Patten and Tim Yeo at the Foreign Office. Even at this late stage, Hurd believed that Mrs Thatcher would battle her way to victory. However, if she fell, he correctly predicted that John Major would be the most likely recipient of the Thatcherite vote.[30]

During his audience with the Prime Minister, Hurd informed her of his continued support, but asked her not to resort to the personalised attacks which she had launched against Michael Heseltine during the first round.[31] But, Kenneth Clarke, Malcolm Rifkind and Chris Patten all made it clear that she risked humiliation if she stood in the second ballot.

By the time Mrs Thatcher realised she could not carry on, there was insufficient time to assess whether John Major or Douglas Hurd should stand. Michael Jopling, the former Chief Whip, suggested to Kenneth Clarke that more than one candidate was needed in order to give the party a wider choice and provide insurance against a barnstorming Heseltine victory in the second ballot.[32] Clarke agreed. At the time, there was no wholly reliable estimate of who was the stronger candidate, Hurd or Major. Tristan Garel-Jones's assessment that Major was going to win was an insufficient basis on which to risk putting Major up directly against Heseltine.

Kenneth Clarke, accompanied by the Deputy Chief Whip, Alastair Goodlad, went to see Hurd. Clarke wanted to make sure that his favoured candidate was willing to stand. Again, Hurd was reluctant. Bruce Anderson's assessment that Hurd would have quite happily bowed out, gracefully supporting a brokered solution in favour of John Major, is probably right. But Clarke told Hurd that there was no time left for soundings, and Hurd confirmed that he would stand against Major if Mrs Thatcher stepped down.[33] Clarke then called John Major to inform him of Hurd's decision, and to persuade Major to stand as well.

For Douglas Hurd, Thursday morning began by observing proprieties, and then rushing around to get his nomination papers in before the twelve-noon deadline. The Cabinet was brought forward to 9 a.m. to allow ministers to go to Lady Home's memorial service. During Mrs Thatcher's final Cabinet, Hurd scribbled an elegant note which became his and Major's joint statement. Hurd tried to catch the eye of Tom King, the Defence Secretary, to ask him if he would act as his proposer on the second ballot, but King failed to cotton-on. In between passing notes and dropping hints, Hurd also paid tribute to the Prime Minister's composure at Paris, but Mrs Thatcher replied that she could cope with business on her final morning, but not with sympathy.[34]

When Cabinet finished, Hurd excused himself from coffee, and immediately secured Tom King, Secretary of State for Defence as his proposer. Minutes later, Heseltine telephoned King to ask for his support, but King explained what had just happened.[35] Despite having worked under Heseltine at Environment, Tom King preferred a candidate experienced in foreign affairs, who could handle the tense situation in the Gulf, in his words, 'with a very steady nerve indeed'.[36] The Defence Secretary was very much an honourable figure who had been annoyed at Heseltine's decision to stand for the Tory leadership on the verge of a possible war in the Gulf.[37] Hurd then asked David Waddington, the Home Secretary, to act as seconder, but he refused. Waddington also turned down the chance to act as seconder to Major's campaign. Tristan Garel-Jones believes that the failure to court Waddington was a crucial blow to Hurd's campaign, because the Home Secretary represented the traditional right, from where it was thought Hurd might gain a number of backers.[38] Both the Hurd and Heseltine campaign teams searched in vain for a figure on the right to 'balance the ticket'. Instead, Hurd asked Chris Patten to act as seconder, giving his ticket a distinctly dampish feel.

The rest of Hurd's campaign team also had a distinctly 'damp'[39] feel to it.

Douglas Hurd with Edward Heath and Teng Hsiao Ping, China, 1974.
(William Waldegrave is on Hurd's left)

At the Great Wall of China with Mrs Thatcher, leader of
the opposition, 1977

Douglas Hurd with the Queen and Francis Pym (right), Foreign Office, 1982

Douglas, Judy and their son, Philip. Philip was born on election night,
June 1983, causing Hurd to miss his count

New Year's Day on the mountains of Mourne in Northern Ireland, with sons
Tom and Alexander, 1985

In County Down with the Bradley family, 1985

On the lake at Chevening with Philip, 1991

In Sarajevo with President Izetbegovic, 1992

Enjoying Argentinian hospitality on the Gibson estançia, 1993

Rajasthan, India, 1994

In Vitez, Bosnia, with British troops, 1994

Hurd sports a new coat, admired by John Sawers
(Principal Private Secretary)

Enjoying a relaxed walk along the Rhine with the German Foreign Minister
Klaus Kinkel and his family, 1995

At Westwell with Judy and their daughter Jessica, 1997

Sir Giles Shaw, Treasurer of the backbench 1922 Committee, who had served under Hurd at the Home Office as Minister of State, was appointed chairman of the campaign team, but the campaign manager was effectively John Patten, another former colleague of Hurd's at the Home Office, while Chris Patten acted as a kind of supervisory guru.[40]

Hurd's candidature received heavy-weight backing when six members of the Cabinet (to Major's seven) declared their support,[41] but there was an absence of right-wingers. Very few of the Ministers of State who declared for Hurd had any significant Thatcherite credentials.[42] There were some notable exceptions among more junior ministers. Michael Fallon, MP for Darlington and Parliamentary Under Secretary of State at Education and Science, was a Thatcherite. David Heathcoat-Amory, Hurd's former PPS at the Home Office and then Parliamentary Under Secretary of State at the Department of the Environment, came on board, as did Tim Eggar, MP for Enfield North. Andrew Mackay, MP for Berkshire East, was the only confirmed convert from the 'Tory right' and no confirmed supporter of Hurd came from the 'populists'. This is interesting. While Hurd put up a respectable showing among the 'neo-liberals', he was clearly disliked by the 'Tory right' and the 'populists'. This seems to date from the row over Hong Kong passports a year earlier. Norman Tebbit made a great deal of fuss at the time (see Chapter 19) and said he was not voting for 'Hong Kong Hurd'.[43] Only one right-wing Hong Kong rebel publicly supported Hurd: the monetarist Nicholas Budgen, MP for Wolverhampton South West. Budgen was on record as admiring Hurd's instincts as a traditional Tory.[44] According to press reports, Budgen had to be calmed down when he told the Hurd campaign team of his plan to denounce Major's record as Chief Secretary to the Treasury.[45]

Attention has focused on the role of Tristan Garel-Jones, then Minister of State at the Foreign Office, who acted as Hurd's campaign whip. Some MPs have since speculated that he may have had one foot in the Hurd campaign and the other in the Major camp.[46] According to Robert Shepherd's account, Garel-Jones knew by the Friday morning that Hurd had secured only sixty votes, around thirty, he thought, coming from Heseltine's vote in the first ballot. His own private estimate was that Major would win with 180 votes, with Heseltine second on 132 and Hurd trailing way behind on 60. Yet, according to Shepherd, he did not inform Hurd of this assessment until the day before the result.[47] But, Hurd's diaries show that the Foreign Secretary was well aware that his own campaign was stuck in the sidings. On Friday, 23 November Hurd started ringing around colleagues and noted in his diary that a bandwagon had started to roll for John Major and that there was no 'denting' that.[48] Hurd's prediction on the Wednesday that the right would vote for Major had proved correct. The following day, Hurd recognised that his campaign was going nowhere:

> 24 Nov. 1990: I obtained Peter Brooke's support by telephone. Little
> progress otherwise. I fear we are stuck, but an agreeable day nonetheless.[49]

The real reason why fellow MPs raised doubts about Garel-Jones's true
allegiances can be easily explained. Within the first twelve hours, the Hurd camp
received the basic number of supporters, around fifty, but quickly became stuck.
When Garel-Jones heard that MPs like Sir Dennis Walters, Sir Charles Morrison
and Sir Ian Gilmour, who had voted for Heseltine on the first ballot, were not
coming across to Douglas Hurd, he knew that the game was up.[50] In fact, Hurd's
own canvassers were very slow to get off the mark. Sir Dennis Walters, in
particular, was a close friend of Hurd's, and yet he was not consulted about his
plans on the Thursday.[51] The view of many of those who had voted for Heseltine
on the first ballot was that Heseltine had had the courage to stand against Mrs
Thatcher, and he had very nearly made it. Hurd, they reasoned, had left it too
late, and they were going to carry on supporting Heseltine. Nigel Lawson claims
that he was not canvassed by the Hurd campaign. Given his close friendship with
Hurd, this seems another glaring omission.[52] In short, Hurd's campaign got off
to a stuttering start and most of the team, including Douglas Hurd, knew the
contest was lost in the first twenty-four hours.

Hurd's first press conference started badly, with an unseemly scrum of
journalists, as they tried to fit into the Map Room at the Foreign Office. The
venue was too small. It was symptomatic of the amateurish and ad hoc way in
which the Hurd campaign was run. Of more significance was Hurd's failure
immediately to match Heseltine's promise to abandon the poll-tax:

> It's clear to me that this should be, on the domestic front, the top priority
> for the new Cabinet. It's an urgent priority. We have to continue to do our
> utmost to make the community charge fairer and more acceptable in the eyes
> of those who have to pay it.[53]

While he realised that the poll-tax had to be abandoned, the Foreign Secretary
viewed the handling of the issue, according to Chris Patten, as 'a question of
seemliness'.[54] Hurd did not want to be seen to be repudiating a key policy plank
of a Cabinet of which he had been a member for so long. Over the weekend,
Chris Patten, the Environment Secretary, dusted off a plan for a complete
overhaul of the poll-tax, and Hurd changed his line in a series of interviews
over the weekend:

> I don't think those changes will be enough and nor does Chris Patten, and
> therefore we have to go to the cupboard for ideas — and this is going to be
> very urgent — and see what's in there.[55]

Finally, over the weekend, the Hurd campaign began to roll. He brought back Edward Bickham, his old special adviser from the Home Office, to handle the media side. On the Monday morning, Hurd enjoyed his only successful press conference of the campaign, making a serious attempt to address the important policy issues of Europe, education and health. Chris Patten and William Waldegrave helped Hurd bring together these policy ideas over the weekend.[56] On Europe, Hurd promised a paper setting out the government's proposals on economic and monetary union ahead of the inter-governmental conferences. Hurd used the fact that William Waldegrave, the Secretary of State for Health, and Kenneth Clarke, Secretary of State for Education, were both on his side, to promote health and education as 'the two great public services'.[57] The line was very much to promise a period of consolidation after Mrs Thatcher's introduction of the internal market in the National Health Service (NHS) and the creation of a national curriculum in Britain's schools. At the same press conference, Clarke delivered a gentle dig at John Major, claiming, 'Britain should not send beginners on to the world stage at the moment' and that Hurd was the man 'to get the big decisions right'.[58] However, The Guardian editorial the following day was unimpressed, accusing Hurd of flannelling 'along an alien washing line of unfamiliar issues'.[59]

It was not merely poor canvassing and lacklustre press conferences which hampered Hurd's candidature. He was immediately put on the defensive when the Major camp delivered the most effective jibe of the campaign: that Hurd was an Old Etonian toff who lacked popular appeal. Tim Yeo, then Hurd's PPS, believes that the Hurd campaign was 'completely out-manoeuvred by that'.[60] Hurd tried to counter the claims of his background when interviewed by Jonathan Dimbleby. It was the most memorable quote from the whole campaign:

> I was brought up on a farm. I don't know how we got into all this. This is inverted snobbery. I thought I was running for Leader of the Conservative Party, not some demented Marxist outfit.[61]

Hurd was perfectly entitled to claim that this was inverted snobbery, but he made the mistake of trying to be lowlier-than-thou. He stressed that his father had been a 'tenant farmer' who would not have been able to afford to send his son to Eton, had Hurd not won a scholarship. His father's five hundred acres, he claimed, were 'not particularly good acres at Marlborough Downs'. Hurd's line about planting potatoes fifteen inches apart for nine pence an hour (see Chapter 1) made his father seem a dirt farmer rather than a well-heeled member of the farming establishment, who later became agricultural correspondent of The Times.[62] His father had been an MP, and was subsequently made a peer, while his grandfather, also an MP, had gone on to receive a knighthood. The unfortunate reality for Hurd was that he looked and sounded like a toff and no matter what he said, the general public perceived him as such. It was a tactical error for Hurd to try to compete with John Major's classless appeal. As Chris Patten has put it:

> How could an old Etonian who was President of the Union at Cambridge make himself sound lowlier than a lad from Brixton who left school at sixteen?[63]

Despite spawning eighteen British Prime Ministers of Great Britain, it is highly unlikely, though not impossible, that an Etonian will ever again become Prime Minister. In February 1995, Matthew Wilson, editor of the Eton Chronicle, wrote an article entitled 'Mundus Contra Etonienses' ('The World Against Etonians') in which he raised that very possibility:

> If public opinion continues to see Eton, beyond all other public schools, as a system of élitism and social injustice, no politician will dare to present the electorate with an Etonian as a potential prime minister. So much for those who insist that an Etonian education is an untold advantage in life.[64]

At first, Hurd seemed exasperated by the media's obsession with images. Interviewed in *The Guardian*, he said:

> I could jump up and down, change my hairstyle and alter my specs, but that's not the point . . . Images, images images. The day politics is dominated by images is the day it goes downhill.[65]

One journalist, at least, saw a positive advantage in Hurd's old-fashioned style. Writing slightly tongue in cheek, Simon Jenkins called upon the electorate:

> Oh give the vote to Barsetshire. Give it to village fêtes and autumn leaves, to damp Cotswold stone and muddy churches, to a novel by the fire and a slice of jam sponge. Give it to honest England and Douglas Hurd would win by a mile. The upwardly mobile Majorettes in their suburban lounges may deride him as the Duke of Omnium. But he is no grandee. He is of Framley Parsonage, lightly rehabbed by Laura Ashley.[66]

After the initial shock of the toff jibe, some of Hurd's supporters tried to turn Hurd's image to their advantage. Chris Patten wrote in the *Daily Telegraph*:

> We should be pleased not surprised to have here a politician always anxious
> to steal ten minutes between the speaking rostrum and the television studio
> to squint through those heavy spectacles at the engravings on the walls of the
> local parish church.[67]

Although Hurd disliked modern image-making techniques, the paradox was that he took great trouble over his appearance during the campaign. At the first main press conference on the Friday morning, he decided to appear in shirt sleeves, in order to present a more relaxed air. Over that weekend (24-25 November), he was photographed at a Red Cross jumble sale. Then he broke the rule that one should never appear with children or animals by being photographed with his two young children, Philip (then seven) and Jessica (five), and their two ponies 'Willow' and 'Betsy'. He even tried manfully to present a popular image by allowing himself to be filmed drinking beer at a constituency supper. Hurd was enough of a politician to care about how he looked and with whom he was seen. At a more serious level, he tried to present himself as the unity candidate, the man with the experience, who would deal authoritatively and in a statesmanlike way with the emerging crisis in the Gulf.[68] The problem was that the image projected failed to win over the voters in the opinion polls and among the narrower electorate of Tory MPs.

Hurd's own television interviews were relaxed and elegant, but once again he was put on the defensive by jibes from the more street-wise Major campaign team, who claimed that Douglas Hurd had insufficient experience in economic matters. This, coupled with the jibe that he was an Old Etonian, meant that his candidature was neutralised from the beginning. Francis Maude, who had worked so closely with Hurd at the Foreign Office a year earlier on the issue of Hong Kong (see Chapter 19), but who was now supporting Major as part of the Treasury team, was mainly responsible for disseminating the line that one could not have a Prime Minister who did not understand economics. For Douglas Hurd, who had never had an economic portfolio, it was a particularly hard charge to counter. Nigel Lawson believes that, 'basically, of all the people at the centre of the government in recent years, he had the least interest in economic policy.'[69]

Hurd had also made an unfortunate remark in 1987, when he admitted that 'the one thing I am not disciplined about is money. I am very much a back-of-the-envelope person.'[70]

Among the disenfranchised sections of the Conservative Party who nevertheless, according to the rules, had to be consulted, Hurd performed badly. Among the constituency associations he secured only 22 constituencies against 65 for Heseltine and an overwhelming 485 for John Major.[71] But he finished top of the poll of Conservative peers, with forty-five backers, against thirty-eight for Major and only seventeen backing Heseltine.[72] Despite being the only aspect of the contest in which Hurd came top, this served to highlight the mistaken perception of Hurd as an aristocratic Tory grandee. Among their Lordships, Hurd secured the heavy-weight support of William Whitelaw, who was concerned about John Major's inexperience.[73] Lord Home of the Hirsel, the former Prime Minister, also came on board, but there was disappointment when Lord Carrington, Hurd's old boss at the Foreign Office, decided to back Michael Heseltine. Despite being a great admirer of Douglas Hurd, Carrington felt he was not enough of 'a party politician in the sense that a prime minister has to be'.[74] In his view Douglas had a measured, rather withdrawn style which suited his being Foreign Secretary but not being Prime Minister. By contrast, Carrington preferred Michael Heseltine, because he had the 'fire and oratory' necessary to appeal to the electorate.[75]

Amongst the press, Hurd could only secure the official support of the *Daily Telegraph* and *The Independent on Sunday*. His friend Charles Moore, then Associate Editor of the *Daily Telegraph*, lent his weight to Hurd's campaign by penning an article in support.[76] Conrad Black, the owner of the Telegraph group, allowed Peregrine Worsthorne to back Major in the *Sunday Telegraph*, whilst at the same time, allowing supportive noises to be made in Hurd's direction. Heseltine could only manage the support of the *Sunday Times* and the *Mail on Sunday*, whilst Major scooped the rest of the Tory press in the shape of the *Sun*, the *News of the World*, the *Daily Mail* and *The Times* (although, as we have seen, Simon Jenkins wrote favourable pieces in *The Times* about Douglas Hurd). *The Independent* and *The Guardian* remained largely neutral, but Hurd received support from two of their experienced journalists, Ian Aitken and Hugo Young. Both stressed Hurd's experience, competence and intellectual capacity for the job of Prime Minister.[77] Both were Labour-supporting intellectuals from the old school with a lingering respect for the traditional Toryism which Douglas Hurd represented.

On Tuesday, 27 November 1990, Hurd entered Committee Room 12 to cast his vote. On his way out, he thanked the *Daily Mirror* for praising the cut of his suits. He would pass on the compliment to his tailor, Craggs of Swindon.

Hurd received a modest 56 votes (15 per cent of the Conservative MPs), whilst Major won with 185 votes (49.7 per cent), with Heseltine on 131 (35.2 per cent). Major had won nineteen fewer votes than Mrs Thatcher, who had been forced to step down. According to the rules, he was also two votes short of the simple majority needed on the second ballot. But Hurd immediately conceded defeat and told the press that his supporters would back Major if a third ballot was needed. In his statement to the press, the Foreign Secretary continued to emphasise that party unity was his priority:

It's been a very good fight, and I send heartfelt thanks to all those who worked so hard for me and all those who voted for me.

My aim throughout has been to help restore unity to the Conservative Party. I think we can now find unity with a broadly based Cabinet working in close consultation with our MPs and our supporters in the country. Having worked closely with John Major I believe in the new circumstances that John Major is the right leader for this task. I know he will be an excellent Prime Minister and he will have my full and unreserved support.[78]

Realising he could not win, Michael Heseltine also conceded defeat, and Cranley Onslow, Chairman of the 1922 Committee, declared John Major the winner, despite his failure to win under the rules.

Why did Hurd lose? One reason why Hurd lost might seem to be that he ran a lacklustre campaign. One of his campaign team has commented that ' "campaign" is too pugilistic a word for what was not a very distinguished effort'.[79] Douglas Hurd was too much of a gentleman who played it by the book and lacked both the necessary hunger for the job and the wily skills to run a hard-nosed campaign. Advised by a member of his campaign team to install more phone lines, he is alleged to have replied, 'What do we need with another one?'[80] William Waldegrave and Chris Patten, while being distinguished ministers, were not politicians with their finger on the pulse of the parliamentary party. In contrast, the Major camp contained more street-fighters. Only one member of the Government Whip's Office is thought to have voted for Douglas Hurd, with the vast majority opting for John Major. In addition, the Major camp had thrusting, media-friendly vipers like David Mellor and Francis Maude who put Hurd on the defensive about his background and his lack of economic experience.

But so far, this account has concentrated on campaign and candidate-centred explanations for Hurd's defeat. The conduct of Hurd's campaign was essentially irrelevant because at no point did he stand a chance of winning – the votes were simply never there. At least none of Hurd's fifty-five backers could be accused of political opportunism or of backing the wrong man for the wrong reasons. If one is seeking to establish a typical profile of a Hurd supporter, according to Philip Cowley, expert on Conservative leadership contests, they were disproportionately damp on economic issues, were members of the Government and were more likely to have been educated at Oxbridge.[81] It is perhaps significant that ten of Hurd's forty-four declared supporters had worked under him as junior ministers and PPSs, while three others, Steven Norris, MP for Epping Forest, Sir Patrick Mayhew, the Attorney-General, and Sir John Wheeler had observed him at close quarters at the Home Office. Another, Peter Blaker, had worked alongside Douglas Hurd as Minister of State at the Foreign

Office in the early 1980s. There was a certain element of admiration for the way in which Hurd ran his departments. The exceptions to this rule were Francis Maude, formerly with Hurd at the Foreign Office (who disagreed with Hurd over Europe), and David Mellor, both of whom backed John Major. Mellor was not impressed by Hurd's performance as a Minster of State at the Home Office, nor by his handling of the Broadcasting Bill as Home Secretary.

Why did John Major win? Part of the answer to that question is that Mrs Thatcher succeeded in persuading the bulk of her supporters to back John Major. Mrs Thatcher was reluctant to support Hurd because, although he had remained loyal to her, he had never been a true Thatcherite, and because of his Foreign Office background, she was always suspicious about his views on Europe. She also suspected he might be inclined to consolidate rather than push ahead with the Thatcher revolution. Instead, as she openly admits in her memoirs, 'There was one more duty I had to perform and that was to ensure that John Major was my successor.'[82] On the first day of the campaign, Hurd was correct in his assessment that Mrs Thatcher's supporters were clambering aboard the John Major bandwagon.

There was also the more general perception of Hurd as someone who would lose the election for the Conservatives because he lacked popular appeal. One MP told a Hurd canvasser that he would not be able to 'take Hurd around one of my council estates'.[83] Nigel Lawson, who failed to persuade Geoffrey Howe to stand, decided to support Michael Heseltine, even though of the three candidates he was personally closest to Hurd and least close to Heseltine. He shared Peter Carrington's view that Hurd lacked the campaigning ability to win the election for the Conservative Party.[84]

This impression was reflected in a series of opinion polls. They clearly showed Major and Heseltine neck and neck, several points ahead of Labour. Alas for Hurd, of the six opinion polls taken between the Friday and Saturday, Hurd averaged a lead over Labour of only 2.25 per cent, whereas Heseltine's 8.5 per cent just beat Major's 8.1 per cent.[85] NOP and Gallup polls held on the Monday both showed Major edging ahead of Heseltine, if only just, and Hurd just beating Labour.[86]

Symbolically at least, Hurd lost partly because he failed, in the words of Hugo Young, 'The Saloon Bar Test'. Young, later a strong critic of Hurd on Europe, was in no doubt that he was witnessing a trend in modern British politics, whereby potential party leaders had to have a classless appeal:

> Could there be a more telling commentary on the condition of England, and of post-Thatcherite Conservatism, than that of Major's very lack of a university education is publicly cited by several of his backers as a reason to support him?

It is for that reason, and reasons like it, that Douglas Hurd is held not to fit the bill. He does not match the stereotype to which, it seems, every modern Tory leader must conform more tightly than was ever the case before classlessness had been heard of. Who would you rather drink a pint with? That is the question that obsesses those whose imagination stretches no further than the saloon bar vote in 1992. A literate man evidently fails the test.[87]

Hurd's immediate reaction to losing was one of genuine disappointment. Members of the Hurd camp recall an awkward silence as the Foreign Secretary absorbed the news. Hurd was not a man used to losing. Not since he had been rejected by Conservative selection committees had he failed to come top. Moreover, this time he had finished a poor third. However, he gathered himself together and wrote in his diary:

27 Nov. 1990: Perhaps I shouldn't have gone for it, but it was an experience not to be missed . . . Quite relieved in fact, but don't regret the escapade.[88]

The following evening, Hurd won a consolation prize in the form of The Spectator's 'Parliamentarian of the Year' award. One of the judges remarked that Hurd 'displays the parliamentary equivalent of the bedside manner in the days when doctors actually called on their patients'.[89] Accepting the award, Hurd reflected on the damaging patrician label:

I have often thought of it as I strolled over my rolling acres – all six of them.[90]

In general, Hurd succeeded in his aim of conducting a civilised contest in which it was the relative merits of the individual candidates which were aired, rather than the internal divisions within the Conservative Party. When the contest was over, Hurd wrote a letter to Geoffrey Howe:

I am content that I had my hat in the ring and perhaps helped to keep the contest within bounds. You too had a difficult role. Although I tried to dissuade you, looking back I now think you were right to resign. You did not plan the avalanche which followed, but if the landscape had to change, better now than next year.[91]

Indeed, compared with the June 1995 and May/June 1997 Conservative leadership contests, the November 1990 contest was a civilised affair, but only just.

In November 1990, the most intelligent, the most well-read, the most qualified and the most experienced of the three candidates for the Conservative leadership contest lost. Even if Heseltine had been in the House of Commons longer – for twenty-four years to Hurd's seventeen – he had not served in any one of the three major offices of state. By contrast, Hurd had served with distinction in two out of the three highest offices of state and Major's claim to have done the same was dented by his relative inexperience and his hesitant spell at the Foreign Office the previous year.

A Hurd premiership would not have greatly differed from that which occurred under John Major – with a number of exceptions. Hurd would have adopted a tougher, more brutal approach to wielding the premiership. He would not have become obsessed with the press or allowed himself to become embittered in the way that John Major did. But perhaps Hurd was never destined to become Prime Minister. So adept did he become at playing the supporting role of the loyal number two under Heath, Thatcher and then Major, that he became stuck with the image. This view is shared by Nigel Lawson:

> He always struck me as somebody who was an absolutely brilliant and reliable and sound number two, that any number one would be lucky to have along side him, [but] not one of nature's number ones.[92]

The misperceptions during the November 1990 Conservative leadership election were crucial to the fate of the Major Government. The right of the party, encouraged by Mrs Thatcher, were led to believe that John Major was 'son of Thatcher', the man to carry on Thatcherism. In this they were grossly mistaken. As the wise old sage William Whitelaw remarked at the time to Kenneth Baker:

> Many will vote for him thinking he is on the right wing. They'll be disappointed and soon find out that he isn't.[93]

Hurd, too, realised that the right would be disappointed. The mistake of Mrs Thatcher and the right in thinking that John Major was 'one of us' stored up enormous trouble for John Major's premiership. The right felt that they had been sold a false prospectus, when in fact they had deluded themselves.

Having half-heartedly tried and failed to become leader, Hurd publicly counted himself out of any subsequent leadership challenges and determined himself to defend John Major's premiership with all the authority at his command. The leadership contest changed the relationship between Major and Hurd from an *entente cordiale* into a full blown alliance. Any threat to the Major premiership would be resisted four-square by Douglas Hurd:

The nature of that contest put me on close terms with the Prime Minister for a long time to come.[34]

If Hurd had been on the shortlist of candidates for a job interview (which he was in a way) he would have failed to secure the post of Prime Minister. One can just imagine the letter from his interviewers, commending him for his performance, but stressing they were looking for a candidate with greater experience of economic matters and more rapport with the electorate. Hurd's curriculum vitae matched him perfectly for the post of Foreign Secretary, but did not quite match the requirements for a modern Prime Minister.

Notes

1. Geoffrey Howe, *Conflict of Loyalty* (Macmillan: London, 1994), p. 647.
2. Ibid., p. 647.
3. *The Guardian*, 6 Nov. 1990.
4. Ibid., 5 Nov. 1990.
5. It is sometimes forgotten that there was a long gap between Geoffrey Howe's resignation on 30 October and his actual resignation speech on 13 November. This was mostly because Howe's resignation came right at the end of the 1989/90 parliamentary session.
6. Diary Readings with Douglas Hurd, 18 Mar. 1997.
7. Ibid.
8. The 'Blue Chips' were members of a dining club established in 1979 by Tristan Garel-Jones, whose membership included the 1979 intake of MPs, who regarded themselves as potential leaders. The membership included John Patten, Chris Patten and William Waldegrave; John Major did not join until 1983.
9. Interview with Tristan Garel-Jones, 19 Nov. 1996.
10. Robert Shepherd, *The Power Brokers: The Tory Party and Its Leaders* (Hutchinson: London, 1991), p. 8; Bruce Anderson, *John Major: The Making of the Prime Minister* (Headline Book Publishing, 2nd edn.: London, 1992), p. 183.
11. Shepherd, *Power Brokers*, p. 57.
12. Baker, *Turbulent Years*, p. 395.
13. Clark, *Diaries* (13 Nov. 1990), p. 347.
14. Ibid. (17 Nov. 1990), p. 349.
15. Peter Jenkins, 'Win or Lose, How can she Unite her Party?', *The Independent*, 20 Nov. 1990.
16. *The Independent*, 17 Nov. 1990.

17. Ibid.

18. Baker, *Turbulent Years*, p. 393.

19. *The Independent*, 17 Nov. 1990.

20. Private information.

21. Ibid.

22. *Sunday Telegraph*, 18 Nov. 1990; see also Mrs Thatcher's interview with Michael Jones, Political Editor of the *Sunday Times*, 18 Nov. 1990.

23. Simon Jenkins, interview with Douglas Hurd, *The Times*, 19 Nov. 1990.

24. Watkins, *Conservative Coup*, p. 7; Baker, *Turbulent Years*, p. 397.

25. Interview with Douglas Hurd, 18 Mar. 1997.

26. *The Independent*, 21 Nov. 1990.

27. Douglas Hurd, 'Chairing from the Front', *The Spectator*, 6 Nov. 1993.

28. Interview with Timothy Yeo, 23 Jul. 1996.

29. Interview with Chris Patten, 22 Jul. 1997.

30. Shepherd, *Power Brokers*, p. 63.

31. Ibid., p. 41.

32. Anderson, *Major*, p. 149; Shepherd, *Power Brokers*, p. 63.

33. Anderson, *Major*, pp. 289–90.

34. Watkins, *Conservative Coup*, p. 26.

35. Shepherd, *Power Brokers*, p. 65.

36. *Daily Telegraph*, 27 Nov. 1990.

37. Michael Crick, *Michael Heseltine* (Hamish Hamilton: London, 1997), p. 35.

38. Interview with Tristan Garel-Jones, 19 Nov. 1996.

39. The seven categories, 'damp', 'wet', 'Tory right', 'pure Thatcherite', 'neo-liberal', 'populist' and 'party faithful' were used by Professor Philip Norton to categorise the various strands in the Conservative Party. Philip Norton, 'The Lady's Not For Turning, But What About the Rest? Margaret Thatcher and the Conservative Party 1979–89', *Parliamentary Affairs*, 43, 1990, (1), pp. 41–58. Briefly, 'neo-liberals' believe in market forces; the 'Tory right' stress moral issues, especially law and order; 'pure Thatcherites' believe in market forces and law and order; 'wets' believe in government intervention in social and economic affairs; 'damps' are share similar beliefs to 'wets' but not so intensely; 'populists' are left-wing on social issues but right-wing on law and order, reflecting majority opinion by the electorate; and 'party faithful' – by far the largest group – support the party rather than any ideology. Collectively, the pure Thatcherites, Tory right and neo-liberals are called 'Thatcherites' and the wets and damps are sometimes grouped together as the 'Critics'; Philip Cowley, 'How Did He Do That? The Second Round of the 1990 Conservative Leadership Contest', *British Elections and Parties Yearbook*, 1996, pp. 198–216.

40. Matthew Carrington (Fulham), Peter Viggers (Gosport), Julian Brazier (Canterbury) and Ann Widdecombe (Maidstone) joined Hurd's campaign team and all four canvassed on his behalf.

41. Hurd's Cabinet backers were Chris Patten (Environment), Kenneth Clarke (Education), William Waldegrave (Health), Malcolm Rifkind (Scotland), Tom King (Defence) and Peter Brooke (Northern Ireland), who waited until the Saturday before declaring his hand.

42. Tristan Garel-Jones (Foreign Office), Virginia Bottomley (Health), John Patten (Home Office), Lynda Chalker (Overseas Development), Douglas Hogg (Trade and Industry) and Tony Baldry (Energy) were all 'damps'.

43. Baker, *Turbulent Years*, p. 395.

44. H. of C. Deb. (6th Series), 31 Mar. 1997, vol. 113, col. 982.

45. *The Guardian*, 27 Nov. 1990.

46. Private information.

47. Shepherd, *Power Brokers*, p. 69; Alan Watkins believes Tristan Garel-Jones refrained from telling Hurd, because he did not want to depress him too early in the contest: Watkins, *Conservative Coup*, p. 199.

48. Diary Readings with Douglas Hurd, 18 Mar. 1997.

49. Ibid.

50. Interview with Tristan Garel-Jones, 19 Nov. 1996.

51. Interview with Timothy Yeo, 23 Jul. 1996.

52. Lawson, *The View from No. 11*, p.1002.

53. *The Independent*, 24 Nov. 1990.

54. Interview with Chris Patten, 22 Jul. 1997.

55. Peter Jenkins, 'He's friendly, but has he got Essex appeal?', *The Independent*, 27 Nov. 1990.

56. Interview with Timothy Yeo, 23 Jul. 1996.

57. *The Independent*, 27 Nov. 1990.

58. *The Guardian*, 27 Nov. 1990.

59. Ibid.

60. Interview with Timothy Yeo, 23 Jul. 1996.

61. Transcript, *On the Record*, BBC1, 25 Nov. 1990.

62. *The Guardian*, 26 Nov. 1990.

63. Interview with Chris Patten, 22 Jul. 1997.

64. Quoted in 'Times Diary', *The Times*, 15 Feb. 1995.

65. *The Guardian*, 26 Nov. 1990.

66. Simon Jenkins, 'Cool Hands in the Kitchen', *The Times*, 26 Nov. 1990.

67. Chris Patten, 'A Man Who Will be More Than Comfortable at the Top', *Daily Telegraph*, 24 Nov. 1990.

68. *The Independent*, 23 Nov. 1990.

69. Interview with Lord Lawson of Blaby, 6 Dec. 1995.

70. 'Peterborough', *Daily Telegraph*, 24 Nov. 1990.

71. Crick, *Heseltine*, p. 358.

72. Stark, *Choosing a Leader*, p. 73.

73. *The Independent*, 26 Nov. 1990.

74. Interview with Lord Carrington, 6 Dec. 1995.

75. Ibid.

76. Charles Moore, 'Hurd is the best suited to take on Thatcher's mantle', *Daily Telegraph*, 24 Nov. 1990.

77. *See The Guardian*: Ian Aitken, 'Tarzan, King or Wimp of the Jungle?', 5 Nov. 1990; Hugo Young, 'When Tory Jaw-Jaw Turns to War War', 15 Nov. 1990; Hugo Young, 'Relieved Party Heads Back To Future in Hope', 23 Nov. 1990; Hugo Young, 'The Best Man Fails the Saloon Bar Test', 27 Nov. 1990.

78. *The Guardian*, 28 Nov. 1990.

79. Private information.

80. Private information.

81. Cowley, 'How did he do That?', op cit., pp. 198–216.

82. Thatcher, *Downing Street Years*, p. 860.

83. Private information.

84. Lawson, *View from Number 11*, pp. 1002–3.

85. Peter Kellner, 'Major Wipes out Heseltine lead in latest polls', *The Independent*, 26 Nov. 1990.

86. Peter Kellner, 'Major Edges Ahead as Vote-Winner', *The Independent*, 27 Nov. 1990.

87. Hugo Young, 'The Best Man Fails the Saloon Bar Test', *The Guardian*, 27 Nov. 1990.

88. Diary Readings with Douglas Hurd, 18 Mar. 1997.

89. The judges were: Noel Malcolm of *The Spectator*, Alan Watkins of *The Observer*, Colin Welch of the *Daily Mail*, Ian Aitken of *The Guardian*, Matthew Parris of *The Times*, and Donald McIntyre of *The Independent*. *The Spectator*, 1 Dec. 1990.

90. *The Independent*, 29 Nov. 1990.

91. Howe, *Conflict of Loyalty*, p. 674.

92. Interview with Lord Lawson of Blaby, 6 Dec. 1995.

93. Baker, *Turbulent Years*, p. 396; Lawson, *View from No. 11*, p. 1002.

94. Interview with Douglas Hurd, 18 Mar. 1997.

16

In the Ascendancy, December 1990–April 1992

John Major's authority as Prime Minister was highest in the country and with his own party during the period between the fall of Margaret Thatcher and the winning of the April 1992 General Election. Mrs Thatcher carped occasionally from the sidelines, but her interventions were regarded more with irritation than outright alarm.

Despite his relative inexperience in foreign affairs, John Major quickly demonstrated his own skills as a committee chairman, and his admirable negotiating skills and fighting qualities. Hurd's diaries consistently reveal admiration for John Major's performance as Prime Minister, much more so than with Edward Heath or Margaret Thatcher. The exception was Hurd's view that John Major was over-sensitive to the opinions of the media. Even as Chancellor of the Exchequer, John Major fretted about how others saw him:

> 8 Nov. 1989: John Major is very worried that *Spitting Image* is about to produce a puppet of him as a poodle. Strangely, he takes this very seriously.[1]

The main foreign policy objective in the early days of the Major premiership was to complete the task of securing Saddam Hussein's withdrawal from Kuwait. The most important political decisions had already been taken by President Bush and Margaret Thatcher: the initial decision to resist aggression; the deployment of troops into Saudi Arabia as a defensive exercise; and the switch in November 1990 to preparations for an offensive operation. The twin priorities for Hurd remained, internationally, to keep the allied coalition together in the face of attempts by Saddam Hussein to create divisions, and, domestically, to maintain the bipartisan consensus in the House of Commons.

On 28 November 1990, as part of his strategy of strengthening the allied coalition, the Foreign Secretary announced the resumption of diplomatic relations with Syria. Diplomatic ties with Damascus had been severed in 1986 after suspected Syrian involvement in the attempt to blow up an El-Al airliner at Heathrow in what became known as the Hindawi affair. However, when Syria sided with the allies against Saddam Hussein, it was in Britain's interest to re-establish ties with Damascus. Responding to questioning about the change of policy, Hurd said he had 'never regarded diplomatic relations with a country as conferring great blessing upon it'.[2] Rather it was 'a hard-headed calculation in British interests that diplomatic relations should be resumed'.[3]

Similar arguments had been deployed to defend the resumption of diplomatic relations with Iran which took place on 27 September 1990. Geoffrey Howe had previously tried to improve relations with Iran, but his initiatives had been set back by the fatwa issued by the Ayatollah Khomeini against the novelist Salman Rushdie on 14 February 1989 after the publication of his book *The Satanic Verses*. While Hurd shared Howe's revulsion at this attack on basic freedoms, Hurd made a series of conciliatory statements to Tehran, designed to build confidence and trust. These included an open letter to Sir Peter Blaker, former Minister of State at the Foreign Office, acknowledging the deep offence caused by Mr Rushdie's book.[4]

The other major reason for resuming diplomatic relations with Tehran was to try to break the log-jam over the British hostages held in the Lebanon, including John McCarthy and the Archbishop of Canterbury's special envoy, Terry Waite. David Waite, brother of Terry Waite, lived in Hurd's constituency, Witney. Hurd arranged a meeting with David Waite along with some of the other hostage families on 20 November 1989, and followed this up with an open letter to David Waite that December which appeared to lessen Britain's insistence on the lifting of the fatwa against Salman Rushdie as a condition for the resumption of diplomatic relations.

Shortly after entering the Foreign Office, Hurd called together a meeting of intelligence officers and departmental heads to brief him on the hostage issue. While he continued to oppose any deals with the terrorists, he instructed the intelligence services to try to identify those figures close to Hezbollah, the terrorist group believed to be holding the hostages in Beirut. Alongside these private initiatives, Hurd pursued a public policy of improving relations with Syria and Iran – the two countries believed to hold influence over the hostage groups in the Lebanon. On 6 February 1991, Hurd would meet with his Syrian opposite number, Farouk al-Shara in London for talks:

> 6 Feb. 1991: A grey, competent man, who speaks his lines well. He's forthcoming about our wretched hostages.[5]

Hurd was instrumental in persuading the EC to lift sanctions against Syria. In October 1993, he met President Assad. Two-and-a half hours later, he was still listening to the Syrian President. Assad, in Hurd's experience, talks longer than any other leader in the world.[6]

It may be regarded as unseemly for Hurd to have been resuming relations with President Assad, a brutal dictator, but Hurd's active line bore fruit with the gradual release of all the British hostages during 1991. Although Hurd sees some validity in the claim that he took a more active line on the hostage issue than Geoffrey Howe, it is only fair to point out that, from November 1990, Hurd had the benefit of a more sympathetic Prime Minister. Mrs Thatcher had refused to budge over the Hindawi affair. Also, Hurd inherited a radically altered power configuration in the Middle East as a result of the end of the Iran-Iraq war and the Iraqi invasion of Kuwait. In short, whereas Geoffrey Howe's hands had been tied, Hurd's had been set free. All Foreign Secretaries experience policy issues over which they strive for years without apparent success, only to see their successors preside over the eventual breakthrough.

There was no breakthrough, however, in bringing the perpetrators of the Lockerbie bombing to justice. From time to time, Hurd thought he had found a way of persuading the Libyan Government to hand over the two suspects for trial in the Scottish courts. He tried to explain to the Libyans that they would receive a fair trial, but they refused, arguing instead for a trial in a neutral venue such as The Hague. Hurd's own view was that the Libyan Government 'simply did not want those two prisoners loose because they did not know what they would say'.[7] Having read the papers on the case from the Procurator Fiscal,[8] Hurd believes there is a case to answer. He did not entertain theories – put forward by Tam Dalyell, Labour MP for Linlithgow, and Sir Teddy Taylor, Conservative MP for Southend East – that the Central Intelligence Agency (CIA) might have been implicated in the shooting of PC Yvonne Fletcher in April 1984, or that Syria or Iran might be involved rather than Libya. The theory is that, because Britain and the US were anxious to restore diplomatic ties with Iran and Syria, efforts were made by the CIA, with possible British collusion, to pin the blame for Lockerbie on Libya instead. In a rare move, Hurd personally drafted and answered an adjournment debate called by Tam Dalyell in an attempt 'to lay to rest certain suspicions and accusations which have arisen',[9] but to no avail. For a time, Tiny Rowland of Lonrho used his influence in Africa to spread rumours of possible Syrian involvement. Rowland became an ally of Libya largely because of his hotel interests there. He even asked the Egyptian Government to offer Cairo as a neutral third country for the trial. On 17 May 1995, Hurd tried to disabuse the Egyptian Government of this idea during a meeting with President Hosni Mubarak in Cairo.

Throughout the Gulf crisis, Hurd wanted to confer the maximum degree of legitimacy at the UN for potential military action. On 11 December 1990, during the second adjournment debate in the House of Commons on the Gulf,[10] Hurd said that, while both front benches accepted that Article 51 of the UN charter provided the legal basis for action, he believed there should be 'an additional political basis'.[11] This had been achieved when the UN Security Council passed Resolution 678, which authorised member states 'to use all necessary means to uphold and implement Security Council Resolution 660 and to restore international peace and security in the area.' The UN set a deadline of 15 January 1991 for the Iraqi withdrawal from Kuwait in compliance with the previous eleven resolutions.

At the turn of the year, Douglas Hurd faced a new threat to the cohesion of the allied coalition. Other members of the European Community, particularly the Germans, the French, the Italians, and the Luxembourgers – who held the EC presidency – were keen to try further diplomatic initiatives with the Iraqis. There was a feeling in several European capitals that the British had given President Bush a virtual blank cheque, and that Britain should use its leverage with the United States to press Bush to give more time for sanctions and diplomacy to work. This view was shared by Edward Heath, who pushed for a distinctively European response to the crisis rather than a wholly American-led action.[12] On 31 December 1990, Hurd tried to persuade Jacques Poos, the Luxembourg Foreign Minister, and Hans-Dietrich Genscher, the German Foreign Minister, that any contact with Iraq should be confined to ambassadorial level.[13] The Foreign Secretary was anxious to avoid any weakening of the line that the Iraqis must withdraw unconditionally in case Saddam saw his chance to provoke a split between Europe and America.

Most alarming for the British was the freelance diplomacy of the French. Traditionally, the French were keen to assert their independence from the policies of the United States. Behind the scenes, the French used the services of an unofficial envoy, Michel Vauzelle, to maintain a line of communication with the Iraqis. At the European Political Co-operation (EPC) meeting on 4 January, Roland Dumas, the French Foreign Minister, floated the idea of linkage between Iraqi withdrawal from Kuwait, and an international peace conference on the Middle East. Then, on 14 January 1991 – the eve of the UN deadline on Iraq – the French, without informing their European allies, tabled new proposals at the UN Security Council along the lines of Dumas's earlier plan. That very day John Major lunched with Mitterrand, but was given no hint of the French plan. However, as Mrs Thatcher accurately predicted to George Bush in Aspen, Colorado back in August, 'Mitterrand will give you trouble until the end, but when the ship sails, she [France] will be there.'[14]

On 15 January 1991 – the day of the deadline on Iraq – the House of Commons held its third adjournment debate since the Iraqi invasion of Kuwait the previous August. In his wind-up speech, Hurd adopted a more hawkish tone by stressing that, despite sanctions, 'Saddam Hussein could hold out for a long time without dramatically affecting his fighting arm, and that is the critical point.'[15] There was a real danger, he claimed, that if the West delayed, it might prove impossible to create another similar coalition against Saddam Hussein.[16]

For the first time since the crisis began, there was disagreement between the two Front Benches. Gerald Kaufman (supported by Denis Healey) cited the evidence of William Webster, the Director of the CIA, that sanctions could be made to work.[17] Meanwhile, in a succession of speeches, Edward Heath, Sir Ian Gilmour, Neil Kinnock, Paddy Ashdown and even Tory loyalist David Howell urged ministers to support the last-minute French initiative. The debate was interrupted by a demonstration from four protestors in the Strangers' Gallery who threw paint bombs of fake blood onto the MPs below. Outside the House of Commons, around 4,000 peace protesters gathered in Parliament Square, but were moved on to Trafalgar Square after scuffles with police. Inside the House of Commons, the voting, again on the adjournment, was again decisively in the Government's favour.[18]

On 18 January 1991, Hurd's attention was diverted by the Iraqi Scud missile attack on Israel. Delivering an emergency Commons statement, the Foreign Secretary pleaded with Israel to exercise restraint in the face of what he termed Saddam Hussein's 'reckless ploy to widen the conflict'.[19] Earlier in the day, he had telephoned the Israeli Foreign Minister, David Levy, urging restraint.

Behind the scenes, all debates on the Gulf War were conducted by mutual agreement between Gerald Kaufman and Douglas Hurd. Up till this point, most debates had been on the adjournment, but Hurd explained to Kaufman that, due to Conservative backbench pressure, he could not avoid a debate on a specific motion. Kaufman asked Hurd to let him see the Government motion before they tabled it, to make sure it was one which the Opposition Front Bench could support. Hurd then discovered that it would be possible for dissident Labour backbenchers to put down an amendment to the Government motion and press a vote. He therefore asked Kaufman to table an amendment. If this was done, then it would be the only amendment called by the Speaker. Thus, the Official Opposition tabled an amendment, varying a Government motion. Kaufman showed Hurd the revision beforehand to make sure his side could support it. So the Government drafted a motion subject to Labour's approval and Labour drafted an amendment subject to the Government's approval.[20] The subsequent vote on 21 January was overwhelmingly in the Government's favour.[21]

A few days after the IRA's mortar attack on Downing Street, Hurd made a third visit in almost as many months to several Middle Eastern countries which lasted from 10 to 14 February. One purpose of this trip was to try to raise money from the Gulf states to finance Britain's war effort, although this was done discreetly. Visits to Japan in September 1990 and March 1991 carried a similar motive.

At the last moment, the Iraqi Government issued a statement at 11.30 a.m. on Friday, 15 February, stating its readiness 'to deal with Security Council Resolution 660 with the aim of reaching an honourable and acceptable political solution, including withdrawal.'[22]

At first sight, the statement appeared to be a limited Iraqi concession, but Hurd interpreted it as a cynical ploy by Saddam Hussein to divide the coalition. The Iraqis appeared to be linking an Arab-Israeli political settlement with withdrawal from Kuwait but the pull-out was not unconditional. Hurd delayed making a statement to the House of Commons so he could be briefed by James Baker on the last-minute initiative launched by the Soviet Foreign Minister, Alexandr Bessmertnykh, with his Iraqi counterpart, Tariq Aziz, in Moscow. There was a high degree of co-ordination between the American and British positions and a corresponding impatience with the French and the Soviets at their attempts to stray from the UN resolutions.

One of the most memorable moments of Hurd's entire ministerial career was being in on the decision of George Bush and his advisers to call off the allied attack on the Iraqi forces retreating to Baghdad. Hurd later claimed that he was in the White House on 27 February 1991 'by a fluke'.[23] In actual fact, Hurd curtailed a long-promised bilateral visit to Portugal. With apologies to the Portuguese, Hurd flew back to London, chartered a plane and, with the benefit of the time difference, arrived in Washington by mid-morning. In the afternoon, Sir Antony Acland, the British Ambassador to Washington, accompanied Douglas Hurd to see the President. At this moment, Kuwait had just been liberated, the Iraqi army was fleeing in disarray to Basra, and the question arose over when to call a ceasefire. George Bush told Hurd that he was about to have a meeting with Brent Scowcroft, his National Security Adviser, Dick Cheney, Defense Secretary, and James Baker, Secretary of State. Since Britain had been throughout such a key ally, the President suggested that Hurd and the British team should stay for the discussion. Colin Powell, Chairman of the Joint Chiefs of Staff, and others were brought in. Douglas Hurd was struck by the informality of George Bush, something which would have been unthinkable back home.

During the meeting, Bush expressed the view that he did not feel he had a mandate to pursue the Iraqis on to Baghdad. He did not believe the American public would stand for the unnecessary loss of life. This view was strongly supported by Colin Powell, who expressed doubts as to whether American pilots would go on strafing the demoralised Iraqis. There was also the diplomatic difficulty of holding the support of Hosni Mubarak of Egypt and

President Assad of Syria. Later in the day, after a series of meetings on Capitol Hill, Hurd was taken aside by James Baker and informed that the hostilities would end at six o'clock that evening.

There was a great deal of soul-searching after the conflict: should the allies have overthrown the regime of Saddam Hussein? Mrs Thatcher was firmly of this view. Hurd disagreed, answering her criticisms in an article for *The Times*:

> First, the coalition explicitly limited its objectives to those set out in UN resolutions, which related to the liberation of Kuwait. These limited objectives were central to rallying the necessary support for military action. Second, had we gone to Baghdad, we would have found ourselves forced to choose and then sustain a new Iraqi government. Once drawn into the morass of Iraqi politics extricating ourselves would have been difficult, our soldiers would have been put at risk and support would have been dissipated.[24]

The Syrians to the West, the Turks to the North, and the Iranians to the East would all have looked for a share of the spoils of a disintegrating Iraq, destabilising the region. The question of an extended American commitment in Iraq was never on the agenda because the American military sought throughout to erase the memory of Vietnam. Their strategy aimed to bring maximum force to bear at the beginning of the conflict (in contrast to the steady escalation of the Vietnam war), combined with a clear exit strategy at the end of the war.

Within weeks of the end of the Gulf War, it became clear to Hurd that President Gorbachev's power was going to be circumvented by the new Russian president, Boris Yeltsin, and that the Soviet Union's republics would secede. On 20 March 1991, responding to these rapidly changing events, Hurd paid a visit to the Ukrainian capital, Kiev, *en route* to Moscow. There, he held talks with Leonid Kravchuk, the Ukrainian President. Hurd listened to Kravchuk in disbelief, as they talked about independence for the Ukraine. Pie in the sky, he thought. Eight months later, Ukraine was independent. The following day in Moscow, Hurd announced Britain was opening a consulate in Kiev. The move was seen as a first step by the British Government to upgrade its diplomatic relations with the Ukraine, without seeking to offend Moscow.

One of the purposes of Hurd's visit to Moscow was to get to know the new Soviet Foreign Minister, Aleksander Bessmertnykh, whom he met on two separate occasions, on 20 and 21 March. Between the two meetings, the Foreign Secretary spoke to President Gorbachev and was charmed again by his style:

> 21 Mar. 1991: Bessmertnykh. Interrupted to see Gorbachev. Listed for 30
> minutes, lasts 70. He has that charm in his mouth. Energetic speech, harsh
> laughter. All about his success at the referendum.[25]

While Gorbachev had received support for the continuation of the Soviet Union
in a referendum, a parallel referendum in favour of strengthening the Russian
presidency had put Boris Yeltsin in the driving seat. Hurd therefore considered
it wise to spend equal time with the Russian President after a further lunchtime
get-to-know meeting with Bessmertnykh:

> 21 Mar. 1991: To Gorky's House to Yeltsin. 80 minutes. Strong touch of
> brutality. No real chance of [Yeltsin] working with Gorbachev.[26]

The rivalry between the two men had been evident since October 1987 when
Gorbachev sacked Yeltsin from the Politburo. Yeltsin was a traditional Russian
strong man who was not naturally disposed to democracy, although he possessed
good political antennae. Gorbachev was urbane, civilised, and charming, and it
was with him that Douglas Hurd's sympathies lay, at least until the Soviet
President's authority was fatally weakened by the August *coup* of 1991.

There was brief respite in March 1991 when Hurd enjoyed a state visit to the
United States, which included a few days sailing around the coast of Florida
aboard the Royal Yacht *Britannia*. After a couple of days of formal engagements
in Washington, the Royal Yacht sailed down to Miami. On one occasion, Hurd
and a few others went ashore in a small boat and were nearly swept up in a
big storm. Subsequently, Douglas Hurd decided to use the incident as the
outline for a short story entitled 'A Suitcase Between Friends' which appeared
in the *News of the World* that summer. The plot centres on a drug runner who
uses the friendship of an Englishwoman, her son and his tutor, as cover for a
drugs-smuggling operation. The character of David, the young ginger-haired
tutor, bears an unmistakable resemblance to Richard Gozney, Hurd's Private
Secretary from Christmas 1990 to February 1993. Later on, 'A Suitcase
Between Friends' formed the title of a book of four short stories, published by
Alhani International Books in 1993. The finished article was something of a
disaster. The book is full of typographical errors, and one of Hurd's speeches
as Foreign Secretary, 'The New Disorder', appears incongruously in the middle
of the book.

In March 1991, a new crisis had erupted in northern and southern Iraq.

Seemingly encouraged by the American CIA to rise up against Saddam Hussein – but with the West unwilling to intervene militarily to overthrow him – the Kurdish rebellions in the north and the Shi'ite rebellions in the south of Iraq around the town of Basra were put down by the Republican Guard. The Kurdish dream of an independent state, known as Kurdistan, had been extinguished long before Saddam Hussein. Its fate had been sealed by the Western powers as far back as 1920 at the Treaty of Sèvres – one of the post-Versailles Treaties – which carved up Kurdish land between Turkey, Syria, Iraq and Iran.

Hurd's attitude was that he did not wish to see civil war leading to the dismemberment of Iraq, but he hoped a coup at the centre of Government might topple Saddam Hussein. On 11 April, during Foreign Office questions, Hurd said that, while he was willing to see more autonomy for the Kurds, it was not realistic to contemplate an independent Kurdish state, given that the Kurds lived mainly in four countries.[27] The West stood aside as Saddam Hussein crushed the rebellion and over a million people fled both northward towards the Turkish border and southward into the marshlands.

The UN faced a refugee crisis, but one which existed within the frontiers of a member state. UN Security Council Resolution 688 condemned the repression of the Kurds, regarding Iraq's actions as a threat to peace in the region, and insisted on immediate access for international relief agencies, but stopped short of authorising enforcement actions. Article 2 (7) of the UN Charter outlined the principle of domestic jurisdiction. The general rule during the Cold War had been to uphold collective security, preventing acts of aggression between states, but refraining (at least officially) from interfering in the internal affairs of member states. The emerging refugee crisis in Iraq blurred the lines between internal and external affairs.

In a move which has been credited by Douglas Hurd to the Prime Minister, Britain decided to float a proposal to organise protected areas, or 'safe havens' for the Kurdish population within northern Iraq. The aims of this policy were to protect the Kurdish people from Saddam Hussein, to provide food and shelter, and to give them the assurance that they need not flee out of Iraq into neighbouring countries. Hurd outlined the change in policy in a speech to the Lord Mayor's Easter Banquet on 10 April, saying that the restrictions imposed by the UN charter not to intervene in the affairs of a member state could no longer be allowed to block the amelioration of mass suffering of the Kurdish population.[28] The British move set an important precedent for similar action in the future to relieve human suffering within states, but as Hurd would discover, there would be far greater complications in Somalia, Rwanda, and Bosnia.

John Major had taken a personal gamble by pursuing a European response to the Kurds. He deserves credit for persuading George Bush to come on board.

Without seeking to question Major's authorship of the safe-haven policy, one must recognise that there was not only a major policy input from Douglas Hurd and Lynda Chalker, the Minister for Overseas Development (who visited Turkey and Iran during the crisis), but also a party political need to project John Major as a world statesman in the run-up to the General Election. Major's high-profile visits to Moscow in March and September 1991, and his visit to China in September, need to be seen in this context. John Major's immediate adviser, Stephen Wall was instrumental in persuading the Prime Minister of the real potential of the plan. Douglas Hurd's part in all this was to give the Prime Minister all the credit for the safe-haven policy:

> My right hon. Friend the Prime Minister launched this initiative and persevered with it for weeks during which many clever people were saying that it was all washed up, had been discredited and could never come to fruition. My right hon. Friend persevered to success.[29]

After a difficult visit to China at the beginning of April 1991 (see Chapter 19), Hurd made yet another visit to the Middle East at the end of the month, touring Egypt, Saudi Arabia, Kuwait, and Jordan. In Cairo, it quickly became clear that his hopes for a regional peace force underpinned by Egypt and Syria were a non-starter, given the swift Eyptian pull-out from Saudi Arabia after the end of hostilities.[30] The Saudis also opted out of plans for a regional peace conference. The Gulf Co-operation Council (GCC) failed to organise themselves. The Omanis felt they could manage on their own. The Qataris were in dispute with the Bahrainis over a gas field, colouring co-operation between them. When Douglas Hurd attended a joint EC-GCC meeting in early 1992, the GCC members were still bickering.

In Saudi Arabia on the Sunday, Hurd faced another long wait to be summoned by King Fahd. The Foreign Secretary and his team went snorkling in the Red Sea. The sea was choppy, but no one was more enthusiastic than Hurd for this rare opportunity to do something sane for one or two hours, away from the diplomatic grind.

Eventually, Hurd and his officials were summoned to the King's palace. King Fahd was renowned for his extended monologues, and it took everything in the officials' power to stay awake. On this occasion, it was no use. After the heat of the day, the snorkling and the strenuous travel from Friday to Sunday, two of Hurd's officials fell asleep. The Saudis always gazed downwards, so no one noticed except for the Foreign Secretary.

From Saudi Arabia, Hurd flew to Kuwait for his first visit to the Emir of Kuwait after the end of the Gulf War:

3 May 1991: Forlorn, broken city. Blazing oil wells. Solid brick curve of the [British] embassy undamaged. Call on the ruler. He becomes animated once I get onto the Palestinians. He is very indignant about the way they have behaved. 75 minutes. We have the best conversation I have experienced with him, which is not saying a great deal [The Emir was renowned for being sombre]. Tell the ruler, advise him must try and keep the country together. Tour some broken buildings . . . Palace, the museum. It's the closed shops and the emptiness which is really depressing. Government shows little signs of grip.[31]

From Kuwait, Hurd flew to Jordan, where he encountered an entirely different atmosphere from the previous two meetings. Although King Hussein of Jordan and the Saudis were still not on speaking terms (relations have been frosty ever since), the King had begun to distance himself from Saddam Hussein.

During July 1991, Hurd's attention shifted to South Africa, where President de Klerk was rapidly ditching the pillars of apartheid. But his task was being hampered by continued violence in the townships between the Zulu Inkatha movement and those supporting the ANC. There was a widespread suspicion in the ANC at the time (justified by later investigations) that sections of the South African security forces were responsible for fuelling violence by Inkatha supporters. These suspicions threatened to derail the talks process between the Government and the ANC, as a follow up to de Klerk's visit to London that April. Britain continued to support the fast-moving, but increasingly precarious, policies of President de Klerk — who was in a position not unlike that of President Gorbachev in the Soviet Union:

22 Apr. 1991: Dine at Number 10 with de Klerk. He is an amazingly wise and brave man. Talks freely. He has almost run out of aces. John Major begins abstractedly. Rallies, then does well.[32]

Hurd's high regard for de Klerk continued in July when they met in Pretoria:

8 Jul. 1991: Continues very impressive. Quick, rational, convincing.[33]

Later that day, in Johannesburg, Hurd met with Nelson Mandela, the ANC president:

8 Jul. 1991: He is strong in physical and mental form. Need to check violence. This encourages false suspicions of conspiracy.[34]

There were differences of emphasis between the two men on sanctions. Hurd wanted a faster pace for the lifting of sanctions to encourage investment when it was most needed, whereas the ANC at its national conference the previous weekend had agreed on a three-phase approach to the relaxation of sanctions, tying each stage to progress on the handover to majority rule.

Early in the morning on the second day, Hurd went swimming. His early-morning swims became a fixture on foreign trips. Whenever a swimming pool or stretch of water could be found, he would go in, regardless of the weather conditions. In July, it is the middle of winter in South Africa, and the water freezing cold. His fit young Private Secretary, Richard Gozney, had gone for a swim but, judging it was just too cold – there was frost on the ground – had decided not to wake the Foreign Secretary. Hurd was quite cross and insisted that he would go for a swim the following morning. Despite the freezing conditions, Hurd and Gozney duly swam three or four lengths.

Hurd might have hoped for a quiet August 1991 after the events of the previous year, but it was not to be so:

> John Major, by nature, wakes up rather earlier than I do, and it was not unusual to be roused by a call from him denouncing some enormity in a newspaper which I had not read. But at about six o'clock one August morning as I snoozed in a remote cottage in Devon he rang to ask my views on the coup attempt in progress in Moscow. The Foreign Office Resident Clerk had not thought to ring me, judging perhaps that there was absolutely nothing I could do about it. It was no use flannelling to the Prime Minister and I confessed total ignorance. He is a nice man and concealed the note of triumph in his voice.[35]

Perhaps Britain, along with other Western powers, had stretched out their support for President Gorbachev for too long. In September 1991, Hurd accompanied the Majors to Moscow. Normally, Hurd coped well with the vast amount of air travel involved in being Foreign Secretary, but on this occasion he was exhausted and had a bad headache:

> 1 Sept. 1991: Straight to Gorbachev. He's brisk and self-confident, as if nothing has happened.[36]

There then followed a meeting between Hurd and all three Baltic Prime Ministers at the British Embassy in Moscow. After the dramatic coup attempt in August, Britain had abandoned its policy of waiting until the Soviets had negotiated separately with the Baltic states. Hurd sought and gained an agreement with other EC foreign ministers to make recognition of the Baltic states a joint EC operation.

Early in his premiership, John Major struck a positive approach to Europe, and with a much more conciliatory style than that of his predecessor. On 11 March 1991, he delivered his now famous speech in Bonn where he told the Germans he wanted Britain to 'be where we belong – at the heart of Europe, working with our partners in building the future'.[37]

In the six months running up to the Maastricht summit, Douglas Hurd set out Britain's position in the talks on political union. By contrast, he played only a minor part in the parallel negotiations on EMU, which were conducted by the Chancellor of the Exchequer, Norman Lamont, with the Prime Minister in overall charge. In advance of the final negotiations, John Major ruled out Britain signing up irrevocably to a single currency when he told the House of Commons on 5 November 1991, 'at this moment, in these circumstances, no'.[38]

As the negotiating process got underway, first the Luxembourgers and then the Dutch put forward draft proposals on political union during their respective presidencies in 1991.[39] Hurd firmly believes that the turning point in the negotiations leading up to the final deal at Maastricht came on 30 September 1991 when ten out of the twelve foreign ministers rejected the Dutch draft treaty proposals on political union.[40] He interpreted the moment as a reverse for the centralising tendencies of the European Community, which had seemed entrenched by the Treaty of Rome and the Single European Act:

> The Dutch being convinced Federalists, became impatient with the way the negotiation was going, the compromise was emerging and they tried to persuade everybody to scrap all that and start on a new, clean Dutch draft, which was clearly federalist, which clearly moved everything steadily towards the centre. The people who basically agreed with them, the Luxembourgers and the Italians, knew at that stage that we would never accept, that others wouldn't accept – the French wouldn't accept on foreign policy – so they said to the Dutch, brave try, no go.[41]

Specifically, the Dutch draft had proposed the granting of new powers to the European Commission to initiate legislation in the field of home affairs. For the first time, the European Parliament would have had the power to veto the decisions of the Council of Ministers. Whilst the continuation of NATO was guaranteed, in future, foreign and security matters would have been decided within the Treaty structure, rather than being organised inter-governmentally. Furthermore, social affairs, health and education would have been subject to majority voting.

Hurd found the draft entirely unacceptable, as did his Minister of State, Tristan Garel-Jones. According to the Dutch press, Garel-Jones had to be peeled off the walls of the Foreign Office when he received the details of the Dutch draft.[42]

At the meeting of foreign ministers, only the Belgians and the Dutch together with the European Commission were in favour of the Dutch proposals. The Danes, the Irish, the Portuguese and the British were firmly against. Crucially, the first four Foreign Ministers to speak were against the plan. First the Portuguese, then the Danes spoke against. The negative attitude of the Luxembourgers was understandable because they were the authors of the previous draft. Then came the important vote of the Italian Foreign Minister, Gianni de Michelis. If he spoke against, the draft was stillborn. Hurd had spoken to Gianni de Michelis in advance. In the words of Tristan Garel-Jones, 'Douglas had done a whipping job on Gianni.'[43] The Italian Foreign Minister, whilst not disagreeing with the text itself, expressed the view that its wording was too ambitious for the present development of the European Community. Thereafter, others who might have been expected to support the text, like the Spanish and the Germans, simply fell into the emerging consensus. The final outcome was ten votes to two.

The rejection of the Dutch draft was a major boost for Hurd's attempts to keep the Conservative Party united in the run-up to the final set of negotiations in December at Maastricht. However, he still faced constant carping from his own party about the dangers of handing over more sovereignty. On the eve of the foreign ministers meeting, he had to endure press reports of Mrs Thatcher's speech on nationhood and the future of Europe, delivered to a Chicago audience as part of her extensive (and highly lucrative) lecture tour of the United States, and Edward Heath's angry reaction to it. But he did not allow Heath or Thatcher's interventions to blow him off course:

> There has been something unreal about some parts of the recent public debate. I have felt sometimes like the soldier in one of those wars recounted by Homer or Virgil. In those epics, the prosaic tasks of the soldier are suddenly interrupted by interventions from on high. Attention passes to the clash of fabled gods, or even goddesses, in the heavens above his head. Naturally and rightly, the thunder holds our attention. But when the lightning and the thunder of the great ones dies away those of us on the ground have to get on with the work.[44]

Hurd's firm view was that, despite all the thunder and lightning emanating from the 'goddess', Mrs Thatcher's track record suggested that she argued vigorously with her European partners and then eventually signed. Hurd has suggested that Mrs Thatcher would have signed an agreement called the Lisbon Treaty, perhaps six months later during the Portuguese presidency in 1992, rather than at Maastricht in December 1991.[45]

Parliamentary and grass-roots discontent with Europe did not reach a peak before Maastricht. When the Prime Minister asked for an endorsement of his negotiating stance before going to Maastricht, only seven Conservative MPs voted against him, with around twenty abstaining. This compares with twenty-two firm votes against on Second Reading. Hurd was able to claim to the Conservative Party Conference faithful in October 1991 that 'we are grown ups in the Community now, no longer frightened by shadows on the wall. We are well able to take care of ourselves and promote Britain's interests.'[46] A motion supporting the Government's stance on Europe was approved comfortably, although a significant minority of delegates voted against.[47]

The negotiations leading up to Maastricht in 1991 were sold by Hurd to the country and the Conservative Party as an imperfect but necessary process which it was better for Britain to sign up to, so that we could be part of the debate beyond Maastricht. His own personal view was that the Maastricht summit came a little too soon after the Single European Act signed in 1986, since that treaty's central goal of completing the single market had not been realised by 1991.[48] Moreover, with the turbulent events taking place in Eastern and Central Europe, Hurd saw that the Community's institutions would need to change again after Maastricht in order to cope with the consequences of enlargement.[49] But, on 5 November 1991, in a speech to the Atlantic Commission at The Hague, Hurd agreed that it was vital that the European Community stick together at a time of transition in the East. He felt that an agreement should be concluded at Maastricht because 'the European agenda is expanding [and] there is no time to rehash this debate.'[50]

Far from adopting an uncritical stance towards European Community institutions, Hurd worried that some of the European Commission's policies might be adversely affecting the lives of ordinary Europeans. Speaking in Brussels the previous day, Hurd made his now famous attack on the European Commission's decision to invoke environmental-impact rules against Whitehall on transport projects:

> It is the apparent wish of the Commission to insist on inserting itself in the nooks and crannies of everyday life which is worrying people.[51]

Hurd felt a stricter demarcation was needed between the areas of the European Commission's competence and those which should be left to the individual states. The notion of 'subsidiarity' became one of Hurd's main negotiating demands at Maastricht.

Three points of note emerge from Hurd's account of the Maastricht summit: his admiration for John Major's negotiating performance; the patient chairing of the summit by the Dutch Prime Minister, Ruud Lubbers; and also that the summit was not pre-cooked. Arriving at the previously unassuming Dutch town,

Hurd wrote:

> 8 Dec. 1991: No one here has the slightest idea if this summit will succeed.
> Prime Minister in full control says 'modestly pessimistic'. So am I.[52]

The following day, Hurd got up in a gloomy mood, as was sometimes his habit:

> 9 Dec. 1991: Prime Minister keeps our end up really well throughout. Is
> tense and longs to demolish bad arguments, but restrains himself.
> Atmosphere is friendly and gradually my mood lifts. [Ruud] Lubbers chairs
> very well . . . lunch with the Queen [of the Netherlands].[53]

One of the characteristics of European summits identified by Hurd – and
applicable to other areas of political life – is the requirement that politicians
suddenly change gear from a tense situation like a European treaty negotiation
to a relaxed lunch with a Head of State or a drink in a Dublin pub, and then
back to the tension of the summit:

> 9 Dec. 1991: PM launches big attack on social chapter. No one takes offence.
> With Richard [Gozney] briefly along the Maas [river]. Frosty sun. The
> Foreign Ministers as usual met separately, act separately. All in the balance.
> Could still fail.[54]

The following morning, Hurd found the Prime Minister again over-concerned
by the reaction of the British press:

> 10 Dec. 1991: A grisly day, but ends in agreement and a great load is lifted.
> Breakfast with the Prime Minister. Breakfast is disgusting and he is in a grim
> mood. Over-influenced, as usual, by the press. Once in harness, he pulls
> steadily all day for agreement and we sustain him. Various small successes. I
> crack the defence point re: WEU, around lunchtime. Social Chapter much
> the worst. Lamont rather mucks up the cohesion discussion, but manages to
> settle the rather more lethal issue of our own EMU stage three protocol.[55]

The British opt-out from the single currency was not pre-ordained. Hurd's view
was that both Major and Lamont were responsible for the single currency opt-
out, but the social chapter opt-out was entirely the Prime Minister:

> The EMU one was Lamont as well, though it doesn't suit him to recall that
> now because he doesn't want the freedom which he then helped us to gain.[56]

In the final gruelling round of talks, Hurd raised a series of secondary points which irritated what he terms the 'great ones', like Kohl and Mitterrand, but were all part of the exercise to get a satisfactory agreement for the British:

> 10 Dec. 1991: Long talk with Lubbers at tea-time . . . final set of bloody little battles in which I become rather unpopular with Kohl and Mitterrand. Final bedraggled result after 1 a.m. Lubbers is the hero. Shrewd and infinitely patient and courteous.[57]

In view of the epic parliamentary struggle over the Maastricht Treaty which followed, Hurd's diary entry noting the favourable reception which the Prime Minister received on his return from Maastricht seems incredible. And yet, it is an accurate account of the mood of the vast bulk of the Conservative Party after Maastricht:

> 11 Dec. 1991: Prime Minister's statement goes well. Party in euphoria over our triumph. The sour right momentarily silenced, discovering for themselves the pillars we have told them about for months. With Norman Lamont talk to a backbench committee.[58]

Of course there is a world of difference between supporting the Prime Minister's deal, and scrutinising the text of the Treaty line by line. But at Maastricht, there is little doubt that the British delegation achieved the majority of their original demands and prevented several policies from being pursued by the federalists. Hurd secured an inter-governmental approach to home affairs, foreign and security policy – the so-called three pillars. For the first time, the principle of subsidiarity was enshrined in the Treaty and the European Court of Justice gained the power to impose fines on member states who broke Community law. In addition, the Court of Auditors was made an institution of the European Community, strengthening its ability to tackle fraud. In the negative sense of preventing things from happening, the European Parliament failed to gain significant powers, except for the British proposal of its greater role in scrutinising the Commission. The major concession made by Britain was the extension of majority voting into several new policy areas. Where Britain fundamentally disagreed, they secured opt-outs on the single currency and the social chapter.

A great deal of the credit for Maastricht must go to Sir John Kerr, the UK's Permanent Representative in Brussels. Kerr is a brilliant tactician. Not for nothing does Tristan Garel-Jones describe him as 'the cleverest man in the Northern Hemisphere'.[59]

John Major, too, proved himself to be an admirable negotiator abroad, and at home appeared to have secured the support of his parliamentary party. But Hurd believes Major's mistake was to say that Maastricht was 'game, set and match' for Britain, because the message was more complicated than that. Yes, it was in Britain's national interest to sign up to parts of Maastricht because it enshrined inter-governmentalism. By allowing other countries to proceed on the social chapter and the single currency, Britain was winning allies at the European table and would be in a stronger position to put forward the British agenda of enlargement, free markets and deregulation. While Hurd believes these were perfectly convincing arguments, they hardly amounted to 'a trumpet call'.[60] This helps explain why there was no publicity campaign after Maastricht to convince the British people of its merits.

Shortly after Maastricht, Hurd conceded ground to the Germans on the recognition of Croatia and Slovenia. A meeting of European foreign ministers took place on 16 December 1991, at which Roland Dumas, the French Foreign Minister, despite being under instructions to resist recognition, was not willing to stand and fight with sufficient force early on in the day's negotiations:

> 16 Dec. 1991: Clear majority upstairs [in the Council before lunch] against immediate recognition. I speak at length after Lord Carrington. [Roland] Dumas inexplicably silent.[61]

It was at this point that the German Foreign Minister, Hans Dietrich Genscher, led the argument in favour of early recognition, supported by the Danes, and to a lesser extent, by the Italians and the Belgians. The Dutch, represented by Hans van den Broek, strongly supported the British and French position. The German Government had strong historical ties with Croatia; the Croatians had sided with Germany in the Second World War. However, there was nothing sinister about the national mood inside Germany. It was simply that, drawing on their deep ties, German public opinion's sympathy lay with the plight of the Croatians. Douglas Hurd recalls Genscher's line of argument:

> You must understand that after all we have inflicted on Europe, we Germans are not going to find ourselves on the morally wrong side of an argument. Here are these people who are actually entitled to independence. They are independent. It's a fact. We are not going to get ourselves into a position where the Serbs are enabled to deny that any longer.[62]

Then the Italian delegation intervened:

16 Dec. 1991: Gianni de Michelis storms and shouts, but actually provides the driving force for compromise. Conditional recognition for January 15.[63]

However, the arguments then began to tilt Genscher's way and Hurd insisted on a break in order to consult with the Prime Minister by telephone, having talked to Dumas, who, in Hurd's opinion, was not going to put up a fight. John Major and Douglas Hurd agreed that Britain should accept a compromise of recognition for 15 January 1992, but with discretion for the Arbitration Commission. The arguments swung one way then the other:

16 Dec. 1991: Genscher accepts then retracts. Finally, a tiny chink of opt-out remains. Hans van den Broek unhappy. Dumas shows signs of fight. Too late after he's already given in. We settle at 1 a.m.[64]

The compromise set a single date of 15 January 1992, on which the European Community would act as one in recognising the two republics, provided a set of criteria had been established. These conditions included respect for human rights and minorities, and undertakings that borders could only be changed by peaceful means. At the insistence of the Greeks, all republics would abandon territorial claims on their EC neighbours. The Greeks were worried about the territorial designs of Macedonia, their northern neighbour. Throughout the wars of the Yugoslav Succession, the Greek Government would, in Hurd's view behave irresponsibly over Macedonia. But the compromise which was so painfully hammered out was swept aside by the Germans on 23 December 1991 when President von Weizsacker wrote a letter of recognition to the Croatians and Slovenians, accepting their vague assurances that the EC's criteria had been met.

Several points emerge from Hurd's account. The British never regarded their opposition to recognition as sacrosanct. In the spring of 1991, Hurd had hoped for some form of loose confederation in Yugoslavia, and been opposed to any secession by the republics, but by 3 July 1991, he appeared to have softened his position:

At the moment – I say 'at the moment' – the two republics [Slovenia and Croatia] – do not satisfy our criteria for recognition, but obviously, we keep an eye on that all the time.[65]

By the time the crucial meeting of Foreign Ministers took place in December, Hurd gave in to strong German pressure as the French failed to put up a fight. This left both Hans van den Broek and Peter Carrington (the EC's peace envoy for the former Yugoslavia) isolated and extremely angry.

It has been suggested by several commentators since, including John Simpson, the BBC's Diplomatic Correspondent, that Britain made a quid pro quo with Germany, whereby Britain gained opt-outs on the single currency and the social chapter, in return for Germany's desire to recognise the two republics. Hurd has denied on several occasions that any such deal was made. Hurd maintains that the Germans would have gone ahead and recognised the two republics unilaterally, which they were perfectly entitled to do. Seeing the tide was shifting his way, President Tudjman of Croatia would not have signed up to Carrington's peace plan anyway. Hurd, the architect of intergovernmentalism at Maastricht, also wanted to avoid the prospect of a damaging split in the EC only a few days after signing an agreement to co-operate intergovernmentally. He believes a united EC position achieved something in the negative sense of 'preventing everybody going off and doing things in rivalry and competition with each other'.[66] There is no evidence of a written or verbal deal. But Hurd and Major were in debt to the Germans. It was clear that Chancellor Kohl's initial brief at Maastricht had mentioned nothing about conceding an opt-out on the single currency to the British. During his evidence to All Souls in March 1996, Hurd admitted that:

> The Germans did draw attention privately to the fact that a fortnight before they had given a certain flexibility, a certain leeway to the British Prime Minister in the Maastricht negotiations.[67]

Hurd wanted to preserve a semblance of unity and simply reconciled himself to the inevitability of the German position. As he said later, the decision was 'a matter of timing rather than principle'.[68]

In their long association, the issue over recognition of Slovenia and Croatia is the only time that Hurd and Carrington have been in fundamental disagreement. Carrington describes the decision to recognise the two republics as 'an absolutely idiotic mistake'.[69] Carrington was understandably angry at Hurd's decision to give way to the Germans, partly because the key to his confederation plan was not to encourage any of the republics to think that they could secede. If you gave two of the six republics their independence, they had no incentive to negotiate with their neighbours and their indigenous ethnic populations. Even more seriously, Carrington argues, giving Croatia and Slovenia their independence gave a green light to other countries to claim their own independence – particularly the multi-ethnic state of Bosnia, comprising Muslims, Croats and Bosnian Serbs – making a civil war inevitable.[70] The Bosnian Serbs held a referendum and decided not to secede from Serbia-Montenegro. President Alija Izetbegovic, the Muslim President of Bosnia, declared this unconstitutional and the country descended into civil war, with

President Milosevic in Serbia-Montenegro funding and supporting the Bosnian Serbs. Peter Carrington believes that there is a line of reasoning running from the December 1991 decision by the EC to recognise Croatia and Slovenia to the Bosnian crisis – a view shared by Labour's then Shadow Foreign Secretary, Gerald Kaufman, but contested by Douglas Hurd.

Lord Carrington's argument rests to some extent on the assumption that the complete break-up of Yugoslavia was preventable, and that some sort of looser confederation could have been made to stick. These assumptions are open to debate. Fearing the break-up of Communism in Yugoslavia, President Milosevic took refuge in aggressive nationalism, provoking conflict with Croatia and Slovenia and re-inventing Serb history through mass propaganda, re-igniting ancient ethnic hatreds. The conflict can be seen as a civil war only in the sense that a former Communist state broke up into ethnic pieces, which at the outset were not yet recognised states. While President Tudjman of Croatia may have taken advantage of the conflict once it began, Milosevic was primarily responsible for the break up of Yugoslavia through his carefully planned aggressive war first with Slovenia and then with Croatia. It is too convenient to bring up ancient animosities to argue that Serbs, Croats and Muslims all shared part of the blame for starting the war, relegating the Balkans in Western European minds to an impenetrable thicket of unsolvable ethnic hatreds. Bosnia had a long history as a multi-ethnic state. It was Milosevic's military support for his criminal allies, Radovan Karadzic and Ratko Mladic, which was largely responsible for starting the so called 'civil war' in Bosnia, not the EC's recognition of Slovenia and Croatia. Realising his Communist state was breaking up into several pieces, Milosevic tried to grab hold of as many of the fragments as he could, and incorporate them into a Greater Serbia. Western European leaders were merely recognising what had already happened on the ground. The real moral issue which preyed on Hurd's mind in the next four years, was whether Europe could have done more to stop the horror of ethnic cleansing taking place inside its own continent. The recognition issue is a red herring; the issue of whether Britain should have taken stronger action, using air power earlier against the Serbs, lies at the heart of the moral dilemma which Hurd faced.

It was incongruous (but typical of his schedule) that on the day the Prime Minister and Douglas Hurd agreed to recognise Croatia and Slovenia (14 January), the Foreign Secretary was about to head off for a visit to India. Douglas Hurd found India a very chaotic country in many respects, but he was always struck by the intelligence and civilised character of its people:

15 Jan. 1992: Admirable debating dinner here [at the High Commission] with Indian notables. They are verbose and trail off into side arguments and

autobiography as do we all, but the intelligent diversity of thought is striking and warming.[71]

In a memorable meeting with Prime Minister P.V. Narasimha Rao, the two men sat in Rao's sunny garden for an hour, discussing important affairs of state. On this occasion, there was more of a meeting of minds on Kashmir than there has been since. The issues of Northern Ireland and Kashmir share the questions of whether or not to shift the border, and how best to ensure that two communities can co-exist in peace. Douglas Hurd brought to the Kashmir problem his knowledge and experience of Northern Ireland, but little progress was actually made.

The trip to India was not as arduous as most. There was even time for a day off to Udaipur in Rajasthan, where Hurd stayed at the Lake Palace Hotel – which features in one of the James Bond movies – with the local maharaja. The maharaja was on his uppers, and pretended to be entertaining guests for the weekend, who were in fact paying guests.

From India, Hurd flew off to Kazakhstan, Ukraine and Russia. President Nazarbayev of Kazakhstan was a firm ruler of one of the largest countries in the world. In January 1992, it was far from clear whether Kazakhstan would return their nuclear weapons to Russia, which they had inherited from the old Soviet Union. It was entirely possible – and alarming to the West – that Kazakhstan, along with the Ukraine and Belarus, might join the exclusive club of nuclear weapons states. However, Nazarbayev came to realise the importance of Western aid and co-operation.

That night, the Foreign Office team were treated to a great banquet, where the head of a beast was brought in. Hurd was asked to carve and apportion bits of the head to his staff. Warming to the task, Douglas Hurd gave the lip to his spokesman and the cheek to his policeman.

The highlight of the Russian visit was an incident in the middle of a meeting with President Yeltsin, who was by this time established in the Kremlin as Russian President. After five minutes, Hurd recalls that a flunkey appeared with a great piece of parchment and a pen. Rather theatrically, Yeltsin apologised and said he had to sign an important decree on the status of the intellectuals in Russia. Here, for the British Foreign Secretary, was a modern-day Tsar signing something of great importance.

Hurd returned home to join in the April 1992 General Election campaign. Hurd enjoys electioneering in a perverse sort of way:

4 Apr. 1992: Bath. Find Chris Patten battling hard but pessimistically. Others more hopeful . . . Swindon . . . this vexing campaign nears its end. Cold intense rain. Like my army career, I find it both disagreeable and

irresistible. Longing for it to be over, yet regretting its passing.[72]

In late March and early April 1992, it turned out to be very cold all the way through the campaign, especially during a trip to Scotland where the Conservatives actually gained two seats.[73] Throughout his time as a senior minister, Hurd took a keen interest in Scottish affairs. Special advisers and private secretaries alike would sigh every time Hurd began another story about his two Scottish grandmothers.[74] More seriously, Hurd was committed to preserving the Union, and supported Ian Lang, the Secretary of State for Scotland's efforts after the General Election to 'take stock' of the Union. *Scotland in the Union: A Partnership for Good* (HMSO, 1993) re-established Scottish Select Committees at Westminster and led to the Scottish Grand Committee making a tour of Scottish cities. But it was all too little and too late to save the status quo.

On 9 April, polling day, Hurd's own result in Witney was a formality, but he increased his majority from 18,464 to 22,568, despite a 2.8 per cent swing to Labour.[75] Nationally, Labour had achieved a modest swing, but it was not enough to unseat the Government and John Major triumphed with an overall majority of twenty-one. Hurd travelled to London to be with the Prime Minister during the celebrations in the early morning of 10 April. Despite the reduced majority, John Major had polled more votes nationally than any previous Conservative leader. Hurd was admiring of the way the Prime Minister had swept his advisers aside, got on his soapbox and fought his own plucky election battle. But of all the Governments since the Second World War, John Major's suffered the shortest post-election honeymoon. Hurd was able to savour victory for the briefest of moments. While on a family outing to a point-to-point meeting on the hillside at Lockinge, on the Berkshire Downs – something which became a family custom – Hurd engaged in a rare and uncharacteristic bout of gloating:

> 20 Apr. 1992: For once, a perfect spring day. Sun gleaming on the massed cars of triumphant Tory England. Saluted still on the wave of election victory.[76]

Notes

1. Diary Readings with Douglas Hurd, 7 Oct. 1997.
2. H. of C. Deb. (6th Series), 28 Nov. 1990, vol. 181, col. 874.
3. Ibid., col. 874.

4. Harvey Morris, 'Why Hurd strode in where Howe had feared to tread', *The Independent*, 9 Aug. 1991.

5. Diary Readings with Douglas Hurd, 18 Mar. 1997.

6. Interview with Douglas Hurd, Westwell, 13 Jun. 1997.

7. Interview with Douglas Hurd, 18 Mar. 1997.

8. Scottish law officer who decides whether to bring forward charges, similar, but not identical to the Director of Public Prosecutions (DPP) in England.

9. H. of C. Deb. (6th Series), 1 Feb. 1995, vol. 253, col. 1058.

10. Again, the House of Commons voted decisively in favour of the Government's policy. The House divided 455 votes to forty-two (excluding tellers) with forty-one Labour MPs defying the Labour whip, along with three Plaid Cymru MPs; H. of C. Deb. (6th Series), 11 Dec. 1990, vol. 182, cols 908–11.

11. Ibid., col. 824.

12. *The Guardian*, 1 Jan. 1991.

13. Ibid.

14. 'Observer', *Financial Times*, 18 Jan. 1991.

15. H. of C. Deb. (6th Series), 15 Jan. 1991, vol. 183, col. 818.

16. Ibid., col. 819.

17. Ibid., cols 810–11 (Kaufman); col. 770 (Healey).

18. The voting was 534 votes to 57. Ibid., cols 821–5. This represented both a higher turnout than the previous two votes, and a rise in support for the Government among Labour MPs (up from 128 to 140). However, this was accompanied by a corresponding rise in Labour dissent (from forty-two to fifty-five). The vote resulted in two Opposition frontbenchers, Maria Fyfe (Glasgow, Maryhill) responsible for women's issues and John McFall (Dumbarton), a whip, resigning their posts. A further six frontbenchers abstained: Tony Banks (London Labour Whip, Social Security), David Blunkett (Environment), John Fraser (Legal Affairs), Joan Lestor (Children), Joan Ruddock (Transport) and Clare Short (Social Security).

19. H. of C. Deb. (6th Series), 18 Jan. 1991, vol. 183, col. 1113.

20. Interview with Gerald Kaufman, 13 Nov. 1996.

21. H. of C. Deb. (6th Series), 21 Jan. 1991, vol. 184, cols 110–13. The motion on 21 January 1991 was carried by 563 votes to 34 (excluding tellers). Among the thirty-six Labour MPs who defied the Labour front-bench line, was Tony Banks, who immediately lost his job as a whip and Front Bench Spokesman on Social Security. The Labour leadership continued to maintain the maximum possible unity in the House of Commons. On 21 February, during a Nationalist Opposition Day, a

Government amendment affirming the aims of British military action was secured by 301 votes to 25; H. of C. Deb. (6th Series), 21 Feb. 1991, vol. 186, cols 489–91.

22. Quoted from H. of C. Deb. (6th Series), 18 Feb. 1991, vol. 186, col. 19.

23. Douglas Hurd, 'First steps on the campaign trail?', *Daily Telegraph*, 7 Oct. 1995. (Book Review, Colin Powell with Joseph E. Persico, *A Soldier's Way: an Autobiography* (Hutchinson: London, 1995)).

24. Douglas Hurd, 'A year the world lived dangerously', *The Times*, 2 Aug. 1991.

25. Diary Readings with Douglas Hurd, 18 Mar. 1997.

26. Ibid.

27. H. of C. Deb. (6th Series), 13 Mar. 1991, vol. 187, col. 931.

28. *The Guardian*, 11 Apr. 1991.

29. H. of C. Deb. (6th Series), 17 Apr. 1991, vol. 189, col. 422.

30. Hurd had outlined a four-point plan for security policy in the Gulf at an EC Foreign Ministers meeting in Luxembourg on 3 February 1991.

31. Diary Readings with Douglas Hurd, 18 Mar. 1997. Hurd was referring to the reported beatings and abductions taking place against Palestinians living in Kuwait, which the Kuwaitis were keen to downplay.

32. Ibid.

33. Ibid.

34. Ibid.

35. Douglas Hurd, 'The Tyranny of Time'.

36. Diary Readings with Douglas Hurd, 18 Mar. 1997.

37. Conservative Research Department, 'Britain at the Heart of Europe', *Politics Today*, 7 Feb. 1992, no. 3, p. 73.

38. H. of C. Deb. (6th Series), 5 Nov. 1991, vol. 198, col. 324.

39. An earlier Luxembourg draft had proposed an inter-governmental approach to home affairs, foreign and security policy, with separate pillars existing outside the existing institutions of the European Community.

40. H. of C. Deb. (6th Series), 21 Nov. 1991, vol. 199, col. 446.

41. Douglas Hurd, quoted from Michael Elliot, 'Nemesis – The Enemy Within', *The Poisoned Chalice*, BBC2, 30 May 1996.

42. Ibid.

43. Interview with Tristan Garel-Jones, 19 Nov. 1996.

44. H. of C. Deb. (6th Series), 26 Jun. 1991, vol. 193, cols 1011–12.

45. Douglas Hurd, 'Chairing from the Front', *The Spectator*, 6 Nov. 1993.

46. *The Guardian*, 9 Oct. 1991.

47. Conservatives never have card votes at their Annual Conferences, so it is

difficult to determine the numbers on either side using proclamation or a show of hands.

48. The Single European Act envisaged completion of the single market by 1 January 1993.
49. H. of C. Deb. (6th Series), 21 Nov. 1991, vol. 199, col. 437.
50. *The Guardian*, 6 Nov. 1991.
51. Ibid., 5 Nov. 1991.
52. Diary Readings with Douglas Hurd, 18 Mar. 1997.
53. Ibid.
54. Ibid.
55. Ibid.
56. Interview with Douglas Hurd, 18 Mar. 1997.
57. Diary Readings with Douglas Hurd, 18 Mar. 1997.
58. Ibid.
59. Interview with Tristan Garel-Jones, 19 Nov. 1996.
60. Interview with Douglas Hurd, Westwell, 13 Jun. 1997.
61. Diary Readings with Douglas Hurd, 18 Mar. 1997.
62. Interview with Douglas Hurd, 18 Mar. 1997.
63. Diary Readings with Douglas Hurd, 18 Mar. 1997.
64. Ibid.
65. H. of C. Deb. (6th Series), 3 Jul. 1991, vol. 194, col. 330.
66. Peter Riddell & Martin Ivens, interview with Douglas Hurd, 'Hurd presses for quicker response to global ills', *The Times*, 21 Apr. 1993.
67. Douglas Hurd, 'A British Overview of the Conflict, All Souls College: Foreign Policy Studies Programme', Seminar Series on Lessons from Bosnia. Hilary Term, 8 Mar. 1996 (Verbatim text of the lecture).
68. H. of C. Deb. (6th Series), 30 May 1992, vol. 208, col. 716.
69. Interview with Lord Carrington, 6 Dec. 1995.
70. Ibid.
71. Diary Readings with Douglas Hurd, 18 Mar. 1997.
72. Ibid.
73. The Conservatives gained Aberdeen, South and won back Kincardine and Deeside which had been lost at a by-election.
74. Private information.
75. *The Times Guide to the House of Commons*, 1992, p. 242.
76. Diary Readings with Douglas Hurd, 18 Mar. 1997.

17

Game, Set and Match:
The Parliamentary Ratification of the
Maastricht Treaty, April 1992–July
1993

On 22 April, Hurd made his first trip abroad since the beginning of the General Election campaign. The visit to Turkey and Greece was carefully planned in advance by Foreign Office officials rather than something which Hurd was compelled to do simply to satisfy the demands of the diplomatic circuit. Hurd believed – and still does – that the European Community had made 'rather a hash' of its relations with Turkey. Despite being a full member of NATO, she had only been half-offered membership of the European Community. Hurd felt it was vital to develop a friendlier dialogue with the Turks 'to stop them scratching away at the Greeks and give them a bit of confidence that we're actually on their side'.[1] There were also good geopolitical reasons for having closer relations with Turkey. Her position resting to the south of the former Soviet Union, to the west and north of the Middle East, and at the eastern end of the Mediterranean made her an important ally. After the April 1992 visit, Hurd arranged a series of talks with the Turks alongside his German opposite number, Klaus Kinkel, to try to move forward the European Community's relations with Turkey.

Hurd's opposite number in Turkey was Hikmet Cetin, whom Hurd thought at first a rather sober man. However, on the evening of 22 April, events took a potentially embarrassing turn. While on a trip up the Bosporus, a gleam came into Cetin's eye as he announced that the party was heading to Asia. Puzzled, Hurd was driven across the bridge into a sleazy area of Istanbul on the Asian side of the river. By this stage, Hurd was becoming alarmed: he thought he was going to a brothel! In the end, the cars drew up outside a restored Pasha's house, where they were entertained by a belly dancer. Much to the relief of the Foreign Secretary, the dancer kept just within the bounds of decency. But as Hurd sat down sleepily, Keith Lowe, a wily detective constable from the Metropolitan police, and a trusted member of Hurd's bodyguard team, spotted a press photographer trying to get a shot of the Foreign Secretary, slumped back in his chair gazing up at a lurid belly dancer. Thanks to the close attention paid by Keith Lowe and Richard Gozney, the photographer's mischief was thwarted:

22 Apr. 1992: A gypsy lady, swathed in garments sings and bestows flowers, but no more. A handsome girl wiggles her almost bare bottom. Safe in bed by 1.30 a.m.[2]

The next day, a somnolent Douglas Hurd travelled to Greece for talks with the Prime Minister, Constantine Mitsotakis:

23 Apr. 1992: He's urbane and charming. I warm to him more than before, but he's tough on Macedonia.[3]

Hurd believes the Greeks behaved very badly over Macedonia by refusing to recognise it, thus making it difficult for the other European Community members to come to her aid. Overall, the Greeks seemed to be more insecure than the Turks over the Cyprus issue. Hurd was worried that, when the leadership of the Greek and Cypriot communities passed to a younger generation, they would never have experienced what it was like to live together in a united island in the days before the Turkish invasion of 1974, and the chances of a long-term settlement would be reduced. In October 1993, he invited Glafkos Clerides, the Greek leader, and Rauf Denktash, the Turkish community leader, for lunch at the Ledra Palace Hotel on the border between the two parts of Cyprus. Hurd chose English food to avoid arguments about the menu.[4] Both his guests were self-confident lawyers who had sparred with one another in the colonial courts in the days of British rule. Both were anxious to show Hurd they wanted to be reasonable, but in reality, neither was willing to shift from their ground. Hurd was in Cyprus on that occasion for the CHOGM to be hosted by the Queen. It was the first visit to Cyprus by a British monarch since Richard the Lionheart in the twelfth century. In Nicosia, the Queen's motorcade was confronted by a group of about 100 Greek extremists. Tear gas had to be used to disperse the crowds. It was a scene straight out of a Hurd novel. At the time, he fretted that the whole visit might be ruined by the television footage back in Britain. Throughout his years as Foreign Secretary, the trivial and the important jostled for his limited time.

Hurd's most important task after the General Election was to secure parliamentary ratification of the Maastricht Treaty. But, on 2 June 1992, disaster struck when the Danes narrowly voted against the Maastricht Treaty.[5] By unhappy coincidence, the Government had been set to proceed with the Committee Stage of the Maastricht Bill the following day (3 June 1992):

> 3 Jun. 1992: A bleak day. The Danish vote creates a huge and unpromising muddle. The Prime Minister rings just before I broadcast [on the *Today* programme on Radio 4], and says I shouldn't mention about proceeding with the Bill today [so Hurd did not mention it]. This is wise. Soon becomes evident that there is no prospect of proceeding this week . . . What Denmark needs, and therefore we all need, [Uffe] Ellemann-Jensen, Danish Foreign Minister tells me at seven in the evening, is time and resolute partners. Hang on to the autumn and there might be another chance. Prime Minister makes a statement. Deals faultlessly with questions. Maastricht yes, proceed with the Bill yes, but not now . . . sit exhausted with him for an hour in his House of Commons room.[6]

The Cabinet decided officially on 4 June to suspend the ratification process in the House of Commons, but as the above diary entry proves, the policy to suspend the Committee stage of the Bill had been decided in effect by the Prime Minister and Douglas Hurd on the morning before. John Major had listened to the advice of the Tory Chief Whip, Richard Ryder, whose assessment was that the Government faced defeat unless it deferred the Treaty. Douglas Hurd has since admitted that he underestimated the extent of the reaction among Conservative MPs to the referendum result, but according to Philip Stephens, Political Editor of the *Financial Times*, he would have resisted any attempt by the Prime Minister to abandon the Treaty.[7]

Early that morning, before Hurd appeared on the *Today* programme and before the Prime Minister telephoned, Hurd rang Tristan Garel-Jones to ask his advice on whether to proceed with the Bill. His Minister of State argued for a Committee Stage the next day and a Bill by the summer. According to Tristan Garel-Jones, Hurd's initial reaction was to go on, but he later deferred to the Prime Minister and the whips. Tristan Garel-Jones believes that the Government should have proceeded with the Bill. The whipping would have been brutal, debates would have been curtailed, but the Government would have avoided bleeding to death for over a year.[8] But that was not John Major's view. He wanted to see a proper parliamentary debate of the Treaty. The problem was that the Prime Minister's honourable instincts were traded at a discount in the increasingly heated atmosphere of Westminster.

Against the Garel-Jones view has to be set the sheer potential size of the Tory backbench rebellion. Some eighty-four Conservative members signed the now famous 'Fresh Start' Early Day Motion.[9] Crucially, Conservative MPs were starting to blame the prolonged economic recession – unemployment was rocketing towards the three million mark – on Britain's membership of the Exchange Rate Mechanism (ERM) and the Maastricht Treaty, which envisaged further steps down the road to a single currency. The ERM was seen as a foretaste of flawed fixed-exchange rates, a view expressed by Lady Thatcher in an interview with Sir David Frost on 28 June 1992.[10]

Despite the decision to delay the Maastricht Bill, Britain had to be seen to be moving towards ratification, without isolating the Danes. Hurd attempted to stick to the line that there would be no abandonment of the Treaty by Britain. In a statement to the House of Commons on his return from a Special Council at Oslo, a joint NATO-EC meeting – which discussed interminably the implications of the Danish referendum result – Hurd promised that Britain would proceed with the Committee Stage of the Maastricht Bill. He refused to set a date, but announced that the House would have an opportunity to debate the implications of the Danish referendum result before the Maastricht Bill was discussed in Committee. He acknowledged that the voters in Denmark had 'given politicians a kick in the pants', but opposed a renegotiation of the Treaty on the grounds that the deal at Maastricht had reversed the centralising tendencies of the European Community and Britain's gains might be lost if the Treaty were unbundled.[11]

In a speech to the European Union of Women in Chelsea on 30 June, Hurd emphasised that Maastricht was the best deal available for Britain, and he raised the stakes by arguing that 'our integrity would be doubted and our influence decreased if we behaved like political spivs, changing our price and our minds at the first opportunity.'[12]

On 1 July 1992, Britain assumed the presidency of the European Community at a critical moment in the Maastricht ratification process. In a statement to the House of Commons, Hurd set out Britain's aims for the next six months. Ratifying Maastricht was listed as the top priority for the British presidency. If Britain could engineer a compromise acceptable to the Danes, so the thinking went, then the really important British aims of completing the single market, entrenching subsidiarity, securing a completion of the Uruguay round of GATT, concentrating on enlargement, developing a common foreign and security policy and obtaining a viable system of financing the Community would be attainable. The Prime Minister's later description of the deal at Edinburgh as a 'Rubik's cube' was accurate; everything would fall into place if the Danes agreed.

The biggest blow to this strategy came when Britain was forced to withdraw from the Exchange Rate Mechanism of the European Monetary System on

Wednesday, 16 September 1992. Black Wednesday, as it became known, was not only a political disaster for the Government and a severe blow to the Prime Minister's authority, it was also a national humiliation.

The real reasons for the presence of Kenneth Clarke, then Home Secretary, and Douglas Hurd on Black Wednesday were partly coincidental and partly deliberate. Coincidentally, Clarke, Hurd, Heseltine, and Richard Ryder had scheduled a meeting that morning with the Prime Minister to discuss British contingency plans in the event of a French 'Non' in the referendum on Sunday, 20 September. By another quirk of circumstance, the Prime Minister had been moved to offices in Admiralty House, while Downing Street's defences were strengthened against terrorist assault following the IRA's mortar attack the previous February. Hurd was familiar with the rooms in Admiralty House having used them to give dinner to Chief Constables during his time as Home Secretary. As was his trait, he would sit admiring the flock wallpaper and the naval pictures in two of the more pleasant rooms.[13] There was no telephone switchboard in the building. In his unrivalled account of Black Wednesday, *Politics and the Pound*, Philip Stephens recalls that, as Britain lost billions on the Foreign exchange markets:

> At one point during the day, three of the government's most important ministers – Hurd, Heseltine and Clarke – found themselves sitting idly in an ante room without even a television set to follow events in the financial markets.[14]

It seems surreal, but ministers holding no economic portfolio took part in the decision to raise interest rates from 10 per cent to 12 per cent. Major was keen to lock his senior ministers into his decision to defend the pound at any cost. As Kenneth Clarke put it, Major's senior ministers were there 'to put our hands in the blood'. Hurd was strongly of the view that if the Government was going to be forced out of the ERM, then they should do so in a way which was reputable and was not seen as sabotaging the outcome of the French referendum on the Sunday (20 September).[15] As Philip Stephens points out (his account is based on the testimony of many of those present):

> Hurd led the argument that the Government must observe all the proprieties. In the words of a colleague, the Foreign Secretary was determined to ensure that it had not 'thrown in the towel at the first squall.'[16]

Clarke, Heseltine and Hurd returned to Admiralty House at 12.30 (fifteen minutes before a larger meeting of ministers at 12.45) and agreed with John Major and Norman Lamont to raise interest rates to 15 per cent. Hurd's diary reveals that much of the afternoon was spent waiting around for events to run their course:

> 16 Sept. 1992: Separate after sandwiches and I walk around the lake with Richard [Gozney]. Then back to Admiralty, hung around gossiping pleasantly in the sunshine [with Ken Clarke] with more sandwiches. Eventually Lamont reports that £5 billion more had been spent and no progress had been made in getting the pound above the floor. So, grumpily we agree to suspension.[17]

It was with a sense of relief that the second interest-rate hike was abandoned later that day. Hurd had been appalled at the sums of money which had been lost. Contrary to press reports at the time, in Hurd's account, the Prime Minister showed no signs of wobbling during the day:

> 16 Sept. 1992: PM and Lamont both calm and I admire their coherence.[18]

The following morning, the Cabinet decided to suspend Britain's membership of the ERM. According to Hurd, there was a good deal of discussion, which now seems incredible, over whether the Government might leave open the possibility of going back into the ERM – a policy which Norman Lamont very much favoured that day in order to avoid a further free fall of the pound – but 'Clarke and I and PM believe this to be unreal for the time being.'[19] A formula was agreed for a statement which said Britain could re-enter 'as soon as conditions allow', but everyone knew that, for the medium-term at least, re-entry into the ERM was a political impossibility.

On Monday, 21 September, the day after the narrow 'Yes' vote in the French referendum, Hurd chaired a bad-tempered meeting of EC Foreign Ministers in Brussels. A row broke out about the Maastricht ratification timetable, with Hurd in effect saying that, just because the French had narrowly voted yes, it was not at all certain if the whole EC project was going to work. These remarks were very badly received by the other foreign ministers. Eventually, Hurd agreed a declaration which actually went further than would have been acceptable at home. He remembers it as 'a thoroughly awkward evening'.[20] Hurd rang John Major that evening. His diary recorded the Prime Minister as being 'much depressed'.[21]

The following day, Hurd flew to New York, and during a briefing with American journalists, commented that Britain's European Community partners were living 'in a fairyland' if they claimed the way to ratification of the Maastricht Treaty had been cleared by the French referendum. Of all the European politicians, only the apocalyptic Jacques Delors, the European Commission President, realised the enormity of the challenges faced by the EC following the currency collapse. The other EC leaders initially failed to comprehend the extent to which Britain's humiliating withdrawal from the ERM led to an adverse reaction among Conservative ministers and their backbenchers – from which Hurd was not immune – to the whole EC project.

The politician who took Britain's humiliation the hardest was John Major: his two main policies – Europe and the economy – which were linked inextricably by the ERM, lay in ruins. Hurd returned from New York on 23 September, to be warned by Stephen Wall that the Prime Minister was seriously considering resignation. Hurd spent the afternoon and the evening with the Prime Minister in various meetings, but latterly alone over a steak. John Major said he felt it was going to be very difficult for him to continue, but Hurd urged him to stay on as Prime Minister. They should both stay on to complete the ratification of the Maastricht Treaty which was in the national interest, but if the Bill were defeated, Hurd's view was that neither he nor the Prime Minister could continue.

The next day, John Major faced the House of Commons for the first time on the ERM issue. Hurd felt that the Prime Minister put his main points across well and gave full marks to Norman Lamont who, according to Hurd's diaries, gave 'an excellent and courageous speech'.[22] However, on the same day, David Mellor, the National Heritage Secretary, resigned in disgrace,[23] to be replaced by Peter Brooke, the former Northern Ireland Secretary. It was only one instance of Hurd's view of Government that the big things have a tendency to be shoved aside for less important matters. During a visit to the Gaza strip in January 1994, Hurd was in Yasser Arafat's scruffy office when John Major telephoned to remonstrate about the Timothy Yeo crisis.[24] It was difficult to explain to John Major that Hurd was actually speaking from the PLO leader's home!

The diplomatic consequences of Britain's withdrawal were most deeply felt in Germany, whose politicians were stung at British accusations, especially from Norman Lamont, that the Germans had refused to come to the aid of the British by cutting German interest rates at the Bath meeting of EC finance ministers on Saturday, 5 September. In fact, the overwhelming evidence suggests that Norman Lamont ran roughshod over the normal rules of European diplomacy by attempting, as chairman of the meeting, to browbeat the German delegation into cutting interest rates. The first Hurd learned of the details of the Bath meeting was when he read a detailed account of it in Philip Stephens's book, several years later.[25] Whatever the real truth, Hurd was the minister charged with repairing the 'extremely damaging' impact of this row on Anglo-German relations.

At the end of September 1992, the row with Germany blew up again when Helmut Schlesinger, the President of the Bundesbank, sent a briefing note to Von Richtofen, the German ambassador in London, which was leaked to Peter

Norman, Economics Editor of the *Financial Times*. The note showed that the French Government had received massive assistance from the Germans to prop up the franc. Schlesinger's note contained a detailed rebuttal of the charges made by Lamont and Major, arguing that the British had been offered a wider realignment by the Germans. In a rare move, Douglas Hurd's name was added by Downing Street to a Treasury rebuttal dated 30 September stating, 'No request was made by the German authorities on that weekend that it too should realign.' Unfortunately, on the day the row blew up, Hurd was in Bonn meeting with his opposite number, Klaus Kinkel. The meeting began with Hurd describing Kinkel as 'direct and friendly and disarming'. In the middle of the meeting, Norman Lamont telephoned from London to let Hurd know about the leak. Hurd commented that the German ambassador had been very unwise and that the British Government was being thrown back into a controversy from which he thought it had been emerging. That evening, Hurd dined with the Prime Minister and his Danish colleague. After the Danes had gone, John Major lapsed into total gloom again.[26]

In party political terms, Hurd played a vital role in holding the Government line until a deal could be hatched with Britain's European partners at the Edinburgh Summit in December 1992. He made a series of speeches urging party unity, but the real showdown with the sceptics came at the Conservative Party Conference at Brighton in October. In the middle of the Conference, Lady Thatcher penned a vitriolic article in *The European* newspaper in which she claimed that the ERM and the Maastricht Treaty would lead to the loss of political and economic freedoms.[27]

Hurd was absolutely determined to face down Conference calls for the abandonment of Maastricht, but privately, he was nervous:

> 6 Oct. 1992: Drive with Judy, rather silently and sleepily to Brighton, trying to insert myself into my speech. All the Home Office anxieties return. Pace up and down the bedroom declaiming. Sandwiches and wine.[28]

Judy played an important supporting role in Hurd's preparation for Conference speeches. Because she could see things from the perspective of a Conference delegate, she became a good judge of which passages or phrases would carry the Conference. On this occasion, they did:

> 6 Oct. 1992: A dramatic debate. The National Union allows free rein including [Norman] Tebbit who makes a poisonous speech against the Prime Minister, who peppers me with 'Give 'em hell' notes throughout the debate. 'Don't worry about causing offence.' After what seems endless debate, reply. This goes better than any speech at Conference before.

Defuse, perhaps even persuade. Lots of radio and TV. Usual telephones.[29]

Hurd kept Major's scribbles of encouragement, written on the back of an envelope. In his speech, the Foreign Secretary warned the Conservative Party that it could break itself over Europe, in the same way as it had over the Corn Laws in the 1840s and over tariff reform in the early part of the twentieth century. Amidst heckling from the audience, he told the Conservative Party to 'give that madness a miss'.[30] There is little doubt that this was the bravest conference speech of his career. Under severe pressure, Hurd drew on his accumulated experience of Conference speeches as Home Secretary to face down the critics in the audience. The following morning, his reaction was one of relief:

7 Oct. 1992: Wake at Brighton for first time in weeks without an incubus. Press excellent, except for a poisonous leader in *The Times* . . . Make a truce with Tebbit.[31]

Hurd's respite was short-lived. The next big diplomatic hurdle on Europe was the Birmingham Summit on 16 October 1992. Yet again, the coverage of the summit was largely drowned out by other less vital issues, this time the sudden row over the President of the Board of Trade, Michael Heseltine's plans to close thirty coal mines. Hurd was 'totally baffled' that the issue of the miners caused such a stir.[32] Perhaps it was the fact that the pit-closure plans came in the trough of an economic recession, triggering in the public − 100,000 joined a march in London − a fresh anxiety about unemployment. But to Hurd, the presence of miners demonstrating outside the National Exhibition Centre (NEC) in Birmingham was just another relatively minor domestic issue getting in the way of the major European questions.

The only silver lining among the clouds was the excellent running of the summit at Birmingham:

16 Oct. 1992: The only good thing about today, is Birmingham herself. Like a lady without beauty, she has organised herself into elegance.[33]

Hurd recalls Chancellor Kohl praising the technical excellence of the summit. Ever since, Hurd has thought that the Conservatives should hold their party conference there.

The main achievement of the summit from the British point of view was to secure a reaffirmation of the principle of subsidiarity. However, Hurd claims he detected a new mood of realism at Birmingham, the beginnings of a shift away from the centralist tendencies of the founding fathers of the European

Community. He tells the story that when the ministers were discussing the subsidiarity declaration, President Mitterrand said that the European Community should only do what it needed to do and it should not deal with matters which did not have to be done at Community level. At this remark, the Italian Foreign Minister, Emilio Colombo, an old salt of the Community, awoke from his slumber, grabbed the microphone and claimed this was a betrayal. A kind of silence ensued. Hurd, forever the optimist, interpreted Mitterrand's remarks as a sign that the argument had begun to move in Britain's favour.[34]

It is important not to understate the significance of Birmingham. Tristan Garel-Jones believes that, at Birmingham, 'for the first time, there was a real question mark over the future survival of the European Community as a whole.'[35] During September 1992, the Federalists had the *élan* knocked out of them, first by the Danish referendum, then by the French referendum and the currency instability. There was a widespread sense of bewilderment in European capitals at the turn of events. It was left to John Major and Douglas Hurd to pick their way around the debris and try to keep the European ship afloat.

But between his impressive chairmanship of summits, John Major was still depressed. On Sunday, 18 October, Hurd wrote in his diary that the Prime Minister was again talking about resigning.[36] After appearing on the *Walden* programme, Hurd spoke three times with the Prime Minister on the telephone, suggesting that he should try a Prime Ministerial broadcast. Such a tactic had rather gone out of fashion. But Hurd felt it was 'an opportunity to speak to the country without the benefit of a [Jeremy] Paxman or a [John] Humphrys'.[37] The Prime Minister can say exactly what he wants to the nation. The idea was not acted upon, but it does provoke comparisons with Hurd's previous – and often unsuccessful – attempts as political secretary to give political advice to Edward Heath.

Apart from one comment praising Norman Lamont's speech in the House of Commons on 24 September, Hurd's diary entries reveal a growing criticism of the Chancellor of the Exchequer around this time. By 19 October, he noted that 'the Chancellor has exhausted his authority.'[38]

John Major was willing to risk his premiership in order to succeed in the crucial paving motion on Maastricht on 4 November. Technically, there was no need for John Major to hold the vote – although he had promised to consult the House again before proceeding with the Bill. However, the Prime Minister felt he had to demonstrate to his European allies before the Edinburgh meeting of the European Council due in December 1992 that he carried with him the full authority of the House of Commons and was also strongly of the view that Parliament should have its proper opportunity to debate the Bill in full. This view did not necessarily chime with the more brutal view emanating from the

Tory Whip's Office that an element of bludgeoning was needed to force the rebels into line.

The Minister responsible for Europe, Tristan Garel-Jones, regarded the paving debate as a no-win exercise. If the Government had lost, then the Prime Minister and Douglas Hurd would have resigned. The Government would have fallen. If the Government had won, they would have gained the privilege of bleeding to death for a few more months. In what he modestly terms 'a too-clever-by-half Garel-Jones wheeze', Tristan Garel-Jones spent a week floating the idea that the Government should invoke Standing Order 91 – relating to Special Standing Committees – if it won the paving debate. Straight after the successful vote, a motion would be put before the House 'that the Maastricht Bill be referred to a Special Standing Committee'. In such a committee, solemn evidence would have been taken, but ultimately the Government would have had a built-in majority, staffing their side with MPs handpicked by the Whip's Office. Of course, it can be argued that the Special Standing Committee was a rarely used device and that referring a constitutional bill upstairs to a committee might well have been interpreted as a sleight of hand, but everyone knew this went on anyway. The wheeze, however, failed to impress the Prime Minister.[39]

The men who assisted Hurd in the task of getting the Maastricht Bill through the House of Commons, were Tristan Garel-Jones, alias 'Mr Europe', the man who co-ordinated the whipping with the Chief Whip, Richard Ryder, and his deputy, David Heathcoat-Amory, who had served as Hurd's PPS at the Home Office from 1987 to 1988. David Davis, as Assistant Whip, acted as messenger relaying to Douglas Hurd and Tristan Garel-Jones the state of opinion in the parliamentary party. Their principal tactics were to steer clear of the irreconcilables – including people like Sir Teddy Taylor (Southend, East), Sir Richard Body (Holland with Boston) and William Cash (Stafford) – and to select the minister or whip who stood the best chance of persuading that particular rebel to change his or her mind. Hurd was not hugely involved on the party management side, but his diary entry for 2 November 1992 does record: 'I wrestle with Ken Baker for his soul . . .'[40]

Meanwhile, John Major and Michael Heseltine made a series of conciliatory noises and concessions to the sceptics.[41] However, on the eve of the vote, Hurd's diary reveals that 'no one in the know believes we will win at 10 tomorrow.'[42]

On the day of the vote, there was much agonising over what the Government would do if it was defeated. According to Hurd, the Prime Minister continued to be very depressed throughout this period. But, against the odds, the Government won the first division on Labour's amendment by six votes, largely due to the votes of Liberal Democrats, with twenty-six Conservative MPs voting against the Government line.[43]

In between the first and second division on the Government's own paving motion, Michael Heseltine, after consulting the Prime Minister, but without consulting Douglas Hurd, made one final critical concession to Michael Cartiss (Great Yarmouth) and Vivian Bendall (Ilford, North) that the Bill's Third Reading would be delayed until after the second Danish referendum. At the time, Hurd did not believe the concession was necessary to gain their votes, and was cross with Michael Heseltine, partly on the grounds that it was his patch and he should have been consulted. Heseltine retorted that Hurd's job was to wind up, which he had done well, while his was to gather in the votes. Hurd did not see it that way. While he may have drunk the champagne along with jubilant colleagues after the vote, he was 'irritated because I thought that an unnecessary concession had been made in a disorderly way'.[44] Given that the Government squeaked home by three votes on the second division, it may be that Hurd's assessment was wrong: the conversions of Cartiss and Bendall were crucial if one assumes that they both intended to vote against the Government on the second vote.[45] More damage was done when Michael Cartiss publicised the concession. John Major later went back on the assurance, saying that the Maastricht Bill's Third Reading would stand irrespective of Denmark's timetable, although at the time it seemed likely (by pure coincidence) that the proposed second Danish referendum would take place in May 1993, before the British ratification process was due to be completed.

Michael Heseltine and Douglas Hurd are of dissimilar political temperaments. Hurd sees Heseltine as 'a swashbuckler' who loves the exhilaration of a crisis.[46] During one of the many crises over Bosnia, Hurd recalls walking along a corridor with Heseltine. While the Foreign Secretary was filled with deep gloom, Heseltine commented: 'Isn't this fun?'; he was plainly relishing the experience of dealing with a crisis.[47] In contrast, Hurd is filled with relief after he has found a way through a difficulty.

The Edinburgh Summit marked the final phase in Britain's troubled presidency of the European Community. At the time, the view of Labour's Shadow Foreign Secretary, Jack Cunningham, that it had been 'an almost unmitigated disaster' seemed to have some validity.[48] Since June, the Government appeared to have been blown off course by the Danish referendum result, the dispute over pit closures, and the humiliating withdrawal from the ERM. Hurd believes that the British salvaged their presidency at Edinburgh. Indeed, he sees the Edinburgh summit as a classic example of what modern diplomacy should be about, and the Prime Minister's finest hour.[49]

On Thursday, 10 December, Hurd attended an early, brief Cabinet in London, before flying to Edinburgh. Prior to the business of the day, Hurd took some time out for a bracing walk up Calton Hill. As Foreign Secretary, Hurd became renowned not only for his love of walking – Edinburgh was one of his favourite cities – but also for his brisk walking pace. Foreign dignitaries would often trail behind in his wake, while London taxi drivers occasionally spotted him fresh from a brisk walk in St James's Park jay-walking across the busy road back to his office in King Charles Street.

Hurd arrived at the Meadowbank Sports Arena, and was impressed to see how the organisers had transformed the venue into a huge press centre. From there, he went to the Caledonian Hotel for a long briefing session with the Prime Minister. Then, as was typical of these summits, Hurd began a round of preliminaries with European colleagues, beginning with an hour with Jacques Delors, the President of the European Commission, during which they argued over the British financing proposals, with Delors describing them as 'mean'.[50] The Edinburgh Summit brought together the Danish problem and the equally thorny issue of the future financing of the European Community. Hurd felt that, for far too long, the budget of the European Community had been allowed to rise inexorably, and that the time had come to rein it back. Crucially, for the outcome of the summit, he was supported in this view by the Germans.

The summit began formally the following morning with what Hurd described in his diary as 'the usual battering first day'.[51] There is a ritual about European summits, whereby the first day is characterised by long-range artillery fire, before everyone gets down to the actual drafting. Morning coffee was taken in the splendour of Holyrood Palace. The palace had been converted into a series of booths and offices: Hurd's office had a crimson four-poster bed, but no one was permitted to catch a quiet nap, regardless of the number of hours they worked.

In the morning, there was 'a sour round on Denmark',[52] concentrating on the problem of how to satisfy the demands of the Danes without amending the Maastricht Treaty (which would have involved the unpalatable prospect of every member state having to go through another difficult round of ratification). The conundrum would be solved by a Frenchman by the name of Pirice, an official on the Secretariat of the Council of Ministers, and a great authority on the complex legal art of drafting treaties. Pirice came up with an ingenious formula that the Community could take a decision, which would have legal force but which would not involve amending the Treaty.

By the middle of the first day, rain was pouring down outside as the Foreign Ministers boarded a bus to take them up to a chilly Edinburgh Castle for a working lunch. Every summit involves plenary sessions, where the leaders and their Foreign Ministers are present, and separate sessions of Foreign Ministers, along with a haphazard series of hastily arranged conclaves between politicians where many of the deals are struck. The Foreign Ministers' own lunchtime meeting appeared to be going well until the Greeks objected to Hurd's proposal to move towards European Union recognition of Macedonia.

In the main plenary session after lunch, the Prime Minister was again in the chair. It quickly became clear to Hurd that although the Danish problem was nearly cracked, the major sticking point remained the future finance of the Community. As was his lot at many of these summits, Hurd tended to mop up on the secondary issues – he secured an agreement on Macedonia with the Greek Prime Minister, Constantine Mitsotakis, on the morning of 12 December – while the Prime Minister addressed the central issues.

Around the time of the summit, the Prime Minister also had to deal with the delicate matter of the separation of the Prince and Princess of Wales. There was some doubt as to whether Princess Diana would attend the official summit dinner for European leaders aboard the Royal Yacht *Britannia*, moored at Leith harbour. However, to her credit, she appeared, and was, as always, very much the centre of attention. Hurd felt a shade guilty that while he and other the European leaders merrily dined aboard the Royal Yacht, the Foreign Office officials were working flat out trying to prepare the groundwork, still not allowed to use the tempting four-poster beds nearby. That night, Hurd believes the Foreign Office machine was being tested to its very limits. As he wrote in his diary that night, 'Success [is] far from assured.'[53]

When the summit officially restarted, everything began to fall into place. First, agreement was reached on Denmark, then subsidiarity and openness. All that remained was the issue of the so-called Cohesion Fund – the structural funds for Spain, Portugal, Ireland and Greece. The Prime Minister proposed a set of figures which the Spanish Prime Minister, Felipe González, found unacceptable. A deal was only struck after Chancellor Kohl bellowed 'Felipe!', summoning González out of the room. The two leaders re-emerged minutes later with the Spanish Prime Minister, according to Hurd, looking rather shaken.

Then, just as everything finally seemed to be agreed, a row broke out at the end of the table between two people whom Hurd had not seen quarrel with one another before – Prime Minister Ruud Lubbers of the Netherlands and his Luxembourg counterpart, Jacques Santer. The spat was over the side issue of the proposed sites of European institutions. The Prime Minister had to adjourn the meeting and sort out the difficulty, while all Hurd needed to do was to secure the right phrasing on the enlargement passages. As a veteran of these summits, Hurd noticed it was characteristic for relatively minor rows to break out just as a deal was on the verge of being struck.

Hurd felt that the Prime Minister had 'played a blinder', and everyone in the British team was on a high. However, while most people were anxious to tie up the press conferences swiftly and get home to their beds, Hurd noticed that Major tended to dally around on these great occasions. It was literally hours before the Prime Minister called the final press conference. Hurd was especially keen to get home to his bed: his waiting VC 10 landed at Brize Norton, a tantalising ten minutes's drive away from his home at Westwell. It was 3.35 a.m. before his head finally hit the pillow.

The biggest remaining obstacle for the British Government was to secure the passage of the Maastricht Bill through the House of Commons. The paving motion of 4 November, although procedurally unnecessary, had given the Government the authority to start the Committee Stage of Maastricht. Few could have imagined that the Commons would spend over two hundred hours debating the Bill, raising major constitutional questions, and forcing the Government into a series of embarrassing evasions and defeats, ultimately leading to the Prime Minister's 'nuclear option', when he announced a vote of confidence after the defeat on the Social Protocol in July 1993.

Douglas Hurd spoke comparatively little during the Committee Stage of the Maastricht Bill, confining his remarks to the debates on intergovernmentalism, subsidiarity, the referendum debate, or when the Government got into difficulties. His most uncomfortable moment during ratification came when he was forced to make a statement to the House of Commons admitting that if Labour's Amendment Number 27 were carried, it would have no effect on the Government's ability to ratify the Treaty.[54] This contradicted earlier statements made by Tristan Garel-Jones on 20 January 1993, based on legal advice from Foreign Office lawyers.

On the morning of 15 February, Hurd went into the Prime Minister's room 'quite bobbish about my coming ordeal [in the House of Commons] but leave depressed.'[55] The Prime Minister was very cross at the Amendment 27 cock-up. Hurd's statement was greeted with hoots of derision from the Labour benches, as Labour's Shadow Foreign Secretary, Jack Cunningham, argued that the Government was using the royal prerogative to ignore Parliament.

While Hurd feels he was never outstanding at the great set piece occasions in the House of Commons, he does feel he had an ability to manage the House when he was called upon to pull the Government out of a hole. By being that bit more open than most ministers, he was able to emerge relatively unscathed. This would later prove useful in mopping up after the Qualified Majority Voting (QMV) compromise in March 1994 (see Chapter 20), and the Pergau Dam affair in November 1994 (see Chapter 22). In July 1993, Labour's European Affairs spokesman, George Robertson, pithily described the Foreign Secretary as 'the chief salesman of the unacceptable'.[56] But while George Robertson proved a consistently good performer across the Dispatch Box and was one of Labour's rising stars, Douglas Hurd was also helped on this occasion and on others by the fact that Jack Cunningham always seemed to miss his punches on these occasions. Hurd never found Cunningham a particularly formidable opponent, unlike his successor, Robin Cook. On the night of 15 February, Hurd wrote:

15 Feb. 1993: I fumble once or twice but keep the House . . . Press will be lethal. Now we have to get the show back on the road.[57]

And the following day:

16 Feb. 1993: Press sour and harsh, but not more than expected. Reaction from colleagues continues to be good. Feel rather relieved.[58]

Besides the formidable task of guiding Maastricht through the Commons, much of Hurd's time at this point was taken up with handling the crisis in Bosnia. In May 1993, Hurd had to persuade the EC's chief negotiator, David Owen, to abandon the Vance-Owen plan in favour of the five-power 'Contact Group' plan, involving Britain, France, Germany, Russia and the United States (see Chapter 18). Contrary to the view of Martin Maginnis and Gerry Adams, Hurd did not play a central part in the Irish peace process. While he consulted regularly with Dick Spring, the Irish Foreign Minister, it was Patrick Mayhew, the Northern Ireland Secretary, and John Major who carried forward the policy. At the time, Hurd was simply too weighed down with the Bosnian issue to play a major part. For example, on 17 May 1993, at a ministerial meeting which decided not to admit Sinn Fein to a delegate conference, Hurd had to leave for a meeting of European Union Foreign Ministers to discuss the Bosnian peace plan.[59]

May 1993 also produced a catalogue of bad news on the domestic front. The local elections were lost along with the Newbury by-election. Good news on inflation (down to 1.3 per cent) and that the Danes had voted 'yes' in their second referendum on Maastricht was drowned by bad. First came the forced resignation of Norman Lamont as Chancellor of the Exchequer. Then stories appeared linking the Conservative MP Michael Mates (Hampshire, East) with the disgraced Polly Peck chairman, Asil Nadir. The situation in June worsened, as the opinion polls showed John Major to be the most unpopular Prime Minister since records began, and Norman Lamont delivered a bitter resignation speech in which he accused the Government of being 'in office but not in power'.[60]

In June 1993, the British Government was condemned by the Opposition for supporting President Clinton's decision to bomb Iraq after allegations that the Iraqis had launched an assassination attempt on George Bush. Hurd defended the action as 'justified and proportionate',[61] but while in Washington the previous month, he had urged restraint, and the bombing seems to have been delayed. The difficulty for Hurd was that he did not have the luxury of tackling each of these difficulties in a neat line, one after the other.

Meanwhile, in Parliament, the European Communities (Amendment) Bill was at last lumbering towards its conclusion, but with one final, dramatic twist. Labour's so-called 'ticking time bomb', Amendment 27, was a device to show Labour supported ratification of the Maastricht Treaty, but only if Britain signed the Social Chapter. Amendment 27 had changed its name since February 1993 due to the initial failure of the Deputy Speaker to accept the amendment for debate during the Committee Stage of the Bill. Labour's amendment reappeared at Report Stage as New Clause 2 and was accepted for debate by the Speaker. The Government accepted the amendment, allowing it to lie dormant until the very end of the parliamentary process, thus creating the ticking time bomb, which was scheduled to go off on 22 July.

At 7 p.m. on the evening of the vote, the Cabinet met in the House of Commons to discuss the options if the Government lost. The meeting began with the Chief Whip, Richard Ryder, reporting pessimistically on the Government's prospects for the vote at 10 p.m. At this point, Kenneth Clarke, the new Chancellor, proposed that the Government should hold a vote of confidence if it lost the vote. Douglas Hurd and the new Home Secretary, Michael Howard, agreed. Howard's support was crucial. Although the new Home Secretary was at heart a Euro-sceptic, he remained a Major loyalist. Howard's support for the vote of confidence had the effect of marginalising Michael Portillo, Peter Lilley and John Redwood, who were, according to Hurd, opposed to the plan. Hurd had talked with the Prime Minister that morning, and knew that he would support the move.

The first vote on Labour's amendment was tied at 317 votes to 317, with Betty Boothroyd bound by convention to support the Government.[62] On the second vote, the Government's own motion was defeated by 324 votes to 316.[63] Another quick Cabinet meeting was held, but the policy had already been agreed. Hurd wrote in his diary:

> 22 Jul. 1993: Tomorrow, the highest wire [We were not at all sure that the rebels would respond].[64]

The comments in square brackets were, unusually for the Hurd diaries, written a few days later to stress that the Government believed it was taking a big gamble, hoping that the rebels would draw back from the precipice of electoral defeat.

The following morning, Hurd appeared on the *Today* programme. At this stage, he was uncertain whether the Government would win. He then had a series of meetings with the rebels, including one with Bill Cash (Stafford) and another with Trevor Skeet (Bedfordshire, North). It became clear by the end of the morning that the resistance of the rebels was crumbling.

While the Prime Minister did not give a very good opening speech, Hurd's wind-up went rather better. He was greeted with an ironic round of applause when he told the House that this was the last speech on the ratification of the Maastricht Treaty.[65] He was relieved to discover that the rebels did not fire a series of volleys at him; all that Michael Spicer (Worcestershire, South) required was a courteous acknowledgement, which Hurd would have given anyway. In the course of his speech, the Foreign Secretary tried to don his party political hat by attacking the Liberal Democrat leader, Paddy Ashdown, for switching his line over the Social Chapter:

> The leader of the Liberal Democrats has the gifts of a master tailor: he is skilled at measuring and fitting his opinions to his audience.[66]

Hurd described the parliamentary struggle over Maastricht as a 'fierce tussle within our own party . . . by a stalwart group, basing themselves on their convinced interpretation of Conservative tradition'.[67] His patience had been tested to the limits:

> I have heartily disagreed with them. I have often wished them to go away, go to bed and to get lost. However, I do not doubt that their struggle will find a remembered place in the annals of parliamentary conflict.[68]

Hurd expressed the hope that the Conservative Party, bolstered by signs of economic recovery, could put behind it 'not just the long, necessary but debilitating debate about Maastricht, but that whole year of roughness and misfortune'.[69] In typical Hurd style, he concluded his wind-up with yet another analogy:

> . . . we have cultivated the land well, despite much rough weather. I believe that we have sown good seed, and that we can now work together to bring in a good harvest.[70]

Douglas Hurd does not believe, as some commentators have claimed, that John Major became a prisoner of the Euro-sceptics. The Prime Minister saw them as assassins, as was evidenced by his description of Michael Portillo, Peter Lilley, and John Redwood as 'bastards' in an off-camera remark to ITN's Michael Brunson just after the vote of confidence on 25 July 1993. But the experience of the ERM withdrawal affected John Major's morale so adversely that he seriously considered resignation. Even when he recovered from his bouts of depression, he still regarded ratification of Maastricht as being in the national interest, but that it was all a bally nuisance.

After September 1992, Hurd found it impossible to persuade John Major to make positive speeches on Europe. Beyond Maastricht, each British reversal at European meetings, particularly at Ioannina in Greece in March 1994, increasingly led the Prime Minister to feel that he could never win in Europe.

Notes

1. Interview with Douglas Hurd, 18 Mar. 1997.
2. Diary Readings with Douglas Hurd, 18 Mar. 1997.
3. Ibid.
4. Interview with Douglas Hurd, Westwell, 13 Jun. 1997.
5. The Danish vote was 49.3 per cent for and 50.7 per cent against, a margin of only 48,000 votes.
6. Diary Readings with Douglas Hurd, Westwell, 13 Jun. 1997.
7. Philip Stephens, *Politics and the Pound*, p. 206
8. Interview with Tristan Garel-Jones, 19 Nov. 1996.
9. 'Future Development of the EEC', *House of Commons Order Paper*, 3 Jun. 1992, Motion. 174. For full list of signatories of Fresh Start and a comparison with those opposing the Government's paving motion in November 1992, *see* Baker, Gamble & Ludlam, 'Whips or Scorpions? The Maastricht Vote and the Conservative Party', *Parliamentary Affairs*, vol. 46, no. 2, Apr. 1993, pp. 151–66.
10. (Transcript) *Breakfast with Frost*, BBC 1, 28 Jun. 1992.
11. H. of C. Deb. (6th Series), 8 Jun. 1992, vol. 209, cols 32–9.
12. *The Guardian*, 1 Jul. 1992.
13. Interview with Douglas Hurd, Westwell, 13 Jun. 1997.
14. Stephens, *Politics and the Pound*, p. 246.
15. Interview with Douglas Hurd, Westwell, 13 Jun. 1997.
16. Stephens, *Politics and the Pound*, p. 250.
17. Diary Readings with Douglas Hurd, Westwell, 13 Jun. 1997.
18. Ibid.
19. Ibid.
20. Interview with Douglas Hurd, Westwell, 13 Jun. 1997.
21. Diary Readings with Douglas Hurd, Westwell, 13 Jun. 1997.
22. Ibid.
23. David Mellor, the National Heritage Secretary, having just staved off resignation over committing adultery, finally had to resign after a scandal involving hospitality during a visit to the Gulf when he was Minister of State at the Foreign Office.
24. The Suffolk South MP had had an extramarital affair. Diary Readings with Douglas Hurd, 13 Jun. 1997.
25. Interview with Douglas Hurd, Westwell, 13 Jun. 1997; Stephens, *Politics*

and the Pound, pp. 228–33.

26. This account is based on a letter from Douglas Hurd to the author, dated 15 Oct. 1997. Hurd consulted his diary entry and produced a summary. This was the only occasion on which this happened.

27. The European, 7 Oct. 1992.

28. Diary Readings with Douglas Hurd, Westwell, 18 Mar. 1997.

29. Ibid.

30. The Guardian, 7 Oct. 1992.

31. Diary Readings with Douglas Hurd, 18 Mar. 1997.

32. Diary Readings with Douglas Hurd, Westwell, 13 Jun. 1997.

33. Ibid.

34. Interview with Douglas Hurd, Westwell, 13 Jun. 1997.

35. Interview with Tristan Garel-Jones, 19 Nov. 1996.

36. Diary Readings with Douglas Hurd, Westwell, 13 Jun. 1997.

37. Interview with Douglas Hurd, Westwell, 13 Jun. 1997.

38. Diary Readings with Douglas Hurd, Westwell, 13 Jun. 1997. During a discussion at Westwell, Douglas Hurd made no attempt to censor his diary entries criticising Norman Lamont.

39. Interview with Tristan Garel-Jones, 19 Nov. 1996.

40. Diary Readings with Douglas Hurd, Westwell, 13 Jun. 1997.

41. Baker, Gamble & Ludlam op. cit., pp. 156–7.

42. Diary Readings with Douglas Hurd, Westwell, 13 Jun. 1997.

43. H. of C. Deb. (6th Series), 4 Nov. 1992, vol. 213, cols 376–85.

44. Interview with Douglas Hurd, Westwell, 13 Jun. 1997.

45. Michael Cartiss (Great Yarmouth) voted with the Government on both motions; Vivian Bendall (Ilford, North) abstained on the first vote and voted with the Government on the second vote.

46. Interview with Douglas Hurd, Westwell, 13 Jun. 1997.

47. Ibid.

48. H. of C. Deb. (6th Series), 24 Nov. 1992, vol. 214, col. 770.

49. Interview with Douglas Hurd, Westwell, 13 Jun. 1997.

50. (10 Dec. 1992) Diary Readings with Douglas Hurd, Westwell, 13 Jun. 1997.

51. (11 Dec. 1992) Ibid.

52. (11 Dec. 1992) Ibid.

53. (11 Dec. 1992) Ibid.

54. H. of C. Deb. (6th Series), 15 Feb. 1993, vol. 219, cols 27–37.

55. Diary Readings with Douglas Hurd, Westwell, 13 Jun. 1997.

56. H. of C. Deb. (6th Series), 23 Jul. 1993, vol. 229, col. 710.

57. Diary Readings with Douglas Hurd, Westwell, 13 Jun. 1997.

58. Ibid.

59. Eamonn Mallie and David McKittrick, *The Fight for Peace: The Secret Story Behind the Irish Peace Process* (Heinemann: London, 1996), pp. 250–1.

60. H. of C. Deb. (6th Series), 9 Jun. 1993, vol. 226, cols 281–5.

61. H. of C. Deb. (6th Series), 28 Jun. 1993, vol. 227, col. 657.

62. The vote was subsequently found to have been 317 to 316 in favour of the Government due to an error in counting by a Conservative whip. The Speaker's casting vote was therefore not necessary.

63. H. of C. Deb. (6th Series), 22 Jul. 1993, vol. 229, cols 602–10.

64. Diary Readings with Douglas Hurd, Westwell, 13 Jun. 1997.

65. H. of C. Deb. (6th Series), 23 Jul. 1993, vol. 229, col. 711.

66. Ibid., col. 713.

67. Ibid.

68. Ibid.

69. Ibid., col. 714.

70. Ibid.

18

Waiting for the Americans:
The Wars of the Yugoslav Succession,
1991–1995

Any historical assessment of Douglas Hurd's tenure as Foreign Secretary will hinge on differing interpretations of his handling of the events in the former Yugoslavia and his policy towards European integration. These two great issues which dominated his last three years at King Charles Street were not mutually exclusive. Both raised fundamental questions about the future shape of Europe after the end of the Cold War, and consideration of one issue affected the response to the other. At the same time that the Yugoslavian crisis was erupting in 1991, Western European leaders were considering at Maastricht how best to move towards closer integration within the European Community, before going on to consider the widening of their membership to include the countries of Eastern Europe. But all at once, they were confronted with a problem in the Balkans at a time when Western European institutions had not evolved sufficiently to address post-Cold War realities. The problem was compounded by a hiatus in American leadership of the Western world at a time when only American military power could have been brought to bear to intervene in the conflict. Hurd realised this, and engaged in a holding operation over the former Yugoslavia, until the Americans were willing to reassume their world role. But that holding operation – along with his valiant attempts to unite the Conservative Party on Europe – had the effect of denting, but never entirely destroying, the favourable reputation he had enjoyed in his first two years as Foreign Secretary.

In the early 1990s, the European Community was primarily an economic and political organisation, and had never been a military organisation. The main vehicle for closer European defence links was the Western European Union (WEU), set up partly to provide a forum which did not impinge on the traditionally neutral states in the European Community, particularly Ireland and Denmark.

The real guarantor of Western European security lay in the North Atlantic Treaty Organisation (NATO). By 1991, whilst everyone could agree with the rhetoric that NATO had to change to reflect the collapse of the Soviet Union, NATO strategy was in limbo between 1989 and 1995. Troop levels were reduced in Central Europe, but the debate about the 'out of area' role of NATO and whether and when the states of Eastern Europe should join the military alliance moved at a snail's pace. In short, NATO was in transition and did not quite know what its future role should be, because its major enemy for the last forty years had departed from the scene. Meanwhile, the Americans increasingly felt that Europe should take more responsibility for its own defence. France, along with Germany, Italy and the Benelux countries, heartily agreed. The French in particular had always been suspicious of American influence — General de Gaulle had taken France out of the military structure of NATO in 1966. When the issue of Yugoslavia arose, they saw it as an opportunity for Europe to act as one to solve a crisis on their own continent without the help of the United States. As David Owen, the EC's peace envoy in the former Yugoslavia has pointed out:

> At first Europe wanted to stand on its own two feet — Yugoslavia was the virility symbol of the Euro-federalists. This was going to be the time when Europe emerged with a single foreign policy and therefore it unwisely shut out an America only too happy to be shut out.[1]

Douglas Hurd, on the other hand, was opposed to the idea that the European Community should develop into a military organisation. While he was willing to concede an enhancement of the WEU, this should run complementary to NATO, not in competition with it. This debate was argued out during the Maastricht negotiations on 9-10 December 1991. The real issue for Hurd was that, having enshrined the idea of intergovernmentalism in foreign and security policy at Maastricht only six days earlier, he could not then be seen to tarnish that concept with European states acting at odds with each other.

Above all, it seems that Hurd wanted to win the debate about the security structures of Europe, and that meant preserving the Atlantic Alliance at all costs — persuading her European partners not to desert the American defence role in Europe. Hurd told the House of Commons in November 1994:

> We must not allow the strains created by Bosnia to disrupt the transatlantic

319

partnership. The danger is there for all to see and I shall work with all my
energy to prevent such disruption.[2]

Hurd's central aim in the former Yugoslavia – that of preserving the Atlantic
Alliance – was made much more difficult by two factors. The first was the
intermittent hiatus that is often caused to the leadership of the Western world
when there is a change-over in the American presidency. A similar problem had
occurred in 1980-81, when, according to Lord Carrington (the erstwhile
Foreign Secretary), America was 'taking a sabbatical', as the Carter
Administration was being replaced by the Reagan administration.[3] During 1991
and 1992, American foreign policy was virtually put on hold as President Bush
discovered that an ungrateful public after the Gulf War was only interested in
domestic economic issues. In such circumstances, the commitment of American
ground troops to Yugoslavia was too risky. America had not fully erased the
memory of Vietnam even after defeating Saddam Hussein. They feared another
quagmire in the former Yugoslavia. The military doctrine of General Colin
Powell was all-pervasive: if America was going to do anything, it had to do
everything.

The second difficulty for the Foreign Secretary was that, when the Clinton
administration came to power in January 1993, it promoted a policy to which
he was implacably opposed: lifting the arms embargo to allow the Bosnian
Muslims to defend themselves. Hurd believes that the Clinton administration
'latched onto the proposal for lifting the arms embargo as being the neatest and
(they thought) the most moral way through the difficulty, partly because it
didn't involve any deployment of American troops.'[4]

It was paradoxical that Hurd's main aim was to preserve the Atlantic Alliance
when that ally was proposing policies which were in conflict with almost every
initiative which Europe and the United Nations developed toward the former
Yugoslavia between 1991 and 1993. The American decision not to send ground
troops to enforce the Vance–Owen plan led to its collapse in May 1993; air
strikes threatened the humanitarian relief effort on the ground; America's
decision not to enforce the arms embargo in November 1994 upset her
European allies and undermined their efforts to prevent the conflict from
spreading. The decision to equip the Croats against the Krajinian Serbs in May
1995 risked widening the conflict, and in effect lifted the arms embargo in
favour of the Croats so that the Serbs were forced to negotiate a settlement.
In the middle of all this, Douglas Hurd tried to ease the Americans on board,
whilst diplomatically ditching most of the previous peace efforts. Arguably, the
policies developed by Europe and the UN between 1991 and 1993 were merely
holding operations until old-fashioned American imperial power was brought to
bear to bring the parties to the negotiating table. But the man whose reputation

suffered as a result of facilitating the progressive handover of the issue to the United States was Douglas Hurd.

There is a powerful counter-argument which suggests that the initial conflict was provoked by President Milosevic in Serbia to save his Communist regime by recourse to crude nationalism and a war of aggression. Faced with a clear case of aggression, albeit against emerging states, the argument runs that Douglas Hurd, more than any other European politician, stood in the way of Western European military intervention against the Serbs. Once the conflict widened, the opportunity to use force diminished, and the conflict descended into a civil war, in which the West (so the argument goes) should have lifted the arms embargo and used air power to hit Serb positions. Again, more than any other politician, Hurd opposed these moves. Indeed, much of Hurd's time during 1993 and 1994 was spent trying to persuade the Clinton Administration and US Congressmen not to lift the arms embargo.

Warren Christopher, the new US Secretary of State, tried to persuade the British Government to change its mind. On the weekend of 2-3 May 1993, Warren Christopher put the Clinton Administration's case for lifting the arms embargo in favour of the Bosnian Muslims to John Major and Douglas Hurd at Chevening, the Foreign Secretary's residence in Kent. But they refused, believing that arming the Bosnian Muslims would have prolonged the war. Lifting the arms embargo would also have endangered the humanitarian relief effort. Britain and France made it clear that in those circumstances their troops would have been withdrawn. As Hurd recalled later, 'that seemed to us to be a simple matter of safety.'[5]

However, because Hurd's main aim was not to create a breach with the Americans, he had to consider other policy options, such as air power:

> This was not because we believed that the use of air power had any magical effect or ever would have. But we saw a place for it, and because of our fourth objective (preventing differences of opinion from undermining the Atlantic Alliance), we were ready to see the increased use of air power to enable the Americans to continue as part of the Contact Group and as part of the Alliance.[6]

Hurd flew to Washington on 21 May 1993 to reach agreement on the five-powered document – comprising Britain, France, Russia, Germany, and the United States – known as the Contact Group plan. The outline plan sought to divide Bosnia into 51 per cent Muslim/Croat areas, with 49 per cent going to the Bosnian Serbs, and five 'grey zones' – captured by the Bosnian Serbs from the Muslims – placed under UN control. Hurd considered the plan during an overnight stay in New York. From there, he telephoned David Owen, who was, according to Hurd, 'morose' because he believed Hurd was ditching the Vance–Owen plan.[7]

The Vance–Owen plan drew its ideas from the Finnish diplomat Martti Ahtisaari. In October 1992, he proposed that Bosnia be divided up into autonomous provinces or 'cantons', allowing refugees to return to their homes. The Vance–Owen plan of January 1993 redefined these cantons, giving them ethnic labels, which, it can be argued, had the effect of breaking the alliance between the Muslims and the Croats, sparking fighting between Croats and Muslims for mixed areas – between Mate Boban's HVO Croat forces and the Muslims – for the towns of Mostar, Gornji Vakuf and Vares. The fighting between Bosnian Croats and Bosnian Muslims weakened the military position of the Bosnian Muslims in the so-called Eastern enclaves, including the towns of Srebrenica and Zepa, which, in spite of being declared UN safe areas, would later be ethnically cleansed by the Bosnian Serbs.

In May 1993, Lord Owen still believed it was possible to impose the Vance–Owen plan on Bosnia, but Hurd and the policy-makers in Washington disagreed. Owen felt the Clinton Administration cut the ground from under his feet by refusing to promise American troops to implement his plan and by devising their own new peace process through the Contact Group plan. One is compelled to agree. When Vance–Owen was put before the self-styled Bosnian Serb Assembly in Pale on 5 May 1993 it was decisively rejected. Hurd was left as the messenger to Owen that his plan was stillborn. Lord Owen recollects that, prior to the telephone conversation with Douglas Hurd on 21 May 1993, he mistakenly received a telegram from the Foreign Office outlining the text of the new Contact Group plan about to be signed in Washington. So, a situation arose where the EC's chief negotiator listened on the telephone, being reassured about the Vance–Owen plan by the British Foreign Secretary, when Lord Owen had the text of the outline agreement designed to ditch his own plan!

Despite Hurd's willingness to dispense with the Vance–Owen plan and accept greater use of air strikes in order to prevent serious damage to the Atlantic Alliance, at no stage was he willing to lift the arms embargo. On 21 June 1994, he flew to Washington for a two-day visit with the aim of getting the new Clinton administration and the key people on Capitol Hill to listen to the British case. He faced an uphill task. Many of the opinion formers and Congressmen who were most interested in Bosnia had formed their views as a result of listening to the reports on CNN news and reading the one-sided accounts in favour of the Bosnian-Muslim case in the East Coast press, most notably those of William Safire in the New York Times. These reports failed to distinguish between Bosnian Serbs and Serbs from other areas, depicting the conflict as a clear case of ethnic cleansing from evil Serbs against innocent Muslims. Hurd spent a couple of days talking to groups of Congressmen to try to explain his view of the nature of the conflict, going into great detail, answering questions. In this task, Hurd was aided by Sir Robin Renwick, Britain's Ambassador to Washington. Just as he had become renowned for his expert hosting of dinners while British Ambassador in Pretoria, Sir Robin established a pattern of inviting a cross-section of Washington politicians and opinion formers to the British Embassy in Washington. On 21 June 1994, for example, according to Hurd's diary, around six senators attended, along with several Congressmen, two or three of the top journalists and a couple of people from the US State Department.[8] This pattern was repeated three or four times when Hurd visited Washington. As he recalls, 'it was a way of being heard in a congenial atmosphere.'[9]

The following day (22 June), Hurd had further meetings with nineteen senators on Capitol Hill, followed by lunch with the Speaker of the House of Representatives, Tom Foley, all with the aim of preventing the Americans from lifting the arms embargo. A Foreign Office insider believes that this explanation/communication role of Hurd's was 'worth its weight in gold'.[10]

But this was a difficult point in the Atlantic Alliance's history. A row broke out at the end of January 1994 during one of Hurd's visits to Washington when President Clinton overrode the State Department and issued a visa to Gerry Adams, President of Sinn Fein. Hurd received the news while attending another of Robin Renwick's dinners at the British Embassy. The following morning, he had a meeting with Vice-President Al Gore, which he described as 'quite rough'.[11] Hurd telephoned John Major in London and found him 'very frustrated'.[12] The main problem by this stage was that Adams had taken the American media by storm. Every network news channel and chat show wanted to speak with him. Foreign Office officials offered up Hurd for the news networks, but he only managed one appearance on CNN. Adams had his day in the sun.

After the Adams visa row, Hurd felt it was important to find an issue where Britain and the US could be seen to be standing together. He was provided with such an opportunity in October 1994 when Saddam Hussein started large-scale troop manouevres on the border with Kuwait. The crisis blew up in the middle of the Conservative Party Conference in Bournemouth. After delivering his Conference speech, Hurd flew out to Kuwait to attend a Gulf Co-operation Council (GCC) meeting. He was pleased to see that Warren Christopher was by his side. Until then, outside countries had never been invited to GCC meetings, so Hurd was keen to cite this as an example of Anglo-American co-operation. The British deployed forces, but the crisis passed as Saddam Hussein backed down.

The show of unity was short-lived. In November 1994, the Clinton administration came under domestic pressure from the Republicans after their victory in the mid-term Congressional elections. With the Republicans in control of both Houses of Congress, and with the Senate Majority leader Bob Dole calling for tougher action on Bosnia, the President announced on 11 November 1994 that the United States would no longer help enforce the arms embargo against the former Yugoslavia. Although there was little military impact – the Americans had only provided two warships for 'Operation Sharpguard' against sixteen from other countries – it caused a sizeable diplomatic rift. The Foreign Office had not been informed in advance: the first they learned of it was from US press reports.

On 13 November, Bob Dole paid a visit to London, in order to sloganise his 'lift and strike' policy idea. Dole's comment that 'the UN should get off NATO's back and let NATO take care of Serbian aggression' privately irritated Hurd and led to a stern public rebuke from his colleague, Malcolm Rifkind, the Defence Secretary. The discussion between Dole and Hurd was a case of each side agreeing to differ.

In the early stages of the conflict in the former Yugoslavia, the main bone of contention between Hurd and the federalists was whether a peace-keeping force should be sent in. The relevant meeting took place on 19 September 1991 at The Hague. European Foreign Ministers met in joint session with the WEU, acknowledging that the EC did not have the structures in place to consider military solutions. The meeting discussed four possible options, ranging from armed escorts for EC peace monitors to sending a fully-fledged peace keeping force of 20,000-50,000 men. Hurd rejected all four options, invoking the British experience in Northern Ireland. Britain, he said had 'particular experience of operations village by village and street by street in Northern Ireland. I can tell you that it is much easier to get troops in than to get them out again.'[13] Throughout, the Foreign Secretary was wary of the appeal of the quick fix.

No European country was talking about sending a military intervention force, in the true sense of the word, backing one side in the conflict against another. They agreed with Hurd's conditions that a durable ceasefire had to be established alongside consent from all parties for the European presence.

Once military intervention was ruled out by the Europeans, the three priorities became: saving lives through humanitarian relief; seeking ways of securing a settlement between the combatants; and preventing the conflict from spreading. These three aims were addressed by combining the efforts of the UN and the EC, first by a London Conference in August 1992 under Peter Carrington, and then through the efforts of Lord Owen and Cyrus Vance.

As the humanitarian problem deteriorated in the summer of 1992, the question arose: should refugees be allowed to arrive in Britain? In most cases, the aim since April 1992 (when the British humanitarian effort began), had been to look after refugees as close to their original homes as possible, so they could re-assimilate more quickly. But in a number of exceptional cases, Lynda Chalker, the Overseas Development Minister, and Douglas Hurd believed that Britain should allow in refugees. The new Home Secretary, Kenneth Clarke, was concerned about the groups of well-meaning Britons travelling across to the Balkans in buses and lorries and bringing back refugees. Clarke recalls:

> I took a much stiffer view of the rules – open to genuine refugees, but applying the normal rules of asylum – whereas the Foreign Office responded to the wave of public pressures.[14]

In July 1992, Douglas Hurd had gone out to the Balkans to assess the humanitarian problem for himself and to get to know the various leaders. The visit took in Slovenia, Croatia, Sarajevo, Belgrade, Macedonia and Albania. In Slovenia, Hurd went to the boundary between Croatia and the UN-protected area, manned by British monitors. There, he was briefed by Barney Mayhew, Sir Patrick Mayhew's son:

> 16 Jul. 1992: Wander into the Nigerian contingent. Shattered villages just returning to life. Visit our field ambulances. On the whole, British effort [is] stronger than its numbers. Disturbing talk with the UN High Commissioner about refugee crisis.[15]

On his arrival in Sarajevo the following day, Hurd was met by the Canadian General, [Lewis] MacKenzie, commander of UN operations in the city, whom Hurd thought was 'biased against the Bosnians'.[16] Hurd was shown round an airport hangar:

> 17 Jul. 1992: Beds, stores, bullet holes. Travel into Sarajevo in a French armoured car. See [Alija] Izetbegovic. A mortar explodes nearby. Followed by a talk . . . Thousands of cameras, broken windows, where the mortar landed on the bread queue.[17]

There was then a muddle about a visit to a hospital. Hurd described it as 'a sort of rushed, incompetent day'.[18] The Foreign Secretary arrived in Belgrade that evening. The British residence was opened for a dinner in honour of the Serbian Opposition leader, Vuk Draskovic, famous for his long beard and voluminous black locks of hair. Britain had pulled out its Ambassador, Peter Hall, some months before, but his house was re-opened especially for everyone not associated with President Milosevic's circle of influence.

The following day (18 July 1992), Hurd met President Milosevic for the first time:

> 18 Jul. 1992: Very hard on self-justification. A stream of untruths about past and present. Debate here both more defensive and more open than at Zagreb.[19]

While Milosevic was undoubtely a rogue, the problem was that he was an extremely clever, plausible rogue. In contrast, the meeting with President Tudjman of Croatia in Zagreb the day before had been altogether more sinister. In his Presidential suite hangs a great picture of Aryan youth in 1930s style German jumpsuits. The fascist history of Croatia could not be disguised.

In parliamentary terms, the Yugoslavian issue was not one which caused a major split between the two main parties. As with most foreign policy issues, the Official Opposition was keen to be seen to be following a bipartisan policy with the Government. However, the three Shadow Foreign Secretaries between 1991 and 1995 were not entirely uncritical of Government policy. Gerald Kaufman confined his criticisms to the slowness of the EC's sanctions escalation, and Britain's caving-in to Germany's demand for recognition of Croatia and Slovenia.[20] His successor, Jack Cunningham, was even more uncritical, agreeing that air strikes might damage the humanitarian effort.[21] There was a difference of viewpoint early on between the late John Smith, the Labour leader, and Jack Cunningham over the use of air strikes – a battle which Cunningham won.[22] Later, Robin Cook attacked the ineffectiveness of the UN safe areas.[23]

But overall, it is significant that at no point during the period 1991 to 1995 did the Official Opposition call a division on the issue. Indeed, there was only one parliamentary division on the former Yugoslavia, on 16 November 1992. The debate was called, not by Labour, but by the Liberal Democrats. Menzies Campbell, then the Liberal Democrat Defence spokesman, led the case for air strikes against the Serbs.[24]

Most of the parliamentary time taken up by the former Yugoslavia was occupied by statements on the latest developments by Douglas Hurd, or sometimes by Malcolm Rifkind, the Defence Secretary, if troops were being committed. This format suited Douglas Hurd's skill of appearing statesmanlike and reassuring, charting a middle way between the interventionists and the 'let them fight it out' groups in the House of Commons. Crudely put, he was able to play one side off against the other.

Mrs Thatcher took a simplistic view of the conflict. Initially, she backed military intervention against the Serbs. On 6 August 1992, Hurd wrote in his diary that he was 'pushed to counter Margaret Thatcher on military intervention in Yugoslavia'.[25] On one occasion, she even telephoned Hurd in the middle of a meeting he was having with the Canadian Foreign Minister to insist that Britain help the Croats. Subsequently, realising that neither the Americans nor any member of the EC supported military intervention, the former Prime Minister called for the lifting of the arms embargo in favour of the Bosnian Muslims. At one point, she compared the West's inaction as being 'a little like an accomplice to slaughter'.[26] Out of past loyalty, Hurd felt he had to listen to these tirades all the same.

One body of opinion in the House of Commons took an interventionist line, which Hurd termed the 'something must be done' brigade. Whilst very few (under twenty) MPs supported sending British troops to fight on the side of the Bosnian Muslims, many more were in favour of air strikes against the Serbs (whom they saw as the main aggressors), combined with the lifting of the arms embargo in favour of the Bosnian Muslims. All the Liberal Democrat MPs, led by the pious and flak-jacketed Paddy Ashdown, sided with sections of the Labour left,[27] and were supported on the Conservative side by Lady Thatcher in the House of Lords and a small, but highly honourable group of Conservative MPs, most notably Sir Patrick Cormack, Chairman of the All-Party Bosnia Group. Outside the Commons, the former Labour leader Michael Foot made a film for the BBC with his director wife, Jill Craigie, entitled *Two Hours from London*, pleading with the West to intervene on the side of the Bosnian Muslims.

But the Labour left was not uniformly in favour of tougher action against the Serbs. Tony Benn urged Britain to stay out of the conflict, while Dennis Skinner (Bolsover) – well known for his anti-German credentials – constantly heckled Hurd to keep out of the Balkans quagmire. Meanwhile, Bob Wareing (Liverpool, West Derby), Chairman of the All-Party British-Yugoslavia Parliamentary Group, took a passionately pro-Serb view.[28]

'Let them fight it out' Conservatives believed that no direct British national interest was involved in Bosnia.[29] However, Hurd experienced little difficulty in responding to their narrow definition of the British national interest. In reply to Nicholas Budgen's charge that Britain was taking on the role of a 'second-class policeman', Hurd replied:

> When, night after night, people see on television destruction and massacre in a European city, most of them do not expect us to send in troops, but they expect us to take some sensible action, if we can, to bring that suffering to an end.[30]

Despite the honourable stand taken by Sir Patrick Cormack, Hurd was in fact more concerned with the dominant mood on the Tory backbenches, which was one of growing unease that Britain was becoming further embroiled in the conflict.[31] As the number of British troops was increased, several MPs began to express their concern during Hurd's statements to the House of Commons.[32] Cyril Townsend (Bexleyheath) summed up the mood of many when he asked Hurd to be 'extremely cautious about getting UNPROFOR and its large British contingent further embroiled in this treacherous and perilous Bosnian bog?'[33]

Hurd, the Prime Minister and the Defence Secretary, Malcolm Rifkind, were actually the most interventionist members of the Cabinet in arguing for humanitarian aid to Bosnia. Hurd recalls that the three ministers who handled the issues from day to day 'constantly found that we were ahead of our colleagues in government . . . we were up against a very natural and strong reserve about growing involvement in Bosnia.'[34] He cites an occasion when Sir John Weston, Britain's Ambassador to NATO, needed instructions on a forward movement for ten o'clock the following morning. Hurd, Major, and Rifkind were in agreement about the move, but they failed to win over other ministers at a fuller Defence and Overseas Policy Committee (OPD) that evening. So, the following morning, the three men engaged in a series of bilateral chats with reluctant Cabinet colleagues, winning over enough of them to send instructions to Sir John Weston only minutes before the NATO meeting began at ten o'clock.[35]

From the end of November 1994 until his retirement in June 1995, Hurd's diaries are punctuated with expressions of anxiety that some fearful incident might occur in which the British or possibly the French might lose a large number of troops. From time to time, his fears seemed justified: in May 1995, British troops, especially around the town of Gorazde, became exposed and overextended. Contingency plans were drawn up for a withdrawal and official sources hinted at a possible UN pull-out. However, according to Hurd, the Prime Minister was very reluctant to pull out of Bosnia, believing that to do so would cause very real harm to the future standing of the United Nations, and also carried the risk that the warring parties might call the UN's bluff. On this issue, Hurd believes the Prime Minister's judgement was proved right and he was wrong.[36] Far from feeling jealous about the American success in producing the Dayton Agreement, Hurd's reaction, he recalls, was one of 'huge relief' that a major disaster involving UN troops had been averted.[37]

In contrast to the caution of his Cabinet colleagues, Hurd recalls he was conscious of a strong media consensus, 'a huge amount of sympathy, fluctuating from event to event, with the underdog – and the underdog was the Bosnian Government or the Bosnian Muslims'.[38] He judges that this opinion was even more prevalent in Germany and the United States, creating a paradox that the countries who were not committing troops in Bosnia were the most vociferous within NATO in arguing for something to be done.[39] The opponents of Douglas Hurd's policy in the former Yugoslavia, headed by Noel Malcolm, argue that German and American opinion was merely putting forward a perfectly credible alternative policy of withdrawing the humanitarian relief effort, arming the Bosnian Muslims and supporting them through the use of air power against the Serbs.

Although Hurd believed the media had a right to bring horrors to the attention of the British public, he told the House of Commons in April 1993:

> Anger and horror are not enough as a basis for decisions. It is a British interest to make a reasoned contribution towards a more orderly and decent world. But it is not a British interest, and it would only be a pretence, to suppose that we can intervene and sort out every tragedy which captures people's attention and sympathy. I have never found the phrase 'something must be done' to be a phrase which carries any conviction in places such as the House or the Government where people have to take decisions . . . Decisions cannot be based on false analogies or on a desire to achieve better headlines tomorrow than today. That is particularly true when decisions affect human life, and more especially still when the lives are those of British servicemen or civilians.[40]

On 9 September 1993, in what became a famous speech to the Travellers' Club, Hurd continued his theme of the dangers of the media identifying glib solutions to complex problems:

> Most of those who report for the BBC, *The Times*, *The Independent*, *The Guardian*, have all been in different ways enthusiasts pushing for military intervention in Bosnia . . . They are founder members of the something-must-be-done club.[41]

His more general thesis, with application to domestic as well as foreign policy, was that the burdens placed on ministers by the need to justify one's actions to the media were getting out of hand. After a typical ministerial statement to the House of Commons, Hurd judged that one could expect to conduct five or six interviews, possibly four for television and two for radio. If a minister refused, then he risked 'critics and commentators' filling the gap. Justification of policy had become as important as its formulation.

Underpinning the speech was Hurd's belief that there were too many critics and commentators only interested in expressing their opinions, and too few people reporting the actual facts. The analogy he chose on this occasion was of a lighthouse. The searchlight of media coverage was not the 'even regular sweep of a lighthouse' but 'patchy and determined by editorial whim'.[42]

Hugo Young, in *The Guardian* made the counter argument that:

> The emotional impact of television's version of reality is assumed to carry a punch which knocks foreign policy-making sideways . . . [but] the very plethora of disasters does more to anaesthetise than awaken the public demand for action.[43]

The way in which the dispute spiralled downwards into faction-fighting had the effect, not of rousing audiences in Britain, but of making Bosnia seem to the majority of British public opinion as a desperately confusing place, a hopeless country from which we should perhaps withdraw our troops and leave them to fight it out.

Other journalists, like John Simpson, the BBC's chief diplomatic correspondent, drew the conclusion that this meant Hurd secretly preferred the system of diplomacy prevalent in the Concert of Europe early last century where diplomacy was carried out behind closed doors, in the virtual absence of media pressure.[44] There is some truth in this, in the sense that Hurd supports the idea of the big powers playing the decisive role in crises of this kind, exemplified by the Contact Group Plan.

Hurd believed that British soldiers were saving lives through the provision of humanitarian relief. His statements to the House of Commons and articles in the press are littered with proud boasts of the number of aid convoys that were reaching besieged cities, the number of tonnes of aid delivered and the total amount of aid spent.[45]

But there are real doubts whether the humanitarian effort actually achieved anything. Rosalyn Higgins, an expert on the UN, believes that it was a mistake to establish a UN operation dedicated to the provision of humanitarian aid without a ceasefire. By choosing not to stop the violence via a military intervention force, she believes that the UN prolonged the suffering.[46] Lord Carrington takes the view that the only way the West could have helped is if it had decided to take either side in what he saw as a civil war, leaving the task of humanitarian relief to the aid agencies.[47] There are also real doubts that aid got through to the people who really needed it. In December 1993, the International Committee of the Red Cross estimated that 90 per cent of emergency aid was being obstructed by the warring parties. Larry Hollingworth, then the co-ordinator of UN convoys, claimed that only one fifth of aid was getting through whereas Hurd put the figure at nearly half.

In January 1994, Hurd paid a visit to Bosnia in order to assess the effectiveness of the aid effort. The Foreign Secretary was taken in a convoy of white UN vehicles through 'Route Diamond', the main track into Bosnia for the aid convoys. As the trip entered the town of Gornji Vakuf, scene of fighting between Muslim and Croat, Hurd climbed aboard a Warrior armoured vehicle, donning a flak jacket and ill-fitting blue UN helmet on his head. He spent the night in the Croat pocket of Vitez at the headquarters of the Coldstream Guards.

Hurd was genuinely moved by the whole experience, and came away from the trip convinced that the British aid effort was indeed saving lives. Hurd is often accused by journalists of being cynical about his fellow man. In fact, Hurd is a resilient optimist who wants to see the best in what people are doing. He admires all those engaged in public service, but especially voluntary service.

On most ministerial visits, VIPs receive a rosy picture from their hosts of what is going on. Hurd has a tendency to talk up policies which in reality are not working quite as well as he thinks. As he entered the base of the Coldstream Guards, he told the waiting media:

It's working, it's working! It's pretty clear that the troops and the ODA (Overseas Development Agency) drivers are actually managing to get more aid through.[48]

Hurd had visited central Bosnia where it is true that the British troops played a major role in brokering a deal between the Muslims and the Croats which led to aid convoys getting through. But had he talked to the aid agencies, he would have heard of the Muslim and Croat road-blocks, the appalling conditions on the mountain roads, and the seizure of much of the aid by the three armies.

Hurd also displayed a consistently high level of optimism about the effectiveness of international sanctions against Belgrade and their ability to persuade President Milosevic of Serbia to break off his links with the Bosnian Serbs. Hurd describes Milosevic as 'one of the cleverest men I have ever had to deal with. He speaks perfect English. His mind moves in a logical way. He is very quick, but very hard and doesn't give.'[49] In an article in The Independent in December 1994, Hurd acknowledged that Milosevic had played a role in starting the original war, but he felt that the Serbian President held the key to achieving peace:

He [Milosevic] is genuinely trying to bring the Bosnian Serbs round. He has seen that only a negotiated settlement will get sanctions lifted and bring the Serbs back into modern Europe.[50]

The hope was that by putting diplomatic, economic and political pressure on

Belgrade, the European Community would succeed in splitting the Serbs. The problem was that, as with most sanctions policies, there were substantial loopholes. Moreover, the European Community's policy was one of gradually increasing the pressure on Serbia: first by withdrawing association agreements, and then by imposing trade penalities. There was no complete ban on oil supplies from the beginning and no comprehensive monitoring of the effectiveness of sanctions until much later. At least Hurd was at the forefront of suggesting new ways of improving sanctions monitoring. He was the first to suggest that a high-powered sanctions co-ordinator should be appointed to 'knock heads together'.[51]

In April 1993, the Foreign Secretary was upbeat in his assessment of the effectiveness of sanctions, asking the House of Commons to believe that there were 'signs – I put it no more strongly than that – that under pressure the leaders in Belgrade are becoming increasingly impatient with the Bosnian Serbs . . . '[52] By December 1993, Hurd described a grave situation in Belgrade, with farmers slaughtering milk cows for food, and inflation running at 20,000 per cent a month. Milosevic, he claimed, was worried.[53] Hurd was aware that sanctions were an imperfect instrument, but there was an element of talking up the impact of the policy.

By April 1994, even Hurd the optimist was willing to admit publicly that he was having some doubt about Milosevic's ability to exert meaningful leverage over the Bosnian Serbs. He told the House of Commons:

> . . . sanctions have achieved a considerable change in the attitude of President Milosevic and the Government in Belgrade. What is in doubt is the chain of influence through Pale and Mr Karadzic, to General Mladic and the Bosnian Serb commanders. From time to time, that influence is exerted. From time to time, it does not exist.[54]

A change of approach was needed. While the Americans began a twin strategy of stopping the Croats and the Muslims from fighting against one another and using air power to convince the Bosnian Serbs to sign up to a peace agreement, Hurd and his French counterpart, Alain Juppé, launched two diplomatic missions to Belgrade, one in July 1994, the other in December 1994, to persuade Milosevic to drop his support for the Bosnian Serbs. Instead of the earlier heavy handed approach, Hurd and Juppé started a 'carrot and stick' strategy, in which they proposed a partial lifting of EC sanctions for 100 days, if Milosevic closed Serbia's frontier with Bosnia.

Franco-British co-operation over Bosnia was just one example of the new security relationship which Hurd was trying to forge with France during 1994. Hurd developed a very good working relationship with Alain Juppé. The two men had similar intellects: both were cerebral and possessed good analytical brains, but Juppé was more brittle than Hurd. On their shared plane journeys to Belgrade, Hurd admired the fact that Juppé was not surrounded by a flurry of briefing papers, but instead consulted just one succinct set of papers covering the relevant Security Council and NATO documents, which the French Foreign Minister memorised during the flight. It confirmed Douglas Hurd's view that the Foreign Office surrounded itself with too much paper.[55] But, what Douglas Hurd does not know until now is that Juppé used to tell the same anecdote, except in reverse. The French Foreign Minister came back from Belgrade complaining that, while the British Foreign Secretary was supplied by this fantastic, comprehensive set of briefing notes, he had next to nothing in his bag, feeling completely unprepared by the Quai d'Orsay![56]

What is in doubt is whether the sanctions policy and all the exhaustive Franco–British diplomacy actually achieved anything. Throughout, Hurd was very keen to keep alive the diplomatic process with Belgrade. Before flying out for the second time, he was interviewed on BBC 1's *On the Record* programme on Sunday, 4 December 1994. As usual, he could not resist using an analogy, this time selecting Robert the Bruce's mythical experience with the spider to say that the West had to try and try again to achieve peace.

It may be that when the Krajinian Serbs came under attack from American-backed Croats in May 1995, Milosevic's decision not to intervene on behalf of the Krajinian Serbs was influenced by the impact sanctions had had on the Serbian economy. In Hurd's view, Milosevic's decision to sign the Dayton agreement was 'a clear success for sanctions'.[57] Hurd also believes there was a broader reason for Milosevic's change of heart:

> There is no doubt from my conversations with Milosevic in 1994 he had not changed his mind about a greater Serbia, but he knew that Serbia, by the policy which he had forced on it, was actually opting out of the kind of life which was opening up for the other countries of central and eastern Europe.[58]

Throughout the conflict, Hurd believed that President Milosevic was a pragmatist, a man he could do business with. However, the supporters of the Bosnian Government, along with the Germans and the Americans, had a special loathing for Milosevic because they saw him as the aggressor who provoked the original war. For that reason, the French and British diplomatic efforts in Belgrade were not picked up with any enthusiasm by the Americans. Hurd believes more could have been done to further the work done by the British and the French at an earlier stage. But, it was more the long-term impact of sanctions on Serbia, and as Hurd has described, the desire of Milosevic to return to international respectability, rather than the diplomatic manoeuvres of Hurd and Juppé, which were decisive in persuading Milosevic to sign up at Dayton.

Some left-wing commentators in Britain have questioned Hurd's ethics in visiting Belgrade in July 1996. In his capacity as Deputy Chairman of NatWest Markets, he tried to persuade President Milosevic to sign contracts with NatWest to privatise Serbia's electricity and oil sectors.[59] It is possible to set this encounter in the context of Milosevic's pragmatic — if belated — desire to embrace capitalism and re-enter European respectability. However, in the eyes of the Bosnian Muslims, the responsibility for starting the war and the ethnic cleansing which followed lies squarely at the door of Milosevic. Therefore, the idea of a former British Foreign Secretary — indeed, one who played a central role in blocking the American and Muslim efforts to lift the arms embargo — trying to cut financial deals with the Serbian President, is, in their view, profoundly distasteful.

In retrospect, Hurd is willing to admit that the dual-key policy of an air effort conducted by NATO and a ground effort conducted by UNPROFOR did not work. The use of air power authorised by NATO after February 1994 did not require a Security Council Resolution, but did require the authority of the United Nations Secretary General, Dr Boutros Boutros Ghali, acting through his special envoy, Yasushi Akashi. Either the UN or NATO could propose air strikes, but both had to agree. On several occasions, General Sir Michael Rose, the then Commander of UNPROFOR, requested air strikes, only to be turned down by Akashi.[60] At the time, Hurd stoutly defended the policy in Parliament, pointing out that:

> We cannot have a situation in which those who are responsible on the ground
> find that those who are responsible in the air are doing something without
> regard to their own information or their own interests, or vice versa.[61]

Hurd also regrets acquiescing with the decision to declare safe areas. UN Security Council Resolution 836 authorised UNPROFOR, 'acting in self-defence, to take the necessary measures, including the use of force, in reply to bombardment against safe areas by any of the parties or to armed incursion into them.'[62]

In contrast to the dual-key policy, which he always defended publicly, on safe areas he told the House of Commons from an early stage that he did not believe that 'the concept of safe havens would be workable'.[63] There were two major problems with the policy. First, the areas were supposed to be de-militarised. Considerable evidence shows that the safe areas were being used by the Muslims as a way of attacking the Serbs. But even allowing for this, the UN had committed itself to defending these areas, and yet member states refused to respond to the UN Secretary General's request for 34,000 extra troops. The only way safe areas would have been defensible is if large numbers of infantry, backed by tanks and heavy artillery, were dug in. At the time, Douglas Hurd defended Britain's decision not to send any further large contingents, emphasising that Britain was already doing her bit.[64] On 7 December 1994, Hurd was again willing to criticise the UN's flawed strategy of declaring an area safe without having the troops in place to make the policy credible.[65] In his later evidence to All Souls, Hurd claimed the documents will eventually show that British representatives at the UN tried to modify the rhetoric, altering the phraseology of the UN resolutions on safe areas, but with the benefit of hindsight, he feels that Britain should have done more to stop the policy from going ahead.[66] Despite Hurd's candour on this point, he is admitting in effect that the British Government should share some of the blame for the genocide which took place after the fall of Srebrenica. The War Crimes Tribunal at The Hague (established by UN Resolution 827) will be responsible for bringing to justice those who perpetrated these crimes against humanity. But, by agreeing a policy which they could not possibly implement, the UN did lasting damage to its own authority.

For a brief moment during the Gulf War, there had been a remarkable spirit of co-operation between Russia and her former enemies in the UN Security Council. The establishment of the Contact Group in May 1993, comprising Britain, France, the United States, Germany and Russia, appeared to keep the Russians consulted. But, as early as February 1994, cracks had started to appear in the new co-operation with Russia. Russia was upset at the growing influence of NATO in the former Yugoslavia, particularly the American-led calls for more air strikes. She was increasingly uneasy at NATO's plans to expand eastwards into the former Warsaw Pact countries via its 'Partnership for Peace' initiative. Old Russian pan-Slavic sympathies were rekindled, and there was a more general rise in Russian nationalism stoked up by the demagogue, Vladimir Zhironovsky. President Yeltsin came under domestic political pressure to take a harder line against NATO air strikes.

The visit to Moscow in mid-February by John Major and Douglas Hurd had been planned long in advance, but it took on a new significance after the mortar attack on Sarajevo market place which killed sixty-eight people. On 15 February 1994, President Yeltsin said he would not allow attempts to solve the Bosnia problem to exclude Russia. Hurd noted in his diary that night:

15 Feb. 1994: It's this sense of being ignored which really damages, and

could be fatal to Yeltsin if we go on doing that.[67]

The Russians then took a unilateral initiative by sending a special envoy, Vitaly Churkin, to make a deal with Radovan Karadzic, the Bosnian Serb leader. Under the deal, 800 Russian troops were sent under the auspices of the UN to oversee the Bosnian-Serb withdrawal of artillery from the hills around Sarajevo. The Russian intervention was a diplomatic triumph for Yeltsin, because it gave Russia a foothold on the ground in Bosnia, thus making more complicated NATO's strategy of using air strikes to deter the Bosnian Serbs.

For Douglas Hurd, the episode illustrated that the best way to handle the Russians was not to give them a veto, but to consult them regularly so they were not surprised or offended at not being informed.[68] In May 1994, Hurd followed this approach on a visit to Murmansk, the Russian Foreign Minister, Andrei Kozyrev's constituency. In October of that year, Hurd accompanied the Queen on a state visit to Russia, the first by a British monarch since 1908. Although the Russian army's bungled intervention in Chechnya cooled relations, Hurd avoided outright condemnation which might have furthered the forces of autocracy in Russia,[69] and throughout developed a good working relationship with Kozyrev.[70]

The horror of ethnic cleansing and alleged war crimes exposed the undeniable moral dimension to the Yugoslavian crisis. Hurd has admitted since his retirement that the Bosnia issue was 'intellectually and ethically tangled'.[71] In the second half of his Foreign Secretaryship, the Bosnian question consumed more intellectual time than any other subject.[72] It is perhaps significant that before he left the Foreign Office he ordered that an official account of the conflict be written, to remain confidential for thirty years. This was partly intended to act as a corrective to the over-emotive accounts which he suspected might be written in the future. But surely it also indicates a high level of lingering doubt as to whether his own policies were right?

Whilst most of Hurd's earlier novels were written for recreation, his Yugoslavian short stories are written with real feeling, raising moral questions about the conflict. In three short stories, Hurd mulls over the causes of the war, the dilemma of whether to send British troops, and the worth of supplying humanitarian aid.

Of all his short stories, Hurd is most proud of 'The Last Day of Summer' – a parable about the consequences of wars fuelled by nationalism.[73] The story is loosely based on a conversation Hurd had with a Bosnian Croat during his visit to Sarajevo in July 1992, who commented that, until the war started, the only quarrel with his Serb neighbour had been over his son kicking a football into his garden.[74]

In the short story, a Bosnian Serb, Borisav, builds a summer house with his Croat neighbour, Mr Tomic. The summer house is a symbol of peace between ethnic groups in the old Yugoslavia. Borisav, visits a local cemetery and looks at the grave stones from the Second World War and more ancient tombstones from the days of Serbia. Borisav/Hurd cannot believe that history is about to repeat itself. A year later, Borisav is forced to register for military service with the Serbs and is asked by the local mayor to clear the town of Croats and Serbs. Borisav has doubts as first his son and then his wife join the Serbian cause. The following morning, a rogue corporal shells the summer house, in which Borisav finds Tomic lying dead. Borisav uses the wood from the shattered summer house to light a funeral pyre for his old friend. He deserts from the army and escapes in a Hercules plane, but as he flies over his town he cannot see the summer house; all hope in Bosnia has been extinguished.

The allegorical tale reveals Hurd's belief that the war in Yugoslavia was not inevitable. Yugoslavia had been a viable nation under a strong but fair Communist leader in the shape of President Tito. Is Hurd asking us to believe that the war which followed the break-up of Yugoslavia was unpredictable, unforeseen, 'absurd' even?[75] 'People had lived together peacefully', he argues – ancient ethnic hatreds need not have resurfaced. But he skips over the causes of the war. In Hurd's troubled mind, the Yugoslavian conflict is much more a tragic morass than an explainable act of aggression which then descended into an impenetrable thicket. The journalist Boris Johnson believes that Hurd is trying to justify his decision to block the sending of a WEU intervention force in September 1991.[76]

Hurd's pangs of conscience were revealed again in 'Ten Minutes to Turn the Devil' which appeared in *The Observer* on 31 January 1993. This time Hurd addresses the dilemma of whether he should have sent British troops to Bosnia. The story is set in a fictional Caucasia and the central character is a Defence Secretary called Richard Smethwick; for these the reader may as well substitute Bosnia and Douglas Hurd. He asks us to see the possible consequences of sending troops to Caucasia/Bosnia. The story opens with Smethwick/Hurd on his way to a Tory Party Conference to face the 'Troops Out Now' movement, set up after the mounting British casualties in Caucasia/Bosnia. The fictional Smethwick wins over his audience by the power of arguments, only to hear after his standing ovation that his brother-in-law, a serving officer in Caucasia/Bosnia, has been killed in action.

But the tale is not intended merely as a vindication of Hurd's decision not to send in British troops to intervene on behalf of the Bosnian Muslims. There is real doubt in Smethwick/Hurd's mind. Smethwick lies on his bed the night before his big speech to conference, pondering the enormity of his decision:

> Nothing in politics, not the pleasures of hard work in office, the excitement
> of good conversation, the small vanities of fame, the sense of occasional
> service, could make up for these moments of lonely fear. It was not as if, in
> these small hours, he was sure that the policy was right.

Partly this quotation refers to Hurd's nervousness before big Party Conference speeches as Home Secretary and then as Foreign Secretary.

The third short story, 'Warrior', is decidedly weaker than the other two. Hurd drew on his visit to Bosnia in January 1994. One of the characters, a Captain, is gently rebuked by Douglas Hurd for reading the latest Mary Stewart novel. On his real visit to Bosnia, Hurd raised his eyebrows when he spotted General Rupert Smith, reading a Mary Stewart novel. The real hero of the tale is Captain Faith Scrymgeour, a woman responsible for showing British journalists around central Bosnia. In particular, she accompanies Jim Boater, an opinionated journalist who sees the conflict as a clear fight between evil Serbs and innocent Muslims. It is perhaps significant that Martin Bell, the BBC journalist, was there in real life during Hurd's January 1994 visit. Boater is roughed up by mixed Croat-Muslim brigands and comes to reject his glib views on the nature of the conflict and sees the worth of the British aid effort in Bosnia. In real life, Martin Bell stuck to his original beliefs.

Captain Faith Scrymgeour expresses Hurd's view that the British were performing useful, practical deeds in central Bosnia. On the day of Jim Boater's arrival, she has to choose between meeting the Croat Mayor of Vitez to reopen a kindergarten – doing – and acting as a guide for the opinionated journalist – the destroyer. Reluctantly she chooses the latter. Her view of the war is Hurd's view; that it was not a:

> war of right against wrong. More like a mess in which politicians and generals
> in all three communities destroyed their own country. Hard to explain, hard
> to forgive. But on the whole the soldiers kept their mouths shut, and the
> journalists' view swept the world. Truth was one of the first casualties of
> this war.

All three stories end with the Hurd view broadly prevailing – most of Hurd's tales end with a doubting individual seeing commonsense, or turning into a true patriot (see account of *Sea Lion* in Chapter 8) – but they still reveal someone who has lasting doubts about the policy decisions he made on the former Yugoslavia. Like Disraeli in the last century, Hurd uses fiction to express his views on political issues. His latest novel, *The Shape of Ice*, is intended to perform a similar function.

On several occasions during the Yugoslavian crisis, Hurd had to address differing constituencies and take policy decisions which, given everyone's reluctance to send a military intervention force in on one side of the conflict, he knew would not bring about a clean solution to the problem. One of Hurd's central aims was to prevent the conflict from spreading. The scope for further escalation into the whole of the Balkan area was considerable. Several countries surrounding the former Yugoslavia had significant national interests involved. Hungary was worried about the plight of ethnic Hungarians in the Vojvodina province. Albania was similarly concerned about Serbian designs on Kosovo, which was 90 per cent Albanian. Disturbances since October 1997 have shown the volatility of the province. Bulgaria supported the independence of Macedonia, while Greece resisted the presence of a Muslim state on its northern border. It was not inconceivable, as the defence analyst Jonathan Eyal pointed out in 1992, to envisage a regional conflict where Romania, traditionally an ally with Serbia against Hungary, teamed up with the Serbs and the Greeks against a loose alliance comprising Bulgaria, Albania and possibly Turkey.[77] Moreover, any attempt by the Americans to arm the Muslims might have dragged in the Russians, given their historic links with their Slavic brothers (although economic and political weakness would have limited Russian support to the covert supply of arms). The conflict was contained, but arguably the cost of this was savage fighting and atrocities within the bounds of the former Yugoslavia. There was clearly a cost in terms of localised brutality. Lord Owen believes that the West succeeded in managing a war, in preventing it from spreading, and preserving the Atlantic Alliance, but the price was a dismembered Bosnia.[78]

The necessity of containing the war was perhaps why Hurd wanted to prevent the arms embargo from being lifted in favour of the Bosnian Muslims. Hurd's way of expressing this argument was, however, unfortunate:

> We would in effect be saying, 'Here are the arms: fight it out'. That is the policy of the level killing field.[79]

The phrase 'level killing field' was intended by Hurd as a neat and powerful phrase to illustrate the folly of arming the Bosnian Muslims. It was an amalgam of two well known sayings: 'level playing fields' were often referred to at European summits; and *The Killing Fields* was the title of a film about the slaughter of thousands of innocent civilians by Pol Pot's Khmer Rouge in Cambodia (formerly Kampuchea) during the 1970s. Hurd wrote his letter to the *Daily Telegraph* from Jakarta, Indonesia. He was using a pertinent example from the region he was visiting and even tested out the phrase on his PPS, David Martin. However, with hindsight, he is willing to admit it was 'too powerful, too vivid an accusation. It upset those most strongly on the side of the Bosnian Muslims.'[80] To describe a 'level killing field' is to infer that the victims can defend themselves and, to those supporting the Bosnian Muslims, the phrase is a contradiction in terms. A few days later, Lady Thatcher slammed it as 'a terrible and disgraceful phrase'.[81] It does seem ill-judged.

On the crucial question of whether he should have committed troops to defend the Muslims, Hurd has shown in one of his short stories that he still has doubts. But if one accepts that all his fellow European leaders were posturing, and that none would have been willing to intervene without a durable ceasefire, then Hurd emerges from the episode in a better light. Perhaps he deserves credit for being honest enough to admit that the venture would be doomed to fail. Nevertheless, the tantalising possibility remains that an intervention force, or more realistically the earlier use of air power, might have prevented later atrocities.

If Hurd's primary aim in September 1991 was to use the Yugoslavian crisis as a pawn in the debate over the future of European security, then he belongs to the nineteenth-century school of diplomacy, with its emphasis on *realpolitik*. Hurd does retain some of the élitism of that era, but one aspect does not fit. Hurd has a strong sense of decency, and even if he did engage in power play (which has not been proved) he sought to make up for it in the genuine attempt to save lives by providing humanitarian relief. Many will continue to argue that the policy may have only served to prolong the suffering, but Hurd's good intentions are surely not in dispute. Unlike others, Hurd did not engage in posturing, but, like the UN troops on the ground in Bosnia, tried instead to do practical things to save lives.

Hurd could have committed Anthony Eden's mistake. Like Hurd, Eden was normally a calm, cool diplomat, but unlike Hurd, Eden ignored his diplomatic training and, as Prime Minister, had a rush of blood to the head over Suez. Eden also misread history, wrongly equating Nasser with Adolf Hitler. Hurd refused to accept the arguments of those who compared the events in the former Yugoslavia with the West's appeasement in the 1930s. Hurd deserves the same credit as Harold Wilson for keeping Britain out of the Vietnam War. Hurd has a strong dislike of war. That is not to say he is in any way a pacifist; he showed his mettle in the Gulf War. But like most born diplomats, he prefers to seek a resolution to conflicts by peaceful means. His solutions are often messy but necessary compromises. His critics see these as fudges which satisfy no one. Over Yugoslavia, the critics believe the crisis required someone of the stature of a Roosevelt or a Churchill, instead they were handed a civil servant. While he has never allowed emotion to influence policy-making, Hurd shows in his more reflective writing that he has the capacity to doubt the wisdom of his actions. He will be left to doubt whether the concept of a Europe embracing both East and West was destroyed by the failure to stop the tragedy in the former Yugoslavia. More time is needed to see whether his central aim of preserving the Atlantic Alliance in the early 1990s better served the security of the whole of Europe, than a Europe acting on its own.

Notes

1. 'Interview with David Owen', *Foreign Affairs*, vol. 72, Spring 1992–93, p. 6.
2. H. of C. Deb. (6th Series), 17 Nov. 1994, vol. 250, col. 134.
3. Lord Carrington, *Reflect on Things Past: The Memoirs of Lord Carrington* (Fontana, Collins: London, 1989, first published 1982), p. 340.
4. Douglas Hurd, 'A British overview of the conflict', *Lessons from Bosnia, All Souls College Foreign Policy Studies Programme*, 8 Mar. 1996 (verbatim text of the lecture).
5. Ibid.
6. Ibid.
7. (21 May 1993), Diary Readings with Douglas Hurd, Westwell, 13 Jun. 1997.
8. Diary Readings with Douglas Hurd, Westwell, 13 Jun. 1997.
9. Interview with Douglas Hurd, Westwell, 13 Jun. 1997.
10. Private information.
11. Diary Readings with Douglas Hurd, Westwell, 13 Jun. 1997.
12. Ibid.
13. *The Guardian*, 20 Sept. 1991.
14. Interview with Kenneth Clarke, 16 Dec. 1996.
15. Diary Readings with Douglas Hurd, 18 Mar. 1997.
16. Ibid.
17. Ibid.
18. Ibid.
19. Ibid.
20. H. of C. Deb. (6th Series), 2 Jun. 1992, vol. 208, col. 715.
21. H. of C. Deb. (6th Series), 19 Apr. 1993, vol. 223, cols 23-25.
22. *The Times*, 20 Apr. 1993; John Smith was more vulnerable to the sensitivities of his backbenchers than Jack Cunningham. On 17 April 1993, eighteen Labour backbenchers wrote an open letter to *The Guardian* denouncing the Government's policy as appeasement and supporting the possible active engagement of ground troops against the Serbs.
23. H. of C. Deb. (6th Series), 7 Dec. 1994, vol. 251, cols 313–14.
24. H. of C. Deb. (6th Series), 16 Nov. 1992, vol. 214, cols 111–13. Only 206 MPs bothered to vote (including tellers) in the final division. The only

Conservative member to vote against the Conservative party line was Patrick Cormack (Staffordshire, South). It should be noted that Liberal Democrat 'Opposition days' are characterised by low attendance.

25. Diary Readings with Douglas Hurd, 18 Mar. 1997.

26. Verbatim text of interview between Baroness Thatcher and Peter Sissons, *The Times*, 14 Apr. 1993.

27. Based on interventions to Douglas Hurd, Andrew Faulds (Warley, East), Clare Short (Birmingham, Ladywood), Peter Hain (Neath), Chris Mullin (Sunderland, South), Dale Campbell-Savours (Workington), David Winnick (Walsaw, North), James Marshall (Leicester, South), Max Madden (Bradford, West) and George Galloway (Glasgow, Hillhead) were among the Labour MPs who favoured a more interventionist line.

28. On 30 October 1997, Bob Wareing was suspended from the House of Commons for refusing to declare a consultancy with a Serbian company.

29. The most vociferous proponents of this 'let them fight it out' view were: Nicholas Budgen (Wolverhampton, South West); Sir Peter Tapsell (Lindsey, East); Nicholas Bonsor (Upminster), Chairman of the House of Commons Select Committee on Defence; and from outside the House between 1992 and 1997, Alan Clark.

30. H. of C. Deb. (6th Series), 30 May 1992, vol. 208, col. 718.

31. A few Labour members shared this wariness, including John Spellar (Warley, West) and Gwyneth Dunwoody (Crewe and Nantwich), who was worried about the fate of the Cheshires.

32. These included David Sumberg (Bury, South) and Sir Anthony Grant (Cambridgeshire, South West).

33. H. of C. Deb. (6th Series), 25 Apr. 1994, vol. 242, col. 28.

34. Douglas Hurd, 'A British overview of the conflict', *Lessons from Bosnia, All Souls College Foreign Policy Studies Programme*, 8 Mar. 1996.

35. Ibid.

36. Interview with Douglas Hurd, Westwell, 13 Jun. 1997.

37. Douglas Hurd, 'A British overview of the conflict', *Lessons from Bosnia, All Souls College Foreign Policy Studies Programme*, 8 Mar. 1996.

38. Ibid.

39. Ibid.

40. H. of C. Deb. (6th Series), 29 Apr. 1993, vol. 223, col. 1178.

41. Quoted from Nicholas Jones, *Soundbites and Spin Doctors: How Politicians Manipulate the Media — And Vice Versa* (Indigo, 2nd edn: London, 1996), pp. 25–6. Interestingly, when Hurd delivered the speech, he omitted reference to the BBC, although it appeared in the original Foreign Office text.

42. Ibid., p. 26.

43. Hugo Young, 'Hurd's world in camera, not in the camera's eye', *The

Guardian, 14 Sept. 1993.

44. John Simpson, 'The Value of News', *The Spectator*, 18 Sept. 1993; Simpson's article was an abridged version of a speech he gave to the Royal Television Society's Huw Wheldon lecture on Thursday, 16 Sept. 1993, in which he defended the British media against Douglas Hurd's accusations of subjectivity in Bosnia.

45. H. of C. Deb. (6th Series), 9 May 1995, vol. 259, col. 587; Douglas Hurd, 'Our chance to end a Bosnian winter of suffering', the *Sunday Times*, 12 Dec. 1993; Douglas Hurd, 'We can, at least, save civilian lives', *The Independent*, 12 Dec. 1994.

46. Rosalyn Higgins, 'The United Nations and the Former Yugoslavia', *International Affairs*, vol. 69, no. 3. (1993), pp. 465–83.

47. Interview with Lord Carrington, 6 Dec. 1995.

48. *The Observer*, 23 Jan. 1994.

49. Interview with Douglas Hurd, Westwell, 13 Jun. 1996.

50. Douglas Hurd, 'We can, at least, save civilian lives', *The Independent*, 12 Dec. 1994.

51. H. of C. Deb. (6th Series), 19 Apr. 1993, vol. 223, col. 22; Peter Riddell & Martin Ivens, 'Hurd presses on for quicker response to global ills', *The Times*, 21 Apr. 1993.

52. H. of C. Deb. (6th Series), 29 Apr. 1993, vol. 223, col. 1770.

53. Douglas Hurd, 'Our chance to end a Bosnian winter of suffering', the *Sunday Times*, 12 Dec. 1993.

54. H. of C. Deb. (6th Series), 25 Apr. 1994, vol. 242, cols 27–28.

55. Douglas Hurd, 'First Thoughts Looking Back from the City', Chatham House Speech, 13 Mar. 1996.

56. Private information.

57. Douglas Hurd, 'A British overview of the conflict', Lessons from Bosnia, All Souls College Foreign Policy Studies Programme, 8 Mar. 1996.

58. Ibid.

59. *Tribune*, 6 Sept. 1996; *Sunday Telegraph*, 1 Sept. 1996.

60. On 8 May 1995, at Butmir, near Sarajevo, General Rose requested air strikes, but was refused by Akashi.

61. H. of C. Deb. (6th Series), 25 Apr. 1994, vol. 242, col. 24.

62. On 6 May 1993, UN Resolution 823 declared the city of Sarajevo and the towns of Tuzla, Gorazde, Bihac and Srebrenica safe areas. Resolution 836 followed on 4 June 1993.

63. H. of C. Deb. (6th Series), 19 Apr. 1993, vol. 223, col. 30.

64. H. of C. Deb. (6th Series), 7 Dec. 1994, vol. 251, col. 323.

65. Ibid., col. 323.

66. Douglas Hurd, 'A British overview of the conflict', *Lessons from Bosnia, All*

Souls College Foreign Policy Studies Programme, 8 Mar. 1996.

67. Diary Readings with Douglas Hurd, Westwell, 13 Jun. 1997.

68. Interview with Douglas Hurd, Westwell, 13 Jun. 1997; *see* also Douglas Hurd , 'A World Role for a Great Power', *The Times*, 20 Apr. 1994.

69. Douglas Hurd, Speech to Stockholm Institute of International Relations, 14 Feb. 1995.

70. Douglas Hurd and Andrei Kozyrev, 'Conditions for Peacekeeping', *Financial Times*, 14 Dec. 1993.

71. Douglas Hurd, 'A British overview of the conflict', Lessons from Bosnia, All Souls College Foreign Policy Studies Programme, 8 Mar. 1996.

72. Ibid.

73. Interview with Douglas Hurd, 22 Jul. 1996.

74. Douglas Hurd, 'Foreword', *A Suitcase Between Friends*, (Alhani: London, 1993), pp. 5–7.

75. Douglas Hurd, 'The Last Day of Summer', *Daily Telegraph*, 19 Sept. 1992.

76. Boris Johnson, 'Douglas Hurd's Public Conscience', *The Spectator*, 17 Apr. 1993.

77. Jonathan Eyal, 'Tremors spread from Yugoslav epicentre', *The Guardian*, 15 Jul. 1992.

78. *Panorama*, BBC1, 30 Oct. 1995.

79. Douglas Hurd, 'Letter to the Editor', *Daily Telegraph*, 5 Apr. 1993.

80. Telephone Conversation with Douglas Hurd, 5 Dec. 1997.

81. Verbatim text of interview between Baroness Thatcher and Peter Sissons, *The Times*, 14 Apr. 1993.

19

Slow Boats and Through Trains: British Policy towards China and Hong Kong, 1989–1997

On his arrival at the Foreign Office, Hurd could claim to possess a deep knowledge and interest in China and Hong Kong, having been posted to Peking in 1954 as a young diplomat, written a novel on the subject — *The Smile on the Face of the Tiger* — in 1968, and having been chosen by Mrs Thatcher in 1977, when she was Leader of the Opposition, to accompany her on her first visit to China. He prefers to refer to the Chinese capital as Peking rather than Beijing. In a typical headmasterly rebuke, Hurd warned the Foreign Affairs Select Committee in December 1993 not to use the word Beijing in its report:

> I know that it is a matter of personal taste, but I do not talk about 'Roma', 'Bruxelles' or 'Moskva', and I do not see any reason to abandon a perfectly reputable English word for a very distinguished Chinese city.[1]

The most revealing aspect of Hurd's attitude towards China and Hong Kong prior to his becoming Foreign Secretary was the historical book which he wrote after leaving the Diplomatic Service, entitled *The Arrow War: An Anglo-Chinese Confusion, 1856–1860* (see Chapter 5). In researching the book, Hurd tapped the rich vein of the diaries left by the Eighth Earl of Elgin, to recount in a scholarly way the two missions led by Elgin which eventually secured British and French diplomatic representation in Peking.

The book is interesting for what it reveals about Hurd's view of the Chinese as a nation. According to Hurd, the Chinese see themselves as the last imperial power, and regard all other nations as inferior. This 'assumption of superiority'[2] as Hurd terms it, meant that the only way to deal with the Chinese in the last century was to compel them, by force if necessary, to treat other nations as their equals. Hurd criticises Elgin for not forcing sufficient concessions from the Chinese in his first mission, which led the Chinese to believe they could ignore Western wishes. A second mission was necessary to end the 'confusion', although given Hurd's account of the 'gunboat diplomacy' which followed – especially the bombing of the Taku forts and the sacking of the Summer Palace – a reviewer at the time wondered whether 'confrontation' would have been a more apt word.[3]

In the last century, a British foreign secretary would have relied to a large extent on the actions of 'the man on the spot', whether he was a Benthamite Governor of Hong Kong bent on promoting the opium trade, or a British businessman eager to move his trading operations further up the Yangtze river. The British Government could thus be drawn into conflicts which were not of its own making. This predicament was largely determined by the time-lag between London and Peking. Whereas in the 1990s, Hurd could discuss matters over the telephone with his officials or visit Peking within a day; in 1856 it took eleven weeks for a message or a mission to reach China. The appointment of Chris Patten in 1992 as a political governor was partially a reversion to the Victorian notion of 'the man on the spot', except that, due to the speed of modern communications, Patten was more readily answerable to the British Cabinet for his actions.

In the 1850s, China was not one of Britain's primary areas of concern. India was the 'Jewel in the Crown' and there could be no greater illustration of this fact than Hurd's own account of Lord Elgin's forced detour to India in 1857 to help put down the mutiny.[4] In 1857, Chinese affairs could be kept on hold. In the 1990s, Britain could not afford to ignore China indefinitely because of the 1997 expiry date on her ninety-nine-year lease of Hong Kong. Moreover, Britain's relative economic and military decline has meant that she can no longer dictate terms to the Chinese. This was the received orthodoxy among pro-China opinion in Britain, especially in relation to British policy towards Hong Kong.

On his arrival at the Foreign Office in October 1989, Hurd faced two controversial issues in Hong Kong, both relating to immigration. The first concerned immigration into Hong Kong. Since the late 1970s, the Hong Kong authorities had operated a generous system of 'first asylum', automatically classifying all Vietnamese boat people as political refugees. At that time, most refugees had fled from South Vietnam, fearing reprisals from the Communists in the North after the withdrawal of the Americans from Saigon in 1975. However, as the Americans tightened their economic blockade of Vietnam in the 1980s, many Vietnamese, especially in the North, experienced growing economic hardship and decided to make the trip to Hong Kong in search of a better standard of living.

By June 1988, the Hong Kong authorities were forced to reconsider their policy. Boat people were now assumed to be either legitimate asylum seekers or economic migrants. In order to cope with the growing influx of boat people, detention centres were set up on the colony's islands. It was hoped that life in these camps would be so cramped and harsh as to discourage new arrivals. This tactic failed, and a policy of voluntary repatriation was instigated. Each asylum seeker underwent a screening process to determine whether the person was an economic migrant or a genuine political refugee.

By mid-1989, it became clear that too few of the boat people were willing to leave voluntarily, while too many were continuing to flood into Hong Kong. In June 1989, a conference on Indo-Chinese Refugees was held in Geneva, at which it was decided to reclassify all boat people as potential illegal immigrants. But no consensus was reached on how to implement the new guidelines. Britain was left with a failed policy of voluntary repatriation, while other countries, especially the Americans, showed no signs of addressing the issue. In July 1989, John Major, then Foreign Secretary, attempted to introduce a policy known as 'involuntary repatriation', an ugly euphemism for forced repatriation.

Whilst Hurd did not face a significant revolt from his backbenchers on the issue of involuntary repatriation,[5] the strongest opposition came from the American State Department. From early December 1989, the Americans sent out diplomatic signals voicing their disapproval. However, Hurd's position vis à vis the American State Department was greatly strengthened by Mrs Thatcher's support for his scheme, which she fully endorsed.[6] She had tried and failed to reach an agreement with President Bush at Camp David on 24 November. The disagreement over repatriation, though not of huge significance for the Atlantic Alliance, came at a time when the Bush administration was focusing its diplomatic efforts on German reunification. It was therefore unfortunate that James Baker, the US Secretary of State – who had stopped over in London on 11 December on his way to Berlin especially to assuage Britain's feeling of being left out – arrived to be told by Hurd and Thatcher that Britain intended to proceed with forced repatriation. According to Hurd's diary, Baker took the news 'calmly' over lunch,[7] but the following day, Marlin Fitzwater, President Bush's press secretary, read out a terse statement declaring that 'involuntary repatriation is unacceptable until conditions improve in Vietnam',[8] urging instead a policy of voluntary repatriation. The American Government neglected to mention that it was their continued economic boycott of Vietnam which was preventing economic conditions from improving, which might have dissuaded the Vietnamese from leaving their homeland.

Timothy Yeo, Douglas Hurd's Parliamentary Private Secretary at the time, claims that the Foreign Secretary faced strong opposition to the policy from his own officials inside the Foreign Office. Yeo claims that there was a crisis meeting on 11 December 1989, just before the aeroplane was due to leave with the first fifty-one Vietnamese on board, at which Hurd's senior officials, including the then Head of the Hong Kong Section and the Head of the Diplomatic Service, entered Hurd's room and demanded that the policy of forced repatriation be reconsidered. Yeo's recollection is that of those present at the meeting, only Hurd and Bob Peirce (then a junior member of Hurd's private office[9]) were in favour of the policy. Francis Maude, the Minister of State responsible, also supported Hurd's stance. A number of Foreign Office officials at the time were concerned about the possible diplomatic fall-out with the United States. Added to that was the traditionally liberal-minded attitude of the Foreign Office in matters relating to immigration. This version is borne out by Hurd's diary entry of 6 December 1989:

> 6 Dec. 1989: Americans begin to heave against repatriation of boat people for Monday night. Antony Acland [British Ambassador in Washington] and Stephen Wall [Private Secretary] much disturbed. The operation tricky and uncertain.[10]

According to Timothy Yeo, Hurd overruled the mandarins, feeling that it was vital to send a signal to the boat people and the international community, particularly the Americans, that Britain was not going to allow the numbers of boat people in Hong Kong to go on rising indefinitely.[11]

On Hurd's retirement from the Foreign Office, he received a letter from one official, now a senior figure in the Diplomatic Service, who confessed that although he had disagreed with the Foreign Secretary over repatriation at the time, in retrospect, he had come to the view that Hurd had been right.[12]

On 12 December, at 3 a.m. Hong Kong time, fifty-one boat people were escorted by some 150 riot police onto Kai Tak Airport where they boarded an aeroplane bound for Hanoi. Later the same day, in London, Hurd made a statement to the House of Commons in which he stressed that the British Government and the Hong Kong authorities had acted in accordance with international law. Voluntary repatriation, he claimed, had failed: the number of refugees had reached 57,000 and unless a signal was sent, tens of thousands more would arrive in Hong Kong in the 1990 sailing season.[13] Hurd announced that Lord (David) Ennals, formerly the champion of African nationalist leaders, and Hurd's own close friend, Timothy Raison (Aylesbury), would be sent out to Hong Kong as independent observers.

Gerald Kaufman, Labour's Shadow Foreign Secretary, attacked the manner of the undercover operation in his usual caustic style. However, on this occasion it was Sir David Steel who delivered the most scathing attack, likening the operation to a 'knock on the door in the middle of the night'.[14]

Hurd's diary account of 12 December involved much more than

consideration of the boat-people issue. By this stage, the wrangles over Hong Kong passports had already started, along with a whole host of other problems:

> 12 Dec. 1989: A gruelling day. Start off on Trident problems. Then a humdinger at No. 10 on Hong Kong passports, at which with F.M.'s [Francis Maude] stalwart support I gained what I wanted. . . . PM sides with us, only D.W. [David Waddington] and N.R. [Nick Ridley] against, but PM wobbly and we must hold to it. Lunch with [the] P[rince] of Wales at K[ensington] Palace alone – To House of Commons anxious, but PM makes excellent fist of statement on Strasbourg. Controlled and positive. I follow on boat people. Scare off Kaufman, get good support but media strongly opposed and will be ructions. Interviews go less well than the Commons. Vote for war crimes legislation.[15]

The reaction in the British press the following day was generally hostile. Leading up to the decision, Bernard Levin penned a series of particularly vitriolic articles in *The Times*, drawing comparisons between involuntary repatriation and the Holocaust.[16] While acknowledging that the press was bad, Hurd wrote in his diary that evening:

> 13 Dec. 1989: Turmoil runs high over boat people. Feel justified in what we did, but feel weary at what is said and written.[17]

International reaction to the unilateral action was for the most part critical, but it was not accompanied by any concrete measures against Britain. Meanwhile, China, which had been informed of the British plan in advance, warmly applauded it. Harbouring a traditional hatred of the Vietnamese, the Chinese wanted the Vietnamese boat people out of Hong Kong before they arrived in 1997.

The British Government did suspend repatriation on 12 December, but only for seven days, pending a vote in the House of Commons the following Tuesday to arrange the necessary finance.[18] The most immediate problem facing the Hong Kong authorities was a series of disturbances in the detention centres.

The Foreign Secretary visited the detention centre on Hei Ling Chau in mid-January 1990 during a trip to Hong Kong. A visit of this kind always carries with it the risk that trouble will flare up because of the presence of a high-profile figure. A peaceful demonstration involving around 3,600 boat people did accompany Hurd's arrival, but posed no threat to his safety – a double eighteen-foot-high perimeter fence separated Hurd from the demonstrators. The Foreign Secretary declined to meet a deputation of demonstrators, but he did accept letters of protest. He was then given a brief tour of the camp. At a press conference afterwards, he acknowledged the lack of space, but claimed the facilities were 'well run by the authorities within the possibilities'.[19] While involuntary repatriation was 'not an agreeable business', it was better, he said, than keeping people in Hong Kong indefinitely.[20]

The report of David Ennals and Tim Raison concluded they had no reason to suppose that the fifty-one repatriated boat people had been classified wrongly. However, David Ennals described as 'gross overkill' the use of three times as many riot police as boat people for the overnight operation.

The repatriation policy took some time to bear fruit. Francis Maude, the Minister of State at the Foreign Office responsible for the region, was sent out to Hanoi in February 1990. But it was June 1991 before the Americans dropped their opposition to negotiations between Britain and Vietnam over involuntary repatriation. Finally, in February 1994, President Clinton took the important step of lifting the economic embargo on Vietnam, creating the economic incentive for the Vietnamese to stay in Vietnam. By September 1994, Hurd was able to make an official visit to Hanoi.

It is ironic that at a time when the Vietnamese boat people were streaming into Hong Kong, many of the top business people were deciding to leave the colony, fearing the consequences of the Chinese takeover in 1997. After the events in Tiananmen Square in June 1989, business confidence in Hong Kong plummeted. Douglas Hurd, and his predecessor, Geoffrey Howe, felt that a package of measures was needed to restore confidence in the colony in order to prevent what he termed 'this haemorrhage of talent'.[21] In a statement to the House of Commons on 20 December 1989, Hurd announced plans to grant the right of abode in the United Kingdom to 50,000 Hong Kong Chinese and their families, involving a total of around 225,000 people. Successful applicants would have to score high marks in a highly controversial 'points system' which favoured professional and business people working in the public and private-sector. The decisive criteria would be 'the value of the individuals' service to Hong Kong and the extent to which people in that category of employment are emigrating'.[22] Extra points would be gained for long service in British institutions and knowledge of English. The granting of applications would be staggered so as to ease administration, and leave scope for new applicants as the 1 July 1997 deadline approached. The prime motivation behind the policy was not to encourage the best brains to flood into Britain, but to persuade them to stay in Hong Kong.

The initial announcement had been delayed due to disagreements between ministers over the exact numbers to be granted passports. Douglas Hurd, supported by his officials in the Foreign Office, hoped for at least 100,000 families, but the Home Office, led by the traditional right-winger David Waddington – whose department would be legally responsible for the scheme

– wanted the lowest possible level of potential immigration into Britain. Mrs Thatcher's own instincts were more with David Waddington than Douglas Hurd. According to an insider, Hurd thought he had secured agreement at 75,000, but Mrs Thatcher finally whittled them down to 50,000.[23]

In contrast to the issue of involuntary repatriation, where the major headache was diplomatic opposition from the United States, Hurd's main obstacle over Hong Kong passports came from within his own party. He could comfortably bat away Gerald Kaufman's charge that the points system was based on status and affluence, because the Shadow Foreign Secretary was not offering any realistic alternative. But Norman Tebbit's attacks carried weight because he represented a powerful strand of opinion in the Conservative Party which was opposed to any large-scale immigration into Britain. In December 1989, Norman Tebbit accused Hurd of breaking the pledges made in the last four Conservative general election manifestos that there would be no further large scale immigration into Britain. Back came Hurd with a stinging reply:

My right honourable Friend knows that, over the past four years, as Home Secretary, I spent a lot of time trying, with his full support, to plug loopholes and to keep our immigration control strict and fair. I earned a good deal of obloquy from Opposition Members for doing so. I do not need any education on the importance of strict immigration control for entry into this country.[24]

Hurd went on to point out that, even if the 50,000 people came with their families, Britain would be securing some of the most talented professional people in the world. The Foreign Secretary pointed to Britain's moral responsibility to the people of Hong Kong:

I put one final point to my right hon. Friend. He was a very successful chairman of our party, and he knows its traditions. This is just about the last main chapter in the story of this country's empire. I am rather keen, and I am sure that my right hon. Friend is rather keen, that that last chapter should not end in a shabby way.[25]

However, this sense of British honour had to be tempered by political realism. Hurd had to strike a balance between three competing objectives: producing a policy which the right-wing of the Conservative Party was willing to stomach, while still being able to achieve his aim of getting the best minds to remain in Hong Kong, and adhering to the traditional Tory view of strict immigration controls.[26]

The bulk of the commentators and columnists in the press condemned the British Government for not granting the right of abode to all Hong Kong

Chinese.[27] The Chinese denounced it as a 'gross violation' of the Joint Declaration. But this was bluster. Hurd's main obstacle remained how to convince the many doubters on his own backbenches. In the run up to the Second Reading vote on the Hong Kong (Nationality) Bill, Francis Maude, the Minister of State at the Home Office responsible for Hong Kong, played a vital role in persuading backbenchers of the merits of the nationality scheme. Maude's views were heeded by the right, because he too hailed from that wing of the party. Doubting MPs were wheeled in to see Maude and Hurd. Several MPs were even taken on trips to Hong Kong.[28]

The day before the crucial Second Reading vote, Hurd was privately feeling far from confident.[29] However, Norman Tebbit badly misread the mood of the country when he claimed in an interview with the *Los Angeles Times* that a large proportion of Britain's Asian population had failed to pass the 'cricket test . . . Which side do they cheer for?' Although the remarks were not directly related to the passports issue, they exposed the Conservative right-wing's real motivation for opposing the Hong Kong (Nationality) Bill. On Second Reading, the Government secured a comfortable majority of ninety-seven. This was despite experiencing a sizeable rebellion from forty-three Conservative MPs, for the reasons for the Government's victory lay elsewhere. Fifty-four Labour MPs failed to vote on Second Reading, despite a three-line whip against the Bill issued by the Labour front bench.[30] There was a general feeling on the Labour left that they could not oppose a bill when their own front bench was refusing to pledge that all Hong Kong citizens should be given the right of abode in the United Kingdom.[31]

Under the Sino-British Joint Declaration of September 1984, negotiated by Geoffrey Howe, Britain agreed to hand back sovereignty to China on 1 July 1997. In the Declaration, the Chinese guaranteed that Hong Kong could continue with a capitalist economy for at least fifty years after 1997, encapsulated in the term 'one country, two systems'. Geoffrey Howe was very proud of the Joint Declaration, seeing it as a triumph of British diplomacy. Realising the overwhelming power of the Chinese, he believed that the British had gained the best possible deal in the circumstances. Britain's chief negotiators, Sir Richard Evans and Sir Percy Cradock, and others, wholeheartedly agreed with this analysis. The consensus view among the China experts, or sinologists, was that Britain should adhere to the idea of a 'through train'; that arrangements made with Britain before 1997 must be those which the Chinese were prepared to sustain after 1997. The Joint Liaison Group (JLG – originally called the Joint Chinese Commission), had been established by the Joint Declaration of 1984 to prepare for the smooth transfer of power. Given that the Joint Declaration envisaged that there would be intensified co-operation between Britain and China in the second half of the period before 1997, it was considered essential by sinologists that good relations were maintained with China in that period: nothing should be allowed to derail the through train. Deng Xiaoping's impressive programme of economic reform in China seemed to provide evidence for the view that China had no intention of tampering with Hong Kong's capitalist system after 1997. However, China's support for economic liberalism was not matched by respect for human rights or tolerance of calls for greater democracy.

The brutal suppression of pro-democracy demonstrators in Tiananmen Square in June 1989 had understandably obliged Her Majesty's Government to put forward a set of measures, of which the passports legislation was only one, which would restore confidence in Hong Kong, while not antagonising Peking. In July 1989, Howe supported moves by the people of Hong Kong to establish a Bill of Rights, which would entrench essential freedoms.[32] Eventually, on 5 June 1991, Hong Kong's Legislative Council (LegCo) approved a Bill of Rights, which was given added international legitimacy by incorporating the United Nations International Convenant on Civil and Political Rights. However, the final shape of the Bill of Rights was not intended to raise the ire of the Chinese. It excluded the right to self-determination, the right to an elected executive and legislative councils and the right of foreigners to fight deportation.[33] Plainly, Hong Kong could not have the right of self-determination if sovereignty was going to revert to China in 1997, and the exclusion of the right to an elected executive reflected a desire not to antagonise China. The failure, however, to grant right of appeals in immigration cases, was simply a matter of self-interest on the part of the Hong Kong authorities themselves: they needed to maintain a strong immigration policy to deter the Vietnamese boat people.

Throughout the period from Hurd's appointment as Foreign Secretary in October 1989 until the appointment of Chris Patten as Governor of Hong Kong in the summer of 1992, Hurd appeared to stick closely to the policy followed by Geoffrey Howe. The reasoning behind this policy was that the Tiananmen Square massacre did not invalidate the Joint Declaration. Britain should not penalise China excessively through trade sanctions because antagonising China was not in the long-term interests of the people of Hong Kong. After a respectable pause in the negotiations, Britain should reopen high-level diplomatic contacts with Peking, and consult in secret with China on matters relating to the political development of Hong Kong.

The first high-level diplomatic move was made by Francis Maude, Minister of State at the Foreign Office, who visited Peking in July 1990.[34] The following month, Hurd penned an article which appeared in *The Times*, floating the idea that it was time to resume talks with the Chinese. Recalling his own spell in Peking from 1954 to 1956, Hurd cited John Foster Dulles's (then US Secretary of State) failed attempt in the 1950s to isolate China from the Western world as evidence that the present policy of isolation was 'manifestly absurd'.[35] There would be 'no pell-mell rush, and no attempt to obliterate the memories of Tiananmen Square',[36] but Hong Kong's future could not be separated from that of the future of China. Much 'patient and often quiet persuasion' (secret negotiation) was needed to achieve what he called 'the best available prospect'.[37]

By late March 1991, Hurd set out his reasons for talking to the Chinese in an article in *The Independent*. The main reason he cited was to intensify co-operation in the second half of the period before 1997 between Britain and China as laid out in the Joint Declaration of 1984. He claimed that the people of Hong Kong wanted Britain to stand up for their rights but in a way that preserved good relations with Peking. The maxim, he wrote, was 'protect us, but please do so without making waves'.[38]

In April 1991, Hurd made a seven-day visit to China and Hong Kong, the highest ranking European Foreign Minister to visit Peking since Tiananmen Square. The main aim of the visit was to hasten progress in the Joint Liaison Group discussions over Hong Kong's new international airport. The British were anxious to start construction of the airport in good time; but the Chinese objected to the use of Hong Kong's reserves to fund it, hoping to inherit a substantial surplus from the British in 1997.

In the midst of the negotiations with the Chinese, Hurd took the weekend off to re-live one of his favourite trips, dating from his days when he had served as a diplomat in China in the 1950s. In 1956, Hurd had scaled Taishan, China's holiest mountain, set in the north-east province of Shandong, with his fellow diplomat Alan Donald, in celebration of Donald's birthday. Thirty-five years on, Donald had risen to British Ambassador to China. But they discovered much had changed. In 1956, they had walked all the way up the mountain to the Temple of the Jade Emperor at the top, sleeping overnight on the temple floor. By 1991, a road had been carved half-way up the mountain, and a chair-lift ferried thousands of tourists from there to the summit, where a new hotel had been built. Casting aside these quicker modes of travel, they walked up the mountain as before. The Shandong authorities had laid on a sixteen-course lunch half-way up the mountain. Walking proved hard going after the lunch, especially since the final third of the journey involved a steady climb of steps. The path leading up to the Azure Cloud temple was lined with shops selling bric-à-brac, but Hurd found the temple itself untouched by the rigours of tourism:

> 7 Apr. 1991: Bells in the cold wind. Worshippers on their knees. Biscuits and money before the shrines.[39]

That evening, the British visitors stayed in the brand new hotel. The staff were smartly decked out in Ivor Novello uniforms and the fittings were lavish, but the central heating system was not working. It was bitterly cold on the top of a mountain, so at the banquet hosted by the Mayor of Taishan, the dinner guests wore overcoats and were given military greatcoats to keep them warm in bed!

In Canton, at talks with the Chinese, Hurd failed to reach any immediate deal for the financing of Hong Kong's new airport, but his visit paved the way for Francis Maude, his Minister of State, to reach a 'Memorandum of understanding concerning the construction of the new airport and related questions' with the Chinese in July 1991. Enough progress was made in the talks to allow John Major to visit China in September 1991 to sign an agreement in principle – although not in detail – on Hong Kong's Final Court of Appeal, the new body which would replace the old functions of the Privy Council.

On the Prime Minister's first visit to China, Hurd again set time aside to soak up the culture of China. During his periodic visits to Peking, he got into the habit of getting up very early in the morning to visit the Temple of Heaven in the southern part of the city. There, according to Hurd, 'You see something of traditional China, before modern China gets to work.'[40]

> 3 Sept. 1991: Ping-pong and shadow boxing, ballroom dancing and tree-punching.[41]

From the Temple of Heaven, Hurd returned to less spiritual matters, accompanying John Major for a long meeting with the Chinese Premier, Li Peng, in the Great Hall of the People:

> 3 Sept. 1991: Prime Minister [John Major] handles human rights issue very well, pressing just a little harder than I would, but I think that is right.[42]

John Major was more vulnerable to domestic political criticism than the Foreign Secretary on the human rights issue, so it was understandable that he voiced his concerns more forcefully. The next day, Hurd engaged in another bout of nostalgia, taking the Prime Minister to the Western hills where he had gone on so many weekend picnics in the 1950s. During their walk, John Major said he wanted Hurd to stay on as Foreign Secretary after the General Election. Hurd accepted and offered two years. In the end, the Foreign Secretary would serve an extra three years. For his part, Hurd continued to be a firm admirer of the Prime Minister. He felt John Major had handled the press conference in Hong Kong and the speech to the Hong Kong Executive Council (ExCo) extremely well. These were always occasions requiring delicate handling because of the need to speak, in effect, to three audiences: British opinion back home, the Chinese, and the Hong Kong people.

Since June 1985, the Chinese had been formulating their own 'mini-constitution' for Hong Kong in the Basic Law Drafting Committee (BLDC). A second draft of the Basic Law had been drawn up by February 1989, but after Tiananmen, the Chinese instigated a 'consultation period', which was in effect a seemly pause to allow the dust to settle. In January 1990, the British Government sought to gain concessions on several articles of the proposed Basic Law, the most significant of which was an increase in the number of directly elected seats to the LegCo.[43] Sir Alan Donald had intensive meetings with Chinese Foreign Ministry officials with the aim of seeking concessions.

As part of these negotiations, Douglas Hurd made a statement to the House of Commons on 16 February 1990, proposing eighteen seats for the LegCo elections in 1991 and 'not below twenty' for 1995. He envisaged an upward slope of directly elected seats, culminating in full direct elections by 2007.[44] Hurd's proposals fell well short of the House of Commons Select Committee Report in June 1989 which recommended a wholly elected LegCo by 1997.[45] In his defence, Hurd followed the line set by Sir Geoffrey Howe by comparing his policy with walking a tightrope between a politically conscious people wanting a faster pace of democracy, and avoiding constant collision with the Chinese Government in the run up to 1997.[46]

In the Basic Law which was eventually promulgated in April 1990 by the Chinese legislature (the National People's Congress), the Chinese agreed to eighteen seats in 1991. The twenty directly elected seats inherited in 1997 from the 1995 elections would go up to twenty-four (40 per cent) in 1995, and thirty seats (half) by 2003, with any further advance after 2007 requiring a two-thirds majority in the LegCo and the consent of the Hong Kong chief executive (to be chosen by China).[47]

The negotiations between Britain and China at the beginning of 1990 on the issue of direct elections to the LegCo appear to have been sealed by an exchange of letters between Douglas Hurd and the Chinese Foreign Minister, Qian Qichen. In order fully to understand the row which subsequently broke out between China and those in Britain who supported the through-train argument on the one hand, and Douglas Hurd, Chris Patten and John Major on the other, it is vital to appreciate that these letters remained a secret until the Chinese Government made their existence public after Chris Patten made his unilateral proposals of October 1992.

Another twist to the story is that Chris Patten did not know of the existence of these letters until the Chinese released them. Sir Percy Cradock, the Prime Minister's adviser on China, was about to retire, and did not mention the letters to Patten during a briefing session before Patten flew out to Hong Kong to take up his post. Sir Percy Cradock believes it is inconceivable that Patten, having been sent out to Hong Kong to ensure the smooth handover of Hong Kong to China, would not have been briefed on these letters, so Cradock saw no need to mention them.[48] Nor did Douglas Hurd inform Patten of the letters. Hurd claims he was not reminded of these letters due to an oversight by junior Foreign Office officials. According to Hurd, it never occurred to officials that there was a read across from one round of negotiations to another.[49] These comments seem to indicate that, whereas there was a secret deal with China over the shape of the 1991 election proposals, Hurd did not believe this bound them for the elections in 1995. The Chinese, on the other hand, believed they still held a secret veto on the second round. Perhaps the Chinese had good reason to expect this: based on the track record of the British Government; since 1984, they had been consulted in secret on every previous set of proposals for the political development of Hong Kong.

However, it was an oversight on the part of the Foreign Office that Chris Patten was not briefed about the letters when framing his controversial proposals. Patten claims that, if one was being 'tidy minded', it would have been 'helpful' to have known about the letters before devising his controversial proposals. But, having read them, he agrees with Hurd that the letters did not commit Britain to secret consultations with the Chinese on any fresh proposals for the LegCo elections in 1995.[50]

Sometime during the first half of 1992, Hurd came to the view that there was an undeniable demand for greater democracy in Hong Kong which could no longer be ignored. Until the Tiananmen Square massacre in June 1989, the people of Hong Kong had paid much more attention to the making of money than the building of democratic institutions. This was perfectly understandable. Immigrant communities tend to pay much more attention to earning a living for themselves and their families than bothering about political matters. But Hurd waited nearly three years before he came to the view that Tiananmen had politicised the people of Hong Kong. In terms of the talks on political development, this meant that the second round of talks would have to be handled differently from the first round in 1991:

> They [Foreign Office officials] should have reminded us of it [the letters], but I don't think that would have altered the principle that we consulted the Chinese, but we didn't consult them in secret. What would I have said in the House of Commons? The situation was different with the second round. There were politicians [in Hong Kong], there was a democratic heart, a democratic system. I don't think it would have been defensible to cook it up behind the scenes.[51]

However, it is undeniable that Hurd had changed his line on China. Prior to Chris Patten's appointment as Governor of Hong Kong, Douglas Hurd's approach towards China and Hong Kong did not deviate one inch from the line followed by British diplomats and Foreign Secretaries since the Sino–British Joint Declaration in 1984. Hurd would, of course, disagree with this analysis. He claims that:

> I had come to the conclusion long before the election in 1992 that the [last] Governor of Hong Kong should be political. I told [the outgoing] David Wilson this. I just felt there would be a lot of issues which might become very sensitive and controversial, and that we really needed a politician.[52]

The other vital consideration was whether a British Foreign Secretary could have appeared before the House of Commons to claim that the people of Hong Kong had no right to be kept informed of the negotiations until they were completed behind closed doors. In a conciliatory letter to Lord Howe of Aberavon dated 4 August 1997, Hurd wrote:

> I do not believe that you in 1992/3 would have stood pat week after week in the House of Commons (and instructed the Governor to do the same in Hong Kong) on the proposition that we were negotiating with the Chinese on proposals for the future of Hong Kong which would only be revealed when the negotiations were complete . . . The effect on majority opinion in Hong Kong of leaving them entirely in the dark would have been deeply damaging. Trust in us would have ebbed away.[53]

This view was later supported by the findings of the Foreign Affairs Select Committee Report in March 1994 when it stated:

> We endorse the decision by the Governor and the British Government that it would not have been right to enter into detailed negotiations with China about the Governor's proposals before they were announced to the people of Hong Kong and to the Hong Kong Legislative Council (LegCo). When Mr Patten took office, no arrangements had been made for elections to LegCo in 1995. It would have been wholly unacceptable for new arrangements affecting the people of Hong Kong not to have been announced in Hong Kong.[54]

In 1991, Hurd had no idea that this political figure in Hong Kong would be Chris Patten. Then the Conservative Party Chairman lost his seat in Bath at the General Election of April 1992. It was John Major who first had the idea of appointing Patten as Governor of Hong Kong, but, according to Douglas Hurd, the Prime Minister then 'blew very cold on the idea' because he did not want his trusted lieutenant – one of his closest friends and political allies – to be so far away.[55] This is also Chris Patten's recollection.[56] However, Hurd, having been informed of the Prime Minister's original idea, remained keen on the idea of Patten becoming Governor, and invited him to a supper at Carlton Gardens in the summer of 1992 during which they explored the idea. Patten did not decide that evening, but after thinking it over at his retreat in France, decided to accept the Prime Minister's offer. According to Patten, 'Douglas Hurd helped to convince an already mostly convinced former MP.'[57]

Patten set out from the start to promote democracy in Hong Kong. He wanted to create a buttress of democratic institutions in the run-up to the Chinese handover in 1997, as he later put it, 'to put some panes of glass on the window',[58] so that if the Chinese subsequently attempted to dismantle these institutions, they would encounter an element of democratic legitimacy. Patten and Hurd's philosophy was that the Hong Kong people should be allowed as much or as little democracy as they wanted; it was not for the British to impose this on them. At the back of the new Governor's mind was the belief that, whilst Britain had given fifty thousand families the right to leave Hong Kong, Britain had a moral responsibility to the other seven million Hong Kong Chinese who would be left behind after 1997. It seems that Patten was sent out to Hong Kong as the head of a team which had a relatively free rein, provided they worked within the framework of the Sino-British Joint Declaration and the Basic Law.

On 7 October 1992, in his first major policy speech since becoming Governor that August, Patten announced his proposals for local elections in 1994 and the main LegCo elections in 1995. The Governor worked within the letter of the Joint Declaration and the Chinese Basic Law and yet was able to broaden substantially the franchise by lowering the overall voting age to eighteen and giving every member of the population a vote at their workplace as well as a vote in their constituency. By virtually granting the right to vote to every citizen in nine extra 'functional constituencies', Patten created nine more directly elected seats in the LegCo in all but name. A similar ingenious pattern was applied to the district board elections – the third and lowest tier of government whose 346 members would then select 10 of the 60 members in the LegCo.

The speech was a unilateral move by Patten, made without engaging in secret negotiations with the Chinese. Patten set out his proposals in the open, letting the Hong Kong people know what was going on, but all along he was willing to negotiate with the Chinese; they were intended as proposals, not as a final set of demands. The Chinese were given advance notice of Patten's speech when Douglas Hurd handed over a text to the Chinese Foreign Minister on 25 September 1992. But the old established procedure of consulting China in secret had been broken, causing consternation in Peking. There was a very real fear among the Chinese leadership that Patten was engaging in a plot to create in Hong Kong a democratic Trojan horse on China's doorstep which would spread to mainland China after 1997, threatening the dominance of the one-party state. Events in Tiananmen Square, then Eastern Europe and then the Soviet Union caused the Chinese leaders to become paranoid about their own survival. In their eyes, Patten had pulled a confidence trick, insulted their honour, and created a democratic time bomb in Hong Kong which might explode after 1997. An unsavoury and, at times, vitriolic hate campaign was launched by the Chinese Government against the new Hong Kong Governor, conducted via the pro-China Hong Kong press and quite openly by leading Hong Kong businessmen. Patten was variously called a 'triple violator', a 'serpent' and a 'running dog'. The Chinese then snubbed Governor Patten on his first visit to China in November 1992. The Chinese even threatened to cancel commercial contracts between the Hong Kong authorities and the private sector, causing sharp falls on the Hang Seng, Hong Kong's stock exchange. The threat was unreal and was removed in January the following year, but this was a diplomatic rift between Britain and China not seen since the cultural revolution in the 1960s.

In response, Hurd defended Governor Patten in an article in the *Sunday Times* on 11 October. While he revealed that he had outlined Pattens's speech to the Chinese Foreign Minister a fortnight beforehand; he reaffirmed:

> But it is the people of Hong Kong who are directly affected by these proposals. They have a right to express their views on their own political system, and not to wait in suspense for months while these ideas are discussed with China.[59]

On 18 November, Patten visited London where the Governor, Hurd, and Major presented a united front to prevent the Chinese from thinking that Patten was isolated. Hurd described Patten's plans as 'skilful', 'well justified' and having his full support.[60] Was Hurd painted into a corner by Patten? It seems inconceivable that a statesman of Hurd's experience would not have been aware of the likely consequences of not consulting China. His book *The Arrow War* shows he understood the Chinese belief in their superiority over other nations. He has commented widely since on the importance which the Chinese attach to the tiniest nuance of diplomatic protocol.[61] It seems Hurd knew full well the implications of what he was doing when he backed Chris Patten. Throughout Patten's difficulties, John Major and Douglas Hurd supported Patten's judgement. There were grumblings in the Foreign Office from officials who believed that Britain was damaging its relationship with China, but the officials always knew that Patten had the support of the Prime Minister and the Foreign

Secretary. In effect, Patten was an *ex officio* member of the British Cabinet, at least the Overseas Defence Committee (OPD). Chris Patten recalls:

> I could not have shaped policy without having his [Hurd's] approval and without having the approval of Cabinet. At every difficult point, he [Hurd] gave me his support.[62]

Within a month of delivering their snub to Patten, the Chinese calmed down sufficiently for there to be talks about talks. As a gesture, the British postponed the publication of their draft electoral legislation, in the hope of positive proposals from the Chinese.[63] Seventeen rounds of fruitless talks ensued. Despite concessions by Patten that he would consider the issue of the 1994 and 1995 elections separately, the Chinese refused to budge. Patten decided to break off the talks and proceed with his own proposals, subject to the approval of the LegCo.

Meanwhile, Chris Patten's proposals caused grave disquiet among an influential section of pro-China ex-diplomats and politicians in London. But while some, like Sir Geoffrey Howe, remained silent, anxious not to upset what was left of the concept of the through train, others felt less restrained. On 8 December 1993, Sir Percy Cradock, Britain's former ambassador to China and a former prime ministerial adviser on China and Hong Kong, told the Foreign Affairs Select Committee that Britain had pursued 'a dangerous and reckless policy' in making their proposals without the consent of the Chinese.[64] The very same morning, Sir Richard Evans and Sir Alan Donald, who had worked with Douglas Hurd in the 1950s, said Britain should have practised private rather than public diplomacy.[65] Sir Edward Heath, also strongly pro-China, opposed the new thinking, later calling the policy 'a complete misjudgement'. He believed that the Chinese would simply reverse Patten's democratic reforms anyway when they took over in 1997, and also it was pointless to make changes which damaged Britain's economic opportunities in the colony and in China itself.[66]

Hurd attempted to keep the bridge open with the Chinese by seeing his opposite number, Qian Qichen, at the neutral venue of the UN headquarters in New York. But it was symptomatic of the poor state of relations by July 1993 that Hurd's meeting with Qian Qichen in Peking was their first meeting in ten months. Stalled talks on political development spilled over into the talks in the Joint Liaison Group, which proceeded so slowly as to be barely discernible.

Hurd continued to raise the issue of human rights with the Chinese, but he tiptoed carefully over the issue of Tibet when the Dalai Lama visited London to lobby support for the cause of the Tibetan people on 12 May 1993:

> 12 May 1993: A clumsy, honourable, eager man. Spilling out in mixed
> Tibetan and English. Modest in his request for support.[67]

Hurd immediately judged the Dalai Lama a good man because his words just spilled out, very unlike the manner of a trained diplomat or a politician. Although the Dalai Lama expressed his fears to Hurd of a 'cultural genocide' in Tibet as a result of large-scale Chinese immigration into the region, he realised it would be unrealistic to press for Tibetan independence, opting instead for negotiations with China over autonomy.[68]

In September 1993, Hurd stepped into the row over the venue for the Olympic Games in the year 2000. At the time, John Major was strongly behind Manchester's bid to host the Olympics, headed by the tireless Manchester businessman, Bob Scott. It was clear however, that Britain was being edged into third place and the contest was developing into a two-horse race between Sydney and Peking. Hurd, interviewed on Australian television during a visit to promote trade and cultural links, said that a Peking victory would be 'poor news, a bad choice'. He hinted at China's questionable human rights record saying, 'I think there are very strong reasons against that. You only have to look at the newspapers to see what they are. I don't think that [China hosting the Games] is a good idea.'[69]

Relations with the Chinese continued to be tense in the early part of 1994. In February, the Chinese Ambassador in London, Mr Ma Yuzhen, met with executives of leading British companies doing business in China and warned them that their business and European business might suffer if the British Government pursued unfavourable policies in Hong Kong. On 8 February, Douglas Hurd responded by telling the Foreign Affairs Select Committee that 'that kind of discrimination' by the Chinese might affect their application to join the General Agreement on Tariffs and Trade (GATT).[70] Mr Ma was subsequently called to the Foreign Office and rebuked by a senior official. At the end of June 1994, Patten's unilateral proposals were put before the LegCo. Despite behind-the-scenes pressure on LegCo members from the Chinese, an amendment which would have watered down the reforms was defeated by only one vote.

In September 1994, Hurd tried to breathe new life into the Joint Liaison Group negotiations, by visiting Hong Kong to talk with Guo Fengmin, head of the Chinese JLG team. The visit was dominated by the row over Jardine Matheson. The Chinese wished to exclude the Matheson group from winning the 'CT9' container contract to build Hong Kong's ninth container terminal. The Chinese had also been angered by Hong Kong's first fully democratic elections which had just taken place for the district boards, the lowest of three tiers of government structures. A year later, the Chinese were forced to witness the sight of Governor Chris Patten emptying ballot papers to be counted in the first LegCo elections. To their annoyance, the pro-democracy parties out-performed the pro-Chinese parties. The Chinese approve of democracy so long as they know the result in advance.

The impression may have been gained from this account that British foreign policy toward China from October 1992 was solely intended to antagonise the Chinese. This was not in fact the case. The issue of the Court of Final Appeal is a good example. In May 1995, Michael Heseltine, President of the Board of Trade, was due to fly out to China with a planeload of British businessmen. The visit was intended to form part of Heseltine's grandiose drive to intervene before breakfast, before lunch, and before tea to help British industry win export contracts abroad. However, simultaneously, Hurd was on the verge of concluding Britain's proposals for the Final Court of Appeal in Hong Kong. Heseltine was anxious that the Court of Final Appeal matter should be finessed and should not interfere with his visit. Chris Patten, on the other hand, wanted to hang tough to get an acceptable agreement. Patten did not feel that increasing trade with China was dependent on kow-towing on Hong Kong, whereas Heseltine seemed to feel it was necessary to mix politics and commerce. According to Hurd, the disagreements between the two men 'got a bit edgy at times'.[71] The trick on the part of Patten and Hurd was to leave Michael Heseltine with the impression that he was 'the godfather of the agreement'.[72] In fact, the compromises were minor and not fundamental to the final deal. Heseltine's trade visit was a success, but Patten felt he had unnecessarily complicated matters.[73]

The most important commercial deals, on the finances for Hong Kong's new airport and container terminal, were signed shortly after Hurd's departure from the Foreign Office. It was purely coincidental that Hurd's successor, Malcolm Rifkind, presided over the agreements for which Hurd had searched in vain. However, the period between October 1992 and June 1995 could be termed 'the years of the snail'. The British Government's moral decision to try to enhance democracy in Hong Kong after Tiananmen Square clearly had an adverse impact on relations with the Chinese and on the negotiations over the transfer of sovereignty in 1997.

While the British Government had been constrained in parliamentary terms from granting right of abode to all Hong Kong Chinese, they felt they had to do something to show that the British were not ending their rule in Hong Kong in a dishonourable way. One might be tempted to accuse them, as Sir Percy Cradock has done, of salving their own consciences at the expense of the people of Hong Kong. But Cradock's view rests on the belief that democracy is not a universal system of government applicable everywhere in the world whereas Patten, Hurd and Major are all strong believers in the ideal of liberal democracy. Just as Major genuinely believed that Parliament should have its say over Maastricht, Patten believed the Hong Kong people deserved to be consulted over their own future. All three were very much in the tradition of Iain Macleod. In the same way that Macleod was determined to bring democracy to Africa as Secretary of State for the Colonies, Hurd, Major and Patten did not want to see one of the final episodes of the British Empire end in a dishonourable way. But with Hong Kong, Britain was engaged in the transfer of sovereignty from one power to another, not granting independence. In the eyes of the China experts, this was the central fact; China would be in total control after 1997. They argued that Patten had put back the cause of democracy in Hong Kong by upsetting the through train. In July 1997, the LegCo which had been elected in 1995 was in effect dismantled, with the pro-democracy legislators refusing to serve on an appointed Chinese body. Presumably, the detractors of Patten believed, like Hurd, that democracy mattered in Hong Kong, but what trust could they have placed in the version of democracy envisaged by the People's Republic of China?

Why did these distinguished persons oppose Patten and Hurd? At one level, as Hugo Young observed, the row within British diplomatic circles involved 'pride of authorship'.[74] The aforementioned pro-China people all had a stake in the framing of the Sino-British Declaration of 1984, which they saw as a triumph of diplomacy, their perfect creation. In Geoffrey Howe's analogy, Hong Kong required to be handled like a delicate vase. Britain should do nothing to upset China in the run-up to 1997. In the view of the friends of China, Chris Patten smashed the delicate vase, damaging the cause of democracy in Hong Kong and Britain's relations with China; and Douglas Hurd, the trained diplomat, instead of stopping him, endorsed the supposedly disastrous shift in policy.

Jonathan Dimbleby's defence of Chris Patten and the liberal democracy he preached, spawned a savage book review of Dimbleby by Lord Howe in the *Sunday Times*. Howe berated Dimbleby, calling him an 'Iago-like accomplice' and drawing comparisons with Prince Charles' allegedly unhappy reaction to Dimbleby's previous biography.[75] There was even talk in other circles of serving a court action on Chris Patten for revealing state secrets to Dimbleby, but the case was never brought forward.

While Douglas Hurd supported the Patten view, he disliked the Dimbleby book, because it stoked up controversy. Hurd's instincts are not to fan the flames of controversy, but to defuse and conciliate. It was not surprising that, after the handover ceremony, he tried to smooth ruffled feathers in a letter to Lord Howe:

Apart from one short pacifying letter in *The Times* I have kept out of the brou-ha-ha. The handover itself was dignified and could have provided a full-stop to argument. I am not an admirer of the Dimbleby book . . . And I do not think it is seemly for you and me to brawl in public, when we have agreed on so much for so long.[76]

No one should doubt that everyone intimately concerned with British policy towards Hong Kong was thinking and acting throughout in the utmost good faith. But Britain had a moral obligation to the people of Hong Kong. Belatedly, Hurd came to this view. Democracy sometimes has to be fought for. Obviously, there were limits. Everyone realised, even Mrs Thatcher buoyed up by the Falklands War in 1982, that Britain was in no position and had no intention of engaging China militarily over Hong Kong, but the more one inflates the Chinese sense of superiority over all other nations, the greater the danger that they will pose a threat to world security. Neither is it possible to isolate China economically, but that does not mean that the West cannot urge upon China the need to respect human rights in Hong Kong as well as Tibet and Taiwan. In retrospect, Britain should have granted right of abode to all Hong Kong Chinese, but this was impossible in party political terms, so it was left to Chris Patten — supported by John Major and Douglas Hurd — to put forward a set of brave but impractical proposals to retain some element of British honour.

Notes

1. H. of C. Deb. (6th Series), 6 Dec. 1993, vol. 234, col. 29.
2. Douglas Hurd, *The Arrow War: An Anglo-Chinese Confusion, 1856-1860* (Collins: London, 1967), p. 72.
3. Peter Fleming, 'Gunboats Galore', *The Spectator*, 20 Oct., 1967.
4. Hurd, *The Arrow War*, pp. 95–108.
5. Philip Goodhart (Beckenham) was the only Conservative MP to oppose the measure in the division lobbies. *see* Div. no. 25, Supplementary Estimates, Class II, Vote 2, Vietnamese Boat People, H. of C. Deb. (6th Series), 19 Dec. 1989, vol. 164, cols 276–9. In an earlier debate, he said he felt that the boat people were being sent back to a closed and totalitarian society, H. of C. Deb. (6th Series), 12 Dec. 1989, vol. 163, col. 865.
6. (8 Dec. 1989) Diary Readings with Douglas Hurd, 26 Feb. 1997.
7. Diary Readings with Douglas Hurd, 7 Oct. 1997.
8. *The Times*, 12 Dec. 1989.
9. Bob Peirce went on to be Chris Patten's political adviser in Hong Kong.
10. Diary Readings with Douglas Hurd, 7 Oct. 1997.
11. Interview with Timothy Yeo, 23 Jul. 1996.

12. Interview with Douglas Hurd, 7 Oct. 1997.

13. Between March 1989 and 31 December 1989, 867 boat people were repatriated by the UN sponsored voluntary repatriation scheme. However, by the end of 1989, a further 7,500 boat people had been 'screened out' as economic migrants.

14. H. of C. Deb. (6th Series), 12 Dec. 1989, vol. 163, col. 873.

15. Ibid.

16. Bernard Levin, 'Resistance we could not endure', *The Times*, 13 Nov. 1989; Bernard Levin, 'An echo of the Holocaust', *The Times*, 7 Dec. 1989.

17. Diary Readings with Douglas Hurd, 26 Feb. 1997.

18. The finance was passed using the procedure known as Supplementary Estimates. H. of C. Deb. (6th Series), 19 Dec. 1989, vol. 164, cols 276–9.

19. Sarah Helm, 'Boat people protest to the grey suits', *The Independent*, 17 Jan. 1990; Andrew McEwen, 'Hurd shrugs off boat people protests', *The Times*, 17 Jan. 1990.

20. *The Times*, 17 Jan. 1990.

21. H. of C. Deb. (6th Series), 20 Dec. 1989, vol. 164, col. 363.

22. Ibid., col. 364.

23. Private information.

24. H. of C. Deb. (6th Series), 20 Dec. 1989, vol. 164, col. 368.

25. Ibid., col. 368.

26. Ibid., col. 374.

27. Kevin Rafferty, 'Shame in a grubby Hong Kong deal', *The Independent*, 19 Dec. 1989.

28. Interview with Timothy Yeo, 23 Jul. 1996.

29. Diary Readings with Douglas Hurd, 26 Feb. 1997.

30. Amongst the sixteen Labour MPs who abstained on the Second Reading vote and then voted with their party on a subsequent 'Committee of the Whole House' vote, nine were members of the left-wing Campaign Group. The nine were Tony Benn (Chesterfield), Dennis Canavan (Falkirk, West), Jeremy Corbyn (Islington, North), Bernie Grant (Tottenham), Ken Livingstone (Brent, East), Max Madden (Bradford, West), Alan Meale (Mansfield), Brian Sedgemore (Hackney South & Shoreditch) and Dennis Skinner (Bolsover).

31. Anthony Bevins, 'Tory Whips divide and win on Hong Kong', *The Independent*, 21 Apr. 1990.

32. H. of C. Deb. (6th Series), 5 Jul. 1989, vol. 165, cols 309–10.

33. *Keesing's Record of World Events*, June 1991, p. 38291.

34. The day before Francis Maude flew out to China, a Cabinet reshuffle took place, but Maude waited until his return from China before taking up his new post as Financial Secretary to the Treasury.

35. Douglas Hurd, 'Why silence will not help Hong Kong', *The Times*, 3 Aug. 1990.

36. Ibid.

37. Ibid.

38. Douglas Hurd, 'An End to Years of the Snail', *The Independent*, 27 Mar. 1991.

39. Diary Readings with Douglas Hurd, 18 Mar. 1997.

40. Interview with Douglas Hurd, 18 Mar. 1997.

41. Diary Readings with Douglas Hurd, 18 Mar. 1997. It is believed that virtue can come from trees, so men can be seen having a kind of boxing match with the trees and the women can be seen hugging them.

42. Ibid.

43. In 1990, Hong Kong was administered by a UK Governor representing the Queen, who presided over an Executive Council, with four *ex-officio* members and ten nominated members, and a Legislative Council (LegCo) consisting of three of the *ex-officio* Executive Council members, seven *ex-officio* members, twenty appointed members, twenty-six elected members, twelve chosen by an electoral college and fourteen by 'functional constituencies'.

44. H. of C. Deb. (6th Series), 16 Feb. 1990, vol. 167, cols 579–80.

45. H.C. 281, Foreign Affairs Select Committee, *Hong Kong*, Second Report, Session 1988–89, 28 Jun. 1989, p. xxviii.

46. H. of C. Deb. (6th Series), 16 Feb. 1990, vol. 167, col. 582.

47. *Financial Times*, 5 Apr. 1990.

48. Jonathan Dimbleby interview with Sir Percy Cradock, *The Last Governor*, Part 2, 'Restraint in Difficult Circumstances', BBC1, 10 Jul. 1997.

49. Ibid.

50. Ibid.

51. Interview with Douglas Hurd, 18 Mar. 1997.

52. Ibid.

53. Letter from Lord Hurd of Westwell to Lord Howe of Aberavon, 4 Aug. 1997.

54. H.C. 37, Foreign Affairs Select Committee, *Relations between the United Kingdom and China in the period up to and beyond 1997*, First Report, Session 1993–94, 23 Mar. 1994, vol. I, p. lxxxvi.

55. Interview with Douglas Hurd, 18 Mar. 1997.

56. Interview with Chris Patten, 22 Jul. 1997.

57. Ibid.

58. Clive James, interview with Governor Chris Patten, Clive James, *Postcard from Hong Kong*, ITV, 27 Aug. 1996.

59. Douglas Hurd, 'Hopes for Hong Kong rest on democracy backed by

Peking', the *Sunday Times*, 11 Oct. 1992.

60. *The Last Governor*. Part 2. 'Restraint in Difficult Circumstances'.

61. (2 Sept. 1991) Diary Readings with Douglas Hurd, 18 Mar. 1997.

62. Interview with Chris Patten, 22 Jul. 1997.

63. The draft had been due to appear in Hong Kong's Official Gazette on 12 February 1993, but Hurd and Patten eventually delayed the publication of their draft legislation until 10 October. H. of C. Deb. (6th Series), 15 Mar. 1993, vol. 221, cols 22–4.

64. H.C. 37, Foreign Affairs Select Committee, *Relations between the United Kingdom and China in the period up to and beyond 1997*, Minutes of Evidence and Appendices, First Report, Session 1993–94, 23 Mar. 1994, vol. II, p. 124.

65. Ibid.

66. H. of C. Deb. (6th Series), 27 April 1995, vol. 258, cols 1008–13.

67. Diary Readings with Douglas Hurd, Westwell, 13 Jun. 1997.

68. *Keesing's Record of World Events*, May 1993, p. 39462.

69. *The Guardian*, 17 Sept. 1993.

70. H.C. 37, Foreign Affairs Select Committee, *Relations between the United Kingdom and China in the period up to and beyond 1997*, Minutes of Evidence and Appendices, First Report, Session 1993–94, 23 Mar. 1994, vol. II, p. 219.

71. Interview with Douglas Hurd, 18 Mar. 1997.

72. Interview with Chris Patten, 22 Jul. 1997.

73. For a fuller account of the Court of Final Appeal episode, *see* Jonathan Dimbleby, *The Last Governor: Chris Patten and the Handover of Hong Kong* (Little, Brown and Company: London, 1997), pp. 276–84.

74. Hugo Young, 'Handover confounds the chorus of elders', *The Guardian*, 1 Jul. 1997.

75. Geoffrey Howe, 'The Smell of Betrayal', the *Sunday Times*, 20 Jul. 1997.

76. Letter from Douglas Hurd to Lord Howe of Aberavon, 4 Aug. 1997.

20

The Sapping of Authority:
Europe and Domestic Policy,
September 1993–December 1994

After a year which the veteran William Whitelaw considered the worst twelve months endured by any government during the postwar period, the priorities for Hurd were to heal the wounds within the parliamentary party caused by the bitter battle over the ratification of the Maastricht Treaty and to develop a policy on Europe around which the party could unite. Increasingly, he confronted a determined band of Euro-sceptics whose constant desire for news headlines undermined Britain's influence and credibility at the European table.

The new Chancellor of the Exchequer, Kenneth Clarke, became a vital ally of Douglas Hurd and the Prime Minister in holding the European policy together. From May 1993 onwards the considerable presence of Clarke as well as Hurd stood in the way of the sceptics' attempts to shift the Prime Minister's policy on Europe. The difficulty was that Kenneth Clarke was not as keen as Hurd and Major to slide further in a Euro-sceptical direction. The demands of the Government's dwindling majority and the desire for unity seemed to require that conciliatory noises be made to the sceptics. However, Clarke realised that the more one conceded to the sceptics, the more they would demand.

In October 1993, Hurd again stressed the imperative of party unity to delegates at the Conservative Party Conference in Blackpool, 'We need a united party which urges us on and declines to use foreign policy as an opportunity for faction.'[1]

However, once again, Hurd faced attacks at the Conference from Lord Tebbit and Bill Cash. Douglas Hurd possessed two precious resources: he was both a figure of authority in the Conservative Party and simultaneously a respected and credible figure in the diplomatic circuit of Europe. But there were limited reserves of both these resources. Each time Hurd conceded the resource of authority at home in the interests of party unity, each time there was another domestic division or defeat, so his stockpile of credibility was diminished in other European capitals. As Norman Tebbit bluntly put it at the Conference, 'Sooner or later there will be a revolt. For while most things can be fudged, eventually a diet of fudge turns the stomach.'[2]

Amid all the divisions at home, Britain did win a vitally important argument at the European table, by securing the completion of the Uruguay Round of the General Agreement on Tariffs and Trade (GATT). In September 1993, Hurd was forced to cut short a visit to Australia, New Zealand and Japan, when the French – wary of upsetting the powerful farm lobby within France – threatened to veto a GATT deal on farm subsidies.

Although the tactic of threatening to boycott the course of EC decision making was used once too often by the British, her European partners knew Hurd was not bluffing when he said, 'if necessary Britain will act alone to ensure that the life of the Community does not continue as usual.'[3] On 21 September 1993, at a meeting of European agricultural, foreign and trade ministers in Brussels, the British view prevailed: there would be no reopening of negotiations between the EC and the United States over farm subsidies (an EC-US accord on farm subsidies had already been signed in November 1992). The Uruguay Round was completed with the British position holding firm: protectionism was put to flight.

This was in contrast to the handling of the issue of Qualified Majority Voting (QMV). The irony was that the British Government was one of the major supporters of the enlargement of the European Community. The Maastricht process had concentrated on deepening rather than widening European integration. Only when Maastricht was ratified did the newly formed European Union really turn its attention to the question of new applicants, especially the countries of Eastern Europe. But these countries needed time to prepare their economies for the rigours of the European single market. The first tranche of new entrants were not fledgling democracies but fully developed Western European economies.

The prospect of four former European Free Trade Area (EFTA) countries, Sweden, Finland and Austria – Norway also applied but later voted against joining – acceding to the European Union was seen as a welcome development by the British Government. There was a strong strand of Euro-scepticism in Scandinavia, and all four countries had efficient economies and agricultural sectors. Despite the vexed issue of fishing quotas with the Scandinavians, all four applicants would be net contributors, and as northern European states, the British Government hoped this would help tilt the balance of power in the

European Union away from the heavily subsidised southern members. However, their forthcoming entry raised the immediate problem of the voting structure of the European Union.

In areas of QMV introduced under the Single European Act – signed by Mrs Thatcher, and extended by the Maastricht Treaty – the balance of voting in the Council of Ministers at the beginning of 1993 was as follows: the most powerful members were Britain, France, Germany and Italy, each wielding ten votes; Spain with eight; Belgium, the Netherlands, Portugal and Greece each with five; Denmark and Ireland with three; and Luxembourg with only two votes, making a total of seventy-six. If a group of states wished to block a proposal, under the rules a 'blocking minority' of twenty-three votes was required. At the end of November 1993, the Belgians, holders of the EU presidency, proposed four votes for Austria and Sweden and three votes for Norway and Finland.

At the Brussels General Affairs Council in December 1993, there was agreement on the number of votes per country, but no agreement on the Belgian proposal for a new blocking minority of twenty-seven, based on the principle known as 'mechanical transposition'. While the proposed blocking minority was almost identical to the previous system (30 per cent as opposed to 30.26 per cent), in practice, the new arithmetic marginally increased the power of smaller states at the expense of larger ones. For instance, under the existing rules, Britain could block a proposal with the aid of one large state (among the top five) and one other smallish state. The Belgian plan, by contrast, meant Britain would need the support of at least two other large states (in the top five), or at least four small states, or one large state and three small ones.

According to David Heathcoat-Amory, the Minister of State who handled the bulk of the day-to-day enlargement negotiations, the Foreign Office handled the negotiations over enlargement by tackling the less serious financial and agricultural issues first, leaving the bigger question of QMV right until the end. A deadline for completion of the accession negotiations was set for 1 March 1994. This deadline came and went, but by 16 March all other aspects of the accession negotiations – including the thorny question of fisheries – had been settled. Only the blocking minority obstacle remained. As David Heathcoat-Amory recalls, 'we were gradually reversing into a corner'.[4] Having been the prime movers of enlargement, any British threats to hold up the timetable at such a late stage of the negotiations – Finland, Sweden, Norway and Austria were scheduled to join on 1 January 1995, and sufficient time was needed to secure the approval of the European Parliament – would have taken the edge off a British diplomatic triumph and would have not been regarded as credible by her European partners. Hurd summed up the mistake in his diary, before flying to Ioannina in northern Greece to settle for a compromise:

25 Mar. 1994: We've put second things first and will suffer grievously.[5]

By the beginning of March 1994, it became increasingly clear to Douglas Hurd that several of Britain's original allies on QMV, particularly the Germans, the French and the Italians – all larger states – were no longer going to defend twenty-three as the blocking minority. Britain's only reliable ally on the issue was Spain. Throughout the QMV crisis, the Spanish stood resolutely beside the British. Hurd was particularly impressed by the robustness of the Spanish Foreign Minister, Javier Solana, and in October 1995, Hurd's support for the idea that Solana should become Secretary General of NATO was partly based on this.[6]

Shorn of his allies, except Spain, and running out of time to settle the issue of QMV, Hurd was worried that Britain would be blamed for holding up enlargement, having initially been its major proponent. The Foreign Secretary began to warn his Cabinet colleagues that he did not expect the issue to be resolved via a straight choice between twenty-three and twenty-seven as a blocking minority. However, his negotiating hands were tied by the defence of twenty-three, which several members of the Cabinet subcommittte known as OPD (E) upheld. Michael Howard, the new Home Secretary, wanted to prevent any moves which increased QMV in home affairs, with particular regard to border controls and immigration. While other Euro-sceptics in the Cabinet, such as Peter Lilley, Michael Portillo and John Redwood, predictably supported Howard, the Cabinet split on QMV did not fall entirely on Europhile/Eurosceptic lines. Michael Heseltine, the President of the Board of Trade wanted to stick to twenty-three as the blocking minority, as did the Chancellor of the Exchequer, Kenneth Clarke. Generally speaking, the Chancellor was one of Douglas Hurd's closest allies on Europe – he had voted for Hurd in November 1990 because he knew what his views on Europe were, but had no idea as to John Major's. But Kenneth Clarke was not a great enthusiast for enlargement. The Chancellor wanted to maintain the balance of weighted voting in favour of the big players in Europe: Britain, France and Germany. He was worried that in future one might reach a situation in which two or three large states might be outvoted by a block of smaller countries, and also hoped to prevent extra economic burdens on social issues.[7] So, the OPD (E) instructed Hurd to defend twenty-three. In retrospect, Hurd feels he should have pressed his case more emphatically with his colleagues at an earlier stage to give himself more flexibility in the negotiations.[8]

On Sunday, 6 March, Hurd flew to Brussels to prepare for a Council of Foreign Ministers meeting the following day. He got into the habit of travelling on a Sunday night so he could have a working supper with Britain's team of permanent officials in Brussels, headed by Sir John Kerr. His diary entry read:

6 Mar. 1994: Worried about tussle on QMV. Hands tied by the OPD (E) requirements. Trapped here in a furious tempest.'

The sudden storm which blew up was perhaps an ominous sign of the troubles which were to follow:

7 Mar. 1994: Speak alongside Solana. Discussion gets nowhere. Adjourns until lunch tomorrow. Worried about QMV.[10]

The following day was Hurd's birthday, but he was not in a mood to celebrate:

8 Mar. 1994: As nasty a birthday as I can recall. Imprisoned in the Charlemagne. No progress on QMV. We argue with the Dutch. No useful compromise to hand. PM and colleagues miscalculate in supposing the Germans would compromise rather than spoil enlargement. They don't move, though we dangle compromises before them.[11]

Amidst the bad news, Hurd was at least pleasantly surprised that the Spanish continued throughout that Council to mount a stubborn defence of twenty-three as the blocking minority. At this point, the Prime Minister and Douglas Hurd moved the seriousness of the issue up a notch, by sending messages to the German Government to the effect that the issue had become very important to the British in domestic political terms. Privately, after failing to shift Kenneth Clarke on the issue, Hurd failed to see a way through the impasse. On Wednesday, 16 March, during one of the many long conversations which Hurd had with the Prime Minister about his position, Hurd said he felt that Britain was becoming like a bank with a run on it; that it was using up valuable credit on an issue which it was not winning, just as a bank does when its customers demand their money.[12] The following morning in Cabinet, the sceptics continued to oppose any concessions, but, largely due to the helpful stand of the Prime Minister, the majority supported giving Hurd a little more flexibility in his forthcoming discussions.

That weekend, Hurd tried to take a day away from the QMV row by going to his weekend residence at Chevening in Kent, and popping across to nearby Eton College. However, the weekend's press continued to be bad. It was becoming increasingly clear after a telephone conversation with Klaus Kinkel, the German Foreign Minister, that the Swedes were bemused that Britain, the strongest supporters of enlargement, appeared to be endangering its timetable. Meanwhile, Kenneth Clarke's intransigence raised the stakes when he declared, 'I don't accept there is any need to move to twenty-seven as a blocking minority.'[13]

Hurd flew to Brussels that evening to check with Sir John Kerr and his team that the Spaniards were still on board. When negotiations restarted the next day, Hurd's mood was more upbeat:

> 22 Mar. 1994: Feel more perky. For an hour, we actually seem to be getting a grip on QMV. Spaniards stay close all day and are a pleasure to work with.[14]

Then things started to go badly wrong. First, Jacques Delors arrived looking 'fatigued and apocalyptic',[15] then a bad lunch ensued during which first the French, then the Dutch and Belgians refused to budge. Hurd was plunged into a deep gloom when he heard news of John Major's ill-judged comments during Prime Minister's Question Time in the House of Commons:

> We are determined to negotiate in Brussels, and to fight Britain's corner just as hard as every other nation would fight for itself. We will not be moved by phoney threats to delay enlargement. There is ample time to complete the enlargement process . . . The right hon. and learned Member for Monklands, East (Mr Smith) is the man who likes to say yes in Europe – Monsieur Oui, the poodle of Brussels.[16]

The Euro-sceptics on the Tory backbenches loved it. Paradoxically, until the Prime Minister's performance, the issue of QMV was not one which had generated a huge degree of passion among the Euro-sceptics. The effect of the Prime Minister's speech was to raise false expectations among backbenchers that a victory over Europe was on the cards. In the great bulk of their dealings together, Hurd remained a firm admirer of the Prime Minister, especially with regard to his performances at the Maastricht and Edinburgh summits. But on this occasion, Hurd was very cross and feels that John Major 'dug us all in deeper'.[17] The Prime Minister had been kept fully informed of the state of the negotiations; he knew all about the difficulties which Hurd was experiencing, and yet he made this unscripted remark. Hurd returned to London and told John Major how he felt about it all, but this just had the effect of plunging the Prime Minister into another one of his bouts of depression. John Major tried to explain that he had become frustrated during PMQs. At Cabinet on Thursday, 24 March, Michael Heseltine said that Hurd should threaten to resign if he did not get his way. Hurd replied that he did not see any need for that. He recalls:

> The whole thing had got completely out of hand. The effort we were making was completely disproportionate to what was involved.[18]

On the Friday (25 March), Hurd gave a speech to the Conservative Central Council at Plymouth, in which he warned that the Conservative Party must not 'scratch away at old wounds':

> Let us stop this divisive nonsense . . . that is yesterday's game; those are yesterday's toys. Let us put them back in the toy cupboard . . . Britain against Europe, *Britannia Contra Mundum*, cannot in our saner moments be our rallying cry. That is not the approach of a party comfortable with its history and comfortable with Britain's proud role in the world. Isolation is not an end in itself. We argue to get the best outcome we can.[19]

Hurd thought 'Britannia Contra Mundum' was one of his better speeches, but it was very badly received in the press the following day. Simon Hoggart, *The Guardian*'s political sketch writer, described Hurd's performance at Plymouth as 'one of the most Eeyorish speeches a Tory conference can have heard.'[20] Afterwards, Hurd gave a series of interviews to radio and television with the aim of preparing his party for an inevitable compromise on QMV. He was reported as saying, 'At the end of the day there is agreement. That is the way the Community works. That's the way it will work this time.'[21] Back in Witney, Tony Picking, Hurd's association chairman, was baying at his MP for weakening Britain's hand abroad.

During every six-monthly presidency of the European Community, EC foreign ministers hold an informal summit, at which they are supposed to ponder grand visions, but invariably some crisis emerges which dogs the meeting. In this case, both the QMV row and the crisis in Bosnia hijacked the discussions. During the informal summits, European foreign ministers were not permitted to take their permanant representatives or press officials with them. So Hurd knew as he flew out to Ioannina, that apart from his PPS John Sawers and wife, Judy, he was very much on his own. His only comfort as the summit began was that the Spanish Foreign Minister, Javier Solana, continued to side with the British.

All these summits have, as has already been explained, periodic breaks in which European leaders engage in a spot of local tourism. As the foreign ministers visited a monastery on the Saturday, Hurd viewed paintings of saints being beheaded and lacerated, all with mild expressions on their faces, and could not help feeling that this was comparable to his present predicament.[22]

On the Sunday morning, Hurd breakfasted alone with Jacques Delors in the dining room of a dingy hotel. The two had always had a good personal relationship. Hurd saw the European Commission President as a deeply serious, intelligent man, who could be counted on to play it straight. Hurd recalls it as being his best conversation with Delors:

> I warned Delors that if we didn't manage ourselves, all of us, a bit better, he would find that before too long, for the first time, one of the main political parties which had advocated membership of the European Community would turn against it. The thing was deteriorating and we just had to be careful about that. It's still a danger now.[23]

In that conversation in a dingy hotel in northern Greece, we see the underlying bedrock of Hurd's belief in the European Community. It was not just a case of Hurd angling for a better deal, it was the British Foreign Secretary warning the European Commission President that the pro-European, Tory establishment consensus on Europe which had lasted since Harold Macmillan was in danger of breaking up. Using all his personal authority and respect among his fellow European leaders, Hurd was urging them to do everything to prevent the Conservative Government from turning against Europe.

Under the compromise agreed at Ioannina later that Sunday (27 March), the blocking minority was officially set at twenty-seven, but in cases where the total number of blocking votes numbered between twenty-three and twenty-six, countries agreed to a cooling-off period of two months during which the proposals could be re-examined. In effect, the Ioannina Compromise is a delaying mechanism, similar to the Luxembourg Compromise of 1966, which had stated that 'on issues very important to one or more member countries, the Council should try to reach unanimity.'[24] In practice, most issues in the European Council are not subject to a vote. As Hurd is fond of describing, the usual pattern is for member states to negotiate and then reach a compromise.

Despite the accession of three new member states into the European Union, the Ioannina Compromise was a temporary sticking-plaster designed to cover over the issue of enlargement until the next Intergovernmental Conference got under way in 1996, without addressing the fundamental question of the future institutional structure of the European Union. The QMV issue was put to one side at the Amsterdam summit of June 1997, but (at the time of writing) Britain seemed to have the firm backing of France on the issue.

Hurd's initial reaction to the deal at Ioannina was favourable:

> 27 March. 1994: It's an advance, ingenious, but will look weak at Westminster.[25]

The Foreign Secretary consulted with the Prime Minister by telephone, but John Major was noncommittal, so Hurd had to say to his fellow European foreign ministers that he would take the deal back home and recommend it to his colleagues. What he could not tell them was whether or not the Cabinet would accept it.

376

Hurd was able to draw on a deep reservoir of respect from other European leaders to secure a compromise which he would be able to take back to London to sell to the Cabinet and to Tory backbenchers. He knew that his Cabinet had to agree by 29 March or face postponement to the Corfu Summit, which, in effect, meant that enlargement would have been delayed for a year. In his view, putting up a fight on twenty-three was not worth the price of damaging British interests by alienating potential new allies, especially the Swedes. During an interview with the BBC on the Sunday, he dampened down talk of his own resignation:

> One only needs to consider resignation if you are fed up with the job, or if
> your colleagues or party, your country as a whole, goes off in a direction
> which one feels oneself unacceptable. I am not in that position at all.[26]

Hurd is not one of life's natural resigners. Nevertheless, if the Cabinet had failed to endorse the compromise he had negotiated or Tory backbenchers had refused to endorse the Government line, the Foreign Secretary's position would have become untenable.

Hurd had to win over a reluctant Prime Minister and an even more reluctant Chancellor of the Exchequer if he stood a chance of getting the Cabinet to agree to the Ioannina Compromise. With this in mind, Hurd's first task on arrival in London was to meet with John Major. Yet again, the Foreign Secretary found his Prime Minister consumed with the adverse reaction in the press:

> 28 Mar. 1994: Prime Minister very melancholy about the press. Impossible
> to proceed . . .[27]

After talking it through, face to face, the Prime Minister suggested to Douglas Hurd that they ask Kenneth Clarke to join them. The Chancellor of the Exchequer arrived, but instead of holding out against a compromise on an issue which he had spent months opposing tooth and nail, Hurd was surprised when Clarke's advice to the Prime Minister was that this was the best deal Britain could have secured. According to Hurd:

> He [Kenneth Clarke] did not pretend to have mastered the details, but was
> prepared to back my judgement that we could not get more.[28]

So, Kenneth Clarke was persuaded to change his mind, and this had the initial effect of plunging the Prime Minister into yet deeper melancholy. But, John Major recovered himself and began to suggest ways in which the deal could be sold to the Cabinet and the House of Commons. In this way, Hurd brought on board his two key allies before the Tuesday meeting of Cabinet.

Hurd's statement to the House of Commons on Monday went surprisingly well. There was, as Hurd noted in his diary, 'no poison from behind', although the Euro-sceptic Tony Marlow (Northampton, North) said to the press that 'Douglas Hurd has poured some cultured treacle on a box of Euro-fudge.'[29] The political sketch writer Matthew Parris rightly commented that Hurd 'just keeps on convincing people'.[30] However, there were limits to the Conservative Party's ability to accept Hurd's line on Europe:

> The day has yet to come – though for a moment he thought it had – when fate hands Mr Hurd a pill he cannot persuade the Tory Party to swallow.[31]

Douglas Hurd was encouraged on Monday, 28 March after a series of telephone conversations between the Foreign Office and the European Commission, as a result of which the European Commission appeared to make some helpful comments on the future conduct of EU social legislation.[32] The following day, the Commission denied that the comments amounted to fresh 'assurances', designed to help Hurd persuade the British Cabinet to swallow the Ioannina Compromise.[33]

Was there a thread running from Hurd's conversation with Delors in the dingy Greek hotel on the Sunday morning through to the 'assurances' from the European Commission the following day? Did the Foreign Secretary use those assurances to persuade his Cabinet colleagues on the Tuesday to accept the Ioannina compromise? From the limited evidence available, it seems that, by making public the telephone contacts with the Commission on the Monday, Hurd was trying to send an important signal – though nothing more – to his Cabinet colleagues and his backbenchers that the European Union need not always be seen as acting against the wishes of the British Government. In that task, he was undoubtedly helped by Jacques Delors, as a result of Hurd's warning to the European Commission President the previous day. Hurd describes Delors' comments in his diary entry on Monday evening as 'mildly helpful'.[34] This suggests that Hurd did not think the comments amounted to firm assurances. It is highly improbable that Hurd felt he was 'sold' a set of assurances by Delors, which the Commission then recanted the next day and which Hurd had used as a device to mislead his Cabinet colleagues into accepting the Ioannina deal. Rather, the comments are more likely to have been an expression of goodwill from Delors after representations made by Hurd not to make life difficult at a moment of domestic political difficulty for the British Government.

The debate over European Commission assurances was a side issue. The main debate at the two-hour Cabinet on 29 March was whether the Prime Minister could have intervened to gain a better deal than Hurd had negotiated. The four main Euro-sceptics – Michael Howard, Michael Portillo, Peter Lilley and most vigorously, John Redwood – argued that the Prime Minister should intervene. Douglas Hurd, backed by Michael Heseltine and Kenneth Clarke, argued it was not possible to gain any more concessions from Britain's European partners. They had already shifted their position to accommodate British objections. The Foreign Secretary said that the other EU members already found it difficult to understand the British objections; they would completely fail to understand if the British Prime Minister went back demanding yet more concessions. Throughout the meeting, John Major, who was extremely upset, refused to argue. Although he had agreed to support Hurd the previous day, deep down, he still believed that he could have gained a better deal. Looking back, Hurd is sure, having talked it through with John Kerr since, that the Prime Minister could not have gained anything more.[35] Because Ioannina was an informal summit of foreign ministers, in which the member states did not have their official apparatus present, there will always be some uncertainty as to whether Hurd gained everything that could have been gained. Ultimately, John Major had to stomach the Ioannina deal because he could not afford to lose the Foreign Secretary, his closest ally.

It seemed, after his own steady performance in the House of Commons on the Monday, and receiving the endorsement of the Cabinet, that Douglas Hurd had succeeded in limiting the damage. However, John Major was savaged by incandescent Euro-sceptics in the House of Commons that afternoon when he gave his own statement on QMV. For the first time since 1963, a Conservative MP – albeit Tony Marlow, a maverick with a penchant for stripey blazers – called for the resignation of the Prime Minister in the House of Commons.[36] There was a widespread perception in the parliamentary party that the Prime Minister had shown weak leadership by giving way at the end. Unfortunately, the Prime Minister had chosen to fight his pitched battle with Europe on ground which he stood no chance of holding. As the rising star of political columnists, Andrew Marr, pointed out in The Independent, 'Symbolic battles are fine – if you win.'[37]

The press reaction the next day was extremely bloody. Most editors ran with fresh stories of possible contenders for the Conservative leadership contest. The Tory press had already turned against John Major after Black Wednesday, but the QMV row increased the vitriol poured on a Prime Minister who seemed less capable than most Tory leaders of ignoring press criticism. Douglas Hurd did not escape either. Woodrow Wyatt's article in The Times ran with the headline, 'HOW HURD BETRAYED BRITAIN', urging the Prime Minister to sack his Foreign Secretary.[38] But the real impact of the row over QMV was to leave the

Prime Minister with virtually no authority in his party other than wielding the threat of electoral suicide.

Douglas Hurd recalls that, while Bosnia was the most difficult issue he faced, because it went on much longer and was much more tragic and much more important, 'as an episode, [the QMV row] was about as bad a few days as I've ever had'.[39]

The former Chancellor of the Exchequer, Kenneth Clarke, is clear that the impact of the QMV row was disastrous for the authority of the Prime Minister, and has real doubts about whether he should have allowed himself to be persuaded by Douglas Hurd that the cause on twenty-three was lost:

> People will look back on it and say it was a total disaster. The reason I feel guilty about it and think it may have been wrong to persuade me to change over was that John [Major] was left terribly exposed . . . When you look back over the last few years to the times when our authority on Europe took a real hammer blow, while it was not quite on the same scale as Black Wednesday, it was a terrible, terrible hammer blow.[40]

However, Douglas Hurd believes that the reason the Prime Minister was so badly mauled by his own party was because he had 'over-exposed himself unnecessarily' with his 'Monsieur Oui' comment at PMQs the previous Thursday.[41] Kenneth Clarke believes that the row did some damage to the unity of the troika on Europe inside the Government between himself, Douglas Hurd and John Major:

> It slightly mixed it up. The start of the episode was my vehemence we should tackle qualified majority voting. The end of the episode was Douglas Hurd's vehemence that we couldn't possibly exclude the Swedes, and the victim was John Major.[42]

Hurd believes the Prime Minister's miserable experience over the QMV row was a crucial turning point in the Prime Minister's thinking on Europe. From then on, John Major felt increasingly that Britain was always going to be a loser in arguments of this kind.[43] It was around this time, at the beginning of April 1994, that the Prime Minister began airing privately the idea of a referendum on the single currency. Despite being temperamentally opposed to referendums, Hurd quickly became persuaded of a referendum on a single currency as a device to reunite the Conservative Party in time for the General Election. It would be two years, however, and Hurd would have retired, before the rest of the Cabinet – particularly Kenneth Clarke and Michael Portillo – could be persuaded to sign up to the idea. That is why Clarke's comment about the troika becoming 'mixed up' is so crucial. Clarke feels that if only the Prime Minister had not been persuaded to back down over QMV, he would have remained more positive on Europe and not warmed to the idea of a referendum.[44]

From March 1994 onwards, there were growing signs that Hurd was becoming frustrated that the Tory Party was failing to put the rows over Maastricht behind it, and that the antics of the Euro-sceptics at home were beginning to reflect on his negotiating credibility at the European table. During a speech to the Lord Mayor's Easter Banquet at the Mansion House on 13 April, he complained, as ever, in a coded way:

> At present we run the risk of intellectual shrinkage as if we despaired of convincing anybody of anything, as if we simply wanted to devise ways of protecting ourselves against a Europe and a world which was bound to run against us.[45]

The theme of being undermined diplomatically because of domestic divisions was one which Hurd would return to after his resignation. Hurd's difficulties were accentuated by a Euro-sceptical Tory press which had turned against the Prime Minister ever since Black Wednesday. They reported at length comments of Euro-sceptics ever eager to enter a television studio, but failed to report in detail a series of pro-European speeches made by Hurd. The hostile press also ensured speculation over John Major's leadership remained simmering perpetually close to boiling point, thus putting the onus on senior ministers, but especially Douglas Hurd, to give media appearances defending the Prime Minister's position. On 25 April 1994, during an interview with Radio 5, he described John Major as 'a man of steel', claiming, 'This chat about the leadership is unreal. Serious politicians are not talking about it inside the government or the party.'[46]

The most immediate electoral test of John Major's authority and Hurd's balancing act on Europe came with the European Election campaign in June 1994. The Foreign Secretary made a deliberate attempt to exclude the Euro-sceptics from the drafting process of the Conservative's European Election Manifesto. A manifesto drafting committee and a strategy committee were established a year in advance of the European Elections. The two committees wanted to avoid the splits which had occurred during the 1989 European Elections campaign when the strategy committee veered off into negative campaigning, typified by the ill-fated 'Diet of Brussels' advertising campaign.[47]

After receiving input from ministers from each government department and Conservative MEPs, the first draft of the European manifesto, totalling around 18,000 words, was written by Maurice Fraser, Hurd's special adviser, Andrew

Lansley, Head of the Conservative Research Department, and Anthony Teasdale, Head of the London Office of the European People's Party (EPP), and handed to the Prime Minister at Easter.

However, there was a hiccup in the drafting process when *The Times* reported on 29 April that the Cabinet had rejected the draft European Manifesto produced by Douglas Hurd.[48] Early in the morning of 29 April, Hurd heard the familiar ring of the telephone:

> 29 Apr. 1994: PM rings about 7 a.m. Concert line about mischievous story in *The Times* about shortening of the manifesto.[49]

In actual fact, a senior group of ministers meeting in early April had judged the draft too long and lacking sufficient political punch. Sarah Hogg, the Head of the Policy Unit at 10, Downing Street, was given the task of shortening the document and making it more party political. But the Euro-sceptics seized on the leak as evidence that the Prime Minister was shifting in a more Euro-sceptical direction. This in turn angered the Euro-enthusiasts, who were not aware at the time that the Euro-sceptics had been successfully excluded from the drafting process by Douglas Hurd.

When *A Strong Britain in a Strong Europe* was agreed upon on 5 May, it put forward Douglas Hurd's agenda of a wider, deregulated, more transparent Europe, with the party-political spin included. After a heavy defeat in the local council elections of 5 May, Douglas Hurd's priority as campaign manager for the European Elections was to prevent a second humiliation for the party and to protect the position of the Prime Minister.

The day after the local election defeat, Douglas Hurd chose a speech to the Polish Parliament in Warsaw as the venue to promote his 'variable geometry' vision of Europe. Hurd spoke of a 'strong Europe of self-confident nation states', and claimed that a 'multi-speed, multi-track, even multi-faceted Europe' was taking shape.[50] Apart from a trailing of the speech in *The Independent*, Hurd's lecture was barely reported.

The Foreign Secretary ran with the theme again at the Scottish Conservative and Unionist Conference at Inverness on 11 May:

> We are increasingly seeing the need for what is known as variable geometry: the idea that the functions of the European Union should be carried out in different ways, often involving different groups of states . . . This is a multi-track, multi-speed, even multi-layered approach.[51]

While the 'Inverness version' of multi-speed, multi-track received far more coverage in the press than the one in Warsaw, its content was overshadowed by comments Hurd made during a press conference. Hurd told reporters that John Major's position was secure whatever the outcome of the European Elections: 'He will continue as Prime Minister. He will not be defeated. He will not resign.'[52]

It seemed that only when Hurd said something which was related to speculation over the Conservative leadership contest did he make the headlines of the newspapers. His multi-speed, multi-track ideas failed to become airborne until they were flown by the Prime Minister in a speech at Ellesmere Port in Cheshire on 31 May. In an article in the *Daily Telegraph*, just before the European Elections, Douglas Hurd reflected on his initial failure to get his message across:

> One of the odd things about politics is the way an argument suddenly reaches a wide audience some time after it is first stated. It is good news that the Prime Minister regained the initiative for the Conservatives with a speech last Tuesday about a multi-track Europe. It is a thought which he and others of us have expounded before. It was the main theme of my speech at the Scottish Party Conference on May 11.[53]

Overall, the Conservative campaign was a low-key affair, partly reflecting the leadership's desire for damage limitation. Also, the untimely death of John Smith on 12 May had the effect of delaying the official start of the campaign for a week, and the distraction of the D-Day commemorations on 6-7 June meant that the only other highlight of the campaign was John Major's attack on street beggars.[54]

In the final ten days of the campaign, Hurd went on the stump, including a sheep show at Wigton in Cumbria. It was just the kind of rural event which Hurd enjoyed. After talking to the local farmers, the Foreign Secretary again confessed his love of electioneering to Donald McIntyre, saying 'Once I've shaken the first hand of a stranger each morning, it sets me up for the day.'[55]

On 9 June, the number of Conservative MEPs was reduced from thirty-two to eighteen, while the Liberal Democrats gained two seats for the first time, and Labour triumphed with sixty-two seats – up from forty-five in 1989. The Conservatives' share of the national vote was 28 per cent, its worst ever result in a national election. All one can say in Hurd's defence is that a semblance of party unity had been maintained during the campaign, and that he had prevented meltdown. Hurd's own assessment of the campaign and the result was that it could have been a lot worse:

> That was the nearest point where I thought we'd got a party consensus on Europe, in that manifesto and in the [European Elections] campaign.

> Although the results were bad, they weren't absolutely awful. I really thought we were making a bit of progress.[56]

As Hurd and Major arrived at the Corfu Summit at the end of June, Britain's European partners were not expecting any major difficulties in securing the appointment of the Belgian Prime Minister, Jean-Luc Deheane, as the new European Commission President, to succeed Jacques Delors. In terms of being committed federalists, Hurd acknowledges there was not much daylight between the views of Jean-Luc Deheane and that of Jacques Santer, the eventual compromise candidate. However, the British objected to the fact that Deheane had been chosen by the French and the Germans without proper consultation. Other countries agreed with the British line, but, with the exception of the Dutch, were not willing to say so publicly. On the morning of Friday, 24 June, John Major hosted an Anglo-Italian breakfast with the new Italian Prime Minister, Silvio Berlusconi and his Foreign Minister, Antonio Martino. During the outdoor breakfast, Berlusconi – whom Hurd describes as 'extremely disarming' – said that while he entirely agreed with Britain on the Deheane issue, he was not willing to disagree with Chancellor Kohl at this his first summit appearance.[57] That evening, separate dinners were held for the foreign ministers and the prime ministers. Hurd recalls that the foreign ministers' dinner finished first, so he walked onto a terrace filled with statues. At that moment, Edouard Balladur, the French Prime Minister, appeared on the terrace, taking a breather from the prime ministers' dinner. Hurd tentatively asked how the meeting was going. 'Très mal!' was the reply.[58] John Major stuck to his guns and vetoed Deheane.

Klaus Kinkel, the German Foreign Minister, was instrumental in securing eventual agreement on the presidency of the European Commission, after shuttling between European capitals. On 30 June, Kinkel had lunch with Douglas Hurd in London. At the time, the issue of BSE reared its head, with the Germans threatening unilateral measures against British beef. However, it would be two years before the main BSE crisis really came to the fore. Despite their disagreements over beef, Hurd's diary impression of the German Foreign Minister was that 'he remains friendly and likeable'.[59] In German political circles, Kinkel is often criticised for not being a good communicator, but Hurd always found him honest and someone who went out of his way to be friendly. Indeed, in the spring of 1995, the Hurds and the Kinkels spent a pleasant weekend walking along the Rhine together.

The arrival of Jacques Santer as European Commission President, the prospect of three new members joining in January 1995, and the insistence by the 'big five' (Britain, France, Germany, Spain, and Italy) that they retain two European Commissioners each meant there was an inevitable shuffling of the pack of the portfolios held by European Commissioners. Most EU Commissioners held more than one portfolio so some subdivision of their responsibilities was needed. As compensation for losing control of security and foreign policy to Jacques Santer, the former Dutch Foreign Minister, Hans van den Broek, was given the task of developing Britain's policy towards Eastern Europe and the former Soviet Union. Unfortunately, this meant splitting up the portfolio held by Britain's European Commissioner, Sir Leon Brittan.

Leon Brittan had played a decisive role in securing the completion of the Uruguay round of GATT, and felt he deserved some reward. The British Government officially backed his candidature for the post of European Commission President, but although Leon Brittan was widely respected in Europe, he was also regarded by some as a haughty, slightly arrogant figure, and was never seen as a front runner for the post. There was a suggestion at the time that John Major's veto of Dehaene in June affected Leon Brittan's fate in the share-out of Commission portfolios in October. The media speculated that other European leaders feared that Sir Leon, under British influence, might have absorbed the new states of Eastern Europe too quickly, scuppering closer union between the fifteen.[60] Neither Douglas Hurd nor David Heathcoat-Amory see a line of argument running from the Dehaene veto to the demotion of Leon Brittan. The most immediate problem for Hurd was to persuade his former Home Office boss, whose pride had been injured somewhat, to stay on as one of the two British Commissioners. A series of telephone calls helped to bring Sir Leon round.[61]

In October 1994, at the Conservative Party Conference at Bournemouth, Hurd warned of the 'siren sounds', particularly from Norman Lamont, contemplating eventual withdrawal from Europe.[62] The centre of gravity in the Conservative Party had shifted in a Euro-sceptical direction. The variable-geometry vision of Douglas Hurd risked being interpreted by the Euro-sceptics as an argument in favour of avoiding any closer integration. When the Prime Minister put forward his own vision of Europe at the William and Mary Lecture at Leiden University on 8 September 1994, European leaders saw it, not as a serious analysis of the kind of Europe which was emerging and should emerge, but as a policy borne out of domestic political necessity.

The pro-European wing of the Conservative Party refused to stay silent in the face of the Prime Minister's apparent concessions to the sceptics. An indication of their restlessness came in late October when they formed the Action Centre for Europe (ACE). Although there was considerable backing from Michael Heseltine and Kenneth Clarke for the new pressure group, the main impetus came from Geoffrey Howe, its first president.[63] Howe was concerned that the pro-European wing of the Conservative Party had stayed too quiet for too long, allowing a Euro-sceptical drift in the Conservative Party.

Essentially, the pattern from this point until Hurd's retirement in June 1995 remained the same: the Euro-sceptics would create a fuss, which would be countered by the pro-Europeans, leaving the Prime Minister and Douglas Hurd seeking new ways of preserving a paper unity for the election. Sensing that Douglas Hurd, his closest ally in Cabinet on Europe, might be thinking of retirement, Kenneth Clarke took to the habit every time he met Douglas Hurd of pleading with the Foreign Secretary not to resign. In the manner of M. Porcius Cato (234-149 BC), who kept warning the Roman Senate about the rise of the Carthaginians after the Second Punic War by saying 'Carthago delenda est' (And Carthage must be destroyed), the Chancellor exhorted to Hurd 'And you must not resign.'[64] From a purely personal point of view, if Hurd went, Clarke knew he would be the next in the sceptics' firing line, which was in fact what happened. However, Clarke also knew that the Government needed to keep someone of Hurd's weight and authority inside the Cabinet.

In between the trimming to the Euro-sceptics there was another bout of General Custer-style bravado from the Prime Minister over the European Communities (Finance) Bill. The legislation arose because of a complex deal reached at the Edinburgh Summit on the future finance of the Community. The authorship of the idea to treat the vote on Second Reading as a vote of confidence is still a matter of conjecture. Kenneth Clarke strongly denies it was his idea and points the finger at Douglas Hurd, while Hurd says he supported the move, but denies it was his original idea. He vaguely remembers a Sunday night supper held by the Prime Minister at which the move was decided, but drew a blank when trying to find a diary entry alluding to the meeting. By 10 November, Hurd was certainly arguing in Cabinet Committee that the Government could not afford the Prime Minister to experience another long-drawn-out Maastricht-style battle over the future finance of the European Union.

The row over the finance of the European Union came at a bad time for the Government in general and for Hurd in particular. On 3 November, the Cabinet agreed to drop plans to privatise the Post Office after more than a dozen Conservative MPs made it clear they would vote against the plan. David Martin, Hurd's PPS, resigned over the issue, also highlighting his opposition to a single currency. On 11 November, Douglas Hurd was accused of acting unlawfully in authorising £234 million in aid towards the Pergau Dam project in Malaysia (see Chapter 22). Meanwhile, the Bosnian crisis continued to occupy the bulk of Hurd's time. On the same day as the Pergau Dam affair surfaced, the United States announced it was no longer enforcing the arms embargo against the former Yugoslavia (see Chapter 18). Then, on 15 November, the Government received a blow to its attempts to secure the passage of the European Communities (Finance) Bill when the European Court of Auditors published a report highlighting waste and fraud amounting to £6 billion. Next, Kenneth Clarke admitted during the debate on 28 November that the Treasury's uprated forecast for Britain's contribution from £1.7 billion to £2.4 billion did not square with his letter to MPs of 11 November when he had used the £1.7 billion figure. Telling the Shadow Chancellor Gordon Brown that he 'honestly couldn't remember'[65] whether he was aware of the new Treasury figures when writing to MPs and that forecasting was an inexact science did not sound convincing.

The fate of the European Communities (Finance) Bill became entangled with the vote on the Finance Bill's provisions for the second stage of increase of VAT on fuel from 8 per cent to 15 per cent.[66] After pursuing the line that the British Government could not break its solemn international commitments, the Government gained a comfortable victory on the Second Reading of the European Communities (Finance) Bill, but the victory proved short-lived.[67] All eight Conservative rebels had the parliamentary whip withdrawn and a ninth, Sir Richard Body (Holland with Boston), voluntarily resigned the party whip in protest.[68] Only eight days later, the Government was defeated over VAT on fuel, partly as a result of the votes against and abstentions by the whipless rebels.[69]

The decision to withdraw the whip from the rebels not only left the Government with a gap in its finances which had to be filled by unpopular increases in beers and spirits, but it was also now listing without an overall majority (temporarily at least). The overall impression was of a Government stripped of its authority, clinging desperately onto power. The Government plight was compounded by the antics of the nine whipless rebels who were presented with a perfect media platform from which to put forward an agenda on Europe whose inevitable consequence would have been Britain's withdrawal from the EU. It was not the case that parliamentary dissent by Conservatives increased dramatically in this period.[70] It was that the outspoken extra-parliamentary antics of the sceptics, egged on by sections of the British media, damaged the Government's negotiating credibility in Europe. Hurd was scathing of the Euro-sceptics' constant craving for media appearances. To some extent, the power wielded by the sceptics was closely linked to the Government's fast declining majority. Had John Major been governing with a majority of forty or over, the influence of the Euro-sceptics would have been negligible. Instead, the Euro-sceptics perceived the Prime Minister as someone who could be persuaded to shift further in their direction on Europe if only they could remove Douglas Hurd as Foreign Secretary and replace him with a Euro-sceptical Foreign Secretary in the shape of Michael Portillo or possibly John Redwood. In short, Douglas Hurd became the Euro-sceptics' Public Enemy Number One.

Notes

1. *The Guardian*, 6 Oct. 1993.
2. Ibid.
3. Ibid., 21 Sept. 1993.
4. Interview with David Heathcoat-Amory, 22 Jul. 1996. This interview took place on the day of David Heathcoat-Amory's resignation as Paymaster General. Heathcoat-Amory claimed he was resigning in order to speak freely against the Government's 'wait and see' policy on the single currency.
5. Diary Readings with Douglas Hurd, Westwell, 13 Jun. 1997.
6. Interview with Douglas Hurd, Westwell, 13 Jun. 1997
7. Interview with Kenneth Clarke, 16 Dec. 1996.
8. Interview with Douglas Hurd, Westwell, 13 Jun. 1997.
9. Diary Readings with Douglas Hurd, Westwell, 13 Jun. 1997.
10. Ibid.
11. Ibid.
12. Ibid.
13. *The Times*, 22 Mar. 1994.
14. Diary Readings with Douglas Hurd, Westwell, 13 Jun. 1997.
15. Ibid.
16. H. of C. Deb. (6th Series), 22 Mar. 1994, vol. 240, col. 134.
17. Interview with Douglas Hurd, Westwell, 13 Jun. 1997.
18. Ibid.
19. *The Guardian*, 26 Mar. 1994.
20. Ibid.
21. *Financial Times*, 26 Mar. 1994.
22. (Sat. 26 Mar. 1994) Diary Readings with Douglas Hurd, Westwell, 13 Jun. 1997.
23. Interview with Douglas Hurd, Westwell, 13 Jun. 1997.
24. Quoted from Anne Daltrop, *Political Realities: Politics and the European Community* (Longman, 2nd edn.: London, 1986), p. 31.
25. Diary Readings with Douglas Hurd, Westwell, 13 Jun. 1997.
26. *The Guardian*, 28 Mar. 1994.
27. Diary Readings with Douglas Hurd, Westwell, 13 Jun. 1997.
28. Letter from Douglas Hurd to the author, 30 May 1998; Clarke claims Hurd persuaded him before the meeting with John Major. Letter from Kenneth Clarke to the author, 15 Jun. 1998.
29. *The Times*, 29 Mar. 1994.
30. Matthew Parris, 'Obedient Tories chew on Dr Hurd's bitter Euro-pill',

The Times, 29 Mar. 1994.

31. Ibid.

32. The European Commission remarks addressed the British objection to social legislation being introduced through the health and safety directive under Article 118A, most notably the working time directive which proposed to introduce a maximum forty-eight-hour working week. There had also been encouraging noises on applying the so-called 'territorial principle' to social legislation: British workers belonging to multinational companies running European works councils would not have legal protection under EU law because of the British opt-out from the Social Chapter. Finally, the Commission seems to have promised to consider a dispute with the UK over grants for retraining workers.

33. *The Guardian*, 30 Mar. 1994.

34. Diary Readings with Douglas Hurd, Westwell, 13 Jun. 1997.

35. Interview with Douglas Hurd, Westwell, 13 Jun. 1997.

36. H. of C. Deb. (6th Series), 29 Mar. 1994, vol. 240, col. 802.

37. *The Independent*, 29 Mar. 1994.

38. *The Times*, 30 Mar. 1996.

39. Interview with Douglas Hurd, Westwell, 13 Jun. 1997.

40. Interview with Kenneth Clarke, 16 Dec. 1996.

41. Interview with Douglas Hurd, Westwell, 13 Jun. 1997.

42. Interview with Kenneth Clarke, 16 Dec. 1996.

43. Interview with Douglas Hurd, Westwell, 13 Jun. 1997.

44. Interview with Kenneth Clarke, 16 Dec. 1996.

45. *The Guardian*, 14 Apr. 1994.

46. Quoted from David Butler & Martin Westlake, *British Politics and European Elections 1994* (Macmillan Press: London, 1995), p. 65.

47. Ibid., p. 100.

48. *The Times*, 29 Apr. 1994.

49. Diary Readings with Douglas Hurd, Westwell, 13 Jun. 1997.

50. *The Independent*, 6 May 1994.

51. *The Independent*, 12 May 1994.

52. *Evening Standard*, 11 May 1994; Hurd's comments made the lead headline of the newspaper.

53. Douglas Hurd, 'Towards a Europe fit for a free Britain', *Sunday Telegraph*, 5 Jun. 1994.

54. *See* Butler & Westlake, *British Politics and European Elections 1994*, pp. 178–9.

55. Donald McIntyre, 'Hurd in his element in marginal pasturelands', *The Independent*, 2 Jun. 1994.

56. Interview with Douglas Hurd, Westwell, 13 Jun. 1997.

57. Ibid.

58. Ibid.

59. (30 Jun. 1994) Diary Readings with Douglas Hurd, Westwell, 13 Jun. 1997.

60. John Palmer, 'The Battle of Brittan', *The Guardian*, 31 Oct. 1994.

61. In September 1994, Douglas Hurd had followed the bipartisan convention of selecting one Commissioner from Her Majesty's Opposition. Neil Kinnock was selected on the retirement of Bruce Millan. There were some rumblings on the Tory backbenches at the decision, but it did not amount to more than background noise. Kinnock's new portfolio covered transport and competition policy.

62. *The Guardian*, 12 Oct. 1994.

63. Other backers of ACE included David Hunt, Leon Brittan and Tim Renton.

64. Interview with Kenneth Clarke, 16 Dec. 1996; Cicero may also have used the phrase when he was being hounded by the Senate.

65. H. of C. Deb. (6th Series), 28 Nov. 1994, vol. 250, col. 396.

66. Norman Lamont's tax-raising budget of 1993 introduced a starting rate for VAT on fuel of 8 per cent, but in the manner of another ticking time bomb, he laid plans for a second stage increase to 15 per cent. Lamont's forced resignation in June 1993 meant that his successor, Kenneth Clarke, was left to attempt to implement the second stage of the increase.

67. On 28 November 1994, Labour's reasoned amendment on the European Communties (Finance) Bill was defeated by 330 votes to 303, with 7 Conservatives abstaining. The Bill was then given a Second Reading by 329 votes to 44 with 1 Conservative abstaining.

68. The eight Conservative rebels who lost the whip were Teresa Gorman (Billericay), Michael Cartiss (Great Yarmouth), Tony Marlow (Northampton, North), Sir Teddy Taylor (Southend, East), Nicholas Budgen (Wolverhampton, South West), Christopher Gill (Ludlow), Richard Shepherd (Aldridge-Brownhills) and John Wilkinson (Ruislip, Northwood).

69. A Labour amendment to force reconsideration of the second increase in VAT was carried by 319 votes to 311. Seven Conservatives (including three whipless rebels) voted against the Government, and a further eight (including five without the whip) abstained. The Government was forced to accept the defeat and cancelled the VAT increase. I am indebted to Professor Philip Norton and Philip Cowley at the University of Hull for this information.

70. Philip Cowley and Philip Norton, 'Are Conservative MPs Revolting? Dissension by Government MPs in The British House of Commons, *1979–96*', Centre for Legislative Studies, [University of Hull] Research Paper, Feb. 1996.

21

Increasing our Weight: Britain in the World

The end of the Cold War heralded a period of uncertainty among British foreign policy opinion formers about Britain's future role in the world. From about 1990 onwards, there was an intense period of rethinking by academics and Government officials alike as they attempted to assess how best Britain should redefine its foreign policy goals in the changed international environment. Would Britain be able to retain her permanent seat on the United Nations Security Council? How would Britain's relationship with the United States be affected by the progressive withdrawal of American troops from Central Europe? To what extent did this mean Britain had to look at new ways of strengthening European Defence? In the future, would Britain's civilian overseas effort have a greater role to play than her military?

Douglas Hurd always disliked George Bush's phrase about a 'New World Order' in the wake of the Gulf War, believing it raised false expectations about the capacity of world institutions to deal with the new types of disorder. In Hurd's view, the Gulf War had been a relatively straightforward case of one state invading another, involving the enforcement of the principle of collective security by the United Nations, but it was atypical: many of the post-Cold War conflicts were civil wars within the boundaries of states, where the UN mandate was blurred, where it was more difficult to separate good from evil and define objectives. On 27 January 1993, in a speech to the Royal Institute of International Affairs at Chatham House, Hurd spoke instead of 'The New Disorder'. Given Britain's limited resources, a balance had to be achieved between intervening whenever there was a tragedy and failing to intervene because Britain's vital national interests were not directly affected. A month later, this approach was summed up in Hurd's pithy comment that British

391

foreign policy should fall 'somewhere between Gladstone and the saloon bar'.[1] Britain's role as a free-trading nation required that she should prevent chaos which disrupted trade, and make a contribution to 'a safer and more decent world'. However, he identified a new difficulty that such tragedies were now visible to the people of the world as a result of the hand-held video cameras of the BBC and CNN. There was a new immediacy about the reporting, and a greater pressure to act:

> The air is full of the eloquence of many Gladstones. Each new tragedy as it
> is revealed brings its Midlothian campaign.[2]

The comment attracted criticism from *The Times*, whose lead article accused the Foreign Secretary of making 'his somewhat dismissive reference to the nuisance value of public outrage at human misery'.[3] But the remark reflected Hurd's real fear that the demands on Britain's armed forces and resources – for example in Bosnia – meant that they risked being overstretched. Hurd was concerned at the Gladstonian streak in America, which condemned the atrocities in Bosnia, but was not willing to put troops on the ground. The new Clinton administration took time to come to terms with what Hurd knew from an early stage, that for the foreseeable future any major international intervention 'will continue to need American support and probably American participation'.[4]

On 27 May 1993, in another speech to the RIIA at Chatham House, Hurd claimed that British embassies and diplomats played a crucial role in promoting British exports:

> In many markets, political and commercial work are intertwined. You do not
> get the contract unless you have mastered the politics and cultivated the
> politicians. You do not do that by fax machines.[5]

During his last two years as Foreign Secretary, Hurd made a determined effort to use the Diplomatic Service as a vehicle for promoting British exports. At Civil Service level, Foreign Office officials were increasingly seconded to work in industry and took unpaid, non-executive directorships in British arms companies such as Vickers and British Aerospace. This policy carried with it the risk of accusations of promoting the arms trade at the expense of human rights. In particular, the journalist John Pilger mounted a relentless campaign of invective and criticism of Douglas Hurd for authorising arms sales to Indonesia, which Pilger alleged were subsequently used against demonstrators in East Timor.[6] It was a difficult balance to strike between the Foreign Office being seen as a stuffy institution, whose officials turned their noses up at business interests, and being accused of supplying arms to unsavoury dictatorships.

While Michael Heseltine, President of the Board of Trade, was by far the most prolific in promoting British exports, during 1994 and 1995 Douglas Hurd stepped up his own department's export-promotion drive. In April 1994, for example, he was accompanied by six British businessmen on a visit to Brazil. The completion of the Uruguay Round of GATT opened up new areas of opportunity for British exporters, such as in Latin America. Hurd's Minister of State, David Heathcoat-Amory, was responsible for bolstering Britain's relations with Latin America.

The key to improving relations with Argentina lay in setting aside the issue of the sovereignty of the Falkland Islands. The two sides agreed to differ, although the Argentinians did stir the waters at one point by offering to buy sovereignty rights from the islanders for a million pounds each. Discussions centred on fishing rights and oil exploration off the Falklands, and improving trading opportunities. In January 1993, Hurd became the first British Foreign Secretary to visit Argentina since the Falklands War. Relations between the two countries were kept in good repair by the British Ambassador, Humphrey Maud, who was on good terms with the Argentinian president, Carlos Menem. Hurd also got on well with his opposite number, Guido Di Tella, a dissident intellectual hailing from the days when Argentina was ruled by the generals. The Argentinian Foreign Minister had lunched in Westwell with Hurd's friends and neighbours across the duck pond, the Gibsons. Mrs Gibson, a leading Bond Street art dealer, owned an *estançia* in Argentina, and, during Hurd's January 1993 visit, he enjoyed two rare nights in a remote location away from the ministerial boxes. He relaxed by going horse-riding for the first time in years and also attended a huge Argentinian barbecue. But the main aim of the trip was to boost British exports.[7]

In September 1994, Hurd embarked on a four-country Asian trade tour. At his first port of call, Thailand, he was accompanied by an entourage of chief executives from British companies eager to win defence, telecommunication and engineering contracts away from Japan (until then the dominant player in Thailand). British exporters had been slow off the mark, but Hurd's visit reflected an impressive growth in trade between Britain and Thailand in recent years.[8] Hurd then flew to the Vietnamese capital, Hanoi, the first visit by a British Foreign Secretary since the end of the Vietnam War. Hurd was anxious to use the restoration of diplomatic ties with Vietnam, made possible by the belated shift in American policy towards Hanoi, as a bridgehead from which to increase British exports. In Japan, Hurd spoke out against protectionism after a meeting with the Japanese Prime Minister, Tomiichi Murayama. His comments reflected the frustration of other countries at Japan's reluctance to open its own domestic market to free trade.

It is clear that Hurd, the free trader, enjoyed these business-orientated trips, even if the image of a sharp-suited businessman did not quite fit his tweedy appearance. However, there was another reason behind Hurd's attempts to highlight the growing commercial role of the Foreign Office. From 1993 onwards, both the Foreign Office's budget and its methods of working came under the intense scrutiny of the Treasury in the shape of the Chancellor of the Exchequer, Kenneth Clarke, and his Chief Secretary, Jonathan Aitken (and later William Waldegrave). Ken Clarke was a firm ally, indeed firm fan of Douglas Hurd. They shared similar views on Europe. But while Clarke has certain liberal views – he is opposed to capital punishment for instance – he is not a limousine liberal in the same way as Douglas Hurd. Clarke is a radical when it comes to shaking up restrictive practices or cosy entrenched interests. His record as Minister of Health in pushing through the internal market, his reputation at Education, and his ill-fated shake-up of police pay and conditions in the Sheehy proposals as Home Secretary showed where his instincts lay. Clarke was unwilling to allow the Foreign Office to escape the rigours of market testing, performance-related pay, executive agencies and budget constraints. In contrast, while Douglas Hurd has shown a willingness to engage in cautious reform, deep down he is a defender of the notion of public service, a protector of professionals, whether they be his teachers in Oxfordshire or Foreign Office officials.

Hurd was concerned that talk of Treasury cuts would undermine morale in the Diplomatic Service. On 24 January 1994, he took the unusual step of addressing a meeting of his department's entire London-based staff to try to reassure them about the future of the pay, conditions and redundancies. The meeting took place in the grand surroundings of the Durbar Court, designed by Matthew Digby Wyatt, architect of the interior of the old India Office adjoining the Foreign Office. Like a headmaster at the end of term, Hurd addressed his pupils on the future challenges of the school, admitting that there would have to be an element of market testing and a ban on overtime for grades of first secretary and above. Behind the scenes, however, Hurd mounted a series of defensive manoeuvres against the Treasury which left Kenneth Clarke exasperated.

Similarly, Hurd's decision to allow BBC cameras into the Foreign Office during 1992 was not just another paragraph in the essay in openness by the Foreign Secretary, but also an attempt to justify the cost of the Foreign Office's relatively modest budget to the Treasury. The True Brits series broadcast on BBC2 during April and May 1994 trumpeted the work of the Foreign Office, stressing that its entire running costs were a modest £1.36 billion compared with £23 billion for Defence and £80 billion for the Department of Social Security.

In his bilateral meetings with Kenneth Clarke over the annual public expenditure round, Hurd also successfully resisted Clarke's attempts to subject the Foreign Office to a fundamental expenditure review. Clarke recalls:

> He [Hurd] was brilliant at defending his office. He could beat off the Treasury. It was all Douglas Hurd, the grand Foreign Secretary, not quite understanding the figures. Normally with colleagues I had great arguments in detail about how much we were spending on x and y . . . Douglas wouldn't get into any detail at all. It was a broad brush thing about diplomatic effort, comparisons with the Germans, our role in the world, strengthening trade.'

Hurd's tactic reminded Ken Clarke of William Whitelaw's entirely bogus act of not quite understanding the figures at the Home Office as a ruse to defend his departmental budget:

> In fact, Douglas has one of the sharpest minds in politics and he knew perfectly well that he was keeping his outfit completely intact: with morale high in the Service, able to bring back the groceries and his Foreign Office exactly as he intended. It was a very class act, Douglas seeing off management efficiency experts at the Treasury.[10]

William Waldegrave, Chief Secretary to the Treasury, has a similar recollection:

> The Treasury reckoned he [Hurd] was worth a good £100m a year to the Foreign Office . . . He was much too subtle to engage in the argument about figures. He argued at a different level, leaving Treasury ministers bemused.[11]

Hurd felt very strongly that in the new post-Cold War environment, Britain needed to reassess its assets, identifying those areas where she could steadily increase her influence in the world. A series of ministerial and Whitehall meetings followed which culminated in a Chequers strategy meeting in January 1995.[12]

Despite the *Options for Change* Defence Review in 1990, there had not been a dramatic peace dividend after the end of the Cold War. The Gulf War intervened, leading to a reprieve for some of the regiments destined to be disbanded or amalgamated. Even the implementation of modest cuts raised the ire of the defence chiefs and voters in several key marginal Conservative seats. Given these sensitivities, at the beginning of 1995, Hurd was willing to accept the view of John Major and Malcolm Rifkind that there should not be another immediate Defence Review. However, the Foreign Secretary increasingly took the view that there should be an enhancement of the civilian side of Britain's overseas effort – the cultural and educational aspects such as the British Council, the BBC World Service, the various Scholarship schemes, trade promotion, development policy – encapsulated in the term 'preventive diplomacy' and, on 13 January at Chequers, he secured an agreement in principle to this effect. No specific sum of money was agreed, but it was decided that this enhancement policy should be taken into account in the forthcoming public-expenditure discussions. The deal which Hurd secured appeared in the minutes of the meeting, specifically in the Prime Minister's summing up. According to Hurd, the Treasury then challenged the minutes, but the Prime Minister sustained them. Hurd believes that in thirty years' time, the public records will show that he had secured an enhancement of the overseas civilian effort of the Foreign Office.[13] And yet, after Hurd retired, the agreement did not operate. Under intense public expenditure constraints, the budget was actually squeezed during Malcolm Rifkind's tenure as Foreign Secretary.

Two years later, as a postscript to this episode, Hurd wrote a letter to the Editor of *The Times*, responding to the news that the new Labour Government was to launch a fresh Defence Review. He stressed that the defence effort was only one element of Britain's overseas effort:

> Politics, trade and security are nowadays closely intertwined. So therefore should be the defence budget and our budgets for diplomacy, aid, trade promotion, the British Council and the BBC. The cost of these civilian components is tiny compared to the military. Maybe the balance should shift in their favour. There was a case against a further review which, as Foreign Secretary, I reluctantly accepted. But now there is to be a review it should encompass the whole of our overseas effort, not just part.[14]

Whilst still in office, Hurd seized the opportunity provided by the forthcoming seventy-fifth Anniversary of the Royal Insititute of International Affairs at Chatham House to launch a Britain in the World Conference. The one-day conference was held at the Queen Elizabeth II Conference Centre on 29 March 1995. Around 700 opinion-formers – dignitaries, academics, businessman, statesmen, Labour politicians, and high-profile British celebrities – met to identify more clearly what Britain was good at in the post-Cold War world, and how it could do those things better.

There may have been an element of Hurd looking to his retirement, seeing the Conference as his parting shot. At the same time, it provided another occasion to extol the great work of the Foreign Office, thereby warding off the vultures at the Treasury. But, Hurd's main reason for holding the conference was to try to shift the debate in Britain beyond that of Europe. Europe was important, but it was not the only area of the world where British interests lay. Post-Maastricht, it was time to lift the Government's horizons a good deal further afield.

The Foreign Secretary signalled the new line in his speech during the Debate on the Address on 17 November 1994, claiming 'we are a European power with interests that reach far beyond Europe.'[15] In that narrow sense, the move was party political, designed to shift the debate away from the Conservative Party's squabbles, but in no sense was it intended as an exercise in Tory triumphalism. The guest list reflected a wide range of opinion: the Conference was chaired in an unfussy manner by James Naughtie, the *Today* programme presenter on Radio Four; the Shadow Foreign Secretary, Robin Cook, was invited; and the inclusion of the ever-acerbic Denis Healey on the guest list ensured that a mood of self-congratulation would not be allowed to prevail.

Nevertheless, Hurd did want the Conference to counter the mood of pessimism and cynicism which appeared to have gripped Britain in the previous few years. It manifested itself in persistently low consumer confidence after a long economic recession, a loss in confidence in the authority of John Major's government after Black Wednesday, a widespread public hostility to politicians of all parties for engaging in adversarial politics and being exposed as hypocrites over sleaze (both financial and sexual) and a general tendency in the press to run down British institutions, such as the monarchy. Both Douglas Hurd and Michael Portillo, from opposite ends of the political spectrum, had given speeches in the previous year, remarking on this tendency to denigrate Britain's cherished institutions.[16] Two weeks before the Conference, Hurd was in Abu Dhabi addressing a meeting of 250 British businessmen who were operating in the Gulf region. During a question and answer session with the businessmen, Hurd claimed that the question from the floor which raised the loudest applause was when one man asked why the British Government was allowing such a negative image of Britain to be portrayed in the media.[17]

In their speeches at the Conference, the Prime Minister, Prince Charles, and Douglas Hurd, all latched onto this theme of national cynicism. Opening the conference, John Major claimed that Britain had focused too narrowly on Europe, and needed to look to the wider world, avoiding what he termed the 'fashionable sniping' at home. He attempted to link the values he admired in Britain – such as the monarchy, parliamentary government, professional armed forces, and the independent judiciary – to success abroad. In the lunchtime session, the Prince of Wales spoke out against 'an approach to life which appears to seek only to denigrate, to decry and to destroy.'[18] Douglas Hurd wanted to see talented people in Britain engaging less in cynicism, and more in constructive activities which would increase Britain's influence in the world. Britain, he said, needed 'to rediscover our self-knowledge and self-confidence'.[19] Of the political columnists, only Andrew Marr picked up the undercurrent of frustration on the part of the governing élite at the prevailing national cynicism.[20] The problem, Marr argued, was that it was the Government and the heads of British institutions themselves – including Prince Charles – which had let the British people down. The subtext was that only by conducting a purge of the existing élite through a wholesale modernisation of the British state (implying a change of government) could the national mood be lifted. That was in fact what happened two years later on the election of a Labour Government. The capacity of the Conservative Government to decide Britain's role in the post-Cold war world had been thwarted by the national humiliation of Black Wednesday. Meanwhile, a left-of-centre political class, which had been denied access to power for a generation, spent its time attacking the prevailing orthodoxy and institutions.

Hurd correctly identified many of these trends: the impatience of the electorate with adversarial politics, the tendency to destroy rather than to do, the need to reassess Britain's post-Cold War priorities – but he was a leading member of a Government which had long since lost authority at home or abroad because of its internal squabbles over Europe, and which was unable to get Britain out of a psychological rut.

While the main purpose behind the Conference was to move the debate away from Europe, at every turn the shrewder speakers harked back to the dangers of Britain failing to play an active part in the European Union. As Hugo Young wrote, the Conference tried to keep Europe off the agenda, 'but could not resist its seepage in every pore'.[21] The message was clear in the *Financial Times* leader the following day:

> If Britain cannot resolve its relationship with its European partners, then it
> is unlikely to have clarity in its relations with the rest of the world.[22]

The whole show was stolen by Dr Henry Kissinger, the former US Secretary of State, who gave a *tour-de-force* lecture concentrating not on Britain's role in the world, but on his vision of America's future relationship with Europe. It took a master of the school of *realpolitik* to spell out the stark reality that Britain's place in the world was relatively insignificant compared to the United States. He put it kindly: Britain had skilfully managed 'the transition from power to influence'.[23] There were, he said, two approaches to European/American relations. The Gaullist model which emphasised central European stability, and the British model which stressed co-operation with the United States. Cheekily, he claimed the special relationship 'was not particularly special in my day. The British role did not depend on the weight it could throw around, but the British made themselves extremely useful.'[24] He said Britain's mistake was not to have entered Europe from the beginning. He wanted Britain to be engaged in Europe but he was against a 'Maastricht-style' bureaucratic Europe which attempted to link Poland with Portugal. What he wanted to avoid was Gaullist policies pursued with British methods. 'That would be a lethal combination,'[25] he said. America should not shift its focus from Britain to Germany, as some Americans were arguing, but Britain's special relationship with America should be transferred to the whole of Europe, with Britain acting as an oiler in the wheels of US-European relations.

In the defence session of the Conference, Britain's role as a major contributor to international peacekeeping was stressed by both the Chief of the Defence Staff, Sir Peter Inge, and by former commander of United Nations forces in Bosnia, Lieutenant General Sir Michael Rose. However, Sir Peter Inge expressed concern that the new emphasis on low-intensity peace-keeping might leave the British armed forces ill-equipped to fight a major war. Sir Michael Rose highlighted the lessons to be learned from previous peacekeeping failures, saying the UN might need to delegate future peacekeeping operations to regional power groupings, such as NATO. Sir Michael's ideas clearly struck a chord with Douglas Hurd. Both wished to place much more emphasis on defining and strengthening rules of engagement and placing greater stress on intervening at an earlier stage in conflicts.

Perhaps the most interesting session of the Conference, which had been divided into four sessions, was the one entitled 'Projecting British values, education and culture.'[26] Hurd's speech earlier in the day had praised this 'cultural diplomacy', highlighting the work of the British Council, the Open University, the various scholarship funds and the BBC World Service, claiming that 'the BBC is the most recognised brand name in the world – after Coca Cola.'[27] The point being made was that the English language was a huge asset which Britain should exploit to the full. Sir David Puttnam, the veteran film-maker, put it succinctly by saying Britain should become the 'university of the world'.[28] One of the statistics constantly bandied about at the time was that Britain's music industry earned more than its steel industry. Perhaps there was not enough emphasis on music, fashion and sport at the Conference – 'Cool Britannia' had yet to pollute British foreign policy.

The Conference succeeded in achieving one of Hurd's objectives: it stimulated a national debate on Britain's future role in the world. A flurry of press articles by academics and political columnists heralded the run-up to the Conference.[29] However, with the benefit of hindsight, Hurd's own view is that while the Conference itself had been a success – the guest list had been impressive and there was a generally favourable reaction in the press – it rather sputtered out after one day:

> Somehow, we should have found a way of keeping that going. Instead of one conference, maybe we should have had them all over the country. I don't know. It was one of those things which was a good breakthrough opening offensive, but not sustained. So people went back to thinking – because we were squabbling about Europe – that was the only thing we were interested in.[30]

Notes

1. H. of C. Deb. (6th Series), 23 Feb. 1993, vol. 219, col. 774.

2. Douglas Hurd, 'The New Disorder', Speech to RIIA, 27 Jan. 1993.

3. Editorial, 'Hurd's Troubled World', *The Times*, 29 Jan. 1993.

4. Douglas Hurd, 'The New Disorder'.

5. *The Times*, 28 May 1993.

6. *See* for example, John Pilger, 'A Class Act to Follow', *New Statesman and Society*, 30 Jun. 1995.

7. Between 1991 and 1995, British exports to Argentina rose by 165 per cent per annum. H. of C. Deb. (6th Series), 3 Jul. 1995, vol. 263, Part I, col. 366.

8. *Financial Times*, 14 Sept. 1994.

9. Interview with Kenneth Clarke, 16 Dec. 1996.

10. Ibid.

11. Interview with William Waldegrave, 17 Dec. 1996.

12. The attendance list for the meeting at Chequers on 13 January comprised Michael Heseltine (Trade and Industry), Kenneth Clarke (Chancellor), Malcolm Rifkind (Defence) William Waldegrave (Chief Secretary to the Treasury), David Hunt (Cabinet policy co-ordination), Field Marshall Sir Peter Inge (Chief of Defence Staff) Richard Needham (Trade Minister) and Baroness Chalker of Wallasey (Minister for Overseas Development).

13. Interview with Douglas Hurd, Westwell, 13 Jun. 1997.

14. Douglas Hurd, 'Letter to the Editor', *The Times*, 31 May 1997.

15. H. of C. Deb. (6th Series), 17 Nov. 1994, vol. 250, col. 145.

16. Douglas Hurd, Speech to Scottish Conservatives, Perth, 4 Nov. 1994; Douglas Hurd, Speech to Oxford Brookes University, 12 Mar. 1993; for Michael Portillo speech, *see The Times*, 15 Jan. 1994.

17. Douglas Hurd, *Newsnight*, BBC 2, 29 Mar. 1995.

18. *The Times*, 30 Mar. 1995.

19. Ibid.

20. Andrew Marr, 'The end of our decline? We shall see', *The Independent*, 30 Mar. 1995.

21. Hugo Young, 'There is a role elsewhere – but not without Europe', *The Guardian*, 30 Mar. 1995.

22. Leader, *Financial Times*, 30 Mar. 1995.

23. Henry Kissinger, 'America's New Special Relationship', *The Times*, 30 Mar. 1995 (an extract of Dr Kissinger's speech to the Britain in the World Conference).

24. Ibid.

25. Ibid.

26. The first three sessions at the conference covered diplomacy and security; trade and economics; and development.

27. *The Times*, 30 Mar. 1995.

28. Ibid.

29. *See* Vincent Cable [Fellow of RIIA], 'Wake up Britain: Europe's not the world', *The Independent*, 27 Mar. 1995; Ian Davidson, 'A Place in the World', *Financial Times*, 29 Mar. 1995; Simon Jenkins, 'Selling Britain Abroad', *The Times*, 29 Mar. 1995; Ian Black, 'Do we Know our Place?', *The Guardian*, 25 Mar. 1995; Richard Dowden & Stephen Castle, 'Who are we in the world?', *The Independent on Sunday*, 26 Mar. 1995.

30. Interview with Douglas Hurd, 13 Jun. 1997.

22

Away from those 'Dam' Headlines: British Development Policy, 1989–1995

Any assessment of Douglas Hurd's contribution to Britain's overseas development policy will always be coloured by his handling of the Pergau Dam affair. The issue was a hangover from Mrs Thatcher's enthusiastic pursuit of arms sales in the Third World in the 1980s rather than a reflection of the Overseas Development Agency's policies in the 1990s. Away from the headlines, Britain shifted from multilateral to bilateral aid, tying aid to good governance. There was a serious attempt, albeit unsuccessful, to revive the Commonwealth, which had been dominated for the previous thirty years by rows over apartheid. In Central and Eastern Europe, and in the new Russian republics, there was an attempt to use British 'know-how' in the drive to promote economic liberalism and stable democracies. In the Third World, Hurd would visit impressive examples of British development policy in action – projects which were a world away from a certain dam being built in Malaysia.

The roots of the Pergau Dam affair date back to a deal secured in September 1988 between the British and Malaysian Governments in which Malaysia agreed to purchase £1.3 billion of defence equipment in return for £234 million of aid to construct a hydroelectric power station in Pergau, northern Malaysia. Concerns were expressed in a series of questions to ministers by Ann Clwyd, Labour's overseas aid spokesperson, as a result of investigations by *The Guardian* newspaper.

It was not until the National Audit Office (NAO) reported on 22 October 1993 as a result of its own impartial investigation that the issue made the headlines. The NAO report concluded that the British taxpayer had paid £56 million more than was necessary for the dam project.[1] The NAO's findings led first to an inquiry by the Public Accounts Committee, and then to an investigation by the Foreign Affairs Select Committee, who looked into the separate issue of whether there had been a linkage between arms and aid.

Meanwhile, the *Sunday Times* newspaper ran a highly damaging campaign against the Malaysian Government, alleging that bribes had been offered to the Malaysian Prime Minister, Dr Mahathir Mohamed, by British contractors for the dam. These allegations had serious trade implications for Britain, as Dr Mahathir announced a ban on British Government contracts in February 1994. Hurd then faced calls for his resignation in November 1994, when the High Court found him guilty of breaching the Government's own guidelines on the use of aid money.

The 1988 deal with the Malaysians had involved a series of payments for the dam project, with the first instalment due in July 1991. Doubts began to grow inside Whitehall as to the project's viability, and in October 1990 a joint team from the Department of Trade and Industry and the ODA concluded that the Pergau dam would not be an economic proposition until 2005 at the earliest.[2] Then, in February 1991, Hurd took the unusual step of overruling the advice of one of his senior civil servants, Sir Timothy Lankester, then the Permanent Secretary at the Overseas Development Agency, and its Chief Accounting Officer, who sent a memorandum to ministers advising against the project because 'it would not be consistent with policy statements by ministers to Parliament about the basic objectives of the aid programme.'[3] Sir Tim later described the dam project as 'a very bad buy and a burden on Malaysian consumers' in his evidence to the Public Accounts Committee, the parliamentary arm of the NAO. Hurd also overrode the objections of his Minister for Overseas Development, Lynda Chalker, who shared Tim Lankester's scepticism about the project:

> I went through all the papers and I was absolutely convinced it was not the right economic solution for Malaysia. They would have been far better to have gone for combined cycle power generation.[4]

Also, had Baroness Chalker thought there was the slightest chance of a project being carried out commercially, she would have 'pressed for a commercial solution, not using taxpayer's money,'[5] and she was advised by her Permanent Secretary that the project was outside the proper use of aid funds. Hurd and Chalker agreed to differ and their differences would not have been made public had it not been for the Select Committee investigation.

Clearly, this was not some decision that appeared on a hard-pressed Minister's desk in the small hours of the morning, signed without full knowledge of the facts. It was revealed that this was the only time since the Conservatives came to power in 1979 that a Foreign Secretary had overruled an aid decision.[6] Hurd even consulted Charles Powell, the Prime Minister's Private Secretary, who referred the matter to John Major. The Prime Minister agreed that Hurd should carry out the undertaking given by Mrs Thatcher to fund the dam project. The Foreign Secretary then issued a written ministerial instruction to Tim Lankester to make the first payment.

All of Hurd's actions flowed from the central fact that he was honouring a promise given by the previous Prime Minister and to have reneged on that agreement would, he believed, have been damaging to Britain's trading relationship with Malaysia, which had already suffered in the early 1980s when Dr Mahathir launched his 'Buy Britain Last' campaign (after Britain introduced higher university fees for Commonwealth students studying in British universities). A British construction firm, Balfour Beatty and Cementation International, won the contract to build the £400 million dam project, £234 million of which was to be paid for out of the ATP (Aid and Trade Provisions) component of the ODA budget. Alan Clark, who had been Mrs Thatcher's top arms salesman as Minister for Defence Procurement, believed that breaking the agreement would 'have an adverse impact on UK relations with Malaysia in general and on the defence relationship in particular'.[7] That meant arms sales.

Of course, Hurd knew in 1991 that Britain had important defence contracts with Malaysia and, in a broad sense, breaking an agreement might damage those defence interests. However, there is a difference between knowing that the arms trade with Malaysia was in the national interest and knowing that the arms deal and the aid deal had become entangled. In making his decision whether to authorise the first payment due for July 1991, Hurd did not consult the papers relating to the 1988 deal, because he simply did not know at the time that the arms deal and the aid deal had become entangled. There are only two question marks which remain over Hurd's judgement. First, should he have overruled the clear advice of his Accounting Officer and his Minister of State – the two people most closely connected with the issue – that the project was an inefficient use of the Aid and Trade Provision (ATP)? On this point, Hurd has made his case that he was honouring a commitment given by Mrs Thatcher. The High Court did not find him guilty on this first point, they simply found him guilty of authorising a use of the aid budget which fell outwith the stated objectives of the ATP.

This leads to the second question: did Hurd know in February 1991 that his actions might fall outwith the scope of the Government's own stated guidelines and if so, should he have sought more detailed legal advice? After being found guilty by the High Court on 10 November 1994, Hurd told Channel Four News that 'the question of whether it was lawful or not was simply not raised at that time.'[8] However, the sentence in Tim Lankester's memo to ministers clearly indicates that 'it would not be consistent with policy statements by ministers to Parliament about the basic objectives of the aid programme.'[9] In effect, the High Court judgement sustained this view. Barry Ireton, the ODA's principal finance officer, also questioned whether the project was within the provisions of the aid budget. In a matter of this importance, there is a strong case for saying that it may have been sage for Hurd to have taken more detailed legal advice.

The main controversy concerning the linkage of arms to aid had very little to do with Douglas Hurd. Hurd only consulted the papers relating to the 1988 deal when he was asked to appear before the Foreign Affairs Select Committee in March 1994. It was George Younger, Mrs Thatcher's Defence Secretary, who signed a defence protocol with the Malaysians in March 1988 mentioning 'aid in support of non-military aspects under this programme'.[10] In his evidence to the Foreign Affairs Select Committee on 2 March, Hurd indirectly blamed George Younger, saying the linkage had been 'irregular and incorrect'.[11] According to Hurd, there had been 'much animated discussion' on Younger's return from Malaysia, and Geoffrey Howe (the then Foreign Secretary) attempted to break the linkage between arms and aid. On 28 June 1988, George Younger wrote back to the Malaysian Minister of Finance, explaining that aid could not be linked to defence sales. Hurd therefore claimed that the final defence agreement signed in September 1988 contained no linkage between arms and aid:

> There was a temporary incorrect entanglement – incorrect in the sense that
> it ran against British policy. There is now no link. Each part of our policies
> has proceeded without being conditional on the other.[12]

Two pieces of evidence appear to contradict Hurd's view that the two policies ran separately. A Foreign Office paper attached to his own memorandum to the Foreign Affairs Select Committee reveals that Mrs Thatcher wrote to Dr Mahathir on 8 August 1988, a month before the final agreement, confirming that civil aid projects would continue. Two months earlier, the British High Commissioner in Kuala Lumpur, Sir Nicholas Spreckley, gave assurances that the letter from George Younger of 28 June 1988 was merely a technical restatement of the original formula contained in protocol which George Younger signed in March 1988. But, it is possible to see why ODA officials did not present Hurd with the 1988 papers when he was making his decision to authorise payments for the dam. Whitehall in effect said that, because the linkage had been severed on paper, no such link existed.

While the British Government may have been able to de-link arms sales from its aid programme, it was required by law to adhere to Section 1 (1) of the

1980 Overseas Development and Co-operation Act which states that the Foreign Secretary can authorise aid 'for the purpose of promoting the development or maintaining the economy of a country or territory outside the United Kingdom, or the welfare of its people, to furnish any person or body with assistance, whether financial, technical or of any other nature.'[13] The World Development Movement (WDM), a London-based organisation representing aid charities such as Oxfam, Christian Aid and various churches and trade union groups, took the Foreign Secretary to court on their narrow interpretation of what, it has to be said, was a very broadly defined Act. A judicial review was granted by Mr Justice Auld in June 1994, and the case came before the High Court on 9 November 1994. It was an uncomfortable time for Douglas Hurd in the British press. The WDM ran advertisements in the national press, carrying a picture of Douglas Hurd, with the unsavoury label, 'The accused'.[14]

In the High Court, Nigel Fleming, QC, the London law firm acting on behalf of the WDM, argued that Hurd had overstepped his powers by acting outwith the terms of the 1980 Act. Stephen Richards, counsel for Douglas Hurd, claimed that the Foreign Secretary had acted upon 'wider considerations', and that projects requiring aid could not be judged as 'economically unsound' because by their very nature they require funds which are not otherwise available in the market place. Lord Justice Rose (presiding) ruled that 'wider considerations' were not germane to the case, and that the first payment of £29.6 million in July 1991 was 'fatally flawed' because there were no economic arguments in favour of it, adding:

> It seems to me if Parliament intended to confer payments for unsound development purposes it could have been expected to say so expressly.[15]

The court judgement confirmed strict parameters for the future provision of British aid; ministers had to abide by their own guidelines. It was also another example of the rise of judicial review cases where the decisions of ministers and government departments are subject to the scrutiny of the courts. It was coincidental, but indicative of the new trend, that the day before the High Court found Hurd guilty, it had ruled against the Home Secretary, Michael Howard, who was found to have acted unlawfully in introducing a new compensation scheme for victims of violent crime.

In the immediate aftermath of the High Court judgement, Hurd faced calls to resign. Robin Cook, Labour's combative new Shadow Foreign Secretary, called the judgement 'a political blow to the government and a personal humiliation to Mr Hurd'.[16] In retrospect, Hurd describes the Pergau affair as 'a fairish nightmare'.[17] The day after the High Court ruling, the Foreign Secretary revealed on BBC Radio Four that he had contemplated resignation. His attitude to crises is calmly to examine what can be achieved and to set about devising a compromise. However, this was the very criticism levelled at him by those calling on him to resign. Adrian Hamilton, commenting in *The Observer* said:

> Honourable though he undoubtedly is, Hurd has made his entire career out of the proposition of doing the best he possibly can under the given circumstances.[18]

Hamilton argued that a purge was needed of the body politic, along the lines of Peter Carrington's sacrifice after the Falklands War.[19] In fact, Hurd listened to the wise advice of colleagues that this was not an affair which would go on running as a permanent political issue. What was needed was someone with his political skills as a defuser to tidy up the debris.

Hurd acted swiftly by launching a prompt review of all ATP provisions in light of the High Court's judgement. In a statement to the House of Commons on 13 December 1994, he revealed that three more ATP projects were found to have fallen outwith the terms of the 1980 Act.[20]

In such instances, where the Government was shown to have made mistakes, Hurd had the advantage of being markedly more open than most of his Cabinet colleagues in revealing where they had gone wrong. Despite being responsible for several policy errors, none of the opprobrium seemed to stick, and his reputation as 'a safe pair of hands' survived intact. Matthew Parris in *The Times*, again latched onto Hurd's happy knack:

> Could a junior minister handle it? No. An Eton and Oxbridge Christopher Reeve is needed: a blend of Jeeves and Wooster with phenomenal powers of difficulty. Only Super Doug could save the day . . . Super Doug got away with it. Again.[21]

However, on this occasion, Hurd refused to make a public apology over the issue. He announced that future payments for the dam would be made from Treasury reserves, not the Overseas Development budget, in accordance with the High court ruling, but he refused to guarantee that cuts would not be made out of the ODA budget after 1996. He argued that the aid budget, as with all government departments, was subject to a public expenditure review. It was a rather miserly decision, and received an angry response from Sir David Steel, the Liberal Democrat's foreign affairs spokesman:

> What is self-evident to the taxpayer is that this money was misused. The taxpayer believes that the limited budget for overseas aid should be used for the proper purpose, and you should reinstate those funds.[22]

Instead of conceding any further ground, Hurd mounted a spirited defence of the British national interest:

> I do not feel penitent at taking a fairly robust view of where the interests of this country lie.[23]

On 17 November 1994, he told the House: We are not prepared to dull the competitive edge of that part of our industry to satisfy people who are well-meaning but ill-informed; people who have no responsibility for the prosperity of the British people or for our ability to earn our living in the world.[24]

The whole Pergau Dam episode raised again the debate between moralism and *realpolitik* in the conduct of foreign affairs. The Foreign Office has always tried to achieve a balance between maintaining good diplomatic and trade relations and observing moral considerations, but there is an inevitable tendency to tip the scales in the direction of the former.

The Pergau Dam affair did not have a long shelf-life. It caused no lasting damage to the Government, other than perhaps adding to the impression of a Government which was dominated by sleaze. Above all, it was a problem inherited from Mrs Thatcher's administration – just one example of the unravelling of her flawed policies, and the demands party loyalty forced on her former colleagues. She based her assessment of the economic viability of the project on a two-day appraisal by the Overseas Development Agency. From then on, the British share of the project spiralled from £68.25 million to £234 million. The scheme owed much more to the 1950s than the 1980s. The days of large, wasteful projects, such as the Aswan Dam, should have been over. But this was never an issue over British aid, but about securing a lucrative arms contract for Britain. The Foreign Affairs Select Committee Report considered it 'reprehensible for the Ministry of Defence to have prepared for, and conducted, negotiations with another country in 1988 without specific reference to the Foreign and Commonwealth Office.'[25] But George Younger and Margaret Thatcher were not going to let an uneconomic project (which was three times what was needed, destroyed rainforests and actually increased the costs of electricity to Malaysian consumers) stand in the way of an arms deal. Mrs Thatcher could argue quite legitimately that she was reviving Britain's industrial fortunes, but it was left to subsequent ministers to pick up the pieces.[26]

After Mrs Thatcher's departure, there was a growing view inside the Foreign Office, shared by Douglas Hurd and Lynda Chalker, that there needed to be an overhaul of Britain's aid policy towards more clearly defined bilateral aid, tied to good governance and respect for human rights and economic liberalism. The shift of emphasis was heralded in speeches made by Lynda Chalker and Douglas Hurd, both on the same day, 6 June 1990, at a Conference on Africa's economic prospects in the 1990s held in Geneva. Hurd told the Conference:

> Countries tending towards pluralism, public accountability, respect for the
> rule of law, human rights and market principles, should be encouraged.

> Countries who persist with repressive policies, with corrupt management, or
> with wasteful and discredited economic systems should not expect us to
> support their folly with scarce aid.[27]

The speech was subsequently converted into an article in a special edition of
Crossbow, the Bow Group's quarterly magazine, in time for the Conservative
Party Conference of October 1990. The West, Hurd wrote, had emerged from
the 'moral fog' which used to excuse the idea that countries at an early stage
of economic development could not afford the luxury of the political and
economic freedoms enjoyed by the West.

Douglas Hurd and Lynda Chalker hoped to use the Commonwealth as a
vehicle via which Britain could promote these ideas. After years of debates over
apartheid – which had provided a kind of glue, uniting all other states against
Britain – the Commonwealth needed a fresh start, a new *raison d'être*. Hurd was
encouraged by the response of the Commonwealth Heads of Government
Meeting (CHOGM) in Harare in October 1991, but subsequently, turbulent
events in Africa led to Hurd feeling that the idea had not really taken off in the
way that he would have hoped.

There was, however, a great deal more success in the ODA projects in South
Africa, where the British aim was to help manage the transition from the
apartheid system to a stable democratic government. Economic measures
concentrated on privatisation schemes, developing local business skills, training
and encouraging British firms to invest in South Africa.

By 1994, the Government of National Unity had been formed under Nelson
Mandela, allowing Britain to pursue Government-to-Government development
projects, and £100 million of development money was ploughed in over the
next three years. In September 1994, Hurd visited a scheme whereby British
army officers trained black South African troops. Similar schemes operated with
the new black South African police force. Education schemes were established
to improve teacher training, and in rural areas, the British aimed to promote
land redistribution and sustainable use of natural resources through the Land
Reform Pilot Programme (LRPP).[28] Overall, the funding in South Africa placed
most emphasis on demonstration projects to act as models for the rest of the
country.

Lynda Chalker and Douglas Hurd were continually frustrated that these
examples of British success in development projects overseas did not make the

headlines back home. The work of the ODA necessarily ranges from carefully designed projects which promote sustainable development interspersed with the need to respond in an ad hoc way to unexpected disasters and international crises which do make the news headlines, such as those which occurred in Somalia and, later, Rwanda.

In September 1992, during Britain's presidency of the European Community, Hurd visited war-torn Somalia with the Danish Foreign Minister, Uffe Ellemann-Jensen, the Portuguese Foreign Minister's deputy, José Barroso, and a senior EC Commissioner, Hans van den Broek. That night, the troika of ministers travelled from Pretoria to Nairobi. The trip to Nairobi was scheduled to take five hours, but the pilot flew out into the Indian Ocean to allow the foreign ministers an extra hour's sleep. From Nairobi, they decamped onto an RAF Hercules – the VC10 was too cumbersome to land in the Somalian capital, Mogadishu – which performed a very low run to avoid the danger of surface-to-air missiles. The three spent the day amid the harrowing scenes. In the period before American intervention, Mogadishu was without electricity, water or any of the normal features of a stable society. Patches of wasteground were being used as makeshift grave sites for the dead. As the head of the troika, Hurd acted as spokesman, fielding questions from reporters. Afterwards, the ministers flew to Kenya to meet with President arap Moi, before flying back to London via Portugal, having spent three out of four nights in an aeroplane.

Hurd greatly enjoyed visiting British development projects in action. On a visit to Bangladesh in January 1995, he learned that the people of northern Bangladesh did not know that when paddy fields were submerged in water, they could rear fish there at the same time. A British project spent relatively small sums of money making the Bangladeshis aware of this technique. A few days later, Hurd flew to Calcutta where he visited a project where an ODA project helped to pave streets and build drainage systems in a slum in Calcutta. The project was small-scale but Hurd was encouraged: once there had been a hovel; people were now engaging in metal work and embroidery. As in South Africa, one of the concepts behind ODA funding was to set up 'demonstration projects', in the hope of encouraging the host government and other aid donors to follow the example set by the British. Hurd has never been a patriot of the flag-waving kind, but he does believe in people who make an active contribution to the worth of their country. Indeed, Douglas Hurd and Lynda Chalker both share a common belief in the value of ordinary men and women becoming involved in voluntary service at home and abroad.

The harder edge to Hurd's view of foreign aid was his belief that it should be directed to opening up new markets for British companies. One aspect of this enlightened self-interest is the ODA's Know-How Fund (KHF) – Britain's programme of bilateral and technical assistance to the countries of Central and

Eastern Europe and Central Asia. According to the KHF's Annual Report of 1995-96, it aims 'to support their transition to pluralist democracy and a market economy by the timely and flexible provision of British skills in a key range of sectors, and by encouraging British investment in the region.'[29] From its first project in Poland in 1989, the Know-How Fund embraced all twenty-seven countries of Central and Eastern Europe and Central Asia.

At a European level, Hurd wanted to persuade the European Commission to repatriate bilateral aid to member states instead of funding multilateral aid. In a speech to the Overseas Development Institute in London on 15 February 1995, Hurd attacked the EU's 'haphazard' aid programme. There was, he said, a lack of co-ordination between a whole host of EU programmes, run by different parts of the Commission. Multilateral aid now accounted for a quarter of all EU aid and the proportion was set to rise to 40 per cent by 1998. This was leading to a squeeze on bilateral aid. While Hurd conceded that there were advantages in bilateral aid – mobilising finance for large infrastructure projects – Britain needed 'to limit the erosion of our bilateral aid', by making a reduced contribution to the European Development Fund. The move was not intended to cut Britain's aid budget or as an 'attack on Brussels', but merely to stress the need to shift away from aid projects towards those which had demonstration value. Britain wanted to get good value for British expertise. Hurd subsequently wrote to the European Commission President, Jacques Delors, urging him to move towards the new policy, with some success.

Hurd's contribution to overseas aid policy was more high-level than hands-on. His February 1995 speech to the Overseas Development Institute (ODI) was his first on development policy in five years. The jury is still out on the success of the shift from multilateral to bilateral aid. Hurd's hopes to revive the Commonwealth, as he freely admits, have yet to be fulfilled. There is an inevitable tension, as was revealed in Kenya and Nigeria, between preserving good diplomatic relations and promoting trading links, and preaching to countries to improve their human rights record.

The most high-profile aspect of British development policy during Douglas Hurd's tenure as Foreign Secretary, the Pergau Dam affair, was a personal, but temporary blow. The project did not typify Britain's overseas development funding, and belonged more to British policy in the 1980s than the new policies of the 1990s. The new watchwords were 'sustainable development', 'good governance', and 'economic liberalism'.

Notes

1. H.C. 908, National Audit Office, *Report by the Comptroller and Auditor General: Pergau Hydro-Electric Project*, 18 Oct. 1993, HMSO, p. 11.
2. *The Independent*, 11 Nov. 1994.
3. Ibid.
4. Interview with Baroness Chalker of Wallasey, 21 Jan. 1997.
5. Ibid.
6. H. of C. Deb. (6th Series), 10 Feb. 1994, vol. 237, written answers, cols 389–90.
7. *The Independent*, 11 Nov. 1994.
8. Transcript, *Channel 4 News*, 10 Nov. 1994.
9. *The Independent*, 11 Nov. 1994.
10. Quoted from Peter Riddell, 'No UK scandal lurks in muddy water of Pergau', *The Times*, 8 Feb. 1994.
11. H.C. 271, Foreign Affairs Select Committee, *Public Expenditure: The Pergau Hydro-Electric Project, Malaysia, The Aid and Trade Provisions and Related Matters*, Third Report, Session 1993–94, vol. I, 13 Jul. 1994, HMSO, p. 39.
12. Ibid., p. 33.
13. Ibid., p. 34.
14. *See* for example, *The Independent*, 10 Nov. 1994.
15. *The Guardian*, 11 Nov. 1994.
16. Ibid.
17. Interview with Douglas Hurd, 20 Jan. 1997.
18. Adrian Hamilton, 'Hurd must fall on his sword', *The Observer*, 13 Nov. 1994.
19. Ibid.
20. A £22 million project for the Ankara metro in Turkey had been designed to reduce road congestion and pollution; a £9.3 million TV studio project in Indonesia was intended to keep people in touch with their government and unite a disparate community; and a £2.9 million contract for flight information facilities in Gaborone, Botswana, was aimed at reducing their dependence on South Africa.
21. Matthew Parris, 'Very nice, well-mannered minister confidently to the rescue', *The Times*, 14 Dec. 1994.
22. H. of C. Deb. (6th Series), 13 Dec. 1994, vol. 251, col. 777.
23. Ibid., col. 780.
24. H. of C. Deb. (6th Series), 17 Nov. 1994, vol. 250, col. 145.
25. H.C. 271, Foreign Affairs Select Committee, *Public Expenditure: The Pergau*

Hydro-Electric Project, Malaysia, p. liv.

26. Mrs Thatcher turned down a request to appear before the Foreign Affairs Select Committee, arguing that Prime Ministers and former Prime Ministers did not appear before Select Committees, except on specific issues. 'Letter to the Committee from Rt. Hon. Baroness Thatcher, OM, PC', 19 May 1994, in H.C.271, Foreign Affairs Select Committee, 'Minutes . . . ', op. cit. vol. II, Appendix 33, p. 332.

27. *The Times*, 7 Jun. 1990.

28. ODA, *Country Aid Programme Statement: South Africa, British Development Division in Southern Africa*, Nov. 1996.

29. ODA, *Partners in Transition, Know How Fund Annual Report 1995/96*, inside cover; I am indebted to Martin Dawson, who was Assistant Private Secretary to Baroness Chalker (as of 28 Jan. 1997) for providing this booklet and several other ODA documents.

23

Public Enemy Number One

The actual story of Hurd's resignation is a great deal more straightforward than most political commentators of the time believed. During a visit to China in September 1991, the Prime Minister had asked Hurd to stay on as Foreign Secretary after the 1992 General Election. Hurd had replied by offering John Major two years.[1] In March 1994, John Major offered Douglas Hurd the role of Deputy Prime Minister, but Hurd declined on the grounds that he wanted to retire some time shortly after his sixty-fifth birthday (which fell on 8 March 1995), but at a moment which would not be politically damaging to the Prime Minister. Hurd stayed on a year longer than he had originally planned for two reasons: to ensure the survival of the Prime Minister and to achieve a semblance of unity in the run-up to the General Election, which would help to ensure the Conservative Party remained in power. This quest for unity required an extremely difficult balancing act on Europe, and ran the risk of failing to satisfy the demands of the Euro-sceptics, while standing accused by the Euro-philes of trimming. The centrepiece of this strategy was the Prime Minister's idea of a referendum on a single currency.

In November 1994, John Major enlisted Douglas Hurd to try to persuade Cabinet colleagues to agree to such a referendum. The first indication that the Foreign Secretary had shifted his position on the referendum issue came in the run-up to the Second Reading vote on the European Communities (Finance) Bill. In an interview on the *Today* programme, Hurd maintained that he was 'temperamentally opposed' to referendums, but it would be up to Parliament 'to decide whether or not there are referendums and if so on what subject.'[2] He tried to broker a Cabinet referendum deal around a commitment to hold a referendum on further European integration but only if significant constitutional issues were at stake. There was a growing belief that the forthcoming Intergovernmental Conference (IGC) in 1996 would not result in major constitutional upheavals.

Hurd's proposal stopped short of committing the Government to a referendum on the single currency, which would have met with resistance from Kenneth Clarke and Michael Heseltine. All through December 1994, the Foreign Secretary tried to persuade Kenneth Clarke, Michael Portillo and Michael Heseltine to come round to the idea, but while Michael Heseltine appeared to be moving closer, at this stage both Clarke and Portillo refused to budge.

By Christmas 1994, Hurd was still not sure about the precise timing of his own departure. Having mulled over the matter, he let it be known at the beginning of January 1995 that he intended to continue as Foreign Secretary 'for the foreseeable future'.

His decision to stay on for the time being persuaded the sceptics to launch a concerted campaign to oust him as Foreign Secretary. It is not known if anyone masterminded the campaign, but the former Chancellor Kenneth Clarke is clear of its purpose:

> It was very well organised. It was all designed to get rid of Douglas Hurd and get a Euro-sceptic Foreign Secretary. He [Hurd] was seen to be the key personality who had to be removed.[3]

On 20 January, speaking on Radio Four's *World at One* programme, Hurd attacked a 'mission statement' issued by eight of the whipless rebels the previous day:

> There are ideas there which I think are unreal in the sense that if we push them, we would be in fact withdrawing from the European Union, cutting ourselves off from the single market or putting ourselves under rules which we didn't have any share in making.[4]

The Euro-sceptics immediately fired back at Hurd with a vitriolic piece by Lord (Alistair) McAlpine in *The Mail on Sunday* entitled 'The Man For all Seasons Whose Time has Finally Run Out'. The irony was that McAlpine had helped Douglas Hurd earlier on in his political career by giving him a directorship at ELEC from 1975 to 1979. As the Treasurer of ELEC, McAlpine had been an enthusiast for European integration, but since resigning as Treasurer of the Conservative Party in 1990, he had turned against Europe, and would later join Sir James Goldsmith's Referendum Party. Referring to Hurd's comments about the Euro-sceptics' mission statement, McAlpine claimed it was not the sceptics whose views were 'unreal', but Douglas Hurd, who was 'the intellect behind a powerful triumvirate of Cabinet colleagues [Hurd, Clarke and Heseltine] who are arm-twisting the Prime Minister into following policies that are out of step with the country, the Conservative Party and, I also believe, his own instincts.'[5] McAlpine proceeded to launch a series of personal attacks on the Foreign Secretary:

> From an early career as a junior diplomat to his present high office of Foreign Secretary, Douglas Hurd has been a man for all seasons. But he is not a man for this season.
>
> Simply it is time for him to go and rest with dignity, in a style that complements his self-appointed role as the Queen Mother of British politics.[6]

Worse was to follow:

> I have watched Hurd as he has slithered from minor functionary to guru, observed him as he has changed political allegiances, marvelled as he always avoided the political custard pies, leaving every meeting without a stain on his strange Loden overcoat. Hurd does not appear a cunning man. His *modus operandi* is not to produce clever wheezes; rather, sensible solutions are his currency. At least, solutions that appear sensible to those around the table – for the very reason that they are usually the solutions they wished to hear. Behind this technique is an overwhelming desire to reach an agreement, regardless of its consequences. Or could it be that the Hurd consensus approach springs in part from a desire to be personally liked – a task at which he succeeds mightily?[7]

It might have been possible for Hurd simply to ignore the bile written by a man who was drifting into the political wilderness, but the Euro-sceptics were able to seize on an incident on Thursday, 26 January when it appeared that a strategy paper by Hurd on the forthcoming IGC had been rejected in Cabinet. In reality, the Foreign Secretary had delivered a preliminary paper to the Cabinet outlining three options for Britain's negotiating stance on the forthcoming IGC: a minimalist approach; go in all guns blazing, intent on reversing the federalist tide; or choose a middle path, the option favoured by Hurd. During the meeting, five Euro-sceptics veered to the maximalist approach and two other ministers, Gillian Shephard and David Hunt, appeared to move in their direction. Hurd's own recollection from his diaries was that his paper was criticised 'quite briskly by [Michael] Howard and [Michael] Portillo' as being too long and that the Prime Minister was 'not over-helpful'.[8] However, there was no sense in which he felt he had received a major rebuff. So he was 'very cross' the following day when *The Times* led with a story that he had received a major rebuff in Cabinet. The story was very similar to that of 29 April 1994 when *The Times* claimed Hurd had been spurned over his draft of the European

Election manifesto (see Chapter 20). Hurd has his own strong suspicions as to which Cabinet colleague briefed *The Times* misleadingly, but he was never able to prove it.

At this point, a less astute politician might have seen the rug pulled from under his feet. However, as he had done with the story over Mrs Thatcher offering Geoffrey Howe his job as Home Secretary in July 1989, Hurd moved quickly to scotch the rumours through a series of briefings with the political correspondents. Because Hurd was not in the habit of crying foul every time the press reported something of which he disapproved – unlike the Prime Minister – when the Foreign Secretary descended from 'on high' to deny a story, the political correspondents sat up and took notice. Hurd also asked and succeeded in getting the Prime Minister to renounce the story. But the harm had been done.

By coincidence, Hurd had thought of announcing publicly that week that he had told the Prime Minister in 1994 that he was going to resign in 1995, but Judy advised him to wait until this particular flurry had blown over. A series of pro-European Conservatives rallied to Hurd's defence, including Sir Edward Heath who appeared on *Frost on Sunday* claiming:

> There's a campaign at the moment against Douglas Hurd to try to do him in, and saying he is going to retire and what a good thing it is and Michael Portillo [should] become Foreign Secretary. Nothing of that sort is going to happen. I know Douglas isn't going to retire.[9]

Hurd's reaction to Heath's intervention was mixed:

> 29 Jan. 1995: Hope it's not too awful [Manner of future resignation]. The siege of my position continues. Ted Heath lumbering to the rescue, but not wholly helpful.[10]

The forceful way in which Sir Edward Heath defended Douglas Hurd was somewhat surprising. Relations between the two men had been cool ever since Heath's initiatives on hostages during the Gulf Crisis. There was no residual resentment on either side, but politically the two men had drifted apart ever since May 1979 when Hurd accepted a ministerial post in Mrs Thatcher's Government, which was seen by Heath as something of a betrayal. Heath's main motivation in supporting Douglas Hurd was to protect the pro-European cause in the Conservative Party on Europe, which had been the cornerstone of his beliefs when he was Prime Minister.

Other pro-European Conservatives rallied to Hurd's defence. Timothy Renton, a former Chief Whip, mocked Michael Portillo:

> He [Portillo] believes that the Earth is still flat, when a lot of navigators
> found a long time ago that it wasn't.[11]

The problem for Douglas Hurd was that, although this support was welcome
in ensuring his survival, it was 'not wholly helpful' because it showed that the
pro-Europeans in the Conservative Party were no longer willing to remain silent
on the issue, risking further divisions inside the parliamentary Conservative
Party. This was demonstrated in a private meeting which Hurd had with several
members of the ninety-strong Positive European Group on Wednesday, 25
January, and publicly by the comments of Ray Whitney (Wycombe), Chairman
of the Positive Europeans, who said:

> We have spent two years deliberately seeking to keep the temperature down.
> But a small minority is going to go on making trouble.[12]

Geoffrey Howe – by this time Lord Howe of Aberavon – was one of the more
influential figures on the pro-European wing of the Conservative Party. He
wrote an article in the *Financial Times* accusing Douglas Hurd and John Major
of leaning too far in the direction of the sceptics. The article, which appeared
on Monday, 30 January, was actually drafted on 26 January, the day before the
disputed Cabinet meeting. Howe was scathing:

> Britain's national interest and the best strategy for pursuing it . . . are being
> subordinated to short-term tactical considerations of party management . . .
> In the search for party unity at any price, UK foreign policy is being dragged
> into a ghetto of sentimentality and self-delusion.[13]

By pursuing an 'opt-out mentality', Britain risked being left out of the European
mainstream, dominated by France and Germany. Instead of pursuing 'the non-
existent unity of a single party', John Major's Government should follow the
pattern of cross-party consensus achieved in securing Britain's entry into Europe
in 1973 and demonstrated again during the referendum campaign in 1975.
Howe claimed that mistakes had been made by John Major's Government in
failing to secure early ratification of Maastricht by means of a cross-party
consensus before and after the Danish vote 'No' vote in June 1992. He attacked
Hurd's 'espousal of a vision of "multi-speed Europe" [which] so easily converts
into Britain stalled in the slow lane of a two-speed Europe'.[14]

Hurd was accused of trimming by the sceptics and the Euro-philes alike. He
described Howe's article as a 'warning shot'. Perhaps sensing the electoral
dangers of moving too far in the direction of the sceptics, he said:

If we depart from the commonsense of that middle ground, we risk not only losing our place in Europe but we risk losing our position in the minds of the British people.[15]

It had been a long day. That morning, Hurd had insisted that the Prime Minister's office issue a statement saying his future as Foreign Secretary was under no threat and accusing the Eurosceptics of running a campaign to destabilise him. The statement from Downing Street also emphasised that Hurd remained in charge of the Cabinet subcommittee process (known as OPD (E)) of formulating the White Paper for the IGC in 1996. According to Hurd's diary, the Prime Minister also ordered ministers off-the-air on Europe.[16] Later that morning, the arch Euro-sceptic, Teresa Gorman (Billericay), told reporters that, while Hurd was a fine politician, 'as far as Europe is concerned, he is yesterday's man. He is peddling ideas that may be important to the Foreign Office or even within the European Council, but they have no contact point with the grassroots of the natural supporters of the Tory Party.'[17] Hurd then gave an impromptu press conference on the steps of the Foreign Office, claiming 'I am clearly today's man and I can see a good many tomorrows.'[18]

The following day, the criticism of Hurd widened into the circles of academia, when William Wallace, a foreign policy expert and Fellow of St Anthony's College, Oxford, wrote a piece for *The Guardian* claiming, 'The unreconciled Right have set the agenda of Tory foreign policy for the past two years, while the Foreign Secretary has trimmed the articulation of policies to their demands.'[19] The piece was accompanied by a brilliant but cruel illustration by Peter Clarke depicting Hurd's famous quiff of hair as an iceberg listing in the water. While Wallace was a well-known supporter of the Liberal Democrats, the article showed that both Eurosceptics and Europhiles were beginning to turn against Hurd by the end of January 1995. That day, *The Guardian* editorial claimed, 'If Douglas Hurd is the out-spoken leader of the European realists, then heaven help code breakers everywhere.'[20]

As well as the bad press, it appeared as if Malcolm Rifkind, the Defence Secretary, was making a pitch for Douglas Hurd's job by tilting in a more Eurosceptical direction. In what became known as his 'Atlantic Community' speech, the Defence Secretary told a meeting of the Royal Institute of International Relations in Brussels on 30 January that ultimate power should remain with the nation state rather than a supranational European Union. Much of the Rifkind agenda was closely allied to Hurd's views: an enlarged combat-ready NATO, including the former countries of Eastern Europe, was pure Douglas Hurd. However, the timing of the speech on Monday, 30 January at the height of the campaign against Hurd led to the press drawing the wrong conclusions from the Defence Secretary's speech.

Within a week, the concerted campaign to oust Hurd had spluttered to a standstill. Judy's advice to her husband not to announce his intention to step down that week had proved sound. If he had done so, it would have looked as if the sceptics had successfully hounded him from office. Instead, Hurd had another chat with the Prime Minister at the beginning of February 1995 during which he said he wanted to retire in July. John Major advised Hurd to note down his intention to retire in a letter so that, when he did stand down as Foreign Secretary, there would be no doubt that Hurd planned to leave in July and that he was not being forced out. Hurd penned a letter to the Prime Minister on 5 February, the existence of which was revealed on the day of Hurd's resignation.

Despite the public squabbles between Cabinet ministers, the preparations for the IGC in OPD (E) had to continue. The Foreign Secretary tried to flesh out his ideas on the future defence of Europe during a speech in Berlin on 28 February. While stressing the primacy of NATO in Western defence, he signalled the need for Europeans to shoulder more responsibility for their own security, given the American disengagement from Europe. In policy terms, this would mean enhancing the role of the Western European Union (WEU).

During 1994, considerable ground was gained by the British in increasing security co-operation with France. In practical terms, the British and French armies had worked successfully alongside each other in Bosnia. In effect, Britain won the security debate in Europe. The future would rest in NATO, with an enhanced role for the WEU to take into account the realities of progressive American disengagement from Europe. The approach would be inter-governmental rather than shifting to qualified majority voting under the Treaty of Rome. The European Commission did not assume a significant role in defence policy, thwarting its plans for the European Union becoming a military organisation. And yet, this major foreign policy success became drowned out by the domestic divisions in the Conservative Party.

In March 1995, Britain failed to side with the Spanish in a fishing dispute with Canada. On 9 March, Canadian patrol vessels seized the Spanish trawler *Estai* off Newfoundland, outside Canada's 200-mile exclusion zone. She was found to have smaller net-mesh sizes than were permitted under the North West Atlantic Fisheries rules. The Spanish Government reacted angrily to the Canadian action, calling on their EU partners to join in trade sanctions against Canada. The Foreign Office felt that the Spanish had overplayed their hand, and Douglas Hurd was keener to play the role of honest broker instead of siding with the EU and Spain. In fact, the British blocked a strong letter of protest from the EU to Canada. While the British response was measured, it intensified the feeling in European capitals that the British Government was increasingly taking an equivocal attitude to its membership of the European Union. On 19 June 1995, Hurd visited Javier Solana in Madrid in attempt to defuse the Canadian fishing dispute and make progress on easing border controls between Spain and Gibraltar.

Earlier in Hurd's Foreign Secretaryship, Tristan Garel-Jones had aired a plan for joint sovereignty of the Rock, but John Major was not willing to entertain the idea. Apart from the perennial smuggling problem, Hurd was concerned about money laundering in Gibraltar, and in September 1994 he had written to Joe Bossano, Chief Minister of Gibraltar, warning him to comply with EU directives or face direct rule from Britain. Bossano was a tough trade unionist, educated at Oxbridge, who was continually stirring things up. In December 1994, Hurd and Solana agreed to hold tripartite talks on illegal trafficking. The discussions were conducted, in Douglas Hurd's words, under the heading of 'two sides of the table, three flags'.[21] The Gibraltarian politicians were permitted to attend, but on the British side, not as a separate negotiating entity.

Back in Britain, the whipless rebels, egged on by the British press, played on the issue of fish, stirring up Cornish fisherman into demanding the scrapping of the Common Fisheries Policy,[22] much to the annoyance of Solana. Instead of ignoring the rebels, the Government's ever dwindling majority meant that they were invited back into the Conservative Party by the end of April.[23]

Hurd's reasons for retiring were partly financial: he wanted to earn some money – before he was too old – to support his young family from his second marriage. Both his children, Jessica and Philip, were being privately educated. The fees at Eton for Philip were considerable. But Hurd had no idea what he could hope to earn outside the Government. On his retirement, his plans were 'totally vague'.[24] He also saw attractions in writing one more novel, together with other writing projects, and some broadcasting. More importantly, there was also the cumulative strain of spending sixteen unremitting years as a minister, ten-and-a-half of them as a senior Cabinet minister. As his diary entries show, his four years as Home Secretary had involved a burdensome workload. During his five-and-a-half years as Foreign Secretary he had submitted himself to a punishing schedule of foreign travel. Throughout, he had enjoyed good health. Recordings of excessive tiredness or illness in his diaries during his Foreign Secretaryship are less frequent than his days as Home Secretary. However, he did injure his back around the time of the Bournemouth Conservative Party Conference in October 1994. A diary entry of the time records him working on his Conference speech 'blurred by aches'.[25] On the rare occasions that Hurd was able to take time off, friends testify that, towards the end of his time as a minister, he was finding it progressively more difficult to unwind away from work.[26] The continuing crisis in Bosnia constantly preyed on his mind – as his short stories reveal. There was also a growing sense of frustration that the credibility of his carefully formulated negotiating positions in the eyes of fellow European leaders was being undermined by the antics of the Eurosceptics at home.

A sign that the Foreign Secretary was growing weary of fending off the sceptics came during Foreign Office questions on 7 June 1995, where out of five questions on the IGC, he answered none, leaving David Davis, his more Eurosceptical Minister of State, to field questions from the Eurosceptics.[27] The political sketch writer Matthew Parris hit the mark with his comment that, 'The barbarians are at the gate.'[28]

Despite his frustrations, Hurd remained determined that he would not leave at a time inconvenient to the Prime Minister. He wanted to ensure that the Prime Minister's position was secure because he believed that only under John Major's leadership – the Prime Minister was more popular than his party – did the Conservative Party retain a slim chance of winning at the forthcoming General Election.

The catalyst for John Major's decision to stand and fight came on 13 June when he addressed the 'Fresh Start' group of Conservative MPs in the House of Commons. There was an unexpectedly large attendance of MPs – around sixty – who arrived with the intention of persuading the Prime Minister to abandon his 'wait and see' policy on the single currency. In a remarkable display of disloyalty, MPs like the former Chancellor Norman Lamont heckled the Prime Minister. John Major came away from the meeting convinced that the sceptics, having rebelled against him for several years, were now out to assassinate him. Hurd gauged the Prime Minister's reaction from the meeting:

14 Jun. 1995: Prime Minister heavily roughed up by loud army of sceptics yesterday. Seems to have held his ground, though much discouraged. Ken Clarke is robust but pessimistic.[29]

Lady Thatcher stoked the fires of dissent by publishing extracts of the second volume of her memoirs, *The Path to Power*. The latter part of the book amounts to a rambling diatribe against Europe and John Major's Government.

On 17 June, the Prime Minister and his Foreign Secretary flew out to Halifax, Nova Scotia to attend the G7 Summit. Between sessions, Hurd again talked to the Prime Minister about resigning. On Tuesday, 20 January, Hurd had another long chat with John Major in which the Prime Minister began exploring the possibility of grasping the nettle and forcing a choice. Hurd set out four options, the last of which suggested Major should seize the initiative and force a vote immediately. The Prime Minister had already considered risking his leadership to restore his authority a year earlier (after the European Elections in June 1994), but had opted instead for a Cabinet reshuffle. This time, he considered that gambling his leadership was worth the risk, given that he would almost certainly face a challenge in the autumn, by which time he might be weakened still further. A pre-emptive strike would not only restore his authority, but also give him an opportunity to relaunch the Government. Hurd strongly supported the stand-and-fight option. The two men then discussed how this decision might be meshed in with Hurd's own plans. It was agreed at that meeting that Hurd would not announce his intention to resign before the Prime Minister had made his final decision.

On 21 June, Hurd faced down the Eurosceptics in the House of Commons for almost the last time as Foreign Secretary. Or rather he faced down the Eurosceptics and the Europhiles. It was indicative of Douglas Hurd's failure to hold the factions of the Conservative Party together that during the debate on the European Union he was not only attacked by sceptics like Iain Duncan-Smith (Chingford), Bernard Jenkin (Colchester), and Nicholas Budgen (Wolverhampton, South West), but also by his former boss, Sir Edward Heath, and Hugh Dykes (Harrow East). Sir Edward referred to Hurd as his 'former assistant' and mocked Hurd's belief that Mrs Thatcher's attitude on Europe had been 'No, maybe, yes'. It was an 'immense reassurance' to know that current ministers would say 'No, no, no' and then say 'Yes' and sign up:

> . . . if that excellent example is followed, we shall achieve all the aims that my right hon. Friend has been describing in his speech. Those who have been niggling away on the Benches behind us will be defeated and we shall all benefit. I thank him very much.[30]

Hurd dealt with the questions with his usual sang-froid, but he perhaps sensed that his careful strategy to unite the Party was coming unstuck.

Later that day, Hurd appeared before the Foreign Affairs Select Committee and delivered what was in effect his last attempt to unify the Party on Europe. Moving beyond his November 1994 speculation about a referendum if major constitutional issues were agreed at the forthcoming IGC, Hurd revealed for the first time in public that he saw arguments for a referendum on a single currency:

> The Prime Minister has made it clear I think in several public statements that he does not rule that out. It is the Government policy. I am personally no friend of referenda but I do see arguments for a referendum on this subject [single currency] if the British Government came to the conclusion that a

single currency was in the national interest. I do see a case for that but that is a personal view.[31]

On Thursday, 22 June, John Major telephoned Hurd from a meeting of European Foreign Ministers in Luxembourg to say he was resigning that afternoon, but the Prime Minister failed to inform the Cabinet that morning, giving John Redwood, the Welsh Secretary, a peg on which to hang his later challenge for the leadership. After Prime Minister's Questions, John Major called a press conference in the rose garden of Number 10 and shocked everyone by saying it was time for his party to 'put up or shut up'. From Luxembourg, Hurd said the decision was 'a brave step by a brave man and a needed step. He's the best Prime Minister for my country and I wish him all success.'[32]

Hurd's own resignation a day later was widely trailed in the Friday morning press. He describes it in his diary as 'a rather happy, straightforward day'.[33] After pondering over breakfast, he saw no reason to delay the announcement of his resignation any further. Hurd stood on the steps of the Foreign Office and told waiting reporters that he wished to avoid his future becoming 'tangled up' in the leadership contest. He was removing himself as an issue in the campaign. With characteristic understatement, he said there had been 'a small minority who, to put it mildly, have made life difficult.'

Hurd's resignation statement read as follows:

> After sixteen years as a minister, eleven of them as a member of the Cabinet and nearly six as Foreign Secretary, I have decided that the time has come to retire.
>
> I have of course consulted with the Prime Minister. I told him in spring 1994 of my wish to retire this summer and I wrote to the Prime Minister in [4] February 1995 confirming that this remained my intention.
>
> I remain a staunch supporter of the Prime Minister, and I have already made clear that I will support him enthusiastically in the election announced yesterday.
>
> I have no doubt that he will be re-elected. I will then continue to back him in whatever way I can from outside government. I will continue as Foreign Secretary until the next reshuffle and after that as an active backbencher.
>
> It has been a huge privilege to work in government during these years.[34]

The Prime Minister's reply was warm and generous, describing his service to the Government as 'incomparable':

You have been, simply and without question, an outstanding Foreign Secretary. You have represented the United Kingdom with massive authority, and have earned deep respect around the world.[35]

Hurd spent the rest of the morning telephoning his sons, heads of agencies and the like. Warren Christopher and Javier Solana telephoned with kind words and then Hurd went to Ludgrove to watch cricket and have a picnic. Hurd thought it fitting that the Prime Minister should telephone him while he was watching cricket. Ironically, Major would emulate Hurd after his May 1997 election defeat by going to the Oval. Hurd was struck by the irony that he had spent months fretting over the timing of his resignation, only for it to pass off so smoothly when he actually went through with it.

The following day, Hurd was given a relatively good set of reviews by the political correspondents and the diplomatic editors. All the old clichés were used: 'patrician, English gentleman' and 'safe pair of hands'.[36] Most of the articles stressed the respect and authority Hurd commanded at home and abroad, but they noted his failure over Bosnia and the progressive sapping of his political authority on the issue of Europe.

It is a rare event in politics for a politician to go at a time of his own choosing. Hurd had not been nudged out in January 1995 by the sceptics. There is little doubt that Hurd added weight and authority to a Cabinet, which, apart from Clarke and Heseltine, was conspicuously lacking in that commodity. The debate over whether Hurd should have stayed on as Foreign Secretary until the General Election is in some senses irrelevant. He simply wanted to retire and was entitled to do so after such a long period as a minister.

Although the accusation was made that Britain was represented by a lame-duck Foreign Secretary at the Cannes Summit, Hurd ignored such calls and enjoyed his swansong. His diary records that the Prime Minister enjoyed himself too, despite the announcement of a challenge by John Redwood:

26 Jun. 1995: PM curiously relaxed, although the Redwood wind blows quite strongly from London.[37]

The departing British Foreign Secretary showed the kind of *gravitas* for which he had become famous, by walking down the steps of his hotel in his dressing gown and going out for a swim in the sea accompanied by his Principal Private Secretary, John Sawers, with the British press watching his every stroke through their long-lens cameras. Later, sporting a pair of dark glasses, along with a more traditional suit and a smart pink silk tie, he went for a walk along the seafront, stopping at a shop to buy some postcards.

In the lead-up to the Conservative leadership result, Hurd had one remaining doubt. Would the Prime Minister agree to stay on if he did not win very convincingly against John Redwood? Hurd's view was that senior ministers should urge John Major to stay on even by a bare majority. Robert Cranbourne, the Prime Minister's campaign manager, was also very strongly of this view. So, what Hurd terms 'a little bit of a conspiracy'[38] was arranged in which those close to the Prime Minister would congratulate him provided he won.

Originally, Hurd said he planned to be on hand by telephone in the Foreign Office to persuade the Prime Minister to stay on. As it turned out, Hurd was with John Major in the upstairs flat in Number 10 when the figures came through: 218 votes for John Major, with 89 votes against, and 22 abstentions or spoilt ballot papers. In Hurd's view, the margin of victory was clear enough. Before John Major could say anything, everyone present said in their different ways, 'Congratulations!', 'Marvellous!', 'Excellent!', 'Well Done!' The Prime Minister did need a few moments of reflection before agreeing unenthusiastically that the figure of 218 was adequate.

In a remarkable piece of perception, Philip Cowley, now a major authority on Conservative leadership contests, penned an article in August 1995 entitled '111 Not Out. The Press and the Conservative Leadership Contest', in which he puzzled why the press pundits, who predicted before the vote that Major would be in trouble if 100 MPs voted against him, all agreed after the vote that the Prime Minister had stengthened his position, despite failing to win over 111 Conservative MPs. He also puzzled over the 'missing twenty minutes' between the announcement of the result and the Prime Minister's appearance outside Number 10. Cowley's tentative conclusion, without the benefit of Hurd's evidence, was to claim that the Major camp had successfully talked up the result with a series of pre-prepared remarks to the waiting media.[39] From Hurd's evidence, we can now also explain the missing twenty minutes. The Prime Minister was not sure whether he wanted to carry on, but his colleagues gave him little choice in the matter.

During his last ministerial duty at the Dispatch Box, Hurd fielded a series of questions on Foreign Office matters. Amid the kind remarks from colleagues, he did not expect Tim Rathbone (Lewes) to comment on his honesty:

> I say that as the only Member of the House, I believe, to have bought a second-hand car from him.[40]

Hurd replied:

> I remember the car to which my hon. Friend referred. I believe that it was an open-roof Sunbeam Rapier. It had to be taken to Long Island [Hurd was a diplomat in New York, 1956–60] for repairs rather too often in its life, but I am glad that it served my hon. Friend well.[41]

Hurd had trimmed his sails over Europe in the noble aim of protecting the Prime Minister's position and achieving a semblance of unity in the Conservative Party in the run-up to the 1997 General Election. His own departure had helped the Prime Minister to win a battle with the sceptics which meant they could no longer conspire to oust him before the 1997 General Election. However, the victory on 4 July was not resounding: the Prime Minister had been backed by only two-thirds of his parliamentary party. Rumours abounded that Michael Heseltine had saved the Prime Minister in exchange for the deputy leadership. The leadership contest bought the Prime Minister a few months of time in which he was able to reshape his Cabinet. Michael Heseltine, as the new Deputy Prime Minister, tried to fill Hurd's place in the troika of ministers seeking to preserve the 'wait and see' policy on the single currency, but Hurd's departure undoutedly weakened the case of the pro-Europeans in Cabinet.

Although Hurd was pleased and relieved at the appointment of Malcolm Rifkind as Foreign Secretary, Rifkind veered off in a more sceptical direction, carried along by the mood of the Conservative Party. As Kenneth Clarke had feared, with Hurd removed from the picture, the Chancellor became the sceptics' new Public Enemy Number One. However, Kenneth Clarke held his ground far more than Hurd had done. Out of office, Hurd would support Clarke's stand against the sceptics. Meanwhile, the Prime Minister searched in vain for a unity over Europe which would hold the Conservative Party together until the General Election.

From September 1992, a section of the Conservative Party lost its senses. There was a widespread view in the Party that further European integration threatened the British way of life, its parliamentary democracy and its cherished institutions. This view gained a wider following during John Major's Government because of his dwindling majority and the deadly association made by Margaret Thatcher and others between the economic recession, Britain's fall-out from the ERM and the whole European experiment. It was the emotional response to this perceived threat which caused the Conservative Party to tear itself apart while in Government. Few were willing to listen to calls for unity when they believed that the future of their country as a free nation was at stake. However, their cause rested on the mistaken belief that Britain, shorn of its Empire, could be a leading influence in the world without integrating with its European partners.

The difficulty was that the actual single-currency experiment devised in the Delors Plan was seen primarily by the French and the Germans as a political project designed to bind their two countries together in an ever closer union. It was a pity that the pros and cons of the single currency were not debated rationally. There were real question marks about the possible adverse effects of artificially binding the economies of diverse countries together. Such an artificial construct could create strains in the system which would lead to high unemployment, structural imbalances, and also political unrest and nationalism if national parliaments were effectively deprived of their role of voting on taxes and spending. Douglas Hurd realised there were flaws in the single-currency experiment, and he came to believe that the plan as constituted was not one which the bulk of his party could accept. However, he was not willing to listen to the sceptics because their ultimate agenda would have led to Britain's withdrawal from the European Union. To have done so would have led to the failure of Britain's foreign policy objective since the premiership of Harold Macmillan: preventing France and Germany from forming an inner core in Europe, from which Britain was excluded. So the policy became 'wait and see'. The Prime Minister was forced to lead a party which became virtually unleadable. For the first time since the heated debate over Tariff Reform at the beginning of the century, the threat of electoral defeat did not persuade Conservative MPs to unite behind their leader. Ideology and emotion held sway over Tory pragmatism.

Notes

1. (4 Sept. 1991) Diary Readings with Douglas Hurd, 18 Mar. 1997.
2. *The Times*, 26 Nov. 1994.
3. Interview with Kenneth Clarke, 16 Dec. 1996.
4. *The Independent*, 21 Jan. 1995.
5. Alistair McAlpine, 'The Man for all Seasons Whose Time Has Finally Run Out', *Mail on Sunday*, 22 Jan. 1995.
6. Ibid.
7. Ibid.
8. (26 Jan. 1995) Diary Readings with Douglas Hurd, Westwell, 13 Jun. 1995.
9. *The Times*, 30 Jan. 1995.
10. Diary Readings with Douglas Hurd, Westwell, 13 Jun. 1997.
11. *Financial Times*, 30 Jan. 1995.
12. *The Independent*, 30 Jan. 1995.
13. Geoffrey Howe, 'A Better European Policy for Britain', *Financial Times*, 30 Jan. 1995.
14. Ibid.
15. Transcript, *Channel Four News*, 30 Jan. 1995.
16. (30 Jan. 1995) Diary Readings with Douglas Hurd, Westwell, 13 Jun. 1997.
17. *The Times*, 31 Jan. 1995.
18. *The Guardian*, 31 Jan. 1995.

19. William Wallace, 'Hurd fails in the sunset', *The Guardian*, 31 Jan. 1995.

20. 'Editorial', *The Guardian*, 31 Jan. 1995; *see* also Hugo Young, 'Tories who play a dirty game of double-talk on Europe', *The Guardian*, 31 Jan. 1995.

21. Interview with Douglas Hurd, 7 Oct. 1997.

22. Seven of the nine whipless rebels, plus Rupert Allason (Torbay) and David Harris (St Ives) had voted against the Government during an Opposition Day debate on fish; H. of C. Deb. (6th Series), 18 Jan. 1995, vol.252, cols 818–22.

23. The whip was restored to eight whipless rebels on 25 April 1995. A ninth, Sir Richard Body (Holland-with-Boston) declined to reapply for the whip, but had rejoined the parliamentary fold by the May 1997 General Election.

24. Letter to the Author from Douglas Hurd, 30 May 1998.

25. Diary Readings with Douglas Hurd, Westwell, 13 Jun. 1997.

26. Private information.

27. H. of C. Deb. (6th Series), 7 Jun. 1995, vol. 261, cols 201–3.

28. Matthew Parris, 'Hurd's subordinate slips his leash to rally barbarian factions', *The Times*, 8 Jun. 1995.

29. Diary Readings with Douglas Hurd, Westwell, 13 Jun. 1997.

30. H. of C. Deb. (6th Series), 21 Jun. 1995, vol. 262, col. 368.

31. H.C. 401, Foreign Affairs Select Committee, 'Minutes Taken Before the Foreign Affairs Committee', *European Union: Preparations for the 1996 Inter-Governmental Conference*, Third Report, Session 1994-95, printed 13 Jul. 1995, HMSO, p. 35.

32. *The Times*, 23 Jun. 1995.

33. Diary Readings with Douglas Hurd, Westwell, 13 Jun. 1997.

34. Quoted from *Daily Telegraph*, 24 Jun. 1995.

35. Quoted from *The Times*, 24 Jun. 1995.

36. *See* Michael Binyon, [Diplomatic Editor of *The Times*] 'English Gentleman earned world respect'; Edward Mortimer, Philip Stephens, Bruce Clark, 'Cabinet patrician sets sail for calmer waters', *Financial Times*, 24–25 Jun. 1995; 'Editorial', *Daily Telegraph*, 24 Jun. 1995.

37. Diary Readings with Douglas Hurd, Westwell, 13 Jun. 1997.

38. Interview with Douglas Hurd, Westwell, 13 Jun. 1997.

39. Philip Cowley, '111 Not Out. The Press and 1995 Conservative Leadership Contest', *Talking Politics*, vol. 8 (1996).

40. H. of C. Deb. (6th Series), 5 Jul. 1995, vol. 263. Part 1, col. 374.

41. Ibid.

24

Heresies of a Dinosaur

After his resignation, Hurd spent four rejuvenating months relaxing with Judy, Philip and Jessica. There was a last weekend spent enjoying the gardens at Chevening and then many happy hours at their country home in Westwell on the edge of the Cotswolds.

On 12 September 1995, it was announced that Douglas Hurd was to join the board of NatWest, then Britain's third largest clearing bank, as Deputy Chairman of its global investment arm, NatWest Markets. The job involved working two days per week for a salary of around £200,000 a year, including around £20,000 for joining the board of NatWest as a non-executive director. Hurd had been approached by Lord Alexander, NatWest's Chairman, in July. By 1995, around 50 per cent of NatWest's business was conducted overseas. Assessing the political risks associated with such investments abroad was seen as important to the financial aspects. It was proposed that Hurd would provide political analysis for the Bank and its customers, and would take on an ambassadorial role, meeting important clients and representing the Bank abroad.

Despite the political dimension to Hurd's new job, there was some surprise among Hurd's former Cabinet colleagues that he had belatedly entered the City of London, without ever having held an economic-related ministerial portfolio. Douglas Hurd could not boast any real experience of the business world.

News of Hurd's appointment came at a time when the issue of financial probity among politicians was being investigated by Lord Nolan's Committee on Standards in Public Life. There seemed to be a wave of public indignation, whipped up by the press, whenever any former minister appeared to be cashing in on public office.

It was predictable that immediately after hearing of Hurd's appointment, Alistair Darling, Labour's City spokesman, criticised the former Foreign Secretary for being 'the latest in a long line of ministers' to desert the Cabinet 'with indecent haste . . . You don't fix up a directorship like that overnight.'[1]

However, two factors ensured that Hurd's appointment was a storm in a teacup. First, Hurd revealed he had contacted Lord Carlisle, Chairman of the Advisory Committee on Business Appointments for Civil Servants, who had advised him to wait three months. In effect, Hurd had followed informal guidelines, even before the Nolan Committee reported and laid down an official set of rules. Second, Hurd was scrupulous in ensuring that there were no hidden perks associated with his salary. There were to be no share options and no pension plan: the whole of his salary would be taken in cash.

The former Foreign Secretary's cause was also helped by a surprising outbreak of commonsense in the quality press. While the *Daily Mail* ran with the front-page headline 'LAUGHING ALL THE WAY TO THE BANK' on 13 September, the following day, *The Times* editorial ran with the headline 'HURD MENTALITY', proclaiming, 'The politics of envy should be directed elsewhere,'[2] and arguing that, while Hurd's political record was hardly blameless:

> The one charge that could not be levelled against him is want of probity. He is an upstanding and conscientious man, sometimes feline but hardly a fat cat. In the last few years of his career, Mr Hurd deserves to be left alone to earn as much money as he can.[3]

Two political commentators also proved unusual allies. The Eurosceptic, William Rees-Mogg, wrote a thoughtful piece on the issue of ministerial pay entitled 'PAY PEANUTS. GET MPs', in which he pointed out that Hurd's net pay as Foreign Secretary (after taking out his salary as an MP) was £34,630 a year, about 7 per cent of the going rate for an equivalent job in the City of London.[4] Surely, Lord Rees-Mogg argued, underpaying ministers meant that people of ability were not attracted into government because they had to sustain financial hardship if they became ministers. Michael White, the Political Editor of *The Guardian*, also came to Hurd's defence, asking two questions:

> Do you really think Douglas Hurd is the shady type who will use insider information for commercial ends? And do you think that, in 1995, a British foreign secretary should be paid £67,819 – the sort of money Nick Leeson used to lose before lunch?[5]

Shortly after joining NatWest, there was speculation in the press that Hurd was among those shortlisted for the post of Secretary General of NATO. The post fell vacant after the incumbent Willy Claes stood trial on corruption charges.[6] Other names aired for the vacancy included Uffe Ellemann-Jensen, the former Danish Foreign Minister, Ruud Lubbers, the Dutch Prime Minister and Volker Ruhe, the German Defence Minister.

Such was the expectation surrounding Hurd that the *Daily Telegraph* leader ran with the headline 'THE MAN FOR NATO', extolling his virtues as an international statesman and claiming it was time he was recalled 'like Cincinnatus from the plough'[7] – rather ignoring the fact that Hurd had retired for good from international diplomacy, and had just settled into his job at NatWest. Also, he wanted to pursue a career as an author and broadcaster. The last thing on his mind was more gruelling foreign travel and endless summitry. Ruud Lubbers emerged as the favoured choice of the Europeans, but the Americans objected. Hurd's friend, Javier Solana, the former Spanish Foreign Minister, finally came through as the compromise candidate, partly on the back of Hurd's recommendation.

But Hurd did not want to stop expounding his views on the future shape of Europe diplomatically and militarily. Giving his Winston Churchill Memorial Lecture in Luxembourg on 14 March 1996, he put forward his ideas on the enlargement of the European Union and the proposed expansion of NATO to the East. He envisaged the admission of Poland, Hungary, the Czech Republic and possibly Slovenia to the EU within five years. Enlargement would, however, have institutional implications. It would not, for instance, be financially possible to extend the 'foolish aspects' of Common Agricultural Policy to Eastern Europe, nor could Spain, Portugal, Greece and Ireland expect to receive substantial transfers from other member states in a Union which admitted countries with an even lower standard of living. The European Union, he said, 'should spend more time and energy securing enlargement than in defending the timetable for a single currency.'[8]

The European Union, he said, needed to fashion a closer relationship with the two strategic powers in Eastern Europe, Turkey and Russia. He did not believe that Russia would revert to its Stalinist days as an external threat to the West, but the path of economic liberalism was not guaranteed to succeed in the short-term. The best way to manage potential upheavals would be for the European Union to develop a common policy towards Russia. This should be by agreement in the intergovernmental sphere, rather than by the rigid application of qualified majority voting:

> We shall go astray if we regard the Common Foreign and Security Policy as a glass palace which is lowered from heaven in the full perfection of Treaty language. If we do that we shall always mourn over panes of broken glass and other grievous imperfections. Where we can find agreement we should act together. Where we cannot agree or do not agree we go separately. But each act of agreement is a brick which will strengthen the whole. Brick by brick, agreement by agreement, the Common Policy can be built.'[9]

The key to reaching an agreement on an inter-governmental basis rested on the larger states assuming the biggest role: it had been no accident or conspiracy that the Contact Group encompassing Britain, France, Germany, the United States and Russia had been formed to try to create a peace agreement in Bosnia.

Hurd was bringing together his ideas of the previous six years. The following month, Hurd returned to the theme of European security in a speech to the Supreme Headquarters Allied Power Europe (SHAPE) Conference in Brussels. He began by reaffirming that NATO should remain the cornerstone of European Defence. The Atlantic Alliance was 'not just a hangover from the Cold War, but a framework for ensuring the future security of all its members'.[10] The old threat of one state invading another had probably had its day. The Gulf War had probably been the last example of that kind, but regional threats still existed. He believed there were few positive lessons to be learned from the experience in Bosnia:

> In particular we have not learned how to intervene successfully in the affairs
> of a state in order to avert a catastrophe such as a dissolution of Yugoslavia,
> without assuming responsibility for the future of that state.[11]

Hurd then returned to the problem of how to assuage Russian fears of the eastward expansion of NATO. While Russia could not be allowed to veto the entry of at least Poland, Hungary and the Czech Republic into an enlarged NATO, she needed to be reassured that NATO's motives were purely defensive. Hurd suggested a Baltic security system, encompassing Latvia, Lithuania and Estonia, as well as Finland and Sweden – two Scandinavian countries who had successfully retained their neutrality during the Cold War. Although these ideas were not outlined in detail, they were a creative response to the dilemma of how to enhance European Security without causing Russia unnecessarily to intensify her old insecurities about her Western borders.

As well as putting forward constructive ideas on the future shape of Europe, as an elder statesman, Hurd became an 'active backbencher' as he had presaged in his resignation letter to the Prime Minister in June 1995. His own views on the single-currency experiment hardened considerably during 1996. In a series of speeches and interviews, he claimed the single currency was a political move, not based on sound economics. Speaking on Radio Four's *World at One* programme at the end of January 1996, he called for a postponement of the single currency, fearing that the proposals as they stood might lead to an unravelling of the single market. However, he always added the rider that, if the single currency proved a success, Britain might have to join in the medium-term to avoid 'a loss of blood' in the City of London.[12] It would be unwise to abandon the Prime Minister's 'wait and see' policy. Only by staying part of the negotiations on a single currency could Britain hope to influence the future direction of European integration.

Along with other pro-European Conservatives, Hurd became deeply worried that the Eurosceptics, egged on by their allies in the Tory press, were attempting to shift the centre of gravity in the Conservative Party towards an agenda on Europe which might lead the Party to advocate withdrawal from the European Union. In April 1996, in a speech to the Scottish Council of the European Movement, Hurd directed his fire against Sir James Goldsmith and his newly formed Referendum Party. Government policy, he said must not be put 'at the mercy of millionaires who play with British politics as a hobby'.[13] The debate on Europe was in danger of going astray. This biographer also detected a degree of personal frustration that, during the latter stages of Hurd's Foreign Secretaryship, the Government's European policy had been undermined by the raucous and inaccurate debate at home; practical ideas put forward by Hurd were discounted at the European table because of the domestic political atmosphere: after so many years trying to keep the Eurosceptics at bay, Hurd was no longer willing to see the Government's policy drift any further in their direction. The motive was to prevent the party of business, the Conservative Party, from turning its back on Europe.[14]

The first signs of Hurd's new willingness to speak out came during the crisis over BSE in March 1996, when he warned John Major against using an empty-chair policy in an attempt to coerce Britain's European partners into removing the ban on British beef exports. Having agreed a compromise framework at the Florence Summit for a staged lifting of the beef ban, Hurd said on London Weekend Television's *Crosstalk* programme that it would be 'counterproductive to get involved in trench warfare'.[15]

Over the summer of 1996, Hurd decided to mount a rearguard action against the onward advance of the Eurosceptical right. Addressing the Conservative Group for Europe's annual meeting and supper at St Ermin's Hotel in London, he said:

> We in the Conservative Group for Europe are a broad church, but once more we have to act as a church militant. We are not attacking anyone but we have to be ready to defend Britain's place in Europe against those who, unwittingly or wittingly, undermine it.[16]

Then, on 19 September 1996, Douglas Hurd signed a letter to the Editor of *The Independent* to mark the fiftieth anniversary of Winston Churchill's speech at the University of Zurich on the future of European co-operation, along with a highly distinguished group of Conservative elder statesmen: Sir Leon Brittan,

Lord Carrington, Sir Edward Heath, Lord Howe of Aberavon and Viscount Whitelaw of Penrith. The 'grandees' claimed that Britain's influence and prosperity in the world depended on her continued membership of the European Union, which should be seen 'as an opportunity not a threat'.[17] In a thinly veiled reference to the Eurosceptics, they asserted that 'the British instinct is to lead, not walk away. Our greatest patriots have never been little Englanders.'[18] The great tragedy was that Britain had not joined the European Community from the beginning, that she had not been there to shape its future course. Ever since the Treaty of Rome, Britain had been playing 'catch up'. She must not make the same mistake again:

> For us now to rule out British membership of a single currency would be to betray our national interest. To countenance withdrawal from the European Union would be to court disaster. To commit ourselves, by contrast, to a positive role in the leadership of Europe is the most fitting tribute we can pay to Churchill's Zurich vision.[19]

That day, Hurd appeared on ITN to claim that, for the past few years, a one-sided battle had been fought on the subject of Europe inside the Conservative Party. The Government's policy on the forthcoming IGC had been agreed by the whole Cabinet in a White Paper in April 1996. The Eurosceptics, he said, could not agree to half of it and then cried foul. The rest of the Conservative Party were expected to remain silent in the face of these silly remarks. That was not going to happen anymore. Hurd's remarks forced political commentators to sit up and take notice because here was a politician normally renowned for his carefully coded remarks stating publicly that things had gone too far.

Hurd's signature to the 'Grandees' Letter' was only the opening shot in a concerted move by the centre and left of the Conservative Party to fight back against the tilt to the right on Europe, taxation and home affairs.

On 25 September, 1996, Hurd was the leading speaker at the St Stephen's Club launch of 'Conservative Mainstream', an umbrella organisation for the three centre-left bodies inside the Conservative Party comprising the little-known Progress Group, the Macleod Group — represented by its leader, Peter Temple-Morris, and his vice-chairman, Sir Geoffrey Johnson Smith — and the Tory Reform Group, whose most prominent members included Michael Heseltine, Kenneth Clarke, Stephen Dorrell, and David Hunt. Despite the claims of the organisers that around fifty MPs attended the launch, journalists present counted only about twenty.

The keynote speech of the one-day conference was delivered by Douglas Hurd. He began with another of his analogies to which his audiences had become familiar over the years:

> The mainstream of Conservative thinking usually flows quietly through peaceful meadows. Those of us who belong to the mainstream do not usually see the need for a great deal of noise about political theory . . . At intervals, however, the stream of the Conservative Party passes through a gorge, and its waters become deeper and more turbulent. These phases pass, and there is nothing particularly wrong with them. We are in such a phase at present. During this phase those of us who belong to the mainstream of the Party need to be more active and articulate. We can no longer afford to take for granted in silence some of the principles in which we believe.[20]

Hurd then turned to the question of Europe. There were huge economic advantages, he said, in Britain belonging to the single market and promoting expansion of the European Union to the East. However Britain's arguments had been 'weakened by the poison and prejudiced nature of our debate here at home'.[21] The Prime Minister had been right to negotiate an opt-out on a single currency at Maastricht. It was a massive decision which required a referendum.

He acknowledged the success of the Government's privatisations, but said it would be foolish for Conservatives to 'believe that elections, whether in Oxfordshire or elsewhere, can be won by reducing income tax against a background of sacked teachers or closed hospital wards.'[22]

Returning to the reasoning behind Conservative Mainstream, he said that Margaret Thatcher and John Major had made enormous strides since 1979. She had proved it was possible after all to take on trade union power, to privatise, and he had achieved growth without high inflation:

> But Conservative wisdom did not begin in 1979. Lessons learned earlier cannot be forgotten if we are to retain the support which we need. After the crushing defeat of 1945 we learned that the Conservative Party could not afford to be identified with a harsh, divisive, mean view of society. We looked in 1945, despite Winston Churchill's leadership and his own generous impulses, like a Party of those who had done well before the War.
>
> The criticism was unfair but no one goes into politics expecting fairness. Winston Churchill, Anthony Eden, Harold Macmillan and Ted Heath drew the right lesson from that defeat. The phrase 'One Nation' is overused, but it contains a vital truth and indeed a warning for the Conservative Party. If our policies and our phrases seem designed to set one part of our nation against another then we shall lose, and deserve to lose, even if it is a majority which might benefit from our success.[23]

Then, in a rare moment of passion which stirred the political correspondents in their seats, he said:

We must not, even in our inner thinking, despair of part of our population as fit only for poverty – or prison.[24]

At one level, Hurd was trying to summon up the spirits of the Conservative past, to give the Conservative Party back its 'One Nation' soul in time for the General Election. The difficulty for the Conservative Party was twofold. First, Tony Blair, the new Labour leader, strove successfully to occupy the 'One Nation' territory previously occupied by the Conservatives. Quite simply, he stole the Tories' 'One Nation' clothes. Second, in the struggle to reverse trade union power in the 1980s, the Conservative Party worshipped too much at the altar of the free market. As someone who has never been an ideologue, Hurd realised the dangers of believing that the free market was a solution for everything. During the Major Governments, Hurd seemed to sense that things had gone too far. At the Conservative Party Conference in October 1993, he warned Conservatives at a Tory Reform Group fringe meeting against being seen by the voters as believing in 'a permanent cultural revolution in the style of Trotsky or Chairman Mao'.[25] But instead of standing out against change in the Major Government, Hurd became convinced of the merits of the market. He supported prisons privatisation and denationalisation of the railways and the Post Office. Here was the contradiction at the heart of Douglas Hurd's speech to Conservative Mainstream. He was trying to revive a Conservative Party which no longer existed. As he admitted in his peroration, he belonged to 'the era of village fêtes and crowded eve-of-poll meetings in Victorian city halls'.[26]

Hugo Young was the only political commentator to tease out the significance of Hurd's speech:

> Some kind of middle way is what most Conservative voters want to believe in, and what every non-Tory with an open mind would prefer to support.[27]

However, Young argued, Hurd's speech had come much too late. The Conservative Party was not going through a phase, but had been polluted by the stain of the European issue. The Conservative centre-left's subtlety was no match for the simplistic nationalism of the sceptics egged on by a media which consistently failed to report the views of pro-European Conservatives:

> Mainstream, alas, can no longer describe the Tory Party. Mainstream is steady, straight, predictable. But the captain, now, is not in command of his ship. I can call spirits from the vasty deep, Hurd seemed to be saying. If the words signified reality, perhaps he could. So could Mr Major. But when he calls for them, they won't come.[28]

In his defence, Douglas Hurd, never fought shy of warning the Conservative Party of being perceived as too extreme. On 10 March 1995, during a speech at Birmingham University, he had indirectly warned against the 'clear blue water' strategy being proposed by Peter Lilley, John Redwood and Michael Portillo. The Conservatives should not sail away from the 'One Nation' ship they occupied, but repel the Blairite boarders:

> Do we actually take to the boats ourselves and row off into the Great Blue Yonder, hoping that some other ship will come into sight? Or do we repel boarders and say that this is our ship; we know how to sail it; we know its destination and please leave our ship or be thrown into the sea?[29]

Since his appointment as Home Secretary in 1993, Michael Howard had pursued populist policies under the slogan 'prison works', stressing punishment by incarceration rather than education and rehabilitation. Although the new policy appeared to result in a fall in the crime figures, critics wondered whether these falls were purely temporary. In the medium term, prisoners would be released, and in the absence of education programmes to try to prevent prisoners from reoffending, the crime figures would rise again. Meanwhile, in the short term, the inexorable rise in the number of convicted prisoners would place an intolerable strain on the prison system. It is not that Hurd is wildly liberal on criminal justice matters. It is more that he feared a return to overcrowding, sparking disturbances similar to those he had experienced as Home Secretary in 1986 (see Chapter 12). The spectre of executive release – releasing prisoners before their allotted time – would then undermine confidence in the whole criminal-justice system. Hurd had refrained from speaking out against Michael Howard because, despite his Eurosceptic beliefs, the Home Secretary had remained loyal to the Prime Minister during the ratification process of the Maastricht Treaty, helping Hurd to dampen down the protests coming from the other Eurosceptics in Cabinet (see Chapter 17). But Michael Howard consistently failed to listen to the advice coming from those responsible for running the criminal justice system – the judges, the police, the probation officers and the prison governors.

The ire of liberal Conservative MPs was stirred into protest with the introduction of the Crime (Sentences) Bill which sought to impose mandatory minimum sentences for burglary (three years) and drug trafficking (seven years). There would also be automatic life sentences for those convicted for a second time of a serious violent or sexual crime such as attempted murder, manslaughter, rape or serious wounding, along the lines of the 'two strikes and you're out' policies in the United States. Howard also proposed to introduce what he termed 'honesty in sentencing' – the notion that a sentence delivered by a judge should be closer to that actually served. The Criminal Justice Act of 1991 had increased the length of sentence a prisoner had to serve before being considered for parole (known as the 'tariff') from a third to one half of his or her sentence. Howard proposed to increase the time spent in prison to 80 per cent before good behaviour could be considered. In effect, the plans would have resulted in judges passing shorter headline sentences because these more closely reflected the actual time a prisoner should serve. The Bill was heralded by the title of the March 1996 White Paper which presaged it: *Protecting the Public.*

During the Second Reading of the Crime (Sentences) Bill, Michael Howard was criticised by an extremely distinguished group of backbenchers from his own side, including the former Home Secretary Kenneth Baker. The criminal had nothing to lose, a point which had already been expressed in an intervention by the former Education Minister Robert Jackson.[30] The former Home Office minister Sir Peter Lloyd also stood up to voice his concerns.[31] The former Northern Ireland Secretary Peter Brooke arose from his seat once more to express his unease as an old Tory that the Government and the judiciary should be at variance.[32]

However, the best speech of the day was delivered by Douglas Hurd. His approach was a classic example of how to criticise a colleague's policies without engaging in *ad hominem* debating or appearing disloyal to one's party. Instead of accusing Michael Howard directly of having recourse to populism he claimed that Home Office issues

> . . . are sometimes portrayed in the press as though they were stages in a desperate race for votes – the assumption being that the public believe that every potential weapon should be outlawed, that every offender should be sent to prison, that the only good sentence is a long sentence and that it is the job of a politician to come as close to that ideal as possible. If that race is set by the media and some sections of opinion, my right hon. and learned Friend the Home Secretary will not and cannot enter such a race in such crude terms.[33]

Hurd went on:

> If we lock up more burglars for longer, they are not capable of burgling while behind bars, so our streets and homes are safer while they are there. That is a significant short-term gain. When their sentences expire, more burglars will enter prison as they are sentenced, under the new arrangements, for longer, but more burglars will leave prison. There will be an increased flow of released offenders onto our streets. Will those people go straight or return to crime?[34]

Hurd feared that proposed cuts in education, probation, and training inside prison – activities which were not 'progressive waffle' – might mean 'that our prisons will turn out more accomplished criminals'.[35] While the Home Secretary was right to place emphasis on the victim, Hurd said he had:

> . . . never understood why the victim is thought to have benefited when we make a mess of treating the offender. The victim of the past offence does not benefit and offences may be committed in the future as a result.[36]

The following day, Hurd felt that the *Daily Telegraph* had misrepresented what he had said, so he penned a letter to its Editor, setting out the real meaning behind his speech. However, his sentence warning that 'if we treat prison simply as a wastepaper basket into which we toss offenders, we are in the medium term putting the public at risk'[37] served only to put his case against the Crime (Sentences) Bill even more emphatically. Here was the quintessential diplomat using strident language to criticise the Home Secretary's recourse to populism.

Despite the thinly veiled criticism of several Tory backbenchers, the old adage applied: never trust a Tory rebellion. No Conservatives voted against the Second Reading of the Bill, and in fact, throughout its stages, only Sir Peter Lloyd was sufficiently roused to cast any dissenting votes against the Government. During the key amendments in the House of Commons, Douglas Hurd's name was not to be seen in the Government's division lobbies. He had chosen not to be present, not wishing to embarrass the Government even by a definite abstention.

As had been commonplace during the 1980s, it was left to their unelected but sensible Lordships to do battle with such an ill-judged piece of Government legislation. On 13 February 1997, their Lordships succeeded in passing an amendment which gave judges discretion in the application of mandatory sentences for burglary and drug trafficking.[38]

Douglas Hurd sat in his House of Commons office on the afternoon of Tuesday, 18 March watching C-span, the parliamentary channel, for an announcement on whether the Government would defy the Lords. He was due to attend a service at St Margaret's for retiring members and their wives, followed by a party hosted by the Speaker, Betty Boothroyd.[39] Even at this stage, Hurd was thinking of taking the easy way out: choosing to be absent for the votes in the House of Commons. Other potential rebels like Kenneth Baker and Peter Lloyd were considering taking stronger action. In the event, the Government backed down in the face of a rearguard action by Lord Ackner, a former Law Lord, and a group of Liberal Democrat peers, whose blocking moves had threatened to put the Government's plans for a Friday prorogation (winding up of Parliament) in jeopardy. Lord Strathclyde, the Government Chief Whip, held a stock-taking adjournment and agreed to accept the amendment.

The crisis was over for the Government, but Hurd had already determined (in January) to argue the case for a more liberal and less populist criminal justice policy. Free from the constraints of the *Daily Mail* tendency, free from the Tory right, he told an interviewer that he did not have to watch his back anymore.[40] On 15 January 1997, it was announced that Hurd was to succeed Jon Snow, the Channel Four newsreader, as Chairman of the Prison Reform Trust in November 1997.

The Prison Reform Trust is a charitable organisation founded in 1981 as a liberal pressure group campaigning for fewer people to be sent to prison unnecessarily and for better conditions and education for prisoners. In many respects, Hurd's decision was his next logical step on criminal-justice policy. On the other hand, it was radical for a former Conservative Home Secretary to join one of Britain's criminal-justice pressure groups. Hurd could not resist chuckling when he recalled that, in September 1986, he had described pressure groups as being 'like serpents constantly emerging from the sea to strangle Laocoön and his sons in their coils';[41] a decade later, he was about to head up one of these groups.

Just before delivering a speech to students at the University of Hull in November 1996, Hurd scribbled down a possible title for his speech: it read 'Heresies of a Dinosaur'.[42] He decided not to use the title but stood up to give his views on the state of the British political system.[43] In a series of speeches around this time, Hurd claimed that Parliament was failing in its role as a legislative body, that there was a narrowing of the political class and a failure to understand how Government actually worked.

Over Christmas 1996, there was a wave of popular pressure on Parliament to change the law on hand-guns in the wake of the Dunblane massacre when Thomas Hamilton ran amok killing sixteen children. Hurd told Sir David Frost that although the emotional response was understandable, that did not mean that Parliament should rush into legislation without a pause for thought.[44] Was the gun-legislation fully thought through? These views were highly unfashionable. Roy Hattersley, sitting on the sofa beside Douglas Hurd, accused him of being a patrician, believing that the public were not fit to decide these matters.[45]

A second issue which deeply concerned Hurd was the report into arms sales to Iraq conducted by Sir Richard Scott. Hurd described it as 'a deeply inadequate description of modern government'.[46] Scott, he said, had been 'elevated to the position of Chief Whig of the Year'.[47] The main purpose of the Scott Report had been to discover whether three innocent men might have been convicted in the Matrix Churchill trial because the Government sat on its hands and refused to make information available to the trial. Despite a campaign waged in the press, that central charge had been roundly dismissed by Scott. Having seen the main allegation fall apart in the face of the evidence, Hurd believed that Scott had become fixated with two secondary points.

One dealt with the issue of ministers issuing public interest immunity certificates with which Hurd had some sympathy. The other issue concerned whether there had been an alteration in the guidelines issued by the then Foreign Secretary, Sir Geoffrey Howe, in judging whether to grant export licences to Iraq. In Sir Richard's view, there had indeed been an alteration in the guidelines by three junior ministers, William Waldegrave, Alan Clark and Lord Trefgarne, of which Parliament had not been informed. Years were spent investigating whether the ministers had made a real alteration in the guidelines or had interpreted the guidelines differently.

Hurd believed that it was a mistake to investigate every minute angle. It was, he claimed, a relatively minor decision which a comparable junior minister would make on average half-a-dozen times a week. Cabinet ministers made such decisions two or three times a night. It was unrealistic of Scott to expect ministers to labour over every decision, given the severe time constraints on ministers. Hurd's maxim was ministers must decide.

Alongside this attack on the capacity to govern, Hurd claimed Britain was experiencing a narrowing of the political class. Instead of aspiring politicians having to pursue a career in business or the law before they entered the House of Commons, Britain was breeding the professional politician, whose only experience prior to becoming an MP was a previous career as a special adviser or a political research assistant. In the twilight of the Major Government, the scandals involving financial sleaze had led to a public clamour against MPs holding any outside interests. Lord Nolan had been appointed to investigate standards in public life. Once more, Hurd took an unfashionable view: Lord Nolan, quite unwittingly, had accelerated a trend towards the narrowing of the political class. Hurd said 'we must not accept such a narrowing of the political system that Ministers come to high office trained principally in the art of being rude to each other in an adversarial system.'[48] Hurd had returned to yet another of his favourite themes.

On 15 November 1995, he had been given the honour of moving the Debate on the Address and chose the theme of the public's distaste for the adversarial system of British politics:

> I do not believe that sleaze and scandal are really what worries people about this Parliament. What worries them most – it worries many thoughtful people – is the sense of empty noise and phoney war.

There used to be in this country a strong and vivid appetite for adversarial politics in the days of Gladstone and Disraeli, or of Gladstone and Lord Randolph. But for one reason or another, that has gone, and there is a real danger that, egged on by the media, all parties in this House – all of us – may play out the old play not realising that beyond the footlights half the audience has crept away, and the other half is sitting there in mounting irritation.[49]

He concluded by predicting that 'political success may well go to those who sound least like politicians'.[50] By the following Christmas he had singled out Kenneth Clarke as the politician of the year because he did not sound like one.[51]

Hurd decided not to become overly involved in campaigning during the 1997 General Election, but he did come to the aid of Lord James-Douglas Hamilton who was battling to save his seat in Edinburgh, West. Hurd spoke in a hall in the drab town of Kirkliston. Only a dozen souls attended, and half of them were members of Lord James's team. The rest of the audience comprised a few local eccentrics and the caretaker of the building. It was a depressing night, and symbolic of the Conservative Party's plight in Scotland at the end of the twentieth century.

For reasons of nostalgia, Hurd decided to walk round Bexley with his old boss Sir Edward Heath, as they had done during the 1970 General Election campaign. They were photographed in Tescos by the press. 'Ted' survived the election, but Lord James did not, as the Conservatives suffered a complete rout in Scotland and Wales, and a hammering (at least in terms of seats) all over Britain.

The gloom inside the Conservative Party after this defeat carried on into the Conservative leadership contest. Hurd supported Kenneth Clarke, believing, as he wrote in a letter to the Editor of the *Daily Telegraph*, that the former Chancellor was someone whose robust style could 'reach people over the heads of most Westminster politicians.'[52]

As we have seen from Hurd's speeches on the political system, he felt strongly that the way Government operated in Britain was not sufficiently understood by the bulk of the electorate. Ministers were not confronted by a neat succession of compartmentalised decisions, as though each could be considered in a cocoon. Instead, the trivial and the important jostle for a minister's limited time. The sheer pace of events – the pell-mell of politics – crowds in on ministers.

Upon his retirement as a minister, Hurd felt the need to express this view of politics in one final novel. While his other novels had been written principally for fun, Hurd wanted to draw from some of his experiences as a minister, using fiction as a way of explaining what governance was really like, in a way similar to one of his heroes, Benjamin Disraeli. *The Shape of Ice* was published by Little, Brown & Company in May 1998.

His decision to write a last novel heralded a part-time career as a broadcaster and writer. From the second half of 1995, he wrote a number of articles and book reviews for the *Daily Telegraph*. He also wrote occasional articles for the Canadian newspaper the *Globe and Mail*, reviving memories of his grandfather's association with the Canadian press.

In October 1995, Hurd came up with the idea of five talks based on places where he had spent periods of his working life. These were the Foreign Office in London, Peking, New York and Rome and the House of Commons.[53] In June and early July 1996, five fifteen-minute programmes were broadcast after the *Today* programme under the series title *Letters from A Diplomat*. The series was well-received, because it brought together two of Hurd's strongest suits: his knack for talking with authority and confidence on radio – although some disliked his rasping voice – and his ability to engage in a brief sketch of a building, a place or a scene, honed by years of drafting in the Foreign Office as an official. The BBC produced a tape of the talks and to the original five talks Hurd added three more: constituency and campaigning, foreign travel, and words and style.

In November 1997, a further series, *The Search For Peace – A Century of Peace Diplomacy*, was broadcast, this time for BBC television. The series – with accompanying book – sought to trace the history of the international community's attempts to find ways of resolving conflicts. Hurd was filmed against various backdrops, including the Somme battlefield, the Foreign Office, and the playing fields of Eton. His central theme was that foreign policy had to be conducted not by idealism or realism, but by a balance between the two. It took Hurd some time to master the voice-overs, fitting exactly what he had to say into a precise number of seconds. As it happens, his declaiming and pacing up and down paid off. But somehow, he was unable to throw off his awkward posture and over-formal style of speaking on television.

The footage dug up by the BBC archive team was one of the best aspects of the series. Hurd was also able to use his enviable connections to interview international statesmen, including George Bush, Robert McNamara and Dr Henry Kissinger. The last of these three was perhaps overused by Hurd, reflecting his admiration, even adoration, of the former US Secretary of State.

The book itself is extremely well-written – there is hardly a wasted word. But it is characteristically broad-brush and lacking in personal input. Its conclusion that foreign policy is about taking two steps forward and three steps back, is perhaps unoriginal. As a highbrow coffee-table book, it lacks either the glossy colour photographs needed to entice the lay person or the depth to satisfy the academics. While it is impressive to think that Hurd wrote the book over the summer of 1997, the finished article lacks polish.

At the time of writing, Hurd had not yet started to write his memoirs, but his intention is to wait perhaps another year before beginning to write. One of his problems is the enormous number of books, photographs, personal papers and letters which he has accumulated almost religiously through the years. There are plans in hand to convert a barn at his Cotswold home into a Hurd library. He may well produce a self-exculpatory book along the lines of Rab Butler's *The Art of the Possible*, in which he will select eight to ten episodes from his political career. Hurd's is the broad-brush approach. The book will be a summary, not a mine of detail from which historians can trawl. Among the chapters will probably be the 1970 General Election, which holds a special place in his affections as a contest, in many ways like 1992, which the experts failed to predict that a young and inexperienced Conservative leader might win. Hurd had served under two such leaders and another remarkable one in between. In all those years, he had managed to survive, while remaining consistently loyal to all three.

Notes

1. *Financial Times*, 13 Sept. 1995.
2. *The Times*, 14 Sept. 1995.
3. Ibid.
4. The Foreign Secretary's gross salary in 1995 was £67,819, with £42,813 allocated for his job as a minister and a reduced salary of £24,985 for his work as an MP, down from the standard £33,189. In effect, Hurd's net pay as Foreign Secretary was £34,630, which is roughly the same as a middle-grade hospital doctor.
5. Michael White, 'Ministers earn their right to Boggins' turn', *The Guardian*, 13 Sept. 1995.
6. Mr Claes was alleged to have been implicated in a £1 million payment made by Italy's helicopter company to his Flemish Socialist Party. Eventually, he was forced to resign in order to fight the charges.
7. *Daily Telegraph*, 21 Oct. 1995.
8. Douglas Hurd, 'Europe in the 21st Century', Speech to SHAPE Conference, Brussels, 25 Apr. 1996.
9. Ibid.
10. Ibid.
11. Ibid.
12. The theme of 'a loss of blood' was used by Hurd in several speeches

during 1996 including H. of C. Deb. (6th Series), 11 Dec. 1996, vol. 287, col. 319.

13. Douglas Hurd, Speech to European Movement's Scottish Council, Edinburgh, 26 Apr. 1996.

14. The author was present at this speech.

15. Transcript, *ITN News*, 2 Jun. 1996.

16. Douglas Hurd, Speech to Conservative Group for Europe, St Ermin's Hotel, London, 11 Jul. 1996.

17. Sir Leon Brittan *et al.*, 'Our national interest lies in E.U. destiny', 'Letter to the Editor', *The Independent*, 19 Sept. 1996.

18. Ibid.

19. Ibid.

20. Douglas Hurd, Speech to Mainstream Conservative Meeting, St Stephen's Club, London, 25 Sept. 1996.

21. Ibid.

22. Ibid.

23. Ibid.

24. Ibid.

25. Douglas Hurd, Speech to Tory Reform Group, Blackpool, 7 Oct. 1993.

26. Douglas Hurd, Speech to Mainstream Conservative Meeting, St. Stephen's Club, London, 25 Sept. 1996.

27. Hugo Young, 'Grandees waving and drowning', *The Guardian*, 26 Sept. 1996.

28. Ibid.

29. Douglas Hurd, Speech to Birmingham University, 10 Mar. 1995; a similar warning had been delivered a year earlier by Hurd in a speech to the Tory Reform Group entitled 'Charting the Clear Blue Water' delivered on 11 Oct. 1994.

30. H. of C. Deb. (6th Series), 4 Nov. 1996, vol. 285, col. 941; col. 913.

31. Ibid., cols 955–7.

32. Ibid., col. 951.

33. Ibid., col. 934.

34. Ibid., col. 935.

35. Ibid., col. 935–6.

36. Ibid., col. 936.

37. Douglas Hurd, 'Letter to the Editor', *Daily Telegraph*, 5 Nov. 1996.

38. H. of L. Deb. (5th Series), 13 Feb. 1997, vol. 578, cols 359–61.

39. Douglas Hurd, 'Five Days in the Life Of . . . ', *The Independent on Sunday*, 23 Mar. 1997.

40. Robert Crampton interview with Douglas Hurd, 'I am not afraid of being called a liberal', *The Times*, 15 Jan. 1997.

41. Douglas Hurd, Lecture to Royal Institute of Public Administration, 19 Sept. 1986.

42. Private information.

43. Douglas Hurd, 'In Place of Polemics', *The Guardian*, 27 Jan. 1997.

44. Douglas Hurd speaking on *Frost on Sunday*, 15 Dec. 1996 (transcript).

45. Roy Hattersley speaking on *Frost on Sunday*, 15 Dec. 1996 (transcript).

46. Douglas Hurd, 'In Place of Polemics', *The Guardian*, 27 Jan. 1997.

47. Ibid.

48. Ibid.

49. H. of C. Deb. (6th Series), 15 Nov. 1995, vol. 267, col. 9.

50. Ibid.

51. Douglas Hurd speaking on *Frost on Sunday*, 15 Dec. 1996 (transcript).

52. Douglas Hurd, 'Letter to the Editor', *Daily Telegraph*, 19 May 1997.

53. I am indebted to Rosemary Scoular of Peters, Fraser & Dunlop for this information.

25

Conclusion

Hurd was able to draw on his experiences of working for Edward Heath to identify the basic problems of governing Britain in the 1970s – that the trade unions had become too powerful. He had the foresight to see that harsh measures would be required along with, in the title words of his book, *An End to Promises*. The difference between Hurd and Thatcher was that he believed this could be achieved by co-operation between the political parties while she articulated an ideology based on confrontation – enforcing her will on the nation. The price paid for the Thatcher revolution was a decline in deference and support for the very institutions which the Conservative party used to represent. Hurd should be remembered as much for his analysis of contemporary events as for what he has done as a politician.

In the early 1980s, Hurd proved to be a competent Minister of State at the Foreign Office because he knew the terrain, having served as a diplomat. He was a poor Minister of State at the Home Office, because he was exposed to detail which ill-suited his broad-brush approach. Plunged into a domestic department about which – initially at least – he knew little, this deficiency was exposed during the passage of the Police and Criminal Evidence Bill. But he was fortunate that his lack of experience in a domestic department was rectified so early in his ministerial career. The experience stood him in good stead when he became Home Secretary in 1985.

Douglas Hurd was a cautious Secretary of State for Northern Ireland, but was filled with the enthusiasm of a minister who had, after several years of waiting, finally made it into Cabinet. He was not afraid to wield power and the brutalities associated with it, developing a tough attitude to countering terrorism and accepting with fortitude the security guards who surrounded him. He should be remembered as one of the architects of the Anglo-Irish Agreement. But again, it is his analysis that the political leaders of Northern

Ireland were too reluctant to come out of their respective trenches – his commentary and analysis of events – which stands out.

Hurd was a listening Home Secretary, who was never better than when dealing with a crisis in a department which is especially vulnerable to the unexpected. His diaries show that, while Hurd did not relish crises (in the manner of a Michael Heseltine), generally speaking, he handled them astutely, particularly the prison riots in the spring of 1986. If anything, as a former diplomat, he was too respectful of the views of those working in the system – the officials, the judges, the policemen, the prison and probation officers. But this was to be expected. Hurd is an establishment Conservative who will always support established authority. Despite his authoritarian streak – shown during his handling of immigration – Hurd had a capacity for liberal reform in criminal justice policy. But much of the Criminal Justice Act of 1991 which he bequeathed to his successors had to be substantially altered by Kenneth Clarke. Throughout his period at the Home Office, Hurd gave speeches bemoaning the dangers of producing too much legislation and yet he presided over a glut of legislation as Home Secretary, much of which – especially the Public Order Act of 1986 – curbed the rights of the individual. Hurd ceded ground to Mrs Thatcher over broadcasting, ending in the flawed Broadcasting Act of 1990. He lacked a large enough following on the Conservative backbenches to allow him to use the authority of his office to stand up to Mrs Thatcher. Instead, he tried to tone down her views and soften her contradictions, leading to instances – such as the broadcasting ban on the IRA – where he regretted the outcome. He was not supine with Mrs Thatcher, but there were limits to how far he could push her. This was shown in the area of official secrets, where Hurd was forced to accommodate the Prime Minister's obsession with secrecy. Hurd's later measures as Foreign Secretary to increase government openness give a more accurate picture of his true instincts on the subject.

On the question of the miscarriages of justice, Hurd moved a little too slowly and relied too much on official accounts of the cases, but he was not inflexible. Moreover, he attempted to deal with the cases of the Birmingham Six and the Guildford Four like a civil servant, trying to set to one side his political role. Throughout his ministerial career, Hurd took very few originating positions, unlike two of the intellectual giants of the 1980s, Geoffrey Howe and Nigel Lawson. This was partly because Hurd has always eschewed ideology and favours compromises based on the balance of the arguments. But his evidence before the Royal Commission into Miscarriages of Justice was decisive in the setting up of the Criminal Cases Review Commission. Hurd's change of mind illustrated his belief in reform if existing laws have been seen to fall into disrepair or disrepute. In that sense, comparisons with Robert Peel are not all that wide of the mark, although Hurd was more effective as a politician than his nineteenth-century counterpart.

449

Comparing Government ministers with their predecessors is something of a parlour game. Perhaps it is unfair to compare Hurd with Home Secretaries who have served short terms of office, such as Kenneth Clarke or David Waddington. Rather, Hurd should be compared with Home Secretaries since the Second World War who have served at least three years and/or enjoyed the luxury of being reappointed after general election victories. It may be instructive to compare Hurd's performance against William Whitelaw and Michael Howard in the former category, and Roy Jenkins and Rab Butler in the latter. On balance, Hurd finishes some way ahead of Michael Howard (who, although formidable, failed to listen to advice) and just ahead of William Whitelaw, because Hurd never lost control of the Conservative Party Conference debates on capital punishment. But while Hurd is firmly in the top flight of Home Secretaries, he finishes some way short of either Rab Butler or Roy Jenkins, the league leaders. Hurd, Butler and Jenkins were all pragmatists, who adopted rational approaches to Home Office issues, drawing on empirical research for their policy ideas. But there were differences. Rab Butler was more indiscreet, more devious than Hurd, while Roy Jenkins took a more liberal attitude to conscience issues such as homosexuality. Above all, Home Secretaries must be willing to listen. Rigid and inflexible Home Secretaries become unstuck because shaping criminal justice policy does not lend itself to dogmatic solutions.

Douglas Hurd was British Foreign Secretary during a period of transition between the end of the Cold War and wherever we are now. It is difficult to analyse where we are, except to mention that the central international institutions with which Britain is concerned – NATO, the United Nations, and the European Union – are only now undergoing radical reform. Between October 1989 and June 1995, the institutions which had been shaped to deal with the Cold War did not substantially alter to deal with the new realities. NATO, its enemy defeated, stood still. The United Nations made a good start with the Gulf War, but hit problems when faced with the dilemma of whether to intervene in civil wars. The European Community enlarged to include three prosperous Western European nations – Sweden, Finland and Austria – but concentrated primarily on deepening Western European integration, while proceeding at a snail's pace in admitting the countries of Eastern Europe. Diplomacy fell far behind the pace of events. Critics of Hurd say he should have imposed his ideas more forcefully on the international stage. Before he left the Foreign Office, Hurd did at least start a debate – at the Britain in the World Conference – about his country's future role. The supposed mistakes which Hurd made, especially over the former Yugoslavia, were as much an indictment of the institutions – especially the sheer number of them – as of the man himself. There were summits, meetings of EU foreign ministers, intergovernmental conferences, more summits. Diplomacy suffered from a plethora of international organisations. Hurd realised this and tried to cut through the morass by involving the big powers – Britain, France, Russia, Germany, the United States (occasionally Japan) and China – in solving disputes. The method was similar to the nineteenth-century Concert of Europe, but with two differences. First, the great powers were no longer interested in old-style imperialism. Second, great-power rivalries and arms races were out, co-operation in the UN Security Council was in. Hurd was a transitional Foreign Secretary in a period between the end of the Cold War and the reshaping of international institutions to take account of this fact. Being a figure who rarely carried ideological baggage to an issue, he was able to react flexibly when confronted with the fluidity of international events. His critics accused him of lacking any firm principles, but as Mrs Thatcher showed over her opposition to German reunification, dogmatism does not work in such circumstances. He was shrewd enough to realise that there was no 'New World Order', merely a 'slow continuous effort to cope with disaster'.[1]

Douglas Hurd cannot easily be compared with any twentieth-century British Foreign Secretary. His instincts on foreign policy hail from the nineteenth-century, but with a realisation that it was part of Britain's interests to create a safer world. British foreign policy, in his words, fell somewhere 'between Gladstone and the saloon bar'. In a number of respects, he was similar in method to Lord Carrington. They were both good chairs of meetings, both disliked detail, both were weak on economic matters, both eschewed ideology, both were respected by officials and neither was addicted to office. They were both good delegators. While Carrington entrusted Hurd with matters of substance in the early 1980s, Hurd delegated tasks successfully with Francis Maude (especially over Hong Kong passports and Vietnam) and William Waldegrave (over the Middle East). Carrington and Hurd both agree that Mrs Thatcher had a tendency to go over-the-top and both disapproved of her abrasive style: over the European budget row in the early 1980s, in Carrington's case, and her attitude to German unification with Douglas Hurd. Hurd learned from Carrington how to handle Mrs Thatcher. It was no good caving in to her initial set of demands. One had to stand one's ground, argue the case, and seek a compromise. On Europe, they were both pragmatic pro-Europeans, rather than federalists. There were also differences between the two men. While Carrington occasionally rowed with the Prime Minister, Hurd rarely lost his cool. While Carrington was an aristocrat, Hurd hailed from the professional middle classes and was a trained diplomat.

Perhaps there are similarities between Hurd and Sir Edward Grey, Foreign Secretary before the First World War, but Grey hailed from the days when Foreign Secretaries were gentleman amateurs. Neither did Grey have to face

the modern-day strains of international travel placed on a Foreign Secretary —
he rarely left Britain. Hurd admires Anthony Eden as a Foreign Secretary, but
did not commit Eden's mistake as Prime Minister of having a rush of blood to
the head over Suez. Hurd stayed out of war in the former Yugoslavia. To have
gone to war would have represented a reversion to imperialism which would
have involved the Russians intervening indirectly on the Serbian side. Hurd took
up far fewer originating positions as Foreign Secretary than either Ernest Bevin
or Geoffrey Howe, but should be considered in the same league. He nearly
matched (but not quite) Geoffrey Howe's reserves of stamina and quiet
advocacy. While Hurd was respected by officials, and exercised a degree of
independence as Foreign Secretary comparable with Ernest Bevin, he was not
held in the same affection. More importantly, their backgrounds, characters and
political styles are so different that the two men cannot be meaningfully
compared.

Politically, Hurd was stronger on strategy than on tactics and political
intrigue, although even his strategy should be defined more as day-to-day
management based on the merits of each policy, rather than a grand vision.
Over his years as a senior minister, Hurd built up a stock of respect in the
House of Commons. He was able to judge the mood in the Chamber and adopt
an air of calm authority. By being more open than most Conservative ministers,
Hurd was able to get the Government out of difficult corners, most notably
Amendment 27 in February 1993 during the ratification of the Maastricht
Treaty, the Ioannina Compromise of March 1994, and the legal muddle over
the Pergau Dam in November 1994 (a mess left by Mrs Thatcher). The problem
was that he was too convincing — so persuasive, in fact, that even if he was
later found to be wrong on an issue, in the actual debate or statement in the
House of Commons (or in his evidence before the Foreign Affairs Select
Committee) he was able to convince most of the people nearly all of the time.
Despite being well respected in the House of Commons, Hurd never had a big
following on the Conservative backbenches in the way that William Whitelaw
or Michael Heseltine had. This left him vulnerable to sacking by Mrs Thatcher.
The fact that he was not sacked indicates either competence or flexibility or a
mixture of both. The real weakness in Hurd's political armoury was exposed
during the November 1990 leadership contest. He was not enough of a party
politician, in the sense of being willing to manoeuvre on his own behalf, or
engage in political intrigue. Neither did Hurd have popular appeal with the
electorate. He was perceived (incorrectly) as an Alec Douglas-Home figure —
aristocratic and old-fashioned — who did not have the charisma to be a
campaigning party leader or Prime Minister. Tactically, he made a mess of
defending the Etonian toff jibe by trying to appear lowlier-than-thou. Above all,
his own natural modesty made him a good number two to John Major, as he

had been to Margaret Thatcher and Edward Heath. Hurd was more of a supportive figure: just as William Whitelaw (especially 1975-86) supported Mrs Thatcher through good times and bad, and Alec Douglas-Home shored up the leadership of Edward Heath (mainly 1965–74), so Hurd supported John Major (1990-95). His other personal qualities – tolerance, civility, self-discipline and a sense of history – made him a good Foreign Secretary, but those qualities did not necessarily suit his being Prime Minister. In Hurd's case, the hunger for the top spot was not there, as it was for Rab Butler, Iain Macleod, Denis Healey, Geoffrey Howe (in his own quiet, determined way) and Michael Heseltine. Hurd loved being Foreign Secretary. He would have become Prime Minister if required to do so by duty, but he never sat awake at night pondering the prospect or plotting how best to get there.

On Europe, Hurd had the sense to see that German unification was inevitable, despite the views of Nicholas Ridley and Margaret Thatcher. At Maastricht in December 1991, he was one of the architects of intergovernmentalism and, along with John Major, helped to put the European Community back on the rails at Edinburgh in December 1992, after a dreadful start to the British presidency. However, by loyally following the Prime Minister's line of trying to be all things to all men – the Europhiles and the Eurosceptics – Hurd allowed the debate on Europe within the Conservative Party to drift too far in a sceptical direction. During the Qualified Majority Voting row in March 1994, he should have used his authority as Foreign Secretary to put his foot down on the issue earlier than he did. Only out of office did he try to restore the balance, but by then it was too late. His speeches on Europe indeed became the heresies of a dinosaur. The problem was that Hurd and his party came up against an issue which went to the very heart of what it is to be a Conservative – a belief in the sovereignty of the United Kingdom. Hurd realises that Britain can no longer be a great power by acting on its own. To do so, it must be at the core of European decision making. At the same time, he is against a single currency because it is a political exercise, rather than one based on purely economic decisions. He realises that to rule out membership of the single currency for the foreseeable future – as William Hague now does – is to risk a 'loss of blood' in the City of London, whose interests Hurd now represents. As Foreign Secretary he increasingly despaired of the Eurosceptics, whose antics undermined his negotiating credibility at the European table, and became deeply concerned that the Conservative Party was about to reject its pro-European credentials, which had been strong since the premiership of Harold Macmillan. The dingy hotel meeting with Jacques Delors at Ioannina in March 1994 brings this out. If Hurd's aim as an establishment Conservative was to prevent the Conservative Party, the party of business, from withdrawing from the European mainstream, then he failed.

Running parallel with Hurd's troubles over Europe were his important speeches on domestic issues. As Foreign Secretary, Hurd would give two or three speeches of real substance per year, setting out his thinking on the future direction of the Conservative Party. He urged the Conservatives not to engage in permanent revolution. He foresaw that the time had come for consolidation. But these pleas were ignored by the right, who wandered off into the clear blue water, instead of standing and fighting on the old Tory 'One Nation' ground. This strategy allowed Tony Blair to steal the old Tory 'One Nation' clothes from under the Conservatives' noses. The Blair jargon about duty and responsibility to our fellow man is pure Douglas Hurd. It is Douglas Hurd, not Tony Blair who is the true exponent of the active citizen.

Hurd should be held up as an example of how to lead one's life as an active citizen, a public servant and as a human being. Essentially, his personal characteristics changed little from his Eton days. His self-discipline, his sense of duty, combined with a dry wit and an acute sense of irony, make him a rounded individual. He was unfailingly courteous to his enemies and critics, and refrained from *ad hominem* debating. Moreover, Hurd belongs to that rare breed of Conservative which actually reads books. He is an intellectual without being obsessed with ideology. Problems are considered on their merits and, eventually, the sensible or balanced policy emerges.

Hurd will never be able to escape being labelled as an archetypal civil servant or diplomat, but that is no bad thing. The public-service ethic is at the forefront of his values. Throughout his life, Hurd has been the active citizen first described in his Tamworth manifesto speech of February 1988. After sixteen years as a senior minister, he was perfectly entitled to earn a higher income through directorships in the City of London. Critics – *The Guardian* and *Private Eye* seem to be fixated with the subject – believe a conflict of interest arose when Hurd used his position with NatWest Markets to try to win commercial contracts from President Milosevic of Serbia. They find it offensive to see the Western politician who, more than any other, stood in the way of lifting the arms embargo in favour of the Bosnian Muslims, supping with the other side. Hurd would argue the realist's case – that Milosevic has seen the light, seen that he must re-enter European respectability if his country is to prosper. The question is whether events in Kosovo prove Milosevic is beyond redemption. But international trade and diplomacy cannot function if the moral high ground is taken on every issue. The rule of thumb is that if one sets out as a government rigidly to apply morality then one generally leaves office or the boardroom accused of hypocrisy when the policy is inevitably relaxed. The present Foreign Secretary, Robin Cook, is discovering this for himself.

Hurd's realism over Milosevic was not mirrored in his attitude to the British handover of Hong Kong to China. He changed his mind sometime between

1991 and 1992, departing from the line painstakingly established by Geoffrey Howe and accepted by most of the former Ambassadors to China and sinologists. Hurd came to believe that preserving British honour – in his words, ensuring that the last major chapter in the British Empire 'should not end in a shabby way' – and nurturing democracy should take precedence over diplomatic realism. The ideal solution would have been to grant the right of abode in Britain to all Hong Kong people, but this was politically impossible in the Conservative Party and with the wider electorate. Given the constraints, Britain did have a moral obligation to the people of Hong Kong, even if the end result was that the 'through train' became derailed and the Chinese dismantled the democratic structures. The fundamental fact remains that, after the Tiananmen Square massacre, there was a clear demand for democracy in the colony, and it would not have been acceptable to the people of Hong Kong (or credible in the House of Commons) to have negotiated the colony's fate in secret. It was not a case of imposing democracy on an unwilling people, but responding to a real demand for it. The only valid criticism against Hurd is that it took him at least two (if not three) years after Tiananmen to come to this view. Given Hurd's knowledge of the Chinese, one can only assume that he was fully aware of the consequences of appointing Chris Patten as a political governor of Hong Kong. The subsequent row with China and within the British foreign-policy-making establishment erupted in such a way that there appeared to be no middle ground. Hurd, forever the defuser, tried to patch things up with Geoffrey Howe, but the differences run deep.

As Foreign Secretary, Hurd carefully courted Turkey and Russia, two pivotal nations at the eastern end of Europe, trying to calm traditional Russian insecurities by regular consultation and by assuaging Turkish worries about not being part of the European mainstream. The military co-operation with the French in Bosnia and their decision to rejoin the military structure of NATO should be regarded as major achievements. For the time being, the British vision of security and defence structures in Europe – intergovernmentalism and the Western European Union (WEU) as the European arm of NATO – rather than the federalist vision, holds sway. While Hurd will be remembered as one of the architects of intergovernmentalism at Maastricht, it may just have been the British desire to win this debate that led to the premature recognition of Croatia and Slovenia and hampered military intervention in Yugoslavia. But recognition by that stage was inevitable and a European-led intervention force without American help would have been likely to end in either an indefinite commitment or a disaster or both. In 1991, only American power was capable of underpinning military operations of this kind (although, with German help, European-led operations may be possible in the future). At the time of the Yugoslavian wars, American leadership was in limbo due to the changeover of the presidency, and the British Government was immersed in fighting and winning a General Election. Even if the subsequent rifts with the Clinton Administration over Bosnia and Ireland caused considerable strains, these were offset to some extent by co-operation in the Gulf region during the Gulf War (with the Bush Administration) and afterwards (with the Clinton Administration), tackling challenges by Saddam Hussein, particularly in October 1994.

Douglas Hurd's sense of history and his natural modesty lead him to conclude, like Harold Macmillan, that there have been many good Foreign Secretaries before and there will be many good ones in the future. He is willing to see that his own importance will be relatively small in the broader sweep of history. In the Major Governments, Douglas Hurd, alongside Kenneth Clarke and Michael Heseltine, stand out as figures of weight in Cabinets which conspicuously lacked it. The second Major Government lost direction after Black Wednesday. Hurd and Clarke deserve credit at least for keeping the ship of state afloat. But while Clarke defended his corner to the end, Hurd perhaps ceded too much ground to the Eurosceptics, leaving the Labour Government with an uphill task in countering the undercurrent of anti-European feeling which has dominated the British press for the last five years.

Hurd's last word as a senior minister in the House of Commons was 'sensible'. Responding to a question about the repatriation of powers from the European Union to the nation states, he said, 'We are still examining exactly what proposals might be sensible.'[2] It would make a fitting epitaph.

Notes

1. *The Times*, 7 Jul. 1995.
2. H. of C. Deb. (6th series), 5 Jul. 1995, vol. 263, Part 1, col. 379.

Index